济南统计年鉴

JINAN STATISTICAL YEARBOOK

2023

（总第41期 NO.41）

济 南 市 统 计 局
国家统计局济南调查队 编

Jinan Municipal Bureau of Statistics
NBS Survey Office In Jinan

中国统计出版社
China Statistics Press

图书在版编目（CIP）数据

济南统计年鉴. 2023 = Jinan Statistical Yearbook 2023 ：汉英对照 / 济南市统计局，国家统计局济南调查队编. -- 北京 ：中国统计出版社，2023.11
ISBN 978-7-5230-0358-9

Ⅰ. ①济… Ⅱ. ①济… ②国… Ⅲ. ①统计资料－济南－2023－年鉴－汉、英 Ⅳ. ①C832.521-54

中国国家版本馆 CIP 数据核字(2023)第 226773 号

济南统计年鉴 2023

作　　者 / 济南市统计局 • 国家统计局济南调查队
责任编辑 / 周小睿
执行编辑 / 刘　琛
装帧设计 / 山东麦德森文化传媒有限公司
出版发行 / 中国统计出版社有限公司
通信地址 / 北京市丰台区西三环南路甲 6 号　邮政编码/100073
发行电话 / 邮购（010）63376909　书店（010）68783171
网　　址 / http://www.zgtjcbs.com/
印　　刷 / 山东麦德森文化传媒有限公司
经　　销 / 新华书店
开　　本 / 890mm×1240mm　1/16
字　　数 / 830 千字
印　　张 / 23.25 彩页 2.75
版　　别 / 2023 年 11 月第 1 版
版　　次 / 2023 年 11 月第 1 次印刷
定　　价 / 396.00 元　Price：396.00 yuan (RMB)

编辑委员会及编辑工作人员

Editorial Board and Editorial Staff

编 辑 说 明

一、《济南统计年鉴2023》是一部全面反映济南市国民经济和社会发展情况的资料性统计年刊。本书收录了济南市及所辖县、区2022年经济和社会发展各方面大量的统计数据，以及历史重要年份的主要统计数据，是认识和研究济南市情、经济和社会发展，制定宏观政策、指导工作的重要工具书。

二、本年鉴以丰富、翔实的统计资料为主，辅以直观的统计图、特载，全面反映了济南市国民经济和社会发展状况。全书统计资料共分为二十二个部分，即：1. 行政区划；2. 人口；3.综合；4. 国民经济核算；5. 劳动就业；6. 固定资产投资；7. 城市公用事业和环境保护；8. 财政、金融和保险；9. 物价；10. 人民生活；11. 农业；12. 工业；13. 建筑业；14. 运输与邮电；15. 国内贸易；16. 对外贸易与国际旅游；17. 科技；18. 教育与文化；19. 体育与卫生；20. 民政司法和其他；特载和附录。各篇末附有《主要统计指标解释》，对主要统计指标的含义、统计范围、统计方法以及历史变动情况作了简要说明。

三、本年鉴中使用的度量衡均采用国际统一标准计量单位，统计口径除特别注明外，均包括济南市区、平阴县、商河县。资料取自济南市统计局、国家统计局济南调查队及有关部门的统计报表。

四、本年鉴中部分数据合计数或相对数由于计量单位取舍不同而产生的计算误差，均未做机械调整。

五、本年鉴表中的符号使用说明：

"空格"表示该项统计指标数据不足本表最小单位数、数据不详或无该项数据；

"-"表示无此项事实；

"#"表示其中的主要项；

"*"或"①"表示本表下有注解。

《济南统计年鉴》自出版以来，受到了社会各界的关心和支持，对此我们深表感谢。同时，欢迎使用《济南统计年鉴2023》，敬请广大读者提出宝贵意见。帮助我们进一步提高统计年鉴编辑工作，更好地为社会各界服务，谢谢！（网址：http://jntj.jinan.gov.cn/）

编 者

2023年10月

EDITOR'S NOTES

Ⅰ. *Jinan Statistical Yearbook2023* is a statistical reference book published yearly that comprehensively reflects the development of Jinan's national economy and society. With a vast amount of statistical data on various aspects of economic and social development in Jinan and the counties and districts under its jurisdiction in 2022, as well as the main statistical data of important historical years, the yearbook is an important reference book for people to understand and study Jinan and its economic and social development, for government to formulate macro policies and guidance work.

Ⅱ. The yearbook is centered on rich and detailed statistical data with intuitive statistical charts and special articles added, comprehensively reflecting Jinan's economic and social development. Statistical data of the yearbook contains 22 parts, namely:1. Division of Administrative Areas;2. Population;3. General Survey;4. National Accounts;5. Labor and Employment;6. Investment in Fixed Assets;7. Urban Public Utilities and Environmental Protection;8. Government Finance、Financial and Insurance;9. Price;10. People's Livelihood;11.Agriculture;12. Industry;13. Construction;14. Transportation, Post and Telecommunications;15. Domestic Trade;16. Foreign Trade and International Tourism;17. Science and Technology;18. Education and Culture;19. Sports and Public Health;20. Social Welfare Civil Administration and Justice; Special Report and Appendix. We edit *Exploratory Notes on Main statistical Indicators* at the end of every article, briefly explaining the meaning, statistical scope, methods and historical changes of the main statistical indicators.III. The units of measurement used in this yearbook are internationally unified and standard measurement units. The statistical caliber includes Jinan City, Pingyin County and Shanghe County unless otherwise noted. The data in this yearbook are from the statistical reports of Jinan Municipal Bureau of Statistics, Jinan Investigation Team of National Bureau of Statistics and relevant departments.

Ⅳ. The statistical discrepancies caused by the unit of measurement in the total or relative numbers of some data in this yearbook are not adjusted.

Ⅴ. Notations used in this yearbook:

"Blank Space" indicates that the statistical index data is not large enough to be measured with the smallest unit in this table, or data are unknown or not available;

"-" means that there is no such fact;

"#" indicates the main item;

"*" or "①" means there are annotations in this table.

Since its publication, *Jinan Statistical Yearbook* has received the concern and support of all sectors of society, for which we are deeply grateful. At the same time, welcome to use *Jinan Statistical Yearbook2023* and offer valuable suggestions, so as to help us further improve the editing of statistical yearbooks and better serve all sectors of society, thank you! (Website: http://jntj.jinan.gov.cn/)

Editor

October 2023

目　　录

特载　Special Report

一　行政区划　Divisions of Administrative Areas

二　人　口　Population

三　综　合　General Survey

四 国民经济核算 National Accounts

五 劳动就业 Labor and Employment

六 固定资产投资 Investment in Fixed Assets

七 城市公用事业和环境保护 Urban Public Utilities and Environmental Protection

八 财政、金融和保险 Government Finance、Financial and Insurance

九 物 价 Price

十　人民生活　People's Livelihood

十一　农　业　Agriculture

十二 工 业 Industry

十三 建筑业 Construction

十四 运输与邮电 Transportation, Post and Telecommunications

十五 国内贸易 Domestic Trade

十六 对外贸易与国际旅游 Foreign Trade and International Tourism

十七　科　技　Science and Technology

十八　教育与文化　Education and Culture

十九　体育与卫生　Sports and Public Health

二十 民政、司法和其他 Social Welfare Civil Administration and Justice

附 录 Appendix

特载

SPECIAL REPORT

济南概况

济南是中国东部沿海经济文化大省-山东省的省会，全国文明城市，黄河流域中心城市，是中国的特大城市和副省级城市之一，是全省的政治、经济、科创、金融、贸易、文化、教育和交通中心，是山东半岛城市群和省会经济圈核心城市。与德州、滨州、淄博、泰安、聊城等市相邻，辖历下、市中、槐荫、天桥、历城、长清、章丘、济阳、莱芜、钢城十区和平阴、商河二县。2022年末常住人口941.5万，现有汉、回、蒙古、满、苗、壮、朝鲜等55个民族。

济南位于山东省中部，地理位置介于北纬36°02′至37°54′、东经116°21′至117°93′之间，面积10244平方公里。南依泰山，北跨黄河，地处鲁中南低山丘陵与鲁西北冲积平原的交接带上，地势南高北低。境内矿产资源丰富，包括铁、煤、花岗岩、耐火粘土、铜、钾、铂、钴等多种有色金属、稀有金属和非金属资源。

自然景色秀丽，名胜古迹众多，是中国历史文化名城之一。尤以泉水遍布、清冽甘美而闻名于世，有“济南泉水甲天下”和“泉城”之美誉。主要风景名胜有趵突泉、黑虎泉、珍珠泉、五龙潭、百脉泉五大泉群，大明湖、千佛山、灵岩寺等文化遗址。

文化底蕴厚重，是中华文明的重要发祥地之一，是齐鲁文化和儒家文化传承弘扬的重要承载地。龙山文化、泉水文化、诗词文化等特色文化融汇交织，拥有城子崖遗址、齐长城遗址等全国重点文物保护单位，是中国非物质文化遗产博览会永久落户地。

综合实力雄厚。2022年，全市地区生产总值达到12027.5亿元，比上年增长3.1%。其中，第一产业增加值420.5亿元，增长3.1%；第二产业增加值4180.2亿元，增长3.2%；第三产业增加值7426.7亿元，增长3.0%，三次产业构成比为3.5∶34.8∶61.7。一般公共预算收入1001.1亿元。年末金融机构本外币各项存款余额25941.0亿元，比上年增长10.7%；金融机构本外币各项贷款余额26112.3亿元，增长12.0%。全年社会消费品零售总额4878.1亿元，比上年下降4.8%。市场主体总量达到149.8万户，“四上”企业数量达到13055家。

区位优势突出。济南北接京津冀、南连长三角、东承环渤海经济圈、西通中原经济区，具有承东启西、衔南接北的区位优势。2022年年末，公路通车里程18294.4公里。其中，高速公路里程795.3公里，增长7.8%。公路货运量2.4亿吨，下降3.3%；货运周转量608.8亿吨公里，增长5.4%。公共交通旅客运输量4.0亿人次。济南机场全年累计完成航班起降7.9万架次，旅客吞吐量824.2万人次，货邮吞吐量13.8万吨。全年货物进出口总额2208.9亿元，比上年增长13.9%。

创新资源富集。2022年，济南拥有山东大学等驻济高校52所，全日制在校大学生67.1万人。新获批全国重点实验室5家，省级重点实验室10家，新备案省级院士工作站10家，新增省级技术创新中心7家。

产业活力较强。2022年，“四新”经济增加值达到4683.7亿元，占GDP比重提高到38.9%。现代高效农业增加值75.5亿元，比上年增长6.7%，占农林牧渔业增加值比重17.1%。全市规模以上高技术制造业实现增加值增长11.1%，领先规模以上工业平均增速9.5个百分点。现代服务业实现增加值4492.3亿元，增长3.7%，占服务业增加值比重提高到60.4%。

民生福祉增强。全年居民人均可支配收入48827元，比上年增长4.5%。其中，城镇居民人均可支配收入59459元，增长3.5%；农村居民人均可支配收入23844元，增长5.6%。年末拥有卫生机构7665个。城市居民最低生活保障标准每月995元；农村居民最低生活保障标准每月770元。

Special Report-1

Overview of Jinan

Jinan is the capital of Shandong Province, a major coastal economic and cultural province in eastern China, and listed as a national civilized city, a central city in the Yellow River Basin and is one of China's megalopolises and deputy provincial cities.It is the political, economic, technological innovation, financial, trade, cultural, educational and transportation center of the whole province, and the core city of urban agglomeration in Shandong Peninsula and provincial economic circle. It has borders with Dezhou, Binzhou, Zibo, Taian and Liaocheng, it has jurisdiction over 10 districts including Lixia, Shizhong, Huaiyin, Tianqiao, Licheng, Changqing, Zhangqiu, Jiyang, Laiwu and Gangcheng, and two counties of Pingyin and Shanghe. By the end of 2022, the city had a permanent resident population of about 9.415 million, with 55 ethnic groups including Han, Hui, Mongolia, Manchu, Miao, Zhuang and Chinese Korean, among others.

Jinan sits in the central part of Shandong province.Located between 36° 02'-37° 54' northern latitude and 116° 21'-117° 93' east of Greenwich, covering an area of 10,244 square kilometers. with Mount Tai to the south and the Yellow River to the north, Jinan is located at the junction of low hills in central and southern Shandong and alluvial plain in northwestern Shandong, and the terrain is high in the south and low in the north. Jinan is rich in mineral resources, including iron, coal, granite, refractory clay, copper, potassium, platinum, cobalt, a variety of non-ferrous metals, rare metals and non-metallic resources.

With beautiful natural scenery and numerous scenic spots and historical sites, it is one of the famous historical and cultural cities in China. Especially, it is famous all over the world for its pervading, clear and sweet springs, and has the reputation of "Jinan Spring is the finest over the world" and "Spring City". The main scenic spots are Baotu Spring, Black Tiger Spring, Pearl Spring, Five Dragons Pond and Baimai Spring, and cultural sites such as Daming Lake, Qianfo Mountain and Lingyan Temple.

Rich in cultural deposits, it is one of the important birthplaces of Chinese civilization, and an important bearing place for the inheritance and promotion of Qilu culture and Confucian culture. Longshan culture, spring culture, poetry culture and other characteristic cultures are intertwined. It has national key cultural relics protection units such as Chengziya Site and Great Wall of Qi remains, and is the permanent settlement of China Intangible Cultural Heritage Expo.

Great comprehensive strength. In 2022, the GDP of the whole city reached 1,202.75 billion yuan, up by 3.1% over the previous year. Therein, the added value of the primary industry amounted to 42.05 billion yuan, up by 3.1%; the added value of the secondary industry amounted to 418.02 billion yuan, up by 3.2%; the added value of the tertiary industry amounted to 742.67 billion yuan, up by 3.0%. The composition ratio of the three industries is 3.5 : 34.8 : 61.7. The general public budget revenue amounted to 100.11 billion yuan. At the end of the year, the balance of the deposits of financial institutions in local currency and foreign currency amounted to 2,594.10 billion yuan, up by 10.7% over the previous year; the balance of various deposits of financial institutions in local currency and foreign currency amounted to 2,611.23 billion yuan, up by 12.0%. The gross amount of retail sales of consumer goods in the whole year was 487.81 billion yuan, down by 4.8% over the previous year. There were totally 1.498 million market entities, and the number of "four-upper" enterprises reached 13,055.

Outstanding location advantages. Jinan is bordered by Beijing-Tianjin-Hebei Region in the north, the Yangtze River Delta in the south, the Bohai Economic Circle in the east and the Central Plains Economic Zone in the west. It has the geographical advantages of connecting the east with the west and linking the south with the north. By the end of 2022, the mileage of highways was 18,294.4 kilometers, of which the mileage of expressways was 795.3 kilometers, up by 7.8%. The freight volume of highways was 240 million tons, down by 3.3%; the freight turnover was 60.88 billion ton-kilometers, up by 5.4%. The number of public transport passengers was 400 million. Jinan Airport completed a total of 79,000 takeoffs and landings; the passenger throughput was 8.242 million; the postal throughput was 138,000 tons. The gross export-import volume of goods in 2022 was 220.89 billion yuan, up by 13.9% over the previous year.

Extensive and concentrated innovative resources. In 2022, there were 52 universities in Jinan, including Shandong University, with 671,000 full-time college students. There were 5 national key laboratories newly approved, 10 provincial key laboratories, 10 provincial academician workstations newly filed and 7 provincial technology innovation centers newly added.

Strong industry vitality. In 2022, the added value of the "four new" economy was up to 468.37 billion yuan, accounting for 38.9% of GDP. The added value of modern efficient agriculture was RMB 7.55 billion, up by 6.7% over the previous year, accounting for 17.1% of the added value of agriculture, forestry, animal husbandry and fishery. The added value of high-tech manufacturing industries above designated size in the whole city increased by 11.1%, which was 9.5 percentage points higher than the average growth rate of industries above designated size. The added value of modern service industry was up to 449.23 billion yuan, up by 3.7%, and the proportion of the added value of the service industry increased to 60.4%.

People's livelihood and well-being have been enhanced. The per capita disposable income of residents in 2022 was 48,827 yuan, up by 8.5% over the previous year. Therein, the per capita disposable income of urban residents was 59,459 yuan, up by 3.5%; the per capita disposable income of rural residents is 23,844 yuan, up by 5.6%. At the end of the year, there were 7,665 health institutions. The minimum living security standard for urban residents was 995 yuan per month; the minimum living security standard for rural residents was 770 yuan per month.

2022年济南市国民经济和社会发展统计公报[1]

济 南 市 统 计 局
国家统计局济南调查队

2022年，面对复杂严峻的国内外形势和多重超预期因素冲击，市委、市政府团结带领全市上下坚持以习近平新时代中国特色社会主义思想为指导，深入学习宣传贯彻党的二十大精神，坚决落实习近平总书记对山东、对济南工作的重要指示要求，完整、准确、全面贯彻新发展理念，主动服务和融入新发展格局，着力推动高质量发展，落实省委、省政府各项决策部署，锚定“勇当排头兵、建设强省会”，高效统筹疫情防控和经济社会发展，高效统筹发展和安全，全市经济总体呈现承压回升、逐步向好态势，综合实力再上新台阶，动能转换取得新突破，重大国家战略加快落地见效，居民生活持续改善提升，新时代中国特色社会主义现代化强省会建设迈出坚实步伐。

一、综合

经济总量迈上新台阶。根据市级生产总值统一核算结果，2022年全市地区生产总值[2]为12027.5亿元，按不变价格计算，增长[3]3.1%，其中，第一产业增加值为420.5亿元，增长3.1%；第二产业增加值为4180.2亿元，增长3.2%；第三产业增加值为7426.7亿元，增长3.0%。三次产业构成比为3.5∶34.8∶61.7。

图1　2012-2022年地区生产总值

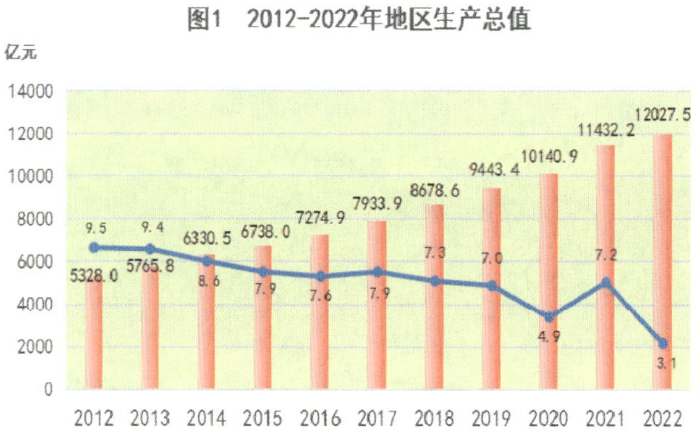

图2　2012年和2022年三次产业比重

人口集聚效应持续显现。年末常住人口941.5万人，比上年末增长0.8%，其中，城镇常住人口699.8万人，占总人口比重（常住人口城镇化率）为74.3%，比上年末提高0.1个百分点。户籍人口819.95万人，增长0.4%。全年申报出生率为7.9‰，申报死亡率为9.7‰，人口自然增长率为-1.9‰。全年人才流入32.6万人，净流入15.8万人。

就业形势保持总体稳定。市场主体增至149.8万户，“四上”[4]单位总数13055家，净增1060家。全年新增城镇就业17.4万人，发放各类稳岗补贴6亿元。实施离校未就业高校毕业生攻坚行动，举办2022年黄河流域优秀大学生创业就业“泉城行”活动，建强创业孵化平台，累计带动就业超过10万人。

居民消费价格涨势平稳。全年居民消费价格指数(CPI)上涨1.4%，比上年回落0.1个百分点。从居民消费的八大类商品及服务项目价格构成看，呈“七涨一降”态势，其中，除居住价格小幅下降0.2%外，交通通信、食品烟酒、生活用品及服务、衣着、其他用品及服务、教育文化娱乐、医疗保健价格分别上涨4.3%、2.3%、1.6%、1.0%、0.7%、0.6%、0.4%。新建商品住宅销售价格同比指数较去年同期涨幅收窄，环比指数小幅波动。

表1　2022年居民消费价格比上年涨跌幅度

指　　标	比上年增长（%）
居民消费价格指数	1.4
食品烟酒	2.3
衣着	1.0
居住	-0.2

指　　标	比上年增长（%）
生活用品及服务	1.6
交通通信	4.3
教育文化娱乐	0.6
医疗保健	0.4
其他用品及服务	0.7

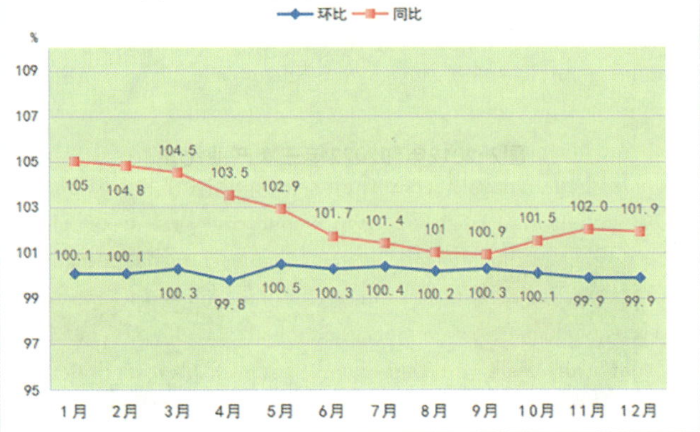

图3　2022年新建商品住宅销售价格指数

重大国家战略加快落地见效。深入落实黄河流域生态保护和高质量发展战略，黄河下游“十四五”防洪工程（济南段）开工建设，黄河防洪工程绿化提升和黄河百里风景区中心景区景观提升工程顺利完工，入选国家再生水利用配置试点城市。济南新旧动能转换起步区加速起势，发展规划获批实施，“1+4+16+N”规划体系逐步完善，创新推出产业正面清单、产业机会清单、重点产业示图、产业准入机制等“四张清单”，黄河大道一期（青银高速以南段）建成通车，山大二院起步区新院、黄河体育中心等公共服务项目加快推进，中科新经济科创园、国际招商产业园等高端平台加快布局，零碳智慧创新运营中心项目荣获“全球人居环境规划设计奖”，比亚迪新能源乘用车项目整车下线，累计签约136个高端优质项目。科创金融改革试验区建设全面推进，设立科技分（支）行等科创金融专营（特色）银行机构20家、科创金融事业部（中心）12个，全市科创板上市企业达到6家，齐鲁科学城科创投资母基金成立，省内首单科创票据、首单科技园区CMBS、首单知识产权融资租赁业务、首单“数字经济”主题公司债券成功落地，本外币合一银行结算账户体系试点、数字人民币试点相继获批。数字济南建设全面铺开，构建起“1+4+N”总体框架体系，统筹数字机关、数字政府、数字经济、数字社会一体推进，入选全国首批数字化绿色化协同转型发展综合试点城市。

新旧动能转换提档升级。创新驱动、智能制造、数字赋能成为加快转型、提升竞争力的核心要素。“四新”经济增加值达到4683.7亿元，占GDP比重为38.9%，占比提高1.2个百分点。“四新”经济投资增长16.8%，增速高于全市13.0个百分点，占全市投资比重为40.1%，占比提高4.5个百分点。全市规模以上高技术制造业实现增加值增长11.1%，领先规模以上工业平均增速9.5个百分点。现代服务业[5]实现增加值4492.3亿元，增长3.7%，领先全部服务业增速0.7个百分点，占服务业增加值比重为60.4%。

二、农业、农村

农林牧渔业总产值稳步增长。全年农林牧渔业总产值784.2亿元，按不变价格计算，增长4.5%，其中，农业总产值526.0亿元，增长4.7%；畜牧业总产值170.2亿元，增长2.7%。农林牧渔业增加值441.6亿元，增长3.6%。

表2　2022年农林牧渔业总产值

指　　标	单位	产值	比上年增长（%）
农林牧渔业总产值	亿元	784.2	4.5
农业	亿元	526.0	4.7
林业	亿元	32.0	0.4
畜牧业	亿元	170.2	2.7
渔业	亿元	8.5	6.0
农林牧渔服务业	亿元	47.5	10.9

农业生产稳中有升。粮食产量再创历史新高，全年粮食播种面积726.9万亩，增长0.2%；粮食总产量296.2万吨，增长1.1%。全年蔬菜总产量712.6万吨，增长3.0%；油料总产量6.6万吨，增长0.4%；水果总产量62.0万吨，增长0.2%。

林业生产保持平稳发展。全年完成造林面积773.3公顷，森林抚育面积5333.3公顷，打造市绿化示范村100个；高质量实施黄河生态保护与修复工程3197亩；大力培育特色优势林业产业，加强经济林新品种引进，改造低产低效园686.7公顷。

畜牧业生产整体向好。全年生猪出栏209.6万头，增长9.2%；牛出栏11.1万头，下降19.4%；羊出栏136.2万头，增长7.4%。全年猪牛羊禽肉总产量29.1万吨，其中猪肉产量16.9万吨，增长9.5%。全年蛋产量27.0万吨，下降11.5%；奶产量43.4万吨，增长3.2%。全年水产品产量1.5万吨，增长5.1%。

表3　2022年主要农产品生产情况

指　　标	单位	面积/产量	比上年增长（%）
粮食总播种面积	万亩	726.9	0.2
棉花种植面积	万亩	4.4	-8.9
油料种植面积	万亩	26.4	0.3
蔬菜种植面积	万亩	149	2.0
实有果园面积	万亩	57.4	-0.3
粮食总产量	万吨	296.2	1.1

指　　标	单位	面积/产量	比上年增长(%)
棉花产量	万吨	0.4	-8.1
油料产量	万吨	6.6	0.4
蔬菜产量	万吨	712.6	3.0
水果产量	万吨	62.0	0.2
生猪出栏	万头	209.6	9.2
牛出栏	万头	11.1	-19.4
羊出栏	万头	136.2	7.4
猪肉产量	万吨	16.9	9.5
牛肉产量	万吨	2.4	-15.6
羊肉产量	万吨	1.9	3.6
禽肉产量	万吨	7.8	9.5
禽蛋产量	万吨	27.0	-11.5
牛奶产量	万吨	43.4	3.2
水产品产量	万吨	1.5	5.1

现代农业质效提升。全年现代高效农业增加值75.5亿元，增长6.7%，占农林牧渔业增加值比重为17.1%，提高0.6个百分点。全年新建“菜篮子”保供园区32个，生猪规模化养殖场达到351家。新建高标准农田27.5万亩，同步发展节水灌溉面积6万亩，水肥一体化推广面积达73.5万亩。省级以上农业知名品牌达到57个，全市“三品一标”农产品有效用标总量达到1699个。特色农产品发展势头良好，章丘大葱、莱芜生姜入选农业农村部农业精品品牌培育计划。长清茶叶、仁风西瓜、曲堤黄瓜、历城草莓等特色农产品不断发展壮大，全年茶叶产量31.3万公斤，大葱71.5万吨，生姜32.3万吨，西瓜29.9万吨，黄瓜120万吨，草莓9.9万吨。聚力种业大发展，全力打造“中国北方种业之都”，全市持证农作物良种企业数量达到73家。

乡村振兴成效明显。全面完成39个省级示范村和129个乡村振兴齐鲁样板村创建任务，创建3个省级乡村振兴示范区。共建成市级田园综合体6个，新认定市级以上示范性新型农业经营主体171家，市级以上农业龙头企业发展到506家，家庭农场、农民合作社分别达到8063家和11796家。健全完善防返贫监测预警机制，共纳入防返贫动态监测对象597户、1594人，全部进行了针对性帮扶。将3.1万脱贫群众纳入全市农村低保和农村特困人员供养范围，全市987个脱贫村全部实现“五通十有”[6]。

三、工业和建筑业

工业加快转型升级。全年全部工业增加值2869.0亿元，增长2.4%。规模以上工业[7]增加值增长1.6%，分经济类型看，公有制经济下降1.4%，非公有制经济增长4.1%；分轻重工业看，轻工业增长7.7%，重工业下降0.1%。41个大类行业中，24个行业实现增加值增长，增长面为58.5%；六大重点行业中，通用设备制造业增长15.4%，石油煤炭加工业增长14.2%，医药制造业增长12.4%，计算机通信设备制造业增长3.1%，黑金属压延加工业、汽车制造业分别下降10.9%、46.7%。

工业企业质效逐步恢复。全年规模以上工业企业完成营业收入8139.9亿元，下降4.1%，年内降幅震荡收窄；利润总额332.5亿元，下降14.8%；营业收入利润率4.1%。41个大类行业中，营业收入超百亿的行业达到16个，合计占规模以上工业企业营业收入的比重为91.6%。黑色金属冶炼和压延加工业营业收入超过千亿规模。

表4　2022年规模以上工业重点行业营业收入增长速度

行业名称	比上年增长（%）
黑色金属冶炼和压延加工业	-13.5
计算机、通信和其他电子设备制造业	11.3
汽车制造业	-44.6
非金属矿物制品业	7.3
电气机械和器材制造业	14.3
石油、煤炭及其他燃料加工业	31.3
医药制造业	10.6
通用设备制造业	2.2
化学原料和化学制品制造业	5.6
金属制品业	-2.6
专用设备制造业	9.2
电力、热力生产和供应业	20.2
农副食品加工业	10.3
黑色金属矿采选业	-10.3
食品制造业	4.4
燃气生产和供应业	26.9

工业产品稳定供应。全年规模以上工业产品产销率97.6%。所生产的306种工业产品中，有123种产品产量实现增长，增长面40.2%，其中，增幅超过20%的产品有59种，占比19.3%。轿车、新能源汽车产量分别达到上年同期的5.1倍、3.8倍，充电桩增长65.3%；卫生防疫用品加速供应，医用口罩7.7亿只，增长47.4%；高附加值产品中，逻辑芯片、锂离子电池产量达到上年同期的5.4、12.9倍，工业机器人增长32.3%。

表5　2022年规模以上工业企业主要产品产量及增长速度

产品名称	单位	产量	增长（%）
鲜、冷藏肉	万吨	16.5	42.3
乳制品	万吨	50.5	-5.9
饮料酒	万千升	26.3	-0.5
合成氨（无水氨）	万吨	20.7	-54.0
聚丙烯树脂	万吨	12.1	15.0
初级形态塑料	万吨	78.0	2.7

产品名称	单位	产量	增长（%）
中成药	吨	7903.6	8.3
水泥	万吨	1354.5	-12.2
石墨及碳素制品	万吨	209.1	12.1
钢材	万吨	2021.4	-4.2
锻件	万吨	128.3	6.3
粉末冶金零件	万吨	1.3	-2.9
发动机	万千瓦	1772.9	-56.6
数控金属切削机床	台	4235	-27.5
气动元件	万件	783.3	-22.4
矿山专用设备	万吨	4.2	3.1
工业机器人	套	3746	32.3
载货汽车	万辆	16.0	-49.9
铁路货车	辆	3765	20.7
变压器	万千伏安	15872.3	3.7
太阳能电池（光伏电池）	万千瓦	4.0	-28.5
电子计算机整机	万台	77.5	-32.6
服务器	万台	77.1	-32.2
集成电路	万块	28964.0	70.7

建筑业实现较快增长。全市具有总承包和专业承包资质的有工作量的建筑业企业1371家，增加189家。全年签订合同额13217.8亿元，增长16.7%，其中，新签合同额6500.9亿元，增长1.8%。实现建筑业总产值4460.8亿元，增长8.1%，其中，国有及国有控股企业产值3430亿元，增长10.5%。房屋施工面积19970.9万平方米，增长2.9%。

四、服务业

新兴服务业引领发展。全年服务业增加值7426.7亿元，增长3.0%。规模以上服务业[8]营业收入增长4.2%，其中，互联网和相关服务、软件和信息技术服务业、专业技术服务业分别增长32.1%、18.2%、15.5%，成为拉动服务业增长的主要力量。新增国家5A级物流企业2家，总数达19家，装卸搬运和仓储业、多式联运和运输代理业营业收入分别增长73.1%、16.8%。

表6　2022年规模以上服务业分门类营业收入情况

门　类	1-12月累计营业收入（亿元）	增速（%）
总计	3631.2	4.2
交通运输、仓储和邮政业	1500.3	-1.8
信息传输、软件和信息技术服务业	786.8	17.2
房地产业（不包含房地产开发经营）	163.4	-0.8
租赁和商务服务业	436.1	11.4
科学研究和技术服务业	508.6	13.2
水利、环境和公共设施管理业	64.2	-4.7
居民服务、修理和其他服务业	24.1	-8.4
教育	24.7	-27.5
卫生和社会工作	50.9	2.4
文化、体育和娱乐业	72.2	-7.7

交通运输业承压企稳。年末公路通车里程数18294.4公里，其中，高速公路里程数795.3公里，增长7.8%。公路货运量2.4亿吨，下降3.3%；货运周转量608.8亿吨公里，增长5.4%。全年累计完成航班起降7.9万架次，下降30.1%；旅客吞吐量824.2万人次，下降39.5%；货邮吞吐量13.8万吨，下降18.1%。年末拥有民用机动车369.2万辆，其中，民用汽车320.3万辆，增长5.9%。公交线路756条，线路总长度15623.2公里，旅客运输量4.0亿人次。轨道交通运营线路3条，长度84.1公里，年客运量5456万人次。

邮政业、电信业平稳运行。邮政行业全年业务收入（不包括邮政储蓄银行直接营业收入）105.4亿元，增长6.2%；业务总量93.3亿元，增长4.4%。快递业务收入82.1亿元，增长5.9%；业务量7.7亿件，下降3.4%。年末移动电话用户1266.0万户，增长4.0%，其中，5G移动电话用户685.2万户，增长47.9%。互联网宽带接入用户501.4万户，增长8.3%。

旅游业、会展业稳步复苏。全年接待国内游客6565.6万人次，恢复到上年同期的80.2%。实现国内旅游收入711.6亿元，恢复到上年同期的72.3%。A级旅游景区85家，其中，5A级旅游景区1家，4A级旅游景区18家。省级旅游度假区2家。推出“泉城夜八点”活动，点亮文旅“夜经济”，获评1个国家级、3个省级夜间文旅消费集聚区。全年举办展会76场，展览面积140万平方米。

五、固定资产投资

投资规模持续扩大。全年固定资产投资增长3.8%，其中，第一产业投资下降2.8%；第二产业投资增长15.1%；第三产业投资增长1.9%。年末亿元以上固定资产投资项目1653个，增加118个，完成投资增长12.4%，其中，五十亿元以上项目43个，完成投资增长13.2%。民间投资占全市投资比重为44.5%。基础设施投资增长17.0%。社会领域投资增长26.5%，高于全市投资增速22.7个百分点。

表7　2022年三次产业投资增速及占比

产业	增长（%）	占固定资产投资比重（%）
固定资产投资	3.8	100.0
第一产业	-2.8	0.4
第二产业	15.1	15.5
第三产业	1.9	84.1

房地产市场低位运行。全年房地产开发完成投资1830.8亿元，下降5.0%，其中，住宅完成投资1247.6亿元，下降7.7%。房屋施工面积8604.9万平方米，下降15.3%，其中，住宅施工面积5338.5万平方米，下降18.8%。房屋竣工面积715万平方米，下降35.9%，其中，住宅竣工面积488.0万平方米，下降38.0%。商品房销售面积1241.9万平方米，下降19.8%，其中，住宅销售面积907.1万平方米，下降30.2%。商品房销售额1514.6亿元，下降22.6%，其中，住宅销售额1221.7亿元，下降29.0%。

六、国内贸易

消费品市场受疫情扰动明显。全年社会消费品零售总额4878.1亿元，下降4.8%，其中，商品零售4194.1亿元，下降4.5%；餐饮收入684.0亿元，下降7.0%。分城乡看，城镇社会消费品零售额4312.2亿元，下降4.9%；乡村社会消费品零售额565.9亿元，下降4.0%。

必需类商品需求稳定。限额以上单位商品零售额中，粮油食品类商品实现零售额182.5亿元，增长8.1%；饮料类商品实现零售额17.7亿元，增长18.1%；烟酒类商品实现零售额43.3亿元，增长2.4%；中西药品类商品实现零售额74.1亿元，增长12.6%。

线上消费蓬勃发展。限额以上批发和零售业单位通过公共网络实现的商品零售额315.8亿元，增长17.4%，占全市限额以上单位零售额的比重为18.1%，占比提高3.1个百分点。

新能源汽车增势较好。限额以上单位新能源汽车实现零售额104.1亿元，增长87.5%，占全市限额以上单位零售额的比重为6.0%，占比提高3.3个百分点。

表8　2022年限额以上批发和零售业单位主要商品零售额及增长速度

商品类别	零售额（亿元）	增长(%)
粮油、食品类	182.5	8.1
饮料类	17.7	18.1
烟酒类	43.3	2.4
服装、鞋帽、针纺织品类	96.5	-19.1
化妆品类	64.1	33.8
金银珠宝类	43.3	-13.2
日用品类	34.2	-38.4
家用电器和音像器材类	117.2	-9.6
中西药品类	74.1	12.6
文化办公用品类	44.2	-17.5
通讯器材类	53.9	-37.2
石油及制品类	174.6	-7.3
汽车类	576.5	-1.2

七、对外经济

进出口保持较快增长。全年货物进出口总额2208.9亿元，增长13.9%，其中，出口1431.8亿元，增长22.0%；进口777.1亿元，增长1.5%。对东盟进出口增长45.9%，对欧盟（不含英国）进出口下降2.6%，对拉丁美洲进出口增长13.1%。对“一带一路”沿线国家和地区进出口增长30.8%，占进出口总额的39.3%。出口商品中，机电产品出口851.6亿元，增长28.8%；农产品出口64.8亿元，增长1.1%。进口商品中，机电产品进口400.9亿元，增长3.3%；农产品进口102.9亿元，增长32.0%。全年经济外向度18.4%，提高1.4个百分点。

利用外资规模显著提升。全市实际使用外资31.4亿美元，增长18.0%，其中，制造业使用外资6.6亿美元，增长148.3%；第三产业使用外资21.9亿美元，增长4.9%。全年实现合同外资78.4亿美元。新批准外商投资项目251个，总投资过亿美元项目22个，总投资过亿美元项目合同外资24.7亿美元。

对外合作领域不断深化。全年对外承包工程新签合同额48.9亿美元，完成营业额40.9亿美元。备案设立境外企业（机构）45家，实际完成投资117.7亿元。派出各类劳务人员4489人。

八、财政和金融

财政收支基本平衡。全年一般公共预算收入1001.1亿元，可比增长8.1%，自然口径下降0.6%，其中，税收收入693.2亿元，可比增长1.0%，自然口径下降10.7%，税收比重为69.2%。一般公共预算支出1225.6亿元，下降5.2%，其中，教育支出251.8亿元，增长18.3%；卫生健康支出134.8亿元，增长20.8%；交通运输支出28.4亿元，增长16.8%，重点事务保障有力。

表9　2022年一般公共预算收入和支出情况

指　标	总量（亿元）	增速（%）
一般公共预算收入	1001.1	-0.6
税收收入	693.2	-10.7
增值税	198.8	-25.8
企业所得税	115.4	-12.6
一般公共预算支出	1225.6	-5.2
教育支出	251.8	18.3
卫生健康支出	134.8	20.8
交通运输支出	28.4	16.8

存贷款余额增量再创新高。年末金融机构本外币各项存款余额25941.0亿元，增长10.7%，较年初增加2504.0亿元；金融机构本外币各项贷款余额26112.3亿元，增长12.0%，较年初增加2799.0亿元。

证券市场稳步发展。年末上市公司数量达到56家，股票58只，全年新增上市及过会企业8家。完成证券交易额5.8万亿元，增长3.1%。在中国证券投资基金业协会登记的私募基金管理机构208家，管理基金711只，管理基金规模1168.4亿元，增长9.7%。

保险业企稳向好。全市保险业实现保费收入631.9亿元，增长6.2%，提高3.8个百分点，其中，财产险保费收入126.8亿元，增长16.1%；人身险保费收入505.2亿元，增长3.9%。

信贷资产质量平稳可控。全市银行业金融机构不良贷款余额234.1亿元，不良贷款率0.9%，低于全省平均水平0.4个百分点。

九、科技、教育、文化、卫生和体育事业

研发投入持续增长。全年研究与试验发展（R&D）经费[9]投入306.7亿元，增长15.5%，其中，基础研究26.8亿元，增长44.9%；试验发展241.3亿元，增长17.4%。R&D经费投入占GDP比重为2.7%，提高0.1个百分点。新认定国家级企业技术中心1家，总数达到30家。新认定省级企业技术中心16家，总数达到236家。

创新能力不断增强。全年万人有效发明专利拥有量48.9件，增长27.5%。发明专利授权量11853件，增长44.4%。技术合同实现交易额613.6亿元，增长29.6%。获得省科学进步奖共90项，其中，自然科学奖二等奖16项，技术发明奖一等奖3项、二等奖4项，科技进步奖一等奖17项、二等奖44项、青年奖5项、国际合作奖1项。全市国家知识产权示范企业、优势企业共计107家。新获批全国重点实验室5家，省级重点实验室10家，新备案省级院士工作站10家，新增省级技术创新中心7家。新备案省级新型研发机构14家，总数达71家；国家科技型中小企业库入库企业达到7613家，增长31%。申报省重大科技创新工程项目立项23项，争取省级财政经费2.4亿元。实施科技型中小企业创新能力提升工程，争取省级项目335项。

教育事业高质量发展。全市普惠性幼儿园覆盖率超过89.0%，公办幼儿园就读幼儿占比超过55.0%。完工中小学校30所，新建学位5万余个。开工新建、改扩建中小学校、幼儿园83所。11所学校斩获全国职业院校技能大赛25个奖项。立项实施市校合作项目95个，支持高校新建产业学院8个。

表10 2022年教育事业基本情况

学校类别	学校数量（所）	在校生（万人）	专任教师（万人）
驻济高等学校	52	67.1	4.2
中等职业学校（不含技工学校）	37	6.5	0.4
技工学校	32	8.5	0.5
普通中学	334	42.1	3.6
小学	608	64.4	4
特殊教育学校	13	0.1	0.1
幼儿园	2190	36.3	2.7

文化事业稳步推进。年末拥有国有艺术表演团体14个，文化馆（站）174个，公共图书馆14个，公共博物馆13个。市级以上文物保护单位437处，其中，国家级30处。城市可统计票房数字影院69家，观众637.6万人次，票房收入2.7亿元。电视人口混合覆盖率为100%，广播人口混合覆盖率为99.7%。建成泉城书房42处，基层综合性文化服务中心覆盖率为100%。

医疗卫生服务能力持续提升。年末共有医疗卫生机构7670个。其中医院283个，在医院中有公立医院99个，民营医院184个；基层医疗卫生机构7293个，其中，镇卫生院49个，社区卫生服务中心（站）399个，门诊部184个，诊所（卫生所、医务室）3073个，村卫生室3588个；专业公共卫生机构54个，其中，疾病预防控制中心14个，卫生监督所（中心）14个。年末卫生技术人员11.4万人，其中，执业医师和执业助理医师4.4万人，注册护士5.2万人。医疗卫生机构床位7.6万张，其中，医院6.6万张，镇卫生院0.4万张。全年总诊疗人次7136.9万人次，出院人数225.9万人。建成社区医院58家，千人口育儿托位数4.15个。中国中医科学院广安门医院济南医院入选国家区域医疗中心项目。济南市入选首批全国婴幼儿照护示范城市和首批健康中国行动创新模式试点城市。

群众体育基础进一步夯实。全年新成立体育社会组织10个，培训社会体育指导员2250人。组织各类全民健身活动（赛事）360次，参与人数300万人次（含线上活动）。获省级及以上金牌287枚，银牌213枚，铜牌217枚。

十、能源、环境、城市建设和安全生产

能源结构不断优化。规模以上工业综合能源消费量下降3.1%，其中，规模以上工业煤炭消费2847.8万吨，增长1.7%；焦炭消费812.7万吨，下降9.4%；天然气消费10.1亿立方

米，增长9.8%。规模以上企业风力发电量21.9亿千瓦时，太阳能发电量3.0亿千瓦时，垃圾焚烧发电量9.5亿千瓦时，生物质发电量6.6亿千瓦时，以上合计发电量占规模以上企业发电量的比重为12.9%，增加0.5个百分点，新能源发电稳步提升。

表11　2022年规模以上企业能源生产情况

指标	单位	生产量	增长（%）
原煤	万吨	48.9	-33.0
发电量	亿千瓦时	318.2	0.8
火力发电量	亿千瓦时	293.3	0.8
垃圾焚烧发电量	亿千瓦时	9.5	0.0
生物质发电量	亿千瓦时	6.6	26.6
风力发电量	亿千瓦时	21.9	-0.1
太阳能发电量	亿千瓦时	3.0	11.9

表12 2022年规模以上工业能源消费情况

指标	累计	增长（%）
煤炭（万吨）	2847.8	1.7
天然气消费量（亿立方米）	10.1	9.8
焦炭（万吨）	812.7	-9.4
汽油（万吨）	0.4	-10.2
柴油（万吨）	3.6	-7.5

全社会用电量稳步增长。全社会用电量499.7亿千瓦时，增长5.1%，其中，居民生活用电量97.6亿千瓦时，增长12.8%。分产业看，第一产业用电量3.5亿千瓦时，增长5.3%；第二产业用电量273.8亿千瓦时，增长2.6%；第三产业用电量124.7亿千瓦时，增长5.4%。工业用电量263.0亿千瓦时，占全社会用电量比重为52.6%，增长2.5%。

表13　2022年全市用电情况

指　标	用电量（亿千瓦时）	增长（%）
全社会用电	499.7	5.1
城乡居民生活用电	97.6	12.8
第一产业用电	3.5	5.3
第二产业用电	273.8	2.6
工业用电	263.0	2.5
第三产业用电	124.7	5.4

生态环境持续改善。空气质量综合指数为4.47，改善4.9%；优良天数比率为65.5%，提高2.8个百分点；细颗粒物（$PM_{2.5}$）浓度为37微克/立方米，改善7.5%；可吸入颗粒物（PM_{10}）年均浓度71微克/立方米，二氧化硫11微克/立方米，二氧化氮31微克/立方米。国控断面好三类水体比例达到100%；小清河出境断面辛丰庄化学需氧量浓度12.8毫克/升，氨氮浓度0.3毫克/升，年均水质首次达到地表水二类标准。区域环境噪声昼间平均等效声级55.0分贝，市区道路交通噪声昼间平均等效声级65.5分贝。

城市建设加快推进。年末城市建成区面积853.9平方公里，增加12.7平方公里。建成区绿地率为37.5%，人均公园绿地面积12.95平方米。全年天然气供气量19.8亿立方米，增长9.9%；液化石油气供气量3.8万吨，增长52.9%。集中供热面积3.3亿平方米，增长9.0%。自来水供水量5.1亿吨，增长1.9%。当年开工建设泉水直饮工程30处，累计完成市民泉水直饮工程56处。生活垃圾无害化处理率为100%。

社会治安保持良好。全年共破获刑事案件19151起，命案现案破案率保持100%，连续12年实现命案全破；八类严重暴力案件破现案率达98.6%，“两盗”案件破案率达75.6%，抓获各类逃犯1693人；打掉黑社会性质组织1个、恶势力犯罪集团7个、恶势力团伙8个。

安全生产形势稳定。全市发生各类生产安全事故134起，下降49.2%，死亡104人，下降35.4%。未发生较大及以上生产安全事故。

十一、居民生活和社会保障

居民收入稳步增长。全市居民人均可支配收入48827元，增长4.5%，分城乡看，城镇居民人均可支配收入59459元，增长3.5%；农村居民人均可支配收入23844元，增长5.6%。农村居民收入增速比城镇居民收入增速快2.1个百分点。城乡居民人均可支配收入比值为2.49，下降0.05。城镇居民恩格尔系数[10]为23.8%，农村居民恩格尔系数为30.5%。

表14 2022年城镇、农村居民人均可支配收入及增长速度

指　标	城镇居民		农村居民	
	2022年（元）	增长（%）	2022年（元）	增长（%）
可支配收入	59459	3.5	23844	5.6
工资性收入	34694	3.4	13138	5.8
经营净收入	3249	3.3	8746	5.5
财产净收入	10078	3.6	506	4.8
转移净收入	11437	3.7	1455	5.2

表15 2022年末每百户居民家庭主要耐用消费品拥有量[11]

指　标	单位	城镇居民	农村居民
家用汽车	辆	66	46
电冰箱(柜)	台	101	97
洗衣机	台	99	93
热水器	台	100	90
空调	台	175	97
彩色电视机	台	103	102

指　　标	单位	城镇居民	农村居民
照相机	台	27	6
计算机	台	79	42
移动电话	部	239	236

社会保障体系更加完善。年末城镇职工基本养老保险参保人数488.6万人，增加15.9万人；职工医疗保险参保人数352.8万人，增加16.6万人；失业保险参保人数235.4万人，增加8.5万人；工伤保险参保人数307.4万人，增加13.9万人；生育保险参保人数245.6万人，增加9.9万人。居民养老保险和医疗保险参保人数分别达到314.9万人和501.9万人。

最低生活保障稳步提升。城市居民最低生活保障标准为995元/月，保障城镇居民0.8万户、1.1万人，发放保障金及各类补贴1.3亿元；农村居民最低生活保障标准为770元/月，保障农村居民5.9万户、8.3万人，发放保障金及各类补贴6.6亿元。城市特困人员基本生活标准为1492元/月，农村特困人员基本生活标准为1356元/月。照料护理标准按照自理、半自理和完全不能自理分别为255元/月、424元/月、847元/月，城市特困保障860人，农村特困保障1.4万人，共发放特困供养救助金及补贴3.4亿元。

救助帮扶有序推进。全市共有社会救助综合服务机构13处，其中救助管理站1处，未成年人救助保护中心1处。培训残疾人3770人次，安置残疾人员就业2770人，帮扶救助残疾人投入资金2.7亿元。

注释：

[1] 2022年统计数据为统计快报数或初步核算数，正式数据以出版的《济南统计年鉴2023》为准。部分数据因四舍五入影响，存在总计与分项合计不等情况。

[2]全市地区生产总值、各产业增加值绝对数按现价计算，增长速度按不变价格计算，当年数据为初步核算数。根据年度核算，对国内生产总值、各产业增加值等相关指标的历史数据进行了修订。

[3]本公报中的增长，如无特殊表述，均为本期数据较上年同期数据的增长率。

[4]“四上”企业指规模以上工业、有资质的建筑业、限额以上批发和零售业、限额以上住宿和餐饮业、房地产开发经营业、规模以上服务业。

[5]现代服务业包括：信息传输、软件和信息技术服务业，金融业，房地产业，租赁和商务服务业，科学研究和技术服务业，水利、环境和公共设施管理业，居民服务、修理和其他服务业，教育，卫生和社会工作，文化、体育和娱乐业。

[6]省扶贫工作重点村“五通十有”是指通路、通电、通水、通广播电视、通信息，有旱涝保收田、有致富项目、有办公用房、有卫生室服务、有农村垃圾处理、有学前教育、有文化活动室、有健身场所、有良好的生态环境、有就业保障措施。

[7]规模以上工业企业指年主营业务收入2000万元及以上的工业法人单位。

[8]规模以上服务业包括：交通运输、仓储和邮政业，信息传输、软件和信息技术服务业，房地产业，租赁和商务服务业，科学研究和技术服务业，水利、环境和公共设施管理业，居民服务、修理和其他服务业，教育，卫生和社会工作，文化、体育和娱乐业。

[9]研究与试验发展（R&D）经费投入相关指标错年使用2021年数据。

[10]恩格尔系数是指食品支出在消费支出中的比重。

[11]数据来自于住户收支与生活状况调查。

资料来源：本公报中黄河流域生态保护和高质量发展战略、企业技术中心数据来自发展改革部门；教育数据来自教育部门；科技数据来自科技部门；电信相关数据来自工业和信息化部门；户籍、社会治安、民用机动车数据来自公安部门；城乡最低生活保障、特困人员救助供养相关数据来自民政部门；财政数据来自财政部门；城镇新增就业、城镇职工保险参保数据来自人力资源和社会保障部门；环境保护相关数据来自生态环境部门；城市建设相关数据来自住房和城乡建设部门；交通运输数据来自交通运输部门；泉水直饮工程建设数据来自城乡水务部门；水产品产量、农业数据来自农业农村部门；林业数据来自园林和林业部门；进出口、展会、新设境外企业、外派劳务人员数据来自商务部门；旅游、文化数据来自文化和旅游部门；卫生数据来自卫生健康部门；安全生产数据来自应急管理部门；知识产权数据来自市场监管部门；体育数据来自体育部门；医疗保险类数据来自医疗保障部门；金融数据来自地方金融监督管理部门；招商引资、外资数据来自投资促进部门；市场主体数据来自行政审批服务部门；物流数据来自口岸物流部门；残疾人保障数据来自残联；邮政、快递数据来自邮政管理部门；居民收入与支出数据、恩格尔系数、价格指数、粮食畜牧数据、城乡家庭主要耐用消费品拥有量来自国家统计局济南调查队；济南新旧动能转换起步区数据来自济南起步区管委会；其他数据均来自市统计局。

Special Report–2

STATISTICAL COMMUNIQUÉ OF THE JINAN MUNICIPAL ON THE 2022 NATIONAL ECONOMIC AND SOCIAL DEVELOPMENT [1]

Jinan Municipal Bureau of Statistics
NBS Survey Office in Jinan

In 2022, the Municipal Party Committee and the Municipal Government, confronted with the complicated and severe domestic and international situation and the impact of multiple factors beyond expectations, united and led the whole city to, by adhering to the guidance of Xi Jinping's Thought on Socialism with Chinese Characteristics for a New Era, thoroughly study, publicize and implement the spirit of the 20th Party Congress, resolutely implement General Secretary Xi Jinping's important instructions and requirements on Shandong and Jinan's work, implement the new development concept in a complete, accurate and comprehensive manner, actively serve and integrate into the new development pattern, put forth effort to boost high-quality development, and implement the decision-making arrangements of the Provincial Party Committee and the Provincial Government; and to consistently emphasize the importance of "being a vanguard and building a strong provincial capital" by effectively balancing the epidemic prevention & control and economic and social development, while also taking into account the overall trend of growth and security. As a result, the city as a whole has showed an economic upturn and a gradual improvement in the face of challenges. Overall, the city has scaled new heights in comprehensive strength, made new breakthroughs in transformation from old growth drivers to new ones, accelerated major national strategies to achieve substantial results, continued to improve and upgrade residents' lives, and taken solid steps in building a strong provincial capital of socialist modernization in the new era.

I. General

The economic aggregate has advanced to new levels. In light of the unified accounting results of municipal GDP, in 2022, the regional GDP of the whole city was [2] RMB 1,202.75 billion, an increase of [3] 3.1% if calculated at constant prices. Therein, the added value of the primary industry was RMB 42.05 billion, up by 3.1%; the added value of the secondary industry was RMB 418.02 billion, up by 3.2%; and the added value of the tertiary industry was RMB 742.67 billion, up by 3.0%. The composition ratio of the three industries was 3.5 : 34.8 : 61.7.

Figure 1 Gross Domestic Product Between 2012to 2022

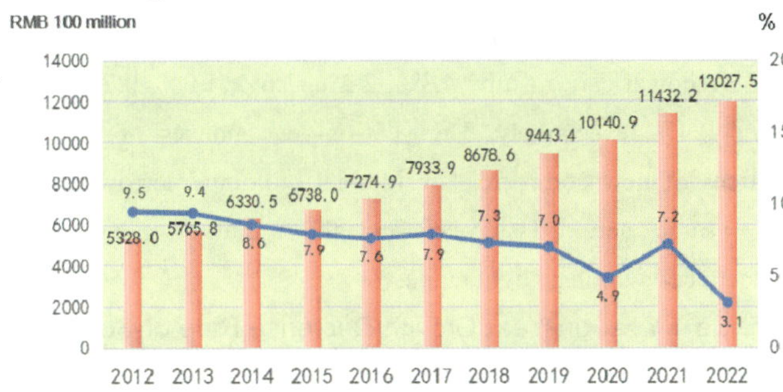

Figure 2 Ratio of Value Addition to the Gross Domestic Product of Primary, Secondary and Tertiary Industries 2012 and 2022

The effect of population aggregation has continued to show. At the end of the year, the resident population was 9.415 million, up by 0.8% over the end of last year, among which the resident population in cities and towns was 6.998 million, accounting for 74.3% of the gross population (urbanization rate of resident population), up by 0.1 percentage point from the end of last year; and the household registered population was 8.1995 million, up by 0.4%; the declared birth rate and the declared death rate of the whole year were declared to be 7.9‰ and 9.7‰ respectively; the growth rate of natural population was -1.9‰; the inflow of talents throughout the whole year was 326,000, with a net inflow of 158,000.

The employment situation has remained generally stable. The number of market players increased to 1.498 million households. The total number of "four-above"[4] enterprises was

13,055, with a net increase of 1,060. In the whole year, 174,000 people were employed in cities and towns, and the subsidies of RMB 600 million for job stabilization were distributed; the city took the action of tackling key problems for unemployed college graduates who left school but were not employed, held the "Spring City Tour" event for outstanding college students in the Yellow River Basin in 2022, and built a strong business incubation platform, driving the employment of more than 100,000 people cumulatively.

Consumer prices have risen steadily. The consumer price index (CPI) of residents rose by 1.4% throughout the year, down by 0.1 percentage point from the previous year. The price composition of eight categories of goods and services consumed by residents took on a trend of "seven rises and one drop", among which, apart from a slight decrease of 0.2% in housing prices, the prices of transportation and communication, food, tobacco and alcohol, daily necessities and services, clothing, other supplies and services, education, culture and entertainment, and medical care rose by 4.3%, 2.3%, 1.6%, 1.0%, 0.7%, 0.6% and 0.4% respectively. The year-on-year indexes of the sales prices of new commercial residential buildings narrowed from the same period last year, and the month-on-month index fluctuated within a slight range.

Table 1 Year-on-Year Growth/Decrease Rate of Consumer Prices Index In 2022

Index	Year-on-year Growth Rate (%)
Consumer Price Index	1.4
Food,Tobacco and Liquor	2.3
Clothing	1.0
Residence	-0.2
Daily Necessities and Services	1.6
Transport Communication	4.3
Education Culture Recreation	0.6
Health Care	0.4
Other Supplies and Services	0.7

FIGURE 3 SALES PRICE INDEX OF NEWLY-BUILT COMERCIAL HOUSING IN 2022

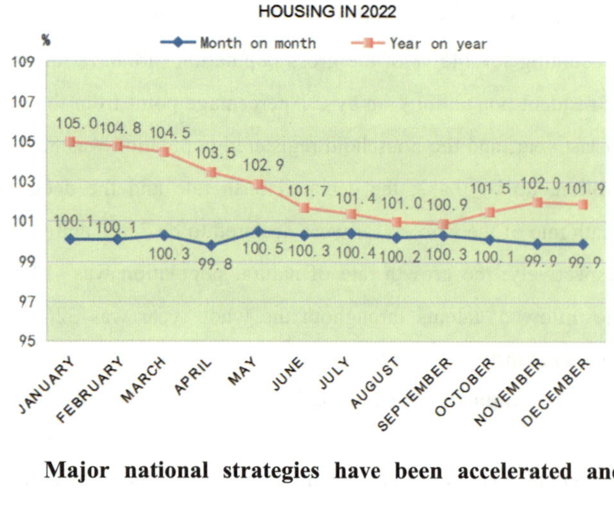

Major national strategies have been accelerated and achieved substantial results. The city thoroughly implemented the strategy of ecological protection and high-quality development in the Yellow River basin. The "14th Five-Year" Flood Control Project (Jinan section) in the lower reaches of the Yellow River started construction, and the Greening and Upgrading Project for Flood Control of the Yellow River and the Landscape Upgrading Project for the Central Scenic Area of the Yellow River Baili Scenic Area were successfully completed; the city was selected as the national pilot city for reclaimed water utilization and allocation; the starting area of transformation from old growth drivers to new ones in Jinan accelerated, and the development plan was approved for implementation; the "1+4+16+N" planning system was gradually perfected, and "four lists" such as the positive list of industries, the list of industrial opportunities, the map of key industries and the industry access mechanism were introduced in an innovative way; the Phase I of Huanghe Avenue (south section of Qingdao-Yinchuan Expressway) was completed and opened to traffic; public service projects such as the new courtyard in the starting area of the Second Hospital of Shandong University and the Yellow River Sports Center were accelerated; the layout of high-end platforms such as New Economy High-Tech Innovative Park of Chinese Academy of Sciences and International Merchants Industrial Park was accelerated; the Zero-carbon Smart Innovation Operation Center Project was granted the "Global Human Settlements Planning & Design Award"; BYD's New Energy Passenger Car Project completed the production of whole vehicles and 136 high-end quality projects were signed cumulatively; the construction of the experimental zone for the reform of finance to science and technology innovation has been comprehensively promoted, with the establishment of 20 banking institutions specializing in finance to science and technology innovation, e.g. science and technology branches (sub-branches), and 12 business departments (centers) of finance to science and technology innovation, and up to 6 listed enterprises of science and technology innovation board in the whole city; the parent fund of investment in science and technology innovation in Qilu Science City was found, and the first science and technology innovation bill, the first science and technology park CMBS, the first intellectual property financing lease business and the first "digital economy" theme corporate bond in the province were successfully implemented; the pilot of local currency-foreign currency integrated bank settlement account system and the pilot of digital RMB were approved in succession; the construction of digital Jinan was rolled out in an all-round way, a "1+4+N"

overall framework system was built; digital authorities, digital government, digital economy and digital society were promoted as a whole; the city was selected as one of the first batch of comprehensive pilot cities in China for digital green coordinated transformation and development.

Transformation from old growth drivers to new ones has been accelerated and upgraded. Innovation driving, intelligent manufacturing and digital empowerment have become the core elements to quicken transformation and enhance competitiveness. The added value of the "four new" economy was up to RMB 468.37 billion, accounting for 38.9% of GDP, with an increase of 1.2 percentage points over the previous year. The "four new" economic investment increased by 16.8%, and the growth rate was 13.0 percentage points higher than that of the whole city, accounting for 40.1% of the whole city's investment, with an increase of 4.5 percentage points over the previous year. The added value of the city's high-tech manufacturing industry above designated size increased by 11.1%, leading the average growth rate of industries above designated size by 9.5 percentage points. The added value of modern service industry [5] was RMB 449.23 billion, up by 3.7%, 0.7 percentage points ahead of the growth rate of all service industries, accounting for 60.4% of the added value of service industry.

II. Agriculture and Rural Areas

The gross value of yield of agriculture, forestry, animal husbandry and fishery has increased steadily. The gross value of yield of agriculture, forestry, animal husbandry and fishery in the whole year was 78.42 billion, up by 4.5% at constant prices, of which the gross value of yield of agriculture was 52.60 billion, up by 4.7%; the gross value of yield of animal husbandry was 17.02 billion, up by 2.7%; and the added value of agriculture, forestry, animal husbandry and fishery was 44.16 billion, up by 3.6%.

Table 2 Gross Output Value of Agriculture, Forestry, Animal Husbandry and Fishery In 2022

Index	Unit	Value of Yield	Year-on-year Growth Rate (%)
Gross output value of agriculture,forestry,animal husbandry and fishery	100 Million Yuan	784.2	4.5
Agriculture	100 Million Yuan	526.0	4.7
Forestry	100 Million Yuan	32.0	0.4
Animal husbandry	100 Million Yuan	170.2	2.7
Fishery	100 Million Yuan	8.5	6.0
Agriculture,forestry, animal husbandry and fishery services	100 Million Yuan	47.5	10.9

Agricultural production has risen steadily. Grain yield scored a record high. In the whole year, the grain sown area of 7.269 million mu, up by 0.2% and the gross yield of grain was 2.962 million tons, up by 1.1%; the gross vegetable yield was 7.126 million tons, up by 3.0%; the gross yield of oil was 66,000 tons, up by 0.4%; and the gross fruit yield was 620,000 tons, up by 0.2%.

Forestry production has maintained steady development. The afforestation covering an area of 773.3 hectares and the forest tending covering an area of 5,333.3 hectares were completed in the whole year, and 100 greening demonstration villages were built in the city; the Yellow River ecological protection and restoration project of 3,197 mu was implemented with high quality; great efforts were made to cultivate forestry industries with distinctive advantages, intensify the introduction of new varieties of economic forests, and transform 686.7 hectares of low-yield and low-efficiency gardens.

The overall production of animal husbandry has tended to a good prospect. 2.096 million pigs were slaughtered in the whole year, up by 9.2%; 111,000 cattle were slaughtered, down by 19.4%; 1.362 million sheep were slaughtered, up by 7.4%; the gross yield of pork, beef, mutton and poultry meat was 291,000 tons, including 169,000 tons of pork, up by 9.5%; the annual yield of eggs was 270,000 tons, down by 11.5%; the yield of milk was 434,000 tons, up by 3.2%; and the annual yield of aquatic products was 15,000 tons, up by 5.1%.

Table 3 Basic Statistics of Major Agricultural Products In 2022

Index	Unit	Area/Yield	Year-on-year Growth Rate (%)
Total sown area of grain	10,000 Mu	726.9	0.2
Cotton planting area	10,000 Mu	4.4	-8.9
Oil planting area	10,000 Mu	26.4	0.3
Vegetable planting area	10,000 Mu	149	2.0
Actual orchard area	10,000 Mu	57.4	-0.3
Total grain output	10,000 Tons	296.2	1.1
Cotton yield	10,000 Tons	0.4	-8.1
Oil yield	10,000 Tons	6.6	0.4

Index	Unit	Area/Yield	Year-on-year Growth Rate (%)
Vegetable yield	10,000 Tons	712.6	3.0
Fruit yield	10,000 Tons	62.0	0.2
Slaughtered Pigs	10 000 Heads	209.6	9.2
Slaughtered Cattle	10 000 Heads	11.1	-19.4
Slaughtered Sheep	10 000 Heads	136.2	7.4
Output of Pork	10,000 Tons	16.9	9.5
Output of Beef	10,000 Tons	2.4	-15.6
Output of Mutton	10,000 Tons	1.9	3.6
Output of Poultry Meat	10,000 Tons	7.8	9.5
Output of Poultry & Eggs	10,000 Tons	27.0	-11.5
Output of Cow Milk	10,000 Tons	43.4	3.2
Output of Aquatic Products	10,000 Tons	1.5	5.1

Modern agriculture has improved both in quality and efficiency. The added value of modern and efficient agriculture was 7.55 billion, up by 6.7%, accounting for 17.1% of the added value of agriculture, forestry, animal husbandry and fishery, 0.6 percentage point higher. In the whole year, 32 new "vegetable basket" parks to guarantee supplies were built, and up to 351 large-scale pig farms were built; 275,000 mu of high-standard farmland was built, the water-saving irrigation area of 60,000 mu was developed simultaneously; the promotion area of water and fertilizer integration was up to 735,000 mu; there were 57 well-known agricultural brands above the provincial level, and up to 1,699 "SAN PIN YI BIAO" agricultural products in the city were effectively indicated; characteristic agricultural products grew with good development momentum, and Zhangqiu green onion and Laiwu ginger were selected into the agricultural boutique brand cultivation plan of the Ministry of Agriculture and Rural Affairs; the characteristic agricultural products such as Changqing tea, Renfeng watermelon, Qudi cucumber and Licheng strawberry continued to grow and develop, with an annual yield of 313,000 kg of tea, 715,000 tons of green onion, 323,000 tons of ginger, 299,000 tons of watermelon, 1.2 million tons of cucumber and 99,000 tons of strawberry; concerted efforts were made to vigorously develop the seed industry and build "the Capital of Seed Industry in Northern China", and there were up to 73 certified enterprises of improved crop seed in the city.

The rural revitalization has achieved remarkable results. 39 provincial-level demonstration villages and 129 rural revitalization Qilu model villages were accomplished in an all-round way, and 3 provincial-level rural revitalization demonstration areas were created; a total of 6 municipal-level pastoral complexes were built, 171 new demonstration agricultural business entities were newly identified, and 506 leading agricultural enterprises were developed above the municipal level; the number of family farms and farmers' cooperatives was up to 8,063 and 11,796 respectively; the monitoring and early warning mechanism for preventing poverty return was perfected, with a total of 597 households and 1,594 people incorporated into the dynamic monitoring of preventing poverty return, and all of them were given targeted assistance; 31,000 people out of poverty were incorporated into the scope of support for people in the rural minimum subsistence guarantee system and exceptionally poor people in rural areas in the city, and all the 987 out-of-poverty villages in the city achieved "five accesses and ten possessions"[6].

III. Industry and Construction

Industrial transformation and upgrading have been accelerated. The gross industrial added value was RMB 286.90 billion, up by 2.4%. The added value of industrial enterprises above designated size [7] increased by 1.6%. Based on economic types, the public economy decreased by 1.4% while the non-public economy increased by 4.1%. With regard to light and heavy industries, light industry increased by 7.7%, while heavy industry decreased by 0.1%. Among the 41 major-category industries, 24 industries achieved value-added growth with a growth rate of 58.5%. Among the six key industries, the manufacture of general purpose equipment increased by 15.4%, the processing of oil and coal increased by 14.2%, the manufacture of medicines increased by 12.4%, the manufacture of computer communication equipment increased by 3.1%, and the processing of ferrous metal calendering and the manufacture of automobiles decreased by 10.9% and 46.7% respectively.

Industrial enterprises have gradually recovered in quality and efficiency. In the whole year, the completed operating revenue of industrial enterprises above designated size was RMB 813.99 billion, down by 4.1%, and the decline fluctuated and narrowed within the year; the gross profit was RMB 33.25 billion, down by 14.8%; and the profit rate of operating revenue was 4.1%. Among the 41 major-category industries, 16 industries had operating revenue exceeding RMB 10 billion, accounting for 91.6% of the operating revenue of industrial enterprises above designated size. The operating revenue of ferrous metal smelting and pressing industries was over RMB 100 billion.

Table 4 Growth Rate of Operating Revenue of Key Industries Above Designated Size In 2022

Industry	Year-on-year Growth Rate (%)
Smelting and Pressing of Ferrous Metals	-13.5
Manufacture of Computers, Communication and Other Electronic Equipment	11.3
Manufacture of Automobiles	-44.6
Manufacture of Non-metallic Mineral Products	7.3
Manufacture of Electrical Machinery and Apparatus	14.3
Processing of Petroleum, Coal and Other Fuels	31.3
Manufacture of Medicines	10.6
Manufacture of General Purpose Machinery	2.2
Manufacture of Raw Chemical Materials and Chemical Products	5.6
Manufacture of Metal Products	-2.6
Manufacture of Special Purpose Machinery	9.2
Production and Supply of Electric Power and Heat Power	20.2
Processing of Food from Agricultural Products	10.3
Mining and Processing of Ferrous Metal Ores	-10.3
Manufacture of Foods	4.4
Production and Supply of Gas	26.9

Industrial products have been in stable supply. The annual production and sales rate of industrial products above designated size was 97.6%. Among the 306 types of industrial products produced, the output of 123 types of products increased by 40.2%, of which 59 types of products increased by more than 20%, accounting for 19.3%; the output of cars and new energy vehicles was up to 5.1 times and 3.8 times of the same period of last year respectively, and the charging pile increased by 65.3%; health and epidemic prevention supplies was in accelerated supply, with 770 million medical masks, up by 47.4%; among high value-added products, the output of logic chips and lithium-ion batteries was up to 5.4 and 12.9 times that of the same period of last year, and industrial robots increased by 32.3%.

Table 5 Output and Growth Rate of Main Products of Industrial Enterprises Above Designated Size In 2022

Product Designation	Unit	Output	Year-on-year Growth Rate(%)
Frozen,Fresh Meat	10,000 Tons	16.5	42.3
Milk Products	10,000 Tons	50.5	-5.9
Liquor	10 000 Kiloliter	26.3	-0.5
Synthetic Ammonia	10,000 Tons	20.7	-54.0
Polypropylene Resin	10,000 Tons	12.1	15.0
Primary Plastic	10,000 Tons	78.0	2.7
Traditional Chemical Medicine	Ton	7903.6	8.3
Cement	10,000 Tons	1354.5	-12.2
Graphite and Carbon Products	10,000 Tons	209.1	12.1
Rolled Steel	10,000 Tons	2021.4	-4.2
Forge Piece	10,000 Tons	128.3	6.3
Sintered Metal Products	10,000 Tons	1.3	-2.9
Engine	10 000kW	1772.9	-56.6
CNC Metal Cutting Machine Tools	Unit	4235	-27.5
Pneumatic Components	10 000 Unit	783.3	-22.4
Mining Equipment	10,000 Tons	4.2	3.1
Industrial Robot	Unit	3746	32.3
Trucks	10,000 Units	16.0	-49.9
Railway Freight Wagons	Unit	3765	20.7
Transformers	10 000 KVA pm	15872.3	3.7
Solar Cells (Photovoltaic Cells)	10 000kW	4.0	-28.5
Computers	10,000 Units	77.5	-32.6
Servers	10,000 Units	77.1	-32.2
Integrated Circuit	10,000 Units	28964.0	70.7

The construction industry has achieved vigorous growth. There were 1,371 construction enterprises eligible for general contracting and professional contracting in the city, with an increase of 189 enterprises; the annual value of signed contracts was RMB 1,321.78 billion, up by 16.7%, of which the value of new contracts was RMB 650.09 billion, up by 1.8%; the gross output value of the construction industry was RMB 446.08

billion, up by 8.1%, among which the output value of state-owned and state-holding enterprises was RMB 343 billion, up by 10.5%; and the construction area of houses was 199.709 million square meters, up by 2.9%.

IV. Service Industry

Emerging service industry has been leading the development. The annual added value of service industry was RMB 742.67 billion, up by 3.0%; the operating revenue increased by 4.2% [8], among which Internet and related services, software and information technology services, and professional and technical services increased by 32.1%, 18.2% and 15.5% respectively, which became the principal force promoting the growth of service industry. Two national 5A-level logistics enterprises were added, and the total number was up to 19, with operating revenue of loading and unloading, warehousing, multimodal transport and transportation agency being 73.1% and 16.8% respectively.

Table 6 Operating Revenue of Service Enterprises Above Designated Size by Sector In 2022

Sector	Operating Revenue (100 Million yuan)	Year-on-year Growth Rate(%)
Total	3631.2	4.2
Transport, Storage and Post	1500.3	-1.8
Information Transmission, Software and Information Technology	786.8	17.2
Real Estate (Excluding Real Estate Development and Operation)	163.4	-0.8
Leasing and Business Services	436.1	11.4
Scientific Research,Technical Services	508.6	13.2
Management of Water Conservancy, Environment and Public Facilities	64.2	-4.7
Services to Households, Repair and Other Services	24.1	-8.4
Education	24.7	-27.5
Health and Social Work	50.9	2.4
Culture, Sports and Recreation	72.2	-7.7

The transportation industry has stabilized under pressure. At the end of the year, the mileage of highways open to traffic was 18,294.4 kilometers, of which the mileage of expressways was 795.3 kilometers, up by 7.8%; the freight volume of highways was 240 million tons, down by 3.3%; the freight turnover was 60.88 billion ton-kilometers, up by 5.4%; 79,000 flights took off and landed in the whole year, down by 30.1%; the passenger throughput was 8.242 million person-times, down by 39.5%; the cargo and mail throughput was 138,000 tons, down by 18.1%. At the end of the year, there were 3,692,000 civil motor vehicles, of which 3,203,000 were civil vehicles, up by 5.9%; 756 bus lines with a gross length of 15,623.2 kilometers, with the passenger throughout of 400 million person-times; and 3 operating lines of rail transit with a length of 84.1 kilometers and an annual passenger volume of 54.56 million person-times.

The postal industry and telecommunications industry have operated smoothly. The annual operating revenue of the postal industry (excluding the direct operating revenue of the Postal Savings Bank of China) was RMB 10.54 billion, up by 6.2%; the gross business volume was RMB 9.33 billion, up by 4.4%; the revenue from express delivery business was RMB 8.21 billion, up by 5.9%; the business volume was 770 million pieces, down by 3.4%. At the end of the year, there were 12.66 million mobile phone users, up by 4.0%, including 6.852 million 5G mobile phone users, up by 47.9%, and 5.014 million Internet broadband access users, up by 8.3%.

The tourism and convention and exhibition industries have recovered steadily. The number of domestic tourists was 65.656 million person-times, up to 80.2% in the same period of last year; the domestic tourism revenue was RMB 71.16 billion, up to 72.3% in the same period of last year. There were 85 A-level scenic spots, including 1 5A-level tourist attraction, 18 4A-level tourist attractions and 2 provincial-level tourist resorts. The activity of "Eight O'clock at Night in Spring City" was launched to light up the "night economy" of cultural tourism, and it was rated as 1 national and 3 provincial-level cultural tourism consumption gathering areas at night. A total of 76 exhibitions were held throughout the year with an exhibition area of 1.4 million square meters.

V. Investment in Fixed Assets

Investment has continued to scale up. The investment in fixed assets increased by 3.8% in the whole year, of which the investment in primary industry decreased by 2.8%; investment in the secondary industry increased by 15.1%; and investment in the tertiary industry increased by 1.9%. At the end of the year, there were 1,653 fixed assets investment projects with a gross investment of over RMB 100 million, with an increase of 118 projects, and the accomplished investment increased by 12.4%, among which 43 projects with a gross investment of over RMB 5 billion, and the accomplished investment increased by 13.2%. Private investment accounted for 44.5% of the city's investment, infrastructure investment increased by 17.0%. Investment in the social sector increased by 26.5%, which was higher than the city's investment growth rate of 22.7 percentage points.

Table 7 Growth Rate and Proportion of Investment In Three Industries In 2022

Industry	Year-on-year Growth Rate(%)	Proportion of investment in fixed assets (%)
Investment In Fixed Assets	3.8	100.0
Primary industry	-2.8	0.4
Secondary industry	15.1	15.5
Tertiary industry	1.9	84.1

The real estate market has been operating at a low level. The investment in real estate development in the whole year was RMB 183.08 billion, down by 5.0%, of which the residential investment was RMB 124.76 billion, down by 7.7%. The construction area of housing was 86.049 million square meters, down by 15.3%, of which the construction area of residence was 53.385 million square meters, down by 18.8%. The construction area of housing was 7.15 million square meters, down by 35.9%, of which the completion area of residence was 4.88 million square meters, down by 38.0%. The sales area of commercial housing was 12.419 million square meters, down by 19.8%, of which the sales area of residence was 9.071 million square meters, down by 30.2%. The sales amount of commercial housing was RMB 151.46 billion, down by 22.6%, of which the sales amount of residence was RMB 122.17 billion, down by 29.0%.

VI. Domestic Trade

The consumer goods market has been obviously disturbed by the epidemic. The gross amount of retail sales of social consumer goods in the whole year was RMB 487.81 billion, down by 4.8%, of which the retail sales amount of commodities was RMB 419.41 billion, down by 4.5%; the catering revenue was RMB 68.40 billion, down by 7.0%. From the perspective of urban and rural areas, the retail sales amount of social consumer goods in cities and towns was RMB 431.22 billion, down by 4.9%; the retail sales amount of consumer goods in rural areas was RMB 56.59 billion, down by 4.0%.

The demand for essential commodities has been stable. Among the retail sales amount of commodities above the norm, the retail sales amount of grain, oil and food commodities was RMB 18.25 billion, up by 8.1%; the retail sales amount of beverage commodities was RMB 1.77 billion, up by 18.1%; the retail sales amount of tobacco and alcohol commodities was RMB 4.33 billion, up by 2.4%; the retail sales amount of Chinese and western pharmaceutical commodities was RMB 7.41 billion, up by 12.6%.

Online consumption has been booming. The retail sales amount of commodities by wholesale and retail units above the norm through public networks was RMB 31.58 billion, up by 17.4%, accounting for 18.1% of the retail sales amount of units above the norm in the whole city, with an increase of 3.1 percentage points over the previous year.

New energy vehicles have been in a good growth trend. The retail sales amount of new energy vehicles by units above the norm was RMB 10.41 billion, up by 87.5%, accounting for 6.0% of the retail sales amount of units above the norm in the whole city, with an increase of 3.3 percentage points over the previous year.

Table 8 Retail Sales Amount and Growth Rate of Main commodities of wholesale and retail units In 2022

Commodity Category	Retail sales (100 Million yuan)	Year-on-year Growth Rate(%)
Grain and Oil, Food	182.5	8.1
Beverages	17.7	18.1
Tobacco and Liquor	43.3	2.4
Clothing, Shoes, Hats and Textiles	96.5	-19.1
Cosmetics	64.1	33.8
Gold, Silver and Jewellery	43.3	-13.2
Articles for Daily Use	34.2	-38.4
Household Appliances and Audio-Visual Equipment	117.2	-9.6
Traditional Chinese and Western Medicine	74.1	12.6
Cultural and Office Goods	44.2	-17.5
Communication Appliances	53.9	-37.2
Petroleum and Related Products	174.6	-7.3
Automobile	576.5	-1.2

VII. Foreign Economy

Imports and exports have maintained a good momentum of rapid growth. The gross export-import volume of goods in the whole year was RMB 220.89 billion, up by 13.9%, of which exports amounted to RMB 143.18 billion, up by 22.0%; imports amounted to RMB 77.71 billion, up by 1.5%. Imports and exports to ASEAN increased by 45.9%, imports and exports to EU (excluding the UK) decreased by 2.6%, and imports and exports to Latin America increased by 13.1%. Imports and exports to countries and regions along the "Belt and Road" increased by 30.8%, accounting for 39.3% of the gross export-import volume. Among the export commodities, the exports of mechanical and electrical products amounted to RMB 85.16 billion, up by 28.8%; the exports of agricultural products was RMB 6.48 billion, up by 1.1%. Among the import commodities, the imports of mechanical and electrical products was RMB 40.09 billion, up by 3.3%; the imports of agricultural products was RMB 10.29 billion, up by 32.0%. The annual economic extroversion was 18.4%, with an increase of 1.4 percentage points over the previous year.

The utilization of foreign capital has scaled up significantly. The actual utilized foreign capital in the whole city was USD 3.14 billion, up by 18.0%, of which the foreign capital of USD 660 million was used for the manufacturing industry, up by 148.3%; the foreign capital of USD 2.19 billion was used for the tertiary industry, up by 4.9%. The contracted foreign capital was USD 7.84 billion in the whole year. There were 251 foreign investment projects newly approved, 22 of which had a gross investment of over USD 100 million, and the contracted foreign capital of projects with a gross investment was over USD 2.47 billion.

The field of foreign cooperation has continuously deepened. In the whole year, the newly signed contracts for foreign contracted projects amounted to USD 4.89 billion, with a turnover of USD 4.09 billion completed. 45 overseas enterprises (institutions) established were put on record, with an actual investment of RMB 11.77 billion, and 4,489 service workers were dispatched overseas.

VIII. Finance

The fiscal revenue and expenditure have been basically balanced. The general public budget revenue of the whole year was RMB 100.11 billion, with a comparable increase of 8.1% and a decrease of 0.6% according to the natural unified standard. Therein, the tax revenue was RMB 69.32 billion, with a comparable increase of 1.0% and a decrease of 10.7% according to the natural unified standard, the proportion of tax revenue was 69.2%. The general public budget expenditure was RMB 122.56 billion, down by 5.2%, of which education expenditure was RMB 25.18 billion, up by 18.3%; health expenditure was RMB 13.48 billion, up by 20.8%; transportation expenditure was RMB 2.84 billion, up by 16.8%, and key affairs were effectively guaranteed.

Table 9 General Public Budget Revenue and Expenditure In 2022

Item	Number (100 Million yuan)	Year-on-year Growth Rate(%)
General Public Budget Revenue	1001.1	-0.6
Tax Revenue	693.2	-10.7
Value-added Tax	198.8	-25.8
Enterprise Income Tax	115.4	-12.6
General Public Budget Expenditure	1225.6	-5.2
Education	251.8	18.3
Health	134.8	20.8
Transport	28.4	16.8

The balance of deposits and loans has set a new record. At the end of the year, the balance of various deposits of financial institutions in local currency and foreign currency was RMB 2,594.10 billion, up by 10.7%, an increase of RMB 250.40 billion over the beginning of the year; the balance of various deposits of financial institutions in local currency and foreign currency was RMB 2,611.23 billion, up by 12.0%, an increase of RMB 279.90 billion over the beginning of the year.

The securities market has developed steadily. At the end of the year, there were up to 56 listed companies, with 58 types of stocks, and 8 listed enterprises and enterprises that applied for IPO and pass the examination of the Issuance Examination Commission were newly added throughout the year. The completed securities transaction volume was RMB 5.8 trillion, up by 3.1%. There were 208 private placement fund management institutions registered in Asset Management Association of China, with 711 types of managed funds, and the scale of managed funds was RMB 116.84 billion, up by 9.7%.

The insurance industry has stabilized and improved. The city's insurance industry achieved the premium revenue of RMB

63.19 billion, up by 6.2%, with an increase of 3.8 percentage points, of which property insurance premium revenue was RMB 12.68 billion, up by 16.1%; personal insurance premium revenue was RMB 50.52 billion, up by 3.9%.

The quality of credit assets has been stable and controllable. The balance of non-performing loans of banking financial institutions in the whole city was RMB 23.41 billion, with a ratio of non-performing loans of 0.9%, which was 0.4 percentage points lower than the provincial average.

IX. Science and Technology, Education, Culture, Health and Sports Cause

R&D investment has continued to rise. The annual investment in the funds of research and experimental development was RMB 30.67 billion, up by 15.5%, of which the basic research amounted to RMB 2.68 billion[9] , up by 44.9%; the experimental development amounted to RMB 24.13 billion, up by 17.4%. The investment in the R&D funds accounted for 2.7% of the GDP, with an increase of 0.1 percentage point over the previous year. There was 1 national enterprise technology center newly recognized, with a total of 30; and 16 provincial enterprise technology centers were newly recognized, with a total of 236.

The innovation capability has been continuously enhanced. In the whole year, there were 48.9 effective invention patents per 10,000 people, up by 27.5%. 11,853 invention patents were granted, up by 44.4%. The transaction volume of technology contracts was RMB 61.36 billion, up by 29.6%. There were 90 provincial scientific progress awards, including 16 second prizes for Natural Science Award, 3 first prizes and 4 second prizes for Technological Invention Award, 17 first prizes and 44 second prizes for Scientific and Technological Award, 5 Youth Awards and 1 International Cooperation Award. There were 107 national intellectual property demonstration enterprises and superior enterprises, 5 newly approved national key laboratories, 10 newly approved provincial key laboratories, 10 newly registered provincial academician workstations and 7 newly added provincial technology innovation centers in the whole city.14 provincial R&D institutions were newly registered, with a total of 71; 7,613 enterprises were in the library of national science and technology small and medium-sized enterprises, up by 31%. 23 provincial major science and technology innovation projects were declared, and RMB 240 million of provincial financial funds was won over. The innovation capability improvement project of science and technology small and medium-sized enterprises was implemented, and 335 provincial projects were won over.

Education cause has achieved high-quality development. The coverage rate of inclusive kindergartens in the whole city was over 89.0%, and the proportion of children enrolled in public kindergartens was over 55.0%. There were 30 primary and secondary schools completed and more than 50,000 degrees newly built. A total of 83 primary and secondary schools and kindergartens were newly built, rebuilt and expanded; 11 schools received 25 awards in the National Vocational College Skills Competition. 95 city-school cooperation projects were established and 8 new industrial colleges were supported.

Table 10 Basic Situation of Education In 2022

School Categories	Number Of Schools (place)	Students At School (10 000 persons)	Full-time teacher (10 000 persons)
Colleges and Universities Stationed in Jinan	52	67.1	4.2
Secondary Vocational Schools (excluding technical schools)	37	6.5	0.4
Vestibule School	32	8.5	0.5
Ordinary Middle School	334	42.1	3.6
Elementary School	608	64.4	4
Special Education School	13	0.1	0.1
Kindergartens	2190	36.3	2.7

Cultural undertakings have been steadily promoted. At the end of the year, there were 14 state-owned art performance groups, 174 cultural centers (stations), 14 public libraries and 13 public museums. There were 437 cultural relics protection units at and above the municipal level, including 30 national-level ones. There were 69 digital cinemas whose box office can be counted, with 6.376 million person-times of audience and box office revenue of RMB 270 million. The mixed coverage rate of TV population and broadcast population were 100% and 99.7% respectively. The constructions of 42 study rooms in the Spring City were completed, and the coverage rate of comprehensive cultural service centers at the grassroots level was 100%.

The capacity of medical and health services has been continuously upgraded. At the end of the year, there were 7,670 medical and health institutions, including 283 hospitals, 99 public hospitals and 184 private hospitals; there were 7,293 medical and health institutions at grass-roots level, including 49 town hospitals, 399 community health service centers (stations), 184 out-patient departments, 3,073 clinics (health centers and medical rooms) and 3,588 village health rooms; there were 54 professional public health institutions, including 14 centers for disease control and prevention and 14 health supervision institutes (centers). At the end of the year, there were 114,000 health technicians, including 44,000 medical practitioners and assistant medical practitioners, and 52,000 registered nurses. There were 76,000 beds in medical and health institutions, including 66,000 beds in hospitals and 4,000 beds in township health centers. In the whole year, 71.369 million person-times received diagnosis and treatments, and 2.259 million person-times were discharged from hospital. There were totally 58 built-up community hospitals and 4.15 childcare places per one thousand people. Guang'anmen Hospital Jinan Hospital, China Academy of Chinese Medical Sciences was selected as the national regional medical center project. Jinan City was selected into the first batch of national infant care demonstration cities and the first batch of pilot cities of the "Healthy China" action innovation model.

The foundation of mass sports has been consolidated to a further extent. There were 10 newly established sports social organizations and 2,250 trained social sports instructors throughout the year. 360 national fitness activities (competitions) were organized with 3 million person-times of participants (including online activities). 287 gold medals, 213 silver medals and 217 bronze medals at and above the provincial level were won.

X. Energy, Environment, Urban Construction and Safety Production

The energy structure has been continuously optimized. The comprehensive energy consumption of industrial enterprises above designated size decreased by 3.1%, of which the coal consumption of industrial enterprises above designated size was 28.478 million tons, up by 1.7%; the coke consumption was 8.127 million tons, down by 9.4%; the natural gas consumption was 1.01 billion cubic meters, up by 9.8%. The power generation capacity of wind energy of enterprises above designated size was 2.19 billion kWh, the power generation capacity of solar energy was 300 million kWh, the power generation capacity of garbage incineration was 950 million kWh, and the power generation capacity of biomass energy was 660 million kWh, totally accounting for 12.9% of the power generation capacity of enterprises above designated size, up by 0.5 percentage point over the previous year. The new energy power generation capacity was steadily raised.

Table 11 Energy Production of Enterprises Above Designated Size In 2022

Item	Unit	Production	Year-on-year Growth Rate(%)
Coal	10,000 tons	48.9	-33.0
Electricity Generation	100 million kWh	318.2	0.8
Thermal Power	100 million kWh	293.3	0.8
Garbage Incineration	100 million kWh	9.5	0.0
Biomass	100 million kWh	6.6	26.6
Wind Power	100 million kWh	21.9	-0.1
Solar Power	100 million kWh	3.0	11.9

Table 12 Energy Consumption of Industrial Enterprises Above Designated Size In 2022

Item	Consumption	Year-on-year Growth Rate(%)
Coal (10,000tons)	2847.8	1.7
Natural Gas (100 million cu.m)	10.1	9.8
Coke (10,000 tons)	812.7	-9.4
Gasoline (10,000 tons)	0.4	-10.2
Diesel Oil (10,000 tons)	3.6	-7.5

The electricity consumption of the whole society has increased steadily. The electricity consumption of the whole society was 49.97 billion kWh, up by 5.1%, of which the electricity consumption of residents was 9.76 billion kWh, up by 12.8%. Viewing by industry, the electricity consumption of the primary industry was 350 million kWh, up by 5.3%; the electricity consumption of the secondary industry was 27.38 billion kWh, up by 2.6%; the electricity consumption of the tertiary industry was 12.47 billion kWh, up by 5.4%. The industrial electricity consumption was 26.30 billion kWh, accounting for 52.6% of the electricity consumption in the whole society, up by 2.5%.

Table 13 Electricity Consumption of the Whole City In 2022

Item	Electricity Consumption (100 million kWh)	Year-on-year Growth Rate (%)
Total Electricity Consumption	499.7	5.1
Household Electricity Consumption	97.6	12.8
Primary industry	3.5	5.3
Secondary industry	273.8	2.6

Item	Electricity Consumption (100 million kWh)	Year-on-year Growth Rate (%)
Industrial Electricity Consumption	263.0	2.5
Tertiary industry	124.7	5.4

The ecological environment has continued to improve. The comprehensive index of air quality was 4.47, an improvement of 4.9%; the ratio of excellent and good days was 65.5%, an increase of 2.8 percentage points over the previous year; the concentration of fine particulate matters ($PM_{2.5}$) was 37 $\mu g/m^3$, an improvement of 7.5%; the average annual concentration of inhalable particulate matters (PM_{10}) was 71 $\mu g/m^3$, that of sulfur dioxide was 11 $\mu g/m^3$, and that of nitrogen dioxide was 31 $\mu g/m^3$. The proportion of three types of water bodies with good state-controlled sections was up to 100%; the chemical oxygen demand concentration of Xinfengzhuang in Xiaoqing River exit section was 12.8 mg/L, the ammonia nitrogen concentration was 0.3 mg/L, and the annual average water quality was up to the Class II standard of surface water for the first time. The daytime average equivalent sound level of regional environmental noise was 55.0 dB, and the daytime average equivalent sound level of urban road traffic noise was 65.5 dB.

Urban construction has been accelerated. At the end of the year, the urban built-up covered an area of 853.9 square kilometers, an increase of 12.7 square kilometers. The Greenery coverage of the built-up was 37.5%, and the per capita green space area of parks was 12.95 square meters. In the whole year, the supply of natural gas was 1.98 billion cubic meters, up by 9.9%; the supply of liquefied petroleum gas was 38,000 tons, up by 52.9%. The central heating covered an area of 330 million square meters, up by 9.0%. The supply of tap water was 510 million tons, up by 1.9%. In that year, the construction of 30 spring direct drinking projects were started, a cumulative number of 56 spring direct drinking projects were completed, and the harmless treatment rate of domestic garbage was 100%.

Public security has maintained well. A total of 19,151 criminal cases were settled in the whole year. The detection rate of murder cases and cases in force remained at 100%, and all murder cases were solved for 12 consecutive years; the detection rate of eight types of serious violence cases was 98.6%, the detection rate of "two-theft" cases was 75.6%, and 1,693 fugitives of various types were arrested; 1 underworld organization, 7 evil criminal groups and 8 evil gangs were destroyed.

Production safety has been in a stable situation. 134 production safety accidents of all types occured in the whole city, down by 49.2%, and 104 people died, down by 35.4%. No major or above production safety accidents occurred.

XI. Residents' Life and Social Security

Residents' income has grown steadily. The per capita disposable income of the city's residents was RMB 48,827, up by 4.5%. By urban and rural areas, the per capita disposable income of urban residents was RMB 59,459, up by 3.5%; the per capita disposable income of rural residents was RMB 23,844, up by 5.6%. The growth rate of rural residents' income was 2.1 percentage points faster than that of urban residents' income. The ratio of the per capita disposable income of urban and rural residents was 2.49, down by 0.05; the Engel coefficient of urban residents[10] was 23.8%, while the Engel coefficient of rural residents was 30.5%.

Table 14 Per Capita Disposable Income and Growth Rates of Urban and Rural Residents In 2022

Item	Urban Residents		Rural Residents	
	2022 (yuan)	Year-on-year Growth Rate (%)	2022 (yuan)	Year-on-year Growth Rate (%)
Disposable Income	59459	3.5	23844	5.6
Income of Wages and Salaries	34694	3.4	13138	5.8
Net Business Income	3249	3.3	8746	5.5
Net Income from Property	10078	3.6	506	4.8
Net Income from Transfer	11437	3.7	1455	5.2

Table 15 At the End of 2022, Number of Major Durable Consumer Goods Owned Per 100 Households [11]

Item	Unit	Urban Residents	Rural Residents
Automobile	Unit	66	46
Refrigerator (cabinet)	Set	101	97
Washing Machine	Set	99	93
Water Heater	Set	100	90
Air Conditioner	Set	175	97
Colour Television Set	Set	103	102
Camera	Set	27	6
Computer	Set	79	42
Mobile Phone	Unit	239	236

The social security system has become more perfect. At the end of the year, there were 4.886 million people engaged in the basic endowment insurance for urban workers, an increase of 159,000 people; 3.528 million employees engaged in medical insurance for workers, an increase of 166,000 people; 2.354 million people engaged in unemployment insurance, an increase of 85,000 people; 3.074 million people engaged in employment injury insurance, an increase of 139,000 people; 2.456 million people engaged in maternity insurance, an increase of 99,000. Up to 3.149 million and 5.019 million people were engaged in endowment insurance for residents and medical insurance respectively.

The minimum living security standard has been steadily enhanced. The minimum living security standard for urban residents was RMB 995/month, with 11,000 urban residents from 8,000 households guaranteed and security funds and various subsidies of RMB 130 million distributed; the minimum living security standard for rural residents was RMB 770/month, with 83,000 rural residents from 59,000 households guaranteed and the security funds and various subsidies of RMB 660 million distributed. The basic living standard for urban people in extreme poverty was RMB 1,492/month, and the basic living standard for rural people in extreme poverty was RMB 1,356/month. In line with the nursing standards of self-care, semi-self-care and completely no self-care, the subsidies were RMB 255/month, RMB 424/month and RMB 847/month respectively, with 860 people in extreme poverty guaranteed in urban areas and 14,000 people in extreme poverty guaranteed in rural areas, and a total of RMB 340 million in support and assistance funds and subsidies were provided for people in extreme poverty.

Assistance and support has been promoted in an orderly manner. There were 13 comprehensive service institutions of social assistance in the whole city, including 1 assistance management station and 1 minor assistance and protection center, training 3,770 person-times of disabled people, arranging 2,770 person-times of disabled people to get employment, and investing RMB 270 million in helping and assisting the disabled.

Notes:

[1] The statistical data for the year 2022 are those of statistical express or preliminary accounting, and the official data are specifically subject to the published *Jinan Statistical Yearbook 2023.* Some data are not equal to the total and the total of sub-items as a result of rounding.

[2] The absolute figures of the regional GDP of the whole city and the added values of various industries were calculated at current prices, the growth rates were calculated at constant prices, and the data of that year were initial accounting figures. According to the annual accounting, the historical data of GDP, added value of various industries as well other related indicators were revised.

[3] All the growth rates in this bulletin are those of the current period in comparison with the same period of last year, unless otherwise stated.

[4] The "four-upper " enterprises refer to industries above designated size, qualified construction industry, wholesale and retail industry above the norm, accommodation and catering industry and real estate development and management industry above the norm, and service industry above designated size.

[5] Modern service industries cover information transmission, software and information technology service industry, financial industry, real estate industry, leasing and business service industry, scientific research and technical service industry, water conservancy, environment and public facilities management industry, residents' service, repair and other service industries, education, health and social work, culture, sports and entertainment.

[6] The "five accesses and ten possessions" of the key villages in the provincial poverty alleviation work refer to the accesses to roads, electricity, water, radio and television and information and the possessions of farmland ensuring stable yields despite drought or excessive rain, projects to get rich, office spaces, health room services, rural garbage disposal, preschool education, cultural activity rooms, fitness centers, good ecological environment and employment guarantee measures.

[7] Industrial enterprises above designated size refer to industrial legal entities with annual revenue of the main business of RMB 20 million or more;

[8] Service industry above designated size includes: transportation, warehousing and postal services, information transmission, software and information technology services, real estate, leasing and business services, scientific research and technical services, water conservancy, environment and public facilities management, residential services, repair and other services, education, health and social work, culture, sports and entertainment.

[9] The indicators related to research and development (R&D) funds use the data of 2021.

[10] Engel's coefficient refers to the proportion of food

expenditure in consumption expenditure.

[11] The data came from the survey of household income and expenditure and living conditions.

Data Source: The data of the Yellow River Basin ecological protection and high-quality development strategy and enterprise technology center in this are from the development and reform departments; the data of education are from the education departments; the data of science and technology are from the science and technology departments; telecommunications-related data are from the industrial and information departments; the data of household registration, social security and civil motor vehicles are from the public security departments; the data in connection with urban and rural minimum living security and assistance and support for people in extreme poverty are from the civil affairs departments; the data of finance are from the financial departments; the data of new employment in cities and towns and insurance for urban employees are from human resources and social security departments; the data in connection with environmental protection are from the ecological environment departments; the data in connection with urban construction are from the housing and urban-rural construction departments; the data of transportation are from the transportation departments; the data of the construction of direct spring drinking projects are from urban and rural water affairs departments; the data of aquatic product output and agriculture are from the agricultural and rural departments; the data of forestry are from the garden and forestry departments; the data of import and export, exhibitions, newly established overseas enterprises and dispatched service workers are from the commercial departments; the data of tourism and culture are from the cultural and tourism departments; the data of health are from the health departments; the data of safety production are from the emergency management departments; the data of intellectual property rights are from the market supervision departments; the data of sports are from the sports departments; the data of medical insurance are from the medical security departments; the data of finance are from local financial supervision and management departments; the data of investment promotion and foreign investment are from the investment promotion departments; the data of market entities are from the administrative examination and approval service departments; the data of logistics are from the port logistics departments; the data of the security of the disabled are from the Disabled Persons' Federation; the data of postal service and express delivery are from the postal administration departments; the data of residents' income and expenditure, Engel coefficient, price index, the data of grain and animal husbandry, and the holding quantity of main durable consumer goods in urban and rural households are from Jinan investigation team of the National Bureau of Statistics; the data of the transformation from old growth drivers to new ones in Jinan Start-up Area are from the Administrative Committee of Jinan Start-up Area; other data are from the Municipal Bureau of Statistics.

2022 年的济南
Jinan in 2022

12027.5
地区生产总值（亿元）
Gross Domestic Product
(100 million yuan)

61.7
第三产业比重 (%)
Proportion of Tertiary
Industry(%)

941.5
常住人口（万人）
Permanent Population
(10 000 persons)

1001.1
一般公共预算收入（亿元）
General Public Budget
Revenue(100 million yuan)

3.8
全社会固定资产投资增长幅度 (%)
Growth Rate Total Investment in
Fixed Assets(%)

327.1
海关进出口总额（亿美元）
Total Value of Imports and
Exports(100 million USD)

128287
人均地区生产总值（元）
Per Capita Gross Domestic
Product(yuan)

4878.1
社会消费品零售总额（亿元）
Total Retail Sale of Consumer
Goods(100 million yuan)

59459
城镇居民人均可支配收入（元）
Per Capita Disposable Income of
Urban Households(yuan)

23844
农村居民人均可支配收入（元）
Per Capita Disposable Income of
Rural Households(yuan)

101.4
居民消费价格指数
Consumer Price Index

济南一日

A Day in Jinan

每日创造

Daily Production

27428.6
一般公共预算收入
（万元 / 天）
General Public Budget Revenue
(10 000 yuan/day)

33577.4
一般公共预算支出
（万元 / 天）
General Public Budget Expenditure
(10 000 yuan/day)

8960.5
海关进出口总额
（万美元 / 天）
Total Value of Imports and Exports
(10 000 USD/day)

39397
公路客运量
（人 / 天）
Highways Passenger Traffic
(person/day)

11521.1
第一产业（万元 / 天）
Primary Industry(10 000 yuan/day)

329519.5
地区生产总值（万元 / 天）
Gross Domestic Product (10 000 yuan/day)

22581
民航客运量
（人 / 天）
Civil Aviation Passenger Traffic
(person/day)

114527.1
第二产业（万元 / 天）
Secondary Industry(10 000 yuan/day)

450
生产汽车
（辆 / 天）
Automobile Manufacturing
(unit/day)

203471.2
第三产业（万元 / 天）
Tertiary Industry(10 000 yuan/day)

8717
发电量
（万千瓦时 / 天）
Power Generating Capacity
(10 000 kWh/day)

19524
蔬菜产量
（吨 / 天）
Output of Vegetables
(ton/day)

8115
粮食产量
（吨 / 天）
Output of Grain Crops
(ton/day)

2112
生产服务器
（台 / 天）
Server Manufacturing
(unit/day)

每日生活
Daily Life

114853.7
批发零售业零售额（万元/天）
Total Retail Sale of Wholesale and Retail Trades (10 000 yuan/day)

743.9
住宿业零售额（万元/天）
Total Retail Sale of Accommodation (10 000 yuan/day)

18049.2
餐饮业零售额（万元/天）
Total Retail Sale of Catering Industry (10 000 yuan/day)

133646.8
社会消费品零售总额（万元/天）
Total Retail Sale of Consumer Goods (10 000 yuan/day)

176
出生人口（人/天）
Population of Birth (person/day)

218
死亡人口（人/天）
Population of Death (person/day)

2674.8
城乡居民生活用电量（万千瓦时/天）
Household Electricity Consumption of Urban and Rural Residents (10 000 kWh/day)

132
登记结婚（对/天）
Registered Marriages (couple/day)

353
城镇非私营单位在岗职工平均工资（元/天）
Average Wages of On-post Staff in Urban Non Private Entities(yuan/day)

64
离婚（对/天）
Divorces (couple/day)

163
城镇居民人均可支配收入（元/天）
Per Capita Disposable Income of Urban Households(yuan/day)

138.7
自来水供水量（万吨/天）
Volume of Water Supply (10 000 tons/day)

98
城镇居民人均消费支出（元/天）
Per Capita Consumer Expenditure of Urban Households(yuan/day)

541.7
天然气供气量（万立方米/天）
Total Natural Gas Supply (10 000 cu.m/day)

7610
生活垃圾清运量（吨/天）
Domestic Waste Removed and Transported(ton/day)

41
农村居民人均消费支出（元/天）
Per Capita Consumer Expenditure of Rural Households(yuan/day)

65
农村居民人均可支配收入（元/天）
Per Capita Disposable Income of Rural Households(yuan/day)

综 合
General

地区生产总值（亿元）

Gross Domestic Product (100 million yuan)

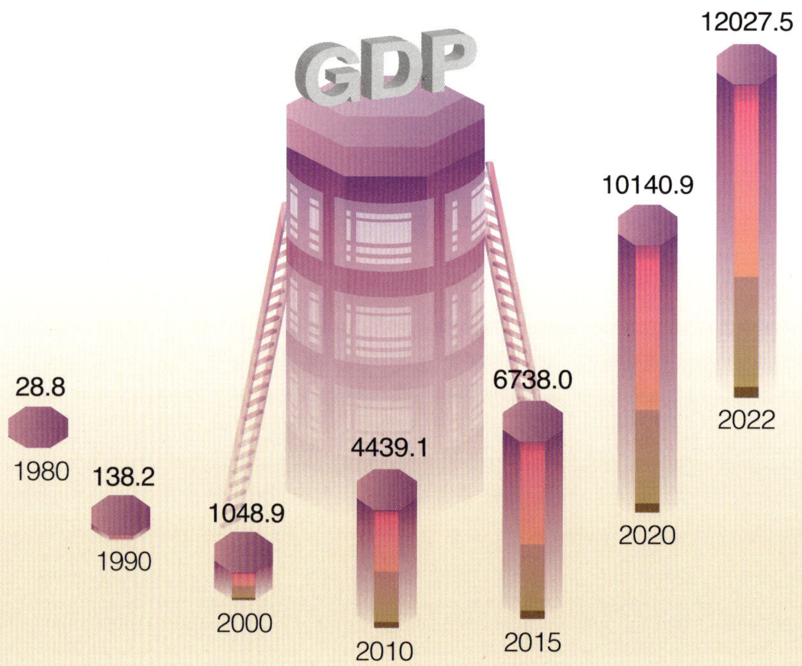

人均地区生产总值（元）

Per Capita Gross Domestic Product (yuan)

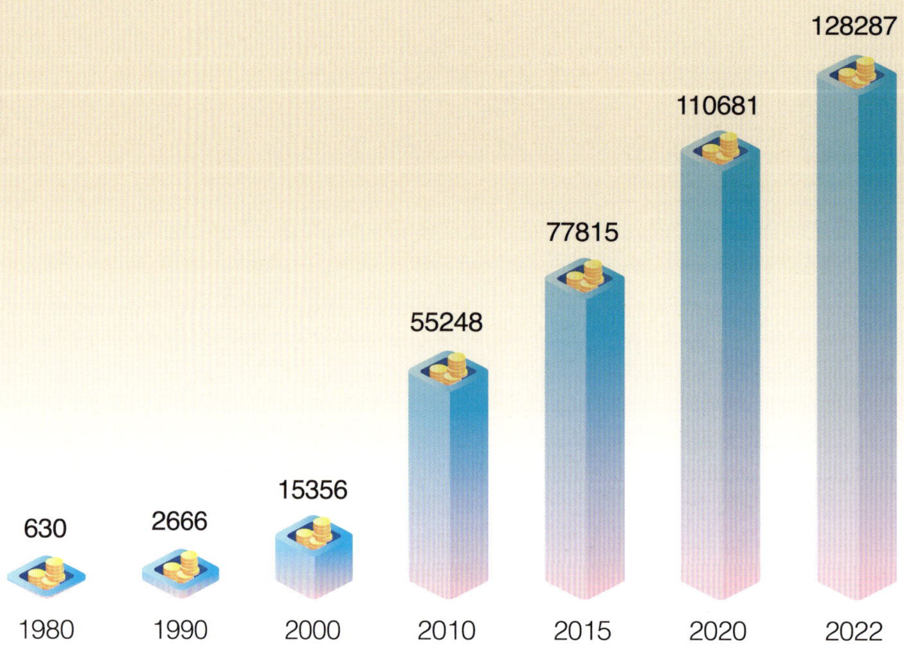

人 口
Population

年末户籍总人口（万人）
Registered Population Year-end (10 000 persons)

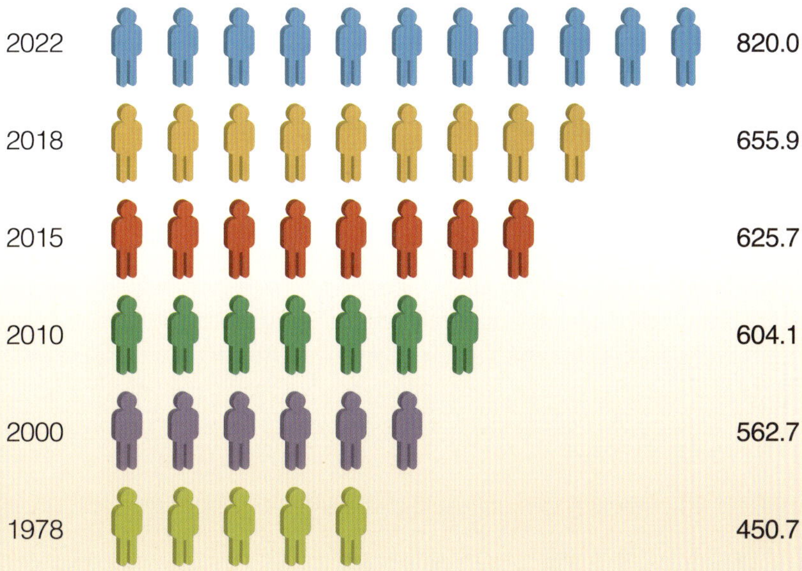

人口自然变动情况（‰）
Natural Changes of Population (‰)

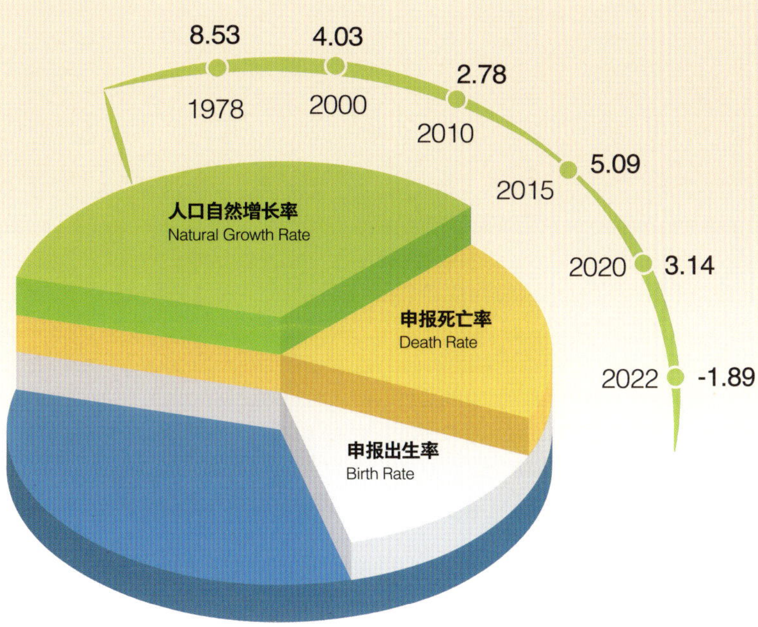

就 业
Employment

全社会从业人员（万人）
Total Employed Persons (10 000 persons)

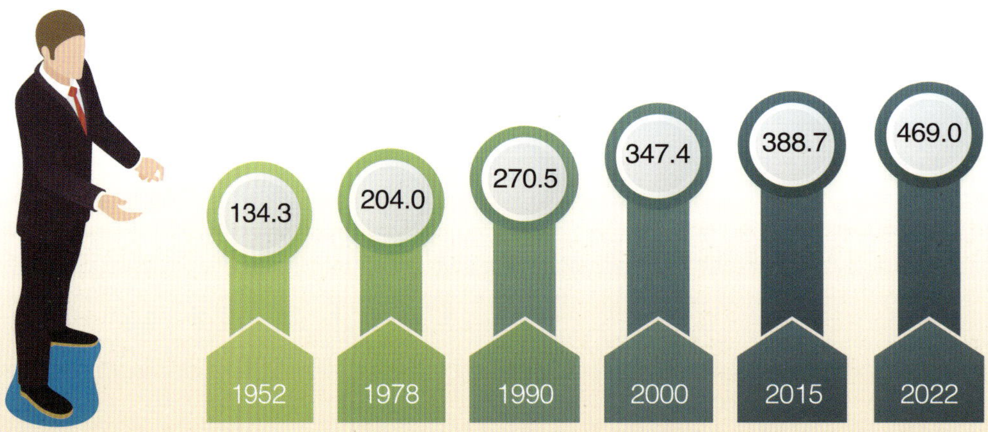

在岗职工平均工资（元）
Average Wage of Staff and Workers (yuan)

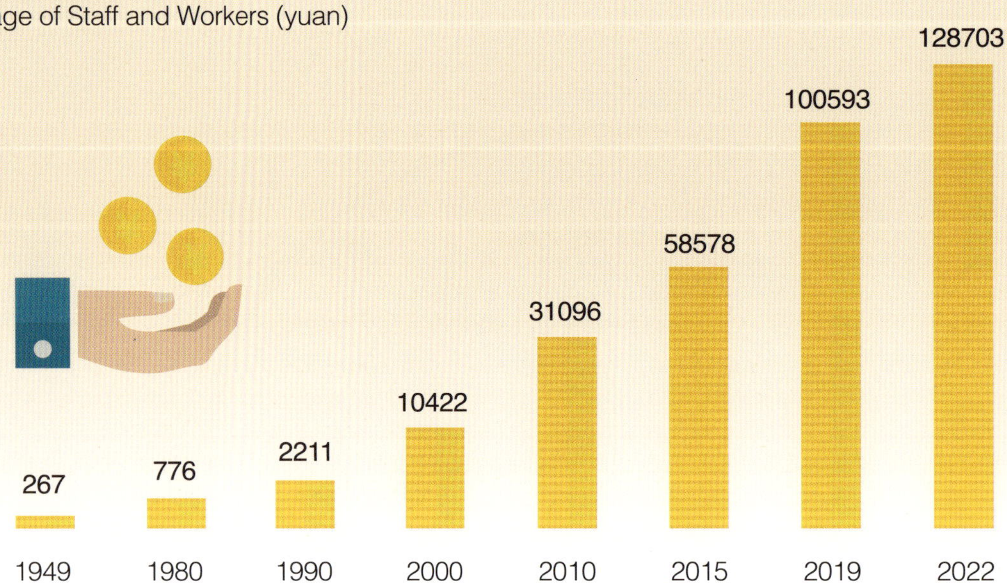

注：1．2006 年以后为法人单位在岗职工口径；2．2019 年以后为城镇非私营单位在岗职工口径。

Notes: 1.The data after 2006 are based on the caliber of on-the-job employees of legal entities.
2.The data after 2019 are based on the caliber of on-post staff in urban non private entities.

财政 金融
Government Finance Financial

一般公共预算收入支出（亿元）
General Public Budget Revenue and Expenditure (100 million yuan)

一般公共预算收入
General Public Budget Revenue

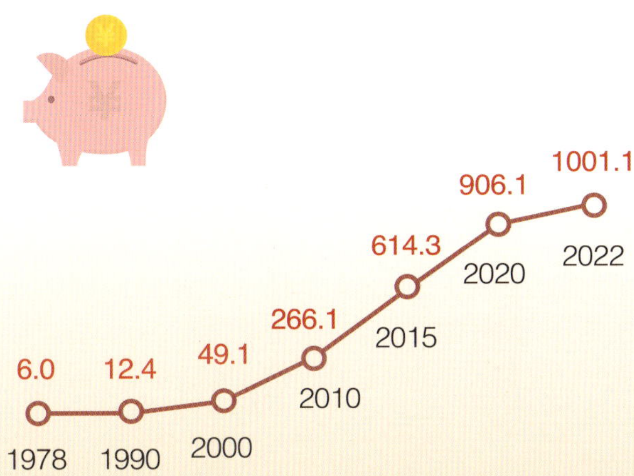

一般公共预算支出
General Public Budget Expenditure

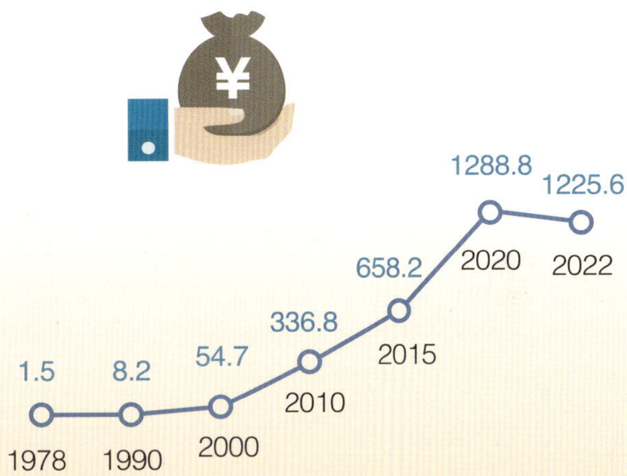

金融机构人民币存、贷款余额（亿元）
The Ending Balance of all Deposits and Loans in RMB of Financial Institutions (100 million yuan)

存
Deposits

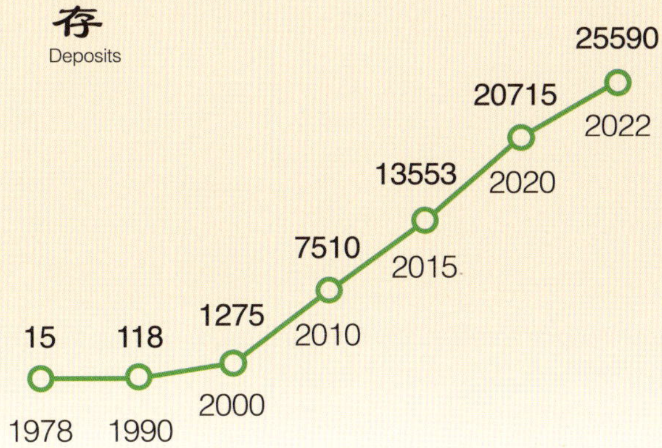

贷
Loans

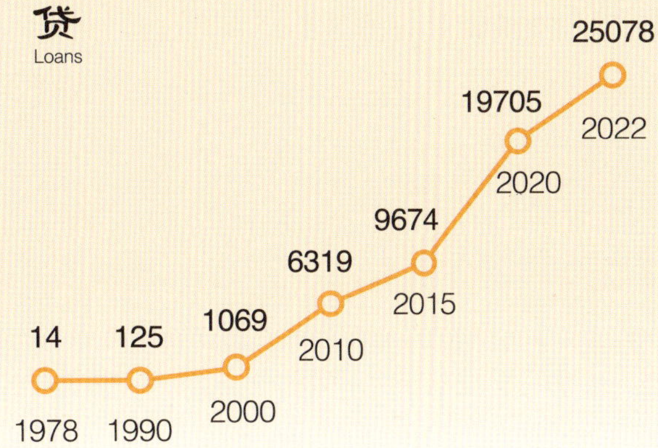

人民生活
People's Livelihood

城乡居民人均可支配收入（元）
Per Capita Disposable Income of Urban and Rural Households（yuan）

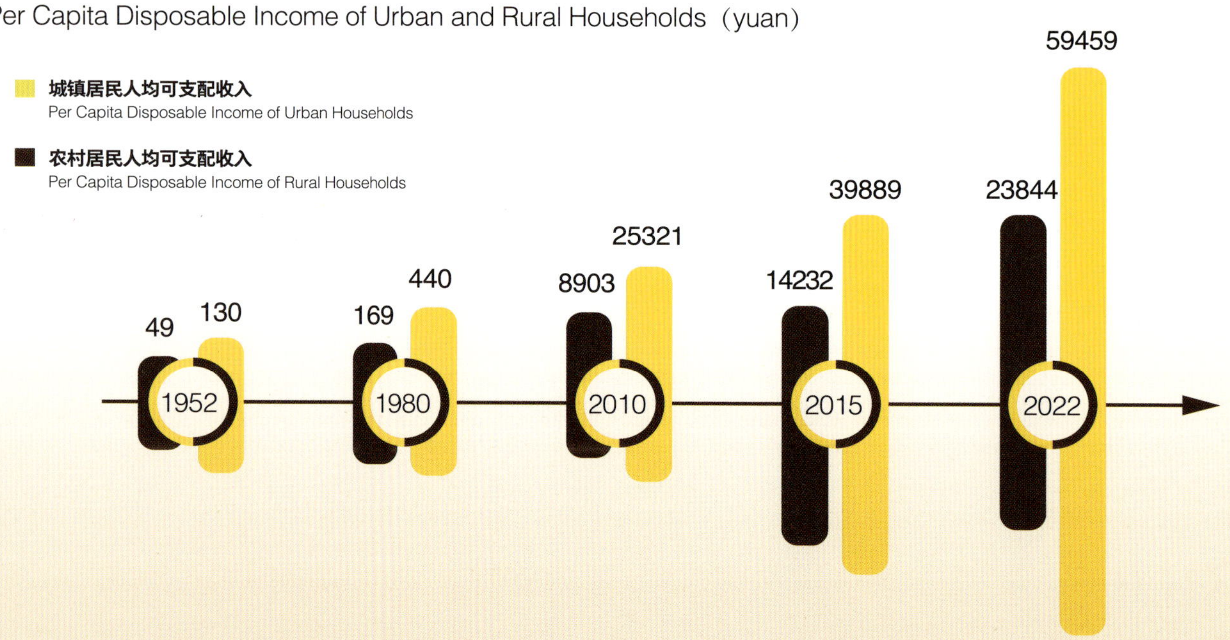

注：城乡一体化改革，2015 年起为城镇居民人均可支配收入和农村居民人均可支配收入口径；之前年份为城市居民人均可支配收入和农民人均纯收入口径。
Note: The urban-rural integration reform has been based on the caliber of per capita disposable income of urban and rural households since 2015; the urban-rural integration reform in previous years was based on the caliber of per capita disposable income of urban households and the per capita net income of farmers.

城乡居民人均消费支出（元）
Per Capita Consumption Expenditure of Urban and Rural Households（yuan）

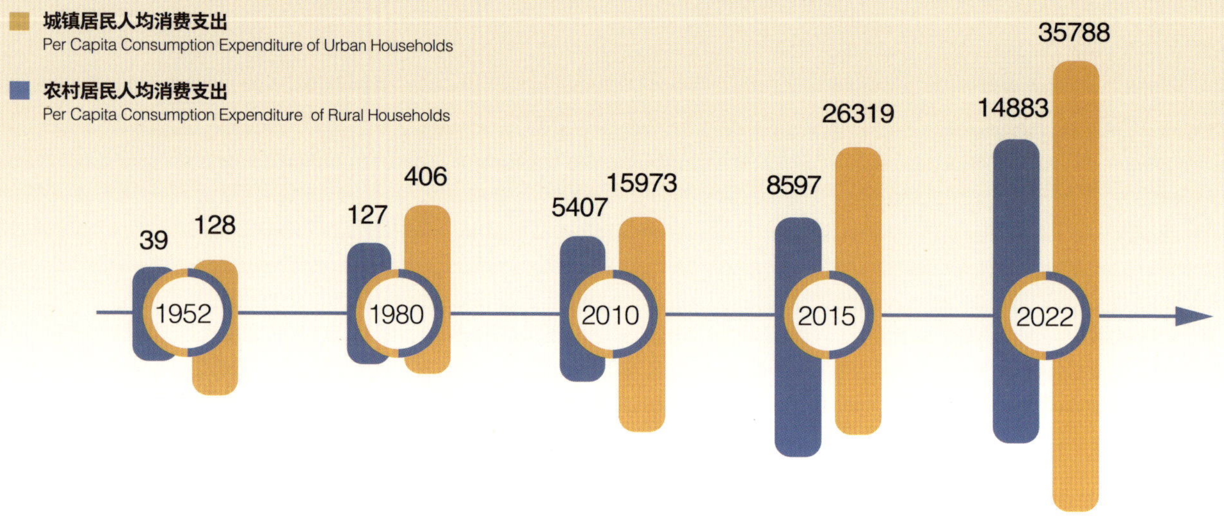

注：从 2015 年开始，本市居民收支调查指标采用新口径。“农村居民人均消费支出”2014 年以前为农民人均生活费支出口径。
Note: Starting from 2015, the city's residents' income and expenditure survey indicators adopt a new caliber. "Per capita consumption expenditure of rural households" was the “per capita living expenses of farmers” before 2014.

城乡居民恩格尔系数（%）

Engel's Coefficient of Urban and Rural Households (%)

城镇居民恩格尔系数

Engel's Coefficient of Urban Households

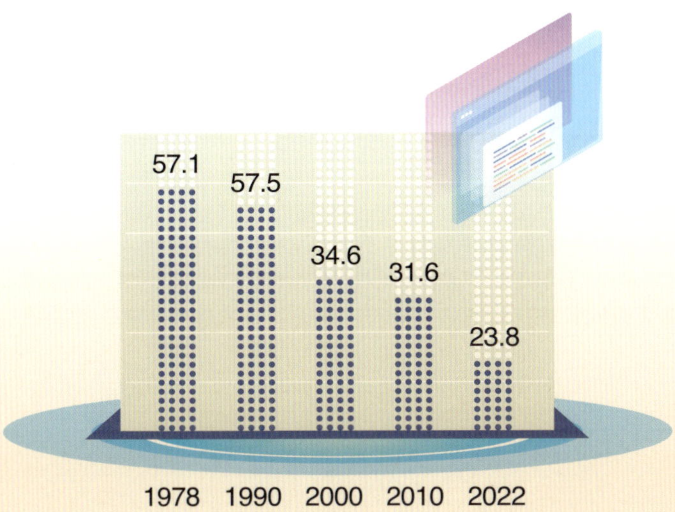

农村居民恩格尔系数

Engel's Coefficient of Rural Households

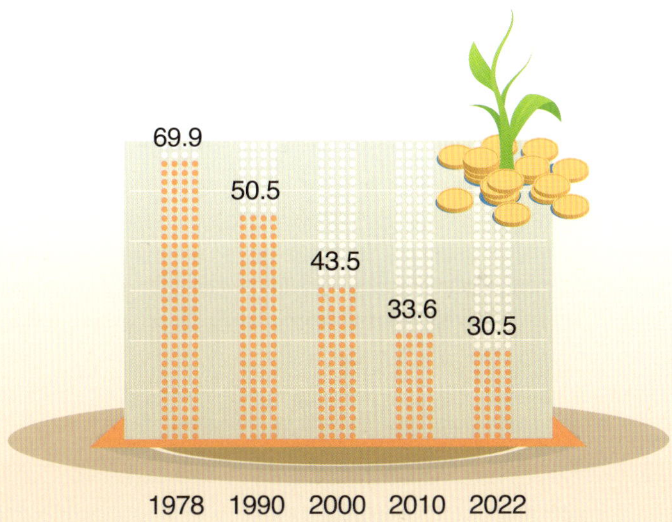

人民币住户存款余额（亿元）

The Balance RMB Household Deposits（100 million yuan）

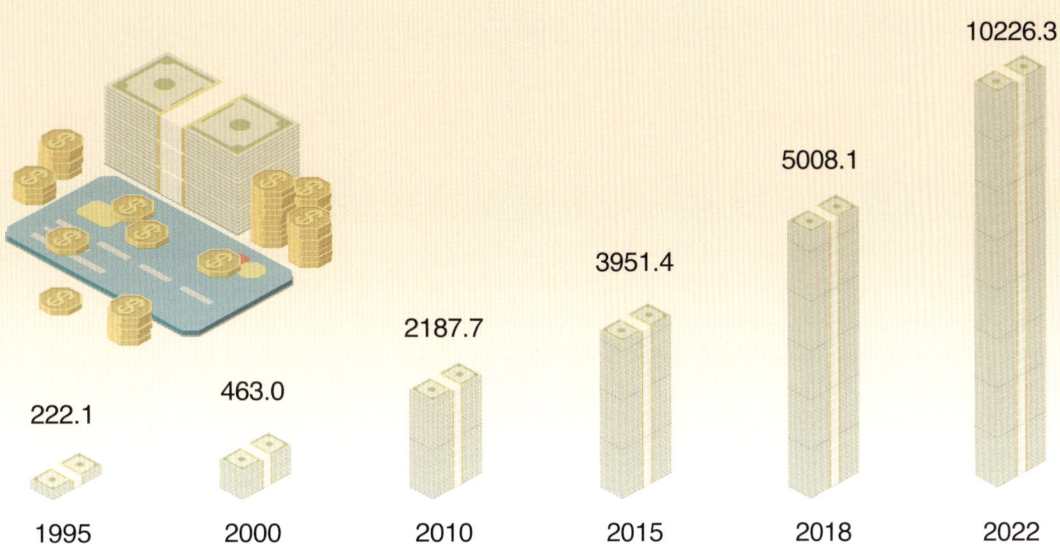

注：2015 年之前为城乡居民人民币储蓄存款余额口径，2015 年调整为住户存款余额口径。
Note: Before 2015, the caliber was the balance of saving deposit (RMB) of urban and rural Households, and has been adjusted to balance held on deposit of households since 2015.

物价
Price

居民消费价格指数与商品零售价格指数（以上年为 100）
Consumer Price Index and Retail Price Index (Preceding Last Year=100)

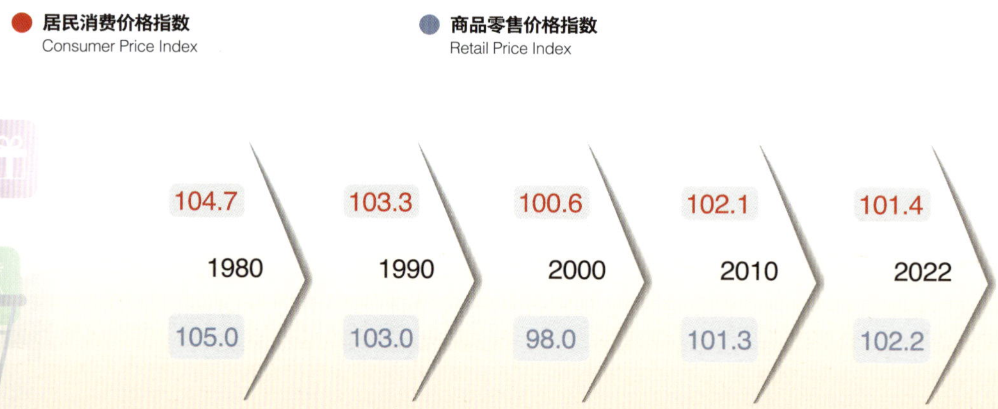

工业生产者出厂价格指数与工业生产者购进价格指数（以上年为 100）
Producer Price Index and Purchasing Price Index for Industrial Products (Preceding Last Year=100)

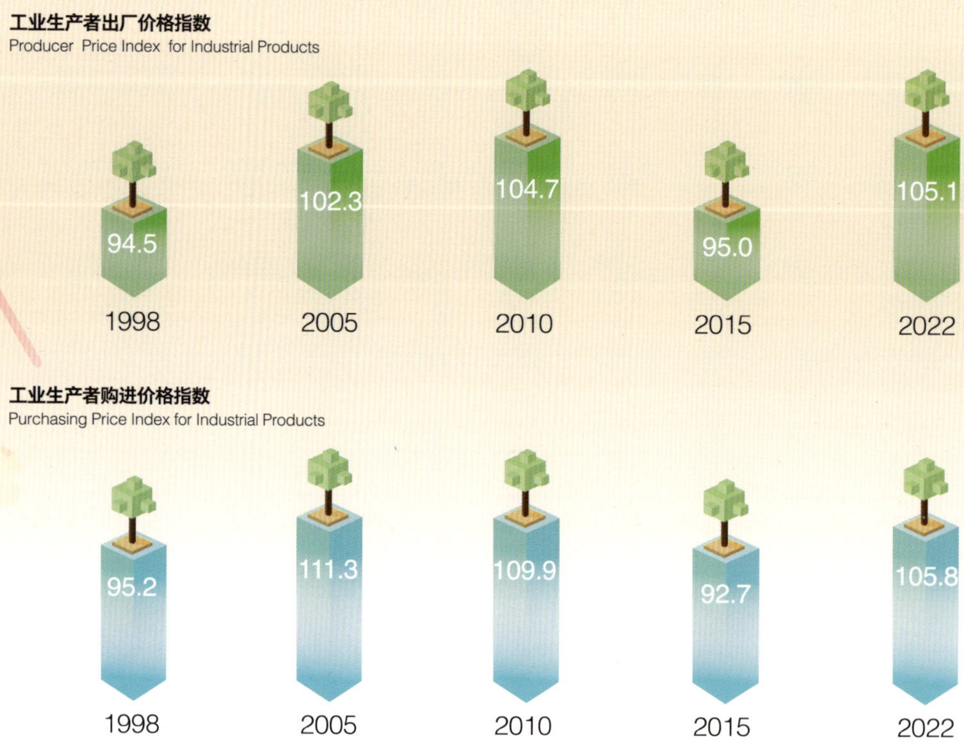

注：2020 年起，“工业生产者出厂价格指数”与“工业生产者购进价格指数”指标为全省数据。
Note: Starting in 2020,the"Producer Price Indices for Industrial Products"and" Purchasing Price Index for Industrial Producer "are province-wide data.

农业
Agriculture

农林牧渔业总产值（亿元）
Gross Output Value of Agriculture, Forestry, Animal Husbandry and Fishery(100 million yuan)

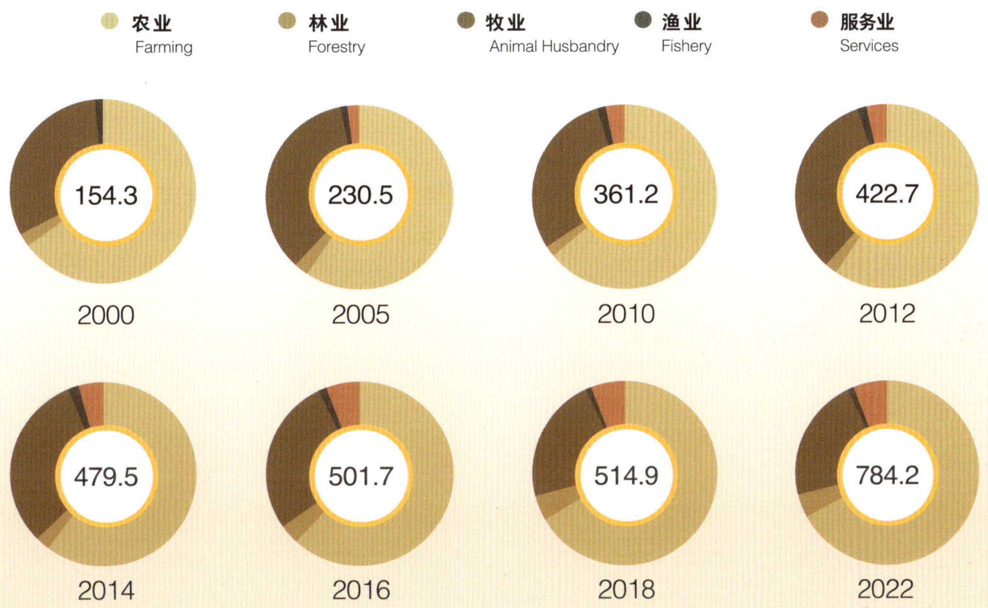

主要农产品产量（万吨）
Output of Main Agricultural Products (10 000 tons)

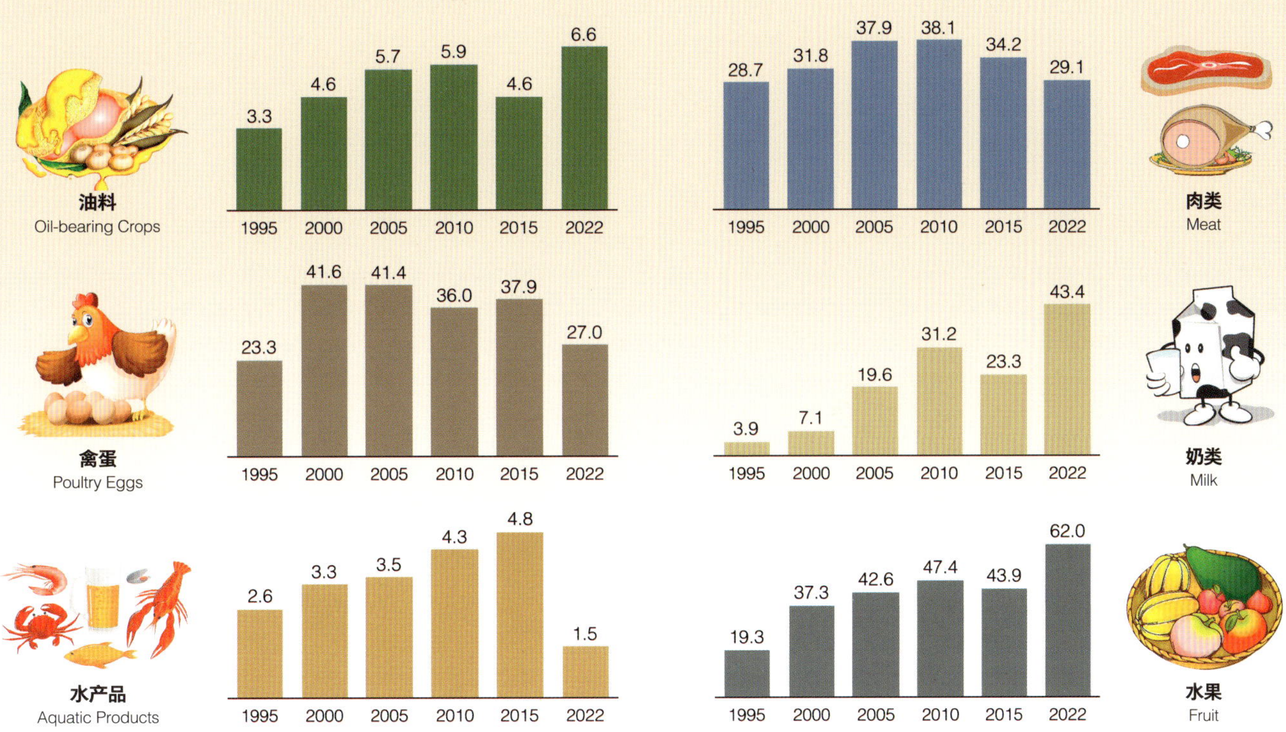

工 业
Industry

规模以上工业营业收入（亿元）
Business Revenue of Industrial Enterprises Above Designated Size (100 million yuan)

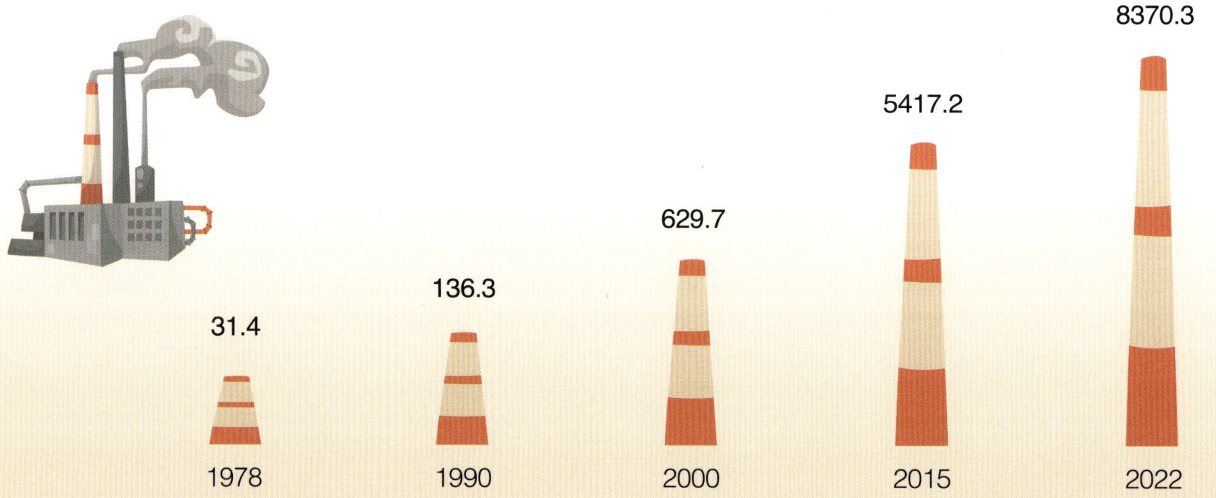

注：2018 年以前为主营业务收入口径。
Note: Before 2018, the main business income caliber.

规模以上工业利税总额（亿元）
Total Profits and Taxes of Industrial Enterprises Above Designated Size (100 million yuan)

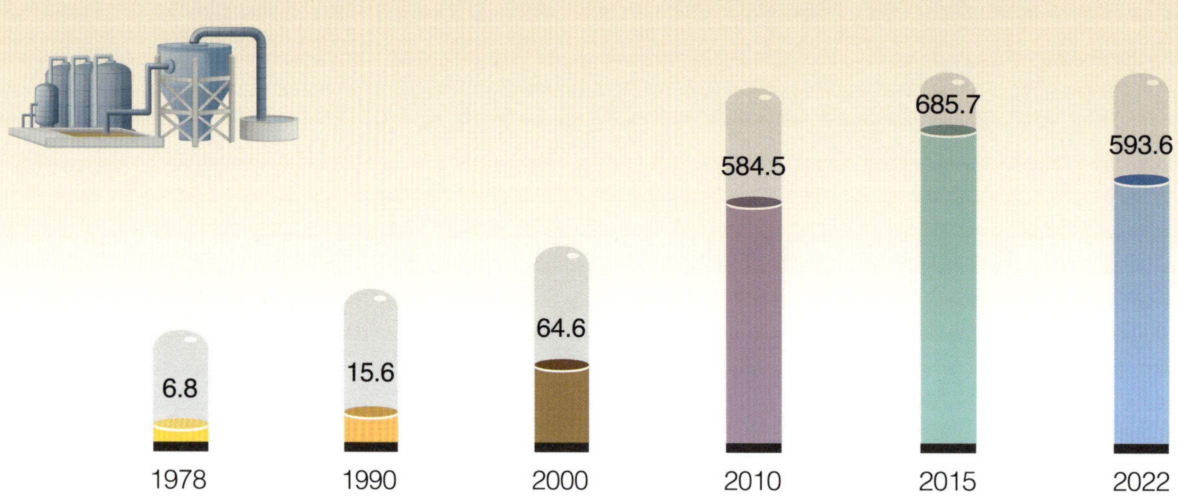

规模以上工业利润总额（亿元）
Total Profits of Industrial Enterprises Above Designated Size (100 million yuan)

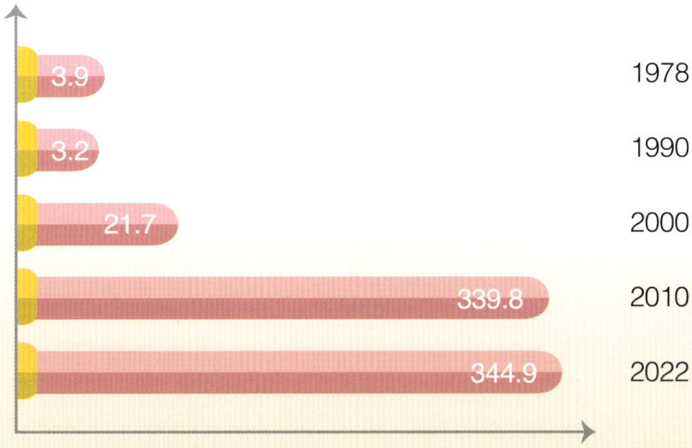

主要工业产品产量
Output of Major Industrial Products

发电量（亿千瓦时）
Power Generating Capacity (100 million kWh)

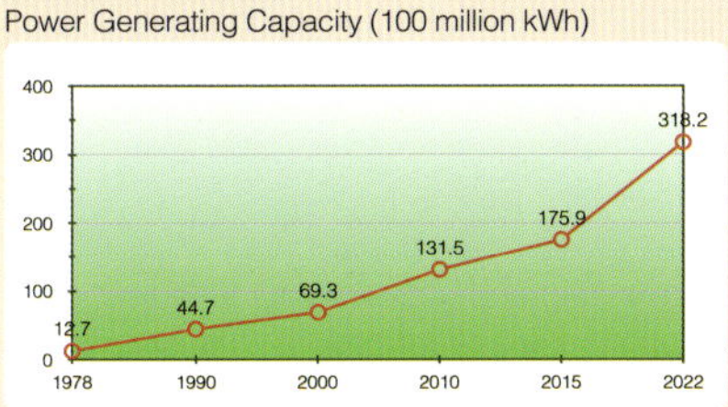

服务器（万台）
Servers (10 000 unit)

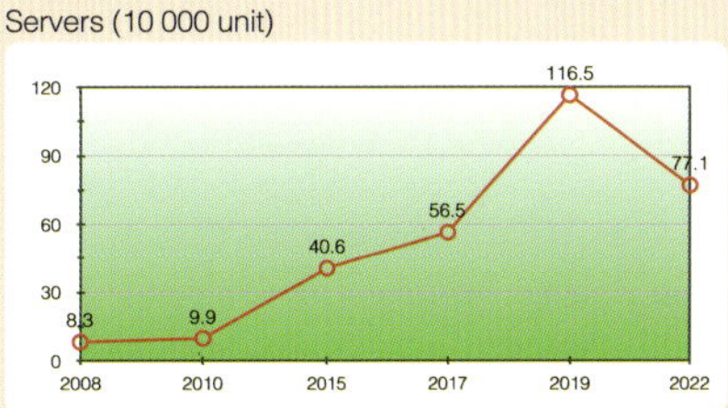

原油加工量（万吨）
Crude Processing Volume (10 000 tons)

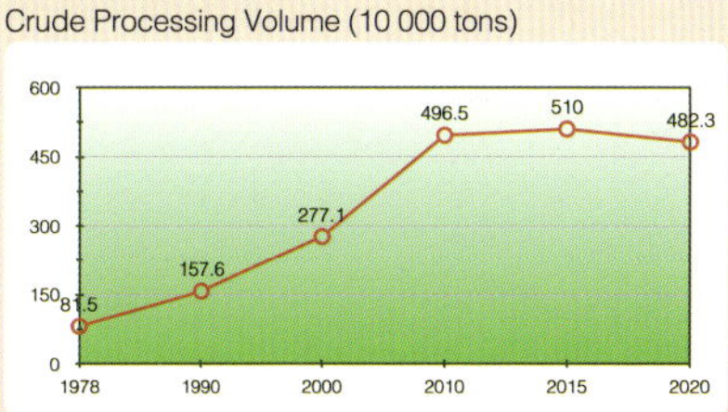

化肥（万吨）
Chemical Fertilizer (10 000 tons)

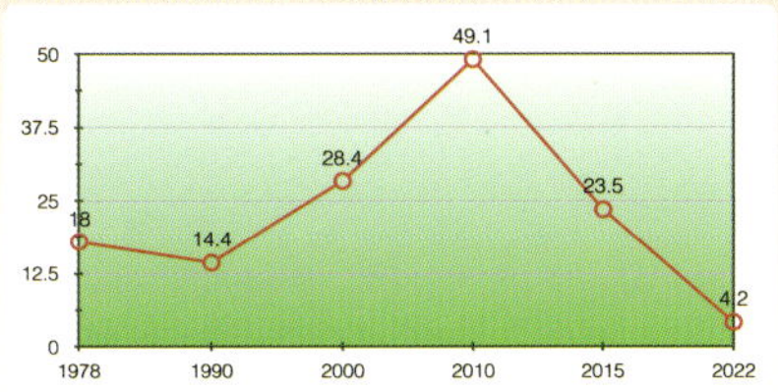

水泥（万吨）
Cement (10 000 tons)

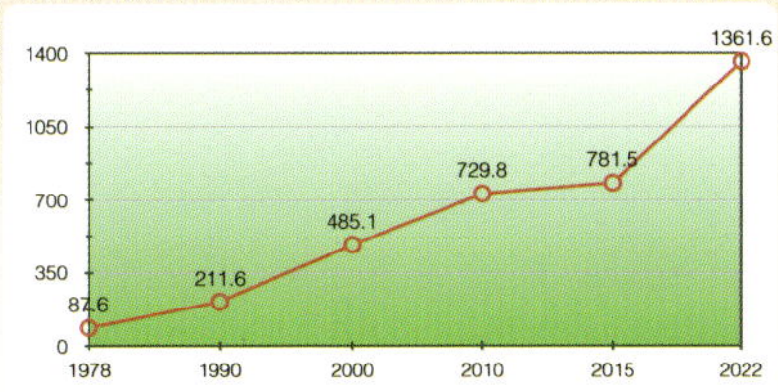

啤酒（万千升）
Beer (10 000 kiloliter)

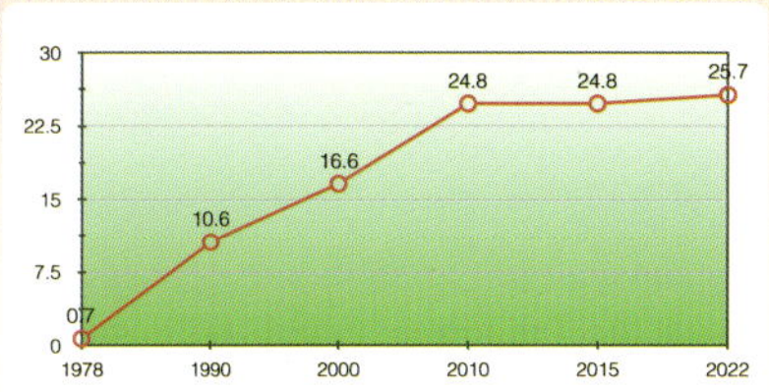

汽车（辆）
Motor Vehicles (unit)

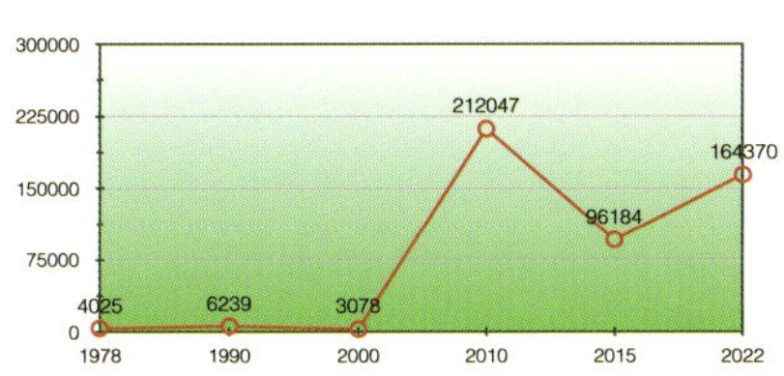

钢（万吨）
Steel (10 000 tons)

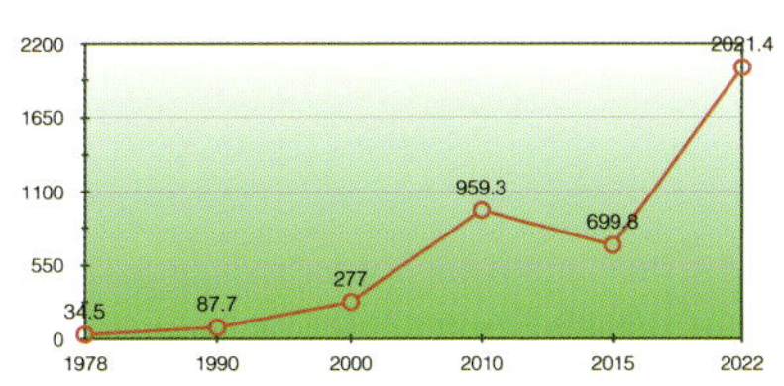

初级形态塑料（万吨）
Primary Plastic (10 000 tons)

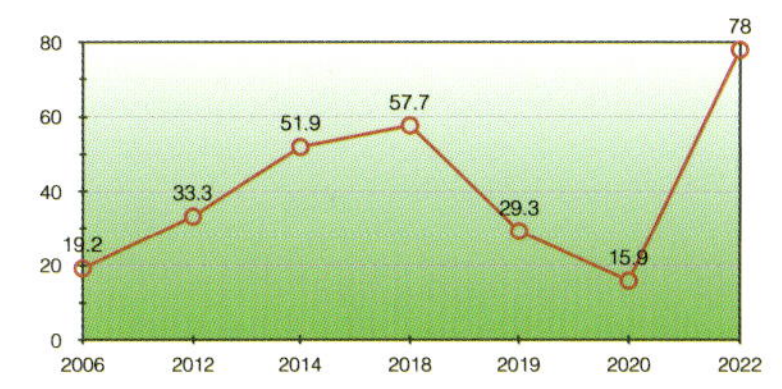

投资
Investment

固定资产投资增长幅度 (%)
Growth Rate of Investment in Fixed Assets(%)

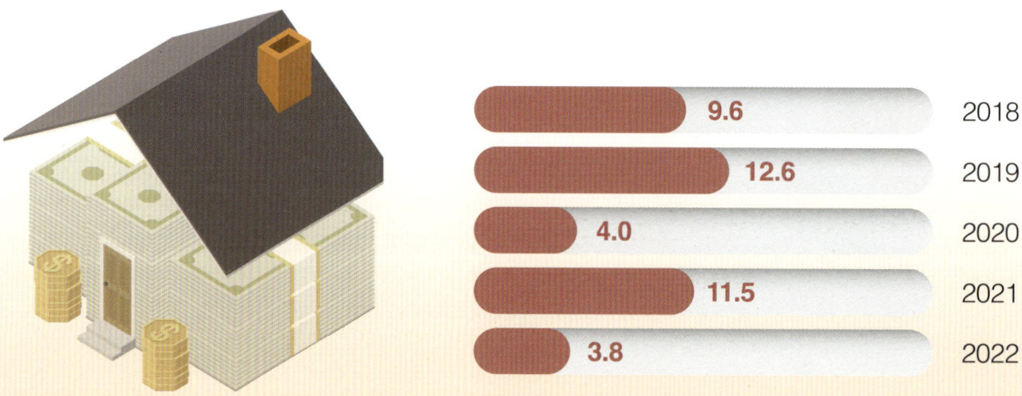

房地产开发投资总额（亿元）
Estate Development Investment(100 million yuan)

贸易外经
Domestic and Foreign Trade

社会消费品零售总额（亿元）
Total Retail Sales of Consumer Goods (100 million yuan)

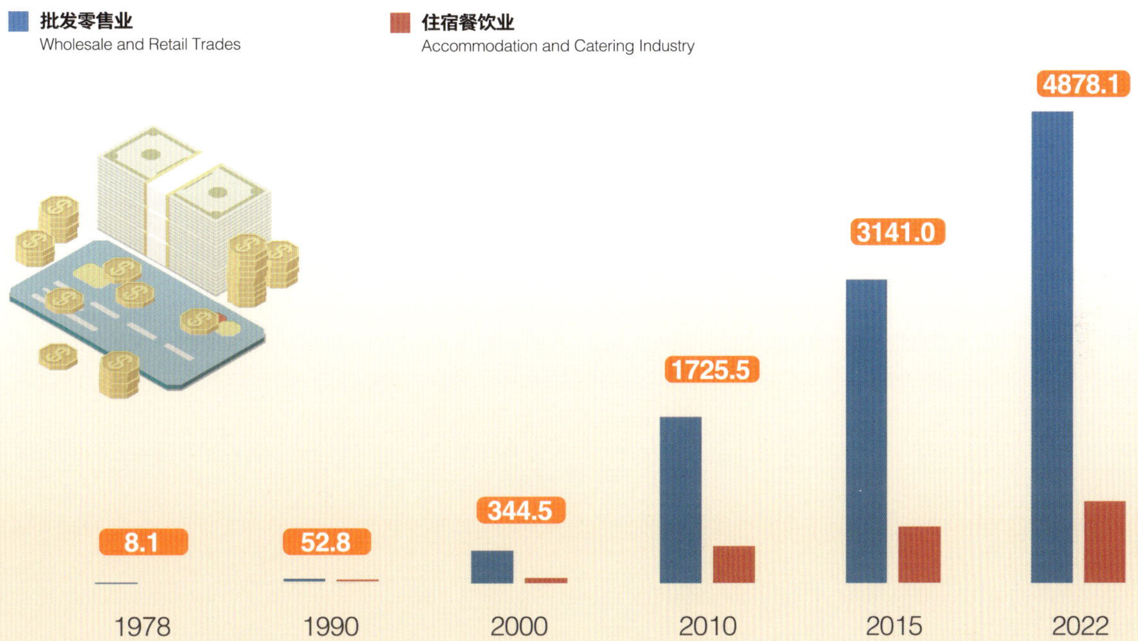

实际使用外资金额（万美元）
Actual Use of Foreign Capital (10 000 USD)

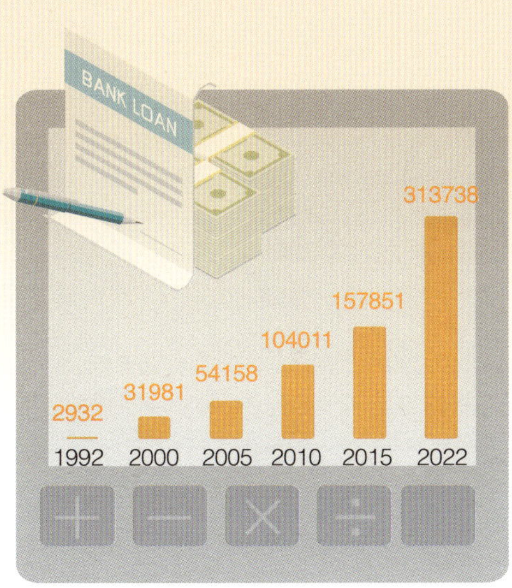

海关进出口总额（万美元）
Total Value of Imports and Exports (10 000 USD)

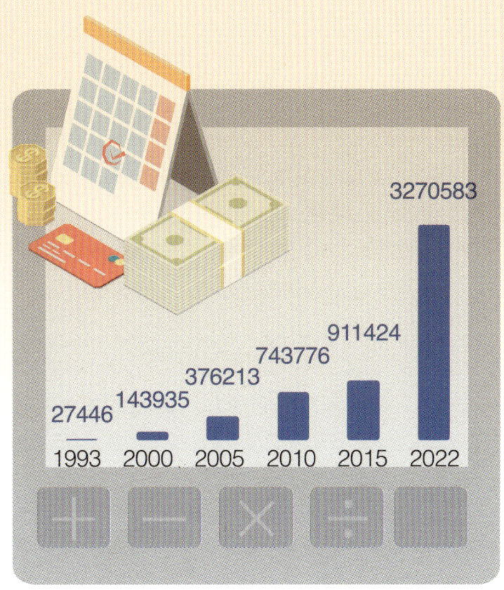

城市建设
Urban Public

全社会用电量（亿千瓦时）
Electricity Consumption (100 million kWh)

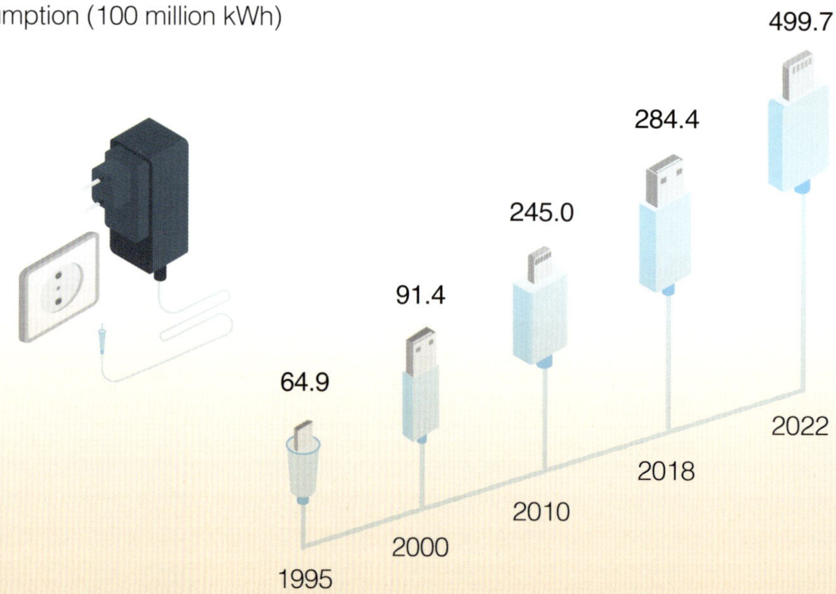

全社会供气量
Total Social Gas Supply

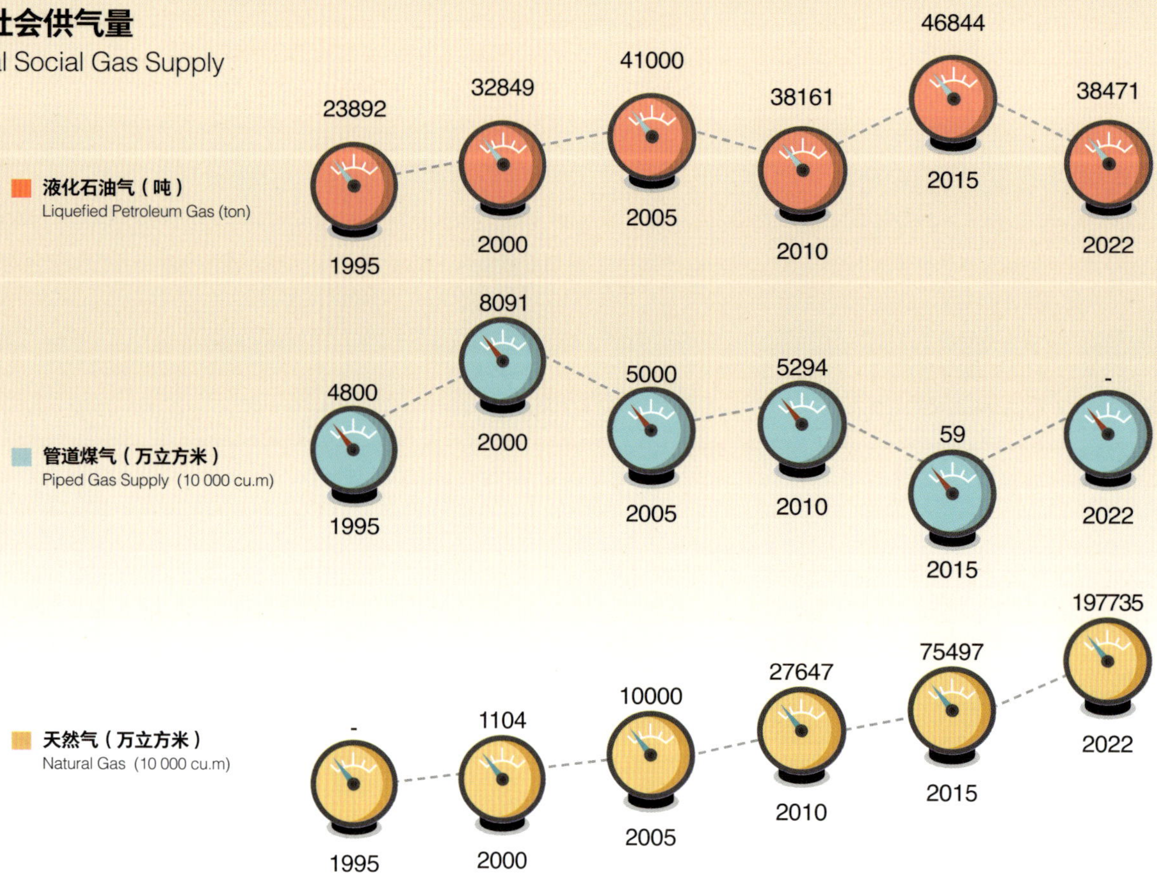

供热面积（万平方米）
Area of Central Heating (10 000 sq.m)

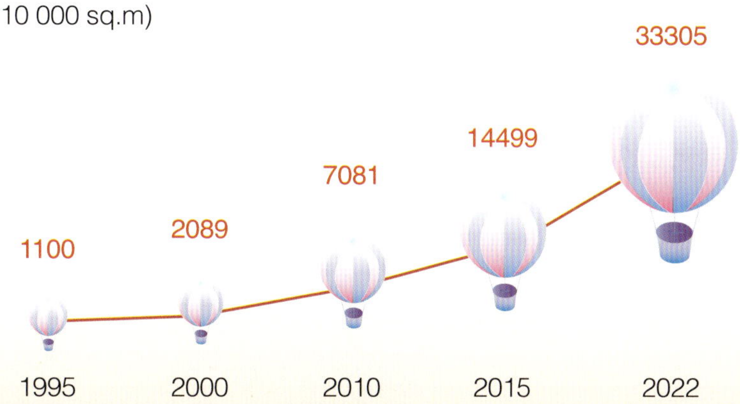

公共交通客运量（万人次）
Public Transportation of Passenger Traffic (10 000 person-times)

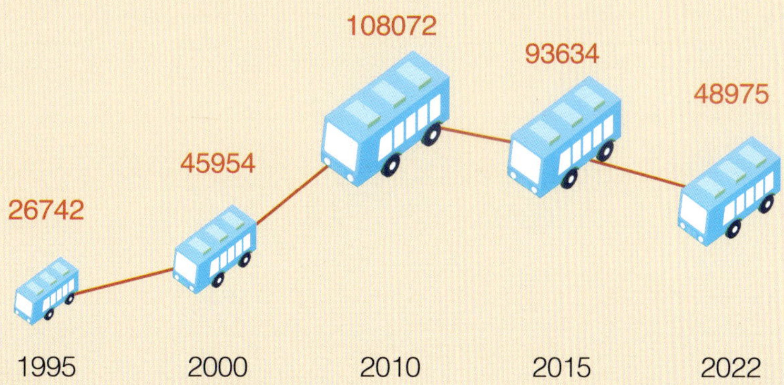

人均公园绿地面积（平方米/人）
Per Capita Public Green Area (sq.m/person)

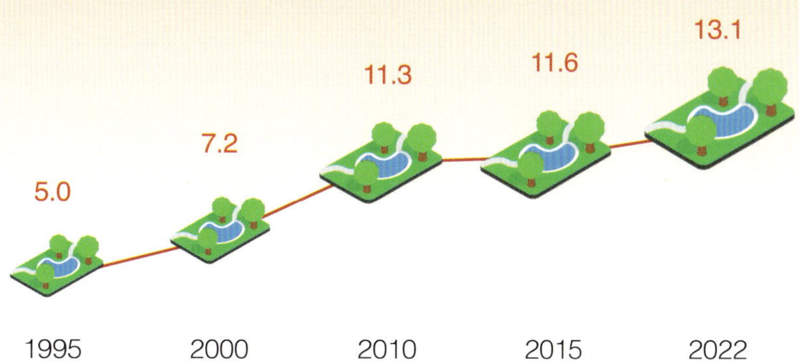

交通 邮电
Transportation Post and Telecommunication

公路通车里程（公里）
Length of Highways in Operation（km）

 # 高速公路（公里）
Expressway（km）

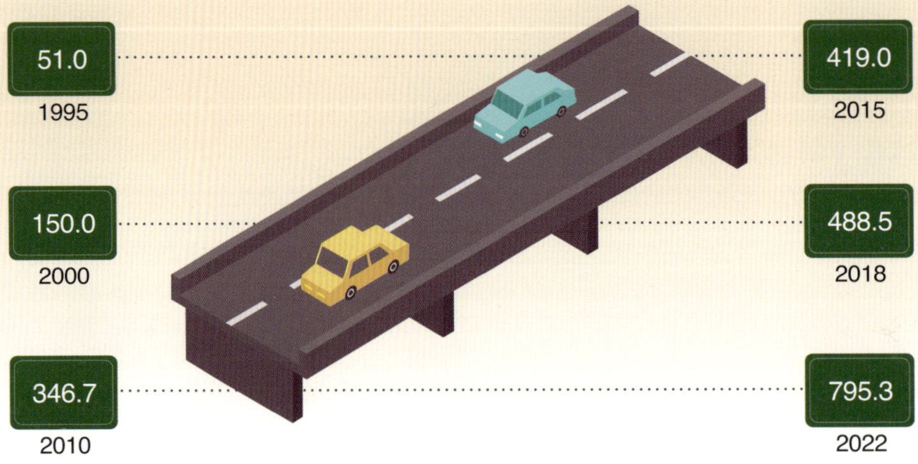

移动电话用户、 宽带互联网接入用户数（万户）
Number of Mobile Telephone Subscribers, Subscribers of Broad Band Internet(10 000 subscribers)

移动电话用户（万户）
Number of Mobile Telephone Subscribers (10 000 subscribers)

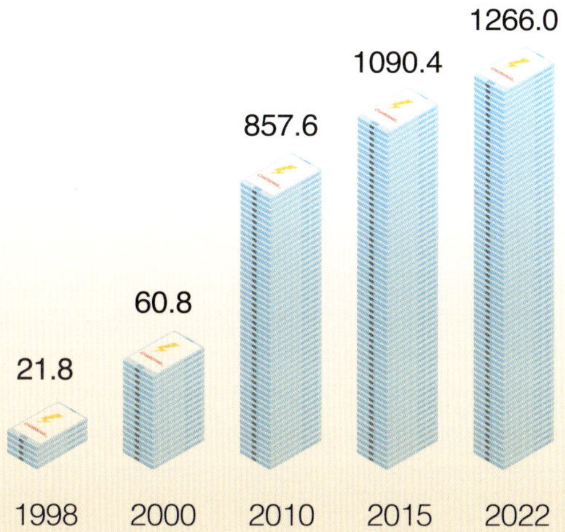

宽带互联网接入用户数（万户）
Subscribers of Broad Band Internet (10 000 subscribers)

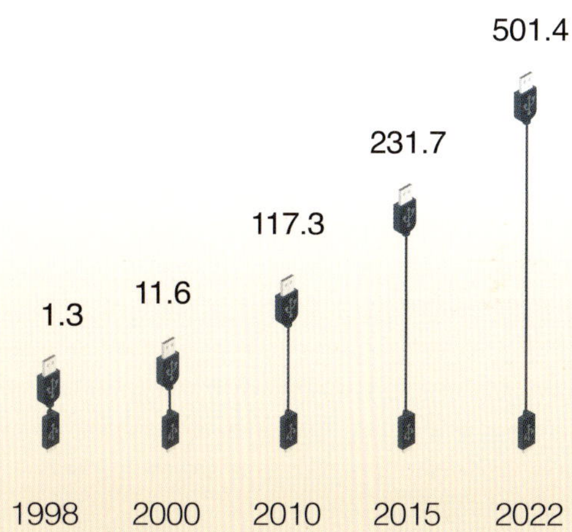

客运量（万人）
Passenger Traffic(10 000 persons)

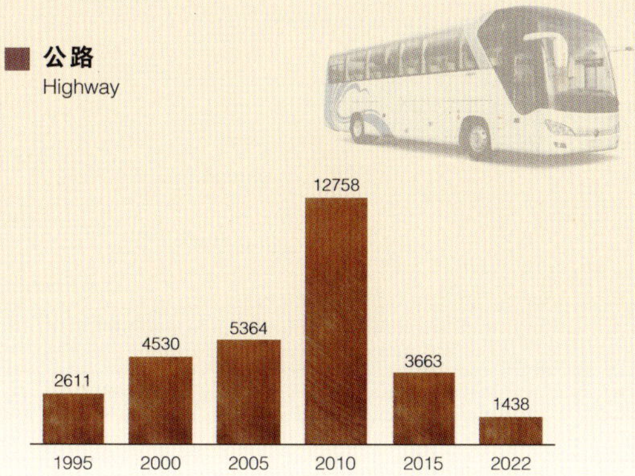

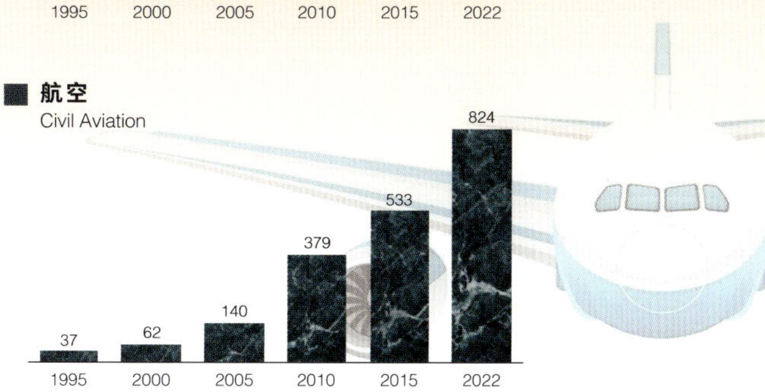

货运量（万吨）
Freight Traffic(10 000 tons)

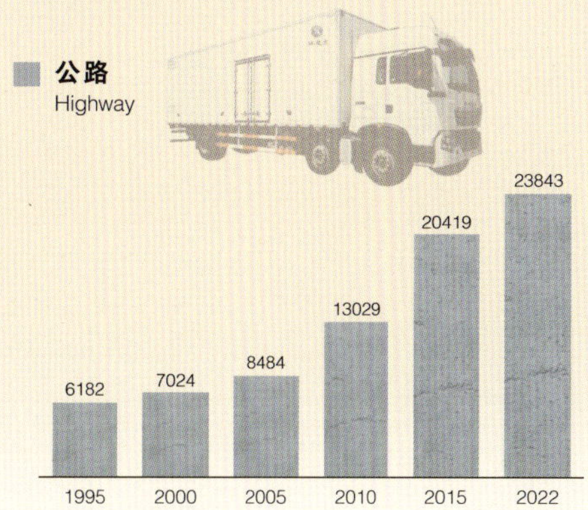

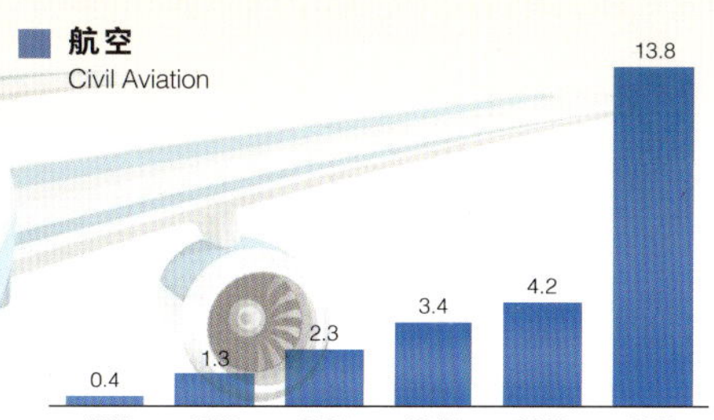

科技 教育 卫生
Science and Technology Education Health

发明专利授权量（件）
The number of invention patents granted(pieces)

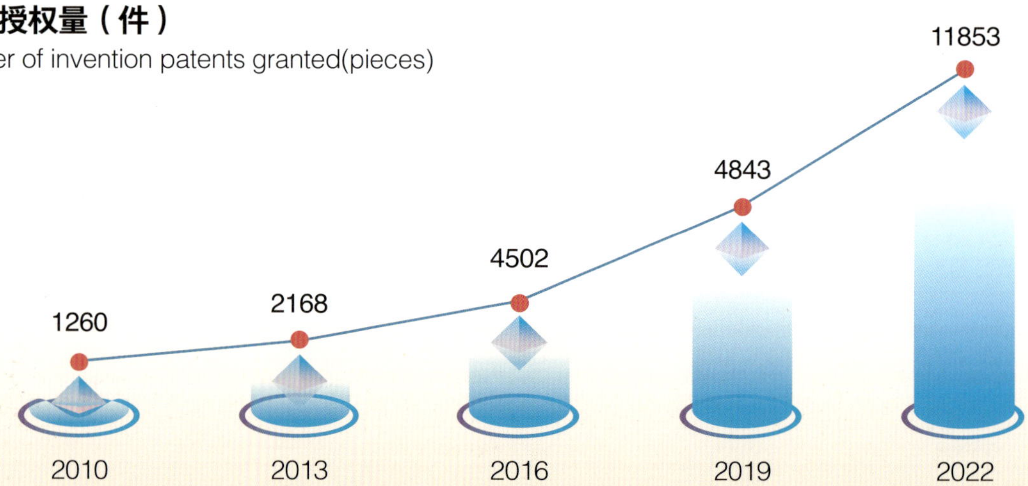

各类学校专任教师（万人）
Full-time Teachers (10 000 persons)

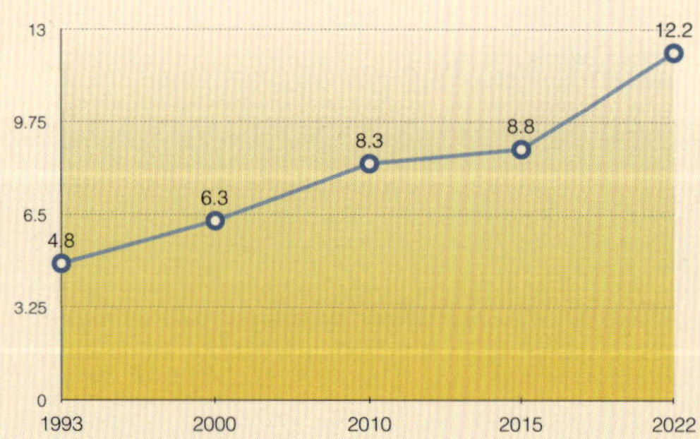

各类学校在校学生（万人）
Total Enrollment (10 000 persons)

每万人拥有医院床位数（张）
Number of Hospitals Beds per 10000 Population (set)

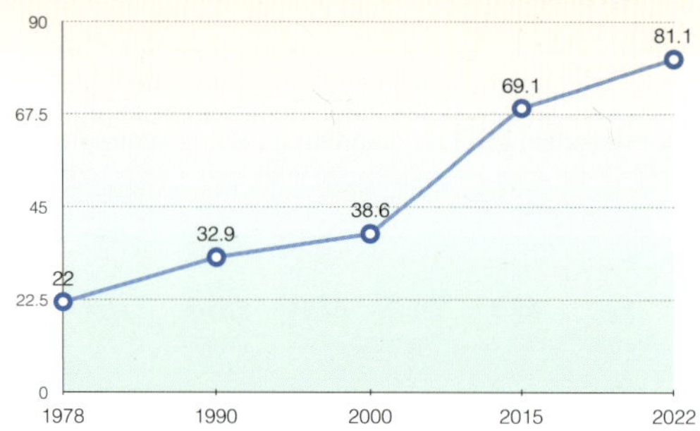

每万人拥有医生数（人）
Number of Doctors per 10000 Population (person)

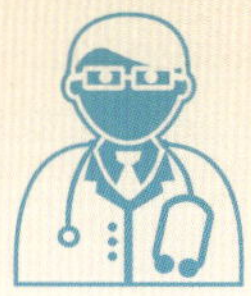

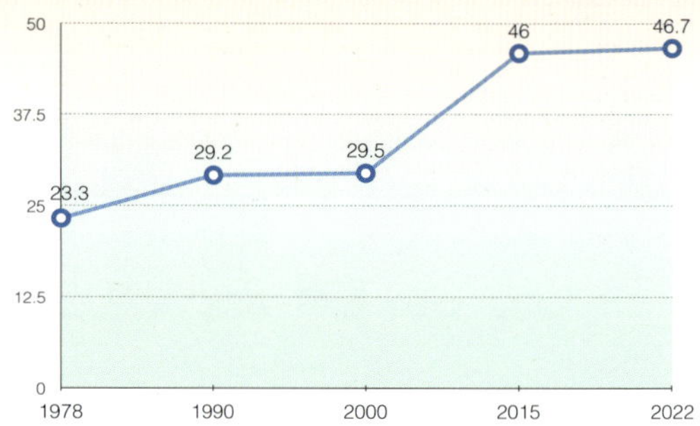

1

行政区划

DIVISIONS OF ADMINISTRATIVE AREAS

1-1 行政区划
Divisions of Administrative Areas

单位：个 (unit)

年份地区	Year and Region	乡 Townships	镇 Towns	街道 Street Communities	村 Village	居委会 Neighborhood committee	土地面积(平方公里) Land Area (sq.km)
全市主要年份							
1989		57	54	53	4710	702	8227
1990		57	54	48	4752	669	8227
1991		57	54	48	4752	670	8227
1992		57	54	48	4759	670	8227
1993		56	55	48	4756	670	8227
1994		55	56	48	4759	670	8227
1995		48	63	49	4723	721	8227
1996		42	68	49	4704	685	8154
1997		42	68	50	4696	616	8154
1998		42	69	50	4711	505	8154
1999		42	69	50	4714	468	8154
2000		42	69	50	4702	416	8154
2001		28	64	54	4677	417	8177
2002		27	65	54	4657	487	8177
2003		27	61	58	4657	487	8177
2004		27	61	58	4657	487	8177
2005		12	53	64	4628	400	8177
2006		11	53	64	4604	487	8177
2007		11	50	73	4563	500	8177
2008		11	50	73	4551	521	8177
2009		11	50	75	4553	522	8177
2010		6	49	86	4552	532	8177
2011		4	51	86	4538	556	8177
2012		4	51	86	4532	586	8177
2013		2	51	90	4548	597	7998
2014		2	51	90	4547	627	7998
2015		2	46	95	4546	641	7998
2016			39	104	4547	669	7998
2017			29	112	4548	711	7998
2018			29	112	4546	740	7998
2019			40	121	5551	847	10244
2020			29	132	5530	861	10244
2021			29	132	4699	992	10244
2022			29	132	4698	1000	10244
2022年分地区							
历下区	Li xia			14		131	101
市中区	Shi zhong			17	77	128	281
槐荫区	Huai yin			16	93	107	152
天桥区	Tian qiao			15	48	153	259
历城区	Li cheng			21	266	99	1301
长清区	Chang qing		2	8	585	60	1209
章丘区	Zhang qiu		1	17	532	61	1719
济阳区	Ji yang		2	8	566	42	1099
莱芜区	Lai wu		7	8	792	69	1740
钢城区	Gang cheng			5	211	41	506
济南高新区	Jinan Gao xin				147	50	
济南起步区(直管)	Jinan Start-up Area (Directly under)				303	5	
南部山区	Nan shan				254		
平阴县	Ping yin		6	2	308	29	715
商河县	Shang he		11	1	516	25	1162

注：1.指标“土地面积”2013年起为第二次全市土地调查数据。
2.本表内数据由相关主管部门提供。

Notes:1. Indicator "land area" is the city land survey data for the second time as of 2013.
2.The data in this table are provided by the relevant authority departments.

1-2 县区所辖镇、街道办事处(2022年末)
Town and Street Communities Under the Jurisdiction(End of 2022)

县区	Region	镇、街道办事处数量(个) Number of Towns and Street Communities (unit)	镇、街道办事处名称 Name of Towns and Street Communities
历下区	Li xia	14	解放路街道办事处 千佛山街道办事处 趵突泉街道办事处 泉城路街道办事处 大明湖街道办事处 东关街道办事处 文化东路街道办事处 建筑新村街道办事处 甸柳新村街道办事处 燕山街道办事处 姚家街道办事处 智远街道办事处 龙洞街道办事处 舜华路街道办事处
市中区	Shi zhong	17	大观园街道办事处 杆石桥街道办事处 四里村街道办事处 魏家庄街道办事处 二七新村街道办事处 七里山街道办事处 六里山街道办事处 舜玉路街道办事处 泺源街道办事处 王官庄街道办事处 舜耕街道办事处 白马山街道办事处 七贤街道办事处 十六里河街道办事处 兴隆街道办事处 党家街道办事处 陡沟街道办事处
槐荫区	Huai yin	16	振兴街街道办事处 中大槐树街道办事处 道德街街道办事处 西市场街道办事处 五里沟街道办事处 营市街街道办事处 青年公园街道办事处 南辛庄街道办事处 段店北路街道办事处 张庄路街道办事处 匡山街道办事处 美里湖街道办事处 兴福街道办事处 玉清湖街道办事处 腊山街道办事处 吴家堡街道办事处
天桥区	Tian qiao	15	无影山街道办事处 工人新村北村街道办事处 工人新村南村街道办事处 天桥东街街道办事处 堤口路街道办事处 北坦街道办事处 制锦市街道办事处 官扎营街道办事处 宝华街街道办事处 纬北路街道办事处 药山街道办事处 北园街道办事处 泺口街道办事处 桑梓店街道办事处 大桥街道办事处
历城区	Li cheng	21	山大路街道办事处 洪家楼街道办事处 东风街道办事处 全福街道办事处 荷花路街道办事处 鲍山街道办事处 唐冶街道办事处 华山街道办事处 王舍人街道办事处 郭店街道办事处 港沟街道办事处 彩石街道办事处 董家街道办事处 唐王街道办事处 孙村街道办事处 巨野河街道办事处 遥墙街道办事处 临港街道办事处 仲宫街道办事处 柳埠街道办事处 西营街道办事处
长清区	Chang qing	10	文昌街道办事处 崮云湖街道办事处 平安街道办事处 五峰山街道办事处 归德街道办事处 张夏街道办事处 万德街道办事处 孝里街道办事处 马山镇 双泉镇
章丘区	Zhang qiu	18	明水街道办事处 双山街道办事处 枣园街道办事处 龙山街道办事处 埠村街道办事处 圣井街道办事处 普集街道办事处 绣惠街道办事处 相公庄街道办事处 文祖街道办事处 官庄街道办事处 曹范街道办事处 宁家埠街道办事处 高官寨街道办事处 白云湖街道办事处 刁镇街道办事处 黄河街道办事处 垛庄镇
济阳区	Ji yang	10	济阳街道办事处 济北街道办事处 回河街道办事处 垛石街道办事处 曲堤街道办事处 崔寨街道办事处 太平街道办事处 孙耿街道办事处 仁风镇 新市镇
莱芜区	Lai wu	15	凤城街道办事处 张家洼街道办事处 高庄街道办事处 鹏泉街道办事处 口镇街道办事处 羊里街道办事处 方下街道办事处 雪野街道办事处 牛泉镇 苗山镇 大王庄镇 寨里镇 杨庄镇 茶业口镇 和庄镇
钢城区	Gang cheng	5	艾山街道办事处 里辛街道办事处 汶源街道办事处 颜庄街道办事处 辛庄街道办事处
平阴县	Ping yin	8	榆山街道办事处 锦水街道办事处 东阿镇 孝直镇 孔村镇 洪范池镇 玫瑰镇 安城镇
商河县	Shang he	12	许商街道办事处 殷巷镇 怀仁镇 玉皇庙镇 龙桑寺镇 郑路镇 贾庄镇 白桥镇 孙集镇 韩庙镇 沙河镇 张坊镇

2

人 口

POPULATION

2-1 主要年份总户数、总人口(户籍人口)
Total Household and Population in Major Years(registered population)

年份 year	年末总户数 (万户) Total year-end Households (10 000 households)	年末总人口 (万人) Total year-end Population (10 000 persons)	按性别分(万人) Grouped by Sex (10 000 persons) 男性 Male	女性 Female	性别比 (女=100) Sex Ratio (Female= 100)	年平均人口 (万人) Annual Average Population (10 000 persons)	比上年增长 (‰) Growth Rate (‰)	人口密度 (人/平方公里) Density of Population (Person/sq.km)
1952	70.19	318.66	157.68	160.98	97.95	315.94	3.30	387
1957	76.44	346.38	170.30	176.09	96.71	343.25	17.40	421
1962	81.45	351.44	174.55	176.89	98.68	350.18	-4.60	427
1965	83.01	373.22	186.08	187.14	99.43	370.24	19.50	454
1970	89.48	407.50	203.16	204.34	99.42	404.17	16.60	495
1975	96.54	437.73	217.82	219.91	99.05	435.15	9.90	532
1976	98.63	442.09	220.89	221.20	99.86	439.91	10.90	537
1977	100.60	445.05	222.46	222.59	99.94	443.57	8.30	541
1978	102.93	450.67	226.31	224.36	100.87	447.86	9.70	548
1979	105.34	456.37	228.57	227.80	100.34	453.52	12.60	555
1980	106.83	458.61	230.47	228.15	101.02	457.49	8.80	557
1981	110.52	467.93	235.35	232.58	101.19	463.27	12.60	569
1982	112.51	474.23	238.99	235.26	101.59	471.08	16.80	576
1983	114.92	479.38	242.02	237.36	101.54	476.81	12.20	583
1984	116.92	483.85	244.32	239.53	102.00	481.62	10.10	588
1985	120.19	488.39	246.86	241.53	102.21	486.12	9.30	594
1986	122.67	494.06	250.09	243.97	102.51	491.23	10.50	601
1987	125.43	501.03	253.95	247.08	102.78	497.55	12.90	609
1988	130.32	507.18	257.22	249.86	102.95	504.11	13.20	616
1989	134.77	513.39	260.79	252.61	103.24	510.29	12.30	624
1990	140.36	523.60	265.91	257.69	103.19	518.50	16.10	636
1991	143.42	527.43	267.78	259.65	103.13	525.52	13.50	641
1992	147.50	530.70	269.46	261.25	103.14	529.07	6.70	645
1993	149.42	533.53	270.77	262.76	103.05	532.12	5.80	649
1994	153.60	537.31	272.76	264.54	103.11	535.42	6.20	653
1995	156.45	542.12	274.98	267.14	102.93	539.72	8.00	656
1996	156.42	543.45	275.59	267.86	102.89	542.79	5.70	666

2-1 续表 continued

年份 year	年末总户数 (万户) Total year-end Households (10 000 households)	年末总人口 (万人) Total year-end Population (10 000 persons)	按性别分(万人) Grouped by Sex (10 000 persons)		性别比 (女=100) Sex Ratio (Female= 100)	年平均人口 (万人) Annual Average Population (10 000 persons)	比上年增长 (‰) Growth Rate (‰)	人口密度 (人/平方公里) Density of Population (Person/sq.km)
			男性 Male	女性 Female				
1997	157.66	549.20	278.30	270.90	102.73	546.33	6.50	674
1998	160.93	553.54	279.91	273.63	102.30	551.37	9.20	679
1999	163.52	557.63	281.71	275.93	102.09	555.59	7.70	684
2000	166.63	562.65	284.19	278.46	102.06	560.14	8.20	690
2001	168.46	569.00	287.39	281.61	102.06	565.83	10.20	696
2002	170.10	575.01	290.58	284.43	102.16	572.00	10.90	703
2003	172.18	582.56	294.04	288.52	101.91	578.78	11.90	712
2004	173.24	590.08	297.25	292.82	101.51	586.32	13.03	722
2005	177.69	597.44	300.42	297.02	101.15	593.76	12.69	731
2006	179.48	603.35	302.72	300.63	100.70	600.39	11.17	738
2007	181.88	604.85	302.87	301.98	100.29	604.10	6.17	740
2008	184.63	603.99	302.00	301.99	100.00	604.42	0.53	739
2009	187.70	603.27	301.26	302.01	99.75	603.63	-1.30	738
2010	190.65	604.08	301.28	302.80	99.50	603.68	0.08	739
2011	193.61	606.64	302.19	304.44	99.26	605.36	2.78	742
2012	195.79	609.21	303.30	305.91	99.15	607.92	4.23	745
2013	199.67	613.25	304.93	308.32	98.90	611.23	5.44	767
2014	201.93	621.61	309.09	312.52	98.90	617.43	15.64	777
2015	203.59	625.73	310.92	314.80	98.77	623.67	10.11	782
2016	205.45	632.83	314.28	318.55	98.66	629.28	9.00	791
2017	208.08	643.62	319.21	324.41	98.40	638.22	14.21	805
2018	216.64	655.90	324.74	331.15	98.06	649.76	19.08	820
2019	270.26	796.74	395.30	401.44	98.47	726.32	21.47	778
2020	276.35	806.72	399.61	407.11	98.16	801.73	12.45	788
2021	283.04	816.61	404.03	412.57	97.93	811.67		797
2022	286.64	819.95	405.11	414.84	97.65	818.28		800

2-2 主要年份市区总户数、总人口(户籍人口)
Total Household and Population of Urban in Major Years(registered population)

年份 year	年末总户数 (万户) Total year-end Households (10 000 households)	年末总人口 (万人) Total year-end Population (10 000 persons)	按性别分(万人) Grouped by Sex (10 000 persons)		年平均人口 (万人) Annual Average Population (10 000 persons)
			男性 Male	女性 Female	
1952	26.46	124.96	63.95	61.01	123.83
1957	29.13	143.17	72.05	71.13	140.11
1962	32.25	153.35	78.52	74.83	154.18
1965	34.03	162.82	83.20	79.62	161.90
1970	37.21	167.82	85.61	82.21	168.51
1975	40.67	178.78	90.83	87.95	177.74
1976	41.59	180.99	91.83	89.16	179.88
1977	42.34	181.49	91.92	89.57	181.24
1978	43.79	186.43	94.70	91.73	183.96
1979	45.33	189.26	96.22	93.04	187.84
1980	46.12	190.01	97.22	92.79	189.63
1981	48.64	194.05	99.37	94.69	192.03
1982	50.60	201.31	101.44	99.87	197.68
1983	52.32	205.48	103.42	102.07	203.39
1984	54.30	209.55	105.57	103.99	207.52
1985	56.88	213.28	107.96	105.33	211.42
1986	58.65	216.98	111.54	105.43	215.13
1987	60.54	221.49	113.79	107.70	219.23
1988	63.03	225.00	115.51	109.39	223.25
1989	65.29	228.88	117.49	111.39	226.94
1990	81.22	283.66	145.29	138.36	
1991	83.30	286.20	146.55	139.65	284.93
1992	85.87	288.52	145.19	143.33	287.36
1993	88.02	291.24	149.07	142.17	289.88
1994	90.10	294.60	150.75	143.85	292.92
1995	92.04	299.20	152.97	146.23	296.90
1996	93.12	302.78	154.58	148.20	300.99
1997	93.90	306.98	156.54	150.44	304.88
1998	96.65	309.90	157.58	152.32	308.44

2-2 续表 continued

年份 year	年末总户数 (万户) Total year-end Households (10 000 households)	年末总人口 (万人) Total year-end Population (10 000 persons)	按性别分(万人) Grouped by Sex (10 000 persons)		年平均人口 (万人) Annual Average Population (10 000 persons)
			男性 Male	女性 Female	
1999	97.74	313.18	159.19	153.99	311.54
2000	99.25	317.20	161.03	156.17	315.19
2001	100.53	322.45	163.73	158.72	319.83
2002	101.62	327.55	166.43	161.12	325.00
2003	102.71	334.80	169.84	164.96	331.18
2004	102.68	341.73	172.91	168.82	338.27
2005	104.87	347.87	175.41	172.45	344.80
2006	106.19	352.29	177.10	175.19	350.08
2007	107.55	352.71	176.70	176.01	352.50
2008	109.26	350.23	175.08	175.15	351.47
2009	111.07	348.24	173.71	174.53	349.24
2010	112.91	348.02	173.19	174.83	348.13
2011	114.75	349.44	173.51	175.93	348.73
2012	116.49	352.17	174.55	177.62	350.81
2013	118.50	355.38	175.86	179.52	353.78
2014	120.33	360.99	178.55	182.44	358.19
2015	121.96	364.54	180.12	184.42	362.77
2016	154.64	473.33	233.74	239.59	418.94
2017	157.42	483.75	238.48	245.27	478.54
2018	182.76	554.13	273.31	280.82	518.94
2019	236.31	695.09	343.90	351.19	689.31
2020	242.04	705.33	348.36	356.97	700.21
2021	248.66	715.55	352.90	362.66	710.44
2022	252.43	719.84	354.40	365.45	717.70

注：1990年以前的数据中不包括长清区。2016年起数据包括章丘区。2018年起数据包括济阳区。 2019年起数据包括莱芜区、钢城区。

Note: The data before 1990 excludes Changqing. The data as of 2016 includes Zhangqiu. The data as of 2018 includes Jiyang. Data after the year of 2019 involves Laiwu and Gangcheng.

2–3 主要年份人口自然变动情况
Natural Change of Population in Major Years

年份 Year	申报出生人口 (人) Population of Birth (person)	申报出生率 (‰) Birth Rate (‰)	申报死亡人口 (人) Population of Death (person)	申报死亡率 (‰) Death Rate (‰)	人口自然增长 (人) Population of Natural Growth (person)	人口自然增长率 (‰) Natural Growth Rate(‰)
1952	72861	23.06	29949	9.48	42912	13.58
1957	108432	31.59	38082	11.09	70350	20.50
1962	108029	30.85	44464	12.70	63565	18.15
1965	121364	32.78	39355	10.63	82009	22.15
1970	111861	27.68	29965	7.41	81896	20.27
1975	82939	19.06	33837	7.78	49102	11.28
1976	70065	15.93	34693	7.89	35372	8.04
1977	67413	15.20	33723	7.60	33690	7.60
1978	69541	15.53	31343	7.00	38198	8.53
1979	72596	16.01	30205	6.66	42391	9.35
1980	60336	13.19	32004	7.00	28332	6.19
1981	70327	15.18	31671	6.84	38656	8.34
1982	74147	15.74	28679	6.09	45468	9.65
1983	56454	11.84	30080	6.31	26374	5.53
1984	61156	12.70	32277	6.70	28879	6.00
1985	55386	11.39	31678	6.52	23708	4.87
1986	69901	14.23	30790	6.27	39111	7.96
1987	86752	17.44	30007	6.03	56745	11.41
1988	78922	15.66	32850	6.52	46072	9.14
1989	76380	14.97	30721	6.02	45659	8.95
1990	66806	12.88	33916	6.54	32890	6.34
1991	59374	11.30	32675	6.20	26699	5.10
1992	52825	9.98	34969	6.61	17856	3.37
1993	46007	8.65	35317	6.64	10690	2.01
1994	49940	9.30	35308	6.60	14632	2.70
1995	54132	10.03	34107	6.32	20025	3.71
1996	58254	10.73	36452	6.71	21802	4.02

2-3 续表 continued

年份 Year	申报出生人口 (人) Population of Birth (person)	申报出生率 (‰) Birth Rate (‰)	申报死亡人口 (人) Population of Death (person)	申报死亡率 (‰) Death Rate (‰)	人口自然增长 (人) Population of Natural Growth (person)	人口自然增长率 (‰) Natural Growth Rate(‰)
1997	62245	11.39	35768	6.55	26477	4.84
1998	62490	11.33	36497	6.64	25893	4.69
1999	55931	10.07	34956	6.29	20975	3.78
2000	62059	11.08	39499	7.05	22560	4.03
2001	55536	9.82	33816	5.98	21720	3.84
2002	57317	10.02	36234	6.33	21083	3.69
2003	54599	9.43	42539	7.35	12060	2.08
2004	60670	10.35	38158	6.51	22512	3.84
2005	60240	10.15	37782	6.36	22458	3.78
2006	57706	9.61	39040	6.50	18666	3.11
2007	58367	9.66	39752	6.58	18615	3.08
2008	59600	9.86	39887	6.60	19713	3.26
2009	56694	9.39	40911	6.78	15783	2.61
2010	67162	11.13	50380	8.35	16782	2.78
2011	66563	11.00	40310	6.66	26253	4.34
2012	71449	11.75	49148	8.08	22301	3.67
2013	69351	11.35	41713	6.82	27638	4.53
2014	110503	17.90	41887	6.78	68616	11.11
2015	73688	11.82	41999	6.73	31689	5.09
2016	91941	14.61	39460	6.27	52481	8.34
2017	113766	17.83	62958	9.86	50808	7.96
2018	94694	14.57	45374	6.98	49320	7.59
2019	101723	12.86	52396	6.62	49327	6.24
2020	83782	10.45	58568	7.31	25214	3.14
2021	66666	8.21	44228	5.45	22438	2.76
2022	64267	7.85	79727	9.74	-15460	-1.89

2-4 分地区户数、人口数(2022年)(户籍人口)
Household and Population by Region(2022)(registered population)

地区	Region	户数 (万户) Households (10 000 households)	人口数 (万人) Population (10 000 persons)	按性别分(万人) Grouped by Sex (10 000 persons)	
				男性 Male	女性 Female
全市	**Total**	**286.64**	**819.95**	**405.11**	**414.84**
市区	Districts	252.43	719.84	354.40	365.45
历下区	Li xia	26.86	77.56	37.64	39.92
市中区	Shi zhong	26.32	69.96	33.91	36.05
槐荫区	Huai yin	18.31	49.03	23.48	25.55
天桥区	Tian qiao	20.20	54.60	26.36	28.24
历城区	Li cheng	41.53	118.71	58.21	60.50
长清区	Chang qing	18.85	56.88	28.31	28.58
章丘区	Zhang qiu	32.22	104.91	51.83	53.08
济阳区	Ji yang	17.79	59.78	30.08	29.71
莱芜区	Lai wu	38.76	98.85	49.48	49.37
钢城区	Gang cheng	11.59	29.56	15.10	14.46
平阴县	Ping yin	13.57	36.65	18.38	18.27
商河县	Shang he	20.65	63.46	32.33	31.13

2–5 分地区人口机械变动情况(2022年)
Mechanical Changes of Population by Region (2022)

地区	Region	迁入人口 (人) Move Into the Population (person)	迁入率 (‰) Move In Rate (‰)	迁出人口 (人) Move Out the population (person)	迁出率 (‰) Move Out Rate (‰)	人口机械增长 (人) Mechanical Growth of Population (person)	人口机械增长率 (‰) Mechanical Growth Rate of Population (‰)
全市	**Total**	**80349**	**9.82**	**31160**	**3.81**	**49189**	**6.01**
市区	Districts	74634	10.40	21144	2.95	53490	7.45
历下区	Li xia	12908	16.76	4341	5.64	8567	11.12
市中区	Shi zhong	9623	13.83	2811	4.04	6812	9.79
槐荫区	Huai yin	11263	23.16	1895	3.90	9368	19.26
天桥区	Tian qiao	8507	15.58	1764	3.23	6743	12.35
历城区	Li cheng	24556	21.00	3715	3.18	20841	17.82
长清区	Chang qing	2149	3.77	1320	2.32	829	1.45
章丘区	Zhang qiu	1978	1.88	1759	1.67	219	0.21
济阳区	Ji yang	1512	2.52	955	1.59	557	0.93
莱芜区	Lai wu	1647	1.66	2002	2.02	-355	-0.36
钢城区	Gang cheng	491	1.65	582	1.96	-91	-0.31
平阴县	Ping yin	1741	4.72	3402	9.23	-1661	-4.50
商河县	Shang he	3974	6.24	6614	10.38	-2640	-4.14

2–6 分地区人口自然变动情况(2022年)
Natural Changes of Population by Region (2022)

地区	Region	申报出生人口 (人) Population of Birth (person)	申报出生率 (‰) Birth Rate (‰)	申报死亡人口 (人) Population of Death (person)	申报死亡率 (‰) Death Rate (‰)	人口自然增长 (人) Population of Natural Growth (person)	人口自然增长率 (‰) Natural Growth Rate (‰)
全市	**Total**	**64267**	**7.85**	**79727**	**9.74**	**-15460**	**-1.68**
市区	Districts	57919	8.05	68253	9.48	-10334	-1.44
历下区	Li xia	6831	8.87	7107	9.23	-276	-0.36
市中区	Shi zhong	5535	7.95	5898	8.47	-363	-0.52
槐荫区	Huai yin	4526	9.31	4544	9.34	-18	-0.04
天桥区	Tian qiao	4381	8.02	6094	11.16	-1713	-3.14
历城区	Li cheng	13522	11.56	8673	7.42	4849	4.15
长清区	Chang qing	4040	7.09	5204	9.13	-1164	-2.04
章丘区	Zhang qiu	6796	6.46	9845	9.36	-3049	-2.90
济阳区	Ji yang	4847	8.09	7142	11.92	-2295	-3.83
莱芜区	Lai wu	5814	5.87	10305	10.40	-4491	-4.53
钢城区	Gang cheng	1627	5.48	3441	11.58	-1814	-6.11
平阴县	Ping yin	2132	5.78	5062	13.73	-2930	-7.95
商河县	Shang he	4216	6.62	6412	10.06	-2196	-3.45

2-7 结婚情况
Number of Marriages

单位：对 (couple)

地区	Region	2018年	2019年	2020年	2021年	2022年
总计	**Total**	**51383**	**52300**	**50521**	**49380**	**48079**
市直	Departments Directly Under the Municipal Government	90				
历下区	Li xia	5763	5456	5634	6196	6382
市中区	Shi zhong	5699	5092	5074	4927	4948
槐荫区	Huai yin	3863	3452	3434	3802	3977
天桥区	Tian qiao	4874	4287	3869	3445	3219
历城区	Li cheng	7419	6809	6094	5591	5742
长清区	Chang qing	4003	3930	3547	3273	3049
章丘区	Zhang qiu	6840	6000	6016	5315	5055
济阳区	Ji yang	4248	3629	3154	2146	2041
莱芜区	Lai wu		4514	4054	3970	3581
钢城区	Gang cheng		1183	1117	1060	995
济南高新区	Jinan Gao xin	2621	2533	2783	2982	3055
济南起步区(直管)	Jinan Start-up Area(Directly under)			560	1312	1181
南部山区	Nan shan				816	991
平阴县	Ping yin	2330	1974	1881	1632	1408
商河县	Shang he	3633	3441	3304	2913	2455

2-8 离婚情况
Number of Divorces

单位：对 (couple)

地 区	Region	2018年	2019年	2020年	2021年	2022年
总计	**Total**	**31611**	**35932**	**36515**	**23837**	**23321**
法院数	**Divorce Case Handled**	**6228**	**7034**	**6887**	**6331**	**6256**
民政数	**Divorces Handled through Civil**	**25383**	**28898**	**29628**	**17506**	**17065**
市直	Departments Directly Under the Municipal Government	19				
历下区	Li xia	3322	3644	3889	2331	2277
市中区	Shi zhong	3288	3441	3785	2254	2268
槐荫区	Huai yin	2362	2416	2530	1701	1704
天桥区	Tian qiao	2810	3031	2936	1665	1656
历城区	Li cheng	3664	4195	4398	2261	2082
长清区	Chang qing	1801	1864	1953	1092	982
章丘区	Zhang qiu	2916	2793	2763	1633	1572
济阳区	Ji yang	1783	1745	1587	652	586
莱芜区	Lai Wu		1418	1220	817	877
钢城区	Gang cheng		502	432	240	292
济南高新区	Jinan Gaoxin	1127	1322	1495	1005	911
济南起步区(直管)	Jinan Start-up Area(Directly under)			269	373	358
南部山区	Nan shan				319	418
平阴县	Ping yin	839	968	938	490	480
商河县	Shang he	1452	1559	1433	673	602

主要统计指标解释

人口数 指一定时点、一定地区范围内的有生命的个人的总和。年度统计的年末人口数指每年12月31日24时的人口数。

出生率（又称粗出生率） 指在一定时期内(通常为一年)一定地区的出生人数与同期内平均人数(或期中人数)之比，用千分率表示。本资料中的出生率指年出生率，其计算公式为：

出生率＝年出生人数／年平均人数×1000‰

式中：出生人数指活产婴儿，即胎儿脱离母体时(不管怀孕月数)，有过呼吸或其他生命现象。年平均人数指年初、年底人口数的平均数，也可用年中人口数代替。

死亡率（又称粗死亡率） 指在一定时期内(通常为一年)一定地区的死亡人数与同期内平均人数(或期中人数)之比，用千分率表示。本资料中的死亡率指年死亡率，其计算公式为：

死亡率＝年死亡人数／年平均人数×1000‰

人口自然增长率 指在一定时期内(通常为一年)人口自然增加数(出生人数减死亡人数)与该时期内平均人数(或期中人数)之比，用千分率表示。计算公式为：

人口自然增长率＝（本年出生人数－本年死亡人数）／年平均人数×1000‰

人口自然增长率＝人口出生率－人口死亡率

人口机械增长率 是反映迁移变动的一个相对指标。它表明一个地区在一定时间内迁入人口数与迁出人口数相抵后的差额与总人口数的比率，用千分率表示。计算公式为：

人口机械增长率=一定时期的迁入迁出人口差额/该时期的平均人口×100%

人口密度 指一定时点，一定地区的人口数与该时点、该地区的面积之比，即一定时点的单位土地面积上的人口数，通常以每平方公里的居民人数来表示：

人口密度＝该地区人口数／该地区土地面积×100%

性别比 反映两性人口间比例的指标，指在总人口中或各年龄组人口中，男性人数与女性人数之比。通常以每100个女性人口相对应的男性人口数。计算公式：

性别比＝男性人口／女性人口×100%

Explanatory Notes on Main Statistical Indicators

Total Population refers to the total number of people alive at a certain point of time within a given area.The annual statistics on total population is taken at midnight, the 31st of December.

Birth Rate (or Crude Birth Rate) refers to the ratio of the number of births to the average population (or mid-year population) during a certain period of time (usually a year), expressed in ‰. Birth rate in the chapter refers to annual birth rate. The following formula is used:

Birth rate = number of births/annual average population *1000‰

Number of births in the formula refers to live births, i.e. when a baby has breathed or showed any vital phenomena regardless of the length of pregnancy.Annual average population is the average of the number of population at the beginning of the year and that at the end of the year. Sometimes it is substituted by the mid-year population.

Death Rate (or Crude Death Rate) refers to the ratio of the number of deaths to the average population (or mid-year population) during a certain period of time (usually a year), expressed in ‰. Death rate in the chapter refers to annual death rate. The following formula is used:

Death rate = number of deaths/annual average population *1000‰

Natural Growth Rate of Population refers to the ratio of natural increase in population (number of births minus number of deaths) in a certain period of time (usually a year) to the average population (or mid-year population) of the same period, expressed in ‰. The following formula is applied:

Natural Growth Rate of Population=(number of births - number of deaths)/ annual average population * 1000‰

Natural Growth Rate of Population=Birth Rate-Death Rate

Mechanical Growth Rate of Population is a relative indicator that reflects changes in the population migration. It shows the ratio of the balance (between the people count moving in and out of a given area) to total population during a certain period of time, expressed in ‰. The following formula is used:

Mechanical growth rate = the balance between people count moving in and out of a given area during a certain period of time/average population * 1000‰

Population Density refers to the ratio of total population in a given area at a certain point of time to the area at this point of time, namely total population per area of land at a certain point of time, expressed in number of residents per square kilometers:

Population density= Total population in the region/Land area in the region*100%

Sex ratio refers to the ratio of male to female population in total population or age groups, male population to per 100 female populations. The following formula is used:

Sex ratio= Male population/Female population*100%

3

综合

GENERAL SURVEY

3-1 国民经济和社会发展总量指标
Principal Aggregate Indicators on National Economic and Social Development

指标	Item	单位 Unit	1978年
面积	Area		
土地面积	Land Area	平方公里(sq.km)	
#建成区面积	Area of Built Districts	平方公里(sq.km)	85
人口	Population		
年末总户数(户籍人口)	Total year-end Households(Household Population)	万户(10 000 households)	102.93
年末总人口	Total year-end Population	万人(10 000 persons)	450.67
#市区	Population	万人(10 000 persons)	186.43
#男性	Male	万人(10 000 persons)	226.31
年末常住总人口	Total Resident Population at the Year-end	万人(10 000 persons)	
就业	Employment		
全社会从业人员	Employed Persons	万人(10 000 persons)	204.04
第一产业	Primary Industry	万人(10 000 persons)	136.30
第二产业	Secondary Industry	万人(10 000 persons)	46.06
第三产业	Tertiary Industry	万人(10 000 persons)	21.68
职工平均工资	Average Wage of Staff and Workers	元(yuan)	578
城镇非私营单位就业人员平均工资	Average Wage of Employed Persons in Urban Non Private Entities	元(yuan)	
城镇非私营单位在岗职工平均工资	Average Wage of Staff and Workers in Urban Non Private Entities	元(yuan)	
城镇私营单位就业人员平均工资	Average Wage of Employed Persons in Urban Private Entities	元(yuan)	
城镇登记失业人员数	Registered Urban Unemployed Persons	万人(10 000 persons)	
城镇登记失业率	Registered Urban Unemployment Rate	%	
国民经济核算	National Accounting		
地区生产总值	Gross Domestic Product	亿元(100 million yuan)	23.60
#非公有制经济	Non-public Economy	亿元(100 million yuan)	
第一产业	Primary Industry	亿元(100 million yuan)	4.16
第二产业	Secondary Industry	亿元(100 million yuan)	13.32
第三产业	Tertiary Industry	亿元(100 million yuan)	6.12
人均地区生产总值	Per Capita GDP	元(yuan)	527
固定资产投资	Investment in Fixed Assets		
固定资产投资	Investment in Fixed Assets	亿元(100 million yuan)	3.19
第一产业	Primary Industry	亿元(100 million yuan)	0.55
第二产业	Secondary Industry	亿元(100 million yuan)	1.15
#工业	Industry	亿元(100 million yuan)	0.75
第三产业	Tertiary Industry	亿元(100 million yuan)	1.29
#房地产投资	Real Estate Investment	亿元(100 million yuan)	
财政税收	Fiscal Tax Revenue		
一般公共预算收入	General Public Budget Revenue	亿元(100 million yuan)	5.90
一般公共预算支出	General Public Budget Expenditure	亿元(100 million yuan)	1.50
地域税收收入	Regional Tax Revenue	亿元(100 million yuan)	

1990年	1995年	2000年	2005年	2010年	2015年	2019年	2020年	2021年	2022年
8227	8227	8154	8177	8177	7998	10244	10244	10244	10244
103	114	120	295	347	497	761	840	841	854
140.36	156.45	166.63	177.69	190.65	203.59	270.26	276.35	283.04	286.64
523.60	542.12	562.65	597.44	604.08	625.73	796.74	806.72	816.61	819.95
232.30	247.57	317.20	347.87	348.02	458.16	695.09	705.33	715.55	719.84
265.91	274.98	284.19	300.42	301.28	310.92	395.30	399.61	404.03	405.11
				681.80	713.20	890.87	924.16	933.61	941.47
270.54	324.22	347.37	360.00	373.70	388.70	492.36	468.90	470.78	469.00
125.73	116.13	109.98	99.10	76.66	71.80	77.42			
87.75	106.68	110.81	114.20	120.20	124.70	154.27			
57.06	101.41	126.58	146.70	176.84	192.20	260.67			
2211	5851	10422	20866	31096	58578				
						97482	104990	114596	123902
						100593	108391	119245	128703
						51530	60348	60914	61538
	2.45	3.90	5.75	5.97	3.20	3.53			
	2.30	3.70	3.86	3.84	2.04	2.01	2.03		
138.24	473.52	944.13	1846.28	3910.53	6100.23	9443.37	10140.91	11413.51	12027.46
		238.32	768.50	1664.43	2599.60				
23.93	67.64	96.02	134.34	215.17	305.39	343.06	361.66	408.77	420.52
67.36	220.37	414.74	847.47	1637.45	2307.00	3265.22	3530.67	3946.10	4180.24
46.95	185.51	433.38	864.47	2057.90	3487.84	5835.09	6248.58	7058.64	7426.70
2666	8773	15356	27338	55248	77815	104180	110681	122873	128287
30.60	112.76	305.95	857.00	1987.44	3498.42				
0.52	3.24	13.57	38.28	68.08	102.52				
14.62	46.26	73.14	362.05	677.28	1217.39				
2.05	45.35	67.72	352.27	667.35	1147.87				
13.94	63.27	219.24	456.67	1242.08	2178.51				
2.18	16.46	50.53	121.09	484.50	1014.14	1576.93	1707.63	1928.00	1830.80
12.40	16.99	49.05	106.15	266.13	614.32	874.19	906.08	1007.61	1001.14
8.20	19.63	54.72	120.66	336.80	658.20	1197.32	1288.80	1293.08	1225.57
	53.49	112.35	231.34	527.70	959.33	1419.58	1369.16	1555.89	1351.69

3-1 续表 1 continued 1

指标	Item	单位 Unit	1978年
国税税收收入	National Tax Revenue	亿元(100 million yuan)	
地税税收收入	Land Tax Revenue	亿元(100 million yuan)	
金融保险	**Finance and Insurance**		
金融机构人民币存款余额	RMB Deposits Balance of Financial Institutions	亿元(100 million yuan)	15.43
#住户存款	Deposits of Households	亿元(100 million yuan)	1.14
金融机构人民币贷款余额	RMB Loans Balance of Financial Institutions	亿元(100 million yuan)	14.08
#短期贷款	Short-term Loans	亿元(100 million yuan)	-
保险金额	Insured Amount	亿元(100 million yuan)	
保费收入	Premium Income	万元(10 000 yuan)	
赔付支出	Claim Payment	万元(10 000 yuan)	
农业	**Agriculture**		
农林牧渔业总产值	Gross Output Value of Farming Forestry, Animal Husbandry and Fishery	亿元(100 million yuan)	6.57
农用机械总动力	total power of agricultural machinery	万千瓦(10 000kW)	69.70
年末实有耕地面积	Actual cultivated Area at Year-end	千公顷(1000 ha)	373.19
粮食总产量	Total Output of Grain	万吨(10 000 tons)	115.38
蔬菜总产量	Total Output of Vegetable	万吨(10 000 tons)	49.19
肉类总产量	Total Output of meat	万吨(10 000 tons)	2.50
奶类总产量	Total Output of Milk	万吨(10 000 tons)	0.40
棉花总产量	Total Output of Cotton	万吨(10 000 tons)	0.51
规模以上工业	**Industry Enterprises above Designated Size**		
单位数	Number of Enterprises	个(unit)	1319
工业总产值	Gross Industrial Output Value	亿元(100 million yuan)	37.67
营业收入	Revenue from Principal Business	亿元(100 million yuan)	31.39
利税总额	Total Profits and Taxes	亿元(100 million yuan)	6.80
利润总额	Total Profits	亿元(100 million yuan)	3.88
资产总计	Total Assets	亿元(100 million yuan)	25.68
所有者权益	Owner's Equities	亿元(100 million yuan)	7.47
建筑业	**Construction**		
资质以上企业个数	Number of Qualification Enterprises	个(unit)	10
建筑业总产值	Gross Output Value of Construction Enterprises	亿元(100 million yuan)	0.68
施工面积	Floor Space under Construction	万平方米(10 000 sq.m)	
竣工面积	Floor Space of Completed	万平方米(10 000 sq.m)	49
其中：住宅	Residential	万平方米(10 000 sq.m)	
交通运输	**Transport**		
货运量	Freight Traffic		
铁路	Railways	万吨(10 000 tons)	2191
公路	Highways	万吨(10 000 tons)	1670
航空	Airways	万吨(10 000 tons)	

1990年	1995年	2000年	2005年	2010年	2015年	2019年	2020年	2021年	2022年
	39.55	72.54	144.20	309.87	494.43	-	-	-	-
	13.94	39.80	87.14	217.82	464.90	-	-	-	-
117.95	438.01	1274.96	3483.34	7510.44	14174.72	18303.20	20714.97	23029.20	25589.51
51.08	222.06	463.04	1024.42	2187.68	3951.42	6438.09	7584.12	8558.43	10226.27
124.76	337.26	1069.31	3259.86	6319.09	11356.78	17624.21	19704.88	22349.91	25077.98
98.50	239.31	527.31	1240.49	1898.61	2692.81	3400.21	3829.14	4329.33	4809.27
						438422	927748	659267	615535
						5322643	6280398	5984712	6324536
						1219250	1603108	2124574	1915636
36.92	114.07	154.30	230.46	361.24	493.04	637.30	671.66	758.41	784.24
183.40	241.20	349.47	426.76	509.68	584.98	543.48	543.48	570.10	594.94
347.56	339.30	333.72	366.99	362.30	358.57	344.82	342.29	342.56	342.88
181.47	252.48	240.27	260.11	289.43	264.55	285.46	290.81	293.07	296.19
126.09	253.54	405.95	529.37	572.05	626.23	671.24	673.73	691.76	712.61
11.38	28.68	31.82	37.93	31.79	34.18	35.86	23.92	27.36	29.10
1.87	3.48	7.09	19.61	31.20	23.27	32.13	41.43	42.10	43.43
5.00	2.91	2.73	3.55	2.94	0.74	0.54	0.42	0.38	0.35
2008	2648	1038	1670	2021	2021	2153	2215	2543	2665
174.89	526.48	680.04	2237.51	4485.61	5339.97	5839.18	6765.08	7591.25	7246.05
136.29	432.17	629.72	2142.84	4497.17	5417.16	6512.66	7575.34	8492.55	8370.30
15.57	53.59	64.62	244.61	584.53	685.71	545.70	659.87	645.49	593.57
3.23	16.30	21.69	131.30	339.76	396.13	310.86	423.31	408.38	344.86
125.25	578.55	958.10	1868.06	3904.42	4987.76	6663.13	7724.85	8494.19	9637.65
36.82	180.86	363.37	630.06	1481.75	2159.78	2743.28	2967.31	3380.30	3779.62
46	141	569	737	739	463	895	1033	1182	1371
12.56	58.78	141.92	462.65	894.30	1663.83	3513.98	3748.12	4126.03	4460.75
269	1030	1611	3298	4655	10189	14955	17090	19410	19971
170	306	701	1400	1306	2039	3418	3323	3730	3128
77	141	396	884	773	1178	2170	1916	2247	1808
3416	3877	5168	7211	9913	15794	20870	23189	22895	24717
3970	6182	7024	8484	13029	20419	28064	22677	24669	23843
	0.4	1.3	2.0	3.4	4.2	6.7	14.7	16.8	13.8

3-1 续表 2 continued 2

指标	Item	单位 Unit	1978年
客运量	Passenger Traffic		
铁路	Railways	万人(10 000 persons)	1302
公路	Highways	万人(10 000 persons)	505
航空	Airways	万人(10 000 persons)	
民用汽车拥有量	Possession of Private Vehicles	辆(unit)	1684
#载客	Passenger Vehicles	辆(unit)	1353
#载货	Trucks	辆(unit)	224
邮电通信	**Post and Telecommunication Services**		
固定电话	Fixed Telephone	万户(10 000 households)	2.68
#城市	Districts	万户(10 000 households)	2.27
移动电话	Mobile Telephone	万户(10 000 households)	
互联网用户	Internet Broad Band	万户(10 000 households)	
国内贸易	**Domestic Trade**		
社会消费品零售总额	Total Retail Sales of Consumer Goods	亿元(100 million yuan)	8.13
#批发零售业	Wholesale and Retail Trade	亿元(100 million yuan)	7.07
#餐饮业	Catering Services	亿元(100 million yuan)	0.29
对外经济和国际旅游	**Foreign Economy and Trade,Tourism**		
全年货物进出口总额(海关)	Total Value of Imports and Exports(Customs)	万美元(10 000 USD)	
进口	Imports	万美元(10 000 USD)	
出口	Exports	万美元(10 000 USD)	
全年货物进出口总额	Total Value of Imports and Exports	亿元(100 million yuan)	
进口	Imports	亿元(100 million yuan)	
出口	Exports	亿元(100 million yuan)	
全年实际使用外资	Total Amount of Foreign Capital Actually Utilized	万美元(10 000 USD)	
全年实现合同外资	Total Amount of Contracted Foreign Capital	万美元(10 000 USD)	
入境游客人数	International Tourists	人(person)	
外国人	Foreigners	人(person)	
港澳台同胞	Chinese Compatriots from Hong Kong Macao and Taiwan Province	人(person)	
国际旅游(外汇)收入	Earnings from International Tourism	亿美元(100 million USD)	
教育	**Education**		
普通高等学校在校生	Total Enrollment of Regular Institutions of Higher Education	万人(10 000 persons)	1.09
普通高等学校专任教师	Full-time Teachers of Regular Institutions of Higher Education	人(person)	2947
中等专业学校在校生	Total Enrollment of Secondary Professional Schools	万人(10 000 persons)	0.68
中等专业学校专任教师	Full-time Teachers of Secondary Professional Schools	人(person)	1020
普通中学在校生	Total Enrollment of Regular Senior Secondary Schools	万人(10 000 persons)	30.61
普通中学专任教师	Full-time Teachers of Regular Senior Secondary Schools	人(person)	19275
小学在校生	Total Enrollment of Regular Primary Schools	万人(10 000 persons)	60.91
小学专任教师	Full-time Teachers of Regular Primary Schools	人(person)	24926

1990年	1995年	2000年	2005年	2010年	2015年	2019年	2020年	2021年	2022年
1438	1519	1693	1924	3327	10681	15745	9797	12164	7322
1801	2611	4530	5364	12758	3663	3244	1209	2024	1438
2.6	37.0	62.0	140.0	379.2	533.1	936.1	1238.5	1361.6	824.2
39748	86766	129204	347687	807378	1541045	2584278	2794278	3025326	3203381
26032	33968	68625	196415	627849	1400588	2370437	2556622	2759683	2925704
12141	47790	56627	71588	117994	123801	194957	224713	250200	261017
9.87	39.18	106.34	258.90	213.30	165.30	148.82	144.78	145.31	147.66
9.12	36.48	83.08	206.30	177.40	141.00	136.30	127.65		
	2.3	60.8	239.0	857.6	1090.4	1122.9	1154.1	1216.3	1266.0
		11.57	74.34	117.30	231.66	392.62	445.48	463.04	501.40
52.82	183.76	344.45	772.65	1725.46	3141.04	4420.41	4469.13	5126.10	4878.11
38.20	134.53	228.75	657.55	1402.27	2648.44	3760.47	3857.01	4388.16	4192.16
2.56	13.35	37.76	108.44	308.11	473.23	632.37	586.62	707.78	658.79
	66587	143935	376213	743776	911424	1630123	1998749	3003034	3270583
	29812	143935	198370	338888	311763	695064	909323	1184182	1157632
	36775	143935	177843	404888	599661	935059	1089426	1818852	2112951
						1103.3	1382.7	1944.2	2208.9
						480.8	627.6	770.1	777.1
						622.5	755.0	1174.1	1431.8
	25294	31981	54158	104011	157851	224249	192456	265840	313738
	47449	44074	112072	120903	303100	683441	585244	968530	784185
20583	54468	103990	120164	230985	332942	456585	108524		
12705	30011	40990	69762	153327	205477	285071	90926		
7878	24457	63000	50402	77658	127465	171514	17700		
0.15	0.19	0.32	0.42	1.14	1.84	2.75	0.33		
3.73	5.66	9.30	38.04	50.53	53.62	76.20	89.85	69.40	67.07
7245	7500	8267	18434	26870	30873	40627	42202	41894	41936
2.51	4.79	5.75	4.79	2.12	1.57	5.68	6.28	6.40	6.49
2890	2890	2916	1578	1334	763	4058	3642	4040	4273
22.45	27.15	33.82	30.91	30.18	30.16	39.35	39.84	40.70	42.10
16065	17621	20585	21915	21943	23643	34177	34796	35587	36165
47.57	49.23	41.40	37.88	38.40	41.44	54.14	57.01	61.00	64.42
26922	27417	27417	25201	24801	25795	36067	37219	38467	39874

3–1 续表 3 continued 3

指标	Item	单位 Unit	1978年
文化	**Culture**		
图书馆藏书量	Number of Books in Library	万册(10 000 copies)	341.0
图书出版种数	Number of Publication	种(kind)	389
图书量	Books	万册(10 000 copies)	20166
报纸量	Newspapers	万册(10 000 copies)	25055
杂志量	Magazines	万份(10 000 copies)	2209
卫生	**Public Health**		
卫生机构数	Number of Health Institutions	个(unit)	1017
#医院及卫生院	Hospitals and Township Hospitals	个(unit)	148
卫生机构床位数	Number of Beds	张(bed)	11496
#医院及卫生院	Hospitals and Township Hospitals	张(bed)	9856
卫生工作人员	Medical Personnel	人(person)	24949
#卫生技术人员	Medical Technical Personnel	人(person)	19198
人民生活	**People's Livelihood**		
城镇居民人均可支配收入	Per Capita Disposable Income of Urban Households	元(yuan)	337.8
城镇居民人均消费支出	Per Capita Consumption Expenditure of Urban Households	元(yuan)	317.9
#食品	Food	元(yuan)	181.6
农村居民人均可支配收入	Per Capita Disposable Income of Rural Households	元(yuan)	110.5
农村居民人均消费支出	Per Capita Consumption Expenditure of Rural Households	元(yuan)	83.2
#食品	Food	元(yuan)	58.2
农民人均住宅居住面积	Rural Residential Area Per Capita	平方米(sq.m)	9.6
社会治安	**Public security**		
交通事故起数	Number of Traffic Accidents	起(case)	
交通事故死伤人数	Deaths and Injuries from Traffic Accidents	人(person)	
交通事故损失折款	Property Losses from Traffic Accidents	万元(10 000 yuan)	
火灾事故起数	Number of Fire Accidents	起(case)	
火灾事故死伤人数	Deaths and Injuries from Fire Accidents	人(person)	
火灾事故损失折款	Property Losses from Fire Accidents	万元(10 000 yuan)	

注：1.“职工平均工资”2006年以前为在岗职工口径，2006年及以后为法人单位在岗职工口径。
2.“建成区面积”为全市口径。
3.工业统计指标1997年及以前统计口径为乡及乡以上工业企业，1998年及以后为全部国有及年销售收入500万元以上工业企业，2011年及以后为年主营业务收入2000万元及以上工业法人单位。
4.货运量、客运量中的“铁路”指标，2013年3月铁路系统改革，铁路系统统计数据按新口径执行；“公路指标”自2014年起交通部门执行新的公路运输量统计方案，调查范围较老口径有所缩小，2014年及2013年数据均为新口径下交通运输部反馈数据。
5.从2015年起，全市居民收支调查指标采用新口径。“农村居民人均可支配收入”2014年以前为农民人均纯收入口径；“农村居民人均生活消费支出”2014年以前为农民人均生活费支出口径。
6.规模以上工业“营业收入”，2018年以前为“主营业务收入”口径。

1990年	1995年	2000年	2005年	2010年	2015年	2019年	2020年	2021年	2022年
476.0	524.6	591.7	725.1	941.2	1195.0				
2001	2603	3851	5389	6586	10234				
31685	39025	38471	27919	26603	43860				
46930	54460	109199	113751	184706	136480				
3321	4579	11177	7195	6995	8572				
1300	1185	1414	2138	5086	5947	7487	7514	7515	7665
178	216	231	246	277	269	351	343	336	329
18214	20747	21698	24695	31947	49311	66623	68831	72832	76367
17216	19534	20830	23524	29844	45195	59697	62072	66258	69642
41444	43648	45166	41499	54711	89117	122370	126681	131269	137111
31130	32848	35669	34129	39366	71778	97532	102172	108401	113536
1619.5	4720.6	8471.3	13578.5	25321.1	39888.7	51912.6	53328.6	57449	59459
1360.1	3830.4	6891.8	9226.6	15973.3	26318.7	33438.7	34390.8	36866	35788
781.6	1823.6	2387.1	3046.9	5051.2	6415.0	7956.3	8071.9	8654	8520
731.1	1812.7	3046.8	4812.3	8903.3	14231.8	19454.2	20432.1	22580	23844
569.8	1373.6	1976.8	2902.8	5406.6	8597.2	12300.3	12946.9	14591	14883
287.7	770.8	860.0	1134.8	1818.3	2775.5	3702.6	3931.3	4446	4538
22.5	24.7	28.6	33.8	40.2	52.6	51.1	50.3	49.8	47.5
509	1231	1306	911	774	2946	3334	3313	3317	3257
518	1345	1364	1186	1121	3885	3925	3747	3631	3771
64	369	357	316	189	840	905	1006	1207	857
309	110	1281	1071	791	2609	4577	4319	5907	5892
67	87	26	3	9	12	12	16	35	13
166	925	471	76	462	1571	1529	2153	6232	3817

Notes: 1. The average salary of employees is the caliber data of employees in the post before 2006, and the caliber data of employees in the legal entity in 2006 and later.

2.The "area of built districts" refers to the entire city.

3. Industrial statistical indicators In 1997 and before, the statistical caliber was industrial enterprises at or above the township level. In 1998 and after, they were all state-owned and with an annual sales income of more than 5 million yuan. In 2011 and beyond, the annual main business income was 20 million yuan and above industrial enterprises legal entities.

4. The "railway" indicator in freight volume and passenger volume, the railway system reform in March 2013, the railway system statistics are implemented according to the new caliber; the "road indicators" since 2014, the transportation department has implemented a new road traffic statistics program. The scope of the survey has been narrower than that of the old one. The data for 2014 and 2013 are the feedback data of the Ministry of Communications under the new caliber.

5. Starting from 2015, the city's residents' income and expenditure survey indicators adopt a new caliber. "per capita disposable income of Rural Residents" was the "per capita net income of Rural Residents" before 2014; "Per capita consumption expenditure of Rural Residents"was the "per capita living expenses of farmers" before 2014.

6."Main operating revenue" of industrial enterprises above designated size adopts the statistical scale of "main operating revenue" before 2018.

3-2 国民经济和社会发展比例和效益指标
Indicators on Proportions and Efficiency in National Economic and Social Development

指标	Item	单位 Unit	1978年	1985年
人口	**Population**			
申报出生率	Birth Rate	‰	15.53	11.39
申报死亡率	Death Rate	‰	7.00	6.52
自然增长率	Natural Growth Rate	‰	8.53	4.87
就业	**Employment**			
就业者负担人口	Dependency of Employed Population	人(person)	2.21	1.99
三次产业从业者比例	Composition of Employed Population			
第一产业	Primary Industry	%	66.8	47.5
第二产业	Secondary Industry	%	22.6	31.0
第三产业	Tertiary Industry	%	10.6	21.5
城镇登记失业率	Registered Unemployment Rate in Urban Areas	%		
国民经济核算	**National Accounting**			
三次产业增加值比例	Composition of Gross Domestic Product			
第一产业	Primary Industry	%		21.1
第二产业	Secondary Industry	%		51.8
第三产业	Tertiary Industry	%		27.1
人均生产总值	Per Capita GDP	元(yuan)		1263
资本形成率(投资率)	Capital Formation Rate	%		
最终消费率(消费率)	Final Consumption Rate	%		
固定资产投资	**Investment in Fixed Assets**			
固定资产投资占生产总值比重	Proportion of Fixed Assets Investment in GDP	%		23.7
财政	**Finance**			
一般公共预算收入占生产总值比重	Proportion of General Public Budget Revenue in GDP	%	25.2	14.5
一般公共预算支出占生产总值比重	Proportion of General Public Budget Expenditure in GDP	%	6.3	5.6
农业	**Agriculture**			
人均耕地面积	Per Cultivated Area	亩(mu)	1.24	1.10
每公顷耕地化肥施用量(折纯)	Consumption of Chemical Fertilizers per Hectare	千克(kg)		225
每公顷播种面积粮食产量	Grain Yield Per Hectare of Sown Area	千克(kg)	2475	3864
机耕率	Machine-cultivated Rate	%		
规模以上工业	**Industry Enterprises above Designated Size**			
产品销售率	Product Sales Rate	%		

1990年	1995年	2000年	2010年	2015年	2019年	2020年	2021年	2022年
12.88	10.03	11.08	11.13	11.82	12.77	10.45	8.21	7.85
6.54	6.32	7.05	8.35	6.73	6.58	7.31	5.45	9.74
6.34	3.71	4.03	2.78	5.09	6.19	3.14	2.76	-1.89
1.94	1.67	1.62	1.62	1.61	1.5	1.3	1.4	1.4
46.5	35.8	31.7	20.5	18.5	15.7			
32.4	32.9	31.9	32.2	32.1	31.3			
21.1	31.3	36.4	47.3	49.4	52.9			
	2.45	3.70	3.84	2.04	2.01	2.03		
17.3	14.3	10.0	5.5	5.0	3.6	3.6	3.6	3.5
48.7	46.5	43.9	41.9	37.8	34.6	34.8	34.7	34.8
34.0	39.2	46.1	52.6	57.2	61.8	61.6	61.7	61.7
2666	8773	15356	55248	77815	104180	110681	122873	128287
39.1	39.5	40.2	52.6	63.0				
37.8	41.9	56.9	46.9	52.3				
22.1	23.8	32.1	50.8	57.3				
9.0	3.6	5.2	15.2	10.1	9.3	8.9	8.8	8.3
5.9	4.1	5.8	16.9	10.8	12.7	12.7	11.3	10.2
1.00	0.94	0.88	0.90	0.87	0.64	0.71	0.63	0.63
330	569	641	646	626	623	599	584	567
4273	5512	5354	6192	6117	5956	6053	6060	6112
					92.0	94.1	96.5	96.6
	97.12	98.24	98.71	98.23	96.80			

3-2 续表 continued

指标	Item	单位 Unit	1978年	1985年
总资产贡献率	Total Asset Contribution Rate	%		
流动资产周转次数	Turnover of Current Asset	次(times)		
邮电通讯业	**Post and Telecommunication Services**			
每百人拥有电话	Number of phones Per 100 Population	部(unit)	0.60	1.26
国内商业	**Domestic Commerce**			
人均消费品零售总额	Total Sales of Consumption Good Per Capita	元(yuan)	182	500
教育	**Education**			
学龄儿童入学率	School-age Children Enrollment Rate	%		99.44
学校教师负担人数	Teacher-student Ratio	人(person)	21.28	16.75
高等教育	Higher Education	人(person)	2.47	6.55
中等教育	Secondary Education	人(person)	16.65	14.46
小学	Primary Schools	人(person)	34.99	20.33
卫生	**Public Health**			
每万人拥有医院卫生院数	Number of Health Institutes per 10000 Population	个(unit)	0.33	0.34
每万人拥有医生数	Number of Doctors per 10000 Population	人(person)	23.3	26.3
每万人拥有医院床位数	Number of Hospitals Beds per 10000 Population	张(bed)	22.0	28.2
市政建设	**City Construction**			
城市人口用水普及率	Coverage Rate of Water Supply	%	99.0	100.0
城市用气普及率	Coverage Rate of Natural Gas Supply	%	17.8	26.3
建成区绿化覆盖率	Coverage Rate of Urban Green Areas	%	12.0	23.0
生活	**Life**			
城镇居民恩格尔系数	Engel's Coefficient of Urban Households	%	57.1	56.5
农村居民恩格尔系数	Engel's Coefficient of Rural Households	%	69.9	51.8

注：1.“一般公共预算收入占生产总值比重”2012年(含)以前为“地方财政收入”口径；“一般公共预算支出占生产总值比重”2012年(含)以前为“地方财政支出”口径。
2.人均生产总值，2000年及以后数据根据全国第四次经济普查修订。

1990年	1995年	2000年	2010年	2015年	2019年	2020年	2021年	2022年
	12.25	8.45	15.98	13.37	8.90	9.11	8.07	6.69
	1.69	1.52	2.11	1.82	1.65	1.61	1.63	1.46
1.89	7.23	18.98	35.31	26.48	18.81	18.06	17.90	18.05
1009	3389	6149	27343	50369	55882	55744	63155	59614
99.03	99.40	99.93	100.00	100.00	100.00	100.00	100.00	100.00
14.20	15.60	15.24	17.40	17.37	15.44	16.58	14.89	14.73
5.15	7.55	11.25	21.76	22.53	18.76	21.29	16.57	15.99
12.99	15.30	16.78	14.72	13.33	12.71	11.00	12.37	12.02
17.67	18.20	15.10	15.48	16.07	15.01	15.32	15.87	16.16
0.34	0.40	0.41	0.46	0.43	0.44	0.43	0.41	0.40
29.2	27.9	29.5	29.1	46.0	43.0	43.7	45.5	46.7
32.9	36.0	38.6	52.9	69.1	74.8	74.8	78.0	81.1
100.0	100.0	100.0	100.0	99.0	100.0	100.0	100.0	100.0
45.7	72.2	90.7	95.5	97.7	100.0	100.0	100.0	100.0
30.0	30.5	36.1	36.9	39.9	41.2	40.7	41.7	41.9
57.5	47.6	34.6	31.6	24.4	23.8	23.5	23.5	23.8
50.5	56.1	43.5	33.6	32.3	30.1	30.4	30.5	30.5

Notes: 1."The proportion of general public budget revenue in total output value" was the caliber of "local financial revenue" before 2012 (inclusive); "The proportion of general public budget expenditure in total output value" was the caliber of "local financial expenditure".

2.Per Capita GDP，The data of 2000 and later are revised data after the Fourth National Economic Census.

3-3 平均每天主要社会经济活动
Selected Indicators on Average Daily Social and Economic Activities

指标	Item	单位 Unit	1978年
每天创造的财富			
地区生产总值(当年价)	Gross Domestic Product	万元(10 000 yuan)	646
第一产业	Primary Industry	万元(10 000 yuan)	114
第二产业	Secondary Industry	万元(10 000 yuan)	365
第三产业	Tertiary Industry	万元(10 000 yuan)	167
一般公共预算收入	General Public Budget Revenue	万元(10 000 yuan)	163
一般公共预算支出	General Public Budget Expenditure	万元(10 000 yuan)	41
固定资产投资	Investment in Fixed Assets	万元(10 000 yuan)	
每天生产主要工、农业产品	**Production of Major Industrial Product and Agricultural Products on Average Daily**		
粮食	Grain	吨(ton)	3161
棉花	Cotton	吨(ton)	14
蔬菜	Vegetable	吨(ton)	1348
猪肉	Pork	吨(ton)	67
奶类	Milk	吨(ton)	11
钢材	Steel	吨(ton)	689
发电量	Electric Energy Capacity	万千瓦时(10 000 kWh)	347
水泥	Cement	吨(ton)	2399
化肥	Chemical Fertilizer	吨(ton)	494
金切机床	Metal-cutting Machine Tools	台(unit)	10
汽车	Motor Vehicles	辆(unit)	12
服务器	Server	台(unit)	-
布	Cloth	万米(10 000 m)	38
每天其他经济活动	**Other Economic Activity on Average Daily**		
最终消费量	Final Consumption	万元(10 000 yuan)	
居民消费	Households Expense	万元(10 000 yuan)	
农业居民	Rural Households	万元(10 000 yuan)	
城镇居民	Urban Households	万元(10 000 yuan)	
政府消费	Government Expense	万元(10 000 yuan)	
社会消费品零售总额	Total Sales of Consumption Good Per Capita	万元(10 000 yuan)	261
公路货运量	Highways Freight Traffic	万吨(10 000 tons)	3.2
公路客运量	Highways Passenger Traffic	万人(10 000 persons)	1.4
自来水供水量	Water Supply	万吨(10 000 tons)	36.9
用电量	Electricity Consumption	万千瓦时(10 000 kWh)	754
市内公共车辆乘客人数	Number of City Bus Passengers	万人次(10 000 person-times)	34.0
实际使用外资额	Total Amount of Foreign Capital Actually Utilized	万美元(10 000 USD)	
港澳台及外国来济旅游人数	Compatriots from Hong Kong Macao and Taiwan and Foreigners	人(person)	
每天人口变动和婚姻	**Daily Population Changes and Marriages**		
出生	Birth	人(person)	191
死亡	Death	人(person)	86
结婚	Marriages	对(couple)	
离婚	Divorces	对(couple)	

注：1."一般公共预算收入"指标1978年到1995年为"地方财政收入"口径，"一般公共预算支出"指标1978年到1995年为"地方财政支出"口径。
2.按照国家统计局经济普查年度数据使用规定，部分涉及国民经济核算的指标数据空缺。

1985年	1990年	1995年	2000年	2010年	2015年	2019年	2020年	2021年	2022年
1682	3787	12973	28657	121618	184603	258722	277074	312699	329519
354	656	1853	2986	6526	8934	9399	9881	11199	11521
872	1845	6038	12793	52563	68959	89458	96796	108112	114527
456	1286	5082	12878	62529	106710	159865	170397	193387	203471
244	339	465	1344	7291	16831	23950	24757	27605	27429
94	224	537	1499	9227	18032	32803	35213	35427	33577
399	838	3089	8382	54450	95847				
4479	4972	6917	6583	7930	7248	7820	7946	8030	8115
136.2	137	79.7	74.7	81	20.2	15	12	10	10
2304	3455	6946	14733	16478	17157	18390	18408	18953	19524
138	215	390	478	597	508	467	350	422	463
23	51	95	194	855	638	880	1132	1153	1190
1197	1576	2856	6507	26857	19852	61793	63839	57690	55381
724	1225	1884	1898	3601	4818	8086	7560	8633	8717
3699	5796	11644	13291	19994	21411	35283	36290	42770	37304
313	396	384	778	1345	644	463	577	458	116
18	14	11	8	6	10	20	29	38	34
31	17	16	8	581	263	481	1077	878	450
				271	1112	3192	3921	3115	2112
50	55	41	45	22	44	11	3	3	2
780	1580	5524	14833	50253	87412				
638	1274	4567	11098	39460	55221				
367	624	1938	3596	5142	7120				
271	650	2629	7502	34317	48101				
142	306	957	3735	10794	32192				
640	1447	5151	9718	49382	93433	121107	122107	140441	133647
6.9	10.9	16.9	19.2	35.7	55.9	94.2	76.5	67.6	65.3
3.1	4.9	7.2	12.4	35.0	10.0	8.9	3.3	5.5	3.9
40	45.3	57.5	76.7	64.5	87.2	121.8	123.0	136.2	138.7
747	1255	1779	2505	6713.3	7238.5	11350.8	11855.2	13020.9	13690.8
62.2	73.3	73.3	125.9	296.1	256.5	272.3	170.6	200.2	134.2
	8.5	69.3	87.6	285.0	432.5	614.4	524.6	728.3	859.6
27	56	149	285	633	912.2	1251.0	298.0		
152	183	148	170	184	202	279	230	183	176
87	93	94	108	138	115	144	160	121	218
	103	137	120	153	138	143	138	135	132
		17	20	50	70	98	100	65	64

Notes: 1. The indicator-"general public budget revenue" was the caliber of "local financial revenue" from 1978 to 1995 and the indicator-"general public budget expenditure" was the caliber of "local fiscal expenditure" from 1978 to 1995.

2. Part of index data regarding national economic accounting is missing according to economic census year data use provisions of National Bureau of Statistics.

3-4 国民经济人均指标
Per Indicators of National Economic

指标	Item	单位 Unit	1978年
地区生产总值	**Gross Domestic Product**	**元(yuan)**	**527**
主要农产品产量	**Output of Major Agricultural Products**		
粮食	Grain	千克(kg)	258
棉花	Cotton	千克(kg)	1.14
猪肉	Pork	千克(kg)	5.44
水果	Fruits	千克(kg)	12.65
禽蛋	Eggs	千克(kg)	
蔬菜	Vegetable	千克(kg)	109.84
牛奶	Milk	千克(kg)	0.88
水产品	Aquatic Products	千克(kg)	0.29
主要工业产品产量	**Output of Major Industrial Products**		
钢材	Steel	千克(kg)	48.1
发电量	Electric Energy Capacity	千瓦小时(kWh)	282.5
水泥	Cement	千克(kg)	195.5
化肥	Chemical Fertilizer	千克(kg)	29.5
服务器	Server	台(unit)	-
布	Cloth	米(m)	30.8
其他经济活动	**Other Economic Activity**		
社会消费品零售总额	Total Sales of Consumption Good Per Capita	元(yuan)	182
一般公共预算收入	General Public Budget Revenue	元(yuan)	133
一般公共预算支出	General Public Budget Expenditure	元(yuan)	33
城乡居民人民币储蓄存款余额	RMB Deposits Balance of Urban and Rural Households	元(yuan)	33
城镇居民人均可支配收入	Per Capita Disposable Income of Urban Households	元(yuan)	338
城镇居民人均消费支出	Per Capita Life Consumption Expenditure of Urban Households	元(yuan)	318
农村居民人均可支配收入	Per Capita Disposable Income of Rural Households	元(yuan)	111
农村居民人均消费支出	Per Capita Life Consumption Expenditure of Rural Households	元(yuan)	83

注：1. "一般公共预算收入" 指标1978年到1995年为"地方财政收入"口径。"一般公共预算支出"指标1978年到1995年为"地方财政支出"口径。
2.从2015年起，全市发布城乡住户调查一体化改革新口径数据，居民收支调查指标与2014年前分别实施的城镇和农村住户调查的调查范围、方法、指标口径、名称有所不同。
3.根据年末反馈人口数据，修订2020年相关数据。

1985年	1990年	1995年	2000年	2010年	2015年	2019年	2020年	2021年	2022年
1263	**2666**	**8773**	**15356**	**55248**	**77815**	**104180**	**110681**	**122873**	**128287**
336	350	468	429	479	424	322	320	316	316
10.22	9.64	5.38	4.87	4.87	2.36	0.61	0.47	0.41	0.37
10.33	15.13	26.33	31.15	36.10	36.46	19.22	14.11	16.60	18.02
14.70	12.88	35.81	66.56	78.58	61.89	70.93	69.64	66.64	66.12
	18.27	41.29	74.29	59.68	56.86	41.22	30.27	32.83	28.79
173.02	243.10	469.77	960.06	996.29	1041.79	756.41	742.39	744.72	760.09
1.76	3.46	6.44	12.65	51.68	46.75	36.21	45.65	45.32	46.32
0.41	1.80	4.72	5.87	7.06	7.63	1.82	1.46	1.51	1.58
69.6	169.1	195.7	424.0	1623.8	1161.8	2541.7	2574.6	2266.9	2156.1
543.9	862.3	1237.0	1231.5	2177.5	2819.9	3326.0	3049.0	3392.2	3393.6
277.9	408.0	728.4	866.1	1208.9	1253.1	1451.2	1463.6	1680.6	1452.3
18.7	23.6	23.0	46.5	80.3	37.7	19.1	23.3	18.0	4.5
-	-	-	-	0.016	0.065	0.1	0.2	0.1	0.1
37.2	38.9	19.9	29.5	13.6	25.7	4.6	1.2	1.2	0.9
500	1009	3468	6332	25577	44243	49812	49245	55185	52031
183	239	315	876	4409	9850	9851	9984	10847	10678
70	158	363	977	5579	10553	13492	14201	13921	13072
236	985	4115	8266	36239	63358	72550	83570	92136	109076
732	1620	4721	8471	25321	39889	51913	53329	57449	59459
704	1369	3830	6892	15973	26319	33439	34391	36866	35788
439	731	1813	3047	8903	14232	19454	20432	22580	23844
330	570	1374	1977	5407	8597	12300	12947	14591	14883

Notes: 1. The indicator-"general public budget revenue" was the caliber of "local financial revenue" from 1978 to 1995 and the indicator-"general public budget expenditure" was the caliber of "local fiscal expenditure" from 1978 to 1995.

2. From 2015, new caliber data about urban and rural household survey integration reform was published by the city and the survey index of residents' income and expenditure was different from survey scope, method, indicator caliber and name of urban and rural residents implemented before 2014.

3.Relevant data in 2020 was revised according to population data at the end of the year.

3-5 国民经济主要指标及占全国、全省比重(2022年)
Main Indicators of National Economy and Their Proportion in China and Shandong Province(2022)

指标	Item	单位 Unit	全国 Country
区划面积	Area	万平方公里(10 000 sq.km)	960
年末总人口	Total year-end Population	万人(10 000 persons)	141175
生产总值(当年价)	Gross Domestic Product	亿元(100 million yuan)	1210207.0
第一产业	Primary Industry	亿元(100 million yuan)	88345.0
第二产业	Secondary Industry	亿元(100 million yuan)	483164.0
第三产业	Tertiary Industry	亿元(100 million yuan)	638698.0
规模以上工业营业收入	Revenue from Business of Industrial Enterprises above Designated Size	亿元(100 million yuan)	1379098.4
规模以上工业利润总额	Total Profits of Industrial Enterprises above Designated Size	亿元(100 million yuan)	84038.5
粮食总产量	Total Output of Grain	万吨(10 000 tons)	68652.8
棉花总产量	Total Output of Cotton	万吨(10 000 tons)	597.7
固定资产投资额	Investment in Fixed Assets	亿元(100 million yuan)	572138.0
公路货物周转量	Highways Freight Turnover	亿吨公里(100 million ton-km)	68958.04
社会消费品零售总额	Total Sales of Consumption Good Per Capita	亿元(100 million yuan)	439733.0
实际使用外资	Total Amount of Foreign Capital Actually Utilized	亿美元(100 million USD)	1891.3
一般公共预算收入	General Public Budget Revenue	亿元(100 million yuan)	203703.0
一般公共预算支出	General Public Budget Expenditure	亿元(100 million yuan)	260609.0
普通本专科在校学生	Enrollment of Regular Institutions of Higher Education	万人(10 000persons)	3659.4
中等职业教育在校学生	Enrollment of Secondary Professional Schools	万人(10 000persons)	1784.7
卫生机构数	Number of Health Institutions	个(unit)	1032918
卫生技术人员	Medical Technical Personnel	万人(10 000persons)	1155.0
#执业(助理)医师	Licensed Doctors	万人(10 000persons)	440.0
城镇居民人均可支配收入	Per Capita Disposable Income of Urban Households	元(yuan)	49283
农村居民人均可支配收入	Per Capita Disposable Income of Rural Households	元(yuan)	20133

全省 Province	济南 Jinan	济南占全国比重 (%) Jinan Account for Proportion of Country (%)	济南占全省比重 (%) Jinan Account for Proportion of Province (%)
15.8	1.0244	0.11	6.48
10162.8	941.5	0.67	9.26
87435.1	12027.5	0.99	13.76
6298.6	420.5	0.48	6.68
35014.2	4180.2	0.87	11.94
46122.3	7426.7	1.16	16.10
108019.9	8370.3	0.61	7.75
4473.2	344.9	0.41	7.71
5543.8	296.19	0.43	5.34
14.5	0.4	0.06	2.41
7912.60	608.80	0.88	7.69
33236.2	4878.1	1.11	14.68
228.7	31.4	1.66	13.72
7104.0	1001.1	0.49	14.09
12131.5	1225.6	0.47	10.10
252.7	67.1	1.83	26.54
133.6	15.0	0.84	11.23
86121	7665	0.74	8.90
87.2	11.4	0.98	13.02
34.68	4.4	1.00	12.68
49050	59459		
22110	23844		

主要统计指标解释

国民经济行业分类 自2017年年报和2018年定期报表开始使用新的《国民经济行业分类》（GB/T4754-2017）。该分类是由国家统计局组织修订，原国家质量监督检验检疫总局和中国国家标准化管理委员会于2017年6月30日发布。这次修订是在2011年分类标准的基础上，结合我国经济活动特点，参照联合国《全部经济活动的国际标准产业分类》（ISIC/Rev.4）进行的。修订后的《国民经济行业分类》（GB/T4754-2017）共有门类20个，大类97个，中类473个，小类1382个。

企业登记注册类型 是以在市场监管部门登记注册的各类企业为划分对象，以市场监管部门对企业登记注册的类型为依据，将企业登记注册类型分为内资企业、港澳台商投资企业和外商投资企业三大类。内资企业包括国有企业、集体企业、股份合作企业、联营企业、有限责任公司、股份有限公司、私营企业和其他企业；港澳台商投资企业和外商投资企业分别包括合资经营企业、合作经营企业、独资经营企业和股份有限公司等。

国有企业 指企业全部资产归国家所有，并按《中华人民共和国企业法人登记管理条例》规定登记注册的非公司制的经济组织。不包括有限责任公司中的国有独资公司。

集体企业 指企业资产归集体所有，并按《中华人民共和国企业法人登记管理条例》规定登记注册的经济组织。

股份合作企业 指以合作制为基础，由企业职工共同出资入股，吸收一定比例的社会资产投资组建，实行自主经营，自负盈亏，共同劳动，民主管理，按劳分配与按股分红相结合的一种集体经济组织。

联营企业 指两个及两个以上相同或不同所有制性质的企业法人或事业单位法人，按自愿、平等、互利的原则，共同投资组成的经济组织。联营企业包括国有联营企业、集体联营企业、国有与集体联营企业和其他联营企业。

有限责任公司 指根据《中华人民共和国公司登记管理条例》规定登记注册，由两个以上、五十个以下的股东共同出资，每个股东以其所认缴的出资额对公司承担有限责任，公司以其全部资产对其债务承担责任的经济组织。有限责任公司包括国有独资公司以及其他有限责任公司。

股份有限公司 指根据《中华人民共和国公司登记管理条例》规定登记注册，其全部注册资本由等额股份构成并通过发行股票筹集资本，股东以其认购的股份对公司承担有限责任，公司以其全部资产对其债务承担责任的经济组织。

私营企业 指由自然人投资设立或由自然人控股，以雇佣劳动为基础的营利性经济组织。包括按照《公司法》、《合伙企业法》以及《个人独资企业法》规定登记注册的私营独资企业、私营合伙企业、私营有限责任公司、私营股份有限公司和个人独资企业。

其他企业 指上述企业之外的其他内资经济组织。

与港澳台商合资经营企业 指港澳台地区投资者与内地企业依照《中华人民共和国外商投资法》及有关法律的规定，按合同规定的比例投资设立，分享利润、分担风险和亏损的企业。

与港澳台商合作经营企业 指港澳台地区投资者与内地企业依照《中华人民共和国外商投资法》及有关法律的规定，依照合作合同的约定进行投资或提供条件设立，分配利润、分担风险和亏损的企业。

港澳台商独资经营企业 指依照《中华人民共和国外商投资法》及有关法律的规定，在内地由港澳台地区投资者全额投资设立的企业。

港澳台商投资股份有限公司 指根据国家有关规定，经商务部（原外经贸部）批准设立，并且其中港、澳、台商的股本占公司注册资本的比例达25%以上的股份有限公司。凡其中港、澳、台商的股本占公司注册资本的比例小于25%的，属于内资中的股份有限公司。

其他港澳台商投资企业 指在中国境内参照《中华人民共和国外商投资法》，依法设立的港、澳、台商投资合伙企业等。

中外合资经营企业 指外国企业或外国人与中国内地企业依照《中华人民共和国外商投资法》及有关法律的规定，按合同规定的比例投资设立，分享利润和分担风险和亏损的企业。

中外合作经营企业 指外国企业或外国人与中国内地企业依照《中华人民共和国外商投资法》及有关法律的规定，依照合作合同的约定进行投资或提供条件设立，分配利润、分担风险和亏损的企业。

外资企业 指依照《中华人民共和国外商投资法》及有关法律的规定，在中国内地由外国投资者全额投资设立的企业。

外商投资股份有限公司 指根据国家有关规定，经商务部（原外经贸部）批准设立，并且其中外资的股本占公司注册资本的比例达25% 以上的股份有限公司。凡其中外资股本占公司注册资本的比例小于25%的，属于内资企业中的股份有限公司。

其他外商投资企业 指在中国境内依照《中华人民共和国外商投资法》，依法设立的外商投资合伙企业等。

Explanatory Notes on Main Statistical Indicators

Industrial Classification of the National Economy The new Industrial Classification of the National Economy (GB/T 4754-2017) is introduced starting from the compilation of 2017 annual statistics and 2018 monthly or quarterly statistics. The revision, based on the 2011 classification, was organized by the National Bureau of Statistics taking into consideration of the characteristics of economic activities in China and the International Standards of the Industrial Classification of All Economic Activities (ISIC/Rev.4) of the United Nations. The new Classification was promulgated by the former National Administration of Quality Supervision, Inspection and Quarantine and the Standardization Administration of the People's Republic of China on June 30, 2017. The revised version of the Industrial Classification of the National Economy (GB/T 4754-2017) is composed of 20 sections, 97 divisions, 473 groups and 1382 classes.

Registration Status of Enterprises (units) Enterprises are classified into 3 categories, namely enterprises with domestic investment, enterprises with investment from Hong Kong, Macao and Taiwan, and enterprises with foreign investment, according to the registration status of an enterprise in market supervision administration. Domestic-invested enterprises include state-owned enterprises, collective-owned enterprises, cooperative enterprises, joint ownership enterprises, limited liability corporations, share-holding corporations Ltd., private enterprises and other enterprises. Included in the enterprises with investment from Hong Kong, Macao and Taiwan and enterprises with foreign investment are joint-venture enterprises, cooperative enterprises, sole-proprietorship enterprises and share-holding corporations Ltd.

State-owned Enterprises refer to non-corporation economic units where the entire assets are owned by the state and which have been registered in accordance with the Regulation of the People's Republic of China on the Management of Registration of Corporate Enterprises. Not included from this category are state sole-proprietorship corporations in the limited liability corporations.

Collective-owned Enterprises refer to economic units where the assets are owned collectively and which have been registered in accordance with the Regulation of the People's Republic of China on the Management of Registration of Corporate Enterprises.

Cooperative Enterprises refer to a form of collective economic units (enterprises) where capitals come mainly from employees as their shares, with certain proportion of capital from the outside, where production is organized on the basis of independent operation, independent accounting for profits and losses, joint work, democratic management, and a distribution system that integrates remuneration according to work with dividend according to capital share.

Joint Ownership Enterprises refer to economic units established by two or more corporate enterprises or corporate institutions of the same or different ownership, through joint investment on the basis of voluntary participation, equality, and mutual benefits. They include state joint ownership enterprises; collective joint ownership enterprises; joint state-collective enterprises; and other joint ownership enterprises.

Limited Liability Corporations refer to economic units established with investment from 2-50 investors and registered in accordance with the Regulation of the People's Republic of China on the Management of Registration of Corporations, each investor bearing limited liability to the corporation depending on its share of investment, and the corporation bearing liability to its debt to the maximum of its total assets. Limited liability corporations include state sole-proprietorship corporations and other limited liability corporations.

Share-holding Corporations Ltd. refer to economic units registered in accordance with the Regulation of the People's Republic of China on the Management of Registration of Corporations, with total registered capital divided into equal shares and additional capitals raised through issuing stocks. Each investor bears limited liability to the corporation depending on the holding of shares, and the corporation bears liability to its debt to the maximum of its total assets.

Private Enterprises refer to profit-making economic units invested and established by natural persons, or controlled by natural persons, using employed labour. Included in this category are private sole-proprietorship enterprise, private partnership enterprise, private limited liability companies, private limited-liability company by shares and individual sole-proprietorship enterprise registered in accordance with the Company Law, the Law on Partnership Business and the Law on Individual Proprietorship Enterprises.

Other Domestic-Invested Enterprises refer to domestic-invested economic units other than those mentioned above.

Joint Venture Enterprises with Hong Kong, Macao and Taiwan are enterprises jointly established by investors from Hong Kong, Macao and Taiwan with enterprises in the mainland of China in accordance with Foreign Investment Law of the People's Republic of China and other relevant laws, where the establishment of the investment and the sharing of profits, taking risks and loss are stipulated in joint venture contracts.

Cooperative Enterprises with Hong Kong, Macao and

Taiwan established by investors from Hong Kong, Macao and Taiwan with enterprises in the mainland of China in accordance with Foreign Investment Law of the People's Republic of China and other relevant laws, where the investment or provision of facilities and the sharing of profits and risks are stipulated under cooperative contracts.

Sole-proprietorship Enterprises with Investment from Hong Kong, Macao and Taiwan refer to enterprises established in the mainland of China with exclusive investment from investors from Hong Kong, Macao and Taiwan in accordance with Foreign Investment Law of the People's Republic of China and other relevant laws.

Share-holding Corporations Ltd. with Investment from Hong Kong, Macao and Taiwan refer to share-holding corporations Ltd. established with the approval from the Ministry of Commerce (the former Ministry of Foreign Trade and Economic Relations) in line with relevant state regulations, where the share of investment from Hong Kong, Macao or Taiwan businessmen exceeds 25% of the total registered capital of the corporation. In case the share of investment from Hong Kong, Macao or Taiwan is less than 25% of the total registered capital, the enterprise is to be classified as domestic-invested share-holding corporation Ltd.

Other Enterprises with Funds From Hong Kong, Macao and Taiwan refer to partnership enterprises with investments from Hong Kong, Macao and Taiwan established within the territory of China in accordance Foreign Investment Law of the People's Republic of China.

Joint Venture Enterprises with Foreign Investment refer to enterprises jointly established by foreign enterprises or foreigners with enterprises in the mainland of China in accordance with Foreign Investment Law of the People's Republic of China and other relevant laws, where the sharing of investment, profits and risks and loss are stipulated in contracts.

Cooperative Enterprises with Foreign Investment refer to enterprises jointly established by foreign enterprises or foreigners with enterprises in the mainland of China in accordance with Foreign Investment Law of the People's Republic of China and other relevant laws, where the investment or provision of facilities and the sharing of profits and taking risks and loss are stipulated in cooperative contracts.

Sole-proprietorship Enterprises with Foreign Investment refer to enterprises established in the mainland of China with exclusive investment from foreign investors in accordance with Foreign Investment Law of the People's Republic of China and other relevant laws.

Share-holding Corporations Ltd. with Foreign Investment refer to share-holding corporations Ltd. established with the approval from the Ministry of Commerce (the former Ministry of Foreign Trade and Economic Relations) in line with relevant state regulations, where the share of investment from foreign investors exceeds 25% of the total registered capital of the corporation. In case the share of foreign investment is less than 25% of the total registered capital, the enterprise is to be classified as domestic-invested share-holding corporation Ltd.

Other Enterprises with Foreign Funds refer to partnership enterprises established within the territory of China in accordance with Foreign Investment Law of the People's Republic of China.

4

国民经济核算

NATIONAL ACCOUNTS

4-1 各时期生产总值(按当年价格计算)
Gross Domestic Product in Each Period(Calculated at Current Prices)

年份 Year	地区生产总值(亿元) Gross Domestic Product (100 million yuan)	其中 of which				人均生产总值(元) Per Capita GDP (yuan)
		第一产业 Primary Industry	第二产业 Secondary Industry	第三产业 Tertiary Industry	#工业 Industry	
1952	3.83	1.45	1.13	1.25	1.09	121
1957	6.66	1.93	2.24	2.50	2.18	194
1962	6.21	1.03	2.43	2.74	2.36	177
1965	9.68	1.88	4.44	3.36	4.34	262
1970	13.61	2.16	7.69	3.76	7.56	337
1975	16.24	2.90	8.65	4.69	8.46	373
"五五"时期						
1976	18.18	3.34	9.98	4.85	9.72	413
1977	19.98	3.58	11.23	5.16	10.98	450
1978	23.60	4.16	13.32	6.12	12.89	527
1979	26.56	5.01	14.77	6.78	14.10	586
1980	28.80	5.96	15.86	6.98	14.24	630
"六五"时期						
1981	31.56	6.56	17.65	7.35	15.11	681
1982	36.06	8.80	18.55	8.70	15.79	765
1983	42.01	11.62	20.48	9.92	17.96	881
1984	47.99	10.35	25.47	12.18	20.10	997
1985	61.37	12.92	31.82	16.63	27.54	1263
"七五"时期						
1986	71.28	14.82	34.48	21.99	28.69	1451
1987	84.54	17.52	40.29	26.74	32.88	1699
1988	114.22	22.23	57.07	34.92	47.49	2266
1989	125.83	23.77	61.52	40.54	54.66	2466
1990	138.24	23.93	67.36	46.95	60.43	2666
"八五"时期						
1991	163.39	25.38	76.56	61.45	67.73	3109
1992	207.84	27.74	98.36	81.73	86.85	3928
1993	270.76	32.66	133.15	104.96	115.36	5088
1994	371.88	49.44	176.82	145.61	154.49	6946
1995	473.52	67.64	220.37	185.51	194.16	8773
"九五"时期						
1996	580.84	74.24	274.93	231.67	238.31	10701
1997	709.95	82.52	327.97	299.46	278.87	12995

4-1 续表 continued

年份 Year	地区生产总值 (亿元) Gross Domestic Product (100 million yuan)	其中 of which 第一产业 Primary Industry	第二产业 Secondary Industry	第三产业 Tertiary Industry	#工业 Industry	人均生产总值 (元) Per Capita GDP (yuan)
1998	802.16	90.20	366.43	345.53	298.41	14549
1999	881.32	92.52	399.80	389.00	318.80	15863
2000	1048.85	109.27	468.23	471.35	379.07	15356
"十五"时期						
2001	1175.98	112.59	499.58	563.81	405.00	17062
2002	1323.06	114.79	572.55	635.72	465.89	19032
2003	1529.34	118.47	687.31	723.56	570.04	21765
2004	1827.84	135.60	858.25	833.99	725.46	25729
2005	2086.44	150.50	1005.54	930.40	859.24	27338
"十一五"时期						
2006	2417.78	161.70	1134.84	1121.24	961.73	31390
2007	2811.23	169.67	1292.43	1349.13	1091.74	36071
2008	3378.97	194.87	1514.48	1669.62	1280.66	42931
2009	3705.96	206.20	1603.76	1896.00	1313.89	46735
2010	4439.05	238.19	1918.55	2282.31	1572.50	55248
"十二五"时期						
2011	4931.10	259.32	2058.29	2613.49	1661.94	60207
2012	5328.00	272.85	2132.64	2922.51	1711.76	63988
2013	5765.76	302.08	2276.14	3187.54	1764.60	68343
2014	6330.51	315.73	2424.33	3590.45	1861.37	74028
2015	6738.01	326.09	2516.99	3894.93	1924.96	77815
"十三五"时期						
2016	7274.94	328.42	2601.27	4345.25	1966.07	82820
2017	7933.87	323.08	2800.42	4810.37	2062.26	89285
2018	8678.64	332.73	2997.08	5348.83	2100.16	96682
2019	9443.37	343.06	3265.22	5835.09	2167.87	104180
2020	10140.91	361.66	3542.73	6236.52	2382.27	110681
"十四五"时期						
2021	11413.51	408.77	3946.10	7058.64	2706.06	122873
2022	12027.46	420.52	4180.24	7426.70	2869.00	128287

注：2000年及以后数据根据全国第四次经济普查修订。
Note: The data of 2000 and later are revised data after the Fourth National Economic Census.

4-2 各时期生产总值环比指数(以上年为100)
Circle Indices of Gross Domestic Product in Each Period(preceding year=100)

年份 Year	地区生产总值 Gross Domestic Product	其中 of which				
		第一产业 Primary Industry	第二产业 Secondary Industry	第三产业 Tertiary Industry	工业 Industry	人均生产总值 Per Capita GDP
1957	97.5	91.7	89.0	112.7	92.3	95.7
1962	105.6	116.7	82.7	121.9	81.3	105.9
1965	120.8	120.4	138.8	105.3	132.9	120.7
1970	113.7	95.9	131.9	100.5	130.8	108.7
1975	139.0	121.5	160.4	117.6	167.8	133.9
"五五"时期						
1976	104.9	93.2	114.6	104.5	113.1	104.6
1977	106.8	95.0	112.3	106.3	113.9	104.7
1978	113.0	99.3	114.2	119.0	111.9	109.1
1979	112.1	120.0	110.5	110.4	109.0	110.8
1980	113.6	124.5	112.5	107.9	105.7	112.6
"六五"时期						
1981	109.5	110.1	111.2	105.1	106.1	108.0
1982	116.0	136.2	106.7	120.2	106.1	114.1
1983	117.0	132.5	110.8	114.5	114.2	115.6
1984	118.4	92.3	128.9	127.3	116.0	117.3
1985	105.4	102.9	103.0	112.6	112.9	104.4
"七五"时期						
1986	110.8	109.4	103.4	126.1	99.4	109.6
1987	112.2	111.9	110.5	115.0	108.4	110.8
1988	119.0	111.8	124.8	115.0	127.2	117.5
1989	103.2	100.1	101.0	108.8	107.8	101.9
1990	108.3	99.2	107.9	114.2	109.0	106.6
"八五"时期						
1991	112.8	101.2	108.5	124.9	107.0	111.3
1992	122.8	105.5	124.0	128.4	123.8	122.0
1993	121.4	109.7	126.1	119.7	123.8	120.7
1994	118.9	131.0	115.0	120.1	115.9	118.2
1995	113.3	121.7	110.9	112.3	111.8	112.4
"九五"时期						
1996	114.9	102.8	116.9	117.0	115.0	114.3

4–2 续表 continued

年份 Year	地区生产总值 Gross Domestic Product	其中 of which 第一产业 Primary Industry	第二产业 Secondary Industry	第三产业 Tertiary Industry	工业 Industry	人均生产总值 Per Capita GDP
1997	119.6	108.8	116.7	126.3	114.5	118.8
1998	113.8	110.1	112.6	116.3	107.8	112.8
1999	113.1	109.5	111.8	115.4	110.6	112.2
2000	112.1	106.1	110.8	114.9	112.2	111.2
“十五”时期						
2001	111.9	104.3	110.3	115.2	111.7	110.9
2002	113.2	102.7	114.8	113.9	115.2	112.2
2003	115.6	102.2	117.8	116.0	120.5	114.4
2004	115.8	108.8	118.9	113.9	122.2	114.5
2005	113.9	106.7	119.0	109.9	119.9	106.0
“十一五”时期						
2006	115.6	105.6	116.5	116.2	118.0	114.5
2007	115.7	100.4	114.9	118.7	115.3	114.3
2008	112.9	104.4	109.5	117.5	109.8	111.8
2009	112.1	104.9	111.2	113.8	109.2	111.3
2010	112.5	104.6	110.1	115.5	109.5	111.0
“十二五”时期						
2011	110.3	104.0	110.8	110.5	110.9	108.2
2012	109.5	104.7	108.9	110.5	108.9	107.7
2013	109.4	103.6	110.9	108.7	108.7	108.0
2014	108.6	103.9	108.0	109.5	107.4	107.1
2015	107.9	103.9	107.1	108.8	106.4	106.5
“十三五”时期						
2016	107.6	104.1	105.9	108.9	105.6	106.0
2017	107.9	103.4	106.8	109.1	106.7	106.7
2018	107.3	102.7	106.1	108.5	104.5	106.3
2019	107.0	101.3	107.8	107.0	104.1	106.0
2020	104.9	102.2	107.0	103.7	108.2	103.7
“十四五”时期						
2021	107.2	107.1	103.2	109.4	104.4	105.7
2022	103.1	103.1	103.2	103.0	102.4	102.1

4-3 分地区生产总值(2022年)
Value of Gross Domestic Product by Region(2022)

单位：亿元 (100 million yuan)

指标	Item	济南市 Total City	历下区 Li xia	市中区 Shi zhong	槐荫区 Huai yin	天桥区 Tian qiao	历城区 Li cheng	长清区 Chang qing	章丘区 Zhang qiu
地区生产总值	**Gross Domestic Product**	**12027.5**	**2282.9**	**1275.6**	**746.8**	**713.3**	**1240.7**	**378.8**	**1120.7**
第一产业	Primary Industry	420.5	0.0	1.8	2.5	1.6	24.6	40.4	97.6
第二产业	Secondary Industry	4180.2	476.8	334.9	213.0	243.9	342.2	171.1	559.1
第三产业	Tertiary Industry	7426.7	1806.2	938.9	531.3	467.8	874.0	167.3	464.0

4-3 续表 continued

单位：亿元 (100 million yuan)

指标	Item	济阳区 Ji yang	莱芜区 Lai wu	钢城区 Gang cheng	济南高新区 Jinan Gao xin	济南起步区(直管) Jinan Start-up Area (Directly under)	南部山区 Nan shan	平阴县 Ping yin	商河县 Shang he
地区生产总值	**Gross Domestic Product**	**237.1**	**1005.3**	**356.4**	**1619.3**	**69.3**	**66.9**	**278.8**	**231.0**
第一产业	Primary Industry	39.6	73.9	12.5	3.6	12.5	10.8	41.3	58.0
第二产业	Secondary Industry	114.1	429.3	240.1	774.3	33.0	14.5	156.3	77.7
第三产业	Tertiary Industry	83.5	502.1	103.8	841.4	23.8	41.6	81.3	95.3

4-4 生产总值(2022年)(分行业，按当年价格计算)
Value of Gross Domestic Product(2022)(Sub Industry, Calculated at Current Prices)

单位：亿元 (100 million yuan)

指标	Item	2022年
地区生产总值	**Gross Domestic Product**	**12027.46**
农、林、牧、渔业	**Agriculture, Forestry, Animal Husbandry and Fishery**	**441.62**
农、林、牧、渔服务业	Services of Agriculture,Forestry,Animal Husbandry and Fishing	21.10
工业	**Industry**	**2869.00**
#开采辅助活动	Mining Support Activities	0.05
#金属制品、机械和设备修理业	Metal Products, Machinery and Equipment Repair Industry	10.39
建筑业	**Construction**	**1321.68**
批发和零售业	**Wholesale and Retail Trade**	**1622.00**
批发业	Wholesale	913.15
零售业	Retail Trade	708.85
交通运输、仓储和邮政业	**Transport, Storage and Post**	**667.53**
住宿和餐饮业	**Hotels and Catering Services**	**154.76**
住宿业	Hotels	15.06
餐饮业	Catering Services	139.70
金融业	**Financial Intermediation**	**1029.80**
房地产业	**Real Estate**	**832.09**
房地产业(K门类)	Real estate industry(K category)	576.78
自有房地产经营活动	Own Real Estate Operating Activities	255.31
其他服务业	**Other Services**	**3088.98**
营利性服务业	Profit service industry	1861.37
非营利性服务业	Non-Profit service industry	1227.61
第一产业	**Primary Industry**	**420.52**
第二产业	**Secondary Industry**	**4180.24**
第三产业	**Tertiary Industry**	**7426.70**

4-5 规模以上服务业企业分行业主要经济指标(2022年)

Main Economic Indicators of Service Enterprises Above Designated Size by Sector (2022)

单位：万元

指标	Item	单位数(个) Number of Enterprises (unit)	固定资产原价 Original Value of Fixed Assets	本年折旧 Depreciation in the Year	折旧率(%) Depreciation Rate (%)
合计	**Total**	**2405**	**58640113**	**2575047**	**4.4**
交通运输、仓储和邮政业	Transport, Storage and Post	357	45303113	1732144	3.8
信息传输、软件和信息技术服务业	Information Transmission, Software and Information Technology	329	7003892	507078	7.2
房地产业	Real Estate	319	1782466	69159	3.9
租赁和商务服务业	Leasing and Business Services	549	1730359	100995	5.8
科学研究和技术服务业	Scientific Research,Technical Services	480	1090161	73225	6.7
水利、环境和公共设施管理业	Management of Water Conservancy, Environment and Public Facilities	41	754402	34051	4.5
居民服务、修理和其他服务业	Services to Households, Repair and Other Services	91	92544	7804	8.4
教育	Education	58	206564	9971	4.8
卫生和社会工作	Health and Social Work	76	242605	21634	8.9
文化、体育和娱乐业	Culture, Sports and Recreation	105	434008	18987	4.4

注：本表中“房地产业”仅包含物业管理、房地产中介服务、房地产租赁经营和其他房地产业四个行业小类。

(10 000 yuan)

营业收入 Business Revenue	税金及附加 Taxes and Other Surcharges	营业利润 Profits from Business	利润总额 Total Profits	应付职工薪酬(本年贷方累计发生额) Total Wages Payable	期末用工人数(人) Number of employees at the end of the period (person)	人均工资(元) Per Capita Wages (yuan)	应交增值税 Value Added Tax Payable
37515837	**186816**	**353558**	**438584**	**8176629**	**592526**	**137996**	**1052998**
14353917	38797	-1066056	-1046408	3205308	179882	178189	484320
8047058	27139	398656	420455	1831212	116279	157484	230993
1889474	34572	42356	65979	478041	74444	64215	61948
4807314	44864	306316	310324	882933	92896	95045	94390
5955981	26044	500811	508201	1190431	71214	167162	137603
534175	5019	56053	56769	93482	12975	72048	15877
259027	615	18998	19028	73359	12005	61107	3927
264757	984	-11642	-15779	95544	7791	122633	6760
604034	880	38393	37192	172381	15382	112067	1404
800101	7902	69673	82824	153940	9658	159391	15775

Note:The "Real Estate" in this table only includes four industry subcategories:property management,real estate intermediary services, real estate leasing operations and other real estate industries.

主要统计指标解释

国内生产总值（GDP） 指一个国家所有常住单位在一定时期内生产活动的最终成果。国内生产总值有三种表现形态，即价值形态、收入形态和产品形态。从价值形态看，它是所有常住单位在一定时期内生产的全部货物和服务价值与同期投入的全部非固定资产货物和服务价值的差额，即所有常住单位的增加值之和；从收入形态看，它是所有常住单位在一定时期内创造的各项收入之和，包括劳动者报酬、生产税净额、固定资产折旧和营业盈余；从产品形态看，它是所有常住单位在一定时期内最终使用的货物和服务价值与货物和服务净出口价值之和。在实际核算中，国内生产总值有三种计算方法，即生产法、收入法和支出法。三种方法分别从不同的方面反映国内生产总值及其构成。

对于一个地区来说，称为地区生产总值或地区 GDP。

三次产业 三次产业的划分是世界上较为常用的产业结构分类，但各国的划分不尽一致。根据《国民经济行业分类》（GB/T 4754—2017）和《三次产业划分规定》，我国的三次产业划分是：

第一产业是指农、林、牧、渔业（不含农、林、牧、渔专业及辅助性活动）。

第二产业是指采矿业（不含开采专业及辅助性活动），制造业（不含金属制品、机械和设备修理业），电力、热力、燃气及水生产和供应业，建筑业。

第三产业即服务业，是指除第一产业、第二产业以外的其他行业。

规模以上服务业法人单位 包括：交通运输、仓储和邮政业，信息传输、软件和信息技术服务业，租赁和商务服务业，科学研究和技术服务业，水利、环境和公共设施管理业，居民服务、修理和其他服务业，教育，卫生和社会工作，文化、体育和娱乐业；以及物业管理、房地产中介服务等行业。

Explanatory Notes on Main Statistical Indicators

Gross Domestic Product (GDP) refers to the final products produced by all resident units in a country during a certain period of time. Gross domestic product is expressed in three different perspectives, namely value, income, and products respectively. GDP in its value perspective refers to the balance of total value of all goods and services produced by all resident units during a certain period of time, minus the total value of input of goods and services of the nature of non-fixed assets; in other words, it is the sum of the value-added of all resident units. GDP from the perspective of income refers to the sum of all kinds of revenue, including compensation of employees, net taxes on production, depreciation of fixed assets, and operating surplus. GDP from the perspective of products refers to the value of all goods and services for final demand by all resident units plus the net exports of goods and services during a given period of time. In the practice of national accounting, gross domestic product is calculated by three approaches, namely production approach, income approach and expenditure approach, which reflect gross domestic product and its composition from different angles.

For a region, it is called as gross regional product(GRP) or regional GDP.

Three Strata of Industry Classification of economic activities into three strata of industries is a common practice in the world, although the grouping varies to some extent from country to country. In China, according to Industrial Classification for National Economic Activities (GB/T 4754—2017) and Rules on Division of Three Strata of Industries, economic activities are categorized into the following three strata of industries:

Primary industry refers to agriculture, forestry, animal husbandry and fishery industries (not including services in support of agriculture, forestry, animal husbandry and fishery industries).

Secondary industry refers to mining and quarrying (not including support activities for mining), manufacturing (not including repair service of metal products, machinery and equipment), production and supply of electricity, heat, gas and water, and construction.

Tertiary industry refers to all other economic activities not included in the primary or secondary industries.

Above State Designated Scale Service Industry Legal Entities include: transportation, warehousing and postal services, information transmission, software, and information technology service industry, leasing and business service, scientific research and technological services, water conservancy, environment and public facility management, resident service, repair and other service industries, education, health and social work, culture, sports and entertainment as well as property management, real estate agency service.

5

劳动就业

LABOR AND EMPLOYMENT

5-1 按三次产业分就业人员及构成
Number of Employed Persons and Structure by Type of Industry

年份 Year	就业人员 (万人) Total Employed Persons (10 000 persons)				构成 (合计=100) Composition in Percentage (Total=100)		
	合计 Total	第一产业 Primary Industry	第二产业 Secondary Industry	第三产业 Tertiary Industry	第一产业 Primary Industry	第二产业 Secondary Industry	第三产业 Tertiary Industry
1952	134.26	109.87	5.86	18.53	81.8	4.4	13.8
1957	144.29	118.65	13.12	12.52	82.2	9.1	8.7
1962	137.58	106.50	16.45	14.63	77.4	12.0	10.6
1965	143.67	107.68	20.96	15.03	74.9	14.6	10.5
1970	161.18	118.15	30.32	12.71	73.3	18.8	7.9
1975	192.59	135.95	41.56	15.08	70.6	21.6	7.8
1978	204.04	136.30	46.06	21.68	66.8	22.6	10.6
1980	214.21	135.16	51.30	27.75	63.1	23.9	13.0
1985	245.32	116.59	76.08	52.65	47.5	31.0	21.5
1990	270.54	125.73	87.75	57.06	46.5	32.4	21.1
1991	276.18	130.36	87.99	57.83	47.2	31.9	20.9
1992	280.19	127.09	85.59	67.51	45.4	30.5	24.1
1993	285.69	124.25	89.91	71.53	43.5	31.5	25.0
1994	303.46	122.62	91.64	89.20	40.4	30.2	29.4
1995	324.22	116.13	106.68	101.41	35.8	32.9	31.3
1996	332.33	107.70	113.91	110.72	32.4	34.3	33.3
1997	337.43	108.17	113.93	115.33	32.0	33.8	34.2
1998	341.63	109.32	113.38	118.93	31.9	33.2	34.9
1999	344.48	109.56	112.98	121.94	31.8	32.8	35.4
2000	347.37	109.98	110.81	126.58	31.7	31.9	36.4
2001	350.10	109.99	109.24	130.87	31.4	31.2	37.4
2002	352.70	108.01	109.14	135.55	30.6	30.9	38.5
2003	355.30	104.90	110.60	139.80	29.5	31.1	39.4

5-1 续表 continued

年份 Year	就业人员 (万人) Total Employed Persons (10 000 persons)				构成 (合计=100) Composition in Percentage (Total=100)		
	合计 Total	第一产业 Primary Industry	第二产业 Secondary Industry	第三产业 Tertiary Industry	第一产业 Primary Industry	第二产业 Secondary Industry	第三产业 Tertiary Industry
2004	358.50	99.30	113.30	145.90	27.7	31.6	40.7
2005	360.00	99.10	114.20	146.70	27.5	31.7	40.8
2006	361.80	99.00	115.20	147.60	27.4	31.8	40.8
2007	364.30	98.80	116.30	149.20	27.1	31.9	41.0
2008	367.36	98.01	116.95	152.40	26.7	31.8	41.5
2009	372.25	97.80	119.15	155.30	26.3	32.0	41.7
2010	373.70	76.66	120.20	176.84	20.5	32.2	47.3
2011	375.50	74.95	120.70	179.85	20.0	32.1	47.9
2012	379.30	74.30	123.10	181.90	19.6	32.5	47.9
2013	382.30	73.40	122.19	186.71	19.20	32.00	48.80
2014	385.70	72.50	123.30	189.90	18.80	31.97	49.24
2015	388.70	71.80	124.70	192.20	18.47	32.08	49.45
2016	394.93	70.90	126.90	197.13	17.95	32.13	49.92
2017	405.38	69.50	129.35	206.53	17.14	31.91	50.95
2018	419.27	68.80	132.17	218.30	16.41	31.52	52.07
2019	492.36	77.42	154.27	260.67	15.72	31.33	52.94
2020	468.90						
2021	470.78						
2022	469.00						

注：2020年起，山东省统计局不再反馈“就业人员”分产业相关数据。
Note:Since 2020, Shandong Provincial Bureau of Statistics will no longer provide relevant data of practitioners by industry.

5-2 主要年份职工工资
Wage of Staff and Workers in Major Years

年份 Year	职工工资总额 (万元) Total Wages of Staff and Workers (10 000yuan)				职工平均工资 (元) Average Wage of Staff and Workers(yuan) (yuan)			
	合计 Total	国有经济 State-owned Units	城镇集体经济 Urban Collective-owned Units	其他经济 Others	合计 Total	国有经济 State-owned Units	城镇集体经济 Urban Collective-owned Units	其他经济 Others
1952	4881	4587	294	-	442	453	324	-
1957	14553	11654	2899	-	586	621	480	-
1962	19412	16409	3003	-	577	607	451	-
1965	20367	16821	3546	-	617	664	461	-
1970	21226	17314	3912	-	549	578	449	-
1975	29239	22662	6577	-	557	615	420	-
1978	37840	28733	9107	-	578	626	465	-
1980	55900	41809	14091	-	776	821	668	-
1985	92092	67756	24330	6	1104	1169	954	894
1986	111934	84269	27643	22	1298	1384	1092	882
1987	126263	96322	29673	268	1422	1515	1185	1603
1988	166206	130287	35515	404	1806	1946	1427	2304
1989	190106	150899	38654	553	2037	2199	1577	2614
1990	210618	166250	43003	1365	2211	2370	1751	2460
1991	229540	181185	46091	2264	2368	2535	1872	2658
1992	267295	214311	49565	3419	2710	2938	2020	2919
1993	327226	264252	54442	8532	3323	3547	2524	3553
1994	465966	371403	67351	27212	4736	5209	2975	4922
1995	581432	465311	79932	36189	5851	6561	3623	5663
1996	700636	562645	89126	48865	7031	7839	4290	6875
1997	792368	636694	67999	57675	7896	8761	4954	7303
1998	717927	578788	68455	70684	8326	9022	5459	7410
1999	756696	608052	67273	81371	9083	9929	5766	7818
2000	857337	639312	59468	158557	10422	11761	6211	8651
2001	950851	713222	60818	176811	11980	13462	7061	9945
2002	1120837	846978	74672	199187	14395	16362	8188	11729
2003	1256160	930392	69554	256214	16027	18197	9331	12942

5-2 续表 continued

年份 Year	职工工资总额 (万元) Total Wages of Staff and Workers (10 000yuan)				职工平均工资 (元) Average Wage of Staff and Workers(yuan) (yuan)			
	合计 Total	国有经济 State-owned Units	城镇集体经济 Urban Collective-owned Units	其他经济 Others	合计 Total	国有经济 State-owned Units	城镇集体经济 Urban Collective-owned Units	其他经济 Others
2004	1420491	1049033	73150	298308	18029	20759	10587	13974
2005	1966782	1126918	77722	762142	20866	24626	11890	18164
2006	2459044	1326412	140974	991658	21808	26550	12332	19305
2007	3086928	1680494	166960	1239474	26085	31910	15763	22500
2008	3735956	2049453	202995	1483509	30798	37191	19296	26645
2009	4241838	2227992	177020	1836825	34544	41239	21365	30368
2010	4695402	2462874	179365	2053164	36833	43339	22593	32740
2011	5569118	2647111	169476	2752531	41959	49342	26646	37851
2012	6458632	2811390	161513	3485729	45924	52845	32180	42294
2013	7927677	2766005	170176	4991497	53650	58842	37264	51891
2014	8464904	2912941	148424	5403539	59534	66810	40170	56945
2015	8885256	3282169	143078	5460009	67112	78733	47013	62283
2016	10068893	3715397	162695	6190800	74834	88887	51370	69107
2017	10694345	3776127	124702	6793516	82192	98770	54790	75814
2018	11496722	3869498	98327	7528898	89168	109052	62941	81935
2019	14170697	4846897	87776	9236024	97482	123249	66047	88204
2020	16196772				104990			
2021	18110031				114596			
2022	19250769				123902			

注：1.本表中1998年及以后年份数据均为在岗职工口径，国有、集体、其他分组按1998年新标准。2006年及以后年份数据为非私营单位从业人员口径。
2.2020年起，国家统计局修订劳动工资统计报表制度，山东省统计局未反馈国有经济、城镇集体经济、其他经济相关分类数据。

Notes:1.In this table, the data for 1998 and subsequent years are the caliber of on-the-job workers, and the data of state-owned, collective and other groups base the new standard in 1998. Data for 2006 and subsequent years are the caliber of employees in non-private units.
2.Since 2020, the National Bureau of Statistics has revised the statistical system of labor wages and salaries, and the Provincial Bureau of Statistics has not given classified data of state-owned economy, urban collective economy and other economies.

5-3 城镇非私营单位就业人员人数(2022年)
Number of Employed Persons in Urban Non-Private Units（2022）

单位：人 (person)

指标	Item	就业人员 Employed Persons	#在岗职工 Employed Staff and Workers
合计	**Total**	**1543425**	**1443007**
按国民经济行业分组	**Grouped by Sector**		
农、林、牧、渔业	Agriculture,Forestry,Animal Husbandry and Fishing	698	689
采矿业	Mining	12169	12070
制造业	Manufacturing	260637	257903
电力、热力、燃气及水生产和供应业	Production and Distribution of Electricity, Heating Power, Gas and Water	18284	17747
建筑业	Construction	272417	225291
批发和零售业	Wholesale and Retail Trade	90220	88351
交通运输、仓储和邮政业	Traffic,Transport,Storage and Post	70333	67680
住宿和餐饮业	Hotels and Catering Services	24363	22151
信息传输、软件和信息技术服务业	Information Transfer, Software and Information Technology Services	80419	80108
金融业	Financial Intermediation	90992	63082
房地产业	Real Estate	67950	66619
租赁和商务服务业	Leasing and Business Services	54337	53160
科学研究和技术服务业	Scientific Research and Development,Technical Services	74200	72933
水利、环境和公共设施管理业	Management of Water Conservancy, Environment and Public Facilities	17468	15750
居民服务、修理和其他服务业	Services to Households, Repair and Other Services	7215	6758
教育	Education	155102	150938
卫生和社会工作	Health and Social Work	105339	102745
文化、体育和娱乐业	Culture,Sports and Entertainment	21329	20265
公共管理、社会保障和社会组织	Public Administration, Social Security and Social Organizations	119952	118765

5-4 城镇非私营单位就业人员工资总额(2022年)
Total Wage Bill of Employed Persons in Urban Non-Private Units(2022)

单位：万元 (10 000 yuan)

指标	Item	就业人员工资总额 Total Wage Bill of Employed Persons	#在岗职工工资总额 Total Wage Bill of Employed Staff and Workers
合计	**Total**	**19250769**	**18648759**
按国民经济行业分组	**Grouped by Sector**		
农、林、牧、渔业	Agriculture,Forestry,Animal Husbandry and Fishing	6867	6852
采矿业	Mining	126292	124909
制造业	Manufacturing	2732648	2710420
电力、热力、燃气及水生产和供应业	Production and Distribution of Electricity, Heating Power, Gas and Water	227272	225588
建筑业	Construction	2825913	2519200
批发和零售业	Wholesale and Retail Trade	844114	831420
交通运输、仓储和邮政业	Traffic,Transport,Storage and Post	842014	829382
住宿和餐饮业	Hotels and Catering Services	137654	134677
信息传输、软件和信息技术服务业	Information Transfer, Software and Information Technology Services	1192881	1191193
金融业	Financial Intermediation	1466979	1311572
房地产业	Real Estate	524122	518812
租赁和商务服务业	Leasing and Business Services	546245	539316
科学研究和技术服务业	Scientific Research and Development,Technical Services	1045298	1035133
水利、环境和公共设施管理业	Management of Water Conservancy, Environment and Public Facilities	145897	139774
居民服务、修理和其他服务业	Services to Households, Repair and Other Services	46346	45328
教育	Education	2424512	2400359
卫生和社会工作	Health and Social Work	1801363	1779002
文化、体育和娱乐业	Culture,Sports and Entertainment	291342	288059
公共管理、社会保障和社会组织	Public Administration, Social Security and Social Organizations	2023010	2017763

5-5 城镇非私营单位就业人员平均工资(2022年)
Average Wage of Employed Persons in Urban Non-Private Units（2022）

单位：元 (yuan)

指标	Item	就业人员平均工资 Average Wage of Employed Persons	#在岗职工平均工资 Average Wage of Employed Staff and Workers
合计	**Total**	**123902**	**128703**
按国民经济行业分组	**Grouped by Sector**		
农、林、牧、渔业	Agriculture,Forestry,Animal Husbandry and Fishing	94976	95447
采矿业	Mining	105486	105183
制造业	Manufacturing	104664	104936
电力、热力、燃气及水生产和供应业	Production and Distribution of Electricity, Heating Power, Gas and Water	125494	126991
建筑业	Construction	101986	108912
批发和零售业	Wholesale and Retail Trade	93270	94094
交通运输、仓储和邮政业	Traffic,Transport,Storage and Post	117989	120605
住宿和餐饮业	Hotels and Catering Services	55493	60792
信息传输、软件和信息技术服务业	Information Transfer, Software and Information Technology Services	146945	147183
金融业	Financial Intermediation	154329	207583
房地产业	Real Estate	76434	77184
租赁和商务服务业	Leasing and Business Services	100343	101302
科学研究和技术服务业	Scientific Research and Development,Technical Services	141595	142630
水利、环境和公共设施管理业	Management of Water Conservancy, Environment and Public Facilities	73482	83496
居民服务、修理和其他服务业	Services to Households, Repair and Other Services	60333	63569
教育	Education	156893	159607
卫生和社会工作	Health and Social Work	174365	176332
文化、体育和娱乐业	Culture,Sports and Entertainment	135450	140959
公共管理、社会保障和社会组织	Public Administration, Social Security and Social Organizations	171289	172452

5-6 社会保障基本情况
Basic Conditions of Social Security

单位：万人 (10 000 persons)

指标	Item	2018年	2019年	2020年	2021年	2022年
职工基本养老保险参保人数	Urban Basic Pension Insurance	331.66	408.33	437.30	472.68	488.62
#企业	Enterpris	306.59	378.63	345.26	441.90	457.23
事业机关	Institution and Government Agency	25.06	29.70	18.99	30.78	31.39
职工基本医疗保险参保人数	Medical Care Insurance	241.54	288.04	313.52	336.20	352.82
参加失业保险人数	Unemployment Insurance	158.29	189.70	213.60	226.91	235.43
工伤保险参保人数	Work Injury Insurance	220.47	262.56	278.60	293.47	307.37
生育保险参保人数	Maternity Insurance	163.97	201.24	213.10	235.77	245.62

注：“职工基本养老保险参保人数”“企业”及“事业机关”包含离退休人员。
Note: The caliber "number of employees with basic endowment insurance", " enterprise" and "business organ" contains the retired after.

主要统计指标解释

单位就业人员　指报告期末最后一日在本单位工作，并取得工资或其他形式劳动报酬的人员数。该指标为时点指标，不包括最后一日当天及以前已经与单位解除劳动合同关系的人员，是在岗职工、劳务派遣人员及其他就业人员之和。就业人员不包括：

(1)离开本单位仍保留劳动关系，并定期领取生活费的人员；

(2)在本单位实习的各类在校学生；

(3)本单位以劳务外包形式使用的人员，如：建筑业整建制使用的人员。

在岗职工　指在本单位工作且与本单位签订劳动合同，并由单位支付各项工资和社会保险、住房公积金的人员，以及上述人员中由于学习、病伤、产假等原因暂未工作仍由单位支付工资的人员。在岗职工还包括：

(1)应订立劳动合同而未订立劳动合同人员(如使用的农村户籍人员)；

(2)处于试用期人员；

(3)编制外招用的人员，如临时人员；

(4)派往外单位工作，但工资仍由本单位发放的人员(如挂职锻炼、外派工作等情况)。

工资总额　指根据《关于工资总额组成的规定》(1990年1月1日国家统计局发布的一号令)进行修订，本单位在报告期内(季度或年度)直接支付给本单位全部就业人员的劳动报酬总额。包括计时工资、计件工资、奖金、津贴和补贴、加班加点工资、特殊情况下支付的工资，是在岗职工工资总额、劳务派遣人员工资总额和其他就业人员工资总额之和。

工资总额是税前工资，包括单位从个人工资中直接为其代扣或代缴的房费、水费、电费、住房公积金和社会保险基金个人缴纳部分等。

工资总额不论是计入成本的还是不计入成本的，不论是以货币形式支付的还是以实物形式支付的，均应列入工资总额的计算范围。

平均工资　指单位就业人员在一定时期内平均每人所得的工资额。它表明一定时期工资收入的高低程度，是反映就业人员工资水平的主要指标。计算公式为：

平均工资=报告期就业人员工资总额/报告期就业人员平均人数

Explanatory Notes on Main Statistical Indicators

Persons Employed in Various Units refer to the total number of employees who work at his unit on the last day and obtain wages or other forms of payment at the end of the reporting period. This indicator is a kind of time point index and it equals to the sum of the number of employed staff and workers, labor dispatch personnel and other employed persons, excluding those who have terminated labor contracts with working unit on or before the last day of the reporting period. Employed persons do not include:

1)persons who have left their working units while keeping their labour contract (employment relation) unchanged and receiving regular alimony;

2)all kinds of enrolled students who do internship in various units;

3)persons employed due to labor outsourcing, for example, persons employed in the organizational system of construction industry.

Employed Staff and Workers refer to persons who signed labor contracts with working units and working units would pay wages, social insurance and housing funds for them. Persons who have their work posts but are temporarily absent from work for reasons of study or on sick, injury or maternal leave and still receive wages from their working units are also included. Employed staff and workers also include:

1)Persons who should have signed the labor contracts but not (like people with rural household registration);

2)Employees on probation;

3)Employees beyond the staffing quota, for example, temporary employees;

4)Employees who are sent to other working units but still obtain wages from their original units (situations like on-the-job placement, expatriated assignment, etc.)

Total Wage Bill It is revised according to the "Provision of Composition of Total Wages" (Order No.1 by National Bureau of Statistics on January, 1st, ,1990), total wage bill refers to the total remuneration payment to all employed persons in various units during the reporting period (by quarter or by year), including hourly-paid wages, piece-rate wages, bonuses, allowance and subsidies, overtime wages and wages paid under special circumstances. It equals to the sum of total wages of employed staff and workers, dispatch labors and other employed persons.

Total wage bill is pre-tax wages, including the room charges, utility bills, housing funds and social insurance paid or withheld by employee's units.

Total wage bill, whether or not included in cost, whether or not paid in money or in kind, shall be included in the calculation of total wage.

Average Wage refers to the average per capita wage during a certain period of time for employed persons. It shows the general level of wage income during a certain period of time and it's one major indicator to reflect the wage level. It is calculated as follows:

Average Wage=Total wage bill of employed persons at reference time/Average number of employed persons at reference time

6

固定资产投资

INVESTMRNT IN FIXED ASSETS

6–1 固定资产投资
Total Investment in Fixed Assets

单位：万元 (10 000 yuan)

指标	Item	2011年	2012年	2013年	2014年	2015年	2016年	2017年
固定资产投资	**Investment in Fixed Assets**	**19343389**	**21860756**	**26383337**	**30634425**	**34984158**	**39743278**	**43635821**
按管理渠道分	**By Management Channels**							
城镇集体以上投资	Above Urban Collective Investment	13059328	14005706	18189147	20297503	23817574	27091510	30334660
房地产开发投资	Real Estate Development Investment	5271575	6633153	7211744	9173706	10141433	11639381	12325712
农村投资	Rural Investment	1012486	1221898	982446	1163216	1025151	1012387	975449
按经济类型分	**Registration Status**							
国有经济	State-owned	7334983	6595774	8770551	6421555	8236033	7175934	8700130
集体经济	Collective-owned	1802483	1920132	2165782	2309282	1809902	1298005	1458316
联营经济	Joint Ownership Units		195897	100213	17820	30882	1808	
股份制经济	Share-holding	5682038	1234405	1448535	5814573	7403146	10826143	12722943
外商投资经济	Fund from Overseas	408736	466383	336618	384940	284944	771449	410019
港澳台投资经济	Fund from Hong Kong,Macao and Taiwan	586347	634574	546675	177167	270022	961601	1129955
个体经济	Self-employed	2956158	3318099	30342	4423319	4447149	6788160	39804
其他经济	Others	572644	1169661	2044857	1912063	2360647	1683680	1002734
按投资用途分	**By Investment Purpose**							
第一产业	Primary Industry	486482	624114	982446	1163216	1025151	1012387	975449
第二产业	Secondary Industry	6073178	7337047	9078831	10985386	12173905	13019930	14418169
#工业	Industry	5767374	7018465	8060463	10410562	11478708	12373806	13176351
第三产业	Tertiary Industry	12783729	13899596	16322060	18485823	21785102	25710961	28242203
投资资金来源	**Fund of Different Sources**							
国家资金	State Appropriations	1317777	1693582	1302138	1240862	691574	1360695	1353707
国内贷款	Domestic Loans	1579846	517431	2173131	341374	73212	3656032	3343213
债券	Bond							40902
利用外资	Overseas Funds	68300	226374	262823	32757	44835	327727	250555
自筹资金	Self-raised Fund	14843051	16405182	19166006	19058000	23594834	28216931	28042143
其他资金	Others	3469710	4139026	5741361	454265	342083	10839004	10267805

注：自2011年起固定资产投资统计口径由50万元调整为500万元。
Note: Statistical caliber of fixed-asset investment as of 2011 was adjusted to RMB 5 million from 0.5 million.

6-2 固定资产投资分类(2022年)
Classification of Investment in Fixed Assets(2022)

指标	Item	固定资产投资额比上年增长(%) Growth rate of Investment in Fixed Assets (%)
本年完成投资	**Investment Completed This Year**	**3.8**
按构成分	**Investment by Structure**	
建筑安装工程	Construction and Installation	2.5
设备工器具购置	Purchase of Equipment and Instruments	35.2
#购置旧设备	Purchase of Second-hand Equipment	-88.8
其他费用	Others	1.7
按产业分	**Grouped by Three Strata of Industry**	
第一产业	Primary Industry	-2.8
第二产业	Secondary Industry	15.1
第三产业	Tertiary Industry	1.9
按登记注册类型分	**By Status of Registration**	
内资	**Domestic Invested**	**2.6**
国有	State-owned	6.3
集体	Collective-owned	51.7
股份合作	Cooperative Enterprises	0.3
私营个体	Private Enterprises	-5.4
港澳台投资	**Investment from Hong Kong,Macao and Taiwan**	**13.0**
#港澳台股份有限公司	Share-holding	161.1
外商投资	**Foreign Invested**	**47.3**
#外商合资经营	Joint Venture	55.7
#外商独资	Enterprises with Sole Fund	52.2
其他	**Others**	**89.4**
按建设性质分	**Investment by Type of Construction**	
新建	New Construction	6.5
扩建	Expansion	58.9
改建和技术改造	Reconstruction and Technical Transformation	-6.0
其他	Others	-4.0
按国民经济行业分	**by Sector**	

6–2 续表 continued

指标	Item	固定资产投资额比上年增长(%) Growth rate of Investment in Fixed Assets (%)
农、林、牧、渔业	Farming, Forestry, Animal Husbandry and Fishery	-13.1
采矿业	Mining	-8.3
制造业	Manufacturing	14.1
电力、热力、燃气及水生产和供应业	Production and Supply of Electricity, Heat, Gas and Water	20.8
建筑业	Construction	-16.6
批发和零售业	Wholesale and Retail Trade	-24.2
交通运输、仓储和邮政业	Transport, Storage and Post	13.1
住宿和餐饮业	Hotels and Catering Services	-14.0
信息传输、软件和信息技术服务业	Information Transmission, Software and Information Technology	-8.2
金融业	Financial Intermediation	32.3
房地产业	Real Estate	-3.6
租赁和商务服务业	Leasing and Business Services	58.1
科学研究和技术服务业	Scientific Research and Technical Services	-30.8
水利、环境和公共设施管理业	Management of Water Conservancy,Environment and Public Facilities	10.0
居民服务、修理和其他服务业	Service to Households, Repair and Other Service	-8.1
教育	Education	-2.6
卫生和社会工作	Health and Social Service	74.2
文化、体育和娱乐业	Culture, Sports and Entertainment	-20.2
公共管理、社会保障和社会组织	Public Management,Social Security and Social Organizations	-30.3
新增固定资产(万元)	**Newly Increased Fixed Assets(10 000 yuan)**	**10161875**
施工项目个数(个)	**Number of Project under Construction(unit)**	**4197**
#新开工	Started This Year	1376
竣工项目个数(个)	**Number of Buildings Completed(unit)**	**889**
房屋施工面积(万平方米)	**Floor Space of Buildings under Construction(10 000 sq.m)**	**8604.93**
#住宅	Residential Buildings	5338.52
房屋竣工面积(万平方米)	**Floor Space of Buildings Completed(10 000 sq.m)**	**714.99**
#住宅	Residential Buildings	488.03

6-3 房地产开发投资分类(2022年)
Classification of Estate Development Investment(2022)

单位：万元 (10 000 yuan)

指标	Item	房地产开发投资 Estate Development Investment
本年完成投资额	**Investment Completed This Year**	**18308037**
按构成分	**Investment by Structure**	
建筑工程	Construction	8861731
安装工程	Installation	384031
设备、工器具购置	Purchase of Equipment and Instruments	24731
其他费用	Others	9037544
按登记注册类型分	**By Status of Registration**	
内资	**Domestic Fund**	**17020338**
国有	State-owned	553779
集体	Collective-owned	
股份合作	Cooperative Enterprises	3817
联营	Joint Ownership	
国有联营	State Joint Ownership	
集体联营	Collective Joint Ownership	
其他联营企业	Other Joint Ownership	
有限责任公司	Limited Liability Corporations	12381798
国有独资公司	State Sole-proprietorship Corporations	1301436
其他有限责任公司	Other Limited Liability Corporations	11080362
股份有限公司	Share-holding Corporations Ltd.	110792
私营	Private	3398423
其它内资	Other Domestic Fund	571729
港澳台投资	**Investment from Hong Kong,Macao and Taiwan**	**1018734**
港澳台商合资经营	Joint-venture	467108
港澳台商合作经营	Cooperative	
港澳台商独资	Sole-proprietorship	460185
港澳台股份有限公司	Share-holding Corporations Ltd.	
外商投资	**Foreign Invested**	**268965**
外商合资经营	Joint-venture	153619
外商合作经营	Cooperative	
外商独资	Sole-proprietorship	96421
外商股份有限公司	Share-holding Corporations Ltd.	18925
其他外商投资企业	Other Foreign Funded Enterprises	
个体经营	**Self-employed**	
新增固定资产	**Newly Increased Fixed Assets**	**4160000**
施工项目个数(个)	**Number of Project under Construction(unit)**	**776**
#新开工	Started This Year	119
竣工项目个数(个)	**Number of Buildings Completed(unit)**	**16**
房屋施工面积(万平方米)	**Floor Space of Buildings under Construction(10 000 sq.m)**	**8604.93**
#住宅	Residential Buildings	5338.52
房屋竣工面积(万平方米)	**Floor Space of Buildings Completed(10 000 sq.m)**	**714.99**
#住宅	Residential Buildings	488.03

6–4 固定资产投资资金来源(2022年)
Investment by Source of Funds (2022)

指标	Item	固定资产投资额比上年增长(%) Growth rate of Investment in Fixed Assets(%)	房地产开发投资(万元) Estate Development Investment (10 000 yuan)
本年资金来源合计	**Total Funds of All Sources**	**-5.2**	**26752041**
上年末结余资金	**Fund Left from Last Year**	**9.4**	**9819285**
本年资金来源小计	**Fund of All Sources in Current Year**	**-8.4**	**16932756**
国家预算资金	State Budget	47.9	
国内贷款	Domestic Loans	-17.1	2245247
债券	Bond	12.8	
利用外资	Foreign Investment	-33.5	
其中：外商直接投资	Foreign Direct Investment		
自筹资金	Self-Raising Funds	4.4	5624670
其中：企、事业单位自有资金	Enterprise and Institutions Own Funds		
其他资金来源	Other Funds	-32.1	668409

6–5 新增主要生产能力和效益(2022年)
Newly Increased Production Capacity and Administrative(2022)

项目 Item	单位 Unit	新增生产能力 Newly Increased This Year
济南市钢城区闫王河水环境综合治理项目	万吨/日(10 000 tons/day)	24
济南市钢城区城区污水综合治理项目	万吨/日(10 000 tons/day)	20
济南市钢城区大汶河西部支流水环境综合治理项目	万吨/日(10 000 tons/day)	20
济南市钢城区大汶河水环境综合治理项目	万吨/日(10 000 tons/day)	17
济南市钢城区颜庄河及支流水环境综合治理项目	万吨/日(10 000 tons/day)	13
济南市历城区彩石水质净化厂	万吨/日(10 000 tons/day)	2
济南市钢城区畜禽粪污资源化利用整县推进项目	万吨/日(10 000 tons/day)	1.3
大冶原水管道改造工程	万吨/日(10 000 tons/day)	0.9

6-6 房地产开发建设情况
Basic Situations of Real Estate Development

单位：万元 (10 000 yuan)

指标	Item	2018年	2019年	2020年	2021年	2022年
计划总投资	**Intended Investment**	**90392774**	**111989855**	**120132064**	**122030897**	**114367104**
本年完成投资	**Investment Completed in Current Year**	**13693456**	**15769302**	**17076304**	**19280018**	**18308037**
按构成分	**Grouped by Use of Funds**					
建筑工程	Construction	7920264	9183871	10195398	9012796	8861731
安装工程	Installation	1409538	1606223	1172528	828597	384031
设备、工器具购置	Purchase of Equipment and Instruments	178895	406018	265076	44903	24731
其他费用	Others	4184759	4573190	5443302	9393722	9037544
#旧建筑物购置费	Purchase of Used Building	196	9701	6041	2211	15800
土地购置	Value of Land Purchased	3780143	4231601	5040479	8497926	8471035
按工程用途分	**Grouped by Use of Buildings**					
住宅	Residential Buildings	9285419	11356997	12043120	13513858	12476265
办公楼	Office Buildings	1047097	1312853	1693130	1433323	2098742
商业营业用房	Buildings for Business Use	1879155	1662057	1693638	1734079	1216401
其他	Others	1481785	1437395	1646416	2598758	2516629
本年新增固定资产	**Newly Increased Fixed Assets**	**4698943**	**3988646**	**5297407**	**7149999**	**4160000**
待开发土地面积(万平方米)	Area of Land Pending for Development (10 000 sq.m)	302.35	455.30	278.98	349.94	272.00
本年土地购置面积(万平方米)	Area of Land Purchased in the Year(10 000 sq.m)	265.91	280.40	106.04	189.99	46.89
房屋施工面积(万平方米)	Floor Space of Buildings under Construction(10 000 sq.m)	9112.05	9979.96	10353.04	10156.54	8604.93
房屋竣工面积(万平方米)	Floor Space of Buildings Completed(10 000 sq.m)	1203.81	1070.03	1272.97	1115.66	714.99
竣工房屋价值	Value of Buildings Completed	3172322	2844724	3321996	3335553	2038727
竣工住宅(套)	Residential Buildings Completed(unit)	70120	60422	77790	64928	40794

6–7 房地产开发公司经营情况
Real Estate Development and Management

单位：万元 (10 000 yuan)

指标	Item	2018年	2019年	2020年	2021年	2022年
开发公司个数(个)	**Number of Real Estate Enterprises(unit)**	**706**	**710**	**704**	**655**	**674**
企业资本金	**Enterprises Funds**	**12994960**	**14920358**	**15884470**	**16394299**	**17588114**
资产与负债	**Assets and Liabilities**					
资产总计	Total Assets	113393735	128868654	136819137	142473813	144643628
负债总计	Total Liabilities	93511277	106654306	113236782	117808688	118769495
所有者权益	Owners' Equity	19882458	22214348	23582355	16394299	25874133
损益情况	**Net Income or Loss**					
经营收入	Business Revenue	12495191	14411472	14853884	18351536	16591169
土地转让收入	Revenues from Land Transfer	952885	150739	344311	339936	228303
商品房销售收入	Revenues from Commercial Housing Sold	11087179	11656310	11934688	15836088	14185254
房屋出租收入	Revenue from House Leasing	90017	99996	109568	170083	133884
其他收入	Others	126592	134461	472363	877906	572082
经营成本	Business Cost	8570149	10131040	11087743	14419864	14049279
经营税金及附加	Taxes and Other Charges	951196	1036931	977022	989222	772482
利润总额	Total Profits	2177983	2287980	1719277	1715428	470150
房屋销售与出租	**House for Sales and Rent**					
本年实际销售房屋面积(平方米)	Floor Space of Commercial Buildings Sold(sq.m)	12346236	12464708	13357486	15481974	12419469
#住宅(平方米)	Residential Buildings(sq.m)	9636143	10206808	11452394	13001987	9070928
本年房屋实际销售额	Total Sale of Commercial Buildings	14737908	13807789	15719460	19569740	15145712
#住宅	Residential Buildings	11728181	11738543	14065259	17216533	12217238
待售房屋面积(平方米)	Floor Space of Waiting For Sold(sq.m)	980301	1064915	1474183	2100169	2481683
#住宅(平方米)	Residential Buildings(sq.m)	542047	635088	906322	1203741	1382209
出租房屋面积(平方米)	Floor Space of House Leasing(sq.m)	1794	39132	2385	1165	76236

6–8 房地产开发公司经营情况(2022年)

Real Estate Development and Management(2022)

单位：万元 (10 000 yuan)

指标	Item	合计 Total	内资企业 Domestic Invested Enterprises 小计 Total	#国有 State–owned	港、澳、台商投资企业 Enterprises with Investment from Hong Kong, Macao and Taiwan	外商投资企业 Foreign Invested Enterprises
开发公司个数(个)	**Number of Real Estate Enterprises(unit)**	**674**	**639**	**171**	**25**	**10**
按资质分	**by Qualification Criteria**					
#一级资质	First Grade	29	28	20	1	
二级资质	Second Grade	135	128	44	5	2
三级资质	Third Grade	63	60	12	1	2
四级资质	Forth Grade	7	6	3	1	
企业资本金	**Enterprises Funds**	**17588114**	**15155507**	**7986231**	**2134091**	**298516**
资产与负债	**Assets and Liabilities**					
资产总计	Total Assets	144643628	137810108	71305382	5442020	1391500
负债总计	Total Liabilities	118769495	114471603	55472084	3264325	1033568
所有者权益	Owners' Equity	25874133	23338505	15833298	2177696	357932
损益情况	**Net Income or Loss**					
经营收入	Business Revenue	16591169	15889021	6554810	551803	150345
土地转让收入	Revenues from Land Transfer	228303	228303	71002		
商品房销售收入	Revenues from Commercial Housing Sold	14185254	13660914	5119494	373996	150345
房屋出租收入	Revenue from House Leasing	133884	68564	36197	65320	
其他收入	Others	572082	564426	421868	7656	
经营成本	Business Cost	14049279	13450697	5544486	437572	161010
经营税金及附加	Taxes and Other Charges	772482	742538	285869	28710	1234
利润总额	Total Profits	470150	512092	322019	-16729	-25213

主要统计指标解释

固定资产投资 指以货币形式表现的在一定时期内建造和购置固定资产的工作量以及与此有关的费用的总称。

房地产开发投资 指房地产开发企业本年完成的全部用于房屋建设工程、土地开发工程的投资额以及公益性建筑和土地购置费等的投资。

国家预算内资金 国家预算包括一般预算、政府性基金预算、国有资本经营预算和社保基金预算。各类预算中用于固定资产投资的资金全部作为国家预算资金填报，其中一般预算中用于固定资产投资的部分包括基建投资、车购税、灾后恢复重建基金和其他财政投资。各级政府债券也应归入国家预算资金。

国内贷款 指报告期固定资产投资项目单位向银行及非银行金融机构借入用于固定资产投资的各种国内借款，包括银行利用自有资金及吸收存款发放的贷款、上级拨入的国内贷款、国家专项贷款（包括煤代油贷款、劳改煤矿专项贷款等），地方财政专项资金安排的贷款、国内储备贷款、周转贷款等。

债券 指企业或金融机构为筹集用于固定资产投资的资金向投资者出具的承诺按一定发行条件还本付息的债务凭证，包括金融债券和企业债券。

利用外资 指报告期收到的境外（包括外国及港澳台地区）资金(包括设备、材料、技术在内)。包括对外借款(外国政府贷款、国际金融组织贷款、出口信贷、外国银行商业贷款、对外发行债券和股票)、外商直接投资、外商其他投资(包括补偿贸易、加工装配由外商提供的设备价款、国际租赁、外商投资收益的再投资资金)。不包括我国自有外汇资金(国家外汇、地方外汇、留成外汇、调剂外汇和国内银行自有资金发放的外汇贷款等)。各类外资按报告期的外汇牌价（中间价）折成人民币计算。

自筹资金 指在报告期内筹集的用于项目建设和购置的资金。包括自有资金、股东投入资金和借入资金，但不包括各类财政性资金、从各类金融机构借入资金和国外资金。

其他资金来源 指在报告期收到的除以上各种资金之外的用于固定资产投资的资金。包括社会集资、个人资金、无偿捐赠的资金及其他单位拨入的资金等。

固定资产投资按国民经济行业分 指根据其从事的社会经济活动性质对各类单位进行的分类。应根据建设项目建成投产后的主要产品种类或主要用途及社会经济活动种类来划分，不能根据项目单位本身的行业类别来划分。如果项目投产后有几种产品，应根据主要产品来确定行业类别。一般情况下，一个建设项目只能属于一种国民经济行业。

固定资产投资按建设性质分 按整个建设项目情况来确定。建设项目的性质一般分为新建、扩建、改建和技术改造、单纯建造生活设施、迁建、恢复、单纯购置。农户投资不划分建设性质。

（1）新建 指从无到有“平地起家”开始建设的项目。现有企业、事业、行政单位投资的项目一般不属于新建。但如有的单位原有基础很小，经过建设后新增的固定资产价值超过该企业、事业、行政单位原有固定资产价值（原值）三倍以上的，也应作为新建。

（2）扩建 指在厂内或其他地点，为扩大原有产品的生产能力（或效益）或增加新的产品生产能力，而增建的生产车间（或主要工程）、分厂、独立的生产线等项目。行政、事业单位在原单位增建业务性用房（如学校增建教学用房、医院增建门诊部、病房等）也作为扩建。

现有企、事业单位为扩大原有主要产品生产能力或增加新的产品生产能力，增建一个或几个主要生产车间（或主要工程）、分厂，同时进行一些更新改造工程的，也应作为扩建。

（3）改建和技术改造 指现有企业、事业单位对原有设施进行技术改造或更新（包括相应配套的辅助性生产、生活福利设施）的建设项目。改建项目包括企业、事业单位为适应市场变化的需要，而改变企业的主要产品种类（如军工企业转民用产品等）的建设项目；原有产品生产作业线由于各工序（车间）之间能力不平衡，为填平补齐充分发挥原有生产能力而增建但不增加主要产品生产能力的建设项目。技术改造是指企业、事业单位在现有基础上用先进的技术代替落后的技术，用先进的工艺和装备代替落后的工艺和装备，以改变企业落后的技术经济面貌，实现以内涵为主的扩大再生产，达到提高产品质量、促进产品更新换代、节约能源、降低消耗、扩大生产规模、全面提高社会经济效益的目的。技术改造具体包括以下内容：机器设备和工具的更新改造；生产工艺改革、节约能源和原材料的改造；厂房建筑和公共设施的改造；保护环境进行的“三废”治理改造；劳动条件和生产环境的改造等。

固定资产投资按构成分

（1）建筑工程 指各种房屋、建筑物的建造工程。这部分投资额必须兴工动料，通过施工活动才能实现，是固定资产投资额的重要组成部分。

（2）安装工程 指各种设备、装置的安装工程。

在安装工程中，不包括被安装设备本身价值。

（3）设备工器具购置 指报告期内购置或自制的，达到固定资产标准的设备、工具、器具的价值。新建单位及扩建单位的新建车间，按照设计或计划要求购置或自制的全部设备、工具、器具，不论是否达到固定资产标准均计入“设备工器具购置”中。

（4）其他费用 指在固定资产建造和购置过程中发生的，除建筑安装工程和设备、工器具购置投资完成额以外的应当分摊计入固定资产投资的费用，不指经营中财务上的其他费用。

新增生产能力(或工程效益)名称 指建成投产项目或工程新增生产能力(或工程效益)的名称。

待开发土地面积 指房地产开发企业经有关部门批准，通过各种方式获得土地使用权，但尚未开工建设的土地面积。

本年土地购置面积 指房地产开发企业本年通过各种方式获得土地使用权的土地面积。房屋施工面积 指报告期内施工的全部房屋建筑面积。

房屋施工面积 指房地产开发企业本年施工的全部房屋建筑面积。包括本年新开工的房屋建筑面积、上年跨入本年继续施工的房屋建筑面积、上年停缓建在本年恢复施工的房屋建筑面积、本年竣工的房屋建筑面积以及本年施工后又停缓建的房屋建筑面积。多层建筑应填各层建筑面积之和。

房屋竣工面积 指房地产开发企业本年按照设计要求已全部完工，达到住人和使用条件，经验收鉴定合格或达到竣工验收标准，可正式移交使用的各栋房屋建筑面积的总和。

商品房销售面积 指房地产开发企业本年出售商品房屋的合同总面积(即双方签署的正式买卖合同中所确定的建筑面积)。

商品房销售额 指房地产开发企业本年出售商品房屋的合同总价款(即双方签署的正式买卖合同中所确定的合同总价)。该指标与商品房销售面积同口径。

Explanatory Notes on Main Statistical Indicators

Total Investment in Fixed Assets refers to the volume of activities in construction and purchases of fixed assets and related fees during a certain period of time, expressed in monetary terms.

Investment in Real Estate Development refers to the investment made by real estate development enterprises in the construction of buildings, development of land, nonprofit buildings and value of land purchased.

Fund from the State Budget State budget consists of general budget, government fund budget, operation budget of state-owned assets and social security fund budget. Funds for investment in fixed assets from various budgets are reported as fund from the state budget, of which, the general budget utilized on fixed assets investment includes investment on infrastructure construction, vehicle purchase tax, post-disaster restoration and reconstruction funds and other financial investment. Government bonds at all levels should also be included.

Domestic Loans refer to loans of various forms borrowed by investing units from banks and non-bank financial institutions during the reference period for the purpose of investment in fixed assets, including loans issued by banks from their self-owned funds and deposit, loans appropriated by higher responsible authorities, special loans by government (including loan for substituting petroleum with coal, special loans for reform-through-labour coal mines), loans arranged by local government from special funds, domestic reserve loan, and revolving loan, etc.

Bond refer to the certificate of indebtedness issued by the enterprise or the financial institution to the investor for raising the capital of fixed-asset investment with capital and interest promised to be repaid as per certain issue terms, including financial bond and enterprise bond.

Foreign Investment refers to overseas (including foreign countries, Hongkong, Macao and Taiwan) funds received during the reference period (covering equipment, materials and technology), including foreign borrowings (loans from foreign governments and international financial institutions, export credit, commercial loans from foreign banks, issue of bonds and stocks overseas), foreign direct investment and other foreign investments (including funds from foreign direct investment income that are reinvested in fixed assets domestically). Excluded from this category is capital in foreign exchanges owned by China (foreign exchanges owned by the central and local governments, foreign exchanges retained by enterprises, foreign exchanges by enterprises through the regulating mechanism, loans in foreign exchanges issued by the Bank of China with its own fund, etc.). In calculating the utilization of foreign capital, foreign currencies are converted into Chinese Renminbi applying the exchange rate (central parity rate) at the end of the reference period.

Self-raised Funds refer to funds for investment in fixed assets received during the reference period by investing units, including investment in fixed assets using own funds of various enterprises and institutions or funds raised from other units other than financial funds, funds borrowed from financial institutions and overseas funds.

Other Funds refer to funds for investment in fixed assets received from sources other than those listed above, including funds raised from individuals and through donations, and funds transferred from other units.

Investment in Fixed Assets by Sector refers to the classification of investment by the nature of social economic activities the investing units are engaged in. The classification of construction projects by sector is determined by the major products or the purpose of the projects when they are put into production or use, and by the nature of their social economic activities, instead of being determined by industrial classification of the project enterprises. The project will be classified according to major product if there are several kinds of products yielded. In general, one project can only be classified into one sector.

Investment in Fixed Assets by Type of Construction Construction projects in general can be classified, by the type of construction, into new construction, expansion, reconstruction and technical transformation, purely construction of living facilities, moving, restoration and purely purchasing. However, investment by type of construction is not applied to investment by real-estate development units and investment by rural households.

(1) New construction in general refers to construction projects, which start from scratch. The existing projects invested by enterprises, institutions and administrative agencies cannot be classified as new construction. In case the size of the existing unit is quite small, and the value of newly added fixed assets is more than three times of the original value, the expansion will be considered as new construction.

(2) Expansion refers to projects of construction of new production workshop, branch factory or independent production line within a factory or in other locations, for the purpose of increasing the production capacity (or improving efficiency) or adding new production capacity. Newly constructed accommodation for the operation of institutions and administrative organizations (such as newly constructed buildings for teaching in schools, buildings for clinics or wards in hospitals, etc.) are also classified as expansion.

Also included in expansion are investments by existing enterprises or institutions in building major production line(s) or branch factory (ies) along with some work on innovation, for the purpose of expanding the production capacity of original products or producing new products.

(3) Reconstruction and technical transformation refers to construction projects by existing enterprises or institutions in innovation

or technical transformation of the old facilities (including auxiliary production equipment and welfare facilities). Also considered as reconstruction is the construction of new workshops by the existing enterprises or institutions to change the variety of products to meet the market demand (such as the production of civil products by defence industries), or to bring the designed production capacity into full play through a more balanced production process on production lines. Technical transformation refers to replacement of old technology or equipment by new technology or equipment, in order to expand the reproduction through improvement of technology contents in production, to improve product quality, to promote new products, to save energy, to reduce consumption, to expand the production scale and to improve overall social-economic efficiency. Contents of technical transformation include: updating of machinery, equipment and tools; reforming production process by using energy or materials saving technology; construction of factory workshops and transformation of public facilities; treatment transformation of "three wastes" (waste gas, waste water and industrial residue) aiming at environmental protection; improvement of working conditions and environment, etc.

Investment in Fixed Assets by Structure

(1) Construction refers to the construction of houses and buildings, also known as work volume of construction. This part of investment can only be achieved through construction activities, it is the major component of the total investment in fixed assets.

(2) Installation refers to the installation of various kinds of equipment and instruments, also known as work volume of installation.

The value of equipment installed itself is not included in the value of installation projects.

(3) Purchase of equipment and instruments refers to the total value of equipment, tools, and instruments purchased or self-produced which come up to the cut-off point for fixed assets during the reference period. Equipment, tools and instruments purchased or self-produced for new workshops by newly established or expanded units are categorized as "purchase of equipment and instruments" no matter whether they come up to the cut-off point for fixed assets.

(4) Other expenses refer to expenses arising during the construction or purchase of fixed assets other than those expenses on construction, installation and purchase of equipment and instruments. Other financial expenses arising in operation are not included.

Newly Increased Production Capacity (or Project Efficiency) refers to the name of new production capacity (or project benefit) of the project or the engineering completed and put into operation.

Area of Land Pending for Development refers to the area of land with its use rights already approved by authorities and obtained by real estate development enterprises but the land development not yet started.

Area of Land Purchased in the Year refers to the area of land with its use rights already obtained in the year by real estate development enterprises.

Floor Space of Buildings under Construction refers to the total space area of the buildings under construction in the year by real estate development enterprises. It includes buildings started in the year, continued from the previous year, suspended in earlier years but restarted in the year, completed in the year, and buildings under construction but suspended in the year. The floor space of a multi-storied building should be the sum of floor space of all the stories.

Floor Space of Buildings Completed refers to the total floor space area of each building completed in the year by real estate development enterprises, which meet the requirements as designed, up to the standard for being resided in and put into use, has been checked and accepted by departments concerned as qualified or up to the standard of buildings completed and can be handed over for putting into use.

Floor Space of Commercial Buildings Sold refers to total contracted area of commercial buildings (i.e. area of floor space as designated in the formal contracts signed by both sides) sold by real estate development enterprises in the year.

Sales of Commercial Buildings refers to the total contracted value (i.e. value of sales/purchase for selling/ purchase of commercial buildings as designated in the contract signed by both sides) received from the sales of the buildings by real estate development enterprises in the year. This indicator has the same statistical coverage as the area of commercial buildings sold.

7

城市公用事业和环境保护

URBAN PUBLIC UNILITIES
AND ENVIRONMENTAL
PROTECTION

7–1 城市道路与公共交通
Basic Statistics on Municipal Engineering and Public Transportation

指标	Item	2018年	2019年	2020年	2021年	2022年
城市道路	**City Roads**					
道路长度(公里)	Length of Roads (km)	5788	6987	7301	7847	8064
道路面积(万平方米)	Area of Roads (10 000 sq.m)	10529	12653	13138	14212	14776
城市桥梁(座)	Number of City Bridges (unit)	1021	1136	978	1004	1044
#立交桥(座)	Interchange (unit)	85	95	79	79	79
路灯(盏)	Number of Streetlights (unit)	195014	213259	185188	204404	231892
人均拥有道路面积(平方米)	Per Capita Road Arae (sq.m)	23.03	20.30	20.66	20.88	21.50
公共交通	**Public Transportation**					
年末营运车辆(辆)	Number of Operating Vehicles (unit)	16644	19676	18915	19219	18134
公共汽车	Buses	6951	8383	8188	8833	7630
#无轨电车	Trolley Buses	106	109	126	126	278
出租汽车	Number of Taxis	9693	11293	10727	10386	10504
客运总量(万人次)	Total Passenger Traffic (10 000 person-times)	89619.7	99389.9	62425.9	73058.0	48974.7
轨道交通	**Rail Traffic**					
配属车辆数(辆)	Number of Vehicles (unit)		204	204	408	408
运营里程(公里)	Length in Operation (km)		47.7	47.7	84.1	84.1
客运总量(万人次)	Total Passenger Traffic (10 000 person-times)		573.5	867.6	5602.9	5455.4

注：2020年，“城市桥梁”使用新统计口径。
Note:In 2020, “Urban Bridge” will be subject to new statistic specifications.

7-2 水、电、气、热供应情况
Basic Statistics on Water, Electricity, Gas and Heating in Cities

指标	Item	单位 Unit	2018年	2019年	2020年	2021年	2022年
自来水	**Water**						
年末水厂生产能力	Production Capacity of Water Supply	万吨/日(10 000 tons/day)	220.27	241.00	243.00	288.90	288.90
年末管线长度	Length of Water Supply Pipelines	公里(km)	5277.13	5703.60	6033.59	7077.25	7531.00
全年供水量	Volume of Water Supply	万吨(10 000 tons)	39226.16	44452.30	45182.90	49712.36	50636.04
人均日生活用水	Per Capita Daily Water Consumption	升(litre)	140.37	134.79	131.58	141.07	143.93
供水普及率	Coverage Rate of Urban Population with Access to Tap Water	%	99.78	100.00	100.00	100.00	100.00
用电量	**Electricity Consumption**						
全社会用电量	Total Electricity Consumption	万千瓦时(10 000 kWh)	2843630	4143022	4338712	4752639	4997126
工业用电量	Industrial Electricity Consumption	万千瓦时(10 000 kWh)	1215034	2215281	2395876	2565881	2630417
城乡居民生活用电量	Household Electricity Consumption	万千瓦时(10 000 kWh)	667505	776162	796871	865304	976315
液化石油气和天然气	**Liquefied Petroleum Gas and Gas**						
液化石油气全年供气量	Total Liquefied Petroleum Gas Supply	吨(ton)	41110.0	45518.0	38353.0	25160.0	38471.0
生活用	Residential Use	吨(ton)	20458	25935	22119	12981	14134
居民用气人口	Population Uses Gas	万人(10 000 persons)	46.81	59.90	52.59	40.70	41.08
天然气供气量	Total Natural Gas Supply	万立方米(10 000 cu.m)	113945.56	143576.00	161034.00	179895.21	197735.00
生产用	Production Use	万立方米(10 000 cu.m)	88821.02	96706.80	113916.82	100508.71	116850.46
生活用	Residential Use	万立方米(10 000 cu.m)	25124.54	46869.20	47117.18	79386.50	80884.54
居民用气人口	Population Uses Gas	万人(10 000 persons)	409.70	560.90	614.20	639.78	646.09
供气普及率	Coverage Rate of Urban Population with Access to Gas	%	99.87	99.97	100.00	100.00	100.00
集中供热	**Central Heating**						
管道长度	Length of Heating Pipelines	公里(km)	7010	8893	10426	12836	14381
供热面积	Heating Area	万平方米(10 000 sq.m)	19834	26073	27740	30465	33305

7-3 环境状况及污染治理情况
Basic Statistics on Environment and Treatment of Pollution

指标	Item	单位 Unit	2018年	2019年	2020年	2021年	2022年
环境质量状况	**Environment Condition**						
环境空气细颗粒物($PM_{2.5}$)浓度年均值	Annual Average Concentration of $PM_{2.5}$	mg/m^3	0.052	0.053	0.047	0.040	0.037
环境空气二氧化硫浓度年均值	Annual Average Concentration of SO_2	mg/m^3	0.017	0.015	0.012	0.011	0.011
环境空气二氧化氮浓度年均值	Annual Average Concentration of NO_2	mg/m^3	0.045	0.041	0.035	0.033	0.031
环境空气可吸入颗粒物(PM_{10})浓度年均值	Annual Average Concentration of PM_{10}	mg/m^3	0.112	0.103	0.086	0.078	0.071
集中式饮用水源地水质达标率	Standard rate of concentrate Water Source Area	%	100.00	100.00	100.00	100.00	100.00
区域环境噪声昼间平均等效声级	Area Whole-day Average Noise Value	分贝(db)	53.3	54.9	54.4	53.8	55.0
道路交通噪声平均等效声级	Traffic Average Noise Value	分贝(db)	69.5	69.6	69.1	68.8	66.5
污染物排放情况	**Discharge of Major Pollutants**						
废水排放总量	Volume of Waste Water Discharged	万吨 (10 000 tons)	28714	29261	46493	49649	
#工业废水排放量	Volume of Industrial Waste Water Discharged	万吨 (10 000 tons)	4770	5120	5886	6084	
化学需氧量排放量	Volume of COD Emission	吨(ton)	19756	19131	49922	44799	
#工业化学需氧量排放量	Volume of Industrial COD Emission	吨(ton)	1433	1425	1744	1557	
氨氮排放量	Volume of Ammonia Nitrogen	吨(ton)	1497	1447	3016	2568	
#工业氨氮排放量	Volume of Industrial Ammonia Nitrogen	吨(ton)	111	78	54	52	
二氧化硫排放量	Volume of Sulphur Dioxide Discharged	吨(ton)	20948	17124	15920	13601	
#工业二氧化硫排放量	Volume of Industrial Sulphur Dioxide Discharged	吨(ton)	16672	13353	11356	9458	
氮氧化物排放量	Volume of Nitrogen Oxides Discharged	吨(ton)	43841	41533	52729	55787	
#工业氮氧化物排放量	Volume of Industrial Nitrogen Oxides Discharged	吨(ton)	41128	38022	25382	22763	
机动车氮氧化物排放量	Volume of Vehicle Nitrogen Oxides	吨(ton)			24814	30628	
烟(粉)尘排放量	Volume of Soot and Dust Discharged	吨(ton)	31345	31258	25871	22580	
#工业烟(粉)尘排放量	Volume of Industrial Soot and Dust Discharged	吨(ton)	22497	22404	13414	11047	

注：1.生态环境部以第二次污染源普查成果为基准，依法组织对2016–2019年污染源统计初步数据进行更新，2018、2019年数据为更新后的数据。根据统计规则，2020年之前未对机动车氮氧化物排放量进行统计。

2.根据生态环境部统一工作安排，2020年开始统计农村生活污水污染物产排量；目前2022年环境统计工作只完成了工业源统计部分，生活源、机动车统计正在开展中，尚未定库。

Notes:1.Based on the results of the Second Pollution Sources Census of China, the Ministry of Ecology and Environment organized to update preliminary statistic data of pollution sources from 2016 to 2019 under laws, and data in 2018 and 2019 are the updated data. According to the statistic rules, the emission of nitrogen oxides from motor vehicles was not counted before 2020.

2.According to the unified work arrangement of the Ministry of Ecology and Environment, the output and discharge of pollutants in rural domestic sewage have been counted since 2020; At present, the environmental statistics work in 2022 has only completed for the statistics of industrial sources, while the statistics of living sources and motor vehicles are undergoing,and the database has not yet been fixed.

7-4 城市园林绿化、环境卫生及其他
Basic Statistics on Parks Green Areas and Urban Sanitation in Cities

指标	Item	单位 Unit	2018年	2019年	2020年	2021年	2022年
园林绿化	**Parks Gardens and Green Areas**						
年末园林绿地面积	Area of Green Space at Year-end	公顷 (ha)	20701.0	28199.3	31087.8	31761.9	32405.1
#公园面积	Area of Parks	万平方米(10 000 sq.m)	3930	3688	3754	4339	4421
人均公园绿地面积	Per Capita Area of Green Space	平方米/人(sq.m/person)	12.6	13.2	13.1	13.0	13.1
建成区绿化覆盖率	Coverage of Green Area	%	40.52	41.18	40.69	41.69	41.94
城市卫生	**Urban Health**						
污水集中处理率	Centralized Sewage Treatment Rate	%	96.59	97.73	98.17	98.20	98.23
清运垃圾	Garbage Clearance	万吨(10 000 tons)	202.64	278.75	278.03	296.96	277.77
公共厕所	Public Lavatory	座 (unit)	1086	1122	1203	1267	1298

主要统计指标解释

年末自来水生产能力 指年底城建部门管理的自来水厂和自备水源的社会单位取水、净化、送水、出厂输水干管等环节的实际生产能力。

供水管道长度 指从送水泵至各类用户引入管之间所有市政管道的长度。不包括新安装尚未使用、水厂内以及用户建筑物内的管道。

供水总量 指公用自来水厂和自备水源的社会单位全年的供水总量，包括有效供水量及损失水量。

生活用水 包括公共服务用水和居民家庭用水。公共服务用水指为城区社会公共生活服务的用水。包括行政事业单位、部队营区和公共设施服务、批发零售业、住宿餐饮业以及社会服务业等单位的用水。居民家庭用水指城市范围内所有居民家庭的日常生活用水。包括城市居民、农民家庭、公共供水站用水。

供水普及率 指报告期末城区用水人口数与城市人口总数的比率。计算公式：

供水普及率=城区用水人口（含暂住人口）/（城区人口+城区暂住人口）*100%

燃气普及率 指报告期末城区使用燃气的城市人口数与城市人口总数的比率。其中燃气包括人工煤气、天然气、液化石油气三种。计算公式为：

燃气普及率=城区用气人口（含暂住人口）/（城区人口+城区暂住人口）*100%

供热管道长度 指从各类热源到热用户建筑物接入口之间的全部蒸汽和热水的管道长度。不包括各类热源厂内部的管道长度。

城市桥梁 指为跨越天然或人工障碍物而修建的构筑物。包括跨河桥、立交桥、人行天桥以及人行地下通道等。

绿地面积 指报告期末用作园林和绿化的各种绿地面积。包括公园绿地、防护绿地、广场用地、附属绿地和位于建成区范围内的区域绿地面积。

公园绿地 向公众开放，以游憩为主要功能，兼具生态、景观、文教和应急避险等功能，有一定游憩和服务设施的绿地。

工业废水排放量 指报告期内经过企业厂区所有排放口排到企业外部的工业废水量。包括生产废水、外排的直接冷却水、废气治理设施废水、超标排放的矿井地下水和与工业废水混排的厂区生活污水，不包括独立外排的间接冷却水(清浊不分流的间接冷却水应计算在内)。

化学需氧量 (COD) 测量有机和无机物质化学分解所消耗氧的质量浓度的水污染指数。废气排放总量 指燃料燃烧和生产工艺过程中排放的各种废气总量，以标准状态下每年万标立方米表示。

二氧化硫排放量 指报告期内企业在燃料燃烧和生产工艺过程中排入大气的二氧化硫总质量。工业中二氧化硫主要来源于化石燃料(煤、石油等)的燃烧，还包括含硫矿石的冶炼或含硫酸、磷肥等生产的工业废气排放。

氮氧化物排放量 指报告期内企业在燃料燃烧和生产工艺过程中排入大气的氮氧化物总质量。

烟(粉)尘排放量 指报告期内企业在燃料燃烧和生产工艺过程中排入大气的烟尘及工业粉尘的总质量之和。烟尘或工业粉尘排放量可以通过除尘系统的排风量和除尘设备出口烟尘浓度相乘求得。

工业粉尘排放量 指企业在生产工艺过程中排放的颗粒物重量。如钢铁企业的耐火材料粉尘、焦化企业的筛焦系统粉尘、烧结机的粉尘、石灰窑的粉尘、建材企业的水泥粉尘等。不包括电厂排放大气的烟尘。

Explanatory Notes on Main Statistical Indicators

Year-end Tap Water Production Capacity refers to actual capacity of such links as water intaking, purification, water carriage and leaving factory water main pipe of the waterworks managed by urban construction department and social unit water source prepared at the end of the year.

Length of Water Supply Pipelines refers to the total length of all municipal pipelines between the water pumps and the user service pipes, excluding pipelines newly installed but not in use yet, pipelines in the water factories, and pipelines in the users' buildings.

Total Volume of Water Supply refers to the total volume of water supplied by water-works (units) during the reference period, including both the effective water supply and loss during the water supply.

Consumption of Water for Daily Use includes consumption of water for public service use and consumption of water for household use. Consumption of water for public service use refers to water consumption for public service in the urban areas, including water consumption of administrative institutions, military barracks, public facilities, wholesale and retail, accommodation and catering industries and social service industry, etc. Consumption of water for household use refers to consumption of water for daily life of all households in cities, including households of urban residents and farmers, and public water supply stations.

Coverage Rate of Urban Population with Access to Tap Water refers to the ratio of the urban population with access to tap water to the total urban population at the end of reference period. The formula is:

Coverage rate of urban population with access to tap water=Urban population with access to tap water/Urban population*100%

Coverage Rate of Urban Population with Access to Gas refers to the ratio of the urban population with access to gas to the total urban population at the end of the reference period. Gas here includes gaswork gas, natural gas and liquefied petroleum gas. The formula is:

Coverage Rate of Urban Population with Access to Gas= Urban population with access to gas/ Urban population*100%

Length of Urban Heating Pipelines refers to the total length of steam or hot water pipelines for sources of heat to the leading pipelines of the buildings of the users, excluding internal pipelines in heat generating enterprises.

Urban Bridges refer to bridges built to cross over natural or man-made barriers, including bridges over rivers, overpasses for traffic and for pedestrians, underpasses for pedestrians, etc.

Area of Green Space refers to the total area occupied for green projects at the end of the reference period, including public recreational green space, protection green land, land for squares, green land attached to institutions, and other green areas.

Public Recreational Green Space refers to green areas open to the public for amusement and rest with the facilities of amusement, rest and services. Its function also includes improving ecology, beautifying landscape, education and preventing and reducing disaster.

Industrial Waste Water Discharged refers to the volume of industrial waste water discharged through all of the drainage system to the outside of factory complex by enterprises during the report period. It includes discharged waste water from production, direct cooling water, waste gas treatment facilities, mine groundwater beyond the standard and domestic sewage mixed with industrial waste water, does not include independently discharged indirect cooling water (voicing split-less indirect cooling water should be taken into account).

Chemical Oxygen Demand (COD) refers to index of water pollution measuring the mass concentration of oxygen consumed by the chemical breakdown of organic and inorganic matter. Total exhaust emission refers to total quantity of various exhaust gases discharged in the process of fuel burning and production which is expressed with 10,000 standard cubic meters each year under the standard state.

SO2 Emission refers to total volume of SO2 discharged into air during the process of fuel combustion and industrial production in enterprises in a given time, and is mainly caused by the combustion of fossil fuel, ore smelting and the discharge of industrial waste gas during the production of sulfuric acid and phosphate fertilizers.

Nitrogen Oxides Emission refers to total volume of nitrogen oxides discharged into air during the process of fuel combustion and industrial production.

Industrial Soot and Dust Emission refers to volume of soot and dust in smoke emitted in process of fuel burning and industrial production in premises of enterprises in the report period. It is calculated by multiplying exhaust volume of dust removal system by dust concentration.

Emission Load of Industrial Dust refers to the weight of particulate matters discharged in the process of production (such as fireproofing dust of the iron and steel enterprise, coke screening system dust of the coke making enterprise, dust of the sintering machine, dust of the lime kiln and cement dust of the building material industry), excluding smoke discharged by the power plant in to the atmosphere.

8

财政、金融和保险

GOVERNMENT FINANCE、FINANCIAL AND INSURANCE

8-1 各时期地方财政收支及指数

Local Government Revenue, Expenditures and Indices in Each Period

年份 Year	一般公共预算收入 (万元) General Public Budget Revenue (10 000yuan)	一般公共预算支出 (万元) General Public Budget Expenditure (10 000yuan)	指数(以上年为100) (Preceding Year=100) 一般公共预算收入 General Public Budget Revenue	一般公共预算支出 General Public Budget Expenditure
1999	460690	497667	119.9	110.8
2000	490485	547210	110.5	110.4
"十五"时期				
2001	596061	703720	121.5	128.6
2002	662511	775046	115.4	110.2
2003	761064	884597	119.6	114.3
2004	890364	1016953	120.9	115.0
2005	1061547	1206643	120.7	118.7
"十一五"时期				
2006	1284388	1469762	121.0	121.8
2007	1570192	1799787	122.3	122.5
2008	1860155	2213190	118.5	123.1
2009	2101923	2599178	113.0	117.4
2010	2661314	3368037	126.6	129.6
"十二五"时期				
2011	3249315	3968831	122.1	117.8
2012	3808218	4656731	117.0	117.3
2013	4820722	5193190	113.9	111.5
2014	5431278	5714138	112.7	110.0
2015	6143172	6581813	113.1	115.2
"十三五"时期				
2016	6412167	7412641	104.4	112.6
2017	6772100	8340600	105.6	112.5
2018	7528162	10183179	111.2	122.1
2019	8741898	11973158	107.2	107.0
2020	9060751	12887953	103.6	107.6
"十四五"时期				
2021	10076073	12930814	111.2	108.4
2022	10011421	12255733	99.4	94.8

注：1.2013年财政部门对一般公共预算收入口径进行调整，2013年一般公共预算收入指数为可比口径。2018年以前为区划调整前数据。
2."一般公共预算收入"与"一般公共预算支出"为预算数据，以下各表同。

Notes:1. In 2013, the financial department adjusted the caliber of general public budget revenue. In 2013, the index of general public budget income index was comparable caliber.Data before the year of 2018 are the data of administrative division before the adjustment.
2."General public budget revenue" and "general public budget expenditure" are estimates, the same for the following tables.

8-2 地方财政收入(2022年)
Local Financial Revenue(2022)

单位：万元 (10 000yuan)

指标	Item	合计 Total	市本级 Cities				县区级 Counties
			小计 Total	市直 Departments Directly Under the Municipal Government	济南起步区(直管) Jinan Start-up Area (Directly under)	南部山区 Nan shan	
一般公共预算收入	**General Public Budget Revenue**	**10011421**	**1820781**	**1725666**	**83737**	**11378**	**8190640**
增值税	Value-added Tax	1987483	23150		18585	4565	1964333
企业所得税	Enterprise Income Tax	1153842	11487		10897	590	1142355
个人所得税	Personal Income Tax	499514	2691		1621	1070	496823
资源税	Resource Tax	66584	175		111	64	66409
城市维护建设税	Tax on City Maintenance and Construction	467445	10768	5665	4090	1013	456677
房产税	Tax on Real Estates	323455	3267		2946	321	320188
印花税	Stamp Tax	176939	2362		2197	165	174577
城镇土地使用税	Holding tax on urban and county land	262875	3825		3564	261	259050
土地增值税	Land Value Added Tax	1170579	2242		1388	854	1168337
车船税	Tax on vehicles and Their Registration	132525	3		2	1	132522
耕地占用税	Farmland Occupation Tax	51544	5944		5944		45600
契税	Contract tax	626154	14897		14811	86	611257
环境保护税	Environmental Protection Tax	11098	25		20	5	11073
专项收入	Specific Revenue	1327924	1021605	1017924	3082	599	306319
行政事业性收费收入	Income from Administrative Fees	458299	213124	210557	2103	464	245175
罚没收入	Penalty and Confiscatory Income	146554	56736	56331	263	142	89818
国有资本经营收入	Profits of State-owned Enterprises	12106					12106
国有资源(资产)有偿使用收入	Revenue of Compensable Use of State-owned Resources (Assets)	921388	282662	269372	12112	1178	638726
捐赠收入	Donation Income	32461	191	191			32270
政府住房基金收入	Government Housing Fund Income	170744	165616	165616			5128
其他收入	Others	10382	11	10	1		10371
政府性基金收入	**Government Funds Income**	**5149105**	**4327429**	**4307469**	**18457**	**1503**	**821676**
#城市基础设施配套收入	Urban Infrastructure Supporting Income	556836	332042	312082	18457	1503	224794

8-3 各区财政收入(2022年)
Financial Revenue by District(2022)

单位：万元

指标	Item	合计 Total	历下区 Li xia	市中区 Shi zhong
一般公共预算收入	**Generai Public Budget Revenue**	**7689343**	**1576360**	**892320**
增值税	Value-added Tax	1871982	368460	177448
企业所得税	Enterprise Income Tax	1093702	274914	153421
个人所得税	Personal Income Tax	486148	134488	68331
资源税	Resource Tax	56445	971	8349
城市维护建设税	Tax on City Maintenance and Construction	444624	98319	35629
房产税	Tax on Real Estates	310228	88906	35144
印花税	Stamp Tax	169725	41807	20565
城镇土地使用税	Holding tax on urban and county land	239571	12371	15192
土地增值税	Land Value Added Tax	1148545	288180	154792
车船税	Tax on vehicles and Their Registration	68191	22054	11553
耕地占用税	Farmland Occupation Tax	41047	1450	104
契税	Contract tax	590025	105308	75597
环境保护税	Environmental Protection Tax	9842	270	256
专项收入	Specific Revenue	291236	64815	21431
行政事业性收费收入	Income from Administrative Fees	226253	10856	23991
罚没收入	Penalty and Confiscatory Income	64325	3165	3264
国有资本经营收入	Profits of State-owned Enterprises	3306		
国有资源(资产)有偿使用收入	Revenue of Compensable Use of State-owned Resources (Assets)	559979	59247	87179
捐赠收入	Donation Income	5857		40
政府住房基金收入	Government Housing Fund Income	5116	697	
其他收入	Others	1731		1
政府性基金收入	**Government Funds Income**	**577716**		
#城市基础设施配套收入	Urban Infrastructure Supporting Income	208978		

(10 000yuan)

槐荫区 Huai yin	天桥区 Tian qiao	历城区 Li cheng	长清区 Chang qing	章丘区 Zhang qiu	济阳区 Ji yang	莱芜区 Lai wu	钢城区 Gang cheng	济南高新区 Jinan Gao xin
501483	**303666**	**1261314**	**234015**	**542042**	**236239**	**416691**	**219825**	**1505388**
137297	76402	223568	48352	119030	63945	114440	100505	442535
51614	44742	106324	14606	23546	28714	43242	10796	341783
29978	22969	48664	7007	43903	7587	11211	7583	104427
329	448	2154	5463	10435	787	15341	6374	5794
24157	17915	50267	9258	22093	10635	21944	15969	138438
21998	17516	24158	8129	19280	6891	15569	9545	63092
7990	9783	18997	3966	10448	4037	9044	6367	36721
13230	11650	31468	14858	54239	14548	30774	15564	25677
44926	28598	382304	42064	64253	11209	26756	1850	103613
2433	1528	7303	3274	5294	5095	7822	1639	196
1916	158	9221	4959	7013	2331	6366	2554	4975
77804	30381	149313	11707	30681	18648	22189	2099	66298
125	201	802	105	1304	157	3795	2618	209
14773	10525	32015	8444	17887	8419	16868	12894	83165
16446	5952	56692	15790	23724	8388	42637	8819	12958
1429	7353	10629	10400	8814	3124	6357	8343	1447
			500			2106	700	
53764	17313	105722	20829	79661	40904	19825	5184	70351
15	7	1453	3780	69	326	167		
			520	247				3652
956		117	3	51	494		108	1
	1917		**15684**	**54156**	**18937**	**351431**	**65566**	**70025**
	1917		13534	49594	17200	47567	11008	68158

8-4 各县财政收入(2022年)
Financial Revenue by County(2022)

单位：万元 (10 000yuan)

指标	Item	合计 Total	平阴县 Ping yin	商河县 Shang he
一般公共预算收入	**General Public Budget Revenue**	**501297**	**300116**	**201181**
增值税	Value-added Tax	92351	53980	38371
企业所得税	Enterprise Income Tax	48653	28653	20000
个人所得税	Personal Income Tax	10675	7064	3611
资源税	Resource Tax	9964	9732	232
城市维护建设税	Tax on City Maintenance and Construction	12053	6886	5167
房产税	Tax on Real Estates	9960	6386	3574
印花税	Stamp Tax	4852	3052	1800
城镇土地使用税	Holding tax on urban and county land	19479	8520	10959
土地增值税	Land Value Added Tax	19792	7169	12623
车船税	Tax on vehicles and Their Registration	64331	23576	40755
耕地占用税	Farmland Occupation Tax	4553	3113	1440
契税	Contract tax	21232	9029	12203
环境保护税	Environmental Protection Tax	1231	1128	103
专项收入	Specific Revenue	15083	8216	6867
行政事业性收费收入	Income from Administrative Fees	18922	13932	4990
罚没收入	Penalty and Confiscatory Income	25493	7113	18380
国有资本经营收入	Profits of State-owned Enterprises	8800	8800	
国有资源(资产)有偿使用收入	Revenue of Compensable Use of State-owned Resources (Assets)	78747	67627	11120
捐赠收入	Donation Income	26413	26017	396
政府住房基金收入	Government Housing Fund Income	12	12	
其他收入	Others	8640	50	8590
政府性基金收入	**Government Funds Income**	**243960**	**98995**	**144965**
#城市基础设施配套收入	Urban Infrastructure Supporting Income	15816	4886	10930

8-5 地方财政支出(2022年)
Local Financial Expenditures (2022)

单位：万元 (10 000yuan)

指标	Item	合计 Total	市本级 Cities				县区级 Counties
			小计 Total	市直 Departments Directly Under the Municipal Government	济南起步区(直管) Jinan Start-up Area (Directly under)	南部山区 Nan shan	
一般公共预算支出	**General Public Budget Expenditure**	**12255733**	**4644468**	**3940467**	**521228**	**182773**	**7611265**
一般公共服务支出	General Public Service	1376335	380449	330944	28350	21155	995886
国防支出	Defence Expenditure	21031	15541	15491		50	5490
公共安全支出	Public Security	658806	492681	489167	1975	1539	166125
教育支出	Education	2518396	588051	526162	15314	46575	1930345
科学技术	Science and Technology	281469	90262	80765	9394	103	191207
文化体育与传媒支出	Culture、Sports and Media	156208	93640	92051	245	1344	62568
社会保障和就业支出	Social Security and Employment	1969359	732192	678101	25310	28781	1237167
医疗卫生与计划生育支出	Health and Family Planning	1348226	609049	569773	14437	24839	739177
节能环保支出	Energy-saving and Environment Protection	262503	99262	91528	4102	3632	163241
城乡社区支出	Urban and Rural Community Affairs	1948958	759037	357368	391874	9795	1189921
农林水支出	Farming、Forestry and Irrigation Affairs	565404	224069	179061	13639	31369	341335
交通运输支出	Transport	284399	226216	220846	51	5319	58183
资源勘探信息等支出	Exploration and Information Affairs	125493	35961	30961	5000		89532
商业服务业等支出	Commerce and Services Affairs	55213	17828	17348	25	455	37385
金融支出	Financial Supervision Affairs	68952	49678	49676		2	19274
援助其他地区支出	Aid to Other Area	35345	16443	16443			18902
自然资源海洋气象等支出	Natural Resources Marine Meteorological	118028	62064	61383	26	655	55964
住房保障支出	Housing Security Affairs	233048	28519	16674	6379	5466	204529
粮油物资储备支出	Grain and Oil Reserves	11165	3966	3966			7199
债务付息支出	Pay Principle and Interest for Public Debt	79549	26748	26748			52801
其他支出	Other Expenditure	53398	52920	47920	5000		478
政府性基金支出	**Government Funds Expenditure**	**11527214**	**7210441**	**5518470**	**1678025**	**13946**	**4316773**
#城乡社区支出	Urban and Rural Community Affairs	6557238	3388441	2212707	1162904	12830	3168797

8-6 各区地方财政支出(2022年)
Local Financial Expenditures by District(2022)

单位：万元

指标	Item	合计 Total	历下区 Li xia	市中区 Shi zhong
一般公共预算支出	**General Public Budget Expenditure**	**6867708**	**961364**	**633019**
一般公共服务支出	General Public Service	906093	163855	90312
国防支出	Defence Expenditure	4451	775	349
公共安全支出	Public Security	133100	30978	12444
教育支出	Education	1739682	267618	236315
科学技术	Science and Technology	189006	11883	2506
文化体育与传媒支出	Culture、Sports and Media	56557	19855	2215
社会保障和就业支出	Social Security and Employment	1099735	138957	95695
医疗卫生与计划生育支出	Health and Family Planning	668295	72309	46052
节能环保支出	Energy-saving and Environment Protection	145902	6470	1147
城乡社区支出	Urban and Rural Community Affairs	1136521	187020	108119
农林水支出	Farming、Forestry and Irrigation Affairs	265580	6926	6286
交通运输支出	Transport	45355	10	80
资源勘探信息等支出	Exploration and Information Affairs	77869	754	2378
商业服务业等支出	Commerce and Services Affairs	34110	798	406
金融支出	Financial Supervision Affairs	18644	9192	60
援助其他地区支出	Aid to Other Area	18539	3010	2407
国土海洋气象等支出	Land and Weather Affairs	50028	4236	3091
住房保障支出	Housing Security Affairs	186252	13978	20454
粮油物资储备支出	Grain and Oil Reserves	5180		
国债还本付息支出	Pay Principle and Interest for Public Debt	44863	24	1065
其他支出	Other Expenditure	478	7	
政府性基金支出	**Government Funds Expenditure**	**3799940**	**482964**	**243631**
#城乡社区支出	Urban and Rural Community Affairs	2789918	258387	187152

(10 000yuan)

槐荫区 Huai yin	天桥区 Tian qiao	历城区 Li cheng	长清区 Chang qing	章丘区 Zhang qiu	济阳区 Ji yang	莱芜区 Lai wu	钢城区 Gang cheng	济南高新区 Jinan Gao xin
438593	**295524**	**992354**	**385007**	**833685**	**363984**	**750603**	**238108**	**975467**
72982	35156	139811	49333	88400	39604	108173	28500	89967
89	249	205	45	1494	43	153	530	519
8740	6303	15731	9602	14017	5466	9841	5057	14921
120584	89263	205211	97220	278955	84121	199845	49588	110962
1536	3402	77469	2508	1224	864	2580	804	84230
2043	1124	6406	3810	8243	3857	6160	1554	1290
95023	75534	118527	103660	139948	94233	145353	36825	55980
63077	34618	108048	42177	94746	41412	106465	30521	28870
8828	6036	1250	9600	23058	9783	11008	6567	62155
28076	17318	227045	9703	44884	24001	28196	24732	437427
7694	4629	27493	27950	45729	33589	78778	16531	9975
60	4	13655	3441	13739	3628	3977	5758	1003
5598	703	2602	2116	30168	2647	2631	3034	25238
1755	287	1843	564	999	448	1641	675	24694
355	47	53	190	122	4	296	4	8321
737	649	2253		5170	267	511	1918	1617
1963	985	14689	5121	5184	2714	5717	6085	243
16847	15460	26459	15004	27724	12265	19989	9492	8580
		1784	933	2003	320	130	10	
1906	2787	498	820	5429	3599	17200	8160	3375
		112	215			144		
262562	**240593**	**564987**	**193549**	**318579**	**188719**	**503856**	**86608**	**713892**
186772	190733	391612	131831	232912	112693	383664	43057	671105

8-7 各县地方财政支出 (2022年)
Local Financial Expenditures by County(2022)

单位：万元 (10 000yuan)

指标	Item	合计 Total	平阴县 Ping yin	商河县 Shang he
一般公共预算支出	**General Public Budget Expenditure**	**743557**	**342878**	**400679**
一般公共服务支出	General Public Service	89793	33357	56436
国防支出	Defence Expenditure	1039	934	105
公共安全支出	Public Security	33025	15410	17615
教育支出	Education	190663	92297	98366
科学技术	Science and Technology	2201	1354	847
文化体育与传媒支出	Culture、Sports and Media	6011	3595	2416
社会保障和就业支出	Social Security and Employment	137432	58740	78692
医疗卫生与计划生育支出	Health and Family Planning	70882	27243	43639
节能环保支出	Energy-saving and Environment Protection	17339	9315	8024
城乡社区支出	Urban and Rural Community Affairs	53400	16865	36535
农林水支出	Farming、Forestry and Irrigation Affairs	75755	43647	32108
交通运输支出	Transport	12828	5565	7263
资源勘探信息等支出	Exploration and Information Affairs	11663	10723	940
商业服务业等支出	Commerce and Services Affairs	3275	1535	1740
金融支出	Financial Supervision Affairs	630	300	330
援助其他地区支出	Aid to Other Area	363	231	132
自然资源海洋气象等支出	Natural Resources Marine Meteorological	5936	3761	2175
住房保障支出	Housing Security Affairs	18277	10874	7403
粮油物资储备支出	Grain and Oil Reserves	2019	519	1500
国债还本付息支出	Pay Principle and Interest for Public Debt	7938	4871	3067
其他支出	Other Expenditure			
政府性基金支出	**Government Funds Expenditure**	**516833**	**176209**	**340624**
#城乡社区支出	Urban and Rural Community Affairs	378879	149520	229359

8-8 金融机构本外币各项存、贷款期末余额

The Ending Balance of all Deposits and Loans in RMB and Foreign Currencies of Financial Institutions

单位：万元 (10 000yuan)

指标	Item	2018年	2019年	2020年	2021年	2022年
金融机构本外币各项存款余额	**The Balance of RMB and Foreign Currencies Deposits in Financial Institutions**	**170601377**	**186460860**	**210649849**	**234369588**	**259410006**
#住户存款	Household Deposits	50672701	64970029	76475384	86204521	102917118
非金融企业存款	Non-financial Corporate Deposits	72213088	77067935	87238924	93393082	93495869
广义政府存款	General Government Deposits	36530329	35087861	36351481	41171421	43285939
非银行业金融机构存款	Non-bank Financial Intermediary Deposits	6729522	7629436	9239886	11598655	18448374
金融机构本外币各项贷款余额	**The Balance of RMB and Foreign Currencies Loans in Financial Institutions**	**160599213**	**187687420**	**207202433**	**233132266**	**261122538**
#住户贷款	Household Loans	37617608	47041192	54682406	61126528	65261003
非金融企业及机关团体贷款	Non-financial Corporate and Institution Loans	109865593	129406853	142485017	162082669	185229003
短期贷款	Short-term Loans	29398790	34665784	38736145	43586160	48464423
中长期贷款	Medium and Long-term Loans	72421049	82655910	91489364	102739117	117226259
票据融资	Bill Financing	4995957	8682607	8566014	11195931	14017627
融资租赁	Finance Lease	2870478	3240815	3592611	3971136	4718117
各项垫款	Bill Financing	179319	161737	100884	590324	802577
非银行业金融机构贷款	Non-bank Financial Intermediary Loans		200000			40000

8-9 金融机构人民币各项存、贷款期末余额
The Ending Balance of all Deposits and Loans in RMB of Financial Institutions

单位：万元 (10 000 yuan)

指标	Item	2018年	2019年	2020年	2021年	2022年
金融机构人民币各项存款余额	**The Balance of RMB Deposits in Financial Institutions**	**165718671**	**183032033**	**207149738**	**230292028**	**255895137**
#住户存款	Household Deposits	50080833	64380943	75841225	85584289	102262713
非金融企业存款	Non-financial Corporate Deposits	70776618	75805636	85613093	91691729	72925888
广义政府存款	General Government Deposits	36493478	34923450	36297466	41156864	43276614
非银行业金融机构存款	Non-bank Financial Intermediary Deposits	6630358	7571079	9193889	11550960	18425891
金融机构人民币各项贷款余额	**The Balance of RMB Loans in Financial Institutions**	**147000678**	**176242063**	**197048849**	**223499074**	**250779821**
#住户贷款	Household Loans	37616195	47038338	54680859	61124765	65258011
非金融企业及机关团体贷款	Non-financial Corporate and Institution Loans	108452714	128277535	141659442	161539618	184738842
短期贷款	Short-term Loans	28659735	34002100	38291441	43293345	48092662
中长期贷款	Medium and Long-term Loans	71747225	82190276	91128303	102488882	117107858
票据融资	Bill Financing	4995957	8682607	8566014	11195931	14017627
融资租赁	Finance Lease	2870478	3240815	3592611	3971136	4718117
各项垫款	Bill Financing	179319	161737	81074	590324	802577
非银行业金融机构贷款	Non-bank Financial Intermediary Loans		200000			40000

8–10 保险业务情况
Insurance Business

指标	Item	2018年	2019年	2020年	2021年	2022年
保险金额(亿元)	**Insurance Amount(100 million yuan)**	**256399**	**438422**	**927748**	**659267**	**615535**
保费收入(万元)	**Premium Income(10 000yuan)**	**4155535**	**5322643**	**6280398**	**5984712**	**6324536**
财产险	Property Insurance	843871	1174143	1255657	1091694	1523355
人身险	Life Insurance	3311664	4148500	5024741	4893017	4801181
赔付支出(万元)	**Claim Payment(10 000yuan)**	**1033980**	**1219250**	**1603108**	**2124574**	**1915636**
财产险	Property Insurance	421493	562261	683340	778634	905599
人身险	Life Insurance	612471	656989	919768	1345940	1010037

注：数据由地方金融监管部门提供。
Note: Data are provided by the Data are provided by the Financial Regulatory Authority

8–11 证券机构及证券交易情况
Institution and Trading Summary for Stocks

单位：亿元 (100 million yuan)

指标	Item	2018年	2019年	2020年	2021年	2022年
注册地在济南证券公司数(个)	**Stocks Institutions in Jinan(Unit)**	**1**	**1**	**1**	**1**	**1**
证券营业部(个)	**Securities Business Department(Unit)**	**87**	**92**	**91**	**120**	**92**
证券交易额	**Trading Volume of Securities Business Department**	**28482**	**36453**	**47753**	**55847**	**57576**
股票	Stock	12126	18621	28606	35660	34147
基金	Fund	2111	2197	3528	2872	3119
债券	Bond	14119	15536	15444	17045	19714
其他	Others	126	99	174	271	593

注：数据由地方金融监管部门提供。
Note: Data are provided by the Data are provided by the Financial Regulatory Authority

主要统计指标解释

一般公共预算收入 指国家财政参与社会产品分配所取得的收入，是实现国家职能的财力保证。主要包括：（1）各项税收：包括国内增值税、国内消费税、进口货物增值税、进口消费品消费税、出口货物退增值税、出口消费品退消费税、企业所得税、个人所得税、资源税、城市维护建设税、房产税、印花税、城镇土地使用税、土地增值税、车船税、船舶吨税、车辆购置税、关税、耕地占用税、契税、烟叶税、环境保护税等。（2）非税收入：包括专项收入、行政事业性收费收入、罚没收入、国有资本经营收入、国有资源（资产）有偿使用收入和其他收入。财政收入按现行分税制财政体制划分为中央本级收入和地方本级收入。

一般公共预算支出 指国家财政将筹集起来的资金进行分配使用，以满足经济建设和各项事业的需要。主要包括：一般公共服务、外交、国防、公共安全、教育、科学技术、文化旅游体育与传媒、社会保障和就业、卫生健康、节能环保、城乡社区、农林水、交通运输、资源勘探工业信息等、商业服务业等、金融、援助其他地区、自然资源海洋气象等、住房保障、粮油物资储备、灾害防治及应急管理、债务付息、债务发行费用等方面的支出。财政支出根据政府在经济和社会活动中的不同职权，划分为中央财政支出和地方财政支出。

各项存款 金融机构资金来源的主要项目，包括住户存款、非金融企业存款、机关团体存款、财政性存款、非银行业金融机构存款和境外存款。

各项贷款 金融机构资金运用的主要项目，包括住户贷款、非金融企业及机关团体贷款、非银行业金融机构贷款和境外贷款。

保险金额 指保险人承担赔偿或者给付保险金责任的最高限额。

Explanatory Notes on Main Statistical Indicators

General Public Budget Revenue refers to income for the government finance through participating in the distribution of social products. It is the financial guarantee to ensure government functioning. The government revenue includes the following main items: (1) Various tax revenues including domestic value added tax (VAT), domestic consumption tax, VAT from imports, consumption tax from imports, VAT rebate for exports, consumption tax rebate for exports, corporate income tax, individual income tax, resource tax, city maintenance and construction tax, house property tax, stamp tax, urban land use tax, land appreciation tax, tax on vehicles and boat operation, ship tonnage tax, vehicle purchase tax, tariffs, farm land occupation tax, deed tax, and tobacco tax, environment protection tax, etc. (2) Non-tax revenue, including special program receipts, charge income of administrative and institutional units, penalty receipts, operating income from government capital, income from use of state-owned resources (assets) and others non-tax receipts.

General Public Budget Expenditure refers to the distribution and use of the funds which the government finance has raised, so as to meet the needs of economic construction and various undertakings. It includes the following main items: expenditure for general public services, expenditure for foreign affairs, expenditure for national defence expenditure for public security, expenditure for education, expenditure for science and technology, expenditure for culture, tourism, sport and media, expenditure for social safety net and employment effort, expenditure for health care, expenditure for energy conservation and environment protection, expenditure for urban and rural community affairs, expenditure for agriculture, forestry and water conservancy, expenditure for transportation, expenditure for resource exploration and industrial information, expenditure for affairs of commerce and services, expenditure for finance, aid to other regions, expenditure for nature resources, ocean and weather, expenditure for housing security, expenditure for grain & oil reserves, expenditure for prevention of disasters and emergency management, interest payment for public debts, expenditure for issuing debts. General public budget expenditure is divided into general public budget expenditure of central government and general public budget expenditure of local government according to the different functions of the governments played in economic and social activities.

Total Deposits are the main items of financial sources of financial institutions, which include deposits of households, deposits of non-financial enterprises, deposits of government departments & organizations, fiscal deposits, deposits of non-banking financial institutions and overseas deposits.

Total Loans are the main items of financial uses of financial institutions, which include loans to households, loans to non-financial enterprises and government departments & organizations, loans to non-banking financial institutions and overseas loans.

Amount Insured refers to the maximum that the insurant will get for the claim of the case insured.

9

物价

PRICE

9-1 主要年份物价指数(以上年为100)
Price Indices in Major Years(Preceding Year=100)

年份 Year	居民消费价格指数 Consumer Price Index	#食品 Food	#服务项目 Services	零售物价指数 Retail Price Index
1951	108.5	105.3	98.7	109.8
1952	101.5	103.9	101.0	101.2
1955	101.6	101.3	103.4	101.4
1956	100.5	100.7	100.6	100.5
1965	107.3	111.5	97.5	108.0
1970	98.4	99.0	100.0	98.3
1971	100.0	100.5	100.0	100.0
1972	100.1	100.3	100.0	100.1
1973	99.5	99.6	97.9	99.7
1974	99.4	99.1	99.9	99.5
1975	100.2	100.0	100.0	100.2
1976	100.4	100.0	100.0	100.4
1977	99.2	99.9	91.2	100.0
1978	100.3	100.3	100.0	100.3
1979	101.1	101.7	100.5	101.1
1980	104.7	107.9	100.0	105.0
1981	101.9	102.2	100.1	102.0
1982	101.1	101.6	100.3	101.2
1983	100.1	100.3	100.9	100.1
1984	101.9	101.1	109.8	101.3
1985	108.7	112.2	103.3	109.1
1986	106.2	107.6	104.9	106.3
1987	109.5	111.9	104.9	109.8
1988	122.4	128.0	108.8	123.4
1989	116.2	111.2	113.5	116.4
1990	103.3	102.6	108.0	103.0
1991	106.7	107.6	106.9	106.7
1992	110.4	108.7	122.2	109.3
1993	114.7	109.8	138.0	112.1

9-1 续表 continued

年份 Year	居民消费价格指数 Consumer Price Index	#食品 Food	#服务项目 Services	零售物价指数 Retail Price Index
1994	124.8	133.9	114.5	122.7
1995	117.3	123.0	115.1	113.2
1996	109.1	109.7	116.2	106.3
1997	102.9	101.8	107.8	101.5
1998	100.9	99.4	119.0	98.9
1999	99.1	97.3	127.6	96.9
2000	100.6	97.9	129.0	98.0
2001	100.3	100.8	106.1	98.8
2002	98.8	100.2	101.3	97.8
2003	99.9	103.6	100.3	98.0
2004	102.5	107.4	101.2	100.6
2005	101.1	102.7	101.2	100.4
2006	100.9	102.4	100.9	100.3
2007	103.9	111.6	101.8	102.2
2008	105.7	115.5	101.8	104.5
2009	100.3	102.7	102.4	98.7
2010	102.1	107.3	100.6	101.3
2011	105.4	111.3	104.4	104.6
2012	102.4	103.6	102.2	101.8
2013	102.8	104.9	102.7	101.3
2014	102.2	103.2	102.9	101.2
2015	101.9	101.4	101.6	100.3
2016	102.7	103.9	103.5	100.8
2017	102.0	98.5	104.2	101.0
2018	102.6	102.8	102.1	102.6
2019	103.3	112.0	101.4	102.5
2020	102.4	112.3	99.0	101.9
2021	101.5	100.5	101.4	101.3
2022	101.4	103.3	100.1	102.2

9-2 主要年份物价指数(以1950年为100)
Price Indices in Major Years(Preceding 1950=100)

年份 Year	居民消费价格指数 Consumer Price Index	#食品 Food	#服务项目 Services	零售物价指数 Retail Price Index
1951	108.5	105.3	98.7	109.8
1952	110.1	109.4	103.7	111.1
1955	117.2	123.7	108.2	118.4
1956	117.8	124.6	108.8	119.0
1965	127.7	141.5	116.9	130.7
1970	123.0	141.6	110.1	126.0
1971	123.0	142.3	110.1	126.0
1972	123.1	142.7	110.1	126.1
1973	122.5	142.1	107.8	125.8
1974	121.8	140.9	107.7	125.1
1975	122.0	140.9	107.7	125.4
1976	122.5	140.9	107.7	125.9
1977	121.5	140.7	98.2	125.9
1978	121.9	141.1	98.2	126.3
1979	123.2	143.5	98.6	127.6
1980	129.0	154.9	98.6	134.0
1981	131.5	158.3	98.7	136.7
1982	132.9	160.8	99.0	138.3
1983	133.0	161.3	99.9	138.5
1984	135.6	163.1	109.7	140.3
1985	147.4	183.0	113.3	153.0
1986	156.5	195.8	118.9	162.7
1987	171.4	219.1	124.7	178.6
1988	209.8	280.4	135.7	220.4
1989	234.8	311.8	154.0	256.5
1990	251.8	319.9	166.3	264.2
1991	268.7	344.2	177.8	281.9
1992	296.6	376.2	217.3	308.1
1993	340.2	413.1	299.8	345.4

9-2 续表 continued

年份 Year	居民消费价格指数 Consumer Price Index	#食品 Food	#服务项目 Services	零售物价指数 Retail Price Index
1994	424.6	570.4	343.3	423.8
1995	498.1	709.7	395.1	479.7
1996	543.4	797.7	459.1	509.9
1997	559.2	782.5	494.9	551.6
1998	564.2	777.8	588.9	545.5
1999	559.1	756.8	751.4	528.6
2000	562.4	740.9	969.3	518.0
2001	564.1	746.8	1028.4	511.8
2002	557.3	748.3	1041.8	500.5
2003	556.7	775.2	1044.9	490.5
2004	570.6	832.6	1057.4	493.4
2005	576.9	855.1	1070.1	495.4
2006	582.1	875.6	1079.7	496.9
2007	604.8	977.2	1099.1	507.8
2008	639.3	1128.7	1118.9	530.7
2009	641.2	1159.2	1145.8	523.8
2010	654.7	1243.8	1152.7	530.6
2011	690.2	1384.7	1203.1	555.1
2012	706.8	1434.5	1229.5	565.1
2013	726.6	1504.8	1262.7	572.4
2014	742.6	1553.0	1299.3	579.3
2015	756.7	1574.7	1320.1	581.0
2016	777.1	1636.1	1366.3	585.6
2017	792.6	1611.6	1423.7	591.5
2018	813.3	1656.7	1453.6	606.8
2019	840.1	1855.5	1473.9	622.0
2020	860.3	2083.7	1459.2	633.8
2021	873.2	2094.1	1479.6	642.1
2022	885.4	2163.2	1481.1	656.2

9–3 分月居民消费价格指数(2022年，以上年为100)

Consumer Price Indices by Month(2022，Preceding Year=100)

指标	Item	全年 Annual	一月 January	二月 February
居民消费价格总指数	**Consumer Price Index**	**101.4**	**100.8**	**100.3**
非食品烟酒价格指数	**Non-food,tobacco and alcohol Price Index**	**101.1**	**101.4**	**101.4**
服务价格指数	**Services Price Index**	**100.1**	**100.8**	**100.3**
工业品价格指数	**Industrial Products Price Index**	**102.3**	**102.1**	**102.7**
消费品价格指数	**Consumer Goods Price Index**	**102.3**	**100.8**	**100.2**
扣除食品和能源价格指数	**Excluding Food and Energy Price Index**	**100.2**	**100.6**	**100.3**
一、食品烟酒	**Food,Tobacco and Liquor**	**102.3**	**99.3**	**97.2**
1.食品	Food	103.3	98.1	95.6
(1)粮食	Grain	103.5	99.7	99.9
(2)薯类	Tuber	108.6	98.4	90.5
(3)豆类	Beans	105.8	106.9	106.0
(4)食用油	Edible Oil	103.9	106.5	107.8
食用植物油	Edible Vegetable Oil	104.3	107.5	108.9
(5)菜及食用菌	Vegetable and Edible Fungi	99.8	100.7	96.2
鲜菜	Fresh Vegetable	99.5	100.1	95.2
(6)畜肉类	Meat of Livestock	95.6	73.3	74.0
猪肉	Pork	89.6	51.4	52.0
(7)禽肉类	Meat of Poultry	103.1	98.3	99.1
(8)水产品	Aquatic Products	105.2	120.5	107.0
(9)蛋类	Poultry & Eggs	110.8	102.0	105.0
鸡蛋	Eggs	111.7	99.8	103.9
(10)奶类	Milk	101.0	100.2	99.2
(11)干鲜瓜果类	Fruits and Nuts	114.0	109.1	102.2
鲜果	Fresh Fruits	115.1	111.7	100.6
(12)糖果糕点类	Candy and Cake	101.8	101.2	101.0
(13)调味品	Flavoring	100.3	98.9	99.1
(14)其他食品类	Other Foods	105.7	105.5	103.2
2.茶及饮料	Tea and Beverages	103.6	100.5	102.9
3.烟酒	Tobacco and Alcohol	102.4	102.2	103.9

三月 March	四月 April	五月 May	六月 June	七月 July	八月 August	九月 September	十月 October	十一月 November	十二月 December
100.9	**101.4**	**101.3**	**101.8**	**102.0**	**101.8**	**102.1**	**101.6**	**101.3**	**102.0**
101.4	**101.2**	**101.1**	**101.2**	**100.8**	**100.8**	**100.9**	**101.0**	**101.1**	**101.2**
99.9	**99.8**	**99.8**	**99.6**	**99.5**	**99.8**	**100.1**	**100.6**	**100.6**	**100.8**
103.1	**103.0**	**102.8**	**103.2**	**102.3**	**102.0**	**101.8**	**101.4**	**101.6**	**101.7**
101.5	**102.5**	**102.3**	**103.3**	**103.7**	**103.2**	**103.4**	**102.3**	**101.8**	**102.7**
100.2	**100.0**	**99.9**	**99.8**	**99.7**	**99.9**	**100.1**	**100.4**	**100.5**	**100.8**
99.5	**101.9**	**101.7**	**103.5**	**105.5**	**104.8**	**105.6**	**103.5**	**102.1**	**104.2**
99.0	102.6	102.5	105.1	108.2	107.1	108.5	105.3	103.2	105.9
101.6	103.2	104.1	105.3	104.2	103.7	105.3	105.8	105.1	103.8
99.7	111.0	118.7	105.0	110.1	119.7	119.0	108.8	109.3	119.0
104.2	105.3	106.8	104.2	106.9	108.1	107.2	105.3	103.9	104.6
108.6	107.9	103.9	100.5	101.8	100.8	102.0	105.0	100.4	103.1
109.7	108.7	104.4	100.8	102.0	100.9	102.0	105.0	100.3	103.1
121.5	123.9	109.7	98.1	112.4	105.5	106.4	79.2	71.1	90.3
122.5	125.5	110.2	97.8	114.8	106.2	106.3	77.3	69.5	89.6
74.6	79.0	84.4	91.2	107.7	108.6	115.6	126.9	122.1	117.0
51.5	60.5	71.5	86.4	117.7	121.5	137.0	164.4	145.4	134.0
96.9	101.3	102.1	103.3	105.4	106.8	107.2	105.7	106.3	106.2
108.3	109.2	102.1	101.0	101.6	102.1	100.5	101.8	104.7	105.9
107.8	113.7	111.1	111.0	112.1	108.5	111.9	118.0	114.3	114.1
109.8	115.4	112.6	111.9	113.1	108.5	112.8	120.5	115.8	115.8
98.4	98.9	102.5	103.7	100.6	102.1	101.3	102.8	100.4	102.1
96.2	106.7	114.9	137.6	124.6	120.4	120.6	114.4	114.2	112.6
93.8	106.3	115.7	143.5	126.5	122.1	122.2	116.2	116.7	114.3
104.2	104.2	103.9	101.1	101.1	101.0	100.3	100.8	101.7	101.5
99.7	100.1	102.0	101.7	104.2	100.1	100.5	98.5	100.2	98.6
104.6	107.7	105.8	107.7	105.5	106.5	108.6	104.9	103.9	104.8
101.9	104.7	104.0	104.3	104.3	104.6	105.1	102.2	104.6	103.9
103.8	102.8	101.7	101.3	102.1	101.8	101.7	102.1	102.4	102.6

9-3 续表 1 continued 1

指标	Item	全年 Annual	一月 January	二月 February
(1)卷烟	Cigarette	100.2	100.0	100.0
(2)酒类	Alcohol	104.3	104.2	107.4
4.在外餐饮	Dining Out	99.6	101.6	99.0
二、衣着	**Clothing**	**101.0**	**100.5**	**100.9**
1.服装	Garments	101.1	101.3	101.6
(1)男式服装	Men's Clothing	101.2	101.1	101.8
(2)女式服装	Women's Clothing	101.5	102.0	102.1
(3)儿童服装	Children's Clothing	100.1	98.9	99.6
(4)衣着材料及配件	Clothing and Accessories	99.9	102.0	101.2
(5)衣着服务费	Clothing service fee	100.0	100.0	100.0
2.鞋类	Footwear	100.2	97.1	98.0
(1)鞋	Shoes	100.2	97.0	97.8
(2)鞋类服务	Footwear Services	104.2	104.6	104.6
三、居住	**Residence**	**99.8**	**101.1**	**100.8**
1.租赁房房租	Rent of Rental Housing	99.8	101.8	101.4
2.住房保养维修及管理	Housing Maintenance and Management	100.4	100.6	100.6
(1)住房装潢材料	Housing Decoration Materials	100.8	101.2	101.2
(2)住房维修管理费用	Housing Maintenance Management Fee	100.0	100.0	100.0
3.水电燃料	Water, Electricity and Fuels	101.8	103.5	103.5
(1)水	Water	100.0	100.0	100.0
(2)电	Electricity	100.0	100.0	100.0
(3)燃气	Gas	104.5	104.1	104.1
(4)其他水电燃料类	Other Fuel	102.8	106.7	106.7
4.自有住房	Self-owned House	99.1	100.5	100.0
四、生活用品及服务	**Articles for Daily Use and Services**	**101.6**	**100.5**	**101.0**
1.家具及室内装饰品	Furniture and Interior Decorations	99.7	99.2	98.5
(1)家具	Furniture	99.7	99.9	99.0
(2)室内装饰品	Interior Decorations	99.8	95.2	95.2
2.家用器具	Home Appliances	102.5	102.4	104.6
(1)大型家用器具	Large Home Appliances	102.2	102.2	104.7
(2)小家电	Small Home Appliances	103.7	103.1	103.5

三月 March	四月 April	五月 May	六月 June	七月 July	八月 August	九月 September	十月 October	十一月 November	十二月 December
100.0	100.0	100.0	100.0	100.0	100.0	100.0	100.0	101.0	101.0
107.3	105.2	103.2	102.4	103.9	103.4	103.2	103.9	103.7	104.0
99.3	99.4	99.4	99.9	99.4	99.8	99.2	99.3	98.8	99.9
100.8	**100.2**	**100.2**	**100.2**	**100.6**	**101.0**	**101.1**	**101.7**	**102.1**	**102.2**
101.0	100.5	100.3	100.1	100.4	101.0	101.2	101.7	102.1	102.2
101.0	100.3	100.1	99.8	100.4	101.4	101.7	102.2	102.4	102.7
101.6	101.3	100.9	101.0	101.2	101.4	101.2	101.6	101.9	102.0
98.8	98.0	98.4	98.3	98.4	100.2	101.5	102.8	103.0	103.4
100.5	100.5	100.5	98.7	98.5	98.5	99.0	99.0	99.9	99.9
100.0	100.0	100.0	100.0	100.0	100.0	100.0	100.0	100.0	100.0
99.8	99.2	99.8	100.5	101.2	100.9	100.7	101.4	102.5	102.1
99.7	99.0	99.7	100.4	101.1	100.8	100.6	101.3	102.5	102.2
104.6	104.6	104.6	104.6	104.6	104.6	104.6	104.6	104.6	100.0
99.6	**99.4**	**99.3**	**99.4**	**99.2**	**99.3**	**99.4**	**99.9**	**100.1**	**100.2**
99.7	99.2	99.3	99.2	98.9	98.8	99.2	99.9	100.4	100.5
100.6	100.5	100.5	100.5	100.5	100.3	100.3	100.3	100.3	99.9
101.2	101.0	101.0	100.9	100.9	100.7	100.7	100.7	100.7	99.9
100.0	100.0	100.0	100.0	100.0	100.0	100.0	100.0	100.0	100.0
103.8	102.9	102.0	102.0	101.8	101.2	100.5	100.2	100.2	100.2
100.0	100.0	100.0	100.0	100.0	100.0	100.0	100.0	100.0	100.0
100.0	100.0	100.0	100.0	100.0	100.0	100.0	100.0	100.0	100.0
106.1	106.1	106.1	106.1	106.1	106.1	104.0	102.0	102.0	102.0
106.7	104.7	102.8	102.8	102.2	101.1	100.0	100.0	100.0	100.0
98.2	98.2	98.2	98.5	98.3	98.6	99.0	99.8	100.0	100.2
101.0	**101.7**	**102.6**	**102.3**	**101.9**	**101.6**	**101.6**	**101.5**	**101.9**	**102.0**
98.8	98.9	99.5	100.3	100.5	100.2	100.1	100.3	100.1	100.1
99.0	99.0	99.0	100.1	100.1	100.1	100.1	100.1	100.1	99.7
97.4	98.5	102.5	101.3	103.0	100.8	99.7	101.3	100.0	102.4
104.6	104.3	104.6	102.6	103.5	102.3	100.7	100.7	99.6	99.8
104.6	104.4	104.6	102.4	103.3	102.0	100.0	100.1	99.2	99.4
104.4	103.8	104.3	104.1	104.3	104.3	104.5	104.5	102.0	102.1

9-3 续表 2 continued 2

指标	Item	全年 Annual	一月 January	二月 February
3.家用纺织品	Home Textiles	97.6	94.6	93.6
(1)床上用品	Bedding Article	97.2	95.2	93.5
(2)窗帘门帘	Curtain	100.0	100.0	100.0
(3)其他家用纺织品	Other Home Textiles	97.7	84.5	87.1
4.家庭日用杂品	Daily Use Household Articles	101.1	100.5	100.8
(1)洗涤卫生用品	Washing Sanitary Articles	100.7	99.9	100.0
(2)厨具餐具茶具	Kitchenware, Tableware, Tea Set	102.9	100.5	100.9
(3)其他家庭日用杂品	Other Daily Use Household Articles	100.7	101.7	102.2
5.个人护理用品	Personal-care Supplies	104.4	97.4	99.6
(1)化妆品	Cosmetics	104.6	95.8	98.6
(2)其他护理用品类	Other Personal-care Supplies	104.1	99.9	101.2
6.家庭服务	Household Services	101.6	105.1	102.7
五、交通通信	**Transport and Communications**	**104.3**	**104.5**	**104.5**
1.交通	Transport	105.8	106.0	106.1
(1)交通工具	Transport Facility	96.9	99.3	98.3
(2)交通工具用燃料	Fuels for Transport Facility	121.1	120.5	123.8
(3)交通工具使用和维修	Use and Maintenance of Transport Facility	100.7	100.0	101.4
(4)交通费	Traffic Fee	106.3	106.2	101.0
2.通信	Communications	99.0	99.2	98.7
(1)通信工具	Communication Tools	97.4	98.0	96.7
(2)通信服务	Communication Services	100.0	100.0	100.0
(3)邮递服务	Mailing Services	100.2	101.0	101.0
六、教育文化娱乐	**Education Culture and Recreation**	**100.6**	**100.0**	**100.1**
1.教育	Education	100.6	101.3	101.3
(1)教育用品	Education Articles	100.6	101.0	101.4
(2)教育服务	Education Services	100.6	101.3	101.3
2.文化娱乐	Culture and Recreation	100.5	97.9	98.2
(1)文娱耐用消费品	Durable Consumer Goods for Culture and Recreation	99.3	99.8	99.2

三月 March	四月 April	五月 May	六月 June	七月 July	八月 August	九月 September	十月 October	十一月 November	十二月 December
92.8	93.9	94.5	99.7	99.1	100.0	101.4	101.4	100.4	101.0
92.5	92.8	93.5	99.6	98.7	99.3	101.4	101.5	100.2	100.0
100.0	100.0	100.0	100.0	100.0	100.0	100.0	100.0	100.0	100.0
88.3	95.7	95.7	100.3	100.7	105.4	102.8	102.8	102.8	110.0
100.6	101.5	102.7	102.5	99.6	100.3	99.7	100.7	101.7	102.5
99.8	100.5	103.0	100.3	98.3	99.7	99.4	100.9	102.3	103.8
100.9	103.4	103.9	108.6	101.6	104.8	101.6	100.7	103.8	104.6
101.7	102.2	101.6	102.5	100.7	98.4	98.9	100.5	99.3	99.0
100.1	102.8	105.3	105.7	105.9	104.5	108.1	106.2	109.2	108.7
98.7	101.7	105.2	105.2	106.2	104.3	110.5	107.1	112.0	110.8
102.2	104.5	105.4	106.6	105.3	104.9	104.5	104.7	104.9	105.5
102.7	102.7	103.1	100.8	100.8	100.8	100.4	100.4	100.4	99.9
105.2	**105.7**	**105.5**	**106.5**	**104.9**	**103.9**	**104.1**	**102.4**	**102.0**	**102.1**
107.0	107.7	107.7	109.1	106.7	105.3	105.4	103.2	102.7	102.6
98.5	97.6	97.6	96.2	96.2	96.0	96.1	95.8	95.8	96.1
124.4	128.7	127.4	133.2	124.5	120.2	119.2	112.4	111.3	110.5
100.2	100.7	100.2	100.8	100.8	100.8	100.8	100.8	100.8	100.8
104.3	103.3	106.1	106.5	106.7	107.2	110.3	108.4	107.3	108.0
99.2	98.7	97.9	97.8	98.5	98.7	99.5	99.8	99.3	100.1
98.0	96.9	95.0	94.5	96.3	96.7	98.8	99.6	98.4	100.1
100.0	100.0	100.0	100.0	100.0	100.0	100.0	100.0	100.0	100.0
100.0	100.0	100.0	100.0	100.0	100.0	100.0	100.0	100.0	100.0
100.8	**100.5**	**100.4**	**99.8**	**99.7**	**100.3**	**100.4**	**101.5**	**101.4**	**101.7**
101.2	101.2	101.2	100.0	100.0	100.0	100.2	100.2	100.2	100.2
100.6	100.5	100.5	100.5	100.6	100.6	100.6	100.5	100.5	100.5
101.3	101.3	101.3	100.0	100.0	100.0	100.2	100.2	100.2	100.2
100.1	99.3	99.0	99.3	99.2	100.7	100.7	103.6	103.4	104.3
98.7	98.9	98.6	98.3	98.7	99.6	99.6	99.9	100.5	100.1

9-3 续表 3 continued 3

指标	Item	全年 Annual	一月 January	二月 February
(2)其他文娱用品	Other Articles	102.4	100.4	102.0
(3)文化娱乐服务	Services for Culture and Recreation	99.2	102.5	103.2
(4)旅游	Touring	101.4	91.0	90.5
七、医疗保健	**Health Care**	**100.4**	**101.2**	**101.0**
1.药品及医疗器具	Medicine and Medical Instruments	99.9	101.7	101.5
(1)中药	Traditional Chinese Medicines	103.2	106.0	106.2
(2)西药	Western Medicines	97.7	100.8	99.1
(3)滋补保健品	Health Products	102.0	101.9	102.7
(4)医疗卫生器具	Medical and Health Equipment	95.8	93.9	100.2
(5)保健器具	Healthcare Apparatus	100.6	101.5	100.0
2.医疗服务	Medical Services	100.7	100.9	100.8
(1)综合医疗类	Comprehensive Health Care	101.7	102.0	102.0
(2)诊断类	Diagnostic	100.0	99.9	99.9
(3)治疗类	Therapeutic	100.9	101.0	101.0
(4)康复类	Rehabilitation	100.7	100.0	100.0
(5)中医医疗服务类	Chinese Medicine Services	101.9	104.7	104.7
(6)其他医疗保健服务	Other Medical Services	100.2	102.7	100.0
八、其他用品及服务	**Other Articles and Services**	**100.7**	**99.3**	**99.8**
1.其他用品	Other Articles	101.3	96.2	101.1
(1)首饰手表	Jewelry Watches	100.4	94.8	101.9
(2)母婴用品	Maternal and Infant Supplies	106.1	98.6	100.9
(3)其他杂项用品	Other Miscellaneous Supplies	100.8	98.0	99.4
2.其他服务	Other Services	100.2	102.3	98.6
(1)在外住宿	Hotel Accommodation	90.6	101.1	78.2
(2)美容美发洗浴	Hairdressing Bath	101.8	105.3	102.2
(3)养老服务	Pension Services	101.1	100.0	100.0
(4)金融及保险服务	Finance and Insurance Services	101.6	101.8	101.8
(5)中介法律及其他服务	Legal Intermediary and Other Service	100.1	100.6	100.6

三月 March	四月 April	五月 May	六月 June	七月 July	八月 August	九月 September	十月 October	十一月 November	十二月 December
102.2	101.8	102.7	102.8	101.9	102.7	102.4	103.4	102.4	104.4
104.9	103.8	103.1	96.2	93.9	94.1	93.9	98.4	97.7	99.5
94.6	93.4	92.9	101.4	104.1	107.9	108.3	111.8	112.3	112.3
101.0	**100.7**	**100.4**	**100.3**	**100.1**	**99.9**	**100.0**	**99.9**	**100.4**	**100.5**
101.4	100.2	99.2	99.7	98.8	98.4	98.6	98.6	100.2	100.0
106.1	105.4	105.4	102.2	102.8	100.9	101.0	101.0	101.0	101.0
98.3	95.8	95.9	96.6	96.7	96.7	96.7	96.7	99.8	99.9
105.1	105.1	101.9	104.7	100.5	100.5	100.5	100.5	100.5	100.5
97.3	97.2	94.2	96.8	93.3	93.6	93.6	96.2	97.1	96.5
100.0	101.5	98.5	100.0	100.0	100.0	103.3	100.0	102.5	100.0
100.8	100.9	100.9	100.6	100.6	100.6	100.6	100.4	100.4	100.8
102.0	102.3	102.3	101.6	101.6	101.6	101.7	101.0	101.0	101.0
99.9	100.0	100.0	100.0	100.0	100.0	100.1	100.1	100.1	100.1
101.0	101.0	101.0	101.0	101.0	101.0	100.7	100.7	100.7	100.7
100.0	100.0	100.0	100.0	100.0	100.0	100.0	100.0	100.0	108.8
104.7	104.7	104.7	100.0	100.0	100.0	100.0	100.0	100.0	100.0
100.0	100.0	100.0	100.0	100.0	100.0	100.0	100.0	100.0	100.0
103.6	**101.7**	**100.2**	**100.0**	**99.3**	**101.0**	**100.7**	**100.9**	**100.7**	**101.8**
104.7	102.4	100.8	100.1	99.2	101.9	100.6	102.2	102.3	104.5
105.7	100.9	98.8	97.5	97.0	101.1	98.6	101.7	102.0	105.5
101.5	103.7	109.9	110.9	107.3	108.4	109.6	109.1	106.8	107.1
104.5	105.1	100.5	100.5	99.9	100.3	100.4	99.9	100.5	100.7
102.6	101.0	99.6	100.0	99.4	100.2	100.9	99.6	99.2	99.3
108.2	93.8	86.0	88.0	84.8	90.7	95.5	85.4	89.7	92.3
103.3	103.3	101.1	101.1	101.1	101.1	101.1	101.1	100.7	100.2
100.0	100.0	101.7	101.7	101.7	101.7	101.7	101.7	101.7	101.7
101.8	101.8	101.8	101.9	101.9	101.9	101.9	101.9	100.0	100.0
100.6	100.6	100.2	99.9	99.7	99.7	99.7	99.7	99.7	99.7

9-4 分月商品零售价格指数(2022年，以上年为100)
Retail Price Indices by Month(2022，Preceding Year=100)

指标	Item	全年 Annual	一月 January	二月 February
商品零售价格指数	Retail Price Index	102.2	101.3	101.3
一、食品	Food	102.3	99.0	96.5
二、饮料、烟酒	Beverages, Tobacco and Alcohol	102.7	101.7	103.6
三、服装、鞋帽	Garments, Shoes and Hats	101.0	100.5	100.9
四、纺织品	Textiles	98.3	96.4	95.0
五、家用电器及音像器材	Household Appliances, Music and Video Equipment	100.9	101.0	102.2
六、文化办公用品	Cultural and Office Appliances	99.7	99.9	98.8
七、日用品	Articles for Daily Use	101.4	99.2	99.6
八、体育娱乐用品	Sports and Recreation Articles	100.2	97.8	99.8
九、交通、通信用品	Transportation and Communication Appliances	97.4	98.7	97.8
十、家具	Furniture	99.7	99.9	99.0
十一、化妆品	Cosmetics	104.5	96.7	99.1
十二、金银饰品	Gold and Silver Ornaments	100.6	93.4	102.5
十三、中西药品及医疗保健用品	Traditional Chinese and Western Medicines and Health Care Articles	99.9	101.7	101.5
十四、书报杂志及电子出版物	Books, Newspapers, Magazines and Electronic Publications	103.0	102.6	102.9
十五、燃料	Fuels	119.2	119.2	121.8
十六、建筑材料及五金电料	Building Materials and Hardware	100.5	100.9	100.9

三月 March	四月 April	五月 May	六月 June	七月 July	八月 August	九月 September	十月 October	十一月 November	十二月 December
102.3	102.8	102.6	103.2	102.9	102.4	102.5	101.6	101.6	102.1
99.0	101.7	101.6	103.7	105.8	105.1	105.9	103.7	102.0	104.3
103.3	103.3	102.3	102.1	102.7	102.6	102.6	102.1	103.0	102.9
100.8	100.2	100.2	100.2	100.6	101.0	101.1	101.7	102.2	102.3
94.0	94.3	94.9	100.1	99.8	100.3	102.1	102.1	100.6	100.4
102.0	101.9	102.1	100.7	101.3	100.8	100.0	100.5	99.4	99.4
98.4	99.2	98.7	98.5	100.0	101.3	100.7	99.8	101.3	100.0
100.5	101.9	103.3	103.2	100.9	101.5	100.9	101.4	101.7	102.5
99.9	99.4	100.0	100.5	99.5	100.5	100.2	101.7	100.3	102.9
98.3	97.6	97.3	96.4	96.7	96.7	97.0	96.7	97.4	97.9
99.0	99.0	99.0	100.1	100.1	100.1	100.1	100.1	100.1	99.7
99.4	102.6	105.4	105.7	106.0	104.5	109.1	106.6	110.2	109.3
107.4	101.4	98.7	96.8	96.2	101.4	98.3	102.2	102.7	107.2
101.4	100.2	99.2	99.7	98.8	98.4	98.6	98.6	100.2	100.0
103.4	102.5	103.4	103.5	103.0	103.0	103.0	103.0	102.7	102.7
123.5	127.4	125.9	130.2	122.1	118.3	116.6	110.1	109.2	108.7
100.9	100.3	100.0	100.4	100.7	100.1	100.3	100.6	100.5	99.9

9-5 主要年份零售商品和服务项目年平均价格
Per Retail and Services Price of Major Years

商品名称	Name	规格等级牌号 Grade	单位 Unit	1978年	1980年	1985年
面粉	Flour	特一	元/千克(yuan/kg)	0.50	0.50	0.50
粳米	Japonica	标一	元/千克(yuan/kg)	0.34	0.34	0.40
小米	Millet	一等	元/千克(yuan/kg)	0.27	0.27	0.44
土豆	Potato		元/千克(yuan/kg)	0.19	0.22	0.30
豆腐	Tofu	水豆腐	元/千克(yuan/kg)	0.16	0.18	0.26
猪肉	Pork	净肉	元/千克(yuan/kg)	1.72	1.95	2.65
牛肉	Beef	净肉	元/千克(yuan/kg)	1.26	1.76	2.91
羊肉	Mutton	净肉	元/千克(yuan/kg)	1.38	1.88	2.80
鸡蛋	Hen's Egg	新鲜完整	元/千克(yuan/kg)	1.58	2.20	2.60
海带	Kelp	盐干一级	元/千克(yuan/kg)	1.18	1.26	1.32
大白菜	Chinese Cabbage	一等	元/千克(yuan/kg)	0.11	0.07	0.09
菠菜	Spinage	一等	元/千克(yuan/kg)	0.08	0.09	0.28
油菜	Oilseed rape	一等	元/千克(yuan/kg)	0.05	0.07	0.26
芹菜	Celery	一等	元/千克(yuan/kg)	1.13	0.11	0.39
韭菜	Chinese Chives	一等	元/千克(yuan/kg)	0.15	0.16	0.54
黄瓜	Cucumber	一等	元/千克(yuan/kg)	0.19	0.18	0.47
西红柿	Tomato	一等	元/千克(yuan/kg)	0.15	0.18	0.53
茄子	Eggplant	一等	元/千克(yuan/kg)	0.14	0.11	0.27
青椒	Green Pepper	一等	元/千克(yuan/kg)	0.23	0.20	0.47
大葱	Allium Fistulosum	一等	元/千克(yuan/kg)	0.11	0.12	0.28
黑木耳	Black Fungus	甲级	元/千克(yuan/kg)	30.00	32.00	34.86
精盐	Salt	再制盐	元/500克(yuan/500g)	0.16	0.16	0.14
酱油	Soy Sauce	二级	元/千克(yuan/kg)	0.22	0.22	0.34
味精	Aginomoto	含麸酸钠80%以上	元/千克(yuan/kg)	10.80	9.68	12.60
绵白糖	Soft Sugar	国产机制一级	元/千克(yuan/kg)	1.60	1.70	1.70
红糖	Brown Sugar	一级	元/千克(yuan/kg)	1.30	1.30	1.30
啤酒	Beer	熟12度瓶装	元/瓶(yuan/unit)	0.58	0.58	0.73
苹果	Apple	一级	元/千克(yuan/kg)	0.82	0.90	1.19
桔子	Orange	一级	元/千克(yuan/kg)	1.30	1.52	2.35
西瓜	watermelon	一级	元/千克(yuan/kg)	0.24	0.28	0.32
香蕉	Banana	一级	元/千克(yuan/kg)	1.46	1.65	1.82
自来水	Tap Water	生活用水	元/吨(yuan/tons)	0.08	0.08	0.09
照明用电	Lighting Electricity	民用220V	元/度(yuan/kWh)	0.18	0.18	0.18
平信	Ordinary Mail	外埠	元/封(yuan/unit)	0.08	0.08	0.08
注射费	Injection Fees	肌肉注射	元/次(yuan/unit)	0.10	0.10	0.10
住院费	Hospitalization Fees	普通床位	元/天(yuan/day)			
学杂费	Tuition and Fees	高中学生	元/学期(yuan/semester)	2.50	2.50	2.50
公园门票	Park Tickets	大明湖	元/张(yuan/unit)	0.03	0.03	0.03
理发	Haircut	男理一级全活	元/次(yuan/unit)	0.30	0.30	0.45
洗澡	Bath		元/次(yuan/unit)	0.24	0.24	0.30
课本	Textbook	高中语文一年级	元/本(yuan/unit)			
银花	Silver	一等	元/千克(yuan/kg)	6.65	8.00	18.00

注：1.大明湖景区2017年开始免费入园。
2.由于居民消费价格是指数比较，所以理发和洗澡所选的规格品与上年不一致，绝对价格无可比性。
3.因消费升级，商品和服务规格变化较大，零售商品和服务项目年平均价格自2019年起停止更新。

1990年	1995年	2000年	2005年	2010年	2013年	2014年	2015年	2016年	2017年	2018年
0.50	2.24	1.78	2.86	4.14	5.07	5.41	5.43	5.46	5.64	8.54
1.04	3.33	2.03	3.08	4.76	5.91	5.91	6.04	6.05	6.00	6.06
1.32	2.66	2.07	3.26	6.99	8.58	14.10	14.63	10.51	11.49	10.87
0.36	1.48	1.48	1.92	4.53	3.61	3.72	3.80	3.84	3.53	3.84
0.70	1.43	1.55	2.14	4.31	5.21	5.99	6.24	5.97	5.88	6.11
5.52	12.91	12.87	14.90	25.18	33.04	30.57	32.37	35.78	35.49	32.88
5.43	12.06	10.99	16.34	36.47	64.52	65.00	66.58	69.02	69.46	69.25
5.91	15.49	15.04	22.07	44.80	75.33	79.23	76.29	76.85	69.67	79.86
4.96	5.99	3.99	5.72	7.48	8.52	10.87	9.25	8.41	8.18	9.75
3.60	5.35	5.36	8.76	19.29	30.35	33.43	32.50	28.87	27.15	25.51
0.13	0.72	0.91	1.64	3.23	2.77	2.29	2.84	2.80	2.41	2.93
0.50	0.90	1.57	2.21	6.69	7.61	6.53	7.91	8.53	7.41	8.81
0.63	1.11	1.26	1.83	5.05	5.84	5.17	6.43	7.14	6.08	7.46
0.60	1.22	1.25	2.28	4.99	5.46	4.07	5.62	5.06	5.13	5.68
1.01	1.80	1.98	2.99	6.55	7.05	6.47	7.42	5.33	4.97	5.59
0.99	2.45	2.53	3.16	5.67	6.26	5.36	5.96	6.03	5.67	7.53
1.02	2.66	2.07	2.90	6.01	6.60	6.37	7.02	6.97	7.24	7.69
0.89	2.67	2.51	3.07	6.05	6.34	5.60	6.14	6.66	6.14	7.48
1.34	4.13	3.15	4.10	6.45	7.48	6.38	8.07	7.61	7.00	9.03
0.54	1.46	1.31	2.51	6.16	6.95	5.94	6.56	9.59	6.44	6.19
48.95	59.16	68.57	65.13	86.80	121.45	128.14	122.59	118.11	122.67	128.34
0.31	0.70	1.10	2.02	1.50	3.83	3.84	4.28	5.17	5.97	6.18
0.68	1.83	2.40	4.53	6.74	7.04	6.75	6.61	7.14	7.05	8.69
16.50	22.81	14.26	15.67	19.33	21.02	21.34	22.19	21.94	22.56	22.92
2.60	6.89	6.12	5.43	9.75	15.15	15.89	16.08	14.38	14.25	15.39
2.21	6.32	5.90	5.54	9.80	15.62	15.54	14.70	15.68	18.29	21.07
1.41	2.13	2.30	2.42	2.61	2.68	2.77	2.76	2.72	2.49	2.62
2.48	3.86	2.72	3.19	8.93	12.04	14.96	15.11	10.86	11.86	11.85
2.27	3.37	2.35	3.30	7.45	10.29	11.97	9.06	10.72	13.86	11.96
0.58	3.20	2.70	3.06	4.72	5.56	5.88	5.57	5.16	5.60	5.26
2.93	4.78	4.05	4.02	6.39	7.28	9.70	7.01	7.04	6.63	8.24
0.19	0.51	1.60	2.78	3.15	3.15	3.15	4.00	4.21	4.21	4.21
0.18	0.29	0.43	0.53	0.55	0.55	0.56	0.56	0.56	0.56	0.56
0.13	0.20	0.80	0.80	1.20	1.20	1.20	1.20	1.20	1.20	1.20
0.20	0.25	1.67	2.00	2.00	2.00	2.00	2.00	2.00	2.00	2.00
2.50	4.00	7.67	15.00	26.67	26.67	23.33	23.33	33.89	36.67	36.67
12.00	49.00	600.00	800.00	800.00	800.00	800.00	800.00	800.00	800.00	800.00
0.30	4.33	13.48	15.63	30.00	30.00	30.00	30.00	30.00		
1.30	5.63	10.00	17.50	20.50	25.00	25.21	25.21	32.38	25.10	27.70
0.58	5.00	8.00	12.00	30.00	38.00	53.00	58.00	58.00	68.00	68.00
2.00	2.55	6.41	4.60	6.47	6.47	6.47	6.47	6.47	6.44	6.39
28.00	70.00	93.00	87.22	325.00	314.10	361.17	352.71	325.00	324.39	403.83

Notes: 1.Daming Lake Scenic spot has been free since 2017.

2.Because the consumer price of residents is an index comparison, the standard products selected for haircut and bath are inconsistent with the previous year, and the absolute price is incomparable.

3.Because of consumption upgrading and large exchanges in commodity and service specifications, the annual average price of retail commodity and service items has not been updated since 2019.

9-6 住宅销售价格指数(2022年，以上月为100)

Sales Price Indices of Residential Buildings(2022,Preceding month=100)

指标	Item	一月 January	二月 February	三月 March	四月 April	五月 May	六月 June
新建住宅	**New Residential Buildings**	**100.1**	**100.1**	**100.3**	**99.8**	**100.5**	**100.3**
新建商品住宅	New Commercial Residential Buildings	100.1	100.1	100.3	99.8	100.5	100.3
90平方米及以下	Buildings below 90sq.m	100.4	100.5	100.5	99.4	101.5	100.0
90-144平方米	Buildings 90-144 sq.m	100.2	100.1	100.3	99.9	100.3	100.2
144平方米以上	Buildings above 144sq.m	99.8	100.0	100.1	99.8	100.5	100.7
二手住宅	**Second-hand House**	**99.7**	**99.8**	**99.9**	**99.2**	**99.6**	**99.9**
90平方米及以下	Buildings below 90sq.m	99.7	99.8	99.9	99.4	99.6	99.5
90-144平方米	Buildings 90-144 sq.m	99.8	99.7	100.0	99.0	99.9	100.1
144平方米以上	Buildings above 144sq.m	100.1	100.1	99.4	99.4	98.8	99.9

9-6 续表 continued

指标	Item	七月 July	八月 August	九月 September	十月 October	十一月 November	十二月 December
新建住宅	**New Residential Buildings**	**100.4**	**100.2**	**100.3**	**100.1**	**99.9**	**99.9**
新建商品住宅	New Commercial Residential Buildings	100.4	100.2	100.3	100.1	99.9	99.9
90平方米及以下	Buildings below 90sq.m	100.0	100.5	100.0	100.6	99.6	99.7
90-144平方米	Buildings 90-144 sq.m	100.3	100.0	100.3	100.1	99.9	99.8
144平方米以上	Buildings above 144sq.m	101.0	100.5	100.3	100.0	100.1	100.2
二手住宅	**Second-hand House**	**99.8**	**99.6**	**99.9**	**99.7**	**99.5**	**99.8**
90平方米及以下	Buildings below 90sq.m	100.0	99.9	99.7	99.9	99.5	99.9
90-144平方米	Buildings 90-144 sq.m	99.9	99.4	99.8	99.8	99.4	99.5
144平方米以上	Buildings above 144sq.m	99.2	99.8	100.6	99.0	100.0	100.3

9-7 住宅销售价格指数(2022年，以上年为100)
Sales Price Indices of Residential Buildings(2022,Preceding year=100)

指标	Item	一月 January	二月 February	三月 March	四月 April	五月 May	六月 June
新建住宅	**New Residential Buildings**	**105.0**	**104.8**	**104.5**	**103.5**	**102.9**	**101.7**
新建商品住宅	New Commercial Residential Buildings	105.0	104.8	104.5	103.5	102.9	101.7
90平方米及以下	Buildings below 90sq.m	105.8	106.0	106.2	105.6	105.8	103.4
90-144平方米	Buildings 90-144 sq.m	104.9	104.4	104.2	103.0	102.4	101.2
144平方米以上	Buildings above 144sq.m	105.2	105.2	104.4	103.9	103.2	102.2
二手住宅	**Second-hand House**	**100.7**	**100.8**	**100.5**	**99.1**	**98.2**	**97.6**
90平方米及以下	Buildings below 90sq.m	101.0	100.5	100.3	99.6	98.6	97.4
90-144平方米	Buildings 90-144 sq.m	101.6	100.9	100.7	98.9	98.2	98.0
144平方米以上	Buildings above 144sq.m	102.0	100.9	100.3	98.9	97.8	97.0

9-7 续表 continued

指标	Item	七月 July	八月 August	九月 September	十月 October	十一月 November	十二月 December
新建住宅	**New Residential Buildings**	**101.4**	**101.0**	**100.9**	**101.5**	**102.0**	**101.9**
新建商品住宅	New Commercial Residential Buildings	101.4	101.0	100.9	101.5	102.0	101.9
90平方米及以下	Buildings below 90sq.m	102.9	102.8	101.8	102.5	103.1	102.8
90-144平方米	Buildings 90-144 sq.m	100.8	100.4	100.5	101.2	101.5	101.4
144平方米以上	Buildings above 144sq.m	102.2	102.0	102.0	102.1	102.7	103.0
二手住宅	**Second-hand House**	**97.0**	**96.4**	**96.7**	**96.6**	**96.6**	**96.5**
90平方米及以下	Buildings below 90sq.m	97.1	96.8	96.6	96.8	97.0	97.1
90-144平方米	Buildings 90-144 sq.m	97.4	96.7	96.9	96.9	96.7	96.3
144平方米以上	Buildings above 144sq.m	95.7	95.3	96.2	95.4	95.8	96.0

9–8 主要年份工业生产者出厂、购进价格指数(以上年为100)

Producer Price Indices for Industrial Products and Purchasing Price Indices for Industrial Producers in Main Years(Preceding year=100)

年份 Year	工业生产者出厂价格指数 Producer Price Indices for Industrial Products	工业生产者购进价格指数 Purchasing Price Indices for Industrial Producer
1998	94.5	95.2
1999	98.9	97.6
2000	104.8	114.5
2001	99.8	101.4
2002	97.9	100.4
2003	103.2	111.2
2004	106.7	116.4
2005	102.3	111.3
2006	100.2	105.6
2007	103.9	105.0
2008	109.2	116.9
2009	96.2	94.3
2010	104.7	109.9
2011	105.3	108.2
2012	98.4	99.4
2013	98.8	97.8
2014	99.0	98.0
2015	95.0	92.7
2016	99.8	99.0
2017	105.7	113.9
2018	104.8	108.3
2019	100.3	98.6
2020	98.1	97.5
2021	110.3	109.5
2022	105.1	105.8

注：2020 年起，“工业生产者出厂价格指数”与“工业生产者购进价格指数”指标为全省数据。

Note:Starting in 2020,the“Producer Price Indices for Industrial Products”and“ Purchasing Price Index for Industrial Producer ”are province-wide data.

主要统计指标解释

居民消费价格指数 是反映一定时期内城乡居民所购买的生活消费品和服务项目价格变动趋势和程度的相对数。

商品零售价格指数 是反映一定时期内城乡商品零售价格变动趋势和程度的相对数。

工业生产者出厂价格指数 是反映一定时期内全部工业产品第一次出售时的出厂价格总水平的变动趋势和变动幅度的相对数。

工业生产者购进价格指数 是反映作为中间投入的原材料、燃料、动力购进价格总水平的变动趋势和变动幅度的相对数。

Explanatory Notes on Main Statistical Indicators

Consumer Price Indices are relative figures reflecting the trend and degree of changes in prices of consumer goods and services purchased by urban and rural households during a given period.

Retail Price Indices are relative figures reflecting the trend and degree of changes in retail prices of commodities during a given period.

Producer Price Indices for Industrial Products are relative figures reflecting the trend and degree of changes in general ex-factory prices of all manufactured goods for first sale during a given period.

Purchasing Price Indices for Industrial Producers are relative figures reflecting changes in the level and degree of purchasing prices such as intermediate input such as raw materials, fuels and power.

10

人民生活

PEOPLE´ S LIVELIHOOD

10-1 人民物质文化生活提高情况
Improvement in People's Material and Cultural Life

指标	Item	单位 unit	1978年
就业	**Employment**		
每一农村劳动力负担人数	Average Dependents Per Labor Force	人(person)	1.70
每一城镇就业者负担人数	Dependents Per Urban Employee	人(person)	1.89
城镇登记失业率	Registered Urban Unemployment Rate	%	
收入与支出	**Income and Expenditure**		
农村居民人均可支配收入	Per Capita Disposable Income of Rural Households	元(yuan)	111
农村居民人均消费支出	Per Capita Consumer Expenditure of Rural Households	元(yuan)	83
农村居民恩格尔系数	Engel's Coefficient of Rural Households	%	69.9
城镇居民人均可支配收入	Per Capita Disposable Income of Urban Households	元(yuan)	338
城镇居民人均消费支出	Per Capita Consumer Expenditure of Urban Households	元(yuan)	318
城镇居民恩格尔系数	Engel's Coefficient of Urban Households	%	57.1
居民储蓄	**Household Savings**		
城乡居民年末储蓄存款余额	Deposits of Urban and Rural Households	亿元(100 million yuan)	1.3
人均储蓄存款余额	Per Capita Savings Balance	元(yuan)	28.5
住房面积	**Area of Building**		
农村人均住房建筑面积	Rural Per Capita Living Space	平方米(sq.m)	9.6
城镇人均住房建筑面积	Urban Per Capita Living Space	平方米(sq.m)	4.1
交通通讯	**Traffic and Communication**		
农村每百户拥有摩托车	Number of Motorcycles Owned by Per 100 Rural Households	辆(unit)	
城镇每百户拥有摩托车	Number of Motorcycles Owned by Per 100 Urban Households	辆(unit)	
城市公用事业	**Urban Utilities**		
供水普及率	Coverage Rate of Urban Population with Access to Tap Water	%	99
每万人拥有公园绿地面积	Green Area of Park Per 10 000 Population	公顷(ha)	1.6
文化生活	**Culture Life**		
农村每百户拥有彩色电视机	Number of Color TV Sets Owned by Per 100 Rural Households	台(set)	-
城镇每百户拥有彩色电视机	Number of Color TV Sets Owned by Per 100 Urban Households	台(set)	-
教育卫生	**Education and Public Health**		
每万人口中在校大学生数	Number of College Students Per 10 000 Population	人(person)	22
每万人拥有卫生技术人员	Number of Health Technical Personnel Per 10 000 Population	人(person)	10.98
每万人拥有医院病床	Number of Beds of Hospitals and Health Centers Per 10 000 Population	张(set)	22.01

注：1.“城镇居民人均消费支出”1990年以前为“生活费支出”。
2.“人均住宅建筑面积”，2009年以前(不含)为“使用面积”口径，2002年以前(不含)为“居住面积”口径。
3.从2015年起，全市发布城乡住户调查一体化改革新口径数据，居民收支调查指标与2014年前分别实施的城镇和农村住户调查的调查范围、方法、指标口径、名称有所不同。(以下相关表同)
4.“农村居民人均可支配收入”2014年以前为“农民人均纯收入”口径。

1990年	2000年	2010年	2018年	2019年	2020年	2021年	2022年
1.61	1.40	1.35	1.4	1.4	1.4	1.3	1.4
1.72	1.71	1.67	1.4	1.5	1.3	1.4	1.4
	3.70	3.84	2.06	2.01	2.03		
731	3047	8903	17924	19454	20432	22580	23844
570	1977	5407	11172	12300	12947	14591	14883
50.5	43.5	33.6	30.5	30.1	30.4	30.5	30.5
1620	8471	25321	50146	51913	53329	57449	59459
1360	6892	15973	32977	33439	34391	36866	35788
57.5	34.6	31.6	23.5	23.8	23.5	23.5	23.8
51.1	463.0	2187.7	5008.1	6438.1	7584.1	8558.4	10226.3
975.5	8229.6	36239.0	77076.2	81389.8	94596.7	105441.9	124972.7
22.5	28.6	40.2	54.3	51.1	50.3	49.8	47.5
7.5	10.5	29.7	46.5	39.0	39.3	39.4	39.7
4.0	61.0	84.9	51.7	58.5	57.7	51.7	50.7
7.7	34.3	13.3	11.6	12.9	13.1	11.1	10.4
100	100	100	99.78	100.00	100.00	100.00	100.00
4	7.2	11.3	12.59	13.20	13.06	12.95	13.14
70.0	125.0	122.2	114.1	113.0	110.0	104.3	101.8
61.3	132.3	115.5	106.0	105.1	105.9	104.8	102.5
71	165	1064	1226	1040	1121	743	820
59.45	63.40	65.20	111.00	109.50	112.80	116.10	120.59
32.88	38.57	52.9	77.0	74.8	74.8	78.0	81.1

Notes: 1. "Per capita living expenditure of urban residents" was "cost of living expenses" before 1990.

2. "Per capita housing area" was the caliber of "usable area" before 2009 (excluding) and was the caliber of "living area" before 2002.

3. Since 2015, the city has released new caliber data for the integrated reform of urban and rural household surveys. The survey indicator of residents' income and expenditure was different from the survey scope, method, index caliber and name of urban and rural households carried out before 2014. (The same below)

4. "Per capita disposable income of rural residents" was the caliber of "rural per capita net income" before 2014.

10-2 各时期城镇居民生活情况
Basic Conditions of Urban Households in Each Period

年份 Year	人均可支配收入(元) Per Capita Disposable Income (yuan)	人均消费支出(元) Per Capita Consumer Expenditure(yuan)		就业者负担人数(人) Average Dependents Per Employee (person)	人均住宅建筑面积(平方米) Per Capita Floor Space (sq.m)
		小计 Total	#人均食品支出 Per Capita Food Expenditure		
1949	64.53	61.30	37.39		4.09
1952	130.00	127.84	77.98		4.11
1957	206.50	194.15	117.69		3.64
1962	201.74	209.84	131.42		3.48
1965	219.51	212.82	131.59		3.31
1970					3.51
1975					3.66
1978	337.80	317.88	181.56	1.89	4.06
1980	440.09	405.53	230.11	1.67	4.22
"六五"时期					
1981	487.19	452.77	256.67	1.73	4.40
1982	502.97	468.03	275.30	1.70	4.57
1983	552.37	484.87	293.32	1.66	4.93
1984	671.89	537.27	326.97	1.69	5.10
1985	783.00	703.82	397.33	1.68	5.21
"七五"时期					
1986	946.46	836.50	474.62	1.70	7.40
1987	1057.48	943.58	534.12	1.73	7.30
1988	1272.83	1150.44	635.11	1.70	7.50
1989	1487.91	1355.64	745.32	1.71	7.50
1990	1619.50	1360.08	781.58	1.72	7.50
"八五"时期					
1991	1854.33	1569.26	896.62	1.71	7.60
1992	2148.49	1781.21	979.03	1.73	7.65
1993	2873.94	2394.03	1146.02	1.74	7.80
1994	3951.94	3224.73	1566.59	1.72	7.90
1995	4720.55	3830.38	1823.64	1.80	8.00
"九五"时期					
1996	5681.49	4422.91	2161.00	1.71	8.00
1997	6261.21	5210.40	2185.11	1.62	8.10
1998	6757.12	5440.10	2179.99	1.61	9.89
1999	7162.48	6415.39	2204.76	1.66	10.00
2000	8471.32	6891.75	2387.06	1.71	10.50

10–2 续表 continued

年 份 Year	人均可支配收入 (元) Per Capita Disposable Income (yuan)	人均消费支出(元) Per Capita Consumer Expenditure(yuan)		就业者负担人数 (人) Average Dependents Per Employee (person)	人均住宅建筑面积 (平方米) Per Capita Floor Space (sq.m)
		小 计 Total	#人均食品支出 Per Capita Food Expenditure		
"十五"时期					
2001	9564.99	7465.04	2386.84	1.74	10.70
2002	10094.13	7818.33	2575.21	1.72	17.83
2003	11012.86	8395.36	2610.75	1.68	18.85
2004	12005.06	8580.54	2784.87	1.65	19.50
2005	13578.46	9226.61	3046.93	1.73	19.55
"十一五"时期					
2006	15340.17	10713.13	3335.31	1.74	20.1
2007	18005.10	12389.69	3900.91	1.72	21.0
2008	20802.17	13904.59	4466.18	1.87	21.5
2009	22721.65	14764.28	4836.78	1.86	29.4
2010	25321.06	15973.32	5051.18	1.67	29.7
"十二五"时期					
2011	28891.97	18045.58	5722.65	1.71	30.3
2012	32569.75	20031.67	6162.16	1.72	
2013	35647.59	21666.94	6624.32		
2014	38762.77	22980.67	6814.14	2.04	
2015	39888.71	26318.72	6415.00	1.80	44.9
"十三五"时期					
2016	43052.16	28536.93	6908.01	1.87	45.5
2017	46642.40	30728.60	7229.30	1.35	47.8
2018	50146	32977	7758	1.4	46.5
2019	51913	33439	7956	1.4	39.0
2020	53329	34391	8072	1.3	39.3
"十四五"时期					
2021	57449	36866	8654	1.4	39.4
2022	59459	35788	8520	1.4	39.7

注：1.可支配收入1983年以前为生活费收入,消费支出1992年以前为生活费支出。
2. "人均住宅建筑面积"，2009年以前(不含)为"使用面积"口径，2002年以前(不含)为"居住面积"口径。

Notes: 1. The disposable income was living expenditure income before 1983, and the consumption expenditure was previously the cost-of-living expenditure before 1992.
2. "Per capita housing area", was the caliber of "usable area" before 2009 (excluding) and was the caliber of "living area" before 2002.

10-3 各时期农村居民生活情况
Basic Conditions of Rural Households in Each Period

年份 Year	人均可支配收入(元) Per Capita Disposable Income (yuan)	人均消费支出(元) Per Capita Consumer Expenditure (yuan)		每一劳动力负担人数(人) Average Dependents Per Labor Force (person)	人均住宅建筑面积(平方米) Per Capita Floor Space (sq.m)
		小计 Total	#人均食品支出 Per Capita Food Expenditure		
1952	49.4	39.2	29.2	1.8	7.5
1957	63.6	57.9	34.8	1.8	7.8
1962	67.7	59.9	36.3	1.8	8.0
1965	92.6	69.7	46.1	1.8	8.2
1970	82.7	67.2	42.2	1.7	8.5
1975	79.1	59.5	40.8	1.7	9.0
1978	110.5	83.2	58.2	1.7	9.6
1980	168.9	127.1	85.8	1.6	10.5
1985	439.2	330.5	171.1	1.6	16.9
1990	731.1	569.8	287.7	1.6	22.5
1991	810.1	610.6	303.7	1.6	23.7
1992	865.3	660.5	335.1	1.6	21.1
1993	1031.4	724.8	371.4	1.6	22.9
1994	1401.0	942.5	511.0	1.6	24.1
1995	1812.7	1373.6	770.8	1.4	24.7
1996	2328.1	1728.1	926.2	1.4	26.9
1997	2600.0	1799.7	922.0	1.4	27.1
1998	2826.4	1872.5	935.9	1.4	27.4
1999	2943.7	1841.2	876.7	1.4	28.3
2000	3046.8	1976.8	860.0	1.4	28.6
2001	3215.7	2057.8	852.5	1.5	29.9
2002	3355.8	2133.9	849.5	1.4	30.6
2003	3619.3	2316.2	900.7	1.4	32.5
2004	4198.7	2543.1	1040.4	1.4	32.9
2005	4812.3	2902.8	1134.8	1.4	33.8
2006	5480.0	3415.3	1199.8	1.4	35.3
2007	6300.1	3789.8	1423.0	1.4	37.3
2008	7180.2	4385.4	1628.2	1.4	38.7
2009	7804.8	4733.1	1686.3	1.4	39.4
2010	8903.3	5406.6	1818.3	1.4	40.2
2011	10411.8	5905.1	2147.3	1.4	41.2
2012	11786.2	6932.2	2465.4	1.4	42.9
2013	13247.6	7798.7	2640.8	1.4	43.9
2014	14726.0	8581.4	2831.4	1.4	
2015	14231.8	8597.2	2775.5	1.4	52.6
2016	15345.6	9396.3	3028.0	1.4	53.8
2017	16593.8	10327.3	3253.2	1.3	55.2
2018	17924	11172	3409	1.4	54.3
2019	19454	12300	3703	1.4	51.1
2020	20432	12947	3931	1.4	50.3
2021	22580	14591	4446	1.3	49.8
2022	23844	14883	4538	1.4	47.5

注：1. “人均可支配收入”2014年以前为“农民人均纯收入”口径。
2. “人均住宅建筑面积”，2009年以前(不含)为“使用面积”口径，2002年以前(不含)为“居住面积”口径。

Notes: 1. "Per capita disposable income" was the caliber of "rural per capita net income" before 2014.
2. "Per capita housing area" was the caliber of "usable area" before 2009 (excluding) and was the caliber of "living area" before 2002 (excluding).

10-4 城镇每百户居民家庭主要耐用消费品拥有量
Main Durable Goods Owned Per 100 Urban Households

单位:台 (set)

商品名称	Item	1995年	2000年	2005年	2010年	2015年	2020年	2021年	2022年
家用汽车(辆)	Automobile(Unit)			5.4	22.7	47.6	58.5	62.1	66.1
摩托车(辆)	Motorcycle(Unit)	13.0	34.3	30.1	13.3	15.1	13.1	11.1	10.4
洗衣机	Washing Machine	91.5	100.0	97.0	93.2	98.5	98.4	98.1	98.6
电冰箱	Refrigerator	92.0	99.3	97.0	96.7	101.8	104.0	100.9	100.5
彩色电视机	Color Television Set	95.0	132.3	126.8	115.5	110.5	105.9	104.8	102.5
空调器	Air Conditioner	16.0	65.0	104.4	121.5	146.3	166.4	172.6	175.3
热水器	Water Heaters	36.5	81.3	79.3	82.0	100.3	100.6	99.5	99.8
照相机	Camera	40.5	76.0	59.2	54.0	56.1	33.8	23.5	26.7
住宅电话(部)	Fixed-line Phones	38.0	86.7	88.6	46.3	54.7	19.2	14.5	10.1
移动电话(部)	Mobile Phones		28.7	145.2	179.7	213.5	225.7	227.6	239.5
计算机	Computer		20.0	54.2	81.0	90.8	83.2	80.2	79.5

10-5 农村每百户居民家庭主要耐用消费品拥有量
Main Durable Goods Owned Per 100 Rural Households

单位:台 (set)

商品名称	Item	2011年	2012年	2013年	2015年	2019年	2020年	2021年	2022年
家用汽车(辆)	Automobile(Unit)					39	37	41	46
摩托车(辆)	Motorcycle(Unit)	71	62	65	79	58	58	52	51
洗衣机	Washing Machine	82	86	88	86	93	91	91	93
电冰箱	Refrigerator	88	91	92	91	99	98	96	97
彩色电视机	Color Television Set	116	118	119	114	113	110	104	102
空调器	Air Conditioner	36	39	46	56	93	90	94	97
热水器	Water Heaters	64	69	69	74	82	86	89	90
照相机	Camera	15	14	16	8	6	3	4	6
住宅电话(部)	Fixed-line Phones	60	58	55	47	21	20	16	9
移动电话(部)	Mobile Phones	175	186	195	214	232	229	230	236
计算机	Computer	36	39	43	40	39	43	42	42

10-6 居民人均可支配收入和消费支出(2022年)
Per Capita Disposable Income and Consumer Expenditure(2022)

单位：元 (yuan)

指标名称	Item	全体居民 All Households	城镇居民 Urban households	农村居民 Rural households
可支配收入	**Disposable Income**	**48827**	**59459**	**23844**
工资性收入	Income of Wages and Salaries	28259	34694	13138
经营净收入	Net Business Income	4890	3249	8746
财产净收入	Net Income from Properties	7221	10078	506
转移净收入	Net Income from Transfers	8457	11437	1455
消费支出	**Consumption Expenditure**	**29547**	**35788**	**14883**
食品烟酒	Food,Tobacco and liquor	7331	8520	4538
衣着	Clothing and Footwear	1674	2069	744
居住	Housing	8622	10929	3200
生活用品及服务	Household Equipments, Furnishings and Services	2066	2538	958
交通通信	Transport and Communications	3889	4572	2284
教育文化娱乐	Education, Culture and Recreation	3146	3845	1503
医疗保健	Health care and Medical Services	2212	2545	1429
其他用品和服务	Miscellaneous Goods and Services	607	770	226

主要统计指标解释

居民可支配收入 指居民可用于最终消费支出和储蓄的总和，即居民可用于自由支配的收入。既包括现金收入，也包括实物收入。按照收入的来源，可支配收入包含四项，分别为：工资性收入、经营净收入、财产净收入和转移净收入。

工资性收入 指就业人员通过各种途径得到的全部劳动报酬和各种福利，包括受雇于单位或个人、从事各种自由职业、兼职和零星劳动得到的全部劳动报酬和福利。

经营净收入 指住户或住户成员从事生产经营活动所获得的净收入，是全部经营收入中扣除经营费用、生产性固定资产折旧和生产税之后得到的净收入。计算公式为：

经营净收入=经营收入-经营费用-生产性固定资产折旧-生产税

财产净收入 指住户或住户成员将其所拥有的金融资产、住房等非金融资产和自然资源交由其他机构单位、住户或个人支配而获得的回报并扣除相关的费用之后得到的净收入。财产净收入包括利息净收入、红利收入、储蓄性保险净收益、转让承包土地经营权租金净收入、出租房屋净收入、出租其他资产净收入和自有住房折算净租金等。财产净收入不包括转让资产所有权的溢价所得。

转移净收入 计算公式为：转移净收入=转移性收入-转移性支出

转移性收入 指国家、单位、社会团体对住户的各种经常性转移支付和住户之间的经常性收入转移。包括养老金或退休金、社会救济和补助、政策性生产补贴、政策性生活补贴、经常性捐赠和赔偿、报销医疗费、住户之间的赡养收入，本住户非常住成员寄回带回的收入等。转移性收入不包括住户之间的实物馈赠。

转移性支出 指调查户对国家、单位、住户或个人的经常性或义务性转移支付。包括缴纳的税款、各项社会保障支出、赡养支出、经常性捐赠和赔偿支出以及其他经常转移支出等。

根据住户收支与生活状况调查，分城镇和农村的居民人均可支配收入等数据的覆盖人群主要变化：一是计算城镇居民人均可支配收入时分母包括了在城镇地区常住的农民工，计算农村居民人均可支配收入时分母不包括在城镇地区常住的农民工；二是由本户供养的在外大学生视为常住人口。

居民消费支出 指居民用于满足家庭日常生活消费需要的全部支出，既包括现金消费支出，也包括实物消费支出。消费支出可划分为食品烟酒、衣着、居住、生活用品及服务、交通通信、教育文化娱乐、医疗保健以及其他用品及服务八大类。

食品烟酒 指用于各种食品和烟草、酒类的支出。

衣着 指与居民穿着有关的支出，包括服装、服装材料、鞋类、其他衣类及配件、衣着相关加工服务的支出。

居住 指与居住有关的支出，包括房租、水、电、燃料、物业管理等方面的支出，也包括自有住房折算租金。

生活用品及服务 指家庭及个人的各类生活品及家庭服务。包括家具及室内装饰品、家用器具、家用纺织品、家庭日用杂品、个人用品和家庭服务。

交通通信 指用于交通和通信工具及相关的各种服务费、维修费和车辆保险等支出。

教育文化娱乐 指用于教育、文化和娱乐方面的支出。

医疗保健 指用于医疗和保健的药品、用品和服务的总费用。包括医疗器具及药品，以及医疗服务。

其他用品及服务 指无法直接归入上述各类支出的其他用品与服务支出。

服务性消费 指住户用于各种生活服务的消费支出，包括餐饮服务、衣着鞋类加工服务、居住服务、家庭服务、交通通信服务、教育文化娱乐服务、医疗服务和其他服务等。

Explanatory Notes on Main Statistical Indicators

Disposable Income of Residents refers to the income of residents for purpose of final expenditure and savings. It includes income both in cash and in kind. By sources of income, disposable income includes four categories: income from wages and salaries, net business income, net income from properties and net income from transfer.

Income from Wages and Salaries refers to remuneration and benefits of all kinds of employed persons, including those employed by other units or individuals, freelance workers, part-time jobs, and sporadic workers.

Net Business Income refers to net income earned by households and their members engaged in production and business activities. It refers to the net income of operating revenue minus operating costs, depreciation of productive fixed assets, and production tax. The formula is:

Net business income = operating revenue-operating costs -depreciation of productive fixed assets-production tax

Net Income from Properties refers to the net income received as returns by households or members through lending of their financial assets, non-financial assets such as housing, to other institutions, households or individuals, minus relevant costs. Net income from properties includes net income of interest, bonus income, net income of saving insurance, net income from transferring management right of contract land, income from lending of housing, income from lending other assets, net converted rents of self-owned housing. Net income from properties do not include premium of transferring ownership of assets.

Net Income from Transfer The formula is:

Net income from transfer = income from transfer - expenditure from transfer

Income from Transfer refers to the regular transfer received from governments, institutions, social organizations to households and between households. It includes old-age and retirement pension, regular donation and compensation, reimbursement of medical fees, supporting income between households, income from non-resident members of households, etc. Income from transfer do not include gifts in kinds between households.

Expenditure from Transfer refers to regular or obligatory transfer paid to government, institutions, households or individuals. It includes tax payment, expenditure on all kinds of social security, supporting expenditure, regular donation, compensation payment and other regular transfer expenditure.

According to Household Survey on Income and Expenditure and Living Conditions, main changes of population coverage of per capita disposable income of urban and rural residents includes: migrant workers residing in urban areas are included in the denominator when calculating per capita disposable income of urban residents, and not included in denominator when calculating per capita disposable income of rural residents; students studying in universities or colleges in other places who are supported by the households are regarded as permanent residents of the households.

Consumption Expenditure of Residents refers to all expenditure of residents for living expenditure to satisfy family daily living. It includes expenditure in cash and in kind. It includes eight categories: food, tobacco and liquor; clothing and footwear; housing; household equipments, furnishings and services; transport and communications; education, culture and recreation; health care and medical services, and miscellaneous goods and services.

Food, Tobacco and Liquor refers to expenditure for food, tobacco and liquor of all kinds.

Clothing and Footwear refers to expenditure related to clothing, including clothes, clothing materials, footwear, other clothing and accessories, processing services related to clothing.

Housing refers to expenditure related to housing, including rents, water, electricity, fuel, property management, as well as imputed rent on owner-occupied dwellings.

Household Equipments, Furnishings and Services refers to expenditure of households and individuals on equipments, furnishings and articles for living purpose and on household services. It includes furniture and interior decoration, home appliances, home textiles, household miscellaneous daily articles, personal articles, and household services.

Transport and Communications refers to expenditure on transport and communication and related services, maintenance and repairs, and vehicle insurance.

Education, Culture and Recreation refers to expenditure on educational, cultural and recreational activities.

Health Care and Medical Services refers to expenditure on drugs, supplies and services of medical and health care. It includes medical appliances and drugs, and medical services.

Miscellaneous Goods and Services refers to expenditure on all other articles and services that can not classified into the above categories.

Service Consumption refers to consumption expenditure of households for various living services, including catering services, clothing and footwear processing services, housing services, household services, transportation and communication services, education, culture and entertainment services, medical services and other services.

11

农 业

AGRICULTURE

11-1 各时期农业主要经济指标
Major Economic Indicators of Agriculture in Each Period

年份 Year	农村劳动力(万人) Rural Labor (10 000 persons)	农林牧渔业总产值(亿元) Gross Output Value of Farming, Forestry,Animal Husbandry and Fishery (100 million yuan)	农业机械总动力(万千瓦) Total Agricultural Machinery Power (10 000 kW)	年末实有耕地面积(千公顷) Actual Cultivated Area (1000 ha)	粮食总产量(万吨) Output of Grain (10 000 tons)	蔬菜总产量(万吨) Output of Vegetables (10 000 tons)	肉类总产量(万吨) Output of Meat (10 000 tons)	粮食单产(千克/公顷) Output Per Hectare of Grain (kg/ha)
1949	106.51	1.50	-	469.85	51.63	10.72	0.24	825
1952	112.35	1.91	-	481.17	62.75	8.61	0.40	960
1957	121.09	2.79	0.32	479.58	67.92	15.86	0.66	1065
1962	108.44	1.33	2.98	412.34	39.74	27.67	0.72	765
1965	111.74	2.61	4.84	410.02	73.80	29.12	1.12	1350
1970	123.91	2.75	14.32	396.49	75.47	31.81	1.21	1470
1975	141.00	4.07	48.04	382.05	100.46	42.00	2.07	2025
1978	140.05	6.57	69.70	373.19	115.38	49.19	2.50	2475
1979	141.60	7.48	80.63	372.45	122.56	49.42	2.92	2610
1980	143.19	7.79	88.45	370.87	116.54	58.13	3.69	2565
"六五"时期								
1981	146.52	11.73	94.47	369.80	121.27	49.85	3.99	2865
1982	149.07	14.47	106.60	369.22	121.13	63.45	4.31	3060
1983	152.39	18.07	112.19	368.45	147.41	65.66	4.66	3570
1984	158.23	19.00	123.92	367.35	160.60	86.91	5.03	3915
1985	162.51	18.36	130.41	357.41	163.50	84.11	5.43	3915
"七五"时期								
1986	165.86	20.91	147.36	353.96	168.16	118.86	6.44	3855
1987	168.56	24.65	156.23	352.18	167.25	101.52	7.13	3945
1988	171.44	34.24	172.89	350.56	167.95	122.83	8.68	4080
1989	173.38	35.14	182.40	349.59	162.45	117.99	9.70	3945
1990	176.83	36.92	183.40	347.56	181.47	126.09	11.38	4273
"八五"时期								
1991	180.09	40.13	191.00	344.76	207.55	146.87	13.50	4779
1992	182.51	45.14	191.50	343.29	198.29	170.61	15.36	4655
1993	183.78	57.81	194.40	341.54	232.21	205.62	19.12	4963
1994	183.42	85.37	207.40	339.97	237.66	226.39	26.14	5237
1995	183.55	114.07	241.20	339.30	252.48	253.54	28.68	5512
"九五"时期								
1996	184.68	117.65	247.07	337.25	267.08	350.36	30.43	5602
1997	186.68	131.69	258.50	335.90	240.34	328.64	24.75	5064
1998	186.54	141.45	273.30	334.83	273.10	344.67	27.38	5634
1999	188.27	148.61	297.55	333.72	279.01	366.78	29.89	5752
2000	189.15	154.30	349.47	333.72	240.27	405.95	31.82	5354

注：1.自2005年始年末实有耕地面积有国土资源局提供，暂无2009年数据。
2.依据2006年农业普查数据，对1997年至2007年蔬菜面积、产量做了相应调整。
3.粮食作物产量、播种面积自2012年开始由山东调查总队反馈。
4.按照国务院农普办要求，由国家统计局山东调查总队根据第三次农业普查数据，对2016-2017年市.县(区)粮食播种面积.单产和总产量等数据进行了修订。
5.依据2016年农业普查数据，对2007年至2017年农林牧渔业总产值做了相应调整。
6.依据2016年农业普查数据，对2008年至2017年蔬菜总产量、肉类总产量做了相应调整。
7.2019年农业数据为区划调整后的数据，以下各表同。
8.由于市农业农村局未提供农业机械类指标数据，2020年延用 2019 年数据。以下相关各表同。
9.根据国家统计局最新报表制度，"农村劳动力"指标2022年起不再进行统计。

11-1 续表 continued

年份 Year	农村劳动力 (万人) Rural Labor (10 000 persons)	农林牧渔业总产值(亿元) Gross Output Value of Farming, Forestry,Animal Husbandry and Fishery (100 million yuan)	农业机械总动力 (万千瓦) Total Agricultural Machinery Power (10 000 kW)	年末实有耕地面积 (千公顷) Actual Cultivated Area (1000 ha)	粮食总产量 (万吨) Output of Grain (10 000 tons)	蔬菜总产量 (万吨) Output of Vegetables (10 000 tons)	肉类总产量 (万吨) Output of Meat (10 000 tons)	粮食单产 (千克/公顷) Output Per Hectare of Grain (kg/ha)
"十五"时期								
2001	189.87	162.27	409.07	331.75	239.08	435.20	33.23	5480
2002	190.98	167.99	410.17	329.35	189.86	478.34	31.87	4440
2003	192.71	180.30	417.43	325.18	220.56	504.81	33.29	5448
2004	191.31	204.39	418.54	324.89	242.74	515.26	35.35	5807
2005	190.21	230.46	426.76	366.99	260.11	529.37	37.93	5932
"十一五"时期								
2006	190.80	247.70	429.62	361.74	267.91	536.28	38.74	6042
2007	191.16	262.51	446.60	358.80	268.01	522.24	31.85	6064
2008	190.45	302.00	466.00	361.33	281.50	520.25	30.22	6230
2009	195.56	318.06	486.00		289.47	560.83	31.39	6246
2010	196.85	361.24	509.68	362.30	289.43	572.05	31.79	6192
"十二五"时期								
2011	197.38	399.90	527.39	361.25	295.84	590.02	32.43	6315
2012	198.74	422.75	538.66	360.28	286.03	606.11	33.22	6285
2013	199.80	470.55	552.06	361.01	266.60	629.54	33.59	5997
2014	199.73	479.50	567.02	360.24	271.19	638.22	34.10	6109
2015	200.45	493.04	584.98	358.57	264.55	626.23	34.18	6117
"十三五"时期								
2016	200.46	501.72	447.83	357.60	275.43	611.25	31.72	5778
2017	198.91	505.08	442.90	355.66	255.57	591.63	32.50	5660
2018	189.10	514.90	454.62	353.65	251.42	527.22	29.82	5659
2019	239.03	637.30	543.48	344.82	285.46	671.24	35.86	5956
2020	222.13	671.66	543.48	342.29	290.81	673.73	23.92	6053
"十四五"时期								
2021	212.69	758.41	570.10	342.56	293.07	691.76	27.36	6060
2022		784.24	594.94	342.88	296.19	712.61	29.10	6112

Notes: 1. Since 2005, the actual cultivated area has been provided by Land Resources Bureau. No data for 2009.
2. According to the data of the agricultural census in 2006, the area and yield of the vegetables from 1997 to 2007 were adjusted accordingly.
3. Grain crop yield and sown area have been reported by Shandong Survey Team since 2012.
4. According to the requirements of Agricultural Census Office of the State Council, Shandong Survey Team of National Bureau of Statistics revised the grain sown area, yield per unit and total yield of each city and country (district) from 2016-2017 based on the data from the third agricultural census.
5. According to the data of the agricultural census in 2016, the total output value of agriculture, forestry, animal husbandry and fishery in the period from 2007 to 2017 was adjusted accordingly.
6. According to the data of the agricultural census in 2016, the total output value of vegetable and meat in the period from 2008 to 2017 was adjusted accordingly.
7.The data of agriculture in 2019 is the adjusted data by the administrative division (the same below).
8.Due to the municipal bureau of agriculture and rural affairs didn't provide data on agricultural machines index, thus the data of 2019 is adopted. The same for the following tables.
9.The index of "rural labor force" will not be counted from 2022 in light of the latest report system of National Bureau of Statistics.

11-2 农村基层组织和农业基本情况
Basic Conditions of Rural Grassroots Units and Agriculture

指标	Item	单位 Unit	2018年	2019年	2020年	2021年	2022年
乡镇数量	Number of Towns	个(Unit)	29	40	29	29	29
#镇	Towns	个(Unit)	29	40	29	29	29
村民委员会	Village Committee	个(Unit)	4546	5551	5530	4699	4698
耕地	Cultivated Land	公顷(ha)	353652	344821	342289	342562	342881
其中：水浇地	Irrigated Land	公顷(ha)	263885	269859	268186	270893	271483
园地	Garden Land	公顷(ha)	25675	101941	102052	101351	99552
林地	Forest Land	公顷(ha)	83947	248283	247879	244444	242315
草地	Pasture Land	公顷(ha)	56879	27048	27300	26994	28903
城镇村及工矿用地	Land for Urban Village, Mining and Manufacturing	公顷(ha)	149020	187602	189766	191113	191650
交通运输用地	Land for Transport Facilities	公顷(ha)	30216	19176	19391	20837	22006
水域及水利设施用地	Land for Water Conservancy Facilities	公顷(ha)	50531	58953	58956	60144	59975
农业机械总动力	Total Agricultural Machinery Power	万千瓦(10 000 kW)	454.62	543.48	543.48	570.10	594.94
农用大中型拖拉机	Large and Medium-sized Tractors	台(set)	20208	23553	23553	25498	27040
农用小型拖拉机	Small Tractors	台(set)	30152	49911	49911	48261	47705
谷物联合收割机	Combine Harvester	台(set)	14380	15746	15746	16838	9364
脱粒机	Thresher	台(set)	19660	27007	27007	25932	25821
农用化肥使用量	Consumption of Chemical Fertilizer	吨(折纯) (ton convert to pure volume)	199591	214814	205007	199919	194361
农药使用量	Pesticides Consumption	吨(ton)	2692.9	3477.5	3231.4	2960.8	2846.5
农作物总播种面积	Total Sown Area of Farm Crops	千公顷(1000 ha)	549.0	615.6	614.3	614.8	617.7

11-3 分地区农村基层组织和农业基本情况(2022年)
Basic Conditions of Rural Grassroots Units and Agriculture by Region（2022）

指标	Item	单位 Unit	济南市 Jinan	历下区 Li xia
乡镇数量	Number of Towns	个(Unit)	29	
#镇	Towns	个(Unit)	29	
村民委员会	Village Committee	个(Unit)	4698	
耕地	Cultivated Land	公顷(ha)	342881	66
其中：水浇地	Irrigated Land	公顷(ha)	271483	9
园地	Garden Land	公顷(ha)	99552	77
林地	Forest Land	公顷(ha)	242315	2565
草地	Pasture Land	公顷(ha)	28903	98
城镇村及工矿用地	Land for Urban Village, Mining and Manufacturing	公顷(ha)	191650	7131
交通运输用地	Land for Transport Facilities	公顷(ha)	22006	86
水域及水利设施用地	Land for Water Conservancy Facilities	公顷(ha)	59975	37
农业机械总动力	Total Agricultural Machinery Power	万千瓦(10 000 kW)	594.9	2.8
农用大中型拖拉机	Large and Medium-sized Tractors	台(set)	27040	47
农用小型拖拉机	Small Tractors	台(set)	47705	485
谷物联合收割机	Combine Harvester	台(set)	9364	14
脱粒机	Thresher	台(set)	25821	17
农用化肥使用量	Consumption of Chemical Fertilizer	吨(折纯) (ton convert to pure volume)	194361	
农药使用量	Pesticides Consumption	吨(ton)	2846.5	
农作物总播种面积	Total Sown Area of Farm Crops	千公顷(1000 ha)	617.7	

市中区 Shi zhong	槐荫区 Huai yin	天桥区 Tian qiao	历城区 Li cheng	长清区 Chang qing	章丘区 Zhang qiu	济阳区 Ji yang	莱芜区 Lai Wu	钢城区 Gang Cheng	平阴县 Ping yin	商河县 Shang he
				2	1	2	7		6	11
				2	1	2	7		6	11
77	93	48	266	585	532	566	792	211	308	516
2987	1534	8061	13204	30325	61913	64278	45649	11126	27324	76415
779	617	7907	9597	17044	46788	63576	25546	2089	21122	76409
2836	362	532	29506	18297	13847	1415	19497	5250	7435	500
9178	1890	3032	42494	40943	37476	9770	53475	15881	17141	8469
969	259	537	3285	4088	7989	544	7204	2006	1431	493
10280	7645	8688	29724	15828	31602	16801	26875	10291	10302	16484
820	1009	989	4415	1879	3248	2083	3727	972	1226	1553
379	2291	3671	4814	4375	8969	12440	8458	2072	2753	9715
12.9	3.9	3.8	51.8	54.1	103.3	122.9	72.0	20.0	50.2	97.4
390	246	217	1764	3139	3790	5919	2403	514	1968	6643
412	288	82	5383	3489	2243	5478	15390	4525	5005	4925
64	110	92	728	846	2238	1636	538	114	509	2475
121	2276		1227	886	2193	7214	6702	1301	705	3179
505	190	2764	10968	11826	43141	28935	23795	3345	13755	55137
20.2	4.2	26.1	243.7	316.8	385.3	594.3	549.7	205.5	128.2	372.6
4.1	2.5	12.7	25.5	56.6	140.7	116.2	60.0	11.3	49.3	138.8

11-4 各时期农林牧渔业总产值(按当年价格计算)

Gross Output Value of Agriculture, Forestry, Animal Husbandry and Fishery in Each Period(Calculated at Current Prices)

单位:亿元 (100 million yuan)

年份 Year	合计 Total	其中 of which 农业 Farming	林业 Forestry	牧业 Animal Husbandry	渔业 Fishery	农林牧渔服务业 Services of Agriculture, Forestry,Animal Husbandry and Fishing
1952	1.91	1.67	0.04	0.18	0.02	-
1957	2.79	2.41	0.09	0.28	0.01	-
1962	1.33	1.18	0.03	0.12		-
1965	2.61	2.25	0.07	0.28	0.01	-
1970	2.75	2.32	0.10	0.32	0.01	-
1975	4.07	3.48	0.13	0.44	0.02	-
1978	6.57	5.63	0.20	0.72	0.02	-
1980	7.78	6.66	0.18	0.93	0.01	-
1985	18.36	14.63	0.75	2.93	0.05	-
“七五”时期						
1986	20.91	16.81	0.79	3.23	0.08	-
1987	24.65	19.50	0.99	4.05	0.11	-
1988	34.24	24.83	1.42	7.67	0.32	-
1989	35.14	25.04	1.24	8.47	0.39	-
1990	36.92	24.70	1.41	10.36	0.45	-
“八五”时期						
1991	40.13	26.44	1.47	11.64	0.58	-
1992	45.14	29.01	1.70	13.71	0.72	-
1993	57.81	36.00	1.98	18.86	0.97	-
1994	85.37	52.36	2.80	29.38	0.83	-
1995	114.07	71.48	2.71	38.69	1.19	-
“九五”时期						
1996	117.65	77.16	3.35	35.25	1.89	-
1997	131.69	87.91	3.86	38.04	1.88	-
1998	141.45	93.56	3.55	42.17	2.17	-
1999	148.61	96.81	3.12	46.27	2.41	-
2000	154.30	100.18	3.64	48.34	2.14	-
“十五”时期						
2001	162.27	105.54	3.27	51.16	2.30	-
2002	167.99	106.27	3.51	55.84	2.37	-
2003	180.30	109.41	4.11	60.90	2.05	3.83
2004	204.39	121.28	4.49	71.87	2.50	4.25
2005	230.46	137.01	5.56	80.56	2.69	4.64
“十一五”时期						
2006	247.72	147.98	6.44	84.86	2.89	5.55
2007	262.51	154.32	7.28	91.33	3.18	6.41
2008	302.00	173.32	10.63	104.53	4.54	8.97

11-4 续表 continued

单位:亿元 (100 million yuan)

年 份 Year	合计 Total	其中 of which				
		农业 Farming	林业 Forestry	牧业 Animal Husbandry	渔业 Fishery	农林牧渔服务业 Services of Agriculture, Forestry,Animal Husbandry and Fishing
2009	318.06	192.96	11.16	98.96	4.79	10.18
2010	361.24	231.08	6.87	106.40	5.31	11.58
"十二五"时期						
2011	399.90	240.80	7.98	131.55	6.05	13.51
2012	422.75	251.57	9.00	139.90	6.88	15.39
2013	470.55	284.66	10.34	149.46	8.01	18.07
2014	479.50	291.94	11.19	147.57	8.76	20.03
2015	493.04	296.93	12.15	153.12	9.32	21.52
"十三五"时期						
2016	501.72	298.63	13.20	156.28	9.88	23.74
2017	505.08	296.75	15.25	159.23	7.80	26.06
2018	514.90	318.55	17.72	141.48	7.28	29.88
2019	637.30	424.04	24.99	144.53	6.79	36.96
2020	671.66	447.15	29.82	149.14	6.10	39.46
"十四五"时期						
2021	758.41	501.98	34.41	170.99	8.20	42.83
2022	784.24	526.03	32.02	170.22	8.48	47.48
2022年分地区Region						
历下区 Li xia						
市中区 Shi zhong	3.31	0.75	0.08	2.28		0.21
槐荫区 Huai yin	4.46	2.97	0.55	0.23	0.56	0.15
天桥区 Tian qiao	2.77	1.30	0.09	1.22	0.08	0.08
历城区 Li cheng	74.11	50.07	9.69	7.09	0.37	6.89
长清区 Chang qing	74.20	51.22	3.32	16.13	0.69	2.85
章丘区 Zhang qiu	184.05	125.11	5.29	39.69	1.42	12.54
济阳区 Ji yang	94.81	71.48	2.41	15.46	1.33	4.13
莱芜区 Lai Wu	133.27	95.24	1.57	30.79	1.71	3.95
钢城区 Gang Cheng	23.11	12.49	1.95	7.51	0.13	1.04
平阴县 Ping yin	78.92	48.73	2.68	20.17	0.56	6.78
商河县 Shang he	111.21	66.67	4.40	29.65	1.62	8.87

注：1.依据2016年农业普查数据，对2007年至2017年农林牧渔业总产值做了相应调整。
2.天桥区农林牧渔业总产值仅包含桑梓店街道农林牧渔业产值。

Notes: 1.According to the data of the agricultural census in 2016, the total output value of agriculture, forestry, animal husbandry and fishery in the period from 2007 to 2017 was adjusted accordingly.
2.The gross output value of agriculture, forestry, animal husbandry and fishery in Tianqiao District only includes the output value of agriculture, forestry, animal husbandry and fishery in Sangzidian Sub-District.

11-5 各时期农林牧渔业总产值指数(以1952年为100)

Gross Output Value Indices of Agriculture, Forestry, Animal Husbandry and Fishery in Each Period(1952=100)

年份 Year	合计 Total	其中 of which			
		农业 Farming	林业 Forestry	牧业 Animal Husbandry	渔业 Fishery
1952	100.00	100.00	100.00	100.00	100.00
1957	116.18	114.55	170.35	119.90	109.96
1962	73.32	74.42	69.10	69.25	20.68
1965	123.31	121.76	147.34	141.38	28.95
1970	151.35	146.28	254.82	184.02	58.65
1975	201.09	196.80	317.61	226.74	78.38
“五五”时期					
1976	198.67	185.64	340.19	269.52	118.70
1977	197.95	190.19	373.20	218.87	56.26
1978	208.10	203.90	304.32	239.93	57.89
1979	233.93	224.05	316.47	293.89	53.70
1980	264.53	259.07	286.30	330.80	43.98
“六五”时期					
1981	279.36	279.29	281.28	377.56	55.36
1982	312.68	308.75	346.83	460.13	51.95
1983	402.03	369.18	434.91	460.59	57.98
1984	493.28	436.59	572.67	651.29	69.52
1985	505.48	460.68	992.56	841.94	161.47
“七五”时期					
1986	531.29	488.47	964.62	857.25	229.32
1987	560.14	506.85	1075.00	960.76	291.92
1988	585.14	510.86	992.11	1191.92	383.08
1989	571.95	483.32	886.96	1320.55	495.30
1990	607.77	449.63	1126.99	1931.15	695.49
“八五”时期					
1991	670.19	488.17	1189.04	2204.93	830.45
1992	712.62	491.78	1298.34	2574.55	1007.33
1993	844.31	566.55	1420.51	3221.58	1209.21
1994	945.74	603.90	1671.10	2864.71	1064.29
1995	1093.57	657.49	1508.72	4905.57	1945.11
“九五”时期					
1996	1197.20	727.03	1818.36	5258.95	2224.25

11-5 续表 continued

年 份 Year	合计 Total	其中 of which			
		农业 Farming	林业 Forestry	牧业 Animal Husbandry	渔业 Fishery
1997	1273.56	820.27	2002.99	5116.96	2202.07
1998	1426.28	914.05	1858.14	5907.41	2516.54
1999	1486.09	934.64	2110.21	6277.65	2639.47
2000	1569.90	991.58	2255.81	6620.62	2441.73
"十五"时期					
2001	1599.32	1005.16	1700.16	6905.18	2646.43
2002	1638.09	997.16	1826.57	7349.57	2712.97
2003	1711.88	1072.24	1977.78	7726.93	2324.25
2004	1804.32	1132.29	1979.76	8121.00	2803.05
2005	1930.62	1188.90	2237.13	8770.68	2802.30
"十一五"时期					
2006	2046.15	1249.31	2454.25	9245.35	3003.10
2007	2046.15	1334.26	2610.83	9006.43	3540.65
2008	2148.45	1422.32	2783.14	9231.59	3204.85
2009	2260.17	1524.73	2964.04	9342.35	3323.43
2010	2367.76	1584.02	1815.08	10311.68	3416.48
"十二五"时期					
2011	2471.94	1658.47	2016.56	10600.40	3508.72
2012	2588.12	1724.80	2216.20	11151.62	3768.36
2013	2689.05	1762.74	2491.01	11809.56	3877.64
2014	2801.99	1845.58	2724.66	12116.60	3916.41
2015	2919.67	1924.93	2986.23	12540.68	4033.90
"十三五"时期					
2016	3045.21	2007.70	3317.70	12967.06	4187.19
2017	3157.88	2126.15	3689.28	13278.26	4203.93
2018	3095.96	2215.44	4105.56	12733.85	4330.04
2019	3123.82	2290.76	5037.52	11587.80	3814.77
2020	3205.04	2361.77	5979.54	11460.33	3715.59
"十四五"时期					
2021	3474.26	2456.24	6942.25	14142.05	5164.67
2022	3630.61	2571.68	6970.01	14523.88	5474.55

11-6 主要农作物播种面积及产量
Sown Areas and Output of Major Farm Crops

指标	Item	2018年	2019年	2020年	2021年	2022年
农作物总播种面积(万公顷)	**Total Sown Area of Crops(10 000 ha)**	**54.90**	**61.56**	**61.43**	**61.48**	**61.77**
粮食作物	Grain Crops	44.43	47.93	48.04	48.36	48.46
谷物	Cereals	43.25	46.33	46.38	46.74	46.71
小麦	Wheat	21.38	21.89	21.73	21.95	21.96
稻谷	Rice	0.14	0.14	0.06	0.08	0.09
玉米	Corn	20.84	23.18	23.53	23.64	23.60
谷子	Millet	0.86	1.09	1.03	1.04	1.05
高粱	Jowar	0.02	0.01	0.01	0.01	0.01
其他	Others	0.01	0.01	0.01	0.01	0.01
豆类	Beans	0.62	0.77	0.77	0.75	0.86
薯类	Tubers	0.56	0.83	0.90	0.88	0.89
油料作物	Oil-bearing Crops	1.02	1.92	1.81	1.75	1.76
#花生	Peanuts	0.90	1.81	1.67	1.62	1.63
棉花	Cotton	0.28	0.38	0.35	0.33	0.30
蔬菜	Vegetable	7.89	10.03	9.86	9.74	9.93
果用瓜	Melon	1.07	0.98	0.96	1.00	1.01
其他作物	Other Farm Crops	0.21	0.32	0.40	0.30	0.31
果园种植面积(万公顷)	**Orchard Area(10 000 ha)**	**3.09**	**3.89**	**3.95**	**3.83**	**3.82**
#苹果	Apple	1.13	1.24	1.20	1.20	1.19
梨	Pear	0.16	0.18	0.19	0.21	0.20
葡萄	Grape	0.11	0.11	0.11	0.11	0.12
桃	Peach	0.72	1.00	1.03	0.97	0.95
农作物总产量(万吨)	**Total Output of Farm Crops(10 000 tons)**					
粮食作物	Grain Crops	251.42	285.46	290.81	293.07	296.19
谷物	Cereals	246.12	276.48	280.74	283.22	286.13
小麦	Wheat	121.78	135.31	137.37	139.25	139.69
稻谷	Rice	1.18	1.21	0.52	0.63	0.66
玉米	Corn	119.82	136.11	139.16	139.56	142.11
谷子	Millet	3.27	3.80	3.64	3.73	3.64
高粱	Chinese Sorghum	0.04	0.03	0.02	0.03	0.02
其他	Other Cereals	0.03	0.03	0.03	0.03	0.02
豆类	Beans	1.67	2.12	2.13	2.05	2.25
薯类	Tubers	3.63	6.86	7.93	7.80	7.80
油料作物	Oil-bearing Crops	4.15	6.57	6.82	6.60	6.62
#花生	Peanuts	3.87	6.31	6.48	6.29	6.34

11-6 续表 continued

指标	Item	2018年	2019年	2020年	2021年	2022年
棉花	Cotton	0.29	0.54	0.42	0.38	0.35
蔬菜	Vegetable	527.22	671.24	673.73	691.76	712.61
果用瓜	Melon	59.65	48.02	49.49	50.54	52.28
水果总产量(万吨)	**Output of Fruits(10 000 tons)**	**42.19**	**62.95**	**63.20**	**61.90**	**61.99**
#苹果	Apple	16.00	20.22	18.92	19.26	19.13
梨	Pear	3.40	4.19	3.80	4.16	4.01
葡萄	Grape	3.00	3.13	3.21	3.33	3.49
桃	Peach	11.86	21.40	21.87	20.12	19.56
杏	Apricot	3.02	4.11	4.01	3.47	3.54
枣(鲜)	Jujube	0.89	1.21	1.01	0.97	1.00
柿子(鲜)	Persimmon	1.24	2.29	2.51	2.63	2.69
山楂	Hawthorn	0.63	2.19	2.80	3.15	3.32
樱桃	Cherry	1.51	2.78	3.82	3.60	3.93
其他	Others	0.64	1.19	0.98	0.90	11.70
农作物单位面积产量(公斤/公顷)	**Output per Hectare of Farm Crops(kg/ha)**					
粮食作物	Grain Crops	5659	5956	6053	6060	6112
谷物	Cereals	5690	5968	6053	6060	6126
小麦	Wheat	5696	6181	6321	6344	6362
稻谷	Rice	8288	8334	8250	7771	7327
玉米	Corn	5748	5872	5914	5903	6022
谷子	Millet	3809	3490	3522	3586	3477
高粱	Chinese Sorghum	2074	1941	1958	2324	2115
其他	Others	3062	2750	2813	2838	2737
豆类	Beans	2716	2747	2784	2738	2630
薯类	Tubers	6462	8248	8835	8886	8766
油料作物	Oil-bearing Crops	4083	3418	3761	3761	3762
#花生	Peanuts	4327	3495	3878	3883	3881
棉花	Cotton	1029	1410	1193	1170	1180
蔬菜	Vegetable	66852	66895	68337	71058	71748
果用瓜	Melon	55628	48797	51472	50569	51520

注：粮食作物产量、播种面积由国家统计局山东调查总队反馈。
Note: Grain crop yield and sown area have been reported by Shandong Survey Team.

11–7 林、牧、渔业生产情况
Basic Statistics on Forestry, Animal Husbandry and Fishery

指标	Item	单位 Unit	2018年	2019年	2020年	2021年	2022年
林业生产	**Production of Forestry**						
造林面积	Forested Area	公顷(ha)	4902	10758	10939	5333	774
四旁植树	Surrounding Tree Planting	万株(10000 trees)	1306	1576	1527	845	1714
育苗面积	Area of Nursery Garden	公顷(ha)	10174	11579	10750	7781	5229
果品产量	Output of Fruits	吨(ton)	555042	686868	653290	643282	568611
木材采伐量	Timber Cut	立方米(cu.m)	283354	355596	298532	223579	189631
牧业生产	**Production of Animal Husbandry**						
大牲畜存栏	Stocked Large Livestock	万头(10 000 heads)	26.30	24.42	15.26	17.18	16.89
#役畜	Draught Animal	万头(10 000 heads)	0.02				
#牛	Cattle	万头(10 000 heads)	26.17	24.27	15.20	17.16	16.86
猪存栏	Stocked Pigs	万头(10 000 heads)	102.95	129.26	122.86	131.95	121.21
羊存栏	Stocked Sheep	万只(10 000 heads)	87.61	100.13	66.01	73.56	77.73
家禽存栏	Stocked Poultry	万只(10 000 heads)	2300.42	3440.94	2523.33	2763.07	2488.34
猪出栏数	Slaughtered Pigs	万头(10 000 heads)	185.59	217.66	157.03	192.00	209.60
羊出栏数	Slaughtered Sheep	万只(10 000 heads)	143.84	164.26	86.91	126.84	136.20
肉类总产量	Output of Meat	吨(ton)	298180	358655	239186	273577	291021

11-7 续表 continued

指标	Item	单位 Unit	2018年	2019年	2020年	2021年	2022年
#猪牛羊肉	Meat	吨(ton)	223735	236601	164537	201638	212521
猪肉	Pork	吨(ton)	155005	170584	128052	154189	168901
牛肉	Beef	吨(ton)	46438	40698	21020	28807	24306
羊肉	Mutton	吨(ton)	22292	25319	15465	18642	19314
禽肉	Poultry Meat	吨(ton)	74164	120194	73887	71686	78492
奶类	Milk	吨(ton)	328412	321323	414297	420987	434263
#牛奶	Cow Milk	吨(ton)	328410	321321	414297	420987	434263
禽蛋	Poultry & Eggs	吨(ton)	332303	365810	274673	304983	269925
#鸡蛋	Eggs	吨(ton)	313234	343650			
渔业生产	**Aquatic Products**						
水产品产量	Total Aquatic Products	吨(ton)	31911	16167	13294	14068	14778
捕捞	Fishing	吨(ton)	289	3513	3291	1187	729
养殖	Cultured	吨(ton)	31622	12654	10003	12881	14049
养殖面积	Breeding Area of Aquatic Products	公顷(ha)	5228	4380	4304	4336	4341
养殖单产	Aquaculture Yield	公斤/公顷(kg/ha)	6049	2889	2324	2971	3236

11-8 分地区主要农作物播种面积及产量(2022年)
Sown Areas and Output of Main Farm Crops by Region(2022)

指标	Item	济南市 Jinan	历下区 Li xia	市中区 Shi zhong
农作物播种总面积(公顷)	**Total Sown Area of Crops(ha)**			
粮食	Grain	484568		4005
谷物	Cereals	467101		3963
小麦	Wheat	219574		1435
稻谷	Rice	902		
玉米	Corn	235985		2399
谷子	Millet	10462		129
高粱	Jowar	94		
其他	Others	83		
豆类	Beans	8568		33
薯类	Tubers	8899		8
油料作物	Oil-bearing Crops	17596		3
#花生	Peanuts	16333		3
棉花	Cotton	2967		7
蔬菜	Vegetable	99321		85
果用瓜	Melon	10147		12
其他作物	Other Farm Crops	3103		
果园种植面积(公顷)	**Orchard Area(ha)**	**38244**		**257**
#苹果	Apple	11913		46
梨	Pear	1982		1
葡萄	Grape	1200		16
桃	Peach	9524		117
农作物产量(吨)	**Total Output of Farm Crops(ton)**			
粮食作物	Grain Crops	2961879		19473
谷物	Cereals	2861335		19341
小麦	Wheat	1396875		8489
稻谷	Rice	6608		
玉米	Corn	1421051		10589
谷子	Millet	36375		263
高粱	Jowar	199		
其他	Other Cereals	227		
豆类	Beans	22532		62
薯类	Tubers	78011		70
油料作物	Oil-bearing Crops	66190		11
#花生	Peanuts	63387		11

槐荫区 Huai yin	天桥区 Tian qiao	历城区 Li cheng	长清区 Chang qing	章丘区 Zhang qiu	济阳区 Ji yang	莱芜区 Lai wu	钢城区 Gang Cheng	平阴县 Ping yin	商河县 Shang he
2153	12388	19768	44307	107682	101008	31497	4325	35294	122138
2029	12347	19092	41426	102630	99839	29366	3671	31143	121594
825	5690	5808	16739	52117	53773	6076	512	17035	59564
550				42	311				
655	6658	11935	21012	47842	45648	22240	2908	12659	62030
		1347	3593	2540	107	1050	251	1446	
		1		90				4	
			83						
100	41	336	1248	2887	1148	322	40	2173	240
24		340	1634	2165	22	1809	614	1979	304
	10	217	3746	1775	304	5135	4075	2328	4
	10	215	3438	1620	262	5124	4075	1582	4
	20	16	93	657	188	386	239	1043	319
148	255	3485	8089	25474	13371	22812	2584	8881	14138
5	8	2027	113	5104	1320	172	82	1026	277
160		4	203	5	48	2		726	1954
15	**266**	**10279**	**3376**	**6182**	**762**	**5672**	**3089**	**7782**	**565**
	36	2989	133	2558	111	718	299	4934	90
5	90	885	45	294	98	269	121	92	82
0	9	95	20	372	43	245	19	296	84
7	112	3757	897	845	407	1016	1964	240	161
13557	70333	104762	265077	632741	625883	194893	24614	198750	811797
13169	70259	100990	245368	605849	622685	175877	19341	178773	809683
5088	34288	34777	98778	328596	345759	38451	3057	96697	402895
4134				284	2189				
3947	35971	61881	129784	269551	274319	135174	15440	77608	406788
		4331	16580	7228	418	2251	844	4460	
		2		189				8	
			227						
238	74	944	3430	7925	3014	770	105	5360	609
150		2827	16279	18967	183	18246	5168	14616	1505
	34	1104	17906	5573	1458	19564	11034	9488	17
	34	1103	17185	5319	1377	19537	11034	7768	17

11-8 续表 continued

指标	Item	济南市 Jinan	历下区 Li xia	市中区 Shi zhong
棉花	Cotton	3501		7
蔬菜	Vegetable	7126121		4168
果用瓜	Melon	522792		805
水果总产量(吨)	**Output of Fruits(ton)**	**619906**		**3825**
#苹果	Apple	191324		1549
梨	Pear	40142		71
葡萄	Grape	34867		630
桃	Peach	195564		1204
杏	Apricot	35414		241
枣(鲜)	Jujube	9966		17
柿子(鲜)	Persimmon	26875		20
山楂	Hawthorn	33168		15
樱桃	Cherry	39256		56
其他	Others	9149		8
农作物单位面积产量(公斤/公顷)	**Output per Hectare of Farm Crops(kg/ha)**			
粮食作物	Grain Crops	6112		4862
谷物	Cereals	6126		4880
小麦	Wheat	6362		5914
稻谷	Rice	7327		
玉米	Corn	6022		4414
谷子	Millet	3477		2042
高粱	Jowar	2115		
其他	Others	2737		
豆类	Beans	2630		1847
薯类	Tubers	8766		8329
油料作物	Oil-bearing Crops	3762		3511
#花生	Peanuts	3881		3511
棉花	Cotton	1180		1125
蔬菜	Vegetable	71748		48806
果用瓜	Melon	51520		64919

注：粮食作物产量、播种面积由国家统计局山东调查总队反馈。
Note: Grain crop yield and sown area have been reported by Shandong Survey Team.

槐荫区 Huai yin	天桥区 Tian qiao	历城区 Li cheng	长清区 Chang qing	章丘区 Zhang qiu	济阳区 Ji yang	莱芜区 Lai wu	钢城区 Gang Cheng	平阴县 Ping yin	商河县 Shang he
	29	23	123	702	225	473	345	1186	387
11439	11217	176336	562076	1907577	1245085	1292961	201550	673935	1039776
216	269	98338	4878	255316	70543	6652	3334	68023	14415
399	**8022**	**111161**	**60132**	**74972**	**22225**	**120470**	**95639**	**105905**	**17155**
8	1025	21669	3263	39043	3621	21816	16838	79962	2530
220	3030	15223	1493	2937	2614	6477	1882	2565	3630
	218	1895	536	11343	1372	5601	505	7690	5077
151	3452	51117	14593	11430	11304	26371	66084	5355	4503
15	130	3091	14664	556	509	12231	746	2535	696
	106	395	348	5690	931	1500	240	400	339
		2534	5979	142	815	14977	1969	418	22
		12068	145	603	148	15821	3661	685	22
5	60	2256	18776	2950	8	10948	2205	1880	111
	1	703	83	60	881	1705	1137	4347	225
6296	5677	5300	5983	5876	6196	6188	5691	5631	6647
6489	5690	5290	5923	5903	6237	5989	5269	5740	6659
6167	6026	5988	5901	6305	6430	6328	5973	5676	6764
7522				6821	7050				
6027	5403	5185	6177	5634	6009	6078	5309	6131	6558
		3215	4614	2846	3900	2145	3360	3085	
		2250		2115				2084	
			2737						
2377	1817	2812	2748	2745	2627	2394	2610	2467	2535
6320		8315	9965	8760	8310	10084	8418	7388	4950
	3500	5093	4781	3140	4804	3810	2708	4075	4469
	3500	5121	4999	3284	5249	3813	2708	4909	4469
	1485	1433	1318	1069	1195	1226	1445	1137	1215
77499	44047	50604	69488	74884	93121	56679	78003	75881	73545
45098	33098	48505	42993	50022	53431	38586	40563	66325	52128

11–9 分地区林、牧、渔业生产情况(2022年)
Basic Statistics on Forestry, Animal Husbandry and Fishery by Region(2022)

指标	Item	单位 Unit	济南市 Jinan	历下区 Li xia	市中区 Shi zhong
林业生产	**Production of Forestry**				
造林面积	Forested Area	公顷(ha)	774		133
四旁植树	Surrounding Tree Planting	万株(10000 trees)	1714	95	119
育苗面积	Area of Nursery Garden	公顷(ha)	5229		24
果品产量	Output of Fruits	吨(ton)	568611		7215
木材采伐量	Timber Cut	立方米(cu.m)	189631		
牧业生产	**Production of Animal Husbandry**				
牛存栏	Stocked Cattle	万头(10 000 heads)	16.86		0.08
猪存栏	Stocked Pigs	万头(10 000 heads)	121.21		0.80
羊存栏	Stocked Sheep	万只(10 000 heads)	77.73		4.94
家禽存栏	Stocked Poultry	万只(10 000 heads)	2488.34		20.27
猪出栏数	Slaughtered Pigs	万头(10 000 heads)	209.60		1.28
羊出栏数	Slaughtered Sheep	万只(10 000 heads)	136.20		6.57
猪牛羊肉产量	Meat	吨(ton)	212521		2498
猪肉	Pork	吨(ton)	168901		1032
牛肉	Beef	吨(ton)	24306		535
羊肉	Mutton	吨(ton)	19314		932
禽肉	Poultry Meat		78492		235
奶类	Milk	吨(ton)	434263		
#牛奶	Cow Milk	吨(ton)	434263		
禽蛋	Poultry & Eggs	吨(ton)	269925		3444
渔业生产	**Aquatic Products**				
水产品产量	Total Aquatic Products	吨(ton)	14778		
捕捞	Fishing	吨(ton)	729		
养殖	Cultured	吨(ton)	14049		
养殖面积	Breeding Area of Aquatic Products	公顷(ha)	4341		
养殖单产	Aquaculture Yield	公斤/公顷(kg/ha)	3236		

槐荫区 Huai yin	天桥区 Tian qiao	历城区 Li cheng	长清区 Chang qing	章丘区 Zhang qiu	济阳区 Ji yang	莱芜区 Lai Wu	钢城区 Gang Cheng	平阴县 Ping yin	商河县 Shang he
	40	137		140		187	100		37
70	20	305	160	275	150	189	60	121	150
		1248	2133	733	439	388	7	72	185
	719	256124	43137	21025	7627	101415	102825	17169	11355
28150	9300	7855	24698	45500	16751	8610	12735	16032	20000
0.04	0.06	0.45	2.00	1.01	1.53	1.14	0.29	2.86	7.40
0.05	1.75	4.52	15.91	17.15	9.48	23.06	11.32	14.98	22.18
0.21	4.65	1.77	6.13	9.70	5.91	19.08	7.11	5.88	12.34
3.92	70.75	136.31	241.30	576.55	178.29	470.97	158.93	275.57	355.48
0.08	2.29	6.20	22.19	34.90	14.33	48.74	18.18	23.12	38.29
0.53	9.47	3.68	8.28	13.22	14.93	30.95	14.64	10.93	22.99
251	3358	6979	20720	33894	16765	48054	17191	21229	41582
67	1752	4997	16983	28866	11944	39225	13649	17632	32755
108	263	1459	2564	2953	2904	4440	1466	2047	5567
75	1344	522	1174	2074	1917	4389	2076	1550	3260
96	2137	2793	3639	17953	7193	19176	4842	8767	11660
	499	9058	58565	6350	41409	2487	2357	90049	223489
	499	9058	58565	6350	41409	2487	2357	90049	223489
1196	8015	22606	38036	59820	18025	33144	16046	28153	41440
1320	474	413	950	1704	3255	3809	229	780	1844
	6	28	76		44	479			96
1320	468	385	874	1704	3211	3330	229	780	1748
124	168	48	346	360	560	1723	270	446	296
10645	2786	8021	2526	4733	5734	1933	848	1749	5905

11–10 主要农副产品产量与上年和历史最高年份比较

Output of Major Agricultural Products in Comparision with Last Year and Maximum Year

单位：万吨 (10 000 tons)

指标	Item	2022年	2021年	历史最高年 Maximum Year 年份 Year	历史最高年 Maximum Year 产量 Output	2022年为历史最高年的% 2022 Account for Historic High	2022年为2021年的% 2022 Account for 2021
农产品产量	**Total Output of Farm Crops**						
粮食总产量	Output of Grain Crops	296.19	293.07	2022	296.19	100.0	101.1
#小麦	Wheat	139.69	139.25	2022	139.69	100.0	100.3
稻谷	Rice	0.66	0.63	2000	9.89	6.7	104.8
玉米	Corn	142.11	139.56	2011	143.96	98.7	101.8
薯类	Tubers	7.80	7.80	1995	23.10	33.8	100.0
经济作物	**Commercial Crop**						
#棉花	Cotton	0.35	0.38	1999	5.00	7.0	91.9
油料花生	Peanuts	6.34	6.29	2020	6.48	97.8	100.7
蔬菜总产量	Output of Vegetable	712.61	691.76	2022	712.61	100.0	103.0
水果总产量	Output of Fruits	52.28	61.90	2020	63.20	82.7	84.5
水产品总产量	**Total Aquatic Products**	**1.5**	**1.4**	**2015**	**4.80**	**31.3**	**106.6**

主要统计指标解释

农林牧渔业总产值 指以货币表现的农、林、牧、渔业全部产品和对农林牧渔业生产活动进行的各种支持性服务活动的价值总量，它反映一定时期内农林牧渔业生产总规模和总成果。

农林牧渔业总产值采用“产品法”进行计算，通常是按农、林、牧、渔业产品及其副产品的产量分别乘以各自单位产品价格求得；少数生产周期较长，当年没有产品或产品产量不易统计的，则采用间接方法匡算其产值；然后将四业产品产值及农林牧渔专业及辅助性活动产值相加即为农林牧渔业总产值。

粮食产量 指日历年度内生产的全部粮食数量。按收获季节包括夏收粮食、早稻和秋收粮食，按作物品种包括谷物、豆类和薯类。其产量计算方法：谷物按脱粒后的原粮计算，豆类按去豆荚后的干豆计算；薯类(包括甘薯和马铃薯，不包括芋头和木薯)1964年以前按每4公斤鲜薯折1公斤粮食计算，从1964年开始改为按5公斤鲜薯折1公斤粮食计算；城市郊区作为蔬菜的薯类(如马铃薯等)按鲜品计算，并且不作粮食统计。1989年以前全国粮食产量数据主要靠全面报表取得，1989年开始使用抽样调查数据。

棉花产量 指全社会棉花的产量。包括春播棉和夏播棉。产量按皮棉计算。不包括木棉。

油料产量 指全部油料作物的生产量。包括花生、油菜籽、芝麻、向日葵籽、胡麻籽（亚麻籽）和其他油料。不包括大豆、木本油料和野生油料。花生以带壳干花生计算。

水产品产量 指渔业（捕捞和养殖）生产活动的最终有效成果，包括全部海水和淡水鱼类、甲壳类（虾、蟹）、贝类、头足类、藻类和其他类渔业产品的最终产量。水产品产量是通过各级渔业主管部门逐级上报取得数据。1995年及以前，贝类中牡蛎按鲜肉计算；蚶、蛤、蛏按5斤鲜品折1斤计算。1996年以后则统一按鲜品计算。

猪、牛、羊、禽肉产量 指当年出栏并已屠宰、除去头蹄下水后带骨肉(即胴体重)的重量。1996年以前为全面统计并逐级上报数据。1996年第一次农业普查以后，根据普查结果，对畜牧业主要年报数据进行了修正。1999年，国家统计局在部分地区开展了猪、牛、羊、禽等主要畜禽品种的抽样调查，并用抽样数据作为国家定案数据使用。未开展抽样调查的地区，仍使用各级统计部门逐级上报数据。2008年，建立了主要畜禽监测调查制度，猪、牛、羊、禽等主要畜禽数据均以抽样调查数为法定数据。

农作物播种面积 指日历年度内收获农作物在全部土地（耕地或非耕地）上的播种或移植面积。凡是本年内收获的农作物，无论是本年还是上年播种，都算为播种面积，但不包括本年播种，下年收获的农作物面积。

农用化肥施用量 指本年内实际用于农业生产的化肥数量，包括氮肥、磷肥、钾肥和复合肥。化肥施用量要求按折纯量计算数量。折纯量是指把氮肥、磷肥、钾肥分别按含氮、含五氧化二磷、含氧化钾的百分之百成份进行折算后的数量。复合肥按其所含主要成分折算。公式为：

折纯量=实物量×某种化肥有效成份含量的百分比

农业机械总动力 指全部农业机械动力的额定功率之和。农业机械是指用于种植业、畜牧业、渔业、农产品初加工、农用运输和农田基本建设等活动的机械及设备。

Explanatory Notes on Main Statistical Indicators

Gross Output Value of Agriculture, Forestry, Animal Husbandry and Fishery refers to the total value of products (expressed in monetary terms) of agriculture, forestry, animal husbandry and fishery, and total value of services in support of agriculture, forestry, animal husbandry and fishery activities. It reflects the total scale and results of agricultural production during a given period.

Gross output value of agriculture is calculated by product method, and is obtained by multiplying the output of each product or by-product by its price, resulting in the output value of each single item. For a small number of products, annual output of which is not available or difficult to get due to the long production (growing) process involved, the output value is estimated through an indirect approach. The sum of output values of all products of agriculture, forestry, animal husbandry and fishery and professional and support activities in agriculture, forestry, animal husbandry and fishery is then equal to the gross output value of agriculture.

Grain Output refers to the total output of grains produced within a calendar year. It includes summer crops, early rice and autumn crops by harvest seasons; and covers cereals, beans and tubers by type of crops. Output of cereals cover husked grain only. Output of beans refers to dry beans without pods. The output of tubers (sweet potatoes and potatoes, not including taros and cassava) are converted with the ratio of 4:1, i.e. 4 kilograms of fresh tubers were equivalent to 1 kilogram of grain before 1964. Since 1964 the ratio has been changed to 5:1. Tubers consumed as vegetables (such as potatoes) in cities and suburbs are calculated as fresh vegetables and their output is not included in the output of grain. Data on grain production before 1989 were obtained through the comprehensive statistical reporting system. Since 1989, data from sample surveys are used.

Cotton Output refers to cotton production in the whole country including cotton planted in spring and in summer. Output is measured as the weight of ginned cotton. Ceiba is not included.

Output of Oil-bearing Crops refers to the total production of oil-bearing crops of various kinds, including peanuts (dry, in shell), rapeseeds, sesame, sunflower seeds, flax seeds, and other oil-bearing crops. Soybeans, oil-bearing woody plants, and wild oil-bearing crops are not included.

Output of Aquatic Products refers to final output actually yielded from fishing production (fishery and breeding), including all output of marine and freshwater fish, crustaceans (shrimps, crabs), shellfish, cephalopod, seaweed and other fishery products. Data on output of aquatic products are reported by fishery agencies level by level. Before 1995, among the shellfish, oyster was counted as fresh meat; and 5 kilograms of ark shell, clams and frogs were equivalent to 1 kilogram of fresh aquatic products; they have all been counted as fresh aquatic products since 1996.

Output of Pork, Beef, Mutton and Poultry refers to the meat of slaughtered hogs, cattle, sheep and goats with head, feet, and offal taken away. Before 1996, data were obtained through bottom-up comprehensive reporting system. The first agricultural census of China in 1996 revealed some discrepancy between the production of animal products from the annual reports and that from the census. Efforts were made to adjust the output value of animal husbandry to make the figures from the annual reports consistent with the census data. Since 1999, the NBS conducted sample surveys in selected regions for the major animal husbandry products, such as hogs, cattle, sheep and goats and fowls, and the data from sample surveys are used as finalized national data. Production of other regions which are not covered by the sample survey is still reported by statistical agencies level by level. A monitoring and survey program was set up in 2008 on main livestock, and data on the main livestock such as hog, cattle, sheep and poultry from the sample survey became the official data.

Sown Area of Crops refers to area of all land (cultivated or non-cultivated area) sown or transplanted with crops that are harvested within the calendar year. All crops harvested within the year are counted as sown area, regardless of being sown in this year or the previous year. Crops sown this year but will be harvested in the coming year are excluded.

Consumption of Chemical Fertilizers in Agriculture refers to the quantity of chemical fertilizers applied in agriculture in the year, including nitrogenous fertilizer, phosphate fertilizer, potash fertilizer, and compound fertilizer. The consumption of chemical fertilizers is calculated in terms of volume of effective components by means of converting the gross weight of the respective fertilizers into weight containing effective component (e.g. nitrogen content in nitrogenous fertilizer, phosphorous pentoxide contents in phosphate fertilizer, and potassium oxide contents in potash fertilizer). Compound fertilizer is converted in regard to its major components. The formula is:

Volume of effective component= physical quantity× effective component of certain chemical fertilizer (%)

Total Power of Agricultural Machinery refers to the total rated capacity of all agricultural machinery. Agricultural machinery refers to the machines and equipment which are used for activities of farming, animal husbandry, fishery, primary processing of agricultural products, agricultural transport and infrastructure construction of farmland.

12

工 业

INDUSTRY

12-1 各时期全部工业基本情况
Basic Statistics on Total Industry in Each Period

年份 Year	全部工业单位数(个) Number of Industrial Enterprises (Unit)		工业总产值(亿元) Gross Industrial Output Value (100 million yuan)		工业增加值(亿元) Value Added of Industry Enterprises (100 million yuan)		国有独立核算工业(万元) State-owned Independent Accounting Industrial (10 000 yuan)	
	合计 Total	#国有单位 State-owned	合计 Total	#国有单位 State-owned	合计 Total	#国有单位 State-owned	利润总额 Total Profits	利税总额 Total Profits and Taxes
1949	52	-	1.20	0.52	0.40	0.15	190	541
1952	92	-	2.97	1.65	1.09	0.52	1616	2761
1957	399	-	6.90	6.13	2.18	1.84	5742	10065
1962	847	286	6.67	5.61	2.36	1.80	3293	8242
1965	724	247	11.99	10.09	4.34	3.39	16246	22906
1970	828	285	23.12	17.93	7.56	5.64	19347	31834
1975	1041	326	26.41	18.87	8.46	5.50	11555	27846
1978	1319	398	39.06	25.87	12.89	7.11	28852	53031
1979	1353	359	42.95	28.90	14.10	8.01	31875	57532
1980	1535	356	45.31	30.37	14.24	8.85	32909	59572
“六五”时期								
1981	1538	350	47.61	31.72	15.11	9.47	35077	62657
1982	1619	357	51.98	33.91	15.79	10.01	32062	64673
1983	1674	369	59.06	36.99	17.96	11.49	35870	60308
1984	1981	325	66.96	39.78	20.10	13.17	45869	83520
1985	2584	477	74.41	44.66	27.54	16.97	61274	112154
“七五”时期								
1986	3005	369	86.93	48.71	28.69	17.53	54804	115006
1987	3957	361	107.63	56.16	32.88	19.40	58715	125775
1988	5252	372	138.05	68.58	47.49	25.09	80173	156056
1989	7655	380	158.53	76.19	54.66	30.51	76571	170703
1990	11020	394	222.63	116.92	60.43	37.11	25084	125522
“八五”时期								
1991	12211	376	245.73	131.35	67.73	43.35	36715	151718
1992	15374	373	303.33	162.35	86.85	48.97	55463	193000
1993	19392	376	448.25	230.93	115.36	69.65	57984	223445
1994	22009	366	614.08	236.40	154.49	69.64	60393	240473
1995	24621	495	752.23	279.16	194.16	83.12	65335	316289
“九五”时期								
1996	32902	425	834.45	260.16	238.31	91.30	79615	337807
1997	33000	325	897.59	263.34	278.87	92.99	95267	343426
1998	32793	227	966.62	234.03	298.41	94.28	42152	292991
1999	29319	211	981.78	212.95	318.80	79.51	-2340	254619
2000	30899	195	994.00	237.14	336.61	81.00	34824	292198
“十五”时期								
2001	34135	169	1090.70	140.44	356.72	64.69	49222	226242
2002	30064	155	1302.00	144.78	410.98	49.16	28011	234986

12-1 续表 continued

年份 Year	全部工业单位数 (个) Number of Industrial Enterprises (Unit)		工业总产值 (亿元) Gross Industrial Output Value (100 million yuan)		工业增加值 (亿元) Value Added of Industry Enterprises (100 million yuan)		国有独立核算工业 (万元) State-owned Independent Accounting Industrial	
	合计 Total	#国有单位 State-owned	合计 Total	#国有单位 State-owned	合计 Total	#国有单位 State-owned	利润总额 Total Profits	利税总额 Total Profits and Taxes
2003	30258	126	1544.50	167.30	494.55	68.80	53363	302975
2004	31163	115	1981.80	150.70	620.14	37.21	-3943	72684
2005	31370	102	2447.51	177.00	786.11	66.49	268573	354111
"十一五"时期								
2006	35370	86	2806.94	193.10	861.48	73.95	315323	458191
2007	36112	76	3389.09	283.32	985.78	103.65	364790	751182
2008	36416	80	4829.16	338.24	1140.14	136.55	418265	853091
2009	37656	77	5096.98	345.44	1191.36	166.36	422898	885006
2010	37521	66	5800.39	404.38	1352.42	284.75	643216	1162785
"十二五"时期								
2011	36750	54	5544.60	478.10	1507.88		561683	1217350
2012	35917	52	5535.25	491.20	1603.08		646193	1401892
2013	38443	30	5711.48	280.63	1690.63		551967	665206
2014	38753	25	5861.98	246.26	1822.11		507491	611865
2015	38793	24	5877.28	204.79	1844.37		517575	571354
"十三五"时期								
2016	34310	16	6059.16	157.83	1878.83		540739	622714
2017	33725	12	6395.21	147.27	2003.10		583734	589999
2018	31270	13	5641.61	15.50	2145.10		-4140	5014
2019					2167.87			
2020					2360.48			
"十四五"时期								
2021					2746.00			
2022					2869.00			

注：1.工业增加值、工业总产值按当年价格计算。
2.1985、1995年因工业普查对教育局校办工厂统计方法的规定，故国有单位较多。
3.2001年后炼油、浪潮、将军等原国有企业陆续改制，故国有数字较以前年份有所减小。
4.2004年第一次经济普查后，统计年鉴包含济南供电公司年报数据。
5.非经济普查年度，除"工业增加值"外，其它指标空缺。

Notes: 1. Industrial value added and total industrial output value are calculated according to the current year's prices.
2. There were many state-owned units in 1985 and 1995 due to the provisions regarding statistical approach for school-run factories of Education Bureau from industrial census.
3. Original state-owned enterprises such as Oil Refining, Inspur and General were subject to restructuring in succession after 2001, so the quantity of state-owned enterprises decreased in comparison to that of previous years.
4. After the economic census for the first time in 2004, statistical yearbook includes annual report data of Jinan Power Supply Company.
5.In years other than the year of economic census, indicators are blank, excluding "Value Added of Industrial Enterprises".

12-2 各时期规模以上工业基本情况

Basic Statistics of Industrial Enterprises Above Designated Size in Each Period

单位：亿元 (100 million yuan)

年份 Year	单位数 (个) Number of Enterprises (unit)	工业总产值 Gross Industrial Output Value	工业增加值 Value Added of Industry Enterprises	营业收入 Business Revenue	利税总额 Total Profits and Taxes	利润总额 Total Profits	资产总计 Total Assets	所有者权益 Owner's Equities
1949	52	1.06	0.40	0.91	0.07	0.03	0.58	0.17
1952	92	2.83	1.02	2.40	0.32	0.18	1.89	0.55
1957	399	6.04	2.08	5.85	1.04	0.60	2.85	0.83
1962	847	6.65	2.15	6.87	0.92	0.39	5.66	1.65
1965	724	11.89	4.07	9.49	2.47	1.73	5.93	1.73
1970	828	22.94	7.29	19.30	3.66	2.22	10.67	3.10
1975	1041	26.16	7.94	19.70	3.47	1.55	17.21	5.01
1978	1319	37.67	9.94	31.39	6.80	3.88	25.68	7.47
1979	1353	38.79	11.18	35.51	7.21	4.13	27.19	7.91
1980	1535	43.60	12.15	36.90	7.51	4.26	29.22	8.50
“六五”时期								
1981	1538	42.26	12.77	39.84	7.98	4.37	31.49	9.20
1982	1619	45.58	13.63	42.94	8.13	4.18	34.52	10.08
1983	1674	49.64	14.86	46.38	8.84	4.74	38.09	11.12
1984	1981	55.95	17.91	52.16	10.46	5.82	41.66	12.16
1985	1915	66.98	23.10	64.76	13.98	7.62	47.09	13.75
“七五”时期								
1986	2036	75.67	24.54	73.98	14.38	7.07	56.79	16.70
1987	2004	88.17	27.24	86.19	15.88	7.52	64.21	18.88
1988	1984	107.76	35.39	113.84	19.65	10.37	81.67	24.01
1989	1993	118.88	43.20	131.86	20.88	9.73	104.34	30.68
1990	2008	174.89	41.63	136.29	15.57	3.23	125.25	36.82
“八五”时期								
1991	1985	194.29	44.84	160.58	18.46	4.97	138.34	40.81
1992	1941	236.37	60.16	200.54	23.48	7.84	167.44	49.39
1993	2156	319.49	104.43	309.91	31.88	10.26	338.15	99.61
1994	2202	414.81	113.71	346.13	41.69	13.61	462.34	136.14
1995	2648	526.48	130.88	432.17	53.59	16.30	578.55	180.86
“九五”时期								
1996	2301	549.40	175.21	494.99	66.82	27.83	705.50	225.53
1997	1843	603.30	194.42	605.81	70.12	26.99	882.36	286.59
1998	1060	593.83	189.88	539.29	58.56	18.62	882.38	297.81
1999	1064	628.59	201.38	579.64	59.17	15.97	931.22	302.21
2000	1038	680.04	219.19	629.72	64.62	21.69	958.10	363.37

注：1.工业增加值、工业总产值按当年价格计算。
2.1997年及以前统计口径为乡及乡以上工业企业，1998年及以后为全部国有及年销售收入500万元以上工业企业，2011年及以后为年主营业务收入2000万元以上工业企业。
3.1991年及以前“工业增加值”指标为“工业净产值”指标。
4.2019年及以前“营业收入”、“营业成本”、“税金及附加”指标为“主营业务收入”、“主营业务成本”及“主营业务税金及附加”指标。以下相关各表同。
5.自2019年起，不再包含省直单位相关数据。以下相关各表同。
6.自2019年起，数据为济南市、莱芜市区划调整后合并数据，之前年度数据为原济南市数据。以下相关各表同。
7.表中的合计数和部分计算数据因小数取舍而产生的误差，均未作机械调整。以下相关各表同。

12-2 续表 continued

单位：亿元 (100 million yuan)

年份 Year	单位数 (个) Number of Enterprises (unit)	工业总产值 Gross Industrial Output Value	工业增加值 Value Added of Industry Enterprises	营业收入 Business Revenue	利税总额 Total Profits and Taxes	利润总额 Total Profits	资产总计 Total Assets	所有者权益 Owner's Equities
“十五”时期								
2001	1015	786.70	252.61	746.92	77.79	28.45	984.71	369.40
2002	1125	1009.04	325.98	917.31	92.71	32.13	1120.60	407.36
2003	1319	1318.54	426.30	1223.76	132.84	54.71	1312.97	440.85
2004	1512	1781.78	560.15	1677.93	175.98	83.68	1473.90	507.63
2005	1670	2237.51	722.11	2142.84	244.61	131.30	1868.06	630.06
“十一五”时期								
2006	1752	2591.65	797.70	2490.94	289.78	153.74	2000.62	702.78
2007	1820	3189.09	926.58	3086.85	358.87	199.73	2337.09	903.87
2008	2016	3862.64	1052.48	3766.93	425.72	220.79	2899.47	1123.03
2009	2156	3950.77	1154.01	3868.70	500.63	275.85	3478.94	1572.11
2010	2021	4485.61	1313.00	4497.17	584.53	339.76	3904.42	1481.75
“十二五”时期								
2011	1417	4028.49		4165.19	453.47	242.63	3932.90	1407.89
2012	1647	4248.29		4454.97	498.24	253.06	4109.29	1582.77
2013	1901	4777.47		4926.11	539.49	312.95	4249.79	1671.91
2014	1984	5253.05		5406.67	606.60	357.82	4564.86	1846.32
2015	2021	5339.97		5417.16	685.71	396.13	4987.76	2159.78
“十三五”时期								
2016	1962	5486.56		5714.29	729.75	421.11	5501.88	2301.94
2017	2051	5770.91		5810.16	686.80	415.23	6319.64	2268.27
2018	1889	4992.28		5192.15	535.39	307.98	5892.64	2386.75
2019	2153	5839.18		6512.66	545.70	310.86	6663.13	2743.28
2020	2215	6765.08		7575.34	659.87	423.31	7724.85	2967.31
“十四五”时期								
2021	2543	7591.25		8492.55	645.49	408.38	8494.19	3380.30
2022	2665	7246.05		8370.30	593.57	344.86	9637.65	3779.62

Notes: 1. Industrial value added and total industrial output value are calculated according to the current year's prices.

2. Industrial statistical indicators In 1997 and before, the statistical caliber was industrial enterprises at or above the township level. In 1998 and after, they were all state-owned and with an annual sales income of more than 5 million yuan. In 2011 and beyond,the annual main business income was 20 million yuan and above industrial enterprises legal entities.

3.The index of "industrial added value" in 1991 and before is "net industrial output value".

4. "Operating income", "operating cost" and "taxes and surcharges" indicators in year 2019 and before refer to "main operating income", "main operating cost" and "main operating taxes and surcharges" (the same below).

5. Since 2019, statistics does not include data of units directly under provincial jurisdiction (the same below).

6. Since 2019, the data used refer to the combined data after the adjustment of administrative division between Jinan City and Laiwu City, and the data before 2019 are data of original Jinan City (the same below).

7. Errors in totals and part of calculations in the table are produced by decimal trade-offs, not mechanically adjusted(the same below).

12-3 各时期主要工业产品产量
Output of Major Industrial Products in Each Period

年份 Year	钢 (万吨) Steel (10 000 tons)	发电量 (亿千瓦小时) Electricity Generation (100 million kWh)	水泥 (万吨) Cement (10 000 tons)	化肥 (万吨) Chemical Fertilizer (10 000 tons)	金切机床 (台) Metal-cutting Machine Tools (unit)	汽车 (辆) Motor Vehicles (unit)	服务器 (万台) Servers (10 000 unit)	布 (万米) Cloth (10 000 m)
1949	-	0.29	0.15	-	40	-	-	2682
1952	-	0.55	1.08	1.62	565	-	-	5104
1957	0.03	1.07	1.29	0.48	2312	-	-	5573
1962	0.57	4.20	4.85	0.81	1140	12	-	2160
1965	0.54	5.65	19.24	3.79	2061	335	-	4853
1970	7.01	11.28	38.06	4.87	4718	1775	-	11665
1975	22.81	11.07	58.48	9.06	3994	3507	-	12547
1978	34.54	12.65	87.55	18.02	3610	4025	-	13806
1979	33.19	11.92	93.77	11.07	3771	4515	-	14300
1980	36.34	11.95	98.86	12.78	4414	5641	-	15236
"六五"时期								
1981	34.23	11.12	96.50	11.62	3336	5099	-	16290
1982	34.96	11.15	104.64	13.23	4262	5993	-	17657
1983	41.24	13.01	112.38	15.37	4816	7249	-	17963
1984	43.80	23.49	117.17	14.53	5533	7947	-	16522
1985	52.64	26.44	135.10	11.44	6686	9400	-	18082
"七五"时期								
1986	57.24	27.01	154.51	12.31	7472	7600	-	12346
1987	64.09	28.83	158.92	13.00	7007	5225	-	20137
1988	75.23	42.97	182.80	13.69	7280	6741	-	19374
1989	81.58	43.98	198.95	14.48	6806	7701	-	21744
1990	87.68	44.71	211.56	14.44	5121	6239	-	20155
"八五"时期								
1991	105.42	56.43	248.33	14.90	5330	7096	-	20119
1992	113.34	61.46	335.61	14.64	7443	8544	-	14896
1993	139.35	69.00	340.35	14.47	6724	10132	-	13205
1994	166.19	66.87	384.00	15.62	3297	9380	-	16062
1995	172.72	68.75	425.02	14.03	4109	5657	-	15046
"九五"时期								
1996	205.49	63.50	379.32	13.73	3855	7125	-	13710
1997	237.70	59.14	392.23	13.89	2526	5656	-	14213
1998	267.33	60.06	379.40	17.29	1508	3615	-	11286

12-3 续表 continued

年份 Year	钢 (万吨) Steel (10 000 tons)	发电量 (亿千瓦小时) Electricity Generation (100 million kWh)	水泥 (万吨) Cement (10 000 tons)	化肥 (万吨) Chemical Fertilizer (10 000 tons)	金切机床 (台) Metal-cutting Machine Tools (unit)	汽车 (辆) Motor Vehicles (unit)	服务器 (万台) Servers (10 000 unit)	布 (万米) Cloth (10 000 m)
1999	265.29	64.24	474.47	22.91	1955	3738	-	14782
2000	277.04	69.29	485.12	28.41	2908	3078	-	16493
“十五”时期								
2001	293.83	69.81	572.28	28.71	3528	7395	-	14107
2002	394.41	69.12	867.71	28.29	4522	12152	-	16027
2003	507.70	77.60	925.20	28.50	6751	19989	-	17040
2004	688.30	74.70	1343.90	40.30	8904	29648	-	16336
2005	1046.60	90.80	1595.70	28.90	7166	42214	-	14018
“十一五”时期								
2006	1131.26	100.14	1960.64	31.44	10057	59242	-	22852
2007	1214.90	130.37	733.98	40.31	9473	100133	-	27469
2008	1123.20	124.25	734.58	48.52	5110	109107	8.3	11786
2009	1051.67	128.76	761.72	57.77	2400	129900	9.7	7500
2010	959.33	131.45	729.79	49.09	2165	212047	9.9	8191
“十二五”时期								
2011	835.80	154.48	824.70	44.20	2024	170717	13.0	11461
2012	694.50	156.60	776.00	55.20	4237	141269	14.7	14908
2013	711.14	162.55	782.20	33.29	4297	165963	17.1	14574
2014	746.20	178.47	832.40	28.60	4902	139751	28.1	14070
2015	699.80	175.87	781.50	23.50	3807	96184	40.6	15539
“十三五”时期								
2016	805.70	177.20	719.80	32.50	4679	124200	46.8	15585
2017	452.03	160.12	604.48	21.00	6013	201883	56.5	16407
2018	160.92	152.90	604.32	20.77	5964	232082	99.6	4032
2019	2144.18	295.10	1287.82	16.91	7237	175488	116.5	4095
2020	2228.91	276.70	1335.88	21.09	8998	394133	143.5	1144
“十四五”时期								
2021	1921.86	315.06	1561.13	16.66	14049	320349	113.7	1099
2022	2021.42	318.16	1361.58	4.23	12518	164370	77.1	808

注：按经济普查规定汽车产量不含底盘。

Note: The automotive output excludes chassis in line with the provisions of economic census.

12-4 规模以上工业主要经济指标(2022年)
Main Economic Indicators of Industrial Enterprises Above Designated Size(2022)

指标	Item	企业单位数(个) Number of Enterprises (unit)	亏损企业数(个) Loss Enterprises (unit)	工业总产值(现价)(亿元) Gross Industrial Output Value (Current Prices) (100 million yuan)	平均用工人数(万人) Annual Average Employees (10 000 persons)
总计	**Total**	**2665**	**663**	**7246.05**	**41.70**
按登记注册类型分组	**by Status of Registration**				
内资企业	Domestic Invested Enterprises	2511	632	6177.77	34.94
国有企业	State-owned Enterprises	34	10	89.21	0.50
中央企业	Central Enterprises	7	1	53.49	0.22
地方企业	Local Enterprises	27	9	35.72	0.28
集体企业	Collective-owned Enterprises	7	3	5.67	0.07
股份合作企业	Cooperative Enterprises	4		109.83	0.20
联营企业	Joint Ownership Enterprises	2		9.82	0.07
国有联营企业	State Joint Ownership Enterprises				
集体联营企业	Collective Joint Ownership Enterprises				
国有与集体联营企业	Joint State-collective Enterprises	1		9.03	0.05
其他联营企业	Other Joint Ownership Enterprises	1		0.79	0.02
有限责任公司	Limited Liability Corporations	690	200	2409.60	14.48
国有独资公司	State Sole Funded Corporations	42	16	207.18	1.59
其他有限责任公司	Other Limited Liability Corporations	648	184	2202.42	12.89
股份有限公司	Share-holding Corporations Ltd.	94	23	1515.58	4.42
私营企业	Private Enterprises	1680	396	2038.06	15.18
私营独资企业	Private-funded Enterprises	53	9	24.43	0.26
私营合伙企业	Private Partnership Enterprises	7	2	1.79	0.02
私营有限责任公司	Private Limited Liability Corporations	1534	361	1866.28	13.81
私营股份有限公司	Private Share-holding Corporations Ltd.	86	24	145.56	1.09
其他企业	Other Enterprises				
港、澳、台商投资企业	Enterprises with Funds from Hong Kong,Macao and Taiwan	65	11	717.30	4.27
合资经营企业	Joint-venture Enterprises	35	6	260.95	1.85
合作经营企业	Cooperative Enterprises				
港澳台商独资经营企业	Enterprises with Sole Investment	27	5	273.11	1.86
港澳台商投资股份有限公司	Share-holding Corporations Ltd.	1		181.87	0.55
其他港澳台商投资企业	Other Enterprises with Funds from Hong Kong, Macao and Taiwan	2		1.36	0.01

12-4 续表 1 continued 1

指标	Item	企业单位数（个） Number of Enterprises (unit)	亏损企业数（个） Loss Enterprises (unit)	工业总产值（现价）(亿元) Gross Industrial Output Value (Current Prices) (100 million yuan)	平均用工人数(万人) Annual Average Employees (10 000 persons)
外商投资企业	Foreign Funded Enterprises	89	20	350.98	2.49
中外合资经营企业	Joint-venture Enterprises	38	9	155.39	1.20
中外合作经营企业	Cooperation Enterprises	1		0.36	0.01
外资企业	Enterprises with Sole Fund	46	11	148.78	1.18
外商投资股份有限公司	Share-holding Corporations Ltd.	3		39.60	0.05
其他外商投资企业	Other Foreign Funded Enterprises	1		6.86	0.06
按轻重工业分	**by Light & Heavy Industry**				
轻工业	Light Industry	668	184	1277.71	11.99
重工业	Heavy Industry	1997	479	5968.34	29.71
按企业规模分	**by Enterprise Size**				
大型企业	Large-sized Enterprises	60	11	3597.31	15.08
中型企业	Medium-sized Enterprises	174	47	1321.45	9.08
小型企业	Small-sized Enterprises	2044	490	2110.99	16.74
微型企业	Micro-sized Enterprises	387	115	216.31	0.80
按工业行业分	**by Sector**				
煤炭开采和洗选业	Mining and Washing of Coal	3	1	6.06	0.21
石油和天然气开采业	Extraction of Petroleum and Natural Gas	3		15.96	0.04
黑色金属矿采选业	Mining and Processing of Ferrous Metal Ores	13	1	119.43	0.81
有色金属矿采选业	Mining and Processing of Non-Ferrous Metal Ores				
非金属矿采选业	Mining and Processing of Non-metal Ores	7	3	11.24	0.04
开采专业及辅助性活动	Professional and Support Activities for Mining				
其他采矿业	Mining of Other Ores				
农副食品加工业	Processing of Food from Agricultural Products	100	39	167.17	0.93
食品制造业	Manufacture of Foods	79	18	161.97	1.77
酒、饮料和精制茶制造业	Manufacture of Liquor, Beverages and Refined Tea	20	8	65.89	0.53
烟草制品业	Manufacture of Tobacco	1		1.58	0.02
纺织业	Manufacture of Textile	56	19	42.04	0.53
纺织服装、服饰业	Manufacture of Textile, Wearing Apparel and Accessories	20	10	12.92	0.49

12-4 续表 2 continued 2

指标	Item	企业单位数(个) Number of Enterprises (unit)	亏损企业数(个) Loss Enterprises (unit)	工业总产值(现价)(亿元) Gross Industrial Output Value (Current Prices) (100 million yuan)	平均用工人数(万人) Annual Average Employees (10 000 persons)
皮革、毛皮、羽毛及其制品和制鞋业	Manufacture of Leather, Fur, Feather and Related Products and Footwear	3	1	1.44	0.02
木材加工和木、竹、藤、棕、草制品业	Processing of Timber, Manufacture of Wood, Bamboo, Rattan,Palm and Straw Products	11	2	7.75	0.07
家具制造业	Manufacture of Furniture	16	6	11.60	0.20
造纸和纸制品业	Manufacture of Paper and Paper Products	45	14	43.66	0.41
印刷和记录媒介复制业	Printing and Reproduction of Recording Media	42	10	47.74	0.69
文教、工美、体育和娱乐用品制造业	Manufacture of Articles for Culture, Education, Arts and Crafts, Sport and Entertainment Activities	28	9	15.84	0.30
石油、煤炭及其他燃料加工业	Processing of Petroleum, Coal and Other Fuels	15	3	413.36	0.30
化学原料和化学制品制造业	Manufacture of Raw Chemical Materials and Chemical Products	128	27	352.75	1.56
医药制造业	Manufacture of Medicines	77	10	405.73	3.46
化学纤维制造业	Manufacture of Chemical Fibres	9	1	17.41	0.11
橡胶和塑料制品业	Manufacture of Rubber and Plastics Products	71	13	39.07	0.48
非金属矿物制品业	Manufacture of Non-metallic Mineral Products	335	95	509.70	3.40
黑色金属冶炼和压延加工业	Smelting and Pressing of Ferrous Metals	47	27	1323.79	2.85
有色金属冶炼和压延加工业	Smelting and Pressing of Non-ferrous Metals	40	11	45.98	0.20
金属制品业	Manufacture of Metal Products	304	59	358.83	3.14
通用设备制造业	Manufacture of General Purpose Machinery	323	63	415.96	4.36
专用设备制造业	Manufacture of Special Purpose Machinery	253	53	313.03	2.61
汽车制造业	Manufacture of Automobiles	127	39	629.33	4.19
铁路、船舶、航空航天和其他运输设备制造业	Manufacture of Railway, Ship, Aerospace and Other Transport Equipments	24	2	75.25	0.70
电气机械和器材制造业	Manufacture of Electrical Machinery and Apparatus	150	33	417.71	2.12
计算机、通信和其他电子设备制造业	Manufacture of Computers, Communication and Other Electronic Equipment	91	33	691.67	1.84
仪器仪表制造业	Manufacture of Measuring Instruments and Machinery	81	12	86.02	0.95
其他制造业	Other Manufacture	5		9.11	0.04
废弃资源综合利用业	Utilization of Waste Resources	12	5	18.80	0.23
金属制品、机械和设备修理业	Repair Service of Metal Products, Machinery and Equipment	9	1	16.25	0.25
电力、热力生产和供应业	Production and Supply of Electric Power and Heat Power	61	24	214.33	1.12
燃气生产和供应业	Production and Supply of Gas	32	7	127.98	0.35
水的生产和供应业	Production and Supply of Water	24	4	31.70	0.38

12-5 规模以上国有及国有控股工业主要经济指标(2022年)

Main Economic Indicators of State-Owned and State-Controlled Industrial Enterprises Above Designated Size(2022)

指标	Item	企业单位数(个) Number of Enterprises (unit)	亏损企业数(个) Loss Enterprises (unit)	工业总产值(现价)(亿元) Gross Industrial Output Value (Current Prices) (100 million yuan)	平均用工人数(万人) Annual Average Employees (10 000 persons)
总计	**Total**	**271**	**66**	**2815.45**	**10.37**
按登记注册类型分组	**by Status of Registration**				
内资企业	Domestic Invested Enterprises	256	64	2654.04	9.29
国有企业	State-owned Enterprises	34	10	89.21	0.50
中央企业	Central Enterprises	7	1	53.49	0.22
地方企业	Local Enterprises	27	9	35.72	0.28
集体企业	Collective-owned Enterprises				
股份合作企业	Cooperative Enterprises				
联营企业	Joint Ownership Enterprises	1		9.03	0.05
有限责任公司	Limited Liability Corporations	200	49	1289.46	6.55
国有独资公司	State Sole Funded Corporations	42	16	207.18	1.59
其他有限责任公司	Other Limited Liability Corporations	158	33	1082.28	4.96
股份有限公司	Share-holding Corporations Ltd.	21	5	1266.34	2.19
私营企业	Private Enterprises				
其他企业	Other Enterprises				
港、澳、台商投资企业	Enterprises with Funds from Hong Kong, Macao and Taiwan	8	1	110.44	0.74
合资经营企业	Joint-venture Enterprises	8	1	110.44	0.74
合作经营企业	Cooperative Enterprises				
港澳台商独资经营企业	Enterprises with Sole Investment				
港澳台商投资股份有限公司	Share-holding Corporations Ltd.				
其他港澳台商投资企业	Other Enterprises with Funds from Hong Kong, Macao and Taiwan				
外商投资企业	Foreign Funded Enterprises	7	1	50.97	0.34
中外合资经营企业	Joint-venture Enterprises	7	1	50.97	0.34
中外合作经营企业	Cooperation Enterprises				
外资企业	Enterprises with Sole Fund				
外商投资股份有限公司	Share-holding Corporations Ltd.				
其他外商投资企业	Other Foreign Funded Enterprises				

12-5 续表 1 continued 1

指标	Item	企业单位数(个) Number of Enterprises (unit)	亏损企业数(个) Loss Enterprises (unit)	工业总产值(现价)(亿元) Gross Industrial Output Value (Current Prices) (100 million yuan)	平均用工人数(万人) Annual Average Employees (10 000 persons)
按轻重工业分	**by Light & Heavy Industry**				
轻工业	Light Industry	40	15	115.33	1.22
重工业	Heavy Industry	231	51	2700.11	9.15
按企业规模分	**by Enterprise Size**				
大型企业	Large-sized Enterprises	24	7	1879.78	5.74
中型企业	Medium-sized Enterprises	51	14	442.41	2.71
小型企业	Small-sized Enterprises	170	41	471.87	1.86
微型企业	Micro-sized Enterprises	26	4	21.39	0.05
按工业行业分	**by Sector**				
煤炭开采和洗选业	Mining and Washing of Coal	1		5.14	0.16
石油和天然气开采业	Extraction of Petroleum and Natural Gas	3		15.96	0.04
黑色金属矿采选业	Mining and Processing of Ferrous Metal Ores	3		20.56	0.43
有色金属矿采选业	Mining and Processing of Non-Ferrous Metal Ores				
非金属矿采选业	Mining and Processing of Non-metal Ores	1		2.54	
开采专业及辅助性活动	Professional and Support Activities for Mining				
其他采矿业	Mining of Other Ores				
农副食品加工业	Processing of Food from Agricultural Products	1		0.20	
食品制造业	Manufacture of Foods	6	2	18.66	0.18
酒、饮料和精制茶制造业	Manufacture of Liquor, Beverages and Refined Tea	3	1	23.15	0.21
烟草制品业	Manufacture of Tobacco	1		1.58	0.02
纺织业	Manufacture of Textile	3	3	2.64	0.06
纺织服装、服饰业	Manufacture of Textile, Wearing Apparel and Accessories	3	2	2.92	0.14
皮革、毛皮、羽毛及其制品和制鞋业	Manufacture of Leather, Fur, Feather and Related Products and Footwear				
木材加工和木、竹、藤、棕、草制品业	Processing of Timber, Manufacture of Wood, Bamboo, Rattan,Palm and Straw Products				
家具制造业	Manufacture of Furniture				

12-5 续表 2 continued 2

指标	Item	企业单位数(个) Number of Enterprises (unit)	亏损企业数(个) Loss Enterprises (unit)	工业总产值(现价)(亿元) Gross Industrial Output Value (Current Prices) (100 million yuan)	平均用工人数(万人) Annual Average Employees (10 000 persons)
造纸和纸制品业	Manufacture of Paper and Paper Products	2	1	2.69	0.02
印刷和记录媒介复制业	Printing and Reproduction of Recording Media	6	1	8.35	0.22
文教、工美、体育和娱乐用品制造业	Manufacture of Articles for Culture, Education, Arts and Crafts,Sport and Entertainment Activities				
石油、煤炭及其他燃料加工业	Processing of Petroleum, Coal and Other Fuels	2		355.42	0.16
化学原料和化学制品制造业	Manufacture of Raw Chemical Materials and Chemical Products	13	3	94.90	0.51
医药制造业	Manufacture of Medicines	4		22.50	0.19
化学纤维制造业	Manufacture of Chemical Fibres	2	1	4.61	0.04
橡胶和塑料制品业	Manufacture of Rubber and Plastics Products	2	2	1.28	0.02
非金属矿物制品业	Manufacture of Non-metallic Mineral Products	28	2	75.26	0.46
黑色金属冶炼和压延加工业	Smelting and Pressing of Ferrous Metals	4	4	685.74	1.43
有色金属冶炼和压延加工业	Smelting and Pressing of Non-ferrous Metals	1		16.05	0.02
金属制品业	Manufacture of Metal Products	15	3	64.93	0.35
通用设备制造业	Manufacture of General Purpose Machinery	20	2	120.28	1.05
专用设备制造业	Manufacture of Special Purpose Machinery	12	4	29.99	0.30
汽车制造业	Manufacture of Automobiles	10	1	138.09	0.73
铁路、船舶、航空航天和其他运输设备制造业	Manufacture of Railway, Ship, Aerospace and Other Transport Equipments	10		60.56	0.50
电气机械和器材制造业	Manufacture of Electrical Machinery and Apparatus	24	7	163.80	0.52
计算机、通信和其他电子设备制造业	Manufacture of Computers, Communication and Other Electronic Equipment	14	4	569.76	0.69
仪器仪表制造业	Manufacture of Measuring Instruments and Machinery	6		22.33	0.15
其他制造业	Other Manufacture	1		2.58	0.01
废弃资源综合利用业	Utilization of Waste Resources	1	1	0.50	
金属制品、机械和设备修理业	Repair Service of Metal Products, Machinery and Equipment	3		10.06	0.19
电力、热力生产和供应业	Production and Supply of Electric Power and Heat Power	37	15	194.48	0.99
燃气生产和供应业	Production and Supply of Gas	13	3	55.47	0.24
水的生产和供应业	Production and Supply of Water	16	4	22.49	0.33

12-6 规模以上私营工业企业主要经济指标(2022年)

Main Economic Indicators of Private Industrial Enterprises Above Designated Size(2022)

指标	Item	企业单位数(个) Number of Enterprises (unit)	亏损企业数(个) Loss Enterprises (unit)	工业总产值(现价)(亿元) Gross Industrial Output Value (Current Prices) (100 million yuan)	平均用工人数(万人) Annual Average Employees (10 000 persons)
总计	**Total**	**1680**	**396**	**2038.06**	**15.18**
按登记注册类型分组	**by Status of Registration**				
内资企业	Domestic Invested Enterprises	1680	396	2038.06	15.18
私营企业	Private Enterprises	1680	396	2038.06	15.18
私营独资企业	Private-funded Enterprises	53	9	24.43	0.26
私营合伙企业	Private Partnership Enterprises	7	2	1.79	0.02
私营有限责任公司	Private Limited Liability Corporations	1534	361	1866.28	13.81
私营股份有限公司	Private Share-holding Corporations Ltd.	86	24	145.56	1.09
其他企业	Other Enterprises				
按轻重工业分	**by Light & Heavy Industry**				
轻工业	Light Industry	421	108	539.29	5.43
重工业	Heavy Industry	1259	288	1498.77	9.75
按企业规模分	**by Enterprise Size**				
大型企业	Large-sized Enterprises	8		578.75	2.70
中型企业	Medium-sized Enterprises	52	13	393.73	2.44
小型企业	Small-sized Enterprises	1333	297	950.28	9.60
微型企业	Micro-sized Enterprises	287	86	115.31	0.44
按工业行业分	**by Sector**				
煤炭开采和洗选业	Mining and Washing of Coal	1	1	0.04	
石油和天然气开采业	Extraction of Petroleum and Natural Gas				

12–6 续表 1 continued 1

指标	Item	企业单位数(个) Number of Enterprises (unit)	亏损企业数(个) Loss Enterprises (unit)	工业总产值(现价)(亿元) Gross Industrial Output Value (Current Prices) (100 million yuan)	平均用工人数(万人) Annual Average Employees (10 000 persons)
黑色金属矿采选业	Mining and Processing of Ferrous Metal Ores	5	1	66.65	0.06
有色金属矿采选业	Mining and Processing of Non-Ferrous Metal Ores				
非金属矿采选业	Mining and Processing of Non-metal Ores	6	3	8.70	0.04
开采专业及辅助性活动	Professional and Support Activities for Mining				
其他采矿业	Mining of Other Ores				
农副食品加工业	Processing of Food from Agricultural Products	69	28	110.15	0.64
食品制造业	Manufacture of Foods	44	9	46.06	0.71
酒、饮料和精制茶制造业	Manufacture of Liquor, Beverages and Refined Tea	8	4	8.61	0.09
烟草制品业	Manufacture of Tobacco				
纺织业	Manufacture of Textile	40	9	19.29	0.21
纺织服装、服饰业	Manufacture of Textile, Wearing Apparel and Accessories	12	6	5.39	0.13
皮革、毛皮、羽毛及其制品和制鞋业	Manufacture of Leather, Fur, Feather and Related Products and Footwear	2	1	0.42	
木材加工和木、竹、藤、棕、草制品业	Processing of Timber, Manufacture of Wood, Bamboo, Rattan,Palm and Straw Products	11	2	7.75	0.07
家具制造业	Manufacture of Furniture	14	5	11.15	0.19
造纸和纸制品业	Manufacture of Paper and Paper Products	35	9	21.78	0.25
印刷和记录媒介复制业	Printing and Reproduction of Recording Media	28	7	21.85	0.34
文教、工美、体育和娱乐用品制造业	Manufacture of Articles for Culture, Education, Arts and Crafts,Sport and Entertainment Activities	22	7	12.95	0.25
石油、煤炭及其他燃料加工业	Processing of Petroleum, Coal and Other Fuels	9	1	22.54	0.09
化学原料和化学制品制造业	Manufacture of Raw Chemical Materials and Chemical Products	79	15	136.23	0.62
医药制造业	Manufacture of Medicines	38	3	216.28	1.87

12-6 续表 2 continued 2

指标	Item	企业单位数(个) Number of Enterprises (unit)	亏损企业数(个) Loss Enterprises (unit)	工业总产值(现价)(亿元) Gross Industrial Output Value (Current Prices) (100 million yuan)	平均用工人数(万人) Annual Average Employees (10 000 persons)
化学纤维制造业	Manufacture of Chemical Fibres	4		1.52	0.02
橡胶和塑料制品业	Manufacture of Rubber and Plastics Products	53	9	27.29	0.32
非金属矿物制品业	Manufacture of Non-metallic Mineral Products	231	68	284.40	1.89
黑色金属冶炼和压延加工业	Smelting and Pressing of Ferrous Metals	35	18	385.98	0.72
有色金属冶炼和压延加工业	Smelting and Pressing of Non-ferrous Metals	36	10	22.13	0.13
金属制品业	Manufacture of Metal Products	210	40	122.35	1.33
通用设备制造业	Manufacture of General Purpose Machinery	222	37	126.83	1.57
专用设备制造业	Manufacture of Special Purpose Machinery	172	31	114.71	1.38
汽车制造业	Manufacture of Automobiles	77	27	50.12	0.83
铁路、船舶、航空航天和其他运输设备制造业	Manufacture of Railway, Ship, Aerospace and Other Transport Equipments	4	1	4.72	0.06
电气机械和器材制造业	Manufacture of Electrical Machinery and Apparatus	85	13	76.72	0.43
计算机、通信和其他电子设备制造业	Manufacture of Computers, Communication and Other Electronic Equipment	41	14	39.16	0.29
仪器仪表制造业	Manufacture of Measuring Instruments and Machinery	55	9	35.84	0.52
其他制造业	Other Manufacture	2		0.82	0.01
废弃资源综合利用业	Utilization of Waste Resources	9	3	10.06	0.06
金属制品、机械和设备修理业	Repair Service of Metal Products, Machinery and Equipment	4	1	1.65	0.04
电力、热力生产和供应业	Production and Supply of Electric Power and Heat Power	9	2	9.01	0.04
燃气生产和供应业	Production and Supply of Gas	7	2	8.93	0.01
水的生产和供应业	Production and Supply of Water	1			0.01

12–7 规模以上工业资产实力(2022年)
Capital Power of Industrial Enterprises Above Designated Size(2022)

单位：亿元

指标	Item	流动资产合计 Current Assets	其中of which 应收账款 Accounts Receivable	存货 Inventories
总计	**Total**	**5714.63**	**1727.82**	**1088.71**
按登记注册类型分组	**by Status of Registration**			
内资企业	Domestic Invested Enterprises	4696.77	1505.44	911.57
国有企业	State-owned Enterprises	121.57	26.56	11.13
中央企业	Central Enterprises	28.54	10.25	5.16
地方企业	Local Enterprises	93.03	16.31	5.97
集体企业	Collective-owned Enterprises	3.38	0.70	1.35
股份合作企业	Cooperative Enterprises	115.61	52.09	11.40
联营企业	Joint Ownership Enterprises	10.68	6.28	2.18
国有联营企业	State Joint Ownership Enterprises			
集体联营企业	Collective Joint Ownership Enterprises			
国有与集体联营企业	Joint State-collective Enterprises	10.59	6.27	2.16
其他联营企业	Other Joint Ownership Enterprises	0.10	0.01	0.02
有限责任公司	Limited Liability Corporations	1979.90	515.35	393.42
国有独资公司	State Sole Funded Corporations	300.68	56.13	56.20
其他有限责任公司	Other Limited Liability Corporations	1679.22	459.22	337.21
股份有限公司	Share-holding Corporations Ltd.	849.84	286.10	189.25
私营企业	Private Enterprises	1615.78	618.35	302.83
私营独资企业	Private-funded Enterprises	14.19	8.48	2.17
私营合伙企业	Private Partnership Enterprises	0.90	0.35	0.17
私营有限责任公司	Private Limited Liability Corporations	1467.28	569.50	266.18
私营股份有限公司	Private Share-holding Corporations Ltd.	133.41	40.02	34.31
其他企业	Other Enterprises			
港、澳、台商投资企业	Enterprises with Funds from Hong Kong,Macao and Taiwan	787.11	148.37	117.96
合资经营企业	Joint-venture Enterprises	268.25	55.91	34.21
合作经营企业	Cooperative Enterprises			
港澳台商独资经营企业	Enterprises with Sole Investment	321.60	58.16	50.63
港澳台商投资股份有限公司	Share-holding Corporations Ltd.	195.48	33.64	32.77
其他港澳台商投资企业	Other Enterprises with Funds from Hong Kong,Macao and Taiwan	1.78	0.66	0.36
外商投资企业	Foreign Funded Enterprises	230.76	74.01	59.18
中外合资经营企业	Joint-venture Enterprises	103.17	30.25	33.34
中外合作经营企业	Cooperation Enterprises	0.37	0.08	0.14
外资企业	Enterprises with Sole Fund	93.19	33.12	23.41
外商投资股份有限公司	Share-holding Corporations Ltd.	25.12	8.05	1.95
其他外商投资企业	Other Foreign Funded Enterprises	8.90	2.51	0.34
按轻重工业分	**by Light & Heavy Industry**			
轻工业	Light Industry	1118.00	319.33	211.07
重工业	Heavy Industry	4596.63	1408.50	877.64
按企业规模分	**by Enterprise Size**			
大型企业	Large-sized Enterprises	2362.86	636.97	429.78
中型企业	Medium-sized Enterprises	1170.71	280.91	256.87
小型企业	Small-sized Enterprises	1961.25	681.86	385.24
微型企业	Micro-sized Enterprises	219.82	128.09	16.82

(100 million yuan)

固定资产净额 Net Fixed Assets	固定资产原价 Original Value of Fixed Assets	流动负债合计 Current Liabilities Total	非流动负债合计 Non-Current Liabilities Total	所有者权益合计 Total Owner's Equities	其中of which 实收资本 Paid-up Capital	其中of which 国家资本 Official Capital
2049.71	**3743.97**	**4999.66**	**858.37**	**3779.62**	**2137.18**	**338.47**
1784.81	3221.49	4107.55	783.71	2927.89	1762.60	326.80
69.19	142.59	110.66	38.65	60.41	36.92	14.85
36.40	70.91	45.95	13.96	11.77	19.29	2.56
32.79	71.68	64.70	24.71	48.64	17.63	12.29
1.55	5.46	2.37	1.11	2.68	0.30	
6.14	8.73	76.37	4.63	49.16	5.49	
0.72	2.14	5.87	1.05	5.62	1.02	1.00
0.38	1.20	5.67	0.97	5.26	1.00	1.00
0.34	0.94	0.20	0.08	0.36	0.02	
1076.41	1817.11	2044.70	439.76	1284.68	764.97	209.28
205.57	346.39	345.27	140.81	196.60	138.03	49.75
870.84	1470.72	1699.43	298.95	1088.08	626.94	159.53
271.29	546.95	538.38	139.95	698.49	202.37	97.37
359.51	698.51	1329.21	158.54	826.86	751.54	4.30
4.40	7.07	14.48	2.36	3.64	3.23	
0.22	0.33	0.73	0.01	0.38	0.30	
311.46	622.93	1203.10	128.46	719.64	704.95	3.87
43.43	68.17	110.90	27.72	103.19	43.05	0.42
178.33	339.61	740.36	36.94	630.19	265.98	9.72
87.53	154.11	190.77	20.44	222.70	97.76	7.27
55.71	133.61	426.34	13.93	278.98	155.15	
34.97	51.73	122.57	2.57	126.99	11.75	2.45
0.12	0.17	0.68	0.01	1.52	1.32	
86.57	182.87	151.76	37.70	221.54	108.60	1.94
40.82	89.37	74.77	24.05	76.63	45.61	1.94
0.03	0.10	0.03	0.01	0.37	0.06	
44.47	90.87	54.51	12.64	110.55	53.64	
0.81	1.53	15.01	0.50	32.26	8.30	
0.43	1.00	7.44	0.51	1.73	1.00	
344.47	605.93	756.75	90.41	985.97	545.42	15.36
1705.24	3138.04	4242.92	767.94	2793.65	1591.76	323.11
1017.74	1926.33	1997.22	400.53	1786.36	623.38	187.32
441.41	779.02	1113.39	163.65	845.77	363.61	77.07
506.07	896.61	1707.65	209.48	1059.19	870.27	65.69
84.49	142.02	181.41	84.70	88.31	279.91	8.39

12-7 续表 continued

单位：亿元

指标	Item	流动资产合计 Current Assets	其中of which 应收账款 Accounts Receivable	存货 Inventories
按工业行业分	**by Sector**			
煤炭开采和洗选业	Mining and Washing of Coal	6.30	0.77	0.23
石油和天然气开采业	Extraction of Petroleum and Natural Gas	32.32	3.16	0.04
黑色金属矿采选业	Mining and Processing of Ferrous Metal Ores	79.77	7.03	7.91
有色金属矿采选业	Mining and Processing of Non-Ferrous Metal Ores			
非金属矿采选业	Mining and Processing of Non-metal Ores	7.20	2.35	2.09
开采专业及辅助性活动	Professional and Support Activities for Mining			
其他采矿业	Mining of Other Ores			
农副食品加工业	Processing of Food from Agricultural Products	67.64	19.94	17.29
食品制造业	Manufacture of Foods	88.86	16.84	20.19
酒、饮料和精制茶制造业	Manufacture of Liquor, Beverages and Refined Tea	51.82	5.93	10.67
烟草制品业	Manufacture of Tobacco	3.17	0.25	0.25
纺织业	Manufacture of Textile	33.54	9.19	8.89
纺织服装、服饰业	Manufacture of Textile, Wearing Apparel and Accessories	12.87	2.18	3.48
皮革、毛皮、羽毛及其制品和制鞋业	Manufacture of Leather, Fur, Feather and Related Products and Footwear	1.76	0.30	0.11
木材加工和木、竹、藤、棕、草制品业	Processing of Timber, Manufacture of Wood, Bamboo, Rattan,Palm and Straw Products	3.42	0.96	1.70
家具制造业	Manufacture of Furniture	7.62	2.77	3.36
造纸和纸制品业	Manufacture of Paper and Paper Products	27.00	6.20	10.79
印刷和记录媒介复制业	Printing and Reproduction of Recording Media	37.28	9.33	7.23
文教、工美、体育和娱乐用品制造业	Manufacture of Articles for Culture, Education, Arts and Crafts,Sport and Entertainment Activities	15.15	2.65	9.28
石油、煤炭及其他燃料加工业	Processing of Petroleum, Coal and Other Fuels	112.01	72.37	14.72
化学原料和化学制品制造业	Manufacture of Raw Chemical Materials and Chemical Products	234.67	35.44	43.99
医药制造业	Manufacture of Medicines	470.03	142.95	68.05
化学纤维制造业	Manufacture of Chemical Fibres	12.69	1.05	3.87
橡胶和塑料制品业	Manufacture of Rubber and Plastics Products	27.65	9.77	7.50
非金属矿物制品业	Manufacture of Non-metallic Mineral Products	537.26	241.14	71.54
黑色金属冶炼和压延加工业	Smelting and Pressing of Ferrous Metals	358.27	65.28	101.52
有色金属冶炼和压延加工业	Smelting and Pressing of Non-ferrous Metals	26.42	10.55	5.92
金属制品业	Manufacture of Metal Products	290.17	92.81	58.31
通用设备制造业	Manufacture of General Purpose Machinery	432.56	122.65	110.54
专用设备制造业	Manufacture of Special Purpose Machinery	381.18	142.86	74.06
汽车制造业	Manufacture of Automobiles	659.22	132.76	110.10
铁路、船舶、航空航天和其他运输设备制造业	Manufacture of Railway, Ship, Aerospace and Other Transport Equipments	60.46	13.87	10.62
电气机械和器材制造业	Manufacture of Electrical Machinery and Apparatus	503.73	190.30	92.54
计算机、通信和其他电子设备制造业	Manufacture of Computers, Communication and Other Electronic Equipment	610.04	248.58	155.32
仪器仪表制造业	Manufacture of Measuring Instruments and Machinery	99.98	34.94	22.08
其他制造业	Other Manufacture	10.82	2.67	3.76
废弃资源综合利用业	Utilization of Waste Resources	12.67	6.17	1.14
金属制品、机械和设备修理业	Repair Service of Metal Products, Machinery and Equipment	17.75	3.72	3.38
电力、热力生产和供应业	Production and Supply of Electric Power and Heat Power	265.00	41.77	16.08
燃气生产和供应业	Production and Supply of Gas	59.01	10.67	6.73
水的生产和供应业	Production and Supply of Water	57.33	15.68	3.40

(100 million yuan)

固定资产净额 Net Fixed Assets	固定资产原价 Original Value of Fixed Assets	流动负债合计 Current Liabilities Total	非流动负债合计 Non-Current Liabilities Total	所有者权益合计 Total Owner's Equities	其中of which 实收资本 Paid- up Capital	其中of which 国家资本 Official Capital
2.87	7.54	16.75	0.03	-6.46	1.42	0.30
6.18	32.47	1.39	9.44	34.64	5.18	3.50
32.26	75.05	105.34	12.33	22.95	32.92	2.40
3.31	5.10	9.47	0.01	2.49	1.55	
19.49	26.92	78.02	5.60	20.61	13.71	0.15
51.79	93.85	53.67	22.37	86.74	43.41	0.59
25.57	55.58	44.34	3.24	55.43	44.79	0.37
1.04	1.83	0.51		3.85	0.95	0.95
15.34	29.81	35.06	4.46	18.03	8.26	0.99
10.58	16.23	12.96	3.50	10.40	3.63	
0.25	0.53	1.65	0.06	0.42	0.11	
1.28	2.28	4.24	0.32	0.99	0.55	
2.57	3.94	9.23	0.48	5.14	4.82	
12.25	23.77	25.33	5.14	15.67	9.77	1.00
21.83	45.35	30.93	3.12	39.02	23.75	6.26
4.34	6.99	13.48	1.45	7.24	5.29	
40.22	114.14	102.16	14.29	50.16	34.32	27.81
144.99	225.78	259.57	55.96	163.03	55.87	8.11
100.79	181.16	213.44	19.20	494.84	325.94	3.64
8.02	12.72	8.35	1.37	16.29	13.15	0.85
8.71	19.26	20.74	2.62	16.40	13.62	1.73
112.23	218.37	581.10	26.19	302.16	316.95	7.03
386.17	785.10	484.07	102.89	266.42	178.06	113.36
4.50	8.21	25.79	1.77	10.42	3.94	0.90
79.82	150.17	227.02	25.85	208.10	68.07	6.88
88.55	178.31	302.00	24.74	280.57	153.24	9.34
59.50	88.52	285.70	24.29	204.31	74.61	6.86
114.81	257.09	542.18	56.30	380.11	148.60	17.19
12.32	28.21	43.03	3.65	60.35	42.12	0.10
98.60	153.94	470.92	28.98	242.65	137.30	19.32
94.15	128.48	392.12	53.68	373.11	148.44	11.81
12.54	22.13	52.72	3.30	73.77	23.41	4.86
1.88	2.56	6.18	0.47	6.54	1.94	1.00
6.06	8.62	16.91	1.86	5.07	3.46	0.84
4.13	8.52	13.44	3.67	10.39	4.83	1.76
361.33	579.76	368.87	240.55	177.80	132.63	63.60
43.32	60.77	60.94	11.67	71.54	25.21	2.78
56.12	84.91	80.06	83.49	48.44	31.35	12.19

12-8 规模以上国有及国有控股工业资产实力(2022年)

Capital Power of State-Owned and State-Controlled Industrial Enterprises Above Designated Size(2022)

单位：亿元

指标	Item	流动资产合计 Current Assets	其中 of which 应收账款 Accounts Receivable	存货 Inventories
总计	**Total**	**1835.86**	**499.35**	**355.64**
按登记注册类型分组	**by Status of Registration**			
内资企业	Domestic Invested Enterprises	1693.60	479.70	337.23
国有企业	State-owned Enterprises	121.57	26.56	11.13
中央企业	Central Enterprises	28.54	10.25	5.16
地方企业	Local Enterprises	93.03	16.31	5.97
集体企业	Collective-owned Enterprises			
股份合作企业	Cooperative Enterprises			
联营企业	Joint Ownership Enterprises	10.59	6.27	2.16
有限责任公司	Limited Liability Corporations	1045.35	248.27	196.97
国有独资公司	State Sole Funded Corporations	300.68	56.13	56.20
其他有限责任公司	Other Limited Liability Corporations	744.67	192.14	140.77
股份有限公司	Share-holding Corporations Ltd.	516.09	198.60	126.96
私营企业	Private Enterprises			
其他企业	Other Enterprises			
港、澳、台商投资企业	Enterprises with Funds from Hong Kong,Macao and Taiwan	109.66	12.65	9.37
合资经营企业	Joint-venture Enterprises	109.66	12.65	9.37
合作经营企业	Cooperative Enterprises			
港澳台商独资经营企业	Enterprises with Sole Investment			
港澳台商投资股份有限公司	Share-holding Corporations Ltd.			
其他港澳台商投资企业	Other Enterprises with Funds from Hong Kong,Macao and Taiwan			
外商投资企业	Foreign Funded Enterprises	32.60	6.99	9.04
中外合资经营企业	Joint-venture Enterprises	32.60	6.99	9.04
中外合作经营企业	Cooperation Enterprises			
外资企业	Enterprises with Sole Fund			
外商投资股份有限公司	Share-holding Corporations Ltd.			
其他外商投资企业	Other Foreign Funded Enterprises			
按轻重工业分	**by Light & Heavy Industry**			
轻工业	Light Industry	95.38	13.70	21.97
重工业	Heavy Industry	1740.48	485.65	333.68
按企业规模分	**by Enterprise Size**			
大型企业	Large-sized Enterprises	938.29	228.89	175.32
中型企业	Medium-sized Enterprises	373.45	95.17	88.05
小型企业	Small-sized Enterprises	489.30	166.10	91.49
微型企业	Micro-sized Enterprises	34.82	9.19	0.77
按工业行业分	**by Sector**			
煤炭开采和洗选业	Mining and Washing of Coal	2.93	0.20	0.13
石油和天然气开采业	Extraction of Petroleum and Natural Gas	32.32	3.16	0.04
黑色金属矿采选业	Mining and Processing of Ferrous Metal Ores	11.58	2.16	1.03

(100 million yuan)

固定资产净额 Net Fixed Assets	固定资产原价 Original Value of Fixed Assets	流动负债合计 Current Liabilities Total	非流动负债合计 Non-Current Liabilities Total	所有者权益合计 Total Owner's Equities	其中 of which	
					实收资本 Paid- up Capital	其中 of which 国家资本 Official Capital
1042.45	**1886.10**	**1878.97**	**490.72**	**1141.65**	**672.18**	**323.44**
993.64	1795.89	1756.44	472.91	1041.80	627.70	314.45
69.19	142.59	110.66	38.65	60.41	36.92	14.85
36.40	70.91	45.95	13.96	11.77	19.29	2.56
32.79	71.68	64.70	24.71	48.64	17.63	12.29
0.38	1.20	5.67	0.97	5.26	1.00	1.00
741.25	1246.30	1268.27	324.10	632.34	476.85	204.55
205.57	346.39	345.27	140.81	196.60	138.03	49.75
535.68	899.92	923.01	183.28	435.74	338.82	154.80
182.82	405.80	371.84	109.18	343.79	112.94	94.05
40.89	73.75	95.54	14.96	83.46	35.10	7.27
40.89	73.75	95.54	14.96	83.46	35.10	7.27
7.92	16.46	26.99	2.85	16.39	9.38	1.72
7.92	16.46	26.99	2.85	16.39	9.38	1.72
40.55	72.97	67.52	11.72	84.65	31.80	12.79
1001.90	1813.13	1811.45	479.00	1056.99	640.38	310.65
654.84	1226.98	1012.51	310.81	628.39	335.11	182.71
207.22	363.47	396.42	72.52	236.89	150.69	76.57
146.12	249.31	445.88	77.20	247.91	169.16	55.78
34.27	46.35	24.16	30.20	28.45	17.23	8.38
2.39	6.56	11.53		-5.37	1.05	0.30
6.18	32.47	1.39	9.44	34.64	5.18	3.50
15.81	42.16	9.91	10.52	28.27	26.83	1.99

12-8 续表 continued

单位：亿元

指标	Item	流动资产合计 Current Assets	其中of which 应收账款 Accounts Receivable	存货 Inventories
有色金属矿采选业	Mining and Processing of Non-Ferrous Metal Ores			
非金属矿采选业	Mining and Processing of Non-metal Ores	2.24	1.51	
开采专业及辅助性活动	Professional and Support Activities for Mining			
其他采矿业	Mining of Other Ores			
农副食品加工业	Processing of Food from Agricultural Products	0.28	0.05	0.15
食品制造业	Manufacture of Foods	13.40	1.64	1.48
酒、饮料和精制茶制造业	Manufacture of Liquor, Beverages and Refined Tea	11.88	0.79	2.65
烟草制品业	Manufacture of Tobacco	3.17	0.25	0.25
纺织业	Manufacture of Textile	2.26	0.44	1.16
纺织服装、服饰业	Manufacture of Textile, Wearing Apparel and Accessories	6.62	0.34	1.33
皮革、毛皮、羽毛及其制品和制鞋业	Manufacture of Leather, Fur, Feather and Related Products and Footwear			
木材加工和木、竹、藤、棕、草制品业	Processing of Timber, Manufacture of Wood, Bamboo, Rattan,Palm and Straw Products			
家具制造业	Manufacture of Furniture			
造纸和纸制品业	Manufacture of Paper and Paper Products	3.17	0.29	0.67
印刷和记录媒介复制业	Printing and Reproduction of Recording Media	10.16	1.91	1.28
文教、工美、体育和娱乐用品制造业	Manufacture of Articles for Culture, Education, Arts and Crafts, Sport and Entertainment Activities			
石油、煤炭及其他燃料加工业	Processing of Petroleum, Coal and Other Fuels	20.87	7.58	8.51
化学原料和化学制品制造业	Manufacture of Raw Chemical Materials and Chemical Products	68.45	3.20	14.48
医药制造业	Manufacture of Medicines	20.85	4.68	3.36
化学纤维制造业	Manufacture of Chemical Fibres	3.78	0.27	2.55
橡胶和塑料制品业	Manufacture of Rubber and Plastics Products	2.44	0.83	1.01
非金属矿物制品业	Manufacture of Non-metallic Mineral Products	75.24	37.86	8.70
黑色金属冶炼和压延加工业	Smelting and Pressing of Ferrous Metals	115.20	1.55	28.69
有色金属冶炼和压延加工业	Smelting and Pressing of Non-ferrous Metals	10.05	5.03	0.63
金属制品业	Manufacture of Metal Products	46.64	11.38	13.21
通用设备制造业	Manufacture of General Purpose Machinery	180.35	34.74	43.58
专用设备制造业	Manufacture of Special Purpose Machinery	64.44	19.80	13.48
汽车制造业	Manufacture of Automobiles	127.19	25.81	12.52
铁路、船舶、航空航天和其他运输设备制造业	Manufacture of Railway, Ship, Aerospace and Other Transport Equipments	49.22	9.50	7.27
电气机械和器材制造业	Manufacture of Electrical Machinery and Apparatus	176.97	60.55	45.97
计算机、通信和其他电子设备制造业	Manufacture of Computers, Communication and Other Electronic Equipment	444.55	208.43	111.73
仪器仪表制造业	Manufacture of Measuring Instruments and Machinery	24.28	8.90	4.48
其他制造业	Other Manufacture	2.14	1.55	0.44
废弃资源综合利用业	Utilization of Waste Resources	0.77	0.42	0.07
金属制品、机械和设备修理业	Repair Service of Metal Products, Machinery and Equipment	11.74	2.20	2.85
电力、热力生产和供应业	Production and Supply of Electric Power and Heat Power	207.86	28.44	14.31
燃气生产和供应业	Production and Supply of Gas	38.11	4.07	4.73
水的生产和供应业	Production and Supply of Water	44.71	9.83	2.92

(100 million yuan)

固定资产净额 Net Fixed Assets	固定资产原价 Original Value of Fixed Assets	流动负债合计 Current Liabilities Total	非流动负债合计 Non-Current Liabilities Total	所有者权益合计 Total Owner's Equities	其中of which 实收资本 Paid- up Capital	其中of which 国家资本 Official Capital
		1.37		1.27	0.08	
0.11	0.25	0.34		0.20	0.30	
2.77	7.08	8.29	0.09	12.34	1.19	0.37
6.38	13.71	9.22	0.76	9.91	6.13	0.37
1.04	1.83	0.51		3.85	0.95	0.95
2.04	3.25	3.43	0.96	1.23	0.74	0.69
5.25	7.21	9.56	0.95	3.41	0.55	
0.58	2.38	0.66	2.16	2.02	1.00	1.00
6.80	15.83	6.40	0.47	12.44	9.11	5.67
31.69	93.33	14.87	7.65	41.35	27.81	27.81
90.41	125.18	158.16	31.88	9.85	13.44	5.01
6.15	9.73	14.89	4.02	17.90	3.28	2.34
5.07	6.15	2.71	1.34	7.50	5.91	0.85
1.25	1.88	1.93	0.57	1.81	1.81	1.73
22.71	42.88	81.10	7.14	35.75	14.55	5.69
299.29	551.92	270.33	75.93	130.36	113.73	113.36
1.50	2.08	10.90	0.34	3.14	0.88	0.88
12.59	21.60	52.27	1.56	13.90	9.56	5.75
16.44	62.41	107.95	8.01	111.99	70.42	7.58
18.69	24.66	74.71	5.42	15.68	19.78	6.69
16.01	44.41	112.13	2.33	39.82	23.44	14.43
10.23	22.18	37.29	3.14	51.44	37.50	0.10
30.67	60.06	169.30	6.50	85.76	63.21	19.22
31.70	44.46	293.18	46.31	213.61	68.20	11.81
3.74	6.86	13.89	0.24	17.96	6.23	4.86
0.59	0.85	1.27		1.47	1.00	1.00
1.16	1.26	1.31	0.04	1.02	1.65	0.84
3.23	7.12	8.23	3.58	8.28	3.57	1.53
305.23	499.35	279.11	175.87	145.54	98.06	62.16
31.40	43.74	42.01	11.06	54.10	18.26	2.78
53.33	81.29	68.81	72.46	29.22	16.81	12.19

12-9 规模以上工业损益及分配(2022年)

Profit, Loss and Distribution of Industrial Enterprises Above Designated Size(2022)

单位：亿元

指标	Item	营业收入 Business Revenue	营业成本 Business Cost
总计	**Total**	**8370.30**	**7190.97**
按登记注册类型分组	**by Status of Registration**		
内资企业	Domestic Invested Enterprises	7198.08	6212.35
国有企业	State-owned Enterprises	86.18	77.95
中央企业	Central Enterprises	48.74	48.59
地方企业	Local Enterprises	37.44	29.36
集体企业	Collective-owned Enterprises	4.84	4.39
股份合作企业	Cooperative Enterprises	108.32	88.52
联营企业	Joint Ownership Enterprises	11.56	9.36
国有联营企业	State Joint Ownership Enterprises		
集体联营企业	Collective Joint Ownership Enterprises		
国有与集体联营企业	Joint State-collective Enterprises	10.75	8.85
其他联营企业	Other Joint Ownership Enterprises	0.81	0.51
有限责任公司	Limited Liability Corporations	2794.96	2502.67
国有独资公司	State Sole Funded Corporations	262.14	253.27
其他有限责任公司	Other Limited Liability Corporations	2532.82	2249.40
股份有限公司	Share-holding Corporations Ltd.	1949.92	1693.58
私营企业	Private Enterprises	2242.29	1835.87
私营独资企业	Private-funded Enterprises	22.44	20.29
私营合伙企业	Private Partnership Enterprises	1.80	1.48
私营有限责任公司	Private Limited Liability Corporations	2083.53	1708.34
私营股份有限公司	Private Share-holding Corporations Ltd.	134.53	105.77
其他企业	Other Enterprises		
港、澳、台商投资企业	Enterprises with Funds from Hong Kong,Macao and Taiwan	822.52	704.15
合资经营企业	Joint-venture Enterprises	294.59	228.13
合作经营企业	Cooperative Enterprises		
港澳台商独资经营企业	Enterprises with Sole Investment	306.70	258.63
港澳台商投资股份有限公司	Share-holding Corporations Ltd.	219.49	216.09
其他港澳台商投资企业	Other Enterprises with Funds from Hong Kong,Macao and Taiwan	1.74	1.30
外商投资企业	Foreign Funded Enterprises	349.70	274.48
中外合资经营企业	Joint-venture Enterprises	146.87	114.50
中外合作经营企业	Cooperation Enterprises	0.39	0.26
外资企业	Enterprises with Sole Fund	154.69	120.41
外商投资股份有限公司	Share-holding Corporations Ltd.	40.54	33.34
其他外商投资企业	Other Foreign Funded Enterprises	7.20	5.97
按轻重工业分	**by Light & Heavy Industry**		
轻工业	Light Industry	1309.14	900.70
重工业	Heavy Industry	7061.17	6290.27
按企业规模分	**by Enterprise Size**		
大型企业	Large-sized Enterprises	4340.34	3741.61
中型企业	Medium-sized Enterprises	1550.73	1328.34
小型企业	Small-sized Enterprises	2225.38	1877.10
微型企业	Micro-sized Enterprises	253.85	243.92

(100 million yuan)

税金及附加 Taxes and Other Charges	销售费用 Selling Expenses	管理费用 Management Expenses	利息费用 Interest Expenses	利润总额 Total Profits	所得税费用 Income Tax Payable	亏损企业 亏损总额 Total Loss of Loss Enterprises	利税总额 Total Profits and Taxes	应交增值税 Value-added Tax Payable
109.37	**259.86**	**242.54**	**68.17**	**344.86**	**48.19**	**114.94**	**593.57**	**139.34**
103.30	218.23	199.72	59.55	240.78	36.88	109.66	457.63	113.55
2.48	0.59	2.99	1.67	-2.66	1.37	9.42	3.06	3.24
0.32	0.25	1.47	1.13	-6.71	0.14	8.01	-4.68	1.71
2.17	0.34	1.52	0.54	4.05	1.23	1.41	7.75	1.53
0.04	0.04	0.33	0.02	-0.11	0.01	0.20	-0.03	0.04
0.15	3.56	1.59	0.15	12.00	1.41		12.92	0.77
0.09	0.31	0.79		0.53	0.04		0.82	0.20
0.06	0.31	0.67		0.39	0.01		0.58	0.13
0.04		0.12		0.14	0.03		0.25	0.07
18.74	57.12	81.90	30.99	55.70	13.56	72.17	116.34	41.90
2.95	5.77	12.37	4.14	-7.89	-0.39	14.67	3.77	8.71
15.78	51.35	69.53	26.85	63.59	13.95	57.50	112.57	33.20
72.95	48.61	33.26	9.31	59.76	5.33	11.40	160.62	27.91
8.86	108.00	78.86	17.40	115.56	15.15	16.47	163.91	39.49
0.08	0.90	0.83	0.20	-0.23	0.10	0.61	0.20	0.35
	0.07	0.11	0.01	0.04		0.01	0.07	0.03
8.05	100.52	69.93	12.84	105.06	14.06	12.64	148.37	35.26
0.72	6.51	7.98	4.35	10.69	0.99	3.22	15.26	3.85
3.77	22.22	26.64	6.83	63.11	5.67	2.63	86.77	19.89
1.86	10.91	11.10	1.00	35.59	6.35	2.09	44.70	7.25
1.35	8.50	13.35	5.30	23.55	-0.12	0.54	29.90	5.00
0.56	2.72	2.06	0.52	3.87	-0.55		12.03	7.60
	0.09	0.13	0.01	0.10			0.14	0.04
2.30	19.41	16.18	1.79	40.97	5.64	2.65	49.17	5.90
1.04	7.94	5.99	1.04	12.53	2.05	1.25	15.97	2.40
	0.01	0.05		0.06	0.01		0.06	
1.11	6.39	9.05	0.74	15.31	3.22	1.39	19.36	2.94
0.12	4.32	0.91	0.01	12.99	0.35		13.46	0.35
0.03	0.74	0.18		0.08			0.32	0.21
9.13	131.22	56.08	6.54	162.57	21.84	9.42	201.59	29.89
100.24	128.64	186.46	61.63	182.29	26.35	105.52	391.98	109.45
83.29	124.74	86.13	26.33	184.31	26.28	37.82	337.27	69.67
10.58	55.91	50.44	16.94	71.34	8.13	30.15	110.65	28.73
14.72	75.56	99.77	22.33	93.92	12.83	33.55	146.07	37.43
0.78	3.65	6.20	2.57	-4.71	0.95	13.42	-0.42	3.51

12-9 续表 continued

单位：亿元

指标	Item	营业收入 Business Revenue	营业成本 Business Cost
按工业行业分	**by Sector**		
煤炭开采和洗选业	Mining and Washing of Coal	7.48	4.76
石油和天然气开采业	Extraction of Petroleum and Natural Gas	16.35	7.29
黑色金属矿采选业	Mining and Processing of Ferrous Metal Ores	185.98	166.21
有色金属矿采选业	Mining and Processing of Non-Ferrous Metal Ores		
非金属矿采选业	Mining and Processing of Non-metal Ores	10.05	7.46
开采专业及辅助性活动	Professional and Support Activities for Mining		
其他采矿业	Mining of Other Ores		
农副食品加工业	Processing of Food from Agricultural Products	179.94	169.17
食品制造业	Manufacture of Foods	166.69	129.07
酒、饮料和精制茶制造业	Manufacture of Liquor, Beverages and Refined Tea	68.22	54.46
烟草制品业	Manufacture of Tobacco	1.68	0.92
纺织业	Manufacture of Textile	47.61	44.15
纺织服装、服饰业	Manufacture of Textile, Wearing Apparel and Accessories	14.38	12.13
皮革、毛皮、羽毛及其制品和制鞋业	Manufacture of Leather, Fur, Feather and Related Products and Footwear	1.32	1.05
木材加工和木、竹、藤、棕、草制品业	Processing of Timber, Manufacture of Wood, Bamboo, Rattan,Palm and Straw Products	7.50	6.73
家具制造业	Manufacture of Furniture	11.20	9.97
造纸和纸制品业	Manufacture of Paper and Paper Products	49.42	42.89
印刷和记录媒介复制业	Printing and Reproduction of Recording Media	48.48	38.96
文教、工美、体育和娱乐用品制造业	Manufacture of Articles for Culture, Education, Arts and Crafts,Sport and Entertainment Activities	16.52	13.03
石油、煤炭及其他燃料加工业	Processing of Petroleum, Coal and Other Fuels	462.89	372.48
化学原料和化学制品制造业	Manufacture of Raw Chemical Materials and Chemical Products	387.42	324.91
医药制造业	Manufacture of Medicines	405.46	161.86
化学纤维制造业	Manufacture of Chemical Fibres	18.43	13.82
橡胶和塑料制品业	Manufacture of Rubber and Plastics Products	38.60	32.06
非金属矿物制品业	Manufacture of Non-metallic Mineral Products	551.74	466.21
黑色金属冶炼和压延加工业	Smelting and Pressing of Ferrous Metals	1694.95	1652.87
有色金属冶炼和压延加工业	Smelting and Pressing of Non-ferrous Metals	51.22	48.46
金属制品业	Manufacture of Metal Products	363.15	306.77
通用设备制造业	Manufacture of General Purpose Machinery	414.37	319.76
专用设备制造业	Manufacture of Special Purpose Machinery	326.22	247.97
汽车制造业	Manufacture of Automobiles	694.77	618.94
铁路、船舶、航空航天和其他运输设备制造业	Manufacture of Railway, Ship, Aerospace and Other Transport Equipments	82.71	68.43
电气机械和器材制造业	Manufacture of Electrical Machinery and Apparatus	475.58	409.91
计算机、通信和其他电子设备制造业	Manufacture of Computers, Communication and Other Electronic Equipment	1006.46	922.46
仪器仪表制造业	Manufacture of Measuring Instruments and Machinery	89.52	58.99
其他制造业	Other Manufacture	8.39	6.43
废弃资源综合利用业	Utilization of Waste Resources	32.06	30.19
金属制品、机械和设备修理业	Repair Service of Metal Products, Machinery and Equipment	21.87	16.66
电力、热力生产和供应业	Production and Supply of Electric Power and Heat Power	230.33	237.55
燃气生产和供应业	Production and Supply of Gas	141.73	132.31
水的生产和供应业	Production and Supply of Water	39.59	33.70

(100 million yuan)

税金及附加 Taxes and Other Charges	销售费用 Selling Expenses	管理费用 Management Expenses	利息费用 Interest Expenses	利润总额 Total Profits	所得税费用 Income Tax Payable	亏损企业亏损总额 Total Loss of Loss Enterprises	利税总额 Total Profits and Taxes	应交增值税 Value-added Tax Payable
0.38	0.08	0.90	0.35	0.28			1.35	0.69
3.04		-0.03	0.29	5.69	1.42		10.18	1.45
2.01	0.25	5.14	1.70	9.66	1.41	0.03	15.68	4.01
0.31	0.15	0.88	0.06	-1.06	0.21	1.40	-0.42	0.33
0.27	4.66	3.71	1.35	1.07	0.42	1.74	1.69	0.35
1.04	8.41	7.19	0.37	19.86	3.29	0.84	25.15	4.25
2.01	4.56	1.84	0.38	4.90	1.30	0.63	8.97	2.06
0.01		0.13		0.55	0.08		0.67	0.11
0.19	0.99	1.87	0.23	-0.86	-0.05	1.19	-0.30	0.37
0.26	1.25	1.60	0.21	-0.61	-0.17	0.80	0.07	0.42
0.01	0.01	0.09		0.06		0.01	0.11	0.04
0.04	0.21	0.19	0.15	0.11		0.01	0.24	0.09
0.07	0.40	0.56	0.07	0.10	0.06	0.23	0.95	0.78
0.23	1.98	2.32	0.31	0.30	0.12	0.74	1.23	0.70
0.34	1.46	3.16	0.31	3.68	0.39	0.23	5.39	1.37
0.11	1.37	0.96	0.34	0.21	0.02	0.14	0.60	0.28
68.58	0.92	4.55	0.81	14.45	4.19	2.83	94.27	11.24
1.74	17.46	11.71	5.79	24.55	1.90	2.81	32.98	6.69
3.06	78.85	20.46	2.06	95.23	12.91	0.96	114.13	15.84
0.12	0.45	0.33	0.07	3.41	0.43	0.05	3.71	0.18
0.20	1.24	2.23	0.21	1.40	0.14	0.33	2.21	0.61
3.85	16.88	23.68	7.22	39.23	5.09	5.32	56.16	13.08
3.88	4.34	14.12	9.37	-22.85	-1.01	28.09	-4.15	14.82
0.13	0.48	0.93	0.22	0.64	0.10	0.14	1.21	0.44
1.67	11.08	11.66	3.12	17.85	2.54	2.45	26.76	7.24
2.91	22.82	25.76	2.23	20.23	3.73	11.15	34.15	11.01
1.42	16.18	15.40	2.59	26.87	1.72	6.84	34.96	6.67
2.76	13.65	21.80	5.19	26.09	1.61	2.66	44.75	15.90
0.60	1.65	5.80	0.05	6.84	0.86	0.02	9.03	1.59
2.14	15.77	15.17	2.13	25.91	1.10	4.92	32.59	4.54
1.32	17.63	14.19	6.28	10.20	0.81	14.85	8.00	-3.52
0.58	7.48	6.61	0.43	11.62	0.93	0.18	15.46	3.26
0.01	0.08	0.26	-0.11	1.41	0.08		1.58	0.16
0.15	0.34	0.79	0.14	0.99	0.12	0.26	2.12	0.98
0.15	0.45	1.74	0.17	1.97	0.17	0.02	2.44	0.32
1.71	1.09	9.01	12.29	-11.39	0.63	20.39	-0.86	8.82
0.23	3.39	3.04	0.43	2.87	1.10	1.96	4.51	1.41
1.84	1.86	2.81	1.36	3.38	0.53	0.72	5.98	0.76

12-10 规模以上国有及国有控股工业损益及分配(2022年)

Profit, Loss and Distribution of State-Owned and State-Controlled Industrial Enterprises Above Designated Size(2022)

单位：亿元

指标	Item	营业收入 Business Revenue	营业成本 Business Cost
总计	**Total**	**3395.34**	**3037.76**
按登记注册类型分组	**by Status of Registration**		
内资企业	Domestic Invested Enterprises	3219.85	2894.26
国有企业	State-owned Enterprises	86.18	77.95
中央企业	Central Enterprises	48.74	48.59
地方企业	Local Enterprises	37.44	29.36
集体企业	Collective-owned Enterprises		
股份合作企业	Cooperative Enterprises		
联营企业	Joint Ownership Enterprises	10.75	8.85
有限责任公司	Limited Liability Corporations	1438.51	1304.76
国有独资公司	State Sole Funded Corporations	262.14	253.27
其他有限责任公司	Other Limited Liability Corporations	1176.37	1051.49
股份有限公司	Share-holding Corporations Ltd.	1684.42	1502.70
私营企业	Private Enterprises		
其他企业	Other Enterprises		
港、澳、台商投资企业	Enterprises with Funds from Hong Kong,Macao and Taiwan	126.15	101.79
合资经营企业	Joint-venture Enterprises	126.15	101.79
合作经营企业	Cooperative Enterprises		
港澳台商独资经营企业	Enterprises with Sole Investment		
港澳台商投资股份有限公司	Share-holding Corporations Ltd.		
其他港澳台商投资企业	Other Enterprises with Funds from Hong Kong,Macao and Taiwan		
外商投资企业	Foreign Funded Enterprises	49.34	41.70
中外合资经营企业	Joint-venture Enterprises	49.34	41.70
中外合作经营企业	Cooperation Enterprises		
外资企业	Enterprises with Sole Fund		
外商投资股份有限公司	Share-holding Corporations Ltd.		
其他外商投资企业	Other Foreign Funded Enterprises		
按轻重工业分	**by Light & Heavy Industry**		
轻工业	Light Industry	118.90	72.89
重工业	Heavy Industry	3276.43	2964.86
按企业规模分	**by Enterprise Size**		
大型企业	Large-sized Enterprises	2338.24	2118.50
中型企业	Medium-sized Enterprises	499.24	422.61
小型企业	Small-sized Enterprises	534.16	477.94
微型企业	Micro-sized Enterprises	23.70	18.71
按工业行业分	**by Sector**		
煤炭开采和洗选业	Mining and Washing of Coal	6.72	4.17
石油和天然气开采业	Extraction of Petroleum and Natural Gas	16.35	7.29
黑色金属矿采选业	Mining and Processing of Ferrous Metal Ores	21.53	13.85

(100 million yuan)

税金及附加 Taxes and Other Charges	销售费用 Selling Expenses	管理费用 Management Expenses	利息费用 Interest Expenses	利润总额 Total Profits	所得税费用 Income Tax Payable	亏损企业亏损总额 Total Loss of Loss Enterprises	利税总额 Total Profits and Taxes	应交增值税 Value-added Tax Payable
87.22	**58.18**	**69.14**	**30.08**	**72.42**	**14.04**	**55.63**	**214.97**	**55.33**
86.18	49.28	62.14	29.54	60.94	11.24	53.50	198.48	51.36
2.48	0.59	2.99	1.67	-2.66	1.37	9.42	3.06	3.24
0.32	0.25	1.47	1.13	-6.71	0.14	8.01	-4.68	1.71
2.17	0.34	1.52	0.54	4.05	1.23	1.41	7.75	1.53
0.06	0.31	0.67		0.39	0.01		0.58	0.13
12.54	24.76	40.74	20.95	27.57	6.18	38.43	66.52	26.41
2.95	5.77	12.37	4.14	-7.89	-0.39	14.67	3.77	8.71
9.58	18.99	28.36	16.80	35.46	6.57	23.76	62.74	17.70
71.10	23.62	17.75	6.92	35.64	3.68	5.65	128.32	21.58
0.68	7.70	3.98	0.44	9.14	2.22	1.84	13.00	3.18
0.68	7.70	3.98	0.44	9.14	2.22	1.84	13.00	3.18
0.36	1.20	3.01	0.10	2.34	0.58	0.30	3.50	0.80
0.36	1.20	3.01	0.10	2.34	0.58	0.30	3.50	0.80
2.04	22.88	5.38	0.86	15.69	2.09	0.99	21.85	4.12
85.18	35.30	63.76	29.22	56.73	11.95	54.64	193.13	51.22
75.85	26.48	35.77	16.75	42.39	9.58	32.21	157.75	39.51
5.20	21.93	17.56	6.86	9.90	-0.26	14.26	26.80	11.70
6.00	9.46	14.97	5.57	16.90	4.10	9.02	25.93	3.03
0.17	0.32	0.84	0.90	3.22	0.62	0.14	4.49	1.10
0.35	0.08	0.86	0.35	0.28			1.26	0.63
3.04		-0.03	0.29	5.69	1.42		10.19	1.45
1.05		1.89	0.18	3.96	0.28		6.68	1.67

12-10 续表 continued

单位：亿元

指标	Item	营业收入 Business Revenue	营业成本 Business Cost
有色金属矿采选业	Mining and Processing of Non-Ferrous Metal Ores		
非金属矿采选业	Mining and Processing of Non-metal Ores	2.85	2.23
开采专业及辅助性活动	Professional and Support Activities for Mining		
其他采矿业	Mining of Other Ores		
农副食品加工业	Processing of Food from Agricultural Products	0.28	0.19
食品制造业	Manufacture of Foods	18.19	10.54
酒、饮料和精制茶制造业	Manufacture of Liquor, Beverages and Refined Tea	26.93	18.99
烟草制品业	Manufacture of Tobacco	1.68	0.92
纺织业	Manufacture of Textile	2.81	2.82
纺织服装、服饰业	Manufacture of Textile, Wearing Apparel and Accessories	3.14	2.74
皮革、毛皮、羽毛及其制品和制鞋业	Manufacture of Leather, Fur, Feather and Related Products and Footwear		
木材加工和木、竹、藤、棕、草制品业	Processing of Timber, Manufacture of Wood, Bamboo, Rattan,Palm and Straw Products		
家具制造业	Manufacture of Furniture		
造纸和纸制品业	Manufacture of Paper and Paper Products	2.89	2.18
印刷和记录媒介复制业	Printing and Reproduction of Recording Media	9.14	6.56
文教、工美、体育和娱乐用品制造业	Manufacture of Articles for Culture, Education, Arts and Crafts, Sport and Entertainment Activities		
石油、煤炭及其他燃料加工业	Processing of Petroleum, Coal and Other Fuels	355.71	266.22
化学原料和化学制品制造业	Manufacture of Raw Chemical Materials and Chemical Products	122.10	97.64
医药制造业	Manufacture of Medicines	21.00	9.55
化学纤维制造业	Manufacture of Chemical Fibres	5.21	4.54
橡胶和塑料制品业	Manufacture of Rubber and Plastics Products	1.16	1.05
非金属矿物制品业	Manufacture of Non-metallic Mineral Products	77.35	63.42
黑色金属冶炼和压延加工业	Smelting and Pressing of Ferrous Metals	802.99	788.33
有色金属冶炼和压延加工业	Smelting and Pressing of Non-ferrous Metals	23.60	22.98
金属制品业	Manufacture of Metal Products	82.55	75.66
通用设备制造业	Manufacture of General Purpose Machinery	120.65	95.37
专用设备制造业	Manufacture of Special Purpose Machinery	31.69	27.23
汽车制造业	Manufacture of Automobiles	141.83	120.06
铁路、船舶、航空航天和其他运输设备制造业	Manufacture of Railway, Ship, Aerospace and Other Transport Equipments	67.80	57.10
电气机械和器材制造业	Manufacture of Electrical Machinery and Apparatus	203.98	181.56
计算机、通信和其他电子设备制造业	Manufacture of Computers, Communication and Other Electronic Equipment	881.87	817.39
仪器仪表制造业	Manufacture of Measuring Instruments and Machinery	25.98	18.78
其他制造业	Other Manufacture	1.69	1.50
废弃资源综合利用业	Utilization of Waste Resources	2.85	2.82
金属制品、机械和设备修理业	Repair Service of Metal Products, Machinery and Equipment	14.40	10.79
电力、热力生产和供应业	Production and Supply of Electric Power and Heat Power	206.04	218.06
燃气生产和供应业	Production and Supply of Gas	62.86	57.92
水的生产和供应业	Production and Supply of Water	29.51	27.30

税金及附加 Taxes and Other Charges	销售费用 Selling Expenses	管理费用 Management Expenses	利息费用 Interest Expenses	利润总额 Total Profits	所得税费用 Income Tax Payable	亏损企业亏损总额 Total Loss of Loss Enterprises	利税总额 Total Profits and Taxes	应交增值税 Value-added Tax Payable
0.01	0.01	0.06	0.04	0.21	0.09		0.31	0.09
	0.02	0.03	0.01	0.03			0.04	0.02
0.11	0.68	0.80	0.02	5.94	0.70	0.17	6.07	0.03
1.11	3.41	0.40	0.02	3.15	0.81	0.04	5.03	0.77
0.01		0.13		0.55	0.08		0.68	0.11
0.02	0.02	0.14	0.01	-0.21		0.21	-0.17	0.02
0.13	0.15	0.82	0.11	-0.01	-0.17	0.08	0.23	0.10
0.04	0.02	0.30		0.27	0.04	0.02	0.33	0.01
0.13	0.40	1.08	0.01	0.78	0.10	0.08	1.41	0.50
68.28	0.17	3.70	0.39	16.90	4.16		96.42	11.24
0.66	10.56	3.21	3.52	4.48	0.40	1.70	6.91	1.76
0.25	7.76	0.79	0.62	3.30	0.25		4.91	1.36
0.05	0.08	0.13		-0.02	-0.03	0.05	0.11	0.08
0.02	0.01	0.17	0.02	-0.17		0.17	-0.19	-0.05
1.23	1.02	3.68	0.87	6.22	1.08	0.02	10.23	2.77
2.41	1.93	7.22	6.00	-16.45	-1.43	16.45	-4.58	9.45
0.07	0.09	0.39	0.13	0.48	0.10		0.71	0.16
0.36	0.79	1.72	0.31	1.04	0.31	0.84	2.85	1.46
1.23	3.97	6.80	0.28	5.26	1.44	5.91	12.64	6.15
0.26	1.31	1.61	1.35	-3.97	-1.64	4.91	-3.02	0.70
0.67	1.31	3.01	0.66	16.26	3.19	0.15	19.83	2.90
0.49	1.31	4.69	0.02	5.63	0.65		7.47	1.35
1.03	4.67	5.45	0.67	2.53	0.09	2.79	7.71	4.15
0.75	11.29	6.65	5.63	16.48	0.72	3.13	12.92	-4.31
0.21	1.32	1.28	0.04	3.99	0.36		5.36	1.16
0.01	0.01	0.04		0.02	-0.01		0.04	0.02
0.02	0.01	0.12	0.04	-0.16		0.16	-0.13	0.02
0.12	0.21	1.48	0.11	0.93	0.09		1.20	0.15
1.39	0.90	6.15	7.17	-11.57	0.23	16.15	-2.39	7.79
0.15	2.83	2.05	0.35	0.29	0.56	1.87	1.40	0.97
1.56	1.85	2.29	0.85	0.31	0.18	0.72	2.53	0.66

12-11 分地区规模以上工业主要经济指标(2022年)

Main Economic Indicators of Industrial Enterprises Above Designated Size By Region(2022)

单位：亿元

指标	Item	全市 Total	历下区 Li xia	市中区 Shi zhong	槐荫区 Huai yin	天桥区 Tian qiao	历城区 Li cheng
企业单位数(个)	**Number of Industrial Enterprises (unit)**	**2665**	**49**	**69**	**73**	**139**	**182**
工业总产值	**Gross Industrial Output Value**	**7246.05**	**438.62**	**304.08**	**199.65**	**189.68**	**410.93**
资产与负债	**Assets and Liabilities**						
资产总计	Total Assets	9637.65	380.44	553.10	368.51	330.58	716.88
流动资产合计	Current Assets	5714.63	170.42	365.14	261.82	178.90	486.89
存货	Inventories	1088.71	20.81	63.86	44.57	37.00	79.18
应收账款	Accounts Receivable	1727.82	31.65	98.53	44.93	52.75	120.87
固定资产净额	Net Fixed Assets	2049.71	127.61	90.21	30.09	101.27	107.24
流动负债合计	Current Liabilities Total	4999.66	182.33	272.67	149.58	193.44	463.12
非流动负债合计	Non-Current Liabilities Total	858.37	52.69	64.83	9.79	57.27	47.56
所有者权益合计	Total Owner's Equities	3779.62	145.42	215.61	209.14	79.87	206.20
实收资本	Paid- up Capital	2137.18	64.92	55.99	54.89	51.90	142.56
国家资本	Official Capital	338.47	38.66	24.96	4.09	13.44	15.10
损益及分配	**Profit,Loss and Distribution**						
营业收入	Business Revenue	8370.30	454.83	378.37	198.35	194.45	440.36
营业成本	Business Cost	7190.97	359.25	357.07	164.11	175.83	359.65
税金及附加	Taxes and Other Charges	109.37	68.67	1.78	1.30	0.94	2.22
管理费用	Management Expenses	242.54	9.23	9.45	8.73	9.25	20.30
利润总额	Total Profits	344.86	15.15	4.95	24.35	5.25	26.78
应交所得税	Income Tax Payable	48.19	4.64	-0.05	1.94	0.82	4.36
亏损企业亏损总额	Total Loss of Loss Enterprises	114.94	4.17	3.10	2.23	4.56	11.53
利税总额	Total Profits and Taxes	593.57	97.20	18.38	32.84	12.60	37.25
本年应交增值税	Value-added Tax Payable	139.34	13.38	11.65	7.19	6.41	8.25

(100 million yuan)

长清区 Chang qing	章丘区 Zhang qiu	济阳区 Ji yang	莱芜区 Lai wu	钢城区 Gang Cheng	平阴县 Ping yin	商河县 Shang he	济南高新区 Jinan gao xin	济南起步区(直管) Jinan Start-up Area (Directly under)	南部山区 Nan shan
213	**583**	**152**	**298**	**147**	**144**	**181**	**377**	**42**	**16**
223.02	**1077.15**	**195.45**	**1096.09**	**880.90**	**385.39**	**202.17**	**1576.94**	**52.11**	**13.87**
611.96	1477.23	289.28	1120.99	727.73	485.41	271.93	2211.96	65.89	25.76
283.03	807.86	172.69	683.82	252.32	302.53	144.07	1546.01	43.71	15.44
59.68	147.07	33.63	140.11	66.90	67.16	34.30	283.48	4.56	6.41
93.10	216.83	36.90	234.84	41.21	68.56	50.42	619.88	13.84	3.51
69.54	313.89	68.40	288.54	368.72	103.72	88.70	281.03	8.89	1.86
364.62	763.40	117.52	700.12	407.95	193.36	116.33	1031.23	25.63	18.37
33.73	119.39	34.15	95.43	84.07	27.62	49.15	162.21	19.37	1.10
213.61	594.44	137.60	325.44	235.71	264.43	106.45	1018.51	20.89	6.30
155.18	284.91	59.08	455.45	160.06	60.32	51.35	525.02	13.57	1.98
7.56	30.15	7.16	33.30	121.90	2.13	2.70	37.09	0.12	0.10
237.57	1113.04	207.89	1496.07	1021.99	418.36	196.22	1939.72	59.56	13.52
196.25	943.87	161.05	1400.65	976.32	340.71	164.25	1530.72	50.98	10.28
1.62	6.73	3.19	5.57	3.99	2.60	2.27	7.61	0.32	0.56
15.21	40.74	9.91	24.30	14.53	13.86	7.12	57.26	1.97	0.68
17.73	43.69	17.89	9.58	-4.14	33.23	12.29	133.67	3.86	0.60
1.78	4.19	3.41	0.64	0.07	6.13	1.67	17.69	0.88	0.04
8.58	16.41	2.51	18.98	17.99	5.03	1.40	17.94	0.44	0.06
24.92	71.10	27.60	29.88	14.06	44.51	17.85	158.31	5.76	1.35
5.57	20.68	6.52	14.73	14.21	8.68	3.29	17.03	1.58	0.19

12-12 规模以上大中型工业企业经营情况(2022年)

Main Indicators of Large and Medium-Sized Enterprises(2022)

单位：亿元

指标	Item	企业单位数(个) Number of Enterprises (unit)	亏损企业数(个) Loss Enterprises (unit)
总计	**Total**	**234**	**58**
按登记注册类型分组	**by Status of Registration**		
内资企业	Domestic Invested Enterprises	188	49
国有企业	State-owned Enterprises	3	1
中央企业	Central Enterprises	2	1
地方企业	Local Enterprises	1	
集体企业	Collective-owned Enterprises		
股份合作企业	Cooperative Enterprises	1	
联营企业	Joint Ownership Enterprises	1	
有限责任公司	Limited Liability Corporations	91	26
国有独资公司	State Sole Funded Corporations	11	6
其他有限责任公司	Other Limited Liability Corporations	80	20
股份有限公司	Share-holding Corporations Ltd.	32	9
私营企业	Private Enterprises	60	13
私营独资企业	Private-funded Enterprises	1	1
私营合伙企业	Private Partnership Enterprises		
私营有限责任公司	Private Limited Liability Corporations	49	11
私营股份有限公司	Private Share-holding Corporations Ltd.	10	1
其他企业	Other Enterprises		
港、澳、台商投资企业	Enterprises with Funds from Hong Kong,Macao and Taiwan	23	3
合资经营企业	Joint-venture Enterprises	13	1
合作经营企业	Cooperative Enterprises		
港澳台商独资经营企业	Enterprises with Sole Investment	9	2
港澳台商投资股份有限公司	Share-holding Corporations Ltd.	1	
其他港澳台商投资企业	Other Enterprises with Funds from Hong Kong,Macao and Taiwan		
外商投资企业	Foreign Funded Enterprises	23	6
中外合资经营企业	Joint-venture Enterprises	12	4
中外合作经营企业	Cooperation Enterprises		
外资企业	Enterprises with Sole Fund	10	2
外商投资股份有限公司	Share-holding Corporations Ltd.		
其他外商投资企业	Other Foreign Funded Enterprises	1	
按轻重工业分	**by Light & Heavy Industry**		
轻工业	Light Industry	72	15
重工业	Heavy Industry	162	43
按企业规模分	**by Enterprise Size**		
大型企业	Large-sized Enterprises	60	11
中型企业	Medium-sized Enterprises	174	47
小型企业	Small-sized Enterprises		
微型企业	Micro-sized Enterprises		
按工业行业分	**by Sector**		
煤炭开采和洗选业	Mining and Washing of Coal	2	

(100 million yuan)

工业总产值(现价) Gross Industrial Output Value (Current Prices)	资产总计 Total Assets	负债合计 Total Liabilities	营业收入 Business Revenue	利润总额 Total Profits	利税总额 Total Profits and Taxes	平均用工人数(万人) Annual Average Employees (10 000 persons)
4918.76	**6306.91**	**3674.78**	**5891.07**	**255.65**	**447.91**	**24.16**
4030.81	4766.97	2832.72	4920.08	180.54	345.77	18.48
36.33	43.93	38.48	33.36	-7.85	-6.52	0.22
35.70	42.58	37.58	32.73	-7.87	-6.49	0.18
0.63	1.35	0.89	0.63	0.02	-0.03	0.04
108.75	128.92	80.62	107.25	11.90	12.77	0.18
9.03	11.90	6.64	10.75	0.39	0.58	0.05
1470.06	2407.38	1556.19	1769.01	41.88	84.86	9.17
130.86	554.33	402.66	171.32	-10.05	-0.97	1.26
1339.20	1853.05	1153.53	1597.70	51.93	85.82	7.91
1434.16	1206.43	598.87	1862.49	50.74	149.19	3.72
972.48	968.41	551.91	1137.22	83.47	104.87	5.14
2.04	4.92	5.55	1.97	-0.40	-0.42	0.05
881.46	858.24	509.36	1060.23	73.67	92.33	4.65
88.98	105.25	37.01	75.02	10.20	12.96	0.44
651.99	1293.43	720.65	740.74	53.86	75.34	3.94
225.49	383.20	183.71	244.03	32.22	40.02	1.68
244.63	658.10	411.81	277.22	17.77	23.30	1.71
181.87	252.12	125.14	219.49	3.87	12.03	0.55
235.96	246.51	121.41	230.25	21.26	26.81	1.73
127.99	140.79	80.38	119.10	10.70	13.33	0.92
101.11	96.04	33.08	103.95	10.48	13.17	0.75
6.86	9.68	7.95	7.20	0.08	0.32	0.06
786.00	1225.16	530.38	804.49	126.26	153.35	7.31
4132.76	5081.75	3144.40	5086.58	129.39	294.56	16.85
3597.31	4184.10	2397.75	4340.34	184.31	337.27	15.08
1321.45	2122.81	1277.04	1550.73	71.34	110.65	9.08
6.02	9.56	16.07	7.38	0.28	1.35	0.21

12-12 续表 continued

单位：亿元

指标	Item	企业单位数（个）Number of Enterprises (unit)	亏损企业数（个）Loss Enterprises (unit)
石油和天然气开采业	Extraction of Petroleum and Natural Gas		
黑色金属矿采选业	Mining and Processing of Ferrous Metal Ores	5	
有色金属矿采选业	Mining and Processing of Non-Ferrous Metal Ores		
非金属矿采选业	Mining and Processing of Non-metal Ores		
开采专业及辅助性活动	Professional and Support Activities for Mining		
其他采矿业	Mining of Other Ores		
农副食品加工业	Processing of Food from Agricultural Products	8	5
食品制造业	Manufacture of Foods	13	2
酒、饮料和精制茶制造业	Manufacture of Liquor, Beverages and Refined Tea	7	1
烟草制品业	Manufacture of Tobacco		
纺织业	Manufacture of Textile	4	1
纺织服装、服饰业	Manufacture of Textile, Wearing Apparel and Accessories	4	3
皮革、毛皮、羽毛及其制品和制鞋业	Manufacture of Leather, Fur, Feather and Related Products and Footwear		
木材加工和木、竹、藤、棕、草制品业	Processing of Timber, Manufacture of Wood, Bamboo, Rattan,Palm and Straw Products		
家具制造业	Manufacture of Furniture	3	1
造纸和纸制品业	Manufacture of Paper and Paper Products	2	1
印刷和记录媒介复制业	Printing and Reproduction of Recording Media	3	
文教、工美、体育和娱乐用品制造业	Manufacture of Articles for Culture, Education, Arts and Crafts, Sport and Entertainment Activities	1	
石油、煤炭及其他燃料加工业	Processing of Petroleum, Coal and Other Fuels	2	1
化学原料和化学制品制造业	Manufacture of Raw Chemical Materials and Chemical Products	10	2
医药制造业	Manufacture of Medicines	17	1
化学纤维制造业	Manufacture of Chemical Fibres		
橡胶和塑料制品业	Manufacture of Rubber and Plastics Products	1	1
非金属矿物制品业	Manufacture of Non-metallic Mineral Products	24	5
黑色金属冶炼和压延加工业	Smelting and Pressing of Ferrous Metals	7	3
有色金属冶炼和压延加工业	Smelting and Pressing of Non-ferrous Metals	1	
金属制品业	Manufacture of Metal Products	15	2
通用设备制造业	Manufacture of General Purpose Machinery	21	6
专用设备制造业	Manufacture of Special Purpose Machinery	13	2
汽车制造业	Manufacture of Automobiles	17	2
铁路、船舶、航空航天和其他运输设备制造业	Manufacture of Railway, Ship, Aerospace and Other Transport Equipments	6	
电气机械和器材制造业	Manufacture of Electrical Machinery and Apparatus	16	3
计算机、通信和其他电子设备制造业	Manufacture of Computers, Communication and Other Electronic Equipment	12	7
仪器仪表制造业	Manufacture of Measuring Instruments and Machinery	5	
其他制造业	Other Manufacture		
废弃资源综合利用业	Utilization of Waste Resources	1	
金属制品、机械和设备修理业	Repair Service of Metal Products, Machinery and Equipment	1	
电力、热力生产和供应业	Production and Supply of Electric Power and Heat Power	7	6
燃气生产和供应业	Production and Supply of Gas	3	1
水的生产和供应业	Production and Supply of Water	3	2

(100 million yuan)

工业总产值(现价) Gross Industrial Output Value (Current Prices)	资产总计 Total Assets	负债合计 Total Liabilities	营业收入 Business Revenue	利润总额 Total Profits	利税总额 Total Profits and Taxes	平均用工人数(万人) Annual Average Employees (10 000 persons)
97.88	126.15	109.34	164.10	7.24	12.43	0.71
56.57	44.85	41.33	67.98	0.39	0.28	0.38
117.51	107.78	46.89	121.35	16.98	20.66	1.12
52.68	49.53	30.39	54.55	4.83	8.14	0.40
12.40	15.62	11.87	18.27	-0.43	-0.27	0.20
6.50	19.56	13.37	8.30	-0.33	0.16	0.37
8.09	9.45	6.73	7.69	0.09	0.85	0.13
13.27	13.10	7.79	16.37	0.21	0.56	0.10
12.09	20.94	9.54	12.77	1.19	1.78	0.27
2.57	6.84	5.74	2.39	0.06	0.22	0.05
386.07	89.71	47.95	418.24	14.45	94.67	0.20
186.03	337.69	230.13	209.12	18.53	23.12	0.77
365.81	656.86	189.67	365.47	89.86	107.13	3.02
1.87	1.68	5.20	1.77	-0.05	-0.06	0.04
239.17	505.56	299.40	273.22	32.78	40.42	1.46
1245.21	798.03	545.00	1604.09	-11.61	5.75	2.50
6.04	9.04	5.55	4.70	0.09	0.14	0.04
157.12	223.88	92.46	146.85	14.69	18.84	1.32
238.71	363.67	174.77	239.33	15.29	24.42	2.12
167.71	294.54	196.14	175.56	15.02	17.82	0.84
551.50	860.75	512.27	618.31	24.49	40.88	3.23
59.65	86.68	37.43	66.41	5.70	7.46	0.53
210.25	405.24	277.88	253.17	7.49	9.95	1.21
460.82	526.59	240.69	753.91	9.62	12.05	1.14
21.85	32.53	16.60	21.31	3.06	3.90	0.24
6.17	7.26	5.44	10.58	0.29	0.52	0.15
7.06	12.64	6.93	6.84	0.73	0.82	0.17
172.20	449.30	334.20	179.81	-13.40	-6.15	0.83
33.81	94.33	44.87	41.12	-1.28	-0.45	0.23
16.14	127.54	113.11	20.10	-0.62	0.53	0.20

12-13 规模以上大中型工业企业一览表(2022年)
Summary of Large and Medium-Sized Enterprises(2022)

企业名称 Name	登记注册类型 Status of Registration	企业规模 Enterprise Size	所属行业 Industry
浪潮电子信息产业股份有限公司	股份有限公司	大型	计算机整机制造
山东钢铁股份有限公司	股份有限公司	大型	钢压延加工
山东泰山钢铁集团有限公司	其他有限责任公司	大型	钢压延加工
中国石油化工股份有限公司济南分公司	股份有限公司	大型	原油加工及石油制品制造
莱芜钢铁集团银山型钢有限公司	其他有限责任公司	大型	钢压延加工
山东富伦钢铁有限公司	私营有限责任公司	大型	钢压延加工
中国重汽集团济南卡车股份有限公司	港澳台商投资股份有限公司	大型	汽柴油车整车制造
齐鲁制药有限公司	私营有限责任公司	大型	化学药品制剂制造
中国重汽集团济南商用车有限公司	港澳台商独资	大型	汽柴油车整车制造
山东泰威冶金材料制造有限公司	私营有限责任公司	中型	铁矿采选
济南市九羊福利钢铁有限公司	私营有限责任公司	大型	炼铁
临工重机股份有限公司	股份合作	大型	矿山机械制造
中国重汽集团济南动力有限公司	港澳台商独资	大型	汽车零部件及配件制造
山东泰山焦化有限公司	其他有限责任公司	中型	炼焦
济南万瑞炭素有限责任公司	私营有限责任公司	中型	石墨及碳素制品制造
济南二机床集团有限公司	其他有限责任公司	大型	金属成形机床制造
华能莱芜发电有限公司	其他有限责任公司	中型	火力发电
山东泰山轧钢有限公司	私营有限责任公司	中型	钢压延加工
重汽(济南)车桥有限公司	与港澳台商合资经营	大型	汽车零部件及配件制造
山东电力设备有限公司	国有独资公司	中型	变压器、整流器和电感器制造
山东圣泉新材料股份有限公司	私营股份有限公司	大型	初级形态塑料及合成树脂制造
济南澳海炭素有限公司	其他有限责任公司	中型	石墨及碳素制品制造
玫德集团有限公司	其他有限责任公司	大型	建筑装饰及水暖管道零件制造
中车山东风电有限公司	其他有限责任公司	中型	发电机及发电机组制造
齐鲁安替制药有限公司	与港澳台商合资经营	大型	化学药品原料药制造
济南热力集团有限公司	国有独资公司	大型	热力生产和供应
济南圣泉集团股份有限公司	股份有限公司	中型	初级形态塑料及合成树脂制造
费斯托气动有限公司	外资企业	大型	气压动力机械及元件制造
伊莱特能源装备股份有限公司	中外合资经营	大型	锻件及粉末冶金制品制造
华熙生物科技股份有限公司	其他有限责任公司	大型	生物药品制造
华能济南黄台发电有限公司	国有	大型	热电联产
济南弗迪电池有限公司	其他有限责任公司	大型	锂离子电池制造
济南伊利乳业有限责任公司	其他有限责任公司	大型	液体乳制造
山东晋控明水化工集团有限公司	其他有限责任公司	大型	有机化学原料制造
济南轻骑铃木摩托车有限公司	中外合资经营	大型	摩托车整车制造
山东安信制药有限公司	与港澳台商合资经营	大型	化学药品原料药制造
山东旺旺食品有限公司	外资企业	大型	液体乳制造
山东海鼎农牧有限公司	私营有限责任公司	中型	其他饲料加工
山东鲁碧建材有限公司	其他有限责任公司	大型	水泥制造

12-13 续表 1 continued 1

企业名称 Name	登记注册类型 Status of Registration	企业规模 Enterprise Size	所属行业 Industry
中国重汽集团济南专用车有限公司	其他有限责任公司	中型	改装汽车制造
济南海川投资集团有限公司	私营有限责任公司	中型	石墨及碳素制品制造
中国石油集团济柴动力有限公司	国有独资公司	大型	内燃机及配件制造
济南热电集团有限公司	国有独资公司	大型	热力生产和供应
华电章丘发电有限公司	其他有限责任公司	中型	热电联产
济南龙山炭素有限公司	私营有限责任公司	中型	石墨及碳素制品制造
济南邦德激光股份有限公司	股份有限公司	大型	金属切割及焊接设备制造
中国重汽集团济南特种车有限公司	其他有限责任公司	中型	汽柴油车整车制造
山东明泉新材料科技有限公司	其他有限责任公司	中型	有机化学原料制造
济南港华燃气有限公司	与港澳台商合资经营	大型	天然气生产和供应业
中车山东机车车辆有限公司	其他有限责任公司	大型	铁路机车车辆制造
山东正泰电缆有限公司	私营有限责任公司	中型	电线、电缆制造
重汽(济南)传动轴有限公司	其他有限责任公司	大型	汽车零部件及配件制造
中粮可口可乐饮料(济南)有限公司	与港澳台商合资经营	大型	碳酸饮料制造
中国重汽集团济南橡塑件有限公司	其他有限责任公司	大型	汽车车身、挂车制造
金雷科技股份公司	股份有限公司	大型	发电机及发电机组制造
齐鲁动物保健品有限公司	私营有限责任公司	大型	兽用药品制造
山东福瑞达生物股份有限公司	股份有限公司	中型	化妆品制造
山东晋控日月新材料有限公司	其他有限责任公司	中型	有机化学原料制造
济南裕兴化工有限责任公司	其他有限责任公司	大型	工业颜料制造
卧龙电气(济南)电机有限公司	与港澳台商合资经营	中型	微特电机及组件制造
山东国舜建设集团有限公司	私营有限责任公司	中型	环境保护专用设备制造
山东省章丘鼓风机股份有限公司	股份有限公司	大型	风机、风扇制造
莱芜泰禾生化有限公司	其他有限责任公司	中型	食品及饲料添加剂制造
山东济华燃气有限公司	与港澳台商合资经营	中型	天然气生产和供应业
济南达利食品有限公司	私营有限责任公司	大型	饼干及其他焙烤食品制造
平阴山水水泥有限公司	与港澳台商合资经营	中型	水泥制造
积成电子股份有限公司	股份有限公司	大型	配电开关控制设备制造
鲁中矿业有限公司	其他有限责任公司	大型	铁矿采选
山东阳光铸业有限公司	其他有限责任公司	中型	炼铁
山东宏济堂制药集团股份有限公司	股份有限公司	大型	中成药生产
山东鲁银新材料科技有限公司	其他有限责任公司	中型	锻件及粉末冶金制品制造
济南水务集团有限公司	国有独资公司	大型	自来水生产和供应
大汉科技股份有限公司	其他有限责任公司	大型	生产专用起重机制造
华润双鹤利民药业(济南)有限公司	其他有限责任公司	大型	化学药品制剂制造
济南迈科管道科技有限公司	港澳台商独资	中型	金属结构制造
济南西门子变压器有限公司	中外合资经营	中型	变压器、整流器和电感器制造
山东省万兴食品有限公司	其他有限责任公司	中型	蔬菜加工
福士汽车零部件(济南)有限公司	外资企业	大型	汽车零部件及配件制造
济南金麒麟刹车系统有限公司	私营有限责任公司	大型	汽车零部件及配件制造

12-13 续表 2 continued 2

企业名称 Name	登记注册类型 Status of Registration	企业规模 Enterprise Size	所属行业 Industry
维达纸业(山东)有限公司	港澳台商独资	中型	机制纸及纸板制造
山东爱普电气设备有限公司	国有与集体联营	中型	其他输配电及控制设备制造
山东山水水泥集团有限公司	港澳台商独资	中型	水泥制造
莱芜钢铁集团泰东实业有限公司	其他有限责任公司	大型	金属废料和碎屑加工处理
济南统一企业有限公司	与港澳台商合资经营	中型	茶饮料及其他饮料制造
浪潮商用机器有限公司	与港澳台商合资经营	中型	计算机整机制造
科兴生物制药股份有限公司	股份有限公司	大型	生物药品制造
山东汉方制药有限公司	私营有限责任公司	中型	中成药生产
国网智能科技股份有限公司	股份有限公司	中型	工业机器人制造
山东捷晶生物科技有限公司	其他有限责任公司	中型	营养食品制造
莱芜钢铁集团莱芜矿业有限公司	其他有限责任公司	大型	铁矿采选
山东水泥厂有限公司	私营有限责任公司	中型	水泥制造
济南顶津食品有限公司	外资企业	中型	瓶(罐)装饮用水制造
济南金威刻科技发展有限公司	其他有限责任公司	中型	金属切割及焊接设备制造
莱钢集团矿山建设有限公司	其他有限责任公司	中型	铁矿采选
济南重工股份有限公司	股份有限公司	中型	矿山机械制造
山东宏业纺织股份有限公司	股份有限公司	中型	棉纺纱加工
济南鑫贝西生物技术有限公司	私营有限责任公司	中型	其他医疗设备及器械制造
山东平阴丰源炭素有限责任公司	其他有限责任公司	中型	石墨及碳素制品制造
济南森峰激光科技股份有限公司	其他有限责任公司	中型	其他专用仪器制造
山东奥太电气有限公司	其他有限责任公司	中型	金属切割及焊接设备制造
山东电工电气日立高压开关有限公司	中外合资经营	中型	配电开关控制设备制造
山东齐发药业有限公司	其他有限责任公司	中型	兽用药品制造
莱芜万兴果菜食品加工有限公司	港澳台商独资	中型	蔬菜加工
山东力诺特种玻璃股份有限公司	股份有限公司	中型	玻璃包装容器制造
西电济南变压器股份有限公司	股份有限公司	中型	变压器、整流器和电感器制造
济南黄河特钢有限责任公司	其他有限责任公司	中型	金属结构制造
济南佳宝乳业有限公司	其他有限责任公司	大型	液体乳制造
山东朗进科技股份有限公司	股份有限公司	中型	制冷、空调设备制造
山东济钢环保新材料有限公司	国有独资公司	中型	建筑用石加工
山东力诺瑞特新能源有限公司	其他外商投资	中型	太阳能器具制造
济南宇飞食品有限公司	私营有限责任公司	中型	禽类屠宰
济南迈克阀门科技有限公司	与港澳台商合资经营	中型	阀门和旋塞制造
济南京华金属制品有限公司	其他有限责任公司	中型	金属结构制造
山东博士伦福瑞达制药有限公司	中外合资经营	中型	化学药品制剂制造
山东太古飞机工程有限公司	与港澳台商合资经营	大型	航空航天器修理
青岛啤酒(济南)有限公司	其他有限责任公司	中型	啤酒制造
山东万祥矿业有限公司	其他有限责任公司	大型	烟煤和无烟煤开采洗选
山东华凌电缆有限公司	其他有限责任公司	中型	电线、电缆制造

12-13 续表 3 continued 3

企业名称 Name	登记注册类型 Status of Registration	企业规模 Enterprise Size	所属行业 Industry
山东明化新材料有限公司	私营有限责任公司	中型	有机化学原料制造
济南天邦化工有限公司	私营有限责任公司	中型	化学农药制造
济南重工集团有限公司	其他有限责任公司	中型	隧道施工专用机械制造
莱芜新希望六和食品有限公司	私营有限责任公司	中型	禽类屠宰
济南和盛热力有限公司	其他有限责任公司	中型	热力生产和供应
山东晨熙智能科技有限公司	私营有限责任公司	中型	包装装潢及其他印刷
山东福牌阿胶股份有限公司	私营股份有限公司	中型	中成药生产
山推建友机械股份有限公司	股份有限公司	中型	建筑材料生产专用机械制造
山东天鹅棉业机械股份有限公司	股份有限公司	中型	棉花加工机械制造
济南沃德汽车零部件有限公司	中外合资经营	大型	汽车零部件及配件制造
济南鲁冠混凝土有限责任公司	私营有限责任公司	中型	水泥制品制造
山东鲁中啤酒原料有限公司	私营有限责任公司	中型	玻璃包装容器制造
山东福贞金属包装有限公司	外资企业	中型	金属包装容器及材料制造
济南新峨嵋实业有限公司	私营有限责任公司	中型	耐火陶瓷制品及其他耐火材料制造
济南泉华包装制品有限公司	与港澳台商合资经营	中型	纸和纸板容器制造
济南弘正科技有限公司	港澳台商独资	中型	摩托车零部件及配件制造
济南二机床铸造有限公司	国有独资公司	中型	黑色金属铸造
济南市莱芜燃气热力有限责任公司	其他有限责任公司	中型	天然气生产和供应业
章丘重型锻造有限公司	私营有限责任公司	大型	锻件及粉末冶金制品制造
山东银鹭食品有限公司	私营有限责任公司	中型	含乳饮料和植物蛋白饮料制造
中孚安全技术有限公司	其他有限责任公司	大型	信息安全设备制造
山东赖氏家具股份有限公司	私营股份有限公司	中型	木质家具制造
济南轻骑标致摩托车有限公司	中外合资经营	中型	摩托车整车制造
山东金沙河面业有限责任公司	私营有限责任公司	中型	小麦加工
山东汇金股份有限公司	股份有限公司	中型	汽车零部件及配件制造
山东山大电力技术股份有限公司	股份有限公司	中型	其他专用仪器制造
山东德源电力科技股份有限公司	股份有限公司	中型	配电开关控制设备制造
济南轻骑大韩摩托车有限责任公司	中外合资经营	中型	摩托车整车制造
济南市冶金科学研究所有限责任公司	其他有限责任公司	中型	有色金属合金制造
山东博科生物产业有限公司	其他有限责任公司	中型	医疗实验室及医用消毒设备和器具制造
山东温岭精锻科技有限公司	私营有限责任公司	中型	锻件及粉末冶金制品制造
安莉芳(山东)服装有限公司	港澳台商独资	大型	运动休闲针织服装制造
泰富特钢悬架(济南)有限公司	其他有限责任公司	中型	弹簧制造
山东天岳先进科技股份有限公司	股份有限公司	中型	电子专用材料制造
山东华氟化工有限责任公司	其他有限责任公司	中型	初级形态塑料及合成树脂制造
齐鲁宏业纺织集团有限公司	其他有限责任公司	中型	棉纺纱加工
济南鲁东耐火材料有限公司	中外合资经营	中型	耐火陶瓷制品及其他耐火材料制造
山东中天华泰新材料有限公司	私营有限责任公司	中型	石墨及碳素制品制造
凯傲(济南)叉车有限公司	中外合资经营	中型	生产专用车辆制造

12-13 续表 4 continued 4

企业名称 Name	登记注册类型 Status of Registration	企业规模 Enterprise Size	所属行业 Industry
济南中燃科技发展有限公司	私营有限责任公司	中型	其他金属加工机械制造
济南中船设备有限公司	私营有限责任公司	中型	船用配套设备制造
山东明仁福瑞达制药股份有限公司	股份有限公司	中型	中成药生产
山东金晔农法食品有限公司	私营有限责任公司	中型	蜜饯制作
山东大旺食品有限公司	外资企业	中型	饼干及其他焙烤食品制造
济南东区供水有限公司	其他有限责任公司	中型	自来水生产和供应
北谷电子有限公司	股份有限公司	中型	其他电子器件制造
山东科源制药股份有限公司	股份有限公司	中型	化学药品原料药制造
山东金钟科技集团股份有限公司	股份有限公司	中型	衡器制造
国机铸锻机械有限公司	其他有限责任公司	中型	铸造机械制造
莱芜莱新铁矿有限责任公司	其他有限责任公司	中型	铁矿采选
山东铂源药业有限公司	其他有限责任公司	中型	化学药品原料药制造
济南宜和食品有限公司	中外合资经营	中型	酱油、食醋及类似制品制造
迈大食品(山东)有限公司	外资企业	中型	饼干及其他焙烤食品制造
山东北辰机电设备股份有限公司	私营股份有限公司	中型	金属压力容器制造
山东鲁信天一印务有限公司	其他有限责任公司	中型	包装装潢及其他印刷
章丘华明水泥有限公司	其他有限责任公司	中型	水泥制造
山东济南发电设备厂有限公司	国有独资公司	中型	发电机及发电机组制造
济南泓泉制水有限公司	其他有限责任公司	中型	自来水生产和供应
山东中维世纪科技股份有限公司	股份有限公司	中型	集成电路制造
济南圣都食品有限公司	私营有限责任公司	中型	肉制品及副产品加工
山东上好佳食品工业有限公司	港澳台商独资	中型	饼干及其他焙烤食品制造
济南晶恒电子有限责任公司	其他有限责任公司	中型	半导体分立器件制造
山东大鲁阁织染工业有限公司	外资企业	中型	棉纺纱加工
山东新华印务有限公司	国有独资公司	中型	书、报刊印刷
济南实达紧固件有限公司	私营股份有限公司	中型	紧固件制造
济南冶金化工设备有限公司	其他有限责任公司	中型	冶金专用设备制造
济南比亚迪半导体有限公司	其他有限责任公司	中型	集成电路制造
济南锅炉集团有限公司	其他有限责任公司	中型	锅炉及辅助设备制造
山东华熙海御生物医药有限公司	外资企业	中型	生物药品制造
济南台有玻璃制品有限公司	其他有限责任公司	中型	日用玻璃制品制造
济南科盛电子有限公司	其他有限责任公司	中型	光电子器件制造
济南三星灯饰有限公司	股份有限公司	中型	智能照明器具制造
平阴鲁西装备科技有限公司	其他有限责任公司	中型	金属压力容器制造
山东新升实业发展有限责任公司	国有独资公司	中型	热电联产
济南有人物联网技术有限公司	私营有限责任公司	中型	通信系统设备制造
神思电子技术股份有限公司	股份有限公司	中型	其他计算机制造
济南世纪创新水泥有限公司	其他有限责任公司	中型	水泥制造
济南方圣混凝土构件有限公司	私营有限责任公司	中型	砼结构构件制造

12-13 续表 5 continued 5

企业名称 Name	登记注册类型 Status of Registration	企业规模 Enterprise Size	所属行业 Industry
山东巧夺天工家具有限公司	私营有限责任公司	中型	其他工艺美术及礼仪用品制造
济南奥图自动化股份有限公司	私营股份有限公司	中型	工业机器人制造
力创科技股份有限公司	私营股份有限公司	中型	供应用仪器仪表制造
中集车辆(山东)有限公司	中外合资经营	中型	汽车用发动机制造
山东莱芜煤矿机械有限公司	国有独资公司	中型	矿山机械制造
济南趵突泉酿酒有限责任公司	其他有限责任公司	中型	白酒制造
济南虫洞智能家居设施有限公司	私营有限责任公司	中型	木质家具制造
中建八局建筑科技(山东)有限公司	国有	中型	金属门窗制造
山东小鸭精工机械有限公司	其他有限责任公司	中型	汽车零部件及配件制造
济南活力食品有限公司	私营独资	中型	肉制品及副产品加工
济南元首针织股份有限公司	股份有限公司	中型	运动休闲针织服装制造
山东九龙新材料有限公司	私营有限责任公司	中型	耐火陶瓷制品及其他耐火材料制造
山东通发实业有限公司	私营有限责任公司	中型	建筑工程用机械制造
山东枣矿中兴慧通轮胎有限公司	其他有限责任公司	中型	轮胎制造
山东宏达科技集团有限公司	私营有限责任公司	中型	金属压力容器制造
济南翼菲自动化科技有限公司	其他有限责任公司	中型	工业机器人制造
山东联海建筑科技股份有限公司	私营股份有限公司	中型	粘土砖瓦及建筑砌块制造
山东大众机械制造股份有限公司	私营股份有限公司	中型	机械零部件加工
莱芜环球汽车零部件有限公司	外资企业	中型	汽车零部件及配件制造
山东越宫钢构件有限公司	其他有限责任公司	中型	金属结构制造
济南市白象科技发展有限公司	其他有限责任公司	中型	冶金专用设备制造
济南明鑫制药股份有限公司	私营股份有限公司	中型	化学药品原料药制造
山东新华泰纺织有限公司	私营有限责任公司	中型	棉纺纱加工
山东裕兴电工器材有限公司	私营有限责任公司	中型	电子元器件与机电组件设备制造
中孚信息股份有限公司	股份有限公司	中型	信息安全设备制造
启征新能源汽车(济南)有限公司	私营有限责任公司	中型	汽车零部件及配件制造
山东仁科测控技术有限公司	私营有限责任公司	中型	实验分析仪器制造
山东百脉泉酒业有限公司	其他有限责任公司	中型	白酒制造
山东云德食品有限公司	私营有限责任公司	中型	酱油、食醋及类似制品制造
济南双凤耐火材料有限公司	私营有限责任公司	中型	隔热和隔音材料制造
济南思迈迩制衣有限公司	私营有限责任公司	中型	其他针织或钩针编织服装制造
山东高速生物工程有限公司	其他有限责任公司	中型	液体乳制造
济阳元首针织有限责任公司	其他有限责任公司	中型	其他针织或钩针编织服装制造
山东华森建材集团有限公司	其他有限责任公司	中型	水泥制品制造
山东欧克家具有限公司	私营有限责任公司	中型	木质家具制造
山东省莱芜市辛庄煤矿有限公司	其他有限责任公司	中型	烟煤和无烟煤开采洗选
山东浪潮智能装备有限公司	国有	中型	计算器及货币专用设备制造
山东豪驰智能汽车有限公司	其他有限责任公司	中型	新能源车整车制造

12-14 主要工业产品生产量(2022年)
Output of Major Industrial Products(2022)

主要工业产品名称	Major Industrial Products above Designated Size	单位 Unit	生产量 Production
铁矿石原矿	Crude Iron ore	万吨 (10 000 tons)	535.2
铁矿石成品矿	Iron ore finished ore	万吨 (10 000 tons)	1945.8
铁精矿	Iron ore concentrate	万吨 (10 000 tons)	1848.1
石灰石	Lime Powder	万吨 (10 000 tons)	1632.7
饲料	Feed	万吨 (10 000 tons)	152.2
鲜、冷藏肉	Frozen,Fresh Meat	万吨 (10 000 tons)	16.5
乳制品	Milk Products	万吨 (10 000 tons)	50.5
液体乳	Liquid Milk	万吨 (10 000 tons)	48.9
酱油	Soy Sauce	万吨 (10 000 tons)	5.9
食品添加剂	Food Additives	万吨 (10 000 tons)	21.6
饲料添加剂	Feed Additive	万吨 (10 000 tons)	5.5
饮料酒	Liquor	万千升 (10 000 kiloliter)	26.3
白酒(折65度，商品量)	Liquor (65 degree discount, commercial quantity)	万千升 (10 000 kiloliter)	0.6
啤酒	Beer	万千升 (10 000 kiloliter)	25.7
饮料	Drinks	万吨 (10 000 tons)	232.9
碳酸型饮料(汽水)	Carbonated Drinks	万吨 (10 000 tons)	65.9
包装饮用水	Bottled Drinking Water	万吨 (10 000 tons)	55.8
果汁和蔬菜汁类饮料	Juice and Vegetable Juice Beverage	万吨 (10 000 tons)	49.5
布	Cloth	万米(10 000 m)	807.5
服装	Garments	万件(10 000 pieces)	4372.3
家具	Furniture	万件(10 000 pieces)	61.7
纸制品	Paper Products	万吨 (10 000 tons)	38.0
瓦楞纸箱	Corrugated Box	万吨 (10 000 tons)	16.6
单色印刷品	Monochrome Print	万令(10 000 ream)	74.8
多色印刷品	Ploychrome Print	万对开色令 (10 000 color folio ream)	1778.5
纯苯	Purified Petroleum Benzin(e)	万吨 (10 000 tons)	9.7
精甲醇	Extracted Methanol	万吨 (10 000 tons)	69.6
合成氨(无水氨)	Synthetic Ammonia	万吨 (10 000 tons)	20.7
农用氮、磷、钾化学肥料(折纯)	Chemical Fertilizer	万吨 (10 000 tons)	4.2
尿素(折含氮100%)	Urea	万吨 (10 000 tons)	4.0
化学农药原药(折有效成分100%)	Chemical Pesticide	吨(ton)	917
涂料	Paint	万吨 (10 000 tons)	11.9
初级形态塑料	Primary Plastic	万吨 (10 000 tons)	78.0
化学试剂	Chemical Reagent	万吨 (10 000 tons)	12.8
表面活性剂	Surface Active Agent	万吨 (10 000 tons)	3.1
合成洗涤剂	Synthetic Detergents	万吨 (10 000 tons)	0.4
化学药品原药	Chemical Medicine	万吨 (10 000 tons)	1.4

12–14 续表 1 continued 1

主要工业产品名称	Major Industrial Products above Designated Size	单位 Unit	生产量 Production
中成药	Traditional Chemical Medicine	吨(ton)	7904
兽用药品	Veterinary Drugs	吨(ton)	19048
化学纤维	Chemical Fiber	万吨 (10 000 tons)	7.6
橡胶轮胎外胎	Rubber Tyre Cover	万条(10 000 tires)	19.8
塑料制品	Plastic Articles	万吨 (10 000 tons)	15.3
硅酸盐水泥熟料	Portland Cement Clinker	万吨 (10 000 tons)	535.2
水泥	Cement	万吨 (10 000 tons)	1361.6
石灰	Lime	万吨 (10 000 tons)	250.4
商品混凝土	Concrete	万立方米(10 000 cu.m)	2817.1
水泥混凝土排水管	Cement and Concrete Drainage Pipes	千米(km)	270.8
水泥混凝土压力管	Cement and Concrete Pressure Pipes	千米(km)	150.0
砖	Brick	亿块(100 million unit)	1.7
钢化玻璃	Stalinite	万平方米(10 000 sq.m)	229.7
中空玻璃	Hollow Glass	万平方米(10 000 sq.m)	177.7
耐火材料制品	Refractory Product	万吨 (10 000 tons)	51.2
石墨及碳素制品	Graphite and Carbon Products	万条(10 000 tires)	209.1
生铁	Cast Iron	万吨 (10 000 tons)	1779.9
粗钢	Crude Steel	万吨 (10 000 tons)	1914.2
钢材	Rolled Steel	万吨 (10 000 tons)	2021.4
钢结构	Steel Structure	万吨 (10 000 tons)	94.2
金属切削工具	Metal Cutting Tool	万吨 (10 000 tons)	371.2
锻件	Forge Piece	万吨 (10 000 tons)	128.3
粉末冶金零件	Sintered Metal Products	万吨 (10 000 tons)	1.3
电站锅炉	Utility Boilers	蒸发量吨 (evaporation ton)	1441
发动机	Engine	万千瓦(10 000kW)	1772.9
汽车用发动机	Automotive Engine	万千瓦(10 000kW)	1677.3
金属切削机床	Metal-cutting Machine Tools	台(unit)	12518
起重机	Lifting Equipment	万吨 (10 000 tons)	17.9
电梯、自动扶梯及升降机	Elevators, Escalators and Lifts	台(unit)	55057
液压元件	Hydraulic Components	万件(10 000 unit)	45.7
气动元件	Pneumatic Components	万件(10 000 unit)	783.3
鼓风机	Air Blower	万台(10 000 unit)	3.5
工商用制冷、空调设备	Commercial Refrigeration Equipment	万台(10 000 unit)	3.1
金属紧固件	Metal Fastener	万吨 (10 000 tons)	4.2
弹簧	Spring	万吨 (10 000 tons)	3.4
矿山专用设备	Mining Equipment	万吨 (10 000 tons)	4.2
金属冶炼设备	Metal Smelting Equipment	万吨 (10 000 tons)	4.9
炼油、化工生产专用设备	Special Equipment for Oil Refining and Chemical Protection	吨(ton)	22586

12-14 续表 2 continued 2

主要工业产品名称	Major Industrial Products above Designated Size	单位 Unit	生产量 Production
农产品初加工机械	Agricultural Primary Processing Machinery	万台(10 000 unit)	1.2
电子工业专用设备	Special Equipment for Electronic Industry	万台(10 000 unit)	17.5
棉花加工机械	Cotton Processing Machinery	台(unit)	844
医疗仪器设备及器械	Medical Instruments	万台(10 000 unit)	17.4
工业机器人	Industrial Robot	套(unit)	3746
汽车	Motor Vehicles	万辆(10 000 unit)	16.4
载货汽车	Trucks	万辆(10 000 unit)	16.0
改装汽车	Modified Cars	万辆(10 000 unit)	2.2
铁路货车	Railway Freight Wagons	辆(unit)	3765
摩托车整车	Motorcycles	万辆(10 000 unit)	44.3
发电机组(发电设备)	Power Generating Equipment	万千瓦(10 000kW)	364.9
电动机	Electromotor	万千瓦(10 000kW)	267.7
变压器	Transformers	万千伏安(10 000 KVA pm)	15872.3
高压开关设备(11万伏以上)	High Voltage Switchgear (over 110,000 volts)	万台(10 000 unit)	0.8
安全、自动化监控设备	Safety and Automatic Monitoring Equipment	台(套)(unit)	21515
通信及电子网络用电缆	Cable for Communications and Electronic Network	万对千米(10 000 couples.km)	3.6
电力电缆	Power Cable	万千米(10 000 km)	7.8
太阳能热水器	Solar Water Heater	万平方米(10 000 sq.m)	154.8
灯具及照明装置	Lamps and Lighting Fixtures	万套(台个)(10 000 unit)	27.0
电子计算机整机	Computers	万台(10 000 unit)	77.5
服务器	Servers	万台(10 000 unit)	77.1
半导体分立器件	Discrete Semiconductor Devices	亿只(100 million unit)	128.8
传感器	Transducer	万只(10 000 unit)	1070.0
集成电路	Integrated Circuit	万块(10 000 unit)	28964.0
电子元件	Eletronic Components	亿只(100 million unit)	27.1
电声器件	Electroacoustic Device	万只(10 000 unit)	1599.0
印制电路板	Print-circuit Board	万平方米(10 000 sq.m)	92.8
工业自动调节仪表与控制系统	Industrial Automatic Instrument and Control System	台(套)(unit)	85226
电工仪器仪表	Electrical Instrument	万台(10 000 unit)	475.6
汽车仪器仪表	Automobile Instrument	万台(10 000 unit)	57.9
钟	Clock	万只(10 000 unit)	59.7
自来水生产量	Tap Water Production	亿立方米(100 million cu.m)	8.4
发电量	Electricity Generation	亿千瓦时(100 million kWh)	318.2
其中：火力发电量	Thermal Power	亿千瓦时(100 million kWh)	293.3
风力发电量	Wind Power	亿千瓦时(100 million kWh)	21.9
垃圾发电量	Garbage Power	亿千瓦时(100 million kWh)	9.5
煤气生产量	Gas Power Generation	亿立方米(100 million cu.m)	215.4

12-15 工业企业能源购进、消费及库存(2022年)

Purchases, Consumption and Inventory of Main Energy Source in Industrial Enterprises(2022)

能源名称	Type of Energy	计量单位 Unit	年初库存量 Beginning Stock	本年购进量 Purchases This Year	本年工业生产消费 Industrial Consumption of This Year	年末库存量 Year-end Stock
能源合计	Total Energy	吨标准煤 (tons of SCE)			50126160	
原煤	Raw Coal	吨(ton)	1047582	18001473	18565612	779436
洗精煤	Cleaned Coal	吨(ton)	198036	6829950	6798940	229045
其他洗煤	Other Cleaned Coal	吨(ton)	215843	2353826	2456540	115130
煤制品	Coal Product	吨(ton)	71510	947459	1046611	84952
焦炭	Coke	吨(ton)	99845	6960938	8126791	196414
天然气	Natural Gas	万立方米 (10 000 cu.m)		123248	100994	
液化天然气	Liquefied Natural Gas	吨(ton)	20	30657	10867	71
氢气	Hydrogen	万立方米 (10 000 cu.m)	0.31	3366	4125	
汽油	Gasoline	吨(ton)	45	3664	3763	13
煤油	Kerosene	吨(ton)	0.23	52	84	1
柴油	Diesel Oil	吨(ton)	1836	39887	36473	2663
液化石油气	Liquefied Petroleum	吨(ton)		1198	1198	
石油焦	Petroleum coke	吨(ton)	12605	2627574	2260683	54993
热力	Heating	百万千焦(mkj)		9753863	10723753	
电力	Electricity	万千瓦时 (10 000 kWh)		1656534	2299393	
城市生活垃圾(用于燃料)	Municipal household waste (for fuels)	吨(ton)	31884	2496634	2071171	18916
生物燃料	Biofuel	吨标准煤 (tons of SCE)	43399	270694	353751	18969
余热余压	Residual heat and residual pressure	百万千焦(mkj)		303885	16403394	
其他燃料	Other Fuel	吨标准煤 (tons of SCE)		126	119	

注:按照经济普查要求，免填能源合计中，年初库存、购进量、年末库存。

Note: According to requirements of economic census, it's unnecessary to fill in inventory and volume of purchase at the beginning of the year and the inventory at the end of the year in the total energy.

12-16 工业分行业主要能源消费量(2022年)
Consumption of Main Energy Source in Industrial Enterprises by Sector(2022)

指标	Item	原煤(吨) Coal(ton)
总计	**Total**	**18565612**
采矿业	**Mining**	
煤炭开采和洗选业	Mining and Washing of Coal	412564
石油和天然气开采业	Extraction of Petroleum and Natural Gas	
黑色金属矿采选业	Mining and Processing of Ferrous Metal Ores	38516
非金属矿采选业	Mining and Processing of Non-Ferrous Metal Ores	
制造业	**Manufacture**	
农副食品加工业	Processing of Food from Agricultural Products	41766
食品制造业	Manufacture of Foods	
酒、饮料和精制茶制造业	Manufacture of Wine, Drinks and Refined Tea	
纺织业	Manufacture of Textile	
纺织服装、服饰业	Manufacture of Textile Wearing Apparel and Finery	
皮革、毛皮、羽毛及其制品和制鞋业	Manufacture of Leather, Fur, Feather and Related Products and Footwear	
木材加工及木、竹、藤、棕、草制品业	Processing of Timbers, Manufacture of Wood, Bamboo, Rattan, Palm, and Straw Products	
家具制造业	Manufacture of Furniture	
造纸及纸制品业	Manufacture of Paper and Paper Products	
印刷和记录媒介复制业	Printing and Reproduction of Recording Media	
文教、工美、体育和娱乐用品制造业	Manufacture of Articles for Culture, Education, Arts and Crafts, Sport and Entertainment Activities	
石油、煤炭及其他燃料加工业	Processing of Petroleum, Coal and Other Fuels	
化学原料及化学制品制造业	Manufacture of Chemical Raw Material and Chemical Products	2175378
医药制造业	Manufacture of Medicines	34691
化学纤维制造业	Manufacture of Chemical Fiber	
橡胶和塑料制品业	Manufacture of Rubber and Plastic	
非金属矿物制品业	Manufacture of Non-metallic Mineral Products	821876
黑色金属冶炼及压延加工业	Manufacture and Processing of Ferrous Metals	2166089
有色金属冶炼及压延加工业	Manufacture & Processing of Non-ferrous Metals	
金属制品业	Manufacture of Metal Products	1173
通用设备制造业	Manufacture of General Purpose Machinery	
专用设备制造业	Manufacture of Special Purpose Machinery	
汽车制造业	Manufacture of Automotive	
铁路、船舶、航空航天和其他运输设备制造业	Manufacture of Railroad,Marine,Aerospace and Other Transportation Equipment	
电气机械及器材制造业	Manufacture of Electrical Machinery & Equipment	
计算机、通信和其他电子设备制造业	Manufacture of Computer, Communications and Other Electronic Equipment	
仪器仪表制造业	Manufacture of Measuring Instrument	
其他制造业	Other Manufacture	
废弃资源综合利用业	Utilization of Waste Resources	
金属制品、机械和设备修理业	Metal Products, Machinery and Equipment Repair Industry	
电力、热力、燃气及水生产和供应业	**Production and Supply of Electric Power and Heat Power**	
电力、热力生产和供应业	Production and Supply of Electric Power and Heat Power	12873559
燃气生产和供应业	Production and Supply of Gas	
水的生产和供应业	Production and Supply of Water	

天然气 (万立方米) Natural Gas (10 000 cu.m)	液化天然气 (吨) Liquefied Natural Gas (ton)	汽油 (吨) Gasoline (ton)	柴油 (吨) Diesel Oil (ton)	热力 (百万千焦) Heating (mkj)	电力 (万千瓦时) Electricity (10 000 kWh)
100994	**10867**	**3763**	**36473**	**10723753**	**2299393**
			193		4135
	11		4		6473
		54	2714	300036	70876
			1346		7444
1740	1157	3	209	273644	17472
4317	465	32	126	1312963	39984
1954		41	11	50978	19053
934				101173	29308
255		10	1	10708	2539
110					257
			7		5497
36		3	30		2131
801	334	38	33	960062	16193
176		128	51	2687	14465
336		30			3171
1458	574	90	187	316284	56324
5704	1628	76	712	3288602	250200
4553	24	108	24	2219345	75790
2227		4	4	78136	9991
244	3	57	160	156912	17837
17979	1511	245	15359	291291	186829
1766	1724	44	5772	190460	701004
119		6	27	13417	7174
10133	3248	236	658	1430	137419
2209	111	635	1527	273	48648
418	30	522	283	20014	19582
2953		74	3104	472724	79359
159	19	147	108	45740	11132
4415	5	234	86	2205	49720
313		280	48	5717	29013
1		423	28	1703	2544
		4			1207
			690		8075
			7		720
35677	21	23	2899	607248	295846
6		109	21		1678
		106	43		70302

主要统计指标解释

工业 指从事自然资源的开采，对采掘品和农产品进行加工和再加工的物质生产部门。具体包括：(1)对自然资源的开采，如采矿、晒盐等(但不包括禽兽捕猎和水产捕捞)；(2)对农副产品的加工、再加工，如粮油加工、食品加工、缫丝、纺织、制革等；(3)对采掘品的加工、再加工，如炼铁、炼钢、化工生产、石油加工、机器制造、木材加工等，以及电力、燃气及水的生产和供应等；(4)对工业品的修理、翻新，如机器设备的修理等。

工业统计调查单位为工业法人单位。

工业法人单位指从事工业生产经营活动的法人单位。工业法人单位应同时具备以下条件：①依法成立，有自己的名称、组织机构和场所，能够独立承担民事责任；②独立拥有（或授权）使用资产，承担负债，有权与其他单位签订合同；③具有包括资产负债表在内的账户，或者能够根据需要编制账户。

国有控股企业 即原来的国有及国有控股企业，根据企业实收资本中国有经济成分的出资人的实际投资情况，或国有经济成分的出资人对企业资产的实际控制、支配程度进行分类。以下情况为国有控股：（1）在企业的全部实收资本中，国有经济成分的出资人拥有的实收资本（股本）所占企业全部实收资本（股本）的比例大于50%的国有绝对控股。(2)在企业的全部实收资本中，国有经济成分的出资人拥有的实收资本（股本）所占比例虽未大于50%，但相对大于其他任何一方经济成分的出资人所占比例的国有相对控股；或者虽不大于其他经济成分，但根据协议规定拥有企业实际控制权的国有协议控股。（3）投资双方各占50%，且未明确由谁绝对控股的企业，若其中一方为国有经济成分的，一律按国有控股处理。

本篇涉及的企业登记注册类型的解释详见综合篇。

资产总计 指企业过去的交易或者事项形成的、由企业拥有或者控制的、预期会给企业带来经济利益的资源。包括企业拥有的土地、办公楼、厂房、机器、运输工具、存货等实物资产和现金、存款、应收账款和预付账款等金融资产。资产一般按流动性分为流动资产和非流动资产。其中流动资产可分为货币资金、交易性金融资产、应收票据、应收账款、预付款项、其他应收款、存货等；非流动资产可分为长期股权投资、固定资产、无形资产及其他非流动资产等。来源于会计“资产负债表”中“资产总计”项目的期末余额数。

流动资产合计 资产满足以下条件之一应归为流动资产：(1)预计在一个正常营业周期中变现、出售或耗用，主要包括存货、应收账款等；（2）主要为交易目的而持有；（3）预计在资产负债表日起一年内（含一年）变现；（4）自资产负债日起一年内，交换其他资产或清偿负债的能力不受限制的现金或现金等价物。包括货币资金、应收票据、应收账款、存货等项目。来源于会计“资产负债表”中“流动资产合计”项目的期末余额数。

负债合计 指企业过去的交易或者事项形成的，预期会导致经济利益流出企业的现时义务。包括银行贷款、借款、应付账款、应付职工工资、应付职工福利费、应交税金等企业负有偿还责任的债务。负债一般按偿还期长短分为流动负债和非流动负债。来源于会计“资产负债表”中“负债合计”项目的期末余额数。

应收账款 指资产负债表日以摊余成本计量的、企业因销售商品、提供服务等经营活动应收取的款项。来源于会计“资产负债表”中“应收账款”项目的期末余额数。

存货 指企业在日常活动中持有以备出售的产成品或商品、处在生产过程中的在产品、在生产过程或提供劳务过程中耗用的材料或物料等，通常包括原材料、在产品、半成品、产成品、商品以及周转材料等。来源于会计“资产负债表”中“存货”项目的期末余额数。

营业收入 指企业从事销售商品、提供劳务和让渡资产使用权等生产经营活动形成的经济利益流入。营业收入包括“主营业务收入”和“其他业务收入”。来源于会计“利润表”中“营业收入”项目的本年累计数。

营业成本 指企业从事销售商品、提供劳务和让渡资产使用权等生产经营活动发生的实际成本。包括企业（单位）在报告期内从事销售商品、提供劳务等日常活动发生的各种耗费。包括“主营业务成本”和“其他业务成本”。来源于会计“利润表”中“营业成本”项目的本年累计数。

销售费用 指企业在销售商品和材料、提供劳务的过程中发生的各种费用，包括保险费、包装费、展览费和广告费、商品维修费、预计产品质量保证损失、运输费、装卸费等以及为销售本企业商品而专设的销售机构（含销售网点、售后服务网点等）的职工薪酬、业务费、折旧费等经营费用。

管理费用 指企业为组织和管理企业生产经营所发生的费用，包括企业在筹建期间内发生的开办费、董事会和行政管理部门在企业经营管理中发生的，或者应当由企业统一负担的公司经费等。来源于会计“利润表”中“管理费用”项目的本年累计数。

利润总额 指企业在一定会计期间的经营成果，是生产经营过程中各种收入扣除各种耗费后的盈余，反映企业在报告期内实现的盈亏总额。来源于会计“利润表”中“利润总额”项目的本年累计数。

平均用工人数 指报告期企业平均实际拥有的、参与本企业生产经营活动的人员数。

Explanatory Notes on Main Statistical Indicators

Industry refers to the material production sector which is engaged in the extraction of natural resources and processing and reprocessing of minerals and agricultural products, including (1) extraction of natural resources, such as mining, salt production (but not including hunting and fishing); (2) processing and reprocessing of farm and sideline produces, such as grain and oil processing, food processing, silk reeling, spinning and weaving and leather making; (3) processing and reprocessing of mineral products, such as steel making, iron smelting, chemicals manufacturing, petroleum processing, machine building, timber processing, and production and supply of electricity, gas and water; (4) repairing and renovating of industrial products such as the machinery.

In industrial surveys, the units of enquiry are industrial corporate units.

Industrial corporate units refer to corporate units engaging in industrial production and operation activities, which meet the following requirements: (1) They are established legally, having their own names, organizations, location, and are able to take civil liability independently; (2) They possess (or are authorized to use) assets independently, assume liabilities and are entitled to sign contracts with other units; (3) They have accounts including the balance sheets or can compile the accounts according to the need.

State-holding Enterprises cover the original state-owned enterprises and state-holding enterprises. They are classified according to the actual investment made by the contributors of state-owned part in the paid-in capital of the enterprises, or the degree of control or dominance of the contributor on the assets of the enterprises. The following cases are regarded as state-holding: (1) Absolute state-holding in which the contributors of state-owned parts possess more than 50% of all the paid-in capital (stocks) of the enterprises; (2) Relative state-holding in which the contributors of state-owned parts possess no more than 50% of the paid-in capital (stocks) of the enterprises, but more than that of any other contributors; or agreed state-holding in which the contributors of state-owned parts possess no more than other contributors but have actual control over the enterprises according to agreements; (3) In case both contributors possess 50% and it is not clear which one is in absolute holding position, the enterprise is regarded as state-holding enterprise if one of the contributor has state-owned elements.

For explanation of types of registration covered in this chapter, please refer to Chapter 1 on General Survey.

Total Assets refer to all resources that are owned or controlled by enterprises through previous trades or transactions, with expectation of making economic profits to enterprises. Included are all assets owned by enterprises such as land, office buildings, factories, machines, vehicles, inventories and other physical assets as well as cash, deposits, accounts receivable, prepayments and other financial assets. Classified by the degree of liquidity, total assets include current assets and non-current assets. Current assets can be classified into monetary capital, trading financial assets, notes receivable, accounts receivable, advanced payments, other receivables and inventories. Non-current assets can be divided into long-term equity investment, fixed assets, intangible assets and other non-current assets. Data on this indicator can be obtained from the year-end figures of total assets in the Balance Sheet of accounting records.

Current Assets refer to the assets that meet one of the following requirements: (1) expected to be cashed, sold or used in a normal operation cycle, mainly including inventory and accounts receivable; (2) owned for transaction purpose mainly; (3) expected to be cashed within one year (including one year) from the day of the Balance Sheet; (4) unlimited cash or cash equivalents that can be exchanged with other assets or capable of settling debts during one year since the day of the Balance Sheet. Included are monetary capital, notes receivable, accounts receivable and inventories. Data on this indicator can be obtained from the year-end figures of total current assets in the Balance Sheet of accounting records.

Total Liabilities refer to payable liabilities of enterprises that are accumulated from earlier transactions with expectation of leaking out of economic profits. Included are debts that enterprises are responsible for repaying such as bank loans, borrowings, accounts payable, wages payable, employee benefits payable, taxes payable, etc. In terms of payment, it can be divided into liquid liabilities and long-term liabilities. Data on this indicator can be obtained from the year-end figures of total liabilities in the Balance Sheet of accounting records.

Accounts Receivable refers to creditor's rights through business activities such as selling goods and providing labor. It comes from the ending balance of accounts receivable in balance sheet.

Inventories refers to finished goods or commodities held in preparation for sale in enterprises' daily activities, goods in the production process, material or the physical materials consumed in the production process or in the process of providing labor, usually include raw materials, goods in the production process, semi-finished products, finished products, goods and materials in flow. It comes from the ending balance of inventory in balance sheet.

Business Revenue refers to the inflow of economic benefits

through production and operation activities of enterprises, such as selling commodities, providing labor services and transferring the right to use of assets. Business revenue includes "revenue from principal business" and " revenue from other business". It comes from current year's cumulative report of "business revenue" items from the "income statement".

Business Cost refers to the actual costs incurred by the enterprises in such production and operation activities as selling commodities, providing labor services and transferring the right to use of assets. It includes various expenditures incurred by enterprises (units) in their daily activities of selling goods and providing labour services during the reporting period. It includes "cost of principal business" and "cost of other business". It comes from current year's cumulative report of "operating cost" items from the "income statement".

Selling Expenses refer to the cost during the sale of goods and materials, providing labour services, including insurance, packing, exhibition fees and advertising fees, merchandise maintenance costs, expected product quality guarantee loss, transportation fees, handling fees, and operating expenses for the sales of the company's products, such as employee compensation, business expenses, depreciation costs for dedicated sales offices (including sales outlets, after-sales service outlets, etc.).

Management Expenses refer to the expenses for the organization and management of enterprise operation, including the start-up costs during the construction of enterprises, funds occurred during enterprises operation by board of directors and executive management in the enterprise management, and other costs to be paid by enterprises. It comes from current year's cumulative amount of management cost in income statement.

Total Profits refer to the operational results in a certain accounting period, and it is the balance of various incomes minus various spendings in the course of operation, reflecting the total profits and losses of enterprises in reference period. Data are obtained from current year's cumulative amount of total profits in the profit statement of the accounting record of enterprise.

Annual Average Employees refer to the number of persons engaged in the production and operation activities of enterprises in the reporting period, which are actually employed by the enterprises.

13

建筑业

CONSTRUCTION

13–1 建筑业主要指标
Main Indicators of Construction Enterprises

指标	Item	单位 Unit	2018年	2019年	2020年	2021年	2022年
企业单位数	Number of Enterprises	个(unit)	507	895	1033	1182	1371
建筑业总产值	Gross Output Value	万元(10 000 yuan)	28234734	35139777	37481222	41260343	44607549
按隶属关系分	by Ownership						
中央属	Central	万元(10 000 yuan)	14747883	17350365	20148118	21677643	24519759
地方属	Local	万元(10 000 yuan)		11793174	10596000	10417195	10155041
省属	Provincial	万元(10 000 yuan)	3039149				
市属	Region	万元(10 000 yuan)	6391344				
县及县以下	County	万元(10 000 yuan)	641220				
其他	Others	万元(10 000 yuan)	3415138	5996238	6737105	9165505	9932748
按工程性质分	by Sector						
建筑工程	Building and Civil Engineering Construction	万元(10 000 yuan)	25182882	31199367	33447869	35981015	38174842
安装工程	Construction Installation	万元(10 000 yuan)	2329541	3015885	3288008	3749267	4594480
其他产值	Others	万元(10 000 yuan)	722311	924525	745346	1530061	1838227
竣工产值	Value of Construction Completed	万元(10 000 yuan)	8691856	12943615	12789160	13373476	12501477
房屋施工面积	Floor Space of Buildings under Construction	万平方米(10 000 sq.cm)	12984	14955	17090	19410	19971
#本年新开工	Started This year	万平方米(10 000 sq.cm)	4842	4705	5349	5621	5223
房屋竣工面积	Floor Space of Buildings Completed	万平方米(10 000 sq.cm)	2366	3418	3323	3730	3128
#住宅	Residential	万平方米(10 000 sq.cm)	1502	2170	1916	2247	1808
所有者权益	Owners' Equity	万元(10 000 yuan)	6269077	8130630	7894051	9363017	12683470
利润总额	Total Profits	万元(10 000 yuan)	810897	1051261	1087848	1360873	1747800
工资总额	Total wages	万元(10 000 yuan)	3480056	3793574	3295738	3454592	4500399

13-2 建筑企业资产实力(2022年)
Assets of Construction Enterprises (2022)

单位：万元

指标 (总承包与专业承包)	Item	流动资产合计 Total Current Assets	#存货 Inventory
总计	**Total**	**50619235**	**4404584**
其中：国有及国有控股企业	State-owned and State-controlled Enterprises	37675766	2084186
一、按登记注册类型分组	**By Status of Registration**		
内资企业	Domestic Invested Enterprises	50605568	4395767
国有企业	State-owned Enterprises	115713	23633
集体企业	Collective-owned Enterprises	91083	15587
股份合作企业	Cooperative Enterprises	100410	76159
联营企业	Joint-owned Enterprises		
其他联营企业	Other Joint Ownership Enterprises		
有限责任公司	Limited Liability Corporations	41045752	2914607
国有独资公司	State Sole-proprietorship Corporations	12067112	663953
其他有限责任公司	Other Joint Ownership Enterprises	28978640	2250654
股份有限公司	Share-holding Corporations Ltd.	1068128	117809
私营企业	Private Enterprises	8184483	1247973
私营有限责任公司	Private Limited Liability Corporations	8050146	1225413
私营股份有限公司	Private Share-holding Corporations Ltd.	134337	22560
港、澳、台商投资企业	Enterprises with Investment from Hong Kong,Macao and Taiwan		
外商投资企业	Foreign Invested Enterprises	13667	8817
中外合资经营企业	Joint-venture Enterprises	5403	1172
外资企业	Enterprises with Sole Fund	8263	7645
二、按国民经济行业分组	**By Sector**		
房屋建筑业	Construction of Buildings	14131063	1749091
土木工程建筑业	Civil Engineering	30936308	1924976
建筑安装业	Construction Installation	2111575	292939
建筑装饰装修和其他建筑业	Building Decoration and Other Construction	3440289	437578
三、按隶属关系分组	**By Ownership**		
中央	Central	20065899	665930
地方	Local	16689182	1595869
其他	Others	13864154	2142786
四、按企业资质等级分组	**By Qualification Criteria**		
施工总承包	Construction Contract	45552783	3704485
特级	Special Grade	26175915	1248294
一级	First Grade	12648176	1205882
二级	Second Grade	3797147	859415
三级及以下	Third Grade and below	2931545	390895
专业承包	Professional Contract	5066452	700099
一级	First Grade	3024908	370836
二级	Second Grade	1400349	249378
三级及以下	Third Grade and below	641195	79885

(10 000 yuan)

固定资产原价 Original Value of Fixed Assets	资产合计 Total Assets	流动负债合计 Current Liabilities	非流动负债合计 Non-Current Liabilities	负债合计 Total Liabilities	所有者权益合计 Owners' Equity
3142827	**61669480**	**46743896**	**2242106**	**48986009**	**12683470**
1969311	47294225	35974238	1952541	37926780	9367445
3139814	61643343	46726545	2242106	48968658	12674684
21088	140095	90697	5740	96437	43658
14075	105668	85604	606	86210	19458
1659	105015	118576		118576	-13561
2295120	50805328	38811882	2053611	40865495	9939833
605112	14743875	11268403	902688	12171092	2572783
1690008	36061454	27543479	1150922	28694404	7367050
41055	1146626	779303	65923	845226	301400
766816	9340611	6840484	116226	6956715	2383896
753201	9185362	6740482	108078	6848565	2336797
13616	155249	100002	8148	108150	47099
3013	26137	17351		17351	8786
142	5408	3567		3567	1840
2871	20729	13783		13783	6946
736051	16031010	11515996	531344	12047342	3983668
1945427	39292412	30530119	1498241	32028363	7264049
250203	2538876	1808822	94636	1903460	635416
211147	3807182	2888958	117884	3006844	800338
1228247	25819414	19751889	1078651	20830540	4988874
808096	20224250	15350556	879441	16229998	3994252
1106484	15625816	11641451	284014	11925471	3700345
2676691	55994774	42557092	2113779	44670875	11323899
1209917	33292884	25743987	1050263	26794250	6498635
803855	14933327	11118280	779565	11897845	3035481
367028	4375486	3390090	30492	3420582	954904
295890	3393077	2304736	253459	2558198	834879
466137	5674706	4186803	128327	4315134	1359572
189938	3345330	2497337	84798	2582136	763195
110258	1559060	1144181	21284	1165466	393594
165941	770316	545286	22246	567533	202783

13-3 建筑业施工产值构成(2022年)
Output Value of Construction Structure(2022)

单位:万元 (10 000 yuan)

指标（总承包与专业承包）	Item	合计 Total	建筑工程 Construction	安装工程 Installation	其他产值 Other Value	竣工产值 Output Value of Completed
总计	**Total**	**44607549**	**38174842**	**4594480**	**1838227**	**12501477**
其中：国有及国有控股企业	State-owned and State-controlled Enterprises	34299552	29841469	3100585	1357498	7749313
一、按登记注册类型分组	**By Status of Registration**					
内资企业	Domestic Invested Enterprises	44605560	38174842	4592510	1838208	12501477
国有企业	State-owned Enterprises	50083	31231	1486	17366	11621
集体企业	Collective-owned Enterprises	36023	36023			25180
股份合作企业	Cooperative Enterprises	24604	24604			2190
联营企业	Joint Ownership Enterprises					
其他联营企业	Other Joint Ownership Enterprises					
有限责任公司	Limited Liability Corporations	37344778	32536022	3333565	1475192	9250972
国有独资公司	State Sole-proprietorship Corporations	12101044	10055950	1899302	145792	2422201
其他有限责任公司	Other Limited Liability Corporations	25243734	22480072	1434263	1329400	6828772
股份有限公司	Share-holding Corporations Ltd.	551908	464369	85634	1905	346044
私营企业	Private Enterprises	6598164	5082594	1171824	343746	2865470
私营有限责任公司	Private Limited Liability Corporations	6520237	5018196	1158799	343242	2851731
私营股份有限公司	Private Share-holding Corporations Ltd.	77928	64398	13025	504	13738
港、澳、台商投资企业	Enterprises with Investment from Hong Kong, Macao and Taiwan					
外商投资企业	Foreign Invested Enterprises	1989		1970	19	
中外合资经营企业	Joint-venture Enterprises	1175		1175		
外资企业	Enterprises with Sole Fund	814		795	19	
二、按国民经济行业分组	**By Sector**					
房屋建筑业	Construction of Buildings	19030302	17481766	1440510	108026	8488950
土木工程建筑业	Civil Engineering	21259402	18111127	1788901	1359374	2574298
建筑安装业	Construction Installation	1818678	444961	1137984	235733	646872
建筑装饰装修和其他建筑业	Building Decoration and Other Construction	2499166	2136988	227084	135094	791357
三、按隶属关系分组	**By Ownership**					
中央	Central	24519759	22140938	2339281	39540	5263911
地方	Local	10155041	8424735	490429	1239877	3490557
其他	Others	9932748	7609169	1764769	558810	3747009
四、按企业资质等级分组	**By Qualification Criteria**					
施工总承包	Construction Contract	40522581	35260721	3664454	1597406	11182245
特级	Special Grade	26394821	24535046	1857067	2708	8013770
一级	First Grade	10029722	7455162	1306972	1267588	1880575
二级	Second Grade	2056076	1718813	224548	112715	555397
三级及以下	Third Grade and below	2041962	1551701	275867	214394	732503
专业承包	Professional Contract	4084968	2914121	930026	240821	1319232
一级	First Grade	2356166	1750494	497651	108021	724401
二级	Second Grade	1254619	809203	344224	101192	431901
三级及以下	Third Grade and below	474182	354423	88151	31608	162929

13-4 建筑企业主要经济指标(2022年)
Main Economic Indicators of Construction Enterprises(2022)

单位：万元 (10 000yuan)

指标(总承包与专业承包)	Item	营业收入 Business Revenue	利税总额 Total Pre-tax Profits	营业利润 Profits from Business	利润总额 Total Profits	应付职工薪酬(本年贷方累计发生额) Total Wages Payable
总计	**Total**	**47851301**	**2563162**	**1737195**	**1747800**	**4500399**
其中：国有及国有控股企业	State-owned and State-controlled Enterprises	36388191	2039810	1525586	1540504	2873120
一、按登记注册类型分组	**By Status of Registration**					
内资企业	Domestic Invested Enterprises	47843189	2563235	1737433	1748060	4498654
国有企业	State-owned Enterprises	99105	1337	-902	-749	9913
集体企业	Collective-owned Enterprises	52745	3645	819	528	6460
股份合作企业	Cooperative Enterprises	39345	2437	436	435	2214
联营企业	Joint Ownership Enterprises					
其他联营企业	Other Joint Ownership Enterprises					
有限责任公司	Limited Liability Corporations	39386282	2125534	1525450	1543168	3423201
国有独资公司	State Sole-proprietorship Corporations	12504203	663785	456296	460427	829049
其他有限责任公司	Other Limited Liability Corporations	26882079	1461749	1069154	1082741	2594152
股份有限公司	Share-holding Corporations Ltd.	601588	40093	29674	29720	55892
私营企业	Private Enterprises	7664126	390189	181955	174958	1000974
私营有限责任公司	Private Limited Liability Corporations	7550733	380351	176794	169558	986897
私营股份有限公司	Private Share-holding Corporations Ltd.	113393	9838	5161	5399	14078
港、澳、台商投资企业	Enterprises with Investment from Hong Kong,Macao and Taiwan					
外商投资企业	Foreign Invested Enterprises	8112	-73	-238	-260	1745
中外合资经营企业	Joint-venture Enterprises	7298	90	-32	-32	731
外资企业	Enterprises with Sole Fund	814	-163	-207	-228	1014
二、按国民经济行业分组	**By Sector**					
房屋建筑业	Construction of Buildings	19292321	1035117	697665	701670	1883051
土木工程建筑业	Civil Engineering	23181828	1253830	903132	910661	2067392
建筑安装业	Construction Installation	2559091	96889	36303	37623	253214
建筑装饰装修和其他建筑业	Building Decoration and Other Construction	2818061	177326	100095	97846	296742
三、按隶属关系分组	**By Ownership**					
中央	Central	24564902	1174852	839189	842776	1746380
地方	Local	11645401	759439	565417	576104	1312805
其他	Others	11640998	628871	332589	328920	1441214
四、按企业资质等级分组	**By Qualification Criteria**					
施工总承包	Construction Contract	42979316	2296194	1605000	1615876	4010418
特级	Special Grade	28111144	1527598	1151449	1156658	2219525
一级	First Grade	9966310	481169	315503	321235	1160343
二级	Second Grade	2329828	145677	77329	77164	306670
三级以下	Third Grade and below	2572034	141751	60719	60819	323880
专业承包	Professional Contract	4871985	266968	132195	131924	489982
一级	First Grade	2865779	140327	60197	62318	259083
二级	Second Grade	1407461	90716	58080	55204	153017
三级以下	Third Grade and below	598744	35924	13919	14402	77882

13-5 施工工程施工面积(2022年)

Number of Floor Space Under Construction(2022)

单位：万平方米 (10 000 sq.m)

指标 (总承包与专业承包)	Item	房屋建筑施工面积 Floor Space under Construction	# 本年新开工面积 Started This Year	房屋建筑竣工面积 Floor Space Completed	# 住宅房屋 Residential	竣工房屋价值(万元) Output Value of Completed (10 000 yuan)
总计	**Total**	**19971**	**5223**	**3128**	**1808**	**8520337**
其中：国有及国有控股企业	State-owned and State-controlled Enterprises	14503	3776	1631	799	5590782
一、按登记注册类型分组	**By Status of Registration**					
内资企业	Domestic Invested Enterprises	19971	5223	3128	1808	8520337
国有企业	State-owned Enterprises					
集体企业	Collective-owned Enterprises	9	2	3		11652
股份合作企业	Cooperative Enterprises	3		1		1464
有限责任公司	Limited Liability Corporations	16485	4352	2133	1128	6808254
国有独资公司	State Sole-proprietorship Corporations	5043	1866	647	313	2096394
其他有限责任公司	Other Limited Liability Corporations	11442	2486	1487	815	4711860
股份有限公司	Share-holding Corporations Ltd.	530	105	175	139	320715
私营企业	Private Enterprises	2944	763	816	541	1378252
私营有限责任公司	Private Limited Liability Corporations	2944	763	816	541	1378252
私营股份有限公司	Private Share-holding Corporations Ltd					
二、按国民经济行业分组	**By Sector**					
房屋建筑业	Construction of Buildings	18173	4722	2913	1731	7884362
土木工程建筑业	Civil Engineering	1569	341	86	8	531067
建筑安装业	Construction Installation	11	3	37	29	21699
建筑装饰装修和其他建筑业	Building Decoration and Other Construction	218	156	92	40	83209
三、按隶属关系分组	**By Ownership**					
中央	Central	11661	3253	1053	485	4279215
地方	Local	4763	950	1082	691	2429577
其他	Others	3547	1020	993	632	1811545
四、按企业资质等级分组	**By Qualification Criteria**					
施工总承包	Construction Contract	19665	5029	2987	1735	8411651
特级	Special Grade	14637	3702	2144	1166	6796538
一级	First Grade	4149	958	587	450	1151870
二级	Second Grade	548	227	117	64	229674
三级及以下	Third Grade and below	332	142	138	55	233570
专业承包	Professional Contract	305	194	141	73	108686
一级	First Grade	143	87	47	10	77740
二级	Second Grade	160	106	93	63	28408
三级及以下	Third Grade and below	2	1	2		2538

13-6 济南市建筑业特级、一级资质企业一览表(2022年)
List of Special and First Class Qualification in the Construction Enterprises of Jinan City(2022)

企业名称 Name	资质等级 Ownership	经济类型 Economic Type	所属行业 Industry
中建八局第二建设有限公司	特级	其他有限责任公司	住宅房屋建筑
山东省建设建工(集团)有限责任公司	特级	私营有限责任公司	住宅房屋建筑
山东省路桥集团有限公司	特级	其他有限责任公司	其他道路、隧道和桥梁工程建筑
中铁十四局集团有限公司	特级	其他有限责任公司	铁路工程建筑
中建八局第一建设有限公司	特级	国有独资公司	住宅房屋建筑
济南二建集团工程有限公司	特级	其他有限责任公司	住宅房屋建筑
中铁铁工城市建设有限公司	特级	其他有限责任公司	住宅房屋建筑
济南城建集团有限公司	特级	其他有限责任公司	铁路工程建筑
济南四建(集团)有限责任公司	特级	其他有限责任公司	住宅房屋建筑
中国电建集团山东电力建设第一工程有限公司	特级	国有独资公司	架线及设备工程建筑
中国电建集团核电工程有限公司	特级	其他有限责任公司	火力发电工程施工
中化学交通建设集团有限公司	特级	其他有限责任公司	公路工程建筑
山东港基建设集团有限公司	特级	其他有限责任公司	住宅房屋建筑
中铁十四局集团第三工程有限公司	特级	其他有限责任公司	铁路工程建筑
山东平安建设集团有限公司	特级	其他有限责任公司	住宅房屋建筑
济南长兴建设集团有限公司	特级	其他有限责任公司	住宅房屋建筑
山东高速工程建设集团有限公司	特级	其他有限责任公司	公路工程建筑
山东三箭建设工程股份有限公司	特级	股份有限公司	住宅房屋建筑
中儒科信达建设集团有限公司	特级	其他有限责任公司	住宅房屋建筑
中铁十局集团有限公司	特级	国有独资公司	铁路工程建筑
山东水总有限公司	一级	国有独资公司	河湖治理及防洪设施工程建筑
山东黄河工程集团有限公司	一级	国有独资公司	港口及航运设施工程建筑
山东省齐鲁装饰设计院	一级	集体企业	公共建筑装饰和装修
山东省装饰集团有限公司	一级	国有独资公司	公共建筑装饰和装修
山东江森机电工程有限公司	一级	私营有限责任公司	管道和设备安装
济南百川建设装饰工程有限公司	一级	私营有限责任公司	公共建筑装饰和装修
山东金至尊装饰工程有限公司	一级	其他有限责任公司	公共建筑装饰和装修
山东省工业设备安装集团有限公司	一级	其他有限责任公司	其他建筑安装
山东省深基建设工程有限公司	一级	国有独资公司	住宅房屋建筑
济南岩土工程公司	一级	国有企业	其他土木工程建筑施工
山东展鸿华商装饰工程有限公司	一级	私营有限责任公司	住宅装饰和装修
鸿鑫工程有限公司	一级	私营有限责任公司	公共建筑装饰和装修
山东正元建设工程有限责任公司	一级	其他有限责任公司	其他房屋建筑业
和瑞滢晞智能产业发展集团有限公司	一级	私营有限责任公司	电气安装
山东华迪智能技术有限公司	一级	其他有限责任公司	其他建筑安装
中炬装饰工程集团有限公司	一级	私营有限责任公司	公共建筑装饰和装修
济南林海装饰工程有限公司	一级	私营有限责任公司	公共建筑装饰和装修
山东省金海龙建工科技有限公司	一级	私营有限责任公司	架线及设备工程建筑
山东天宝建设集团有限公司	一级	其他有限责任公司	住宅房屋建筑
山东海威装饰工程有限公司	一级	私营有限责任公司	公共建筑装饰和装修
山东省水利工程局有限公司	一级	国有独资公司	河湖治理及防洪设施工程建筑
山东豪庭建设集团有限公司	一级	私营有限责任公司	公共建筑装饰和装修
中铁十四局集团电气化工程有限公司	一级	国有独资公司	架线及设备工程建筑
山东省建设建工集团装饰装璜有限公司	一级	其他有限责任公司	公共建筑装饰和装修
济南百士岩土工程有限公司	一级	其他有限责任公司	市政道路工程建筑

13-6 续表 1 continued 1

企业名称 Name	资质等级 Ownership	经济类型 Economic Type	所属行业 Industry
山东高速齐鲁建设集团有限公司	一级	其他有限责任公司	其他房屋建筑业
山东高速路桥装备工程有限公司	一级	其他有限责任公司	市政道路工程建筑
山东祥地建筑工程有限公司	一级	私营有限责任公司	其他房屋建筑业
万得福实业集团有限公司	一级	其他有限责任公司	公共建筑装饰和装修
山东华埠特克智能机电工程有限公司	一级	其他有限责任公司	其他未列明建筑业
山东华悦建筑工程有限公司	一级	私营有限责任公司	公共建筑装饰和装修
济南政和消防工程有限公司	一级	私营有限责任公司	电气安装
神州瑞宸建设集团有限公司	一级	私营有限责任公司	公共建筑装饰和装修
山东环城城建工程有限公司	一级	其他有限责任公司	其他未列明建筑业
山东奥深智能工程有限公司	一级	私营有限责任公司	其他未列明建筑业
山东剑锋消防工程有限公司	一级	私营有限责任公司	管道和设备安装
山东宇宸建设工程有限公司	一级	私营有限责任公司	管道和设备安装
山东德铭工程建设有限公司	一级	私营有限责任公司	住宅装饰和装修
济南舜联建设集团有限公司	一级	私营有限责任公司	其他房屋建筑业
济南易通城市建设集团股份有限公司	一级	股份有限公司	市政道路工程建筑
永隆装饰工程有限公司	一级	私营有限责任公司	公共建筑装饰和装修
瑞森新建筑有限公司	一级	私营有限责任公司	其他房屋建筑业
中国山东对外经济技术合作集团有限公司	一级	其他有限责任公司	住宅房屋建筑
山东同霖节能科技有限公司	一级	私营有限责任公司	建筑幕墙装饰和装修
山东百安建设工程有限公司	一级	其他有限责任公司	管道和设备安装
山东印象照明科技股份有限公司	一级	股份有限公司	其他电力工程施工
山东宏晨智能工程有限公司	一级	私营有限责任公司	市政道路工程建筑
佳泽睿安集团有限公司	一级	私营有限责任公司	公路工程建筑
山东嘉嘉装饰有限公司	一级	其他有限责任公司	建筑幕墙装饰和装修
山东圣恩城市建设工程有限公司	一级	私营有限责任公司	工矿工程建筑
山东省城建工程集团公司	一级	股份合作企业	住宅房屋建筑
山东鲁建工程集团有限公司	一级	其他有限责任公司	住宅房屋建筑
济南万泰建筑装饰工程有限公司	一级	私营有限责任公司	住宅装饰和装修
山东省邮电工程有限公司	一级	其他有限责任公司	架线及设备工程建筑
海瑞林建设有限公司	一级	私营有限责任公司	公共建筑装饰和装修
山东金桥保安器材有限公司	一级	私营有限责任公司	电气安装
山东泰山建工发展集团有限公司	一级	其他有限责任公司	住宅房屋建筑
山东土地集团建设投资有限公司	一级	其他有限责任公司	公共建筑装饰和装修
山东泉景建设有限公司	一级	其他有限责任公司	住宅房屋建筑
山东费尔消防技术工程有限公司	一级	私营有限责任公司	电气安装
山东涌泉安全科技有限公司	一级	私营有限责任公司	其他建筑安装
济南昌汇建筑工程有限公司	一级	私营有限责任公司	其他未列明建筑业
山东鼎森集团有限公司	一级	其他有限责任公司	住宅房屋建筑
山东恒霖建设工程有限公司	一级	私营有限责任公司	住宅房屋建筑
山东宏雁电子系统工程有限公司	一级	私营有限责任公司	电气安装
山东华森建筑消防项目管理有限公司	一级	私营有限责任公司	电气安装
山东世纪装饰工程股份有限公司	一级	私营股份有限公司	住宅装饰和装修
山东美德隆建设有限公司	一级	私营有限责任公司	住宅房屋建筑
山东宜佳美建设集团有限公司	一级	私营有限责任公司	其他建筑安装
济南宏铁建筑装饰工程有限公司	一级	其他有限责任公司	住宅装饰和装修
山东今生缘建筑装饰工程有限公司	一级	私营有限责任公司	建筑幕墙装饰和装修

13-6 续表 2 continued 2

企业名称 Name	资质等级 Ownership	经济类型 Economic Type	所属行业 Industry
济南华海建设集团有限公司	一级	私营有限责任公司	住宅房屋建筑
济南凯诚消防自控设备有限公司	一级	其他有限责任公司	电气安装
济南普利供水工程有限公司	一级	其他有限责任公司	管道工程建筑
山东顺河路桥工程有限公司	一级	其他有限责任公司	市政道路工程建筑
中铁十四局集团第四工程有限公司	一级	国有独资公司	铁路工程建筑
济南超卓建筑工程有限公司	一级	私营有限责任公司	住宅装饰和装修
山东海灏装饰设计工程有限公司	一级	私营有限责任公司	住宅装饰和装修
山东通海建设集团有限公司	一级	私营有限责任公司	公共建筑装饰和装修
中铁十四局集团隧道工程有限公司	一级	其他有限责任公司	铁路工程建筑
山东坚瑞建设股份有限公司	一级	股份有限公司	其他未列明建筑业
山东中大净化工程有限公司	一级	私营有限责任公司	其他建筑安装
山东清尚科源建设集团有限公司	一级	私营有限责任公司	住宅装饰和装修
山东昌利建设集团有限公司	一级	私营有限责任公司	水源及供水设施工程建筑
中铁济南工程技术有限公司	一级	其他有限责任公司	铁路工程建筑
山东送变电工程有限公司	一级	其他有限责任公司	架线及设备工程建筑
山东三盛防水工程有限公司	一级	私营有限责任公司	环保工程施工
山东深博建筑工程有限公司	一级	私营有限责任公司	管道和设备安装
山东省机械施工有限公司	一级	其他有限责任公司	场地准备活动
山东润霖消防工程有限公司	一级	私营有限责任公司	电气安装
济南四建集团智能消防工程有限责任公司	一级	其他有限责任公司	其他建筑安装
中海(山东)净化工程有限公司	一级	私营有限责任公司	公共建筑装饰和装修
山东省公路桥梁建设集团有限公司	一级	其他有限责任公司	公路工程建筑
山东汇通建设集团有限公司	一级	国有独资公司	市政道路工程建筑
中铁十局集团电务工程有限公司	一级	其他有限责任公司	铁路工程建筑
济南黄河路桥建设集团有限公司	一级	国有独资公司	市政道路工程建筑
山东福思特建筑装饰有限公司	一级	私营有限责任公司	建筑幕墙装饰和装修
山东汇友市政园林集团有限公司	一级	国有独资公司	其他未列明建筑业
山东建科特种建筑工程技术中心有限公司	一级	其他有限责任公司	其他房屋建筑业
山东建勘集团有限公司	一级	国有独资公司	场地准备活动
济南消防工程有限公司	一级	其他有限责任公司	电气安装
辉瑞(山东)环境科技有限公司	一级	私营有限责任公司	公共建筑装饰和装修
山东福缘来装饰有限公司	一级	私营有限责任公司	住宅装饰和装修
中铁十局集团第一工程有限公司	一级	其他有限责任公司	公路工程建筑
山东济铁工程建设集团有限公司	一级	其他有限责任公司	铁路工程建筑
山东康桥交通科技有限公司	一级	私营有限责任公司	市政道路工程建筑
山东润豪建设工程有限公司	一级	私营有限责任公司	公路工程建筑
山东省高速养护集团有限公司	一级	其他有限责任公司	其他道路、隧道和桥梁工程建筑
千庭景观建设有限公司	一级	私营有限责任公司	市政道路工程建筑
中国铁路通信信号集团济南工程有限公司	一级	其他有限责任公司	架线及设备工程建筑
济南建设设备安装有限责任公司	一级	其他有限责任公司	管道和设备安装
山东舜联城市建设发展有限公司	一级	私营有限责任公司	园林绿化工程施工
山东昌舜岩土工程有限公司	一级	私营有限责任公司	场地准备活动
普利置业集团股份有限公司	一级	股份有限公司	住宅房屋建筑
山东黄河顺成水利水电工程有限公司	一级	国有独资公司	管道工程建筑
山东中恒建设集团有限公司	一级	私营有限责任公司	住宅房屋建筑
济南建工总承包集团有限公司	一级	其他有限责任公司	住宅房屋建筑

13-6 续表 3 continued 3

企业名称 Name	资质等级 Ownership	经济类型 Economic Type	所属行业 Industry
山东盛顺装饰有限公司	一级	私营有限责任公司	住宅装饰和装修
山东群雄建设工程有限公司	一级	私营有限责任公司	公共建筑装饰和装修
济南昊兴市政工程有限公司	一级	私营有限责任公司	管道工程建筑
山东金岛消防安全工程有限公司	一级	私营有限责任公司	电气安装
山东省大通公路工程有限责任公司	一级	其他有限责任公司	公路工程建筑
沃尔德建筑装饰集团股份有限公司	一级	私营股份有限公司	住宅装饰和装修
山东鸿图科技有限公司	一级	私营有限责任公司	其他建筑安装
山东林垄幕墙装饰有限公司	一级	其他有限责任公司	住宅装饰和装修
奥斯福集团有限公司	一级	私营有限责任公司	电气安装
山东彩旺建设有限公司	一级	私营有限责任公司	电气安装
山东电建建设集团有限公司	一级	其他有限责任公司	架线及设备工程建筑
济南一建集团有限公司	一级	国有独资公司	住宅房屋建筑
济南东元改建加固工程有限公司	一级	私营有限责任公司	其他房屋建筑业
中铁建黄河投资建设有限公司	一级	国有独资公司	城市轨道交通工程建筑
山东鲁控建设集团有限公司	一级	其他有限责任公司	住宅房屋建筑
山东德才建设有限公司	一级	其他有限责任公司	公共建筑装饰和装修
水电六局华东建设有限公司	一级	国有独资公司	住宅房屋建筑
山东省建设高压容器有限公司	一级	其他有限责任公司	管道和设备安装
山东志坚建筑工程有限公司	一级	私营有限责任公司	其他房屋建筑业
山东众联恒信工程集团有限公司	一级	私营有限责任公司	场地准备活动
山东泰景楼宇安全技术有限公司	一级	私营有限责任公司	其他未列明建筑业
山东铁信建设集团有限公司	一级	其他有限责任公司	住宅房屋建筑
山东宏岳消防工程有限公司	一级	私营有限责任公司	其他建筑安装
嘉林建设集团有限公司	一级	私营有限责任公司	建筑幕墙装饰和装修
山东亚特尔集团股份有限公司	一级	股份有限公司	管道和设备安装
山东亿威市政工程有限公司	一级	其他有限责任公司	市政道路工程建筑
山东昶博建筑工程有限公司	一级	私营有限责任公司	其他房屋建筑业
山东大禹水务建设集团有限公司	一级	其他有限责任公司	水源及供水设施工程建筑
山东黄金集团建设工程有限公司	一级	国有独资公司	住宅房屋建筑
济南能源工程集团有限公司	一级	国有独资公司	管道和设备安装
山东益德净化工程有限公司	一级	私营有限责任公司	环保工程施工
山东鑫龙装饰工程有限公司	一级	私营有限责任公司	公共建筑装饰和装修
齐鲁建工建设发展集团有限公司	一级	其他有限责任公司	公路工程建筑
山东长箭建设集团有限公司	一级	其他有限责任公司	住宅房屋建筑
山东汇富建设集团有限公司	一级	私营有限责任公司	住宅房屋建筑
山东长泰建设集团工程有限公司	一级	私营有限责任公司	住宅房屋建筑
山东润诚机电工程有限公司	一级	私营有限责任公司	电气安装
中广核宏达环境科技有限责任公司	一级	其他有限责任公司	环保工程施工
山东福源设备安装有限公司	一级	私营有限责任公司	管道和设备安装
山东福源建设集团有限公司	一级	私营有限责任公司	管道和设备安装
山东信兴建设发展有限公司	一级	其他有限责任公司	其他建筑安装
济南利宸泽建筑工程有限公司	一级	私营有限责任公司	住宅房屋建筑
济南振华岩土工程有限责任公司	一级	私营有限责任公司	提供施工设备服务
济南章丘三建弘信建筑有限公司	一级	私营有限责任公司	住宅房屋建筑
章丘市第二建筑安装(集团)有限责任公司	一级	其他有限责任公司	住宅房屋建筑
济南通达公路工程有限公司	一级	国有独资公司	公路工程建筑

13-6 续表 4 continued 4

企业名称 Name	资质等级 Ownership	经济类型 Economic Type	所属行业 Industry
山东泰实建筑工程有限公司	一级	私营有限责任公司	住宅房屋建筑
山东博科建筑工程有限公司	一级	其他有限责任公司	住宅房屋建筑
山东科发建设工程有限公司	一级	其他有限责任公司	建筑幕墙装饰和装修
济南金曰公路工程有限公司	一级	其他有限责任公司	公路工程建筑
中铁十四局集团建筑工程有限公司	一级	其他有限责任公司	住宅房屋建筑
山东兴发建筑工程有限公司	一级	其他有限责任公司	住宅房屋建筑
山东津单幕墙有限公司	一级	私营有限责任公司	建筑幕墙装饰和装修
山东国宸装饰工程有限公司	一级	其他有限责任公司	公共建筑装饰和装修
山东三箭建设工程管理有限公司	一级	私营有限责任公司	住宅房屋建筑
山东济开建设有限公司	一级	私营有限责任公司	住宅房屋建筑
秦恒建设科技有限公司	一级	私营有限责任公司	节能工程施工
济南万达建筑安装工程有限公司	一级	其他有限责任公司	住宅房屋建筑
山东欧瑞装饰有限公司	一级	其他有限责任公司	住宅装饰和装修
远大建设工程有限公司	一级	私营有限责任公司	公共建筑装饰和装修
中道华泰建设集团有限公司	一级	私营有限责任公司	其他房屋建筑业
山东洁昕建筑装饰工程设计有限公司	一级	私营有限责任公司	公共建筑装饰和装修
山东大成正合建筑工程有限公司	一级	私营有限责任公司	住宅房屋建筑
山东北成环境工程有限公司	一级	私营有限责任公司	环保工程施工
山东洪雨防水工程有限公司	一级	私营有限责任公司	其他未列明建筑业
山东莱芜建设集团有限公司	一级	其他有限责任公司	住宅房屋建筑
山东泰东公路工程有限公司	一级	其他有限责任公司	公路工程建筑
山东莱芜创艺装饰集团有限公司	一级	其他有限责任公司	住宅装饰和装修
莱芜市庚鑫市政工程有限公司	一级	其他有限责任公司	管道和设备安装
山东中安消防设施维修有限公司	一级	私营有限责任公司	其他未列明建筑业
山东万和中盛幕墙有限公司	一级	私营有限责任公司	建筑幕墙装饰和装修
济南蓝海建设工程有限公司	一级	其他有限责任公司	市政道路工程建筑
山东力盟电力电子有限公司	一级	私营有限责任公司	其他建筑安装
山东正顺建设集团有限公司	一级	私营有限责任公司	住宅房屋建筑
莱芜钢铁集团建筑安装工程有限公司	一级	其他有限责任公司	其他建筑安装
济南市宏强建设有限公司	一级	私营有限责任公司	其他房屋建筑业
济南铸诚建筑工程集团有限公司	一级	其他有限责任公司	住宅房屋建筑
济南成运建筑工程有限公司	一级	私营有限责任公司	其他建筑安装
山东宏业发展集团有限公司	一级	私营有限责任公司	架线及设备工程建筑
山东清华康利城市照明研究设计院有限公司	一级	其他有限责任公司	电气安装
山东华尔泰建筑工程有限公司	一级	私营有限责任公司	电气安装
山东启方科技有限公司	一级	其他有限责任公司	电气安装
山东蓝润建筑工程有限公司	一级	私营有限责任公司	电气安装
山东飞马消防工程有限责任公司	一级	私营有限责任公司	电气安装
中直科创股份有限公司	一级	股份有限公司	建筑幕墙装饰和装修
山东省亘基工程有限公司	一级	私营有限责任公司	其他房屋建筑业
山东万林建设工程有限公司	一级	私营有限责任公司	住宅装饰和装修
山东华德隆建设有限公司	一级	私营有限责任公司	建筑幕墙装饰和装修
山东铁迅建设工程有限公司	一级	私营有限责任公司	电气安装
山东航空港建设工程有限公司	一级	其他有限责任公司	其他土木工程建筑施工
山东青亦蓝装饰工程有限公司	一级	私营有限责任公司	公共建筑装饰和装修

13-6 续表 5 continued 5

企业名称 Name	资质等级 Ownership	经济类型 Economic Type	所属行业 Industry
山东天石集团有限公司	一级	私营有限责任公司	建筑幕墙装饰和装修
山东信达建设工程有限公司	一级	私营有限责任公司	其他房屋建筑业
济南信高工程技术有限公司	一级	私营有限责任公司	电气安装
山东太平洋环保股份有限公司	一级	私营股份有限公司	其他建筑安装
山东鲁光信息工程有限公司	一级	私营有限责任公司	电气安装
山东省鲁美建材装饰有限公司	一级	私营有限责任公司	建筑幕墙装饰和装修
山东安泰智能工程有限公司	一级	其他有限责任公司	电气安装
山东省建设建工集团消防工程有限公司	一级	私营有限责任公司	电气安装
阿郎装饰股份有限公司	一级	私营股份有限公司	公共建筑装饰和装修
山东千业建设工程有限公司	一级	私营有限责任公司	建筑幕墙装饰和装修
山东双利电子工程有限公司	一级	其他有限责任公司	电气安装
山东华盛特克科技有限公司	一级	私营有限责任公司	电气安装
山东水发鲁润水务科技有限公司	一级	其他有限责任公司	环保工程施工
山东天启智能工程有限公司	一级	私营有限责任公司	其他未列明建筑业
七彩建设发展有限公司	一级	私营有限责任公司	公共建筑装饰和装修
山东鑫联通信科技有限公司	一级	私营有限责任公司	电气安装
济南市市政工程建设集团有限公司	一级	国有独资公司	市政道路工程建筑
雪山集团有限公司	一级	私营有限责任公司	管道和设备安装
中建五局(山东)投资建设有限公司	一级	国有独资公司	住宅房屋建筑
森鹏建设集团有限公司	一级	私营有限责任公司	公共建筑装饰和装修
山东佑安消防系统有限公司	一级	私营有限责任公司	其他建筑安装
山东富力达建筑科技有限公司	一级	私营有限责任公司	建筑幕墙装饰和装修
山东博安智能科技股份有限公司	一级	私营股份有限公司	电气安装
济南金宇公路产业发展有限公司	一级	其他有限责任公司	公路工程建筑
万旭宏业集团有限公司	一级	私营有限责任公司	住宅装饰和装修
山东思达特信息科技有限公司	一级	私营有限责任公司	电气安装
中国电建集团山东电力建设有限公司	一级	国有独资公司	火力发电工程施工
山东天翼安全技术有限公司	一级	私营有限责任公司	电气安装
优士科技发展有限公司	一级	私营有限责任公司	电气安装
山东宇顺建筑工程有限公司	一级	私营有限责任公司	住宅房屋建筑
山东省建设集团有限公司	一级	私营有限责任公司	其他房屋建筑业
济南川丽德市政建设工程有限公司	一级	私营有限责任公司	住宅房屋建筑
中宝鼎盛建设集团有限公司	一级	私营有限责任公司	住宅房屋建筑
山东奥邦交通设施工程有限公司	一级	其他有限责任公司	其他建筑安装
山东惠诚建筑有限公司	一级	私营有限责任公司	其他房屋建筑业
山东建华土木有限公司	一级	私营有限责任公司	住宅房屋建筑
中交未名环保有限公司	一级	其他有限责任公司	市政道路工程建筑
山东众海工程有限公司	一级	私营有限责任公司	其他建筑安装
国舜绿建科技有限公司	一级	其他有限责任公司	其他房屋建筑业
山东英士力建设工程集团有限公司	一级	私营有限责任公司	公共建筑装饰和装修
起航(山东)投资建设集团有限公司	一级	其他有限责任公司	市政道路工程建筑
山东盛桥实业集团有限公司	一级	其他有限责任公司	其他建筑安装
山东国创装饰工程有限公司	一级	私营有限责任公司	住宅装饰和装修
济南佳宸装饰安装有限公司	一级	私营有限责任公司	公共建筑装饰和装修

主要统计指标解释

建筑业统计单位 指从事房屋、构筑物建造和设备安装活动的法人企业。建筑业法人企业应具有建筑业资质并能够独立核算，同时还应具备以下条件：①依法成立，有自己的名称、组织机构和场所，能够承担民事责任；②独立拥有和使用资产，承担负债，有权与其他单位签订合同；③独立核算盈亏，能够编制资产负债表。

建筑业总产值 是以货币形式表现的建筑业企业在一定时期内生产的建筑业产品和提供服务的总和。建筑业总产值包括：

（1）建筑工程产值：指列入建筑工程预算内的各种工程价值。

（2）安装工程产值：指设备安装工程价值以及将预制部品部件安装成建筑工程产品的价值，不包括被安装设备本身的价值。

（3）其他产值：建筑业总产值中除建筑工程、安装工程以外的产值。包括房屋构筑物修理产值、非标准设备制造产值、总包企业向分包企业收取的管理费以及不能明确划分的施工活动所完成的产值。

房屋施工面积 指报告期内施工的全部房屋建筑面积，包括本期新开工的房屋建筑面积、上期跨入本期继续施工的房屋建筑面积、上期停缓建在本期恢复施工的房屋建筑面积、本期竣工的房屋建筑面积及本期施工后又停缓建的房屋建筑面积。

房屋竣工面积 指报告期内房屋建筑按照设计要求已全部完工，达到住人和使用条件，经验收鉴定合格或达到竣工验收标准，可正式移交使用的各栋房屋建筑面积的总和。

Explanatory Notes on Main Statistical Indicators

Statistical Units in the Construction Industry refer to corporate enterprises engaged in the construction of buildings and structures and in the installation of equipment. A corporate construction enterprise should have qualification certificates with independent accounting system, and should meet the following 3 requirements: a) being set up in line with relevant legal basis, having its full name, organization and location, and capable of taking civil liabilities; b) independently possessing and using its assets and assuming its liabilities, and entitled to sign contracts with other institutions; c) making independent accounts of its profits and losses, and capable of compiling its own balance sheet.

Gross Output Value of Construction refers to total of construction products and services, expressed in monetary terms, produced or rendered by construction and installation enterprises during a given period of time. It includes:

(1) Output value of construction projects: the value of projects covered by the project budgets;

(2) Output value of installation projects: the value of the installation of equipment, and the value of installing prefabricated components into construction engineering products (excluding the value of the equipment to be installed);

(3) Other output values: the output value of construction industry apart from that of construction projects and installation projects. It includes: output value of repair of buildings and structures; output value of manufacturing of non-standard equipment; overhead expenses received by contracted enterprises from the sub-contracted enterprises, and the completed output value of construction activities for which there is no clear definition.

Floor Space of Buildings under Construction refers to the total floor space area of buildings under construction in the reference period. It includes buildings new started; buildings started earlier and continued during the reference period; buildings suspended earlier but restarted during the reference period; buildings completed during the reference period; and buildings under construction but suspended during the reference period.

Floor Space of Buildings Completed refers to the total floor space area of buildings that have been completed in the reference period in accordance with the requirements of the design, up to the standard for accommodation or putting into use, and have been checked and accepted by departments concerned as qualified or up to the standard of buildings completed and can be handed over for putting into use.

14

运输与邮电

TRANSPORTATION, POST AND TELECOMMUNICATIONS

14–1 邮电业务量
Business Volume of Postal Services and Telecommunication Services

指标	Item	单位 unit	2018年	2019年	2020年	2021年	2022年
国内分类业务量	**Domestic Classified Business Volume**						
固定电话数	Number of Fixed Telephone	万户(10 000 subscribers)	135.27	148.82	144.78	145.31	147.66
年末市内电话	Urban Fixed Telephone at Year-end	万户(10 000 subscribers)	118.70	136.30	127.65		
年末农村电话	Rural Fixed Telephone at Year-end	万户(10 000 subscribers)	16.47	12.20	2.78		
年末住宅电话	Number of Household Telephone at Year-end	万户(10 000 subscribers)	67.64	25.56	14.26		
年末移动电话用户	Number of Mobile Telephone Subscribers at Year-end	万户(10 000 subscribers)	1013.65	1122.86	1154.06	1216.34	1266.04
4G电话用户数	4G Mobile Phone Subscribers	万户(10 000 subscribers)	725.01	888.81	922.67	750.03	570.94
宽带互联网接入用户数	Broadband Subscribers of Internet	万户(10 000 subscribers)	344.7	392.6	445.5	463.0	501.4
每百人互联网用户数	Number of Internet User per 100 Population	户/百人 (subscriber/100 persons)	53.05	49.63	55.56	57.05	61.27
邮电局所	Post & Telecommunication offices	处(unit)	207	252	252	253	253
国际及港澳分类业务量	**International.Hong kong and Macao Classified Business Volume**						
函件	Letters	万件(10 000 pcs)	51.95	45.75	13.02	3.54	1.11
包件	Packages	万件(10 000 pcs)	0.76	0.60	0.60	3.72	0.24

注：按照山东省通信管理局发布的通信业发展情况，年末市内电话、年末农村电话、年末住宅电话等指标不再进行统计。

Note:According to the development of communication industry released by Shandong Communications Administration, data of local telephone, rural telephone and residential telephone indicators at the end of year are not counted.

14-2 交通运输业基本情况
Basic Conditions of Transport

指标	Item	2018年	2019年	2020年	2021年	2022年
客运量（万人）	**Passenger Traffic (10 000 persons)**					
铁路	Railways	14547.7	15745.1	9797.4	12163.7	7321.5
公路	Highways	3149.0	3244.0	1209.0	2024.0	1438.0
民航	Civil Aviation	894.1	936.1	1238.5	1361.6	824.2
旅客周转量（亿人公里）	**Passenger-Kilometers (100 million passenger-km)**					
铁路	Railways	784.6	795.3	431.9	523.9	313.3
公路	Highways	52.9	54.1	17.1	39.6	29.6
民航	Civil Aviation	368.5	376.5	256.3	268.6	136.2
货运量（万吨）	**Freight Traffic (10 000 tons)**					
铁路	Railways	18728.0	20869.8	23188.8	22895.4	24716.7
公路	Highways	25571.0	28064.0	22677.0	24669.0	23843.0
民航	Civil Aviation	5.6	6.7	14.7	16.8	13.8
货物周转量（亿吨公里）	**Freight Ton-Kilometers (100 million ton-km)**					
铁路	Railways	1288.4	1460.5	1566.1	1682.1	1831.5
公路	Highways	474.0	561.4	516.4	577.4	608.8
公路通车里程(公里)	**Length of Highways in Operation(km)**					
公路通车里程	Length of Highways in Operation	12637.7	17770.9	18117.2	18200.1	18294.4
#高速公路	Expressway	488.5	653.6	737.8	737.8	795.3
有铺装、简易铺装路面	Paved Roads	12579.4	17290.0	18117.2	18200.1	18294.4
未铺装路面	UnPaved Roads	58.3	480.9			
民用航空	**Civil Aviation**					
执行航线(条)	Perform Routes(line)	182	198	208	185	180
通航城市(个)	Navigable Cities(unit)	96	120	91	100	104
起降架次(架次)	Plane Flights(Sorties)	126828	129994	102375	112746	78775
民用汽车拥有量(辆)	**Possession of Civil Motor Vehicles(unit)**					
民用汽车拥有量	Possession of Civil Motor Vehicles	2160748	2584278	2794278	3025326	3203381
私人汽车	Private Vehicles	1948815	2332421	2512357	2705622	2857295
载客汽车	Passenger Vehicles	1978951	2370437	2556622	2759683	2925704
#大型	Large	14002	15767	15535	15330	14900
载货汽车	Trucks	166277	194957	224713	250200	261017
#重型	Heavy	36720	41904	46148	51609	51772
其他汽车	Others	15520	18884			
专项作业车	Special Operation vehicles			12943	15443	16660
摩托车	Motorcycle	133743	258382	329477	405497	473433
挂车	Trailer	9851	12538	14842	15590	15307

注：1.铁路系统统计数据来自中国铁路济南局集团有限公司。
2.2020年起，因公安部“公安交通管理综合应用平台”调整，修改了机动车报表统计口径，增加“专项作业车”等部分车型的统计，不再提供“其它”类汽车保有量。
3.2020年起，民航客运量、货运量统计口径调整为出港和进港合计数。
4.2021年交通运输部采用新的公路货运统计方法，对2020年公路货运量、公路货物周转量数据进行了修正。

Notes:1. Statistical data of railway system comes from China Railway Jinan Group Co., Ltd.
2.Since 2020, due to the adjustment of the “Public Traffic Management Integrated Application Platform”, the statistical caliber of motor vehicles statement is varied, the statistics on “special motor vehicle” is supplemented, while “Population of Other Vehicles” is not listed longer.
3.Since 2020, the passenger transport volume of civil aviation, and the statistical caliber of freight traffic volume are adjusted as the total number of departures and arrivals.
4. In 2021, the Ministry of Transport adopted a new statistic method for road freight, and revised the data of road freight volume and road freight turnover in 2020.

14-3 规模以上交通运输、仓储和邮政业企业财务指标(2022年)
Main Financial Indicators of Transport,Storage and Postal Services above Designated Size(2022)

单位:万元 (10 000 yuan)

指标	Item	交通运输、仓储和邮政业 Transport,Storage and Postal Services
单位数(个)	Number(unit)	357
年初存货	Inventory at Beginning of year	224309
流动资产合计	Current Assets	13857683
其中：应收账款	Accounts Receivable	1649948
存货	Inventories	240027
固定资产原价	Original Value of Fixed Assets	45303113
本年折旧	Depreciation in the Year	1732144
资产总计	Total Assets	97256037
负债合计	Total Liabilities	49636448
所有者权益合计	Owners' Equity	47619589
营业收入	Business Revenue	14353917
营业成本	Business Cost	14263429
税金及附加	Taxes and Other Charges	38797
销售费用	Sales Expenses	121773
管理费用	Management Expenses	667144
研发费用	Research and Development Expenses	26606
财务费用	Financial Expenses	1101512
投资收益	Investment Interests	355861
其他收益	Other Revenues	348643
营业利润	Profits from Business	-1066056
营业外收入	Profits from Non-Business	74321
营业外支出	Expense from Non-Business	54673
利润总额	Total Profits	-1046408
所得税费用	Income Tax Expense	108528
应付职工薪酬(本年贷方累计发生额)	Total Wages Payable	3205308
应交增值税	Value-added Tax Payable	484320
期末用工人数(人)	Number of employees at the end of the period(person)	179882

14-4 分地区公路交通(2022年)
Road Transportation by Region(2022)

单位：公里 (km)

指标	Item	济南市 Jinan	其中 of which		
			市区 Districts	平阴县 Ping yin	商河县 Shang he
公路通车里程	Length of Highways in Operation	18294.4	14568.4	1044.6	2681.4
#高速公路	Expressway	795.3	701.8	60.8	32.7
有铺装、简易铺装路面	Paved Road	18294.4	14568.4	1044.6	2681.4

主要统计指标解释

公路里程 指报告期末公路的实际长度。统计范围：包括城间、城乡间、乡（村）间能行驶汽车的公共道路，公路通过城镇街道的里程，公路桥梁长度、隧道长度、渡口宽度。不包括城市街道里程，断头路里程，农（林）业生产用道路里程，工（矿）企业等内部道路里程。统计原则：按已竣工验收或交付使用的实际里程计算；两条或多条公路共同经由同一路段的重复里程，只计算一次。

货(客)运量 指在一定时期内，各种运输工具实际运送的货物重量(旅客数量）。货运按吨计算，客运按人计算。货物不论运输距离长短、货物类别，均按实际重量统计。旅客不论行程远近或票价多少，均按一人一次客运量统计；半价票、儿童票也按一人统计。

货物(旅客)周转量 指在一定时期内，由各种运输工具运送的货物(旅客)数量与其相应运输距离的乘积之总和。该指标可以反映运输业生产的总成果，也是编制和检查运输生产计划，计算运输效率、劳动生产率以及核算运输单位成本的主要基础资料。计算货物周转量通常按发出站与到达站之间的最短距离，也就是计费距离计算。计算公式为：

货物（旅客）周转量=∑（货物（旅客）运输量×运输距离）

民用汽车拥有量 指报告期末，在公安交通管理部门按照《机动车注册登记工作规范》，已注册登记领有民用车辆牌照的全部汽车数量。汽车拥有量统计的主要分类：根据汽车结构分为载客汽车、载货汽车及其他汽车；根据汽车所有者不同分为个人(私人)汽车、单位汽车；根据汽车的使用性质分为营运汽车、非营运汽车；根据汽车大小规格不同，载客汽车分为大型、中型、小型和微型，载货汽车分为重型、中型、轻型和微型。

移动电话用户 指在电信运营企业营业网点办理开户登记手续，通过移动电话交换机进入移动电话网，占用移动电话号码的各类电话用户。包括各类签约用户、智能网预付费用户、无线上网卡用户。

固定电话用户 指在电信企业营业网点办理开户登记手续并已接入固定电话网上的全部电话用户。

Explanatory Notes on Main Statistical Indicators

Length of Highways refers to the actual length of highways at the end of reference period. It covers public roads running vehicles between cities, between urban and rural areas, and between townships (villages), as well as highways passing through streets at small cities and towns, length of bridges and tunnels, width of ferry piers. It does not include the length of streets in cities, dead end highways, the length of streets built for agricultural (forest) production and inside factories (mines). Mileage can only be included when the road is completed, checked and accepted or put into operation. If two or more highways use the same section, the length of the section is counted only once.

Freight (Passenger) Traffic refers to the weight of freight (number of passengers) transported with various means within a specific period of time. Freight transport is calculated in tons and passenger traffic is calculated in terms of number of persons. Freight transport is calculated in terms of the actual weight of the goods, irrespective of the type of freight and distance of transport. Passenger traffic is calculated by the principle that one person can be counted only once in one trip, irrespective of travelling distance and ticket price. The passengers who travel with a discounted ticket or a children ticket is also calculated as one person.

Freight Ton-kilometres (Passenger-kilometres) refers to the sum of the product of the volume of transported cargo (passengers) multiplied by the transport distance. AS an indicator to reflect the achievement of the transportation industry, this is an important indicator to show the total results of the transport industry; to prepare and examine the transport plan; and to serve as the main basic data for calculating the efficiency, labour productivity and unit cost of transport. Normally, the shortest distance between the departure station and the destination station (i.e., the payable distance) is the basis in calculating the freight ton-kilometres. The formula is as follows:

Freight Ton-kilometres (Passenger-kilometres) = Σ(freight (passenger) traffic* distance of transportation)

Possession of Civil Motor Vehicles refer to the total numbers of vehicles at the end of the reference period that are registered and received vehicles license according to the Working Regulations for Motor Vehicle Registration formulated by the transport management offices. Motor vehicles are classified into different categories. By the structure of motor vehicles, they are divided into passenger vehicles, trucks and others; by ownership, into private vehicles and vehicles for the unit's use; by usage, into business vehicles and non-business vehicles; and by size of vehicles, into large passenger vehicles, medium-sized passenger vehicles, small passenger vehicles and mini passenger vehicles, heavy trucks, light-heavy trucks, light trucks and mini-trucks.

Mobile Phone Subscribers refer to persons who have gone through registration procedures in the operation outlets of enterprises engaged in telecommunications and are hence connected with the mobile phone communication network through the mobile phone switchboards and occupy mobile phone numbers. Included are various types of contracted subscribers, prepaid users for intelligent network and wireless network card users.

Fixed Telephone Subscribers refer to all subscribers who have gone through registration procedures in the operation outlets of enterprises engaged in telecommunications and are hence connected to the local telecommunications service provider through fixed line network.

15

国内贸易

DOMESTIC TRADE

15-1 各时期分行业社会消费品零售
Total Retail Sales of Consumer Goods by Section in Each Period

单位:万元 (10 000 yuan)

年份 Year	社会消费品零售总额 Total Retail Sales of Consumer Goods						
	总计 Total	批发零售业 Wholesale and Retail Trade	住宿业 Hotels	餐饮业 Catering Services	制造业 Manufacturing	其他 Others	农民对非农业居民 Farmers to Non-agricultural Residents
1949	11426	7312		556	3514		44
1952	22248	16985		1223	3592		448
1957	34568	29279		1935	2381	3	970
1962	41436	35784		1655	2946	266	785
1965	40795	36470		1829	1856	287	353
1970	42993	39397		1537	1468	321	270
1975	60105	53239		2565	2914	1217	170
1978	81335	70661		2907	5120	2222	425
1979	96036	80703		4000	9060	823	1450
1980	119775	95121		4392	16489	1299	2474
"六五时期"							
1981	135236	103303		5388	21353	2157	3035
1982	152094	116241		8165	21398	2778	3512
1983	167948	127884		9225	23569	2953	4317
1984	200301	150233		11342	29563	4506	4657
1985	243080	181867		14823	32342	5535	8513
"七五时期"							
1986	294102	219730		17880	35565	5456	15471
1987	331504	240192		20305	45386	8963	16658
1988	425984	300090		30808	60463	12300	22323
1989	484392	343978		28634	71653	9729	30398
1990	528221	382047		25599	71505	10886	38184
"八五时期"							
1991	597989	424836		27443	78452	14186	53072
1992	711774	535080		37096	77951		61647
1993	985251	723914		56059	80101		125177
1994	1426472	1037687		86141	99621		203023
1995	1837618	1345321		133501	115105		243691
"九五时期"							
1996	2234590	1570947		176100	141201		346342
1997	2568584	1744014		216727	177219		430624
1998	2834024	1893486		255616	207595		477327

15-1 续表 continued

单位:万元 (10 000 yuan)

年份 Year	社会消费品零售总额 Total Retail Sales of Consumer Goods 总计 Total	批发零售业 Wholesale and Retail Trade	住宿业 Hotels	餐饮业 Catering Services	制造业 Manufacturing	其他 Others	农民对非农业居民 Farmers to Non-agricultural Residents
1999	3092091	2043078		305333	225132		518548
2000	3444527	2287545		377550	233128		546304
"十五时期"							
2001	3857141	2574216		485494	237545		559886
2002	4321225	2935804		613178	231947		540296
2003	5115396	4373831		741565			
2004	6689452	5691288	57973	940191			
2005	7726458	6575543	66490	1084425			
"十一五时期"							
2006	8974064	7571831	78098	1324135			
2007	10526639	8791908	86322	1648409			
2008	12922856	10684195	96391	2142271			
2009	15254265	12710608	105378	2438279			
2010	17254574	14022650	150810	3081114			
"十二五时期"							
2011	20231045	16338362	175067	3717616			
2012	23235965	18740304	187466	4308195			
2013	26338714	22006709	177160	4154845			
2014	28640303	24120903	182090	4337310			
2015	31410419	26484428	193710	4732280			
"十三五时期"							
2016	34350723	28971634	210316	5168774			
2017	37525226	31658152	228909	5638165			
2018	40910775	34521369	248418	6140988			
2019	44204092	37604716	275686	6323691			
2020	44691335	38570115	255049	5866171			
"十四五时期"							
2021	51260961	43881612	301524	7077825			
2022	48781082	41921612	271524	6587946			

注：1992年至2019年社会消费品零售总额及分组数据根据第四次全国经济普查数据进行了修订。
Note: Total retail volume of social consumption and grouping data from 1992 to 2019 are revised according to the fourth national economic census.

15-2 限额以上批发零售业法人企业商品销售情况(2022年)

Sales of Commo-dities by Enterprises above Designated Size of Wholesale and Retail Trade(2022)

单位:万元 (10 000 yuan)

指标	Item	商品销售总额 Total Sales of Commodities 合计 Total	批发 Wholesale	零售 Retail
总计	**Total**	**128240007.8**	**111741911.3**	**16498096.5**
批发业	**Wholesale Trade**	**113144613.2**	**110314080.4**	**2830532.8**
农、林、牧、渔产品批发	Wholesale of Agricultural, Forestry, Livestock and Fishery Products	1573183.2	1548690.4	24492.8
食品、饮料及烟草制品批发	Wholesale of Food, Beverages and Tobaccos	5641477.9	5057668.6	583809.3
纺织、服装及家庭用品批发	Wholesale of Textiles, Wearing Apparel and Household Articles	2972680.4	2661132.1	311548.3
文化、体育用品及器材批发	Wholesale of Culture, Sports Appliances and Equipments	4522968.1	3601112.4	921855.7
医药及医疗器材批发	Wholesale of Medicines and Medical Appliances	10960916.6	10905443.1	55473.5
矿产品、建材及化工产品批发	Wholesale of Mineral Products, Building Materials and Chemical Products	73027369.3	72421072.6	606296.7
机械设备、五金产品及电子产品批发	Wholesale of Machinery, Hardware and Electronic Products	13812288.7	13492307.8	319980.9
贸易经纪与代理	Trade Broker and Agency	46471.4	46471.4	
其他批发业	Other Wholesale not Classified Elsewhere	587257.6	580182.0	7075.6
内资企业	Domestic Invested Enterprises	103666566.3	101297452.6	2369113.7
国有企业	State-owned Enterprises	6988053.7	6977983.9	10069.8
集体企业	Collective-owned Enterprises	6011.8	6011.8	
股份合作企业	Cooperative Enterprises			
联营企业	Joint Ownership Enterprises	5644.0	5644.0	
有限责任公司	Limited Liability Corporations	44986941.5	43899237.2	1087704.3
股份有限公司	Share-holding Corporations Ltd.	1636144.6	1617762.6	18382.0
私营企业	Private Enterprises	50037266.0	48784308.4	1252957.6
其他企业	Other Enterprises	6504.7	6504.7	
港、澳、台商投资企业	Enterprises with Investment from Hong Kong, Macao and Taiwan	4333754.7	4333754.7	
外商投资企业	Foreign Invested Enterprises	5144292.2	4682873.1	461419.1

15-2 续表 continued

单位:万元 (10 000 yuan)

指标	Item	商品销售总额 Total Sales of Commodities		
		合计 Total	批发 Wholesale	零售 Retail
零售业	**Retail Trade**	**15095394.6**	**1427830.9**	**13667563.7**
综合零售	General Retail	2151616.3	108180.3	2043436.0
食品、饮料及烟草制品专门零售	Special Retail of Food, Beverages and Tobaccos	673727.9	175057.1	498670.8
纺织、服装及日用品专门零售	Special Retail of Textiles, Garments and Daily Consumer Articles	447168.4	50654.0	396514.4
文化、体育用品及器材专门零售	Special Retail of Culture, Sports Appliances and Equipments	331985.4	38251.2	293734.2
医药及医疗器材专门零售	Special Retail of Medicines and Medical Appliances	793082.1	40962.4	752119.7
汽车、摩托车、零配件和燃料及其他动力销售	Retail of Motor Vehicles, Motorcycles, Parts, and Fuel and Other Powers	7121980.3	456401.1	6665579.2
家用电器及电子产品专门零售	Special Retail of Household Electric Appliances and Electronic Products	882840.4	379768.8	503071.6
五金、家具及室内装饰材料专门零售	Special Retail of Hardware, Furniture and Interior Decoration Materials	94085.7	4806.2	89279.5
货摊、无店铺及其他零售业	Stalls, Non-shop and Other Retails	2598908.1	173749.8	2425158.3
内资企业	Domestic Invested Enterprises	13550306.9	1392699.2	12157607.7
国有企业	State-owned Enterprises	292053.1	13569.5	278483.6
集体企业	Collective-owned Enterprises	21021.2		21021.2
股份合作企业	Cooperative Enterprises	138787.3	160.7	138626.6
联营企业	Joint Ownership Enterprises			
有限责任公司	Limited Liability Corporations	3787732.1	592164.5	3195567.6
股份有限公司	Share-holding Corporations Ltd.	1116435.5	49190.2	1067245.3
私营企业	Private Enterprises	8191506.8	737614.3	7453892.5
其他企业	Other Enterprises	2770.9		2770.9
港、澳、台商投资企业	Enterprises with Investment from Hong Kong, Macao and Taiwan	842660.4	6235.3	836425.1
外商投资企业	Foreign Invested Enterprises	702427.3	28896.4	673530.9

15-3 限额以上批发零售贸易企业资产实力(2022年)
Capital Power of Enterprises above Designated Size of Wholesale and Retail Trade(2022)

单位：万元

指标	Item	法人企业数 (个) Number of Corporation Enterprises (unit)
总计	**Total**	**5059**
批发业	**Wholesale Trade**	**3951**
农、林、牧、渔产品批发	Wholesale of Agricultural, Forestry, Livestock and Fishery Products	86
食品、饮料及烟草制品批发	Wholesale of Food, Beverages and Tobaccos	250
纺织、服装及家庭用品批发	Wholesale of Textiles, Wearing Apparel and Household Articles	213
文化、体育用品及器材批发	Wholesale of Culture, Sports Appliances and Equipments	122
医药及医疗器材批发	Wholesale of Medicines and Medical Appliances	428
矿产品、建材及化工产品批发	Wholesale of Mineral Products, Building Materials and Chemical Products	1940
机械设备、五金产品及电子产品批发	Wholesale of Machinery, Hardware and Electronic Products	863
贸易经纪与代理	Trade Broker and Agency	4
其他批发业	Other Wholesale not Classified Elsewhere	45
内资企业	Domestic Invested Enterprises	3913
国有企业	State-owned Enterprises	37
集体企业	Collective-owned Enterprises	1
股份合作企业	Cooperative Enterprises	
联营企业	Joint Ownership Enterprises	1
有限责任公司	Limited Liability Corporations	524
股份有限公司	Share-holding Corporations Ltd.	26
私营企业	Private Enterprises	3322
其他企业	Other Enterprises	2
港、澳、台商投资企业	Enterprises with Investment from Hong Kong, Macao and Taiwan	19
外商投资企业	Foreign Invested Enterprises	19

(10 000 yuan)

流动资产合计 Total Current Assets	其中 of which	固定资产原价 Original Value of Fixed Assets	累计折旧 Accumulated depreciation	其中 of which	资产总计 Total Assets	负债合计 Total Liabilities	所有者权益合计 Total Owners' Equities	其中 of which
	存货 Inventories			本年折旧 Depreciation in the Year				实收资本 Paid-up Capital
53194380.1	**7013392.3**	**3863109.2**	**1604104.2**	**277128.4**	**63697591.5**	**50481444.9**	**13512549.0**	**8761473.4**
46305179.7	**5681817.7**	**2439678.3**	**965739.5**	**165926.6**	**53989254.8**	**42358700.5**	**11605178.1**	**7329345.1**
621107.0	133554.6	66142.7	28041.1	2116.2	786711.0	493969.2	292713.8	171276.5
2053229.5	765004.6	303383.8	136594.0	14690.8	2439803.9	1659036.0	779977.4	367303.8
1897844.9	407239.8	141819.8	44524.0	7024.3	2171245.1	1865017.8	305778.7	181885.6
2485372.5	433475.5	396484.9	141423.2	17029.8	3215410.4	2217986.3	997424.2	335312.6
7053035.9	864170.8	395348.9	160604.9	34190.2	7909503.5	6664297.7	1231930.0	836503.2
23951762.3	1926772.7	718160.2	282541.8	58768.7	28530543.5	21874128.4	6653193.4	4534169.2
7995448.0	1115525.9	391672.2	165941.7	30584.9	8660287.5	7384628.4	1268047.4	860852.9
18152.3	3193.7	502.9	364.2	43.6	18391.1	11402.1	6989.0	4000.0
229227.3	32880.1	26162.9	5704.6	1478.1	257358.8	188234.6	69124.2	38041.3
42054949.1	4853612.5	2254717.4	882098.3	144413.0	49377169.1	40686959.4	8664833.5	5781072.4
3180707.8	432148.2	55438.9	11401.0	2562.9	3393795.2	2443331.1	950464.1	362113.9
1079.2	121.6	48.3	29.0		1156.0	545.1	610.9	50.0
3793.7	1853.7	24.3	10.9	3.0	3807.2	3342.6	464.6	50.0
18511944.1	2046644.8	1184027.7	455412.7	68686.7	23116985.6	18725537.5	4382950.5	3130357.1
3572602.6	74569.2	44397.0	11126.3	1483.4	4073629.4	3683174.9	390454.5	180511.5
16783926.1	2298275.0	970781.2	404118.4	71677.0	18786900.1	15831021.3	2939000.2	2107489.9
895.6					895.6	6.9	888.7	500.0
3159235.6	651304.6	47412.4	16632.4	3773.6	3216998.4	2660624.6	556373.8	475639.2
1090995.0	176900.6	137548.5	67008.8	17740.0	1395087.3	-988883.5	2383970.8	1072633.5

15-3 续表 continued

单位：万元

指标	Item	法人企业数（个）Number of Corporation Enterprises (unit)
零售业	**Retail Trade**	**1108**
综合零售	General Retail	81
食品、饮料及烟草制品专门零售	Special Retail of Food, Beverages and Tobaccos	111
纺织、服装及日用品专门零售	Special Retail of Textiles, Garments and Daily Consumer Articles	77
文化、体育用品及器材专门零售	Special Retail of Culture, Sports Appliances and Equipments	57
医药及医疗器材专门零售	Special Retail of Medicines and Medical Appliances	62
汽车、摩托车、零配件和燃料及其他动力销售	Retail of Motor Vehicles, Motorcycles, Parts, and Fuel and Other Powers	410
家用电器及电子产品专门零售	Special Retail of Household Electric Appliances and Electronic Products	148
五金、家具及室内装饰材料专门零售	Special Retail of Hardware, Furniture and Interior Decoration Materials	26
货摊、无店铺及其他零售业	Stalls, Non-shop and Other Retails	136
内资企业	Domestic Invested Enterprises	1086
国有企业	State-owned Enterprises	13
集体企业	Collective-owned Enterprises	9
股份合作企业	Cooperative Enterprises	5
联营企业	Joint Ownership Enterprises	
有限责任公司	Limited Liability Corporations	222
股份有限公司	Share-holding Corporations Ltd.	11
私营企业	Private Enterprises	824
其他企业	Other Enterprises	2
港、澳、台商投资企业	Enterprises with Investment from Hong Kong, Macao and Taiwan	9
外商投资企业	Foreign Invested Enterprises	13

(10 000 yuan)

流动资产合计 Total Current Assets	其中 of which 存货 Inventories	固定资产原价 Original Value of Fixed Assets	累计折旧 Accumulated depreciation	其中 of which 本年折旧 Depreciation in the Year	资产总计 Total Assets	负债合计 Total Liabilities	所有者权益合计 Total Owners' Equities	其中 of which 实收资本 Paid-up Capital
6889200.4	**1331574.6**	**1423430.9**	**638364.7**	**111201.8**	**9708336.7**	**8122744.4**	**1907370.9**	**1432128.3**
2852041.9	154263.3	705905.6	317009.5	45648.1	4175240.5	3573059.8	602116.5	321641.7
241800.7	50011.0	77404.8	33718.8	3518.2	301564.4	211662.3	89902.1	67011.9
256090.4	77096.7	45917.5	14821.0	2250.9	375657.9	318223.4	70114.0	94954.6
236817.1	100033.5	33156.4	16164.9	2563.2	288698.1	160838.5	127859.6	49306.6
605116.1	127283.5	26690.0	15643.7	2792.7	760297.8	557989.9	202307.9	72225.9
1846604.6	653344.0	439422.5	209068.9	48911.1	2715590.3	2453108.3	570878.0	600710.1
310573.2	60578.9	12875.9	5538.4	976.1	415171.2	325393.6	90060.9	91959.4
49192.6	9439.2	43551.6	12647.7	2227.2	110979.6	72111.4	38868.2	45170.3
490963.8	99524.5	38506.6	13751.8	2314.3	565136.9	450357.2	115263.7	89147.8
6627879.0	1234644.8	1228558.5	549169.4	99352.5	9015321.7	7683812.0	1653288.3	1204069.7
121271.4	30761.6	11348.4	5713.5	1290.3	150368.0	129457.4	20910.6	13390.6
6385.5	2002.8	1595.7	839.5	35.9	7640.0	2557.3	5082.7	1074.3
21300.8	5609.0	7099.7	4525.8	517.1	27724.5	15447.7	12276.8	4753.9
1239683.9	307574.9	457265.1	175207.7	37077.4	1894767.7	1300598.9	596373.0	450183.8
2318176.4	82062.8	378807.3	183741.9	28803.4	3271571.5	3130534.3	450306.3	105974.4
2920751.7	806488.7	372442.3	179141.0	31628.4	3662800.7	3105194.3	567911.7	628612.7
309.3	145.0				449.3	22.1	427.2	80.0
102275.3	39990.9	68421.4	38895.4	4685.5	189684.1	122034.6	67649.5	24093.4
159046.1	56938.9	126451.0	50299.9	7163.8	503330.9	316897.8	186433.1	203965.2

15-4 限额以上批发零售贸易企业损益及分配(2022年)

Profit Loss and Distribution of Enterprises above Designated Size of Wholesale and Retail Trade(2022)

单位:万元

指标	Item	法人企业数(个) Number of Corporation Enterprises (unit)	主营业务收入 Revenue from Principal Business	营业成本 Business Cost
总计	**Total**	**5059**	**113051177.8**	**108538314.6**
批发业	**Wholesale Trade**	**3951**	**100119765.4**	**97019851.4**
农、林、牧、渔产品批发	Wholesale of Agricultural, Forestry, Livestock and Fishery Products	86	1461034.2	1425596.2
食品、饮料及烟草制品批发	Wholesale of Food, Beverages and Tobaccos	250	5062523.6	4596012.1
纺织、服装及家庭用品批发	Wholesale of Textiles, Wearing Apparel and Household Articles	213	2559487.0	2470478.0
文化、体育用品及器材批发	Wholesale of Culture, Sports Appliances and Equipments	122	4194143.8	3782558.0
医药及医疗器材批发	Wholesale of Medicines and Medical Appliances	428	9755103.4	8978695.5
矿产品、建材及化工产品批发	Wholesale of Mineral Products, Building Materials and Chemical Products	1940	63861243.6	63317816.6
机械设备、五金产品及电子产品批发	Wholesale of Machinery, Hardware and Electronic Products	863	12648805.0	11894067.4
贸易经纪与代理	Trade Broker and Agency	4	42894.8	39310.6
其他批发业	Other Wholesale not Classified Elsewhere	45	534530.0	515317.0
内资企业	Domestic Invested Enterprises	3913	91447566.5	88645433.4
国有企业	State-owned Enterprises	37	6115681.8	6130503.2
集体企业	Collective-owned Enterprises	1	5364.8	5251.6
股份合作企业	Cooperative Enterprises			
联营企业	Joint Ownership Enterprises	1	4994.7	4244.8
有限责任公司	Limited Liability Corporations	524	39346671.5	38257635.6
股份有限公司	Share-holding Corporations Ltd.	26	1438328.1	1385200.0
私营企业	Private Enterprises	3322	44530021.4	42856357.8
其他企业	Other Enterprises	2	6504.2	6240.4
港、澳、台商投资企业	Enterprises with Investment from Hong Kong, Macao and Taiwan	19	4108956.7	3881967.0
外商投资企业	Foreign Invested Enterprises	19	4563242.2	4492451.0

(10 000 yuan)

税金及附加 Taxes and Other Charges	销售费用 Sales Expenses	管理费用 Management Expenses	财务费用 Financial Expenses	营业利润 Profits from Business	利润总额 Total Profits	所得税费用 Income Tax Expense	应付职工薪酬(本年贷方累计发生额) Total Wages Payable	应交增值税 Value-added Tax Payable
270098.1	**2849168.2**	**1544096.9**	**300328.5**	**888160.0**	**971523.2**	**208728.6**	**1694433.7**	**649072.3**
223835.1	**1602573.0**	**1150823.7**	**225984.3**	**804693.1**	**873588.1**	**155293.2**	**1105723.2**	**497799.5**
445.0	13977.1	20290.1	12336.9	2223.2	14058.4	1965.1	15175.6	1462.1
131854.7	150674.6	166591.7	7883.3	122532.4	121621.7	30759.7	130977.5	63810.9
2497.9	109033.7	53725.0	4429.0	13706.5	17344.6	4463.5	57028.1	24523.2
7249.5	134448.0	123849.3	3463.9	152599.1	156565.6	6191.1	153555.4	12589.0
22167.1	436090.9	212639.8	42319.6	176325.8	174857.3	26566.6	234001.5	127811.6
44595.7	409302.5	328462.3	166860.8	87341.7	114991.5	24541.8	242913.1	133070.8
14442.8	335898.8	235988.5	-10418.1	243456.7	267297.3	60204.2	265047.2	127989.0
9.8	2512.7	521.5	239.6	460.3	477.0	23.7	453.6	96.3
572.6	10634.7	8755.5	-1130.7	6047.4	6374.7	577.5	6571.2	6446.6
214138.8	1444926.3	1045573.3	276787.9	723025.8	792405.6	120436.8	1007560.9	444483.0
5376.9	21763.0	14629.7	12176.4	43273.7	43168.7	10651.3	24620.2	16822.6
1.1		42.1	-0.9	70.8	70.8	1.8	16.4	14.3
10.6	308.1	165.1	0.7	271.3	289.2	8.9	302.1	142.4
171554.3	428491.7	400721.8	111835.5	511291.9	539965.1	60757.5	473950.7	171704.1
1203.9	19595.6	16246.9	22894.6	2152.0	2945.8	1228.4	17332.1	6379.0
35991.9	974679.4	613662.5	129880.4	165894.4	205894.3	47787.2	491232.8	249420.6
0.1	88.5	105.2	1.2	71.7	71.7	1.7	106.6	
4003.0	99631.4	60655.1	-63548.3	104944.3	103531.6	24088.6	57804.6	25898.7
5693.3	58015.3	44595.3	12744.7	-23277.0	-22349.1	10767.8	40357.7	27417.8

15-4 续表 continued

单位:万元

指标	Item	法人企业数(个) Number of Corporation Enterprises (unit)	主营业务收入 Revenue from Principal Business	营业成本 Business Cost
零售业	**Retail Trade**	**1108**	**12931412.4**	**11518463.2**
综合零售	General Retail	81	1454902.3	1206451.2
食品、饮料及烟草制品专门零售	Special Retail of Food, Beverages and Tobaccos	111	604860.9	518478.5
纺织、服装及日用品专门零售	Special Retail of Textiles, Garments and Daily Consumer Articles	77	365370.6	289611.1
文化、体育用品及器材专门零售	Special Retail of Culture, Sports Appliances and Equipments	57	304542.4	253407.9
医药及医疗器材专门零售	Special Retail of Medicines and Medical Appliances	62	715875.1	536708.1
汽车、摩托车、零配件和燃料及其他动力销售	Retail of Motor Vehicles, Motorcycles, Parts, and Fuel and Other Powers	410	6338044.6	5961753.5
家用电器及电子产品专门零售	Special Retail of Household Electric Appliances and Electronic Products	148	775131.1	719610.8
五金、家具及室内装饰材料专门零售	Special Retail of Hardware, Furniture and Interior Decoration Materials	26	89300.3	68323.5
货摊、无店铺及其他零售业	Stalls, Non-shop and Other Retails	136	2283385.1	1964118.6
内资企业	Domestic Invested Enterprises	1086	11541118.1	10351971.4
国有企业	State-owned Enterprises	13	267007.2	251854.9
集体企业	Collective-owned Enterprises	9	18673.7	16976.4
股份合作企业	Cooperative Enterprises	5	117426.0	110316.9
联营企业	Joint Ownership Enterprises			
有限责任公司	Limited Liability Corporations	222	3272208.3	2926365.6
股份有限公司	Share-holding Corporations Ltd.	11	536173.7	463683.0
私营企业	Private Enterprises	824	7326858.3	6580059.3
其他企业	Other Enterprises	2	2770.9	2715.3
港、澳、台商投资企业	Enterprises with Investment from Hong Kong, Macao and Taiwan	9	755811.6	698772.0
外商投资企业	Foreign Invested Enterprises	13	634482.7	467719.8

(10 000 yuan)

税金及附加 Taxes and Other Charges	销售费用 Sales Expenses	管理费用 Management Expenses	财务费用 Financial Expenses	营业利润 Profits from Business	利润总额 Total Profits	所得税费用 Income Tax Expense	应付职工薪酬(本年贷方累计发生额) Total Wages Payable	应交增值税 Value-added Tax Payable
46263.0	**1246595.2**	**393273.2**	**74344.2**	**83466.9**	**97935.1**	**53435.4**	**588710.5**	**151272.8**
15575.2	296423.0	79492.9	14816.8	51392.6	51869.2	7875.2	159304.4	29855.2
1569.2	26887.0	15902.2	837.6	43157.4	42356.1	11406.4	25623.5	9174.6
1664.8	65024.3	20037.6	9986.8	-9392.4	-4406.8	1321.2	32383.1	6253.5
4396.4	31276.8	14790.0	2702.9	9416.2	9850.8	1677.9	22842.1	4579.6
1514.7	140507.3	31763.9	4791.2	14000.1	13393.8	3709.1	71138.5	13972.5
17080.8	325670.1	140380.7	36403.8	-19384.6	-12958.6	19114.9	198999.7	51836.4
358.3	39096.6	22187.1	2627.5	-3860.8	-3257.4	149.7	22140.7	3895.1
777.9	10238.4	11769.1	1815.2	-3443.9	-3266.5	34.5	7944.9	1919.4
3325.7	311471.7	56949.7	362.4	1582.3	4354.5	8146.5	48333.6	29786.5
38471.9	1061295.9	352959.3	64055.7	82928.3	95860.0	42976.1	528786.5	129883.1
334.7	12685.3	8690.1	3430.0	-1373.1	-1395.6	724.1	10952.3	1706.8
44.2	605.9	1450.0	3.4	-308.0	-282.7	5.6	775.7	134.4
620.8	3441.2	2199.1	300.2	4317.7	2809.1	1143.8	2328.7	1066.7
11239.8	279974.8	103505.1	25178.5	47212.9	51956.2	22500.5	146806.6	50983.3
8641.5	128640.0	29955.1	1333.9	44610.5	45526.9	2385.4	68465.0	11817.4
17590.9	635947.1	207119.7	33809.7	-11546.2	-2768.4	16216.7	299348.6	64174.5
	1.6	40.2		14.5	14.5		109.6	
5173.9	37883.0	6109.2	1970.1	18729.6	18722.5	5967.1	23899.9	5271.7
2617.2	147416.3	34204.7	8318.4	-18191.0	-16647.4	4492.2	36024.1	16118.0

15-5 限额以上餐饮业主要经济指标(2022年)

Main Economic Indicators of Enterprises above Designated Size of Catering Services (2022)

单位：万元

指标	Item	法人企业数(个) Number of Corporation Enterprises (unit)	资产总计 Total Assets	负债合计 Total Liabilities	所有者权益 Owners' Equities
总计	**Total**	**611**	**782599.6**	**600317.4**	**182930.0**
正餐服务	Restaurant	330	520835.4	394833.3	126668.9
快餐服务	Fast Food	246	218201.7	161244.9	56937.8
饮料及冷饮服务	Beverages and Cold Drinks	4	5541.9	11937.3	-6395.4
餐饮配送及外卖送餐服务	Catering Distribution and Delivery Service	28	21516.5	15601.7	5914.8
其他餐饮业	Others	3	16504.1	16700.2	-196.1
内资企业	Domestic Invested Enterprises	607	740812.6	548797.0	191897.2
国有企业	State-owned Enterprises	15	191743.5	63278.3	128465.2
集体企业	Collective-owned Enterprises	1	812.7	328.3	
股份合作企业	Cooperative Enterprises	1	2772.6	1883.9	888.7
联营企业	Joint Ownership Enterprises	1	1865.8	364.6	1501.2
有限责任公司	Limited Liability Corporations	78	194808.6	146516.0	50314.9
股份有限公司	Share-holding Corporations Ltd.	1	4813.2	2590.1	2223.1
私营企业	Private Enterprises	510	343996.2	333835.8	8504.1
其他企业	Other Enterprises				
港、澳、台商投资企业	Enterprises with Investment from Hong Kong, Macao and Taiwan	3	41779.3	50746.5	-8967.2
外商投资企业	Foreign Invested Enterprises	1	7.7	773.9	

(10 000 yuan)

其中 of which 实收资本 Paid-up Capital	主营业务收入 Revenue from Principal Business	营业成本 Business Cost	销售费用 Sales Expenses	管理费用 Management Expenses	财务费用 Financial Expenses	营业利润 Profits from Business	利润总额 Total Profits	应付职工薪酬(本年贷方累计发生额) Total Wages Payable
123333.1	**649778.3**	**370541.9**	**197859.6**	**112525.0**	**9755.4**	**-25586.8**	**-19206.7**	**172061.6**
80961.9	359811.5	186398.6	117576.0	87212.7	7483.7	-29878.3	-24643.2	98349.0
36737.9	229995.6	138374.8	74097.4	15484.6	2128.1	6299.0	7335.9	59768.9
300.0	14527.5	9666.7	3176.1	1341.6	53.7	304.3	242.1	2924.6
4768.3	35539.4	27821.3	1993.9	7737.6	67.6	-2139.2	-2052.5	8889.7
565.0	9904.3	8280.5	1016.2	748.5	22.3	-172.6	-89.0	2129.4
118535.0	598848.0	351220.8	169802.5	109705.8	8290.1	-25495.8	-18947.2	154084.4
17786.0	28637.0	16577.0	5505.2	14228.9	-461.7	-6770.3	-4273.9	14815.4
		81.1	49.1	107.5	79.4	55.8	70.9	
876.9	1445.3	533.7	571.9	380.6	-0.1	-43.9	-17.1	380.9
1500.0	2918.0	2776.2	7.4	76.5	-0.2	57.7	69.5	929.0
31022.1	156014.6	101582.9	36923.9	30076.0	3605.1	-6660.2	-5339.8	42253.5
3000.0	3319.9	1250.1	294.6	3074.0	1.1	-1309.9	-830.7	1318.5
64350.0	406513.2	228419.8	126450.4	61762.3	5066.5	-10825.0	-8626.1	94387.1
4798.1	50930.3	19163.6	27703.1	2819.2	1461.9	-11.8	-143.1	17977.2
		157.5	354.0		3.4	-79.2	-116.4	

15-6 限额以上住宿业主要经济指标(2022年)

Main Economic Indicators of Enterprises above Designated Size of Hotels Services(2022)

单位：万元

指标	Item	法人企业数(个) Number of Corporation Enterprises (unit)	资产总计 Total Assets	负债合计 Total Liabilities	所有者权益 Owners' Equities
总计	**Total**	**263**	**1043995.8**	**1027767.3**	**17469.4**
旅游饭店	Tourist Hotel	58	676848.2	550732.9	126115.3
一般旅馆	General Hotels	186	251990.8	298216.0	-45460.1
民宿服务	Home Lodging Services	1	5427.8	2873.1	2554.7
露营地服务	Campground Services				
其他住宿业	Others	18	109729.0	175945.3	-65740.5
内资企业	Domestic Invested Enterprises	261	1032169.3	1020348.4	13061.8
国有企业	State-owned Enterprises	16	452105.4	352978.9	99126.5
集体企业	Collective-owned Enterprises	2	16232.4	21608.1	-5375.7
股份合作企业	Cooperative Enterprises	2	18142.6	16124.6	2018.0
联营企业	Joint Ownership Enterprises				
有限责任公司	Limited Liability Corporations	47	228410.2	327408.6	-98998.4
股份有限公司	Share-holding Corporations Ltd.	3	2196.0	1396.7	799.3
私营企业	Private Enterprises	190	315079.5	300831.2	15489.2
其他企业	Other Enterprises	1	3.2	0.3	2.9
港、澳、台商投资企业	Enterprises with Investment from Hong Kong, Macao and Taiwan	1	11325.3	6299.6	5025.7
外商投资企业	Foreign Invested Enterprises	1	501.2	1119.3	-618.1

(10 000 yuan)

其中 of which 实收资本 Paid-up Capital	主营业务收入 Revenue from Principal Business	营业成本 Business Cost	销售费用 Sales Expenses	管理费用 Management Expenses	财务费用 Financial Expenses	营业利润 Profits from Business	利润总额 Total Profits	应付职工薪酬(本年贷方累计发生额) Total Wages Payable
153860.3	**315832.9**	**145962.3**	**130040.8**	**111597.4**	**5370.8**	**-60989.3**	**-56604.0**	**115513.2**
87654.2	158367.0	69849.8	75995.2	54236.0	-959.3	-34232.1	-31582.5	72953.0
59336.7	135975.4	51802.8	46629.2	46767.8	2937.7	-11149.4	-9297.6	33600.5
2373.2	207.8	220.3	6.5	5.8		-25.6	-25.6	66.0
4496.2	21282.7	24089.4	7409.9	10587.8	3392.4	-15582.2	-15698.3	8893.7
149040.3	311169.6	145679.1	127685.0	109543.8	5389.4	-61268.7	-56863.4	113379.3
47159.3	75647.3	29598.3	42297.1	29684.2	-4233.1	-17384.3	-15345.9	42154.9
1883.4	3100.7	899.4	4136.8	1004.9	-5.6	-2826.9	-2824.0	1054.7
1558.7	2762.8	1309.5	1084.4	1138.3	244.4	-1023.3	305.8	798.1
35543.4	95369.6	50280.8	38844.2	38526.9	4404.4	-25933.4	-25971.3	38843.2
1480.0	2414.2	306.3	1984.3	138.3	45.6	-60.8	-57.9	412.2
61415.5	131704.0	63201.2	39338.2	38964.7	4933.7	-14040.8	-12971.0	30061.9
	171.0	83.6		86.5		0.8	0.9	54.3
4320.0	3526.0	242.6	1298.8	1779.0	-16.8	-75.7	-106.4	1761.9
500.0	1137.3	40.6	1057.0	274.6	-1.8	355.1	365.8	372.0

15-7 限额以上住宿业和餐饮业法人企业经营情况(2022年)

Main Indicators of Enterprises above Designated Size of Hotels and Catering Services(2022)

指标	Item	法人企业数(个) Number of Corporation Enterprises (unit)	从业人员期末人数(人) Engaged Persons at Year-end (person)
总计	**Total**	**874**	**44726**
住宿业	**Hotels**	**263**	**15705**
旅游饭店	Tourist Hotel	58	8345
一般旅馆	General Hotels	186	5522
民宿服务	Home Lodging Services	1	11
露营地服务	Campground Services		
其他住宿业	Others	18	1827
内资企业	Domestic Invested Enterprises	261	15510
国有企业	State-owned Enterprises	16	3926
集体企业	Collective-owned Enterprises	2	220
股份合作企业	Cooperative Enterprises	2	141
联营企业	Joint Ownership Enterprises		
有限责任公司	Limited Liability Corporations	47	5716
股份有限公司	Share-holding Corporations Ltd.	3	68
私营企业	Private Enterprises	190	5425
其他企业	Other Enterprises	1	14
港、澳、台商投资企业	Enterprises with Investment from Hong Kong, Macao and Taiwan	1	144
外商投资企业	Foreign Invested Enterprises	1	51
餐饮业	**Catering Services**	**611**	**29021**
正餐服务	Restaurant	330	16869
快餐服务	Fast Food	246	9778
饮料及冷饮服务	Beverages and Cold Drinks	4	360
餐饮配送及外卖送餐服务	Catering Distribution and Delivery Service	28	1722
其他餐饮业	Others	3	292
内资企业	Domestic Invested Enterprises	607	26003
国有企业	State-owned Enterprises	15	1983
集体企业	Collective-owned Enterprises	1	
股份合作企业	Cooperative Enterprises	1	80
联营企业	Joint Ownership Enterprises	1	144
有限责任公司	Limited Liability Corporations	78	6231
股份有限公司	Share-holding Corporations Ltd.	1	295
私营企业	Private Enterprises	510	17270
其他企业	Other Enterprises		
港、澳、台商投资企业	Enterprises with Investment from Hong Kong, Macao and Taiwan	3	3018
外商投资企业	Foreign Invested Enterprises	1	

营业额(万元) Business Revenue (10 000 yuan)	其中 of which 客房收入 From Hotel Rooms	餐费收入 From Meals	商品销售收入 Revenue from Commodities	其他收入 Other Revenue	客房数(间) Number of Room (room)	床位数(张) Number of Beds (bed)	餐位数(位) Number of Dining-seats (seat)	年末餐饮营业面积(平方米) Operating Area of Catering Enterprises at Year-end (sq.m)
1029697.6	**234653.5**	**693304.2**	**23551.9**	**78188.0**	**52476**	**79472**	**373146**	**1901087**
338672.5	**184773.5**	**98301.4**	**8423.3**	**47174.3**	**41696**	**61004**	**91705**	**986507**
172803.7	67341.8	68348.8	6372.4	30740.7	11256	17485	53741	359690
142590.0	105180.3	21043.7	1207.1	15158.9	26832	37858	30813	569855
207.8	207.8				50	60		
23071.0	12043.6	8908.9	843.8	1274.7	3558	5601	7151	56962
333742.1	182207.2	97366.6	8420.0	45748.3	41267	60354	90665	968007
81649.6	27377.9	32999.0	4070.9	17201.8	3918	6008	9977	124143
3408.0	2056.9	1225.6		125.5	454	789	2450	7707
2839.6	675.1	2049.6		114.9	337	660	1600	6000
104653.3	52868.8	32555.8	2841.3	16387.4	10338	16060	44874	248347
2548.1	2287.8	241.5	11.9	6.9	368	531	242	14045
138470.8	96768.0	28295.1	1495.9	11911.8	25773	36178	31522	563075
172.7	172.7				79	128		4690
3724.7	1373.7	925.0		1426.0	330	490	1000	16000
1205.7	1192.6	9.8	3.3		99	160	40	2500
691025.1	**49880.0**	**595002.8**	**15128.6**	**31013.7**	**10780**	**18468**	**281441**	**914580**
386533.2	49724.6	308590.0	4730.1	23488.5	10752	18416	179117	672454
241384.5		232483.3	3872.4	5028.8			95779	196471
15344.1		14651.0	357.5	335.6			301	1539
37492.2	155.4	30364.0	6168.6	804.2	28	52	3012	33016
10271.1		8914.5		1356.6			3232	11100
636644.4	49880.0	543901.6	13716.3	29146.5	10780	18468	273551	885497
32357.0	9871.5	15870.6	1873.2	4741.7	1698	3097	6084	47525
402.6	402.6							
1531.5	598.0	915.1	18.4		188	357	380	1000
3093.1		3093.1					5000	2000
165828.1	9865.7	139448.2	5370.5	11143.7	2198	3635	72444	220811
3636.6	596.6	2922.6		117.4	245	320	650	3700
429795.5	28545.6	381652.0	6454.2	13143.7	6451	11059	188993	610461
53918.7		50639.2	1412.3	1867.2			7890	29083
462.0		462.0						

15-8 销售过亿元的商品交易市场一览表(2022年)

Large Commodity Markets with Transaction Value over 100 Million Yuan (2022)

市场类别 Category	市场数量 (个) Market Quantity (unit)	市场总摊位 (个) Number of booths (unit)	年末出租摊位数 (个) Number of rent booths at Year-End (unit)	年末营业面积 (平方米) Operating Area at Year-End (sq.m)	年成交额 (万元) Annual Turnover (10 000 yuan)
总计	**26**	**19035**	**17545**	**1620939**	**6597447**
工业消费品综合市场	3	3736	3294	119450	214642
农产品综合市场	2	2555	2505	177800	306432
金属材料市场	2	192	185	45000	565391
水产品市场	2	2022	1802	121200	3680000
蔬菜市场	3	1264	1194	95810	340583
干鲜果品市场	1	258	258	61000	242640
茶叶市场	2	800	605	90000	140030
服装市场	1	2730	2730	199000	142058
鞋帽市场	1	889	775	19925	115200
小商品市场	1	1510	1505	45500	108960
家具市场	5	2074	1928	419316	239251
汽车市场	1	70	70	130000	307260
机动车零配件市场	2	935	694	96938	195000

主要统计指标解释

社会消费品零售总额 指企业（单位、个体户）通过交易直接售给个人、社会集团非生产、非经营用的实物商品金额，以及提供餐饮服务所取得的收入金额。个人包括城乡居民和入境人员，社会集团包括机关、社会团体、部队、学校、企事业单位、居委会或村委会等。

商品销售额 指对本单位以外的单位和个人出售的商品金额（包括售给本单位消费用的商品，含增值税）。商品销售包括：（1）售给个人和社会集团消费用的商品；（2）售给农业、工业、建筑业、服务业等国民经济各行业用于生产、经营用的商品，包括售予批发和零售业作为转卖或加工后转卖的商品；（3）对国（境）外直接出口的商品。不包括：（1）未通过买卖行为付出的商品，如因机构变动移交给其他企业单位的商品、借出的商品、归还受其他单位委托代保管的商品、付出的加工原料和赠送给其他单位的样品等；（2）促销返券所销售的、不计入营业收入的商品；（3）经本单位介绍，由买卖双方直接结算，本单位只收取手续费的业务；（4）未发生所有权转移的商品预付卡销售，如加油卡；（5）汽车维修、电话卡销售等服务性经济活动；（6）购货退回的商品；（7）商品损耗和损失；（8）出售本单位自用的废旧物资；（9）期货交易商品；（10）自来水供应企业、电力企业、天然气供应企业提供的水、电、气。

批发业 指向其他批发或零售单位（含个体经营者）及其他企事业单位、机关团体等批量销售生活用品、生产资料的活动，以及从事进出口贸易和贸易经纪与代理的活动，包括拥有货物所有权，并以本单位（公司）的名义进行交易活动，也包括不拥有货物的所有权，收取佣金的商品代理、商品代售活动；还包括各类商品批发市场中固定摊位的批发活动，以及以销售为目的的收购活动。

零售业 指百货商店、超级市场、专门零售商店、品牌专卖店、售货摊等主要面向最终消费者（如居民等）的销售活动，以互联网、邮政、电话、售货机等方式的销售活动，还包括在同一地点，后面加工生产，前面销售的店铺（如面包房）；谷物、种子、饲料、牲畜、矿产品、生产用原料、化工原料、农用化工产品、机械设备（乘用车、计算机及通信设备除外）等生产资料的销售不作为零售活动；多数零售商对其销售的货物拥有所有权，但有些则是充当委托人的代理人，进行委托销售或以收取佣金的方式进行销售。

住宿业 指为旅行者提供短期留宿场所的活动，有些单位只提供住宿，也有些单位提供住宿、饮食、商务、娱乐一体的服务，不包括主要按月或按年长期出租房屋住所的活动。

餐饮业 指通过即时制作加工、商业销售和服务性劳动等，向消费者提供食品和消费场所及设施的服务。

住宿餐饮业营业额 指住宿和餐饮业单位在经营活动中，因提供服务或销售商品等取得的全部收入（含增值税），收入主要来源于提供客房、餐费服务、商品销售和其他服务，如商务服务。不包括多产业法人企业附营的其他行业产业活动单位的餐费收入、商品销售收入等各项收入。其中，客房收入指住宿和餐饮业单位在经营活动中因提供住宿服务取得的收入（含增值税）。不包括多产业法人企业附营的其他行业产业活动单位的客房收入。餐费收入指本单位为顾客提供就餐服务取得的收入（含增值税）。包括：经烹饪、调制加工后出售的各种食品，如主食、炒菜、凉拌菜等的收入。不包括多产业法人企业附营的其他行业产业活动单位的餐费收入。

亿元以上商品交易市场 指年成交额在亿元及以上的商品交易市场。商品交易市场是指经有关部门和组织批准设立，有固定场所、设施，有经营管理部门和监管人员，若干市场经营者入内，常年或实际开业三个月以上，集中、公开、独立地进行生活消费品、生产资料等现货商品交易以及提供相关服务的交易场所，包括各类消费品市场、生产资料市场等。

Explanatory Notes on Main Statistical Indicators

Total Retail Sales of Consumer Goods refer to the revenue received by enterprises (units, self-employed individuals) through direct sales of non-production and non-business physical commodities to individuals and social institutions, and revenue from providing catering services. Individuals include rural and urban households, population from abroad, social institutions include government agencies, social organizations, military units, schools, institutions, neighbourhood (village) committees, etc.

Total Sales of Commodities refer to value of commodities sold by the establishments to other establishments and individuals (including goods sold for self consumption, including VAT). The commodities include: (1) commodities sold to individuals and social groups for their consumption; (2) commodities sold to establishments in all industries for their production and operation, including agriculture, industry, construction, and catering services, including commodities sold to wholesale and retail establishments for re-selling, with or without further processing; (3) commodities for direct export to abroad. Excluded are (1) extended commodities without trading, such as goods handed over to other enterprises and institutions because of the change of organizations, lent goods, return of goods kept for others, extended processing materials and samples donated to others, (2) goods sold by coupon rebates that are not included in business income, (3) goods of direct settlement between buyer and seller with handling fees introduced by others, (4) prepaid cards for goods without transfer of ownership, such as gas cards, (5) Service-oriented economic activities such as automobile maintenance and telephone card sales, (6) goods returned after purchase, (7) damaged and spoiled goods, (8) waste and used goods of self-use, (9) futures trading commodities, (10) water, electricity and gas supplied by water supply enterprises, electric power enterprises and natural gas supply enterprises.

Wholesale Trade refers to the activities of selling wholesale commodities for daily use and capital goods to other enterprises of wholesale and retail trades (including self-employed individuals) and other enterprises, institutions and government agencies and organizations, and the activities of engaging in import and export and acting as a trade agent. The wholesaler may have the ownership of the commodities for wholesale and trade in the name of its own (a company), and the wholesaler can act as commission agent or commodity broker without the ownership of commodities. Also included are the wholesale activities at the fixed stalls in wholesale market and the acquisition for sales purpose.

Retail Trade refers to the activities of department stores, supermarkets, franchised stores, brand stores, retail stalls and on-the-spot-making-selling stores selling commodities to the final consumers (residents) by any means, including internet, post, telephone, sales machine. It also includes shops with sales and production located in the same places (such as bakeries). Retail trade excludes the activities of sales of capital goods such as grain, seed, feed, livestock, mineral products, raw material for production, industrial chemicals, chemical products for agricultural use, machine and equipment (excluding vehicles, computers and communication equipment). Most retailers have the ownership of commodities to sell, but some are acting as agents or brokers to make transactions for a commission.

Hotel Services refer to short-term accommodation services provided to visitors. Some units may provide only accommodation while others provide a combination of accommodation, meals, business services and recreational facilities. It excludes activities related to the provision of long-term primary residences, typically leased on a monthly or annual basis.

Catering Services refer to the activities of providing foods, serving locations and facilities to customers through instant processing, commercial sales and service-type labor.

Hotels and Catering Services Business Revenue refers to total revenue (including VAT) of hotels and catering services received from providing services or selling commodities through business activities. Revenue comes mainly from providing hotels, catering services, selling of commodities and other services, such as commodity services. It does not include revenue from providing meals or selling of commodities by establishments affiliated to other multi-industrial corporate enterprises. Income from hotel rooms refers to income (including VAT) of hotels and catering services by providing lodging services through business activities. Income from meals refers to income (including VAT) from providing catering services, including selling of cooked or prepared foods, such as staple food, cooked dishes, or cold dishes. It does not include income from meals provided by establishments affiliated to other multi-industrial corporate enterprises.

Large Commodity Markets with Transaction Value over 100 Million Yuan refers to the commodity markets with an annual transaction at and above 100 million. The commodity markets refer to markets approved and managed by related departments, where there are fixed sites, facilities, managers and administrative offices, where there are a certain number of traders to operate for at least three months or all the year, where the commodities, including articles for daily consumption and capital goods and services, are traded in a centralized, independent and open way. Such markets include markets for daily goods, markets of capital goods, etc.

16

对外贸易与国际旅游

FOREIGN TRADE AND INTERNATIONAL TOURISM

16-1 海关进出口商品总额
International Trade in Goods of Customs

单位:万美元 (10 000 USD)

指标	Item	2022年进出口总额 Total Value of Imports and Exports in 2022	其中 of which 出口 Export	其中 of which 进口 Import	2021年进出口总额 Total Value of Imports and Exports in 2021	其中 of which 出口 Export	其中 of which 进口 Import
总　额	**Total**	**3270583**	**2112951**	**1157632**	**3003034**	**1818852**	**1184182**
按贸易方式分	**By Trade**						
一般贸易	General Trade	2850676	1907650	943025	2590983	1597762	993221
援助物资	Aid Material	563	563		705	705	
捐赠物资	Donation Material	38	38		6	6	
补偿贸易	Compensation Trade						
来料加工装配贸易	Processing and Assembling Trade with Sent Materials	37853	20451	17401	59551	28137	31414
进料加工贸易	Processing Trade with Imported Materials	93405	65819	27586	61413	46805	14608
对外承包工程出口货物	Export of Contracted projects	28588	28588		16904	16904	
投资设备	Investment Goods	576		576			
出料加工贸易	Export Processing Trade	189	40	149	421	118	303
海关特殊监管区域进口设备	**Import of Equipment in Special Customs Supervision Area**	**1523**		**1523**	**2912**		**2912**
海关特殊监管区域物流货物	**Logistics Freight of Equipment in Special Customs Supervision Area**	**161415**	**76549**	**84866**	**193999**	**96898**	**97100**
易货贸易	Barter Trade						
保税监管场所进出境货物	**Bonded Supervision Entry and Exit Goods**	**90154**	**9643**	**80511**	**60657**	**26908**	**33749**
来料加工装配进口设备	Imported Equipment for Processing Incoming Materials						
租赁贸易	Leasing Trade				9000		9000
其他贸易	Other Trade	5602	3608	1994	6483	4608	1875
按运输方式分	**By Ways of Transport**						
水路运输	Waterway Transport	2207442	1542729	664714	1907055	1298080	608975
铁路运输	Railway Transport	43620	32514	11106	52574	41049	11525
公路运输	Road Transport	383667	112339	271328	480124	95500	384623
航空运输	Air Transport	448944	239107	209837	447506	278333	169172
邮件运输	Mail Transport	2731	2162	569	4500	3617	884
其他运输	Others	184179	184101	78	111275	102273	9002
按企业性质分	**By Natural of Enterprises**						
国有企业	State-owned Enterprises	602175	83282	518894	535528	54929	480599
集体企业	Collective-owned Enterprises	108507	55582	52925	132501	36683	95818
外商投资企业	Foreign Funded Enterprises	586799	478062	108738	575302	424111	151190
中外合资	Joint-venture Enterprises	146890	123243	23647	147062	114148	32914
中外合作	Cooperation Enterprises	996	996		1347	1347	
外商独资	Enterprises with Sole Fund	438913	353823	85090	426892	308616	118276
其他	Others	2695	2158	537	4505	3603	902

16-2 主要国别(地区)海关进出口商品总额
International Trade in Goods of Customs by Country (Region)

单位：万美元 (10 000 USD)

国别(地区)	Country (region)	2022年进出口总额 Total Value of Imports and Exports in 2022	其中 of which 出口 Export	进口 Import	2021年进出口总额 Total Value of Imports and Exports in 2021	其中 of which 出口 Export	进口 Import
总额	**Total**	**3270583**	**2112951**	**1157632**	**3003034**	**1818852**	**1184182**
亚洲	**Asia**	**1648022**	**1046603**	**601420**	**1456614**	**892916**	**563698**
中国香港	Hong Kong, China	61502	61382	120	76806	76660	147
印度	India	79340	62359	16980	69230	48972	20259
印度尼西亚	Indonesia	70375	60235	10140	49056	41975	7081
日本	Japan	97666	62500	35166	117113	62878	54234
马来西亚	Malaysia	275168	131332	143837	195194	97008	98186
巴基斯坦	Pakistan	16517	16243	274	26960	26944	15
菲律宾	Philippines	80111	61982	18128	74305	53232	21073
卡塔尔	Qatar	3974	3667	306	3984	3723	262
沙特阿拉伯	Saudi Arabia	34240	26093	8148	40291	34872	5419
新加坡	Singapore	132400	115528	16872	61122	50751	10372
韩国	Republic of Korea	146160	107184	38976	144128	108777	35351
泰国	Thailand	100017	45470	54547	94887	26083	68804
土耳其	Türkiye	19382	19077	305	15475	15125	350
阿拉伯联合酋长国	The United Arab Emirates	69271	65336	3934	47454	44205	3250
越南	Vietnam	110899	76735	34164	87131	72482	14648
中国台湾	Taiwan, China	96461	18982	77478	146026	29957	116069
非洲	**Africa**	**256896**	**233868**	**23028**	**225055**	**209351**	**15704**
埃及	Egypt	11724	11522	202	12055	11990	66
南非	South Africa	22792	14429	8363	25570	14691	10878
尼日利亚	Nigeria	32866	32660	206	38311	38131	180
欧洲	**Europe**	**481058**	**356325**	**124733**	**470155**	**332983**	**137172**

16-2 续表 continued

单位：万美元 (10 000 USD)

国别(地区)	Country (region)	2022年进出口总额 Total Value of Imports and Exports in 2022	其中 of which 出口 Export	进口 Import	2021年进出口总额 Total Value of Imports and Exports in 2021	其中 of which 出口 Export	进口 Import
比利时	Belgium	9998	9043	955	10419	9624	795
英国	United Kingdom	35402	30351	5052	41315	36404	4910
德国	Germany	94358	49407	44951	102427	52244	50184
法国	France	24474	20501	3973	26098	20211	5888
意大利	Italy	26050	21805	4245	24316	18013	6304
荷兰	Netherlands	32801	29101	3700	33880	24602	9279
西班牙	Spain	18891	16576	2315	25269	18696	6573
芬兰	Finland	4014	2308	1706	3133	2015	1118
瑞典	Sweden	8315	3036	5279	8670	2630	6040
瑞士	Switzerland	10125	1679	8446	8346	1818	6528
俄罗斯	Russia	92228	76742	15487	81821	71166	10655
拉丁美洲	**Latin America**	**329536**	**154963**	**174574**	**299353**	**119216**	**180138**
阿根廷	Argentina	21820	8064	13756	14424	7659	6765
巴西	Brazil	142368	38455	103913	137045	32170	104875
智利	Chile	34206	12725	21481	52816	11833	40984
墨西哥	Mexico	39659	38919	741	21223	20002	1221
北美洲	**North America**	**331678**	**240222**	**91456**	**302882**	**218852**	**84031**
加拿大	Canada	73413	56067	17346	56433	38694	17739
美国	United States	253150	184135	69015	242830	180130	62700
大洋洲	**Oceanic**	**222844**	**80970**	**141873**	**248095**	**45535**	**202561**
澳大利亚	Australia	200519	72969	127550	224624	37561	187063
新西兰	New Zealand	18514	4191	14323	19696	4459	15238

16-3 海关进出口商品分类金额
International Trade in Goods by HS Section and Division of Customs

单位：万美元 (10 000 USD)

商品分类	Commodity (by HS Section and Division)	2022年 出口 Export	2022年 进口 Import	2021年 出口 Export	2021年 进口 Import
总　额	**Total**	**2112951**	**1157632**	**1818852**	**1184182**
活动物；动物产品	**Live Animals; Animal Products**	**1146**	**118455**		
活动物	Live Animals				
肉及食用杂碎	Meat and Edible Met Offal		87568		65057
鱼、甲壳动物、软体动物及其他水生无脊椎动物	Fish and Crustacean,Mollusc and Other Aquatic Invertebrates	10	24856		17161
乳品；蛋品；天然蜂蜜；其他食用动物产品	Dairy Produce; Birds' Eggs; Natural Honey; Edible Products of Animal Origin, not Elsewhere Specified or Included	104	5626		
其他动物产品	Products of Animal Origin, not Elsewhere Specified or Included	1032	404	1169	131
植物产品	**Vegetables Products**	**58457**	**23865**		
活树及其他活植物；鳞茎、根及类似品；插花及装饰用簇叶	Live Tree and Other Plants; Bulbs, Roots and the Like; Cut Flowers and Ornamental Foliage	50	49		
食用蔬菜、根及块茎	Edible Vegetables and Certain Roots and Tubers	31568	97	35467	150
食用水果及坚果；柑桔属水果或甜瓜的果皮	Edible Fruit and Nuts; Peel of Citrus Fruit or Melons	18313	166	19806	188
咖啡、茶、马黛茶及调味香料	Coffee, Tea, Mate and Spices	8159	2659	14164	3213
谷　物	Cereals		2928		4247
制粉工业产品；麦芽；淀粉、菊粉；面筋	Products of The Milling Industry; Malt; Starches; Inulin; Wheat Gluten		3374		
含油子仁及果实；杂项子仁及果实；工业用或药用植物；稻草、秸秆及饲料	Oil Seeds and Oleaginous Fruits; Miscellaneous Grains, Seeds and Fruit; Industrial or Medicinal Plants; Straw and Fodder	234	14551		
虫胶；树胶、树脂及其他植物液、汁	Lac; Gums, Resins And Other Vegetables Saps and Extracts	90	27	64	33
编结用植物材料；其他植物产品	Vegetables Plaiting Materials; Vegetables Products Not Elsewhere Specified or Included	42	15		
动、植物油、脂及其分解产品；精制的食用油脂；动、植物蜡	**Animal or Vegetables Fats and Oils and their Cleavage Products; Prepared Edible Fats; Animal or Vegetables Waxes**	**3424**	**1196**	**22**	**1746**
动、植物油、脂及其分解产品；精制的食用油脂；动、植物蜡	Animal or Vegetables Fats and Oils and their Cleavage Products; Prepared Edible Fats; Animal or Vegetables Waxes	3424	1196	22	1746
食品；饮料、酒及醋；烟草、烟草及烟草用品的制品	**Prepared Foodstuffs; Beverages, Spirits And Vinegar; Tobacco and Manufactured Tobacco Substitutes**	**33317**	**5221**		
肉、鱼、甲壳动物、软体动物及其他水生无脊椎动物的制品	Preparations of Meat,of Fish or of Crustaceans,Molluscs or other Aquatic Invertebrates	285	173		
糖及糖食	Sugars and Sugar Confectionery	602	2865	388	524
可可及可可制品	Cocoa and Cocoa Preparations	70	100	31	121

16–3 续表 1 continued 1

单位：万美元 (10 000 USD)

商品分类	Commodity (by HS Section and Division)	2022年 出口 Export	2022年 进口 Import	2021年 出口 Export	2021年 进口 Import
谷物、粮食粉、淀粉或乳的制品；糕饼点心	Preparations of Cereals, Flour, Starch or Milk; Pastry-Cooks' Products	4252	9	3585	22
蔬菜、水果、坚果或植物其他部分的制品	Preparations of Vegetables, Fruit, Nuts or Other Parts of Plants	18868	81	19969	785
杂项食品	Miscellaneous Edible Preparations	3580	388	2651	611
饮料、酒及醋	Beverages, Spirits and Vinegar	1234	774	34	1923
食品工业的残渣及废料；配制的动物饲料	Residues and Waste from The Food Industries; Prepared Animal Fodder	733	833	833	124
烟草、烟草及烟草代用品的制品	Tobacco and Manufactured Tobacco Substitutes	3694			
矿产品	**Mineral Products**	**2951**	**292428**		
盐；硫磺；泥土及石料；石膏料、石灰及水泥	Salt; Sulphur; Earths and Stone; Plastering Materials, Lime and Cement	223	1398	583	1453
矿砂、矿渣及矿灰	Ores, Slag and Ash	1	197692	2	295918
矿物燃料、矿物油及其蒸馏产品；沥青物质；矿物蜡	Mineral Fuels, Mineral Oils and Products of Their Distillation; Bituminous Substances; Mineral Waxes	2727	93338	110	17841
化学工业及其相关工业的产品	**Products of The Chemical or Industries Allied**	**186921**	**18281**		
无机化学品；贵金属、稀土金属、放射性元素及其同位素的有机及无机化合物	Inorganic Chemicals; Organic or Inorganic Compounds of Precious Metals, of Rare-Earth	9987	802	5927	487
有机化学品	Organic Chemicals	89405	6775	75904	3247
药品	Pharmaceutical Products	35886	1382	29431	1505
肥料	Fertilizers	7083		1061	
鞣料浸膏及染料浸膏；鞣酸及其衍生物；染料、颜料及其他着色料;油漆及清漆;油灰及其他类似胶粘剂；墨水、油墨	Tanning or Dyeing Extracts; Tannins and Their Derivatives; Dyes, Pigments and Other Colouring Matter; Paints and Varnishes; Putty and Other Mastics; Inks	14865	548	19323	618
精油及香膏；芳香料制品及化妆盥洗品	Essential Oils and Retinoid; Perfumery, Cosmetic or Toilet Preparations	930	2076	854	245
肥皂、有机表面活性剂、洗涤剂、润滑剂、人造蜡、调制蜡、光洁剂、蜡烛及类似品、塑型用膏、“牙科 用蜡”及牙科用熟石膏制剂	Soap,Organic Surface-Active Agents,Washing Preparations, Lubricating Preparations, Artificial Waxes, Prepared Waxes, Polishing or Scouring Preparations, Candles and Similar Articles, Modelling Pastes, "Dental Waxes" And Dental Preparations With a Basis of Plast	1853	622	1371	489
蛋白类物质；改性淀粉；胶；酶	Albuminoidal Substances; Modified Starches; Glues; Enzymes	1962	1097	1809	1322
炸药；烟火制品；火柴；引火合金；易燃材料制品	Explosives; Pyrotechnic Products; Matches; Pyrophoric Alloys; Certain Combustible Preparations				
照相及电影用品	Photographic or Cinematographic Goods	159	1695	96	384
杂项化学产品	Miscellaneous Chemical Products	24790	3282	18006	5007
塑料及其制品；橡胶及其制品	**Plastics and Articles Thereof Rubber and Articles Thereof**	**91503**	**27957**		
塑料及其制品	Plastics and Articles Thereof	82164	23007	68832	23052
橡胶及其制品	Rubber and Articles Thereof	9339	4950	9084	4362

16-3 续表 2 continued 2

单位：万美元 (10 000 USD)

商品分类	Commodity (by HS Section and Division)	2022年		2021年	
		出口 Export	进口 Import	出口 Export	进口 Import
生皮、皮革、毛皮及其制品；鞍具及挽具；旅行用品、手提包及类似容器、动物肠线(蚕胶丝除外)制品	**Raw Hides and Skins, Leather, Fur Skins and Articles Thereof; Saddlery and Harness; Travel Goods, Handbags and Similar Containers; Articles of Animal Gut (Other Than Silk-Worm Gut)**	**21345**	**407**		
生皮(毛皮除外)及皮革	Raw Hides and Skins(Other Than Fur Skins) and Leather	79	371	72	118
皮革制品；鞍具及挽具；旅行用品、手提包及类似容器；动物肠线(蚕胶丝除外)制品	Articles of Leather; Saddlery and Harness; Travel Goods, Handbags and Similar Containers; Articles of Animal Gut (Other Than Silk-Worm Gut)	21193	36	17592	36
毛皮、人造毛皮及其制品	Fur Skins and Artificial Fur; Manufactures Thereof	73		2239	
木及木制品；木炭；软木及软木制品；稻草、秸秆、针茅或其他编结材料制品；篮筐及柳条编结品	**Wood and Articles of Wood; Wood Charcoal;Cork and Articles of Cork; Manufactures of Straw, of Esparto or of Other Plaiting Materials; Basket Ware and Wickerwork**	**9306**	**4853**		
木及木制品；木炭	Wood and Articles of Wood; Wood Charcoal	6914	4853	8172	11590
软木及软木制品	Cork and Articles of Cork	14		11	
稻草、秸秆、针茅或其他编结材料制品；篮筐及柳条编结品	Manufactures of Straw, of Esparto or of Other Plaiting Materials; Basket Ware and Wickerwork	2378		2821	
木浆及其他纤维状纤维素浆；回收(废碎)纸或纸板；纸、纸板及其制品	**Pulp of Wood or of Other Fibrous Cellulosic Material; Waste and Scrap of Paper or Paperboard; Paper and Paperboard and Articles Thereof**	**16353**	**42659**		
木浆及其他纤维状纤维素浆；回收(废碎)纸或纸板	Pulp of Wood or of Other Fibrous Cellulosic Material; Waste and Scrap of Paper or Paperboard	129	39187	43	43197
纸及纸板；纸浆、纸或纸板制品	Paper and Paperboard; Articles of Paper Pulp, of Paper or Paperboard	14759	3167	12505	4962
书籍、报纸、印刷图画及其他印刷品；手稿、打字稿及设计图纸	Printed Books, Newspapers, Pictures and Other Products of The Printing Industry; Manuscripts, Typescripts and Plans	1464	305	1087	154
纺织原料及纺织制品	**Textiles and Textile Articles**	**118376**	**6225**		
蚕丝	Silk	18		20	
羊毛、动物细毛或粗毛；马毛纱线及其机织物	Wool, Fine or Coarse Animal Hair;Horsehair Yarn and Woven Fabric	3	126	18	33
棉花	Cotton	2537	4544	4968	2157
其他植物纺织纤维；纸纱线及其机织物	Other Vegetables Textile Fibres; Paper Yarn and Woven Fabrics of Paper Yarn	25		48	1
化学纤维长丝	Man-Made Filaments	4369	364	5406	262
化学纤维短纤	Man-Made Short Fibres	10894	509	9142	547
絮胎、毡呢及无纺织物；特种纱线；线、绳、索、缆及其制品	Wadding, Felt and Nonwoven; Special Yarns; Twine, Cordage, Ropes and Cables and Articles Thereof	8201	205	7648	381
地毯及纺织材料的其他铺地制品	Carpets and Other Textile Floor Coverings	4206	32	4415	42
特种机织物；簇绒织物；花边；装饰毯；装饰带；刺绣品	Special Woven Fabrics; Tufted Textile Fabrics; Lace; Tapestries; Trimmings; Embroidery	2187	45	1759	75
浸渍、涂布、包覆或层压的纺织物；工业用纺织制品	Impregnated, Coated, Covered or Laminated Textile Fabrics; Textile Articles of a Kind Suitable for Industrial Use	1342	68	1504	57

16–3 续表 3 continued 3

单位：万美元 (10 000 USD)

商品分类	Commodity (by HS Section and Division)	2022年		2021年	
		出口 Export	进口 Import	出口 Export	进口 Import
针织物或钩编织物	Knitted or Crocheted Fabrics	956	109	1143	86
针织或钩编的服装及衣着附件	Articles of Apparel and Clothing Accessories, Knitted or Crocheted	33056	21	35505	32
非针织或非钩编的服装及衣着附件	Articles of Apparel and Clothing Accessories, not Knitted or Crocheted	32686	105	46225	160
其他纺织制成品；成套物品；旧衣着及旧纺织品；碎织物	Other Made Up Textile Articles; Sets; Worn Clothing And Worn Textile Articles; Rags Articles; Rags	17896	98	22067	51
鞋、帽、伞、杖、鞭及其零件；已加工的羽毛及其制品；人造花；人发制品	**Footwear, Headgear, Umbrellas, Sun Umbrellas, Walking-Sticks, Seat-Sticks, Whips, Riding-Crops and Parts Thereof; Prepared Feathers and Articles Made Therewith; Artificial Flowers; Articles of Human Hair**	**19379**	**52**		
鞋靴、护腿和类似品及其零件	Footwear, Gaiters and The Like; Parts of Such Articles	10104	42	10674	86
帽类及其零件	Headgear and Parts Thereof	1575	9		
雨伞、阳伞、手杖、鞭子、马鞭及其零件	Umbrellas, Sun Umbrellas, Walking-Sticks, Seat-Sticks, Whips, Riding-Crops And Parts Thereof	523		335	1
已加工羽毛、羽绒及其制品；人造花；人发制品	Prepared Feathers and Down and Articles Made of Feathers or of Down; Artificial Flowers; Articles of Human Hair	7177		9727	
石料、石膏、水泥、石棉、云母及类似材料的制品；陶瓷产品；玻璃及其制品	**Articles of Stone, Plaster, Cement, Asbestos, Mica or Similar Materials; Ceramic Products; Glass and Glassware**	**52598**	**1629**		
石料、石膏、水泥、石棉、云母及类似材料的制品	Articles of Stone, Plaster, Cement, Asbestos, Mica or Similar Materials	14654	124	10493	188
陶瓷产品	Ceramic Products	15246	411	11429	2022
玻璃及其制品	Glass and Glassware	22698	1094	24381	1151
天然或养殖珍珠、宝石或半宝石、贵金属、包贵金属及其制品；仿首饰；硬币	**Natural or Cultured Pearls, Precious or Semi-Precious Stones, Precious Metals, Metals Clad With Precious Metal and Stones, Precious Metals, Metals Clad With Precious Metal and Articles Thereof; Imitation Jewellery; Coin**	**7786**	**35**	**8330**	**90**
天然或养殖珍珠、宝石或半宝石、贵金属、包贵金属及其制品；仿首饰；硬币	Natural or Cultured Pearls, Precious or Semi-Precious Stones, Precious Metals, Metals Clad With Precious Metal and Stones, Precious Metals, Metals Clad With Precious Metal and Articles Thereof; Imitation Jewellery; Coin	7786	35	8330	90
贱金属及其制品	**Base Metals and Articles of Base Metal**	**245747**	**28446**	**213947**	**46916**
钢　　铁	Iron and Steel	81691	1284	70726	524
钢铁制品	Articles of Iron or Steel	123651	2843	107645	2710
铜及其制品	Copper and Articles Thereof	3658	21010	3897	36398
镍及其制品	Nickel and Articles Thereof	43	49	37	1161
铝及其制品	Aluminium and Articles Thereof	15832	2559	15173	4612
铅及其制品	Lead and Articles Thereof		4	24	1
锌及其制品	Zinc and Articles Thereof	72	27	102	32
锡及其制品	Tin and Articles Thereof	1		2	

16-3 续表 4 continued 4

单位：万美元 (10 000 USD)

商品分类	Commodity (by HS Section and Division)	2022年		2021年	
		出口 Export	进口 Import	出口 Export	进口 Import
其他贱金属、金属陶瓷及其制品	Other Base Metals; Cermets; Articles Thereof	150	214	251	261
贱金属工具、器具、利口器、餐匙、餐叉及其零件	Tools, Implements, Cutlery, Spoons and Forks, of Base Metal; Parts Thereof of Base Metal	10164	208	8060	963
贱金属杂项制品	Miscellaneous Articles of Base Metal	10485	249	8030	254
机器、机械器具、电气设备及其零件；录音机及放声机、电视图像、声音的录制和重放设备及其零件、附件	**Machinery and Mechanical Appliances; Electrical Equipment; Parts Thereof; Sound Recorders and Reproducers, Television Image and Sound Recorders and Reproducers; and Parts and Accessories of Recorders and Reproducers; and Parts and Accessories of Such Artic**	**702529**	**515878**	**573016**	**519589**
核反应堆、锅炉、机器、机械器具及其零件	Nuclear Reactors, Boilers, Machinery and Mechanical Appliances; Parts Thereof	379772	320965	343994	343127
电机、电气设备及其零件；录音机及放声机、电视图像、声音的录制和重放设备及其零件、附件	Electrical Machinery and Equipment and Parts Thereof; Sound Recorders and Reproducers, Television Image and Sound Recorders and Reproducers, and Parts and Accessories of Such Articles	322756	194913	229023	176462
车辆、航空器、船舶及有关运输设备	**Vehicles, Aircraft, Vessels And Associated Transport Equipment**	**377455**	**7369**	**302843**	**16008**
铁道及电车道机车、车辆及其零件；铁道及电车道轨道固定装置及其零件、附件；各种机械(包括电动机械)交通信号设备	Railway or Tramway Locomotives, Rolling-Stock and Parts Thereof; Railway or Tramway Track Fixtures And Fittings and Parts Thereof; Mechanical(Including Electro-Mechanical) Traffic Signalling Equipment of All Kinds	5267	509	796	356
车辆及其零件、附件，但铁道及电车道车辆除外	Vehicles Other Than Railway or Tramway Rolling-Stock, and Parts and Accessories Thereof	368757	1071	296777	1850
航空器、航空器及其零件	Aircraft, Spacecraft, and Parts Thereof	2017	5691	4160	13771
船舶及浮动结构体	Ships, Boats and Floating Structures	1414	98	1111	31
光学、照相、电影、计量、检验、医疗或外科用仪器及设备、精密仪器及设备；钟表；乐器；上述物品的零件、附件	**Optical, Photographic, Cinematographic, Measuring, Checking, Precision, Medical or Surgical Instruments and Apparatus; Clocks And Watches; Musical Instruments; Parts and Accessories Thereof**	**37057**	**61385**	**30400**	**59741**
光学、照相、计量、检验、医疗或外科用仪器及设备、精密仪器及设备；上述物品的零件、附件	Optical, Photographic, Cinematographic, Measuring, Checking, Precision Medical or Surgical Instruments and Apparatus; Parts and Accessories Thereof	32496	61374	26470	59725
钟表及其零件	Clocks and Watches and Parts Thereof	2959	12	2435	15
乐器及其零件、附件	Musical Instruments; Parts and Accessories of Such Articles	1601		1495	1
武器、弹药及其零件、附件	**Arms and Ammunition; Parts and Accessories Thereof**	**1**		**1**	**405**
武器、弹药及其零件、附件	Arms and Ammunition; Parts and Accessories Thereof	1		1	405
杂项制品	**Miscellaneous Manufactured Articles**	**92672**	**618**	**92063**	**99**
家具；寝具、褥垫、弹簧床垫、软坐垫及类似的填充制品；	Furniture; Bedding, Mattresses, Mattress Supports, Cushions and Similar Stuffed Furnishings	40837	570	44661	30
玩具、游戏品、运动用品及其零件、附件	Toys, Games and Sports Requisites; Parts and Accessories Thereof	40609	17	39687	69
杂项制品	Miscellaneous Manufactured Articles	11227	31	7715	
艺术品、收藏品及古物	**Works of Art, Collectors' Pieces and Antiques**	**37**	**73**	**33**	
特殊交易品及未分类商品	**Commodities and Transactions not Classified According to Kind**	**30991**	**598**	**10464**	**950**

16-4 按企业性质分海关进出口商品总额(2022年)
International Trade in Goods of Customs by Type of trade(2022)

单位：万美元

指标	Item	合计 Total	国有企业 State-owned Enterprises
进口商品总额	**Total Value of Imports**	**1157632**	**518894**
一般贸易	General Trade	943025	454317
来料加工装配贸易	Processing and Assembling Trade with Sent Materials	17401	
进料加工贸易	Processing Trade with Imported Materials	27586	1911
租赁贸易	Leasing Trade		
海关特殊监管区域进口设备	Import of Equipment in Special Customs Supervision Area	1523	
海关特殊监管区域物流货物	Logistics Freight of Equipment in Special Customs Supervision Area		
投资设备	Investment Goods		
保税监管场所进出境货物	Bonded Supervision Entry and Exit Goods	165378	63332
国际无偿援助和捐赠物资	International Aid and Material Donations		
其他贸易	Others	1994	53
出口商品总值	**Total Value of Exports**	**2112951**	**83282**
一般贸易	General Trade	1907650	48954
国际无偿援助和捐赠物资	International Aid and Material Donations	563	207
来料加工装配贸易	Processing and Assembling Trade with Sent Materials	20451	
进料加工贸易	Processing Trade with Imported Materials	65819	9540
对外承包工程出口货物	Export of Contracted projects	28587	8178
保税监管场所进出境货物	Bonded Supervision Entry and Exit Goods	86191	16361
海关特殊监管区域物流货物	Logistics Freight of Equipment in Special Customs Supervision Area		
其他贸易	Others	3608	42

(10 000 USD)

外商投资企业 Foreign Funded Enterprises				集体企业 Collective-owned Enterprises	其他 Others
小计 Total	中外合作 Cooperation Enterprises	中外合资 Joint-venture Enterprises	外商独资 Enterprises with Sole Fund		
108783	**23647**		**85090**	**52925**	**537**
58990	9644		49346	529245	
16978	37		16941		
18209	1851		16358		
			1523		
576			576		
11778	11696		81		
685	418		267		
478062	**123243**	**996**	**353823**	**55582**	**2158**
403769	102383	996	300390	55545	
19704	1076		18628		
32229	10551		21678	1	
				36	
21477	9019		12458		
883	214		669		

16–5 历年海关进出口总额
Total Imports and Exports of Customs in Major Years

单位：万美元 (10 000 USD)

年份 Year	进出口总额 Total Value of Imports and Exports	进口总额 Total Value of Imports	出口总额 Total Value of Exports
1993	27446	21371	6075
1994	41746	23579	18167
1995	66587	29812	36775
1996	91347	48193	43154
1997	104230	52862	51368
1998	79943	45096	34847
1999	96125	60199	35926
2000	143935	86827	57108
2001	150143	90746	59397
2002	149264	79755	69509
2003	201554	117980	83545
2004	304678	167373	137305
2005	376213	198370	177843
2006	438930	194981	243949
2007	621804	278277	343527
2008	802699	342979	459720
2009	565704	260998	304706
2010	743776	338888	404888
2011	1041422	436966	604456
2012	913286	341844	571442
2013	957442	409126	548316
2014	1048867	442950	605917
2015	911424	311763	599661
2016	1086259	352229	734030
2017	1130449	379887	750562
2018	1318209	463119	855090
2019	1630123	695064	935059
2020	1998749	909323	1089426
2021	3003034	1184182	1818852
2022	3270583	1157632	2112951

16–6 利用外资情况
Utilization of Foreign Capital

单位：万美元 (10 000 USD)

指标	Item	2018年	2019年	2020年	2021年	2022年
新批外商投资企业个数(个)	**Newly Established Foreign Investment Enterprises(unit)**	**239**	**228**	**203**	**330**	**251**
外商直接投资	Foreign Direct Investments	239	228	203	330	251
合同外资金额	**Total Amount of Contracted Foreign Capita**	**556119**	**683441**	**585244**	**968530**	**784185**
外商直接投资	Foreign Direct Investments	556119	683441	585244	968530	784185
实际使用外资	**Total Amount of Foreign Investment Actually Utilized**	**272847**	**224249**	**192456**	**265840**	**313738**
外商直接投资	Foreign Direct Investments	272847	224249	192456	265840	313738

16–7 对外经济技术合作
Economic Cooperation with Foreign Countries or Regions

单位：万美元 (10 000 USD)

指标	Item	2018年	2019年	2020年	2021年	2022年
对外承包和劳务合作合同金额	**Contracted Value of Contracted Projects and Labour Services**	**565706**	**573114**	**439945**	**660562**	**488850**
对外承包	Contracted Projects	565706	573114	439945	660562	488850
对外承包和劳务合作营业额	**Value of Turnover of Contracted Projects and Labour Services**	**408427**	**408820**	**427206**	**410022**	**409203**
对外承包	Contracted Projects	408427	408820	427206	410022	409203
外派劳务人数(人)	**Dispatched Workers(person)**	**6586**	**8047**	**11996**	**8608**	**4489**
境外投资企业数(个)	**Number of Overseas Investment Enterprises(unit)**	**50**	**79**	**77**	**60**	**45**
中方实际投资额	**China Actual Investment**	**102434**	**110798**	**191321**	**174208**	**174978**

16-8 旅游住宿单位接待入境游客
Received Inbound Tourists by Hotels

指标	Item	2018年	2019年	2020年	2021年	2022年
入境游客人数(人次)	**Number of Inbound Tourists(person-time)**	**398721**	**456585**	**108524**		
外国人	Foreigners	247086	285071	90926		
#日本	Japan	23123	28653	2674		
菲律宾	Philippines	2901	3500	1446		
新加坡	Singapore	17503	18092	2729		
韩国	Republic of Korea	37432	41390	5536		
美国	United States	26325	29556	20623		
加拿大	Canada	6970	7859	1836		
英国	United Kingdom	11602	12910	7623		
德国	Germany	17706	19384	2557		
法国	France	8000	8893	1555		
意大利	Italy	5524	6069	583		
瑞士	Switzerland	1216	1348	156		
澳大利亚	Australia	10762	12422	3783		
新西兰	New Zealand	2078	2113	815		
港澳和台湾同胞	Chinese Compatriots from Hong Kong Macao and Taiwan Province	151635	171514	17700		
#台湾同胞	Chinese Compatriots from Taiwan Province	72667	87086	4355		
入境游客人天数(人天)	**Number of Days on Inbound Tourists(person-day)**	**1086701**	**1276852**	**265436**		
外国人	Foreigners	683730	806837	187665		
港澳和台湾同胞	Chinese Compatriots from Hong Kong Macao and Taiwan Province	402971	959122	77773		
#台湾同胞	Chinese Compatriots from Taiwan Province	265047	317730	45873		
旅游外汇收入(亿美元)	**Foreign Exchange Income of Tourism(100 million USD)**	**2.23**	**2.75**	**0.33**		
#商品性收入	Commercial Income	0.6	0.7	0.08		
附:平均每天来济国际旅游人数(人次)	Number of Tourists Per Day(person-time)	1092	1251	296.51		
星级宾馆客房出租率(%)	Star Hotel Room Rate(%)	63.4	62.0	47.51	50.57	42.69

注：1.2018年起接待入境游客包含了过夜游客和一日游游客。
2.根据省文化和旅游厅统一安排，2021年起暂停测算、公布和使用入境旅游数据。

Notes:1.Starting in 2018, Inbound Tourists Include Overnight Visitors and Day-trippers.
2.According to the unified arrangement of the Provincial Department of Culture and Tourism, the measurement, publication and use of inbound tourism data have been suspended since 2021.

16-9 济南与国外结成友好城市一览表(2022年末)
Foreign Friendly Cities of Jinan(End of 2022)

国别	Country	城市	City	缔结日期 Day
日本	Japan	和歌山市(和歌山县首府)	Wakayama	1983.01.14
英国	United Kingdom	考文垂市(英国汽车工业故乡，制造业中心之一)	Coventry	1983.10.03
美国	United States	萨克拉门托市(加利福尼亚州首府)	Sacramento	1985.05.29
日本	Japan	山口市(山口县首府)	Yamaguchi	1985.09.20
加拿大	Canada	里贾纳市(萨斯喀彻温省省会)	Regina	1987.08.10
巴布亚新几内亚	Papua New Guinea	莫尔斯比港(巴布亚新几内亚首都)	Port Moresby	1988.09.28
韩国	Republic of Korea	水原市(京畿道首府)	Suwon Special	1993.10.27
俄罗斯	Russia	下诺夫哥罗德市(下诺夫哥罗德州首府)	Nizhny novgorod	1994.09.25
芬兰	Finland	万达市(欧洲机场城市、芬兰第四大城市)	Vantaa	2001.08.27
法国	France	雷恩市(布列塔尼大区首府)	Rennes	2002.07.17
澳大利亚	Australia	郡德勒普市(西澳洲新兴教育科技中心)	Joondalup	2004.09.04
德国	Germany	奥格斯堡市(施瓦本地区首府)	Augsburg	2004.10.10
乌克兰	Ukraine	哈尔科夫市(哈尔科夫州首府)	Kharkiv	2007.05.23
以色列	Israel	卡法萨巴市(沙龙地区中心城市)	Kfar Saba	2009.05.11
白俄罗斯	Belarus	维捷布斯克市(维捷布斯克州首府)	Vitebsk	2009.09.20
佛得角	Cape Verde	普拉亚市(佛得角首都)	Praia	2009.09.22
巴西	Brazil	波多韦柳市(朗多尼亚州首府)	Porto Velho	2011.10.13
土耳其	Türkiye	马尔马里斯市(地中海沿岸港口城市和旅游胜地)	Marmaris	2011.10.21
白俄罗斯	Belarus	明斯克市苏维埃区 (白俄罗斯首都明斯克市历史最悠久的区之一)	Soviet region of Minsk	2012.08.03
印度尼西亚	Indonesia	徐图利祖市(东爪哇省泗水市机场城市、新兴经济城市)	Sidoarjo	2012.09.21
保加利亚	Bulgaria	卡赞勒格市(保加利亚玫瑰精油生产中心)	Kazanlak	2013.08.29
墨西哥	Mexico	萨博潘市(哈利斯科州经济首府)	Zapopan	2014.04.18
意大利	Italy	奇维塔韦基亚市(欧洲第三大客运港)	Civitavecchia	2015.08.28
格鲁吉亚	Georgia	库塔伊西市(格鲁吉亚西部历史名城和第二大工业城市)	Kutaisi	2016.05.26
印度	India	那格浦尔市(印度地理中心城市、马哈拉施特拉邦第二首府)	Nagpur	2017.12.05
埃塞俄比亚	Ethiopia	阿尔巴门奇市(格穆戈法省首府、泉水之城)	Arba Minch	2018.09.06
斯洛文尼亚	Slovenia	马里博尔(斯洛文尼亚第二大城市、欧洲足球强市)	Maribor	2019.09.26

16-10 济南市与各友好城市交流
Jinan City Exchanges with Sister Cities

单位：批数、人次 (batch.person-time)

指标	Item	2018年	2019年	2020年	2021年	2022年
接待来访团组	**Receive Visitors**					
批　数	Batch	206	-	-	-	-
人　次	Number	1730	-	-	-	-

注：本表指标为“–”的，部门相关统计制度中已经不在进行统计。
Note: The indicator “-” in this table means statistics are no longer in the relevant statistical system of the department.

主要统计指标解释

海关进出口商品总额 指实际进出我国关境的货物总金额。包括对外贸易实际进出口货物，来料加工装配进出口货物，国家间、联合国及国际组织无偿援助物资和赠送品，华侨、港澳台同胞和外籍华人捐赠品，租赁期满归承租人所有的租赁货物，进料加工进出口货物，边境地方贸易及边境地区小额贸易进出口货物，中外合资企业、中外合作经营企业、外商独资经营企业进出口货物和公用物品，到、离岸价格在规定限额以上的进出口货样和广告品(无商业价值、无使用价值和免费提供出口的除外)，从保税仓库提取在中国境内销售的进口货物，以及其他进出口货物。该指标可以观察一个国家在货物贸易方面的总规模。我国规定出口货物按离岸价格统计，进口货物按到岸价格统计。

外商投资 是指国外及港澳台地区的法人和自然人在中国大陆地区以现金、实物、无形资产、股权等方式进行投资。其中，外商直接投资是指国外及港澳台地区投资者在非上市公司中的全部投资及在单个外国投资者所占股权比例不低于10%的上市公司中的投资。

对外承包工程 根据《对外承包工程管理条例》，对外承包工程是指中国的企业或者其他单位承包境外建设工程项目的活动。

对外劳务合作 指组织劳务人员赴其他国家或地区为国外的企业或机构工作的经营性活动。

入境游客 指报告期内来中国（大陆）观光、度假、探亲访友、就医疗养、购物、参加会议或从事经济、文化、体育、宗教活动的外国人、港澳台同胞等游客（即入境旅游人数）。统计时，入境游客按每入境一次统计1人次。入境游客包括入境过夜游客和入境一日游游客。

国际旅游收入 指入境游客在中国（大陆）境内旅行、游览过程中用于交通、参观游览、住宿、餐饮、购物、娱乐等全部花费。

Explanatory Notes on Main Statistical Indicators

Import and Export of Goods refer to the value of commodities actually imported or exported across the border of China. They include the actual imports and exports through foreign trade, imported and exported goods under the processing and assembling trades and materials, supplies and gifts as aid given gratis between governments and by the United Nations and other international organizations, and contributions donated by overseas Chinese, compatriots in Hong Kong and Macao and Chinese with foreign citizenship, leasing commodities owned by tenant at the expiration of leasing period, the imported and exported commodities processed with imported materials, commodities trading in border areas, the imported and exported commodities and articles for public use of the Sino-foreign joint ventures, cooperative enterprises and ventures with sole foreign investment. Also included are import or export of samples and advertising goods for which CIF or FOB value are beyond the permitted ceiling (excluding goods of no trading or use value and free commodities for export), imported goods sold in China from bonded warehouses and other imported or exported goods. The indicator of the total imports and exports at customs can be used to observe the total size of external trade in a country. In accordance with the stipulation of the Chinese government, exports are calculated at FOB, while imports are calculated at CIF.

Foreign Investment refers to investment in China by legal or natural persons of foreign countries and of Hong Kong, Macao and Taiwan, in the form of cash、physical assets、intangible assets and equity and others. Foreign direct investment refers to investment by investors from foreign countries and from Hong Kong, Macao and Taiwan in a non-listed company, or the investment of over 10 percent or more in a listed company.

Overseas Contracted Projects refer to activities of contracting overseas construction projects by Chinese enterprises or any other units, which are stipulated in the Regulations on Administration of Foreign Contracted Project.

Overseas Labour Services refer to operational activities of organizing labour force to go abroad providing services to foreign enterprises or agencies.

Overseas Visitor Arrivals refer to the number of tourists of foreigners, Chinese compatriots from Hong Kong, Macao and Taiwan who come to China (mainland) within the reference period for sight-seeing, vacation, visiting relatives, medical treatment, shopping, attending conference, or to engage in economic, cultural, sports and religious activities (namely the number of overseas visitor arrivals). In compiling statistics, each arrival is counted as one person-time. Overseas visitor arrivals includes inbound overnight tourists and one-day tourists.

Foreign Exchange Earnings from International Tourism refer to the total expenditure of overseas visitors during their stay in the mainland of China on transportation, sighting, accommodation, food, shopping and entertainment.

17

科技

SCIENCE AND TECHNOLOGY

17–1 科技综合情况
Basic Statistics on Scientific and Technological Activities

指标	Item	单位 Unit	2017年	2018年	2019年	2020年	2021年
R&D活动单位	R&D Activity Units	个(Unit)	964	821	1089	1209	1455
R&D人员全时当量	Full-time Equivalent of R&D Personnel	人年(man-years)	57506	59995	52153	53677.5	61894.1
R&D经费支出	Expenditure on R&D	万元(10 000 yuan)	1851538.7	2085980.1	2255264.6	2654629.1	3067048.7
#基础研究	Basic Research	万元(10 000 yuan)	152909.2	144105.1	173425.2	184501.6	267574.4
#应用研究	Applied Research	万元(10 000 yuan)	208526.4	246533.3	304343.7	414305.5	386592.1
#试验发展	Experimental Development	万元(10 000 yuan)	1490103.1	1695281.7	1777495.7	2055822.1	2412882.4
#日常性支出	Daily Expenditure	万元(10 000 yuan)	1636821.4	1843653.3	2010202.7	2373932.1	2788617.4
人员劳务费	Staff Service Fee	万元(10 000 yuan)	616187.2	763134.5	695510.6	864042.4	975737.2
#资产性支出	Capital Expenditure	万元(10 000 yuan)	214717.4	242326.8	233015.5	277874.7	278431.3
仪器设备	Instrument and Equipment	万元(10 000 yuan)	188836.8	236760.3	218192.1	263337.9	229617.0
R&D经费外部支出	External Expenditure on R&D	万元(10 000 yuan)	70569.2	79731.3	107132.1	218149.6	269409.6
科技成果情况	Statistics on S&T Results						
专利申请数	Number of Patent Applications	件(piece)	19645				
#发明专利申请数	Inventions	件(piece)	12027				
拥有发明专利数	Number of Invention Patents Owned	件(piece)	20059				
科技项目(课题)情况	Statistics on S&T Projects						
项目(课题)数	Number of Projects	项(item)	27666				
项目参加人员折合全时	Participants (Full-time Equivalent	人年(man-years)	46457.1				

注：1.2018年数据为行政区划调整前口径，以下各表同。
2. “科技成果情况”2018年起，省统计局未反馈相关数据。

Notes: 1. Data used in 2018 is the statistical scale before the adjustment of administrative division (the same below).
2."Statistics on S&T Results" since 2018, the Shandong provincial Bureau of Statistics has not provided relevant data.

17-2 科技投入情况(2021年)
Basic Statistics on Science and Technology Investment(2021)

指标	Item	单位 Unit	合计 Total	科研机构 Research Institutions	高等院校 Higher Education Institutions	规模以上工业 Industrial Enterprises Above Designated Size	其他 Others
有R&D活动单位数	**Number of Enterprises with R&D Activities**	**个(unit)**	**1455**	**74**	**71**	**979**	**331**
R&D人员	**R&D Personnel**	**人(Person)**	**99150**	**6735**	**31345**	**43040**	**18030**
#研究人员	Research Personnel	人(Person)	55900	4797	26829	15314	8960
R&D人员折合全时当量	**Full-time Equivalent of R&D Personnel**	**人年(man-years)**	**61894**	**6021**	**15531**	**28712**	**11630**
基础研究	Basic Research	人年(man-years)	10273	1304	8791	142	36
应用研究	Applied Research	人年(man-years)	10343	1535	6205	1260	1343
试验发展	Experimental Development	人年(man-years)	41279	3182	534	27309	10254
R&D经费支出	**Expenditure on R&D**	**万元(10 000 yuan)**	**3067049**	**319857**	**403039**	**1704514**	**639639**
基础研究	Basic Research	万元(10 000 yuan)	267574	74161	165673	4960	22781
应用研究	Applied Research	万元(10 000 yuan)	386592	70509	206383	47377	62322
试验发展	Experimental Development	万元(10 000 yuan)	2412882	175187	30982	1652177	554537
日常性支出	**Routine Expenses**	**万元(10 000 yuan)**	**2788617**	**193479**	**353549**	**1630751**	**610838**
#人员劳务费	Labor Cost	万元(10 000 yuan)	975737	110891	101947	414755	348144
资产性支出	**Assets Expenditure**	**万元(10 000 yuan)**	**278431**	**126378**	**49489**	**73763**	**28802**
#仪器和设备	Instrument and Equipment	万元(10 000 yuan)	229617	88709	44530	68888	27490

17-3 规模以上工业企业科技活动情况(2021年)

Basic Statistics on Science and Technology Activities of Industrial Enterprises Above Designated Size(2021)

单位:个 (unit)

指标	Item	企业数 Number of Enterprises	#有R&D活动单位数 Number of Enterprises with R&D Activities	企业办科技机构数 Statistics on S&T Institutions
总计	**Total**	**2548**	**979**	**332**
按登记注册类型分	**By Status of Registration**			
内资企业	Domestic Invested Enterprises	2399	917	304
国有企业	State-owned Enterprises	38	9	2
集体企业	Collective-owned Enterprises	7	2	1
股份合作企业	Cooperative Enterprises	4	1	
联营企业	Joint Ownership Enterprises	2		
有限责任公司	Limited Liability Corporations	630	259	105
国有独资公司	State Sole-proprietorship Corporations	37	16	10
其他有限责任公司	Other Limited Liability Corporations	593	243	95
股份有限公司	Share-holding Corporations Ltd.	85	65	34
私营企业	Private Enterprises	1633	581	162
私营独资企业	Private Sole-proprietorship Enterprises	49	5	1
私营合伙企业	Private Partnership Enterprises	6	1	
私营有限责任公司	Private Limited Liability Corporations	1499	521	143
私营股份有限公司	Private Share-holding Corporations Ltd.	79	54	18
其他企业	Other Enterprises			
港、澳、台商投资企业	Enterprises with Funds from Hong Kong,Macao and Taiwan	59	18	9
合资经营企业	Joint-venture Enterprises	29	10	4
合作经营企业	Cooperative Enterprises	1		
独资经营企业	Sole-proprietorship Enterprises	27	7	5
投资股份有限公司	Share-holding Corporations Ltd.	1		
其他港澳台投资企业	Other Enterprises with Funds from Hong Kong, Macao and Taiwan	1	1	
外商投资企业	Foreign Funded Enterprises	90	44	19
中外合资经营企业	Joint-venture Enterprises	38	23	9
中外合作经营企业	Cooperative Enterprises	3	1	
外资企业	Sole-proprietorship Enterprises	44	16	9
外商投资股份有限公司	Share-holding Corporations Ltd. with Foreign Investment	5	4	1
其他外商投资企业	Other Foreign Funded Enterprises			
按工业行业大类分	**By Sector**			
煤炭开采和洗选业	Mining and Washing of Coal	3		
石油和天然气开采业	Extraction of Petroleum and Natural Gas	3		
黑色金属矿采选业	Mining and Processing of Ferrous Metal Ores	12	3	4
有色金属矿采选业	Mining and Processing of Non-Ferrous Metal Ores			
非金属矿采选业	Mining and Processing of Nonmetal Ores	10	1	
开采专业及辅助性活动	Professional and Support Activities for Mining			

17-3 续表 continued

单位:个 (unit)

指标	Item	企业数 Number of Enterprises	#有R&D活动单位数 Number of Enterprises with R&D Activities	企业办科技机构数 Statistics on S&T Institutions
其他采矿业	Mining of Other Ores			
农副食品加工业	Processing of Food from Agricultural Products	102	19	11
食品制造业	Manufacture of Foods	74	25	9
酒、饮料和精制茶制造业	Manufacture of Wine, Drinks and Refined Tea	20	4	2
烟草制品业	Manufacture of Tobacco	2	2	1
纺织业	Manufacture of Textile	50	17	3
纺织服装、服饰业	Manufacture of Textile Wearing Apparel and Finery	23	1	1
皮革、毛皮、羽毛及其制品和制鞋业	Manufacture of Leather, Fur, Feather & Its Products and Footwear	4	1	
木材加工和木、竹、藤、棕、草制品业	Processing of Timbers, Manufacture of Wood,Bamboo, Rattan, Palm, and Straw Products	11	3	
家具制造业	Manufacture of Furniture	15	1	
造纸和纸制品业	Manufacture of Paper and Paper Products	46	9	2
印刷和记录媒介复制业	Printing, Reproduction of Recording Media	43	14	5
文教、工美、体育和娱乐用品制造业	Manufacture of Culture, Education,Arts and crafts, Sport and Entertainment Goods	24	9	2
石油、煤炭及其他燃料加工业	Processing of Petroleum, Coal and Other Fuels	14	7	1
化学原料和化学制品制造业	Manufacture of Chemical Raw Material and Chemical Products	119	60	26
医药制造业	Manufacture of Medicines	73	49	29
化学纤维制造业	Manufacture of Chemical Fiber	10	6	3
橡胶和塑料制品业	Manufacture of Rubber and Plastic	68	20	6
非金属矿物制品业	Manufacture of Non-metallic Mineral Products	312	69	24
黑色金属冶炼和压延加工业	Manufacture and Processing of Ferrous Metals	44	14	6
有色金属冶炼和压延加工业	Manufacture & Processing of Non-ferrous Metals	37	16	4
金属制品业	Manufacture of Metal Products	283	83	29
通用设备制造业	Manufacture of General Purpose Machinery	300	148	38
专用设备制造业	Manufacture of Special Purpose Machinery	248	135	35
汽车制造业	Manufacture of Automotive	128	49	17
铁路、船舶、航空航天和其他运输设备制造业	Manufacture of Railroad,Marine,Aerospace and Other Transportation Equipment	26	12	4
电气机械和器材制造业	Manufacture of Electrical Machinery & Equipment	150	80	24
计算机、通信和其他电子设备制造业	Manufacture of Computer, Communications and Other Electronic Equipment	80	52	20
仪器仪表制造业	Manufacture of Measuring Instrument	81	55	21
其他制造业	Other Manufacture	6		
废弃资源综合利用业	Comprehensive Utilization of Waste	9	3	
金属制品、机械和设备修理业	Metal Products, Machinery and Equipment Repair Industry	6	2	1
电力、热力生产和供应业	Production and Supply of Electric Power and Heat Power	59	7	3
燃气生产和供应业	Production and Supply of Gas	32	1	
水的生产和供应业	Production and Supply of Water	21	2	1

17-4 规模以上工业企业技术改造及引进吸收(2021年)

Innovation and Resorb of Industrial Enterprises Above Designated Size(2021)

单位：万元 (10 000 yuan)

指标	Item	技术改造经费支出 Expenditure for Technical Renovation	引进国外技术经费支出 Expenditure for Acquisition of Foreign Technology	引进技术的消化吸收经费支出 Expenditure for Assimilation of Technology	购买国内技术经费支出 Expenditure for Purchase of Domestic Technology
总计	**Total**	**525790**	**80310**	**24**	**42779**
按登记注册类型分	**By Status of Registration**				
内资企业	Domestic Invested Enterprises	513002	71810	24	38138
国有企业	State-owned Enterprises	3847			
集体企业	Collective-owned Enterprises	3375			
股份合作企业	Cooperative Enterprises				
联营企业	Joint Ownership Enterprises				
有限责任公司	Limited Liability Corporations	225655	5185		18822
国有独资公司	State Sole-proprietorship Corporations	103467			
其他有限责任公司	Other Limited Liability Corporations	122189	5185		18822
股份有限公司	Share-holding Corporations Ltd.	137299	125	14	34
私营企业	Private Enterprises	142825	66501	10	19282
私营独资企业	Private Sole-proprietorship Enterprises	1234			
私营合伙企业	Private Partnership Enterprises				
私营有限责任公司	Private Limited Liability Corporations	86981	66501	10	19282
私营股份有限公司	Private Share-holding Corporations Ltd.	54611			
其他企业	Other Enterprises				
港、澳、台商投资企业	Enterprises with Funds from Hong Kong, Macao and Taiwan	9821	234		4234
合资经营企业	Joint-venture Enterprises	9237	234		4234
合作经营企业	Cooperative Enterprises				
独资经营企业	Sole-proprietorship Enterprises	584			
投资股份有限公司	Share-holding Corporations Ltd.				
其他港澳台投资企业	Other Enterprises with Funds from Hong Kong,Macao and Taiwan				
外商投资企业	Foreign Funded Enterprises	2968	8267		407
中外合资经营企业	Joint-venture Enterprises	2081	8267		5
中外合作经营企业	Cooperative Enterprises				
外资企业	Sole-proprietorship Enterprises	886			402
外商投资股份有限公司	Share-holding Corporations Ltd. with Foreign Investment				
其他外商投资企业	Other Foreign Funded Enterprises				
按工业行业大类分	**By Sector**				
煤炭开采和洗选业	Mining and Washing of Coal				
石油和天然气开采业	Extraction of Petroleum and Natural Gas				
黑色金属矿采选业	Mining and Processing of Ferrous Metal Ores	4108			
有色金属矿采选业	Mining and Processing of Non-Ferrous Metal Ores				
非金属矿采选业	Mining and Processing of Nonmetal Ores	463			
开采专业及辅助性活动	Professional and Support Activities for Mining				

17-4 续表 continued

单位：万元 (10 000 yuan)

指标	Item	技术改造经费支出 Expenditure for Technical Renovation	引进国外技术经费支出 Expenditure for Acquisition of Foreign Technology	引进技术的消化吸收经费支出 Expenditure for Assimilation of Technology	购买国内技术经费支出 Expenditure for Purchase of Domestic Technology
其他采矿业	Mining of Other Ores				
农副食品加工业	Processing of Food from Agricultural Products	326			104
食品制造业	Manufacture of Foods	2624			
酒、饮料和精制茶制造业	Manufacture of Wine, Drinks and Refined Tea	180			200
烟草制品业	Manufacture of Tobacco	97350			
纺织业	Manufacture of Textile	3916			
纺织服装、服饰业	Manufacture of Textile Wearing Apparel and Finery				
皮革、毛皮、羽毛及其制品和制鞋业	Manufacture of Leather, Fur, Feather & Its Products and Footwear				
木材加工和木、竹、藤、棕、草制品业	Processing of Timbers, Manufacture of Wood,Bamboo, Rattan, Palm, and Straw Products				
家具制造业	Manufacture of Furniture	8			5
造纸和纸制品业	Manufacture of Paper and Paper Products	230			
印刷和记录媒介复制业	Printing, Reproduction of Recording Media	3280			
文教、工美、体育和娱乐用品制造业	Manufacture of Culture, Education,Arts and crafts, Sport and Entertainment Goods	535			
石油、煤炭及其他燃料加工业	Processing of Petroleum, Coal and Other Fuels	34335			34
化学原料和化学制品制造业	Manufacture of Chemical Raw Material and Chemical Products	84473			
医药制造业	Manufacture of Medicines	74642	66734		25473
化学纤维制造业	Manufacture of Chemical Fiber	33			
橡胶和塑料制品业	Manufacture of Rubber and Plastic	2333			
非金属矿物制品业	Manufacture of Non-metallic Mineral Products	6464			
黑色金属冶炼和压延加工业	Manufacture and Processing of Ferrous Metals	108831			
有色金属冶炼和压延加工业	Manufacture & Processing of Non-ferrous Metals	2042			
金属制品业	Manufacture of Metal Products	8448			2
通用设备制造业	Manufacture of General Purpose Machinery	10805	125	14	402
专用设备制造业	Manufacture of Special Purpose Machinery	10580		10	26
汽车制造业	Manufacture of Automotive	10523			40
铁路、船舶、航空航天和其他运输设备制造业	Manufacture of Railroad,Marine,Aerospace and Other Transportation Equipment	3569	8754		2
电气机械和器材制造业	Manufacture of Electrical Machinery & Equipment	9863			
计算机、通信和其他电子设备制造业	Manufacture of Computer, Communications and Other Electronic Equipment	27896	4697		16424
仪器仪表制造业	Manufacture of Measuring Instrument	5226			53
其他制造业	Other Manufacture				
废弃资源综合利用业	Comprehensive Utilization of Waste				
金属制品、机械和设备修理业	Metal Products, Machinery and Equipment Repair Industry	2102			
电力、热力生产和供应业	Production and Supply of Electric Power and Heat Power	10197			15
燃气生产和供应业	Production and Supply of Gas				
水的生产和供应业	Production and Supply of Water	407			

17-5 规模以上工业企业技术资源(2021年)

Technical Resources of Industrial Enterprises Above Designated Size(2021)

指标	Item	R&D经费支出(万元) Expenditure on R&D (10 000 yuan)	新产品销售收入(万元) Sales Revenue of New Products (10 000 yuan)	研究与试验发展(R&D)人员(人) R&D Personnel (Person)	R&D人员折合全时当量(人年) Full-time Equivalent of R&D Personnel (man-years)
总计	**Total**	**1704514**	**30893382**	**43040**	**28712**
按登记注册类型分	**By Status of Registration**				
内资企业	Domestic Invested Enterprises	1485726	26045674	37968	25670
国有企业	State-owned Enterprises	51982	13404	1414	809
集体企业	Collective-owned Enterprises	1874	9441	72	59
股份合作企业	Cooperative Enterprises	142	87	70	32
联营企业	Joint Ownership Enterprises				
有限责任公司	Limited Liability Corporations	569160	8101071	14961	10946
国有独资公司	State Sole-proprietorship Corporations	33867	1368386	1145	900
其他有限责任公司	Other Limited Liability Corporations	535293	6732685	13816	10046
股份有限公司	Share-holding Corporations Ltd.	348660	11660252	7981	5212
私营企业	Private Enterprises	513909	6261420	13470	8612
私营独资企业	Private Sole-proprietorship Enterprises	740	6895	48	35
私营合伙企业	Private Partnership Enterprises	49	4302	7	3
私营有限责任公司	Private Limited Liability Corporations	476701	5626670	11989	7563
私营股份有限公司	Private Share-holding Corporations Ltd.	36420	623553	1426	1012
其他企业	Other Enterprises				
港、澳、台商投资企业	Enterprises with Funds from Hong Kong, Macao and Taiwan	144542	3739312	2279	1456
合资经营企业	Joint-venture Enterprises	45241	799869	1440	1011
合作经营企业	Cooperative Enterprises				
独资经营企业	Sole-proprietorship Enterprises	98768	2939442	826	434
投资股份有限公司	Share-holding Corporations Ltd.				
其他港澳台投资企业	Other Enterprises with Funds from Hong Kong, Macao and Taiwan	533		13	11
外商投资企业	Foreign Funded Enterprises	74246	1108396	2793	1586
中外合资经营企业	Joint-venture Enterprises	31712	565452	1054	705
中外合作经营企业	Cooperative Enterprises	32	703	2	1
外资企业	Sole-proprietorship Enterprises	21460	214459	1343	675
外商投资股份有限公司	Share-holding Corporations Ltd. with Foreign Investment	21042	327782	394	204
其他外商投资企业	Other Foreign Funded Enterprises				
按工业行业大类分	**By Sector**				
煤炭开采和洗选业	Mining and Washing of Coal				
石油和天然气开采业	Extraction of Petroleum and Natural Gas				
黑色金属矿采选业	Mining and Processing of Ferrous Metal Ores	22608	221074	129	105
有色金属矿采选业	Mining and Processing of Non-Ferrous Metal Ores				
非金属矿采选业	Mining and Processing of Nonmetal Ores	2614	20895	74	45
开采专业及辅助性活动	Professional and Support Activities for Mining				

17-5 续表 continued

指标	Item	R&D经费支出(万元) Expenditure on R&D (10 000 yuan)	新产品销售收入(万元) Sales Revenue of New Products (10 000 yuan)	研究与试验发展(R&D)人员(人) R&D Personnel (Person)	R&D人员折合全时当量(人年) Full-time Equivalent of R&D Personnel (man-years)
其他采矿业	Mining of Other Ores				
农副食品加工业	Processing of Food from Agricultural Products	5226	97176	291	192
食品制造业	Manufacture of Foods	14023	162724	1020	623
酒、饮料和精制茶制造业	Manufacture of Wine, Drinks and Refined Tea	2579	37236	165	95
烟草制品业	Manufacture of Tobacco	589	872603	66	24
纺织业	Manufacture of Textile	7566	147116	332	192
纺织服装、服饰业	Manufacture of Textile Wearing Apparel and Finery	64	57015	4	2
皮革、毛皮、羽毛及其制品和制鞋业	Manufacture of Leather, Fur, Feather & Its Products and Footwear	386	9640	55	31
木材加工和木、竹、藤、棕、草制品业	Processing of Timbers, Manufacture of Wood,Bamboo, Rattan, Palm, and Straw Products	1665	21465	43	37
家具制造业	Manufacture of Furniture	215	2085	6	3
造纸和纸制品业	Manufacture of Paper and Paper Products	7967	77880	220	164
印刷和记录媒介复制业	Printing, Reproduction of Recording Media	5829	130253	456	355
文教、工美、体育和娱乐用品制造业	Manufacture of Culture, Education,Arts and crafts, Sport and Entertainment Goods	2681	40303	136	79
石油、煤炭及其他燃料加工业	Processing of Petroleum, Coal and Other Fuels	20906	218578	210	136
化学原料和化学制品制造业	Manufacture of Chemical Raw Material and Chemical Products	64899	1359208	1742	1128
医药制造业	Manufacture of Medicines	253031	2467994	5000	3430
化学纤维制造业	Manufacture of Chemical Fiber	10459	15935	161	114
橡胶和塑料制品业	Manufacture of Rubber and Plastic	9009	109121	372	240
非金属矿物制品业	Manufacture of Non-metallic Mineral Products	40634	1222449	1392	907
黑色金属冶炼和压延加工业	Manufacture and Processing of Ferrous Metals	296171	3029451	4465	2284
有色金属冶炼和压延加工业	Manufacture & Processing of Non-ferrous Metals	9051	79161	383	302
金属制品业	Manufacture of Metal Products	73550	1310605	2513	1736
通用设备制造业	Manufacture of General Purpose Machinery	135581	1398240	5340	3736
专用设备制造业	Manufacture of Special Purpose Machinery	94649	1495911	3281	2355
汽车制造业	Manufacture of Automotive	137496	7264332	2512	1236
铁路、船舶、航空航天和其他运输设备制造业	Manufacture of Railroad,Marine,Aerospace and Other Transportation Equipment	9956	378942	398	265
电气机械和器材制造业	Manufacture of Electrical Machinery & Equipment	120877	1863490	2853	1858
计算机、通信和其他电子设备制造业	Manufacture of Computer, Communications and Other Electronic Equipment	257389	6286064	5204	4156
仪器仪表制造业	Manufacture of Measuring Instrument	41318	407139	2075	1566
其他制造业	Other Manufacture		86		
废弃资源综合利用业	Comprehensive Utilization of Waste	775		54	28
金属制品、机械和设备修理业	Metal Products, Machinery and Equipment Repair Industry	2662	45436	393	283
电力、热力生产和供应业	Production and Supply of Electric Power and Heat Power	50879	38066	1558	940
燃气生产和供应业	Production and Supply of Gas	130		21	5
水的生产和供应业	Production and Supply of Water	1081	5711	116	63

17–6 规模以上工业企业科技活动项目(2021年)

Technology Project Activities of Industrial Enterprises Above Designated Size (2021)

指标	Item	R&D经费支出(万元) Expenditure on R&D (10 000 yuan)	新产品开发项目数(项) Projects for New Products Development (unit)	新产品开发经费支出(万元) Expenditure on new products Development (10 000 yuan)
总计	**Total**	**1704514**	**10852**	**2066344**
按登记注册类型分	**By Status of Registration**			
内资企业	Domestic Invested Enterprises	1485726	9889	1670289
国有企业	State-owned Enterprises	51982	596	52939
集体企业	Collective-owned Enterprises	1874	8	2005
股份合作企业	Cooperative Enterprises	142	2	647
联营企业	Joint Ownership Enterprises			
有限责任公司	Limited Liability Corporations	569160	3052	629155
国有独资公司	State Sole-proprietorship Corporations	33867	283	46617
其他有限责任公司	Other Limited Liability Corporations	535293	2769	582538
股份有限公司	Share-holding Corporations Ltd.	348660	1073	368095
私营企业	Private Enterprises	513909	5158	617448
私营独资企业	Private Sole-proprietorship Enterprises	740	21	1804
私营合伙企业	Private Partnership Enterprises	49	6	323
私营有限责任公司	Private Limited Liability Corporations	476701	4643	557640
私营股份有限公司	Private Share-holding Corporations Ltd.	36420	488	57680
其他企业	Other Enterprises			
港、澳、台商投资企业	Enterprises with Funds from Hong Kong, Macao and Taiwan	144542	432	317110
合资经营企业	Joint-venture Enterprises	45241	233	55425
合作经营企业	Cooperative Enterprises			
独资经营企业	Sole-proprietorship Enterprises	98768	190	260821
投资股份有限公司	Share-holding Corporations Ltd.			
其他港澳台投资企业	Other Enterprises with Funds from Hong Kong, Macao and Taiwan	533	9	864
外商投资企业	Foreign Funded Enterprises	74246	531	78945
中外合资经营企业	Joint-venture Enterprises	31712	213	33964
中外合作经营企业	Cooperative Enterprises	32	14	812
外资企业	Sole-proprietorship Enterprises	21460	158	24243
外商投资股份有限公司	Share-holding Corporations Ltd. with Foreign Investment	21042	146	19925
其他外商投资企业	Other Foreign Funded Enterprises			
按工业行业大类分	**By Sector**			
煤炭开采和洗选业	Mining and Washing of Coal			
石油和天然气开采业	Extraction of Petroleum and Natural Gas			
黑色金属矿采选业	Mining and Processing of Ferrous Metal Ores	22608	27	16943
有色金属矿采选业	Mining and Processing of Non-Ferrous Metal Ores			
非金属矿采选业	Mining and Processing of Nonmetal Ores	2614	6	1471
开采专业及辅助性活动	Professional and Support Activities for Mining			

17-6 续表 continued

指标	Item	R&D经费支出(万元) Expenditure on R&D (10 000 yuan)	新产品开发项目数(项) Projects for New Products Development (unit)	新产品开发经费支出(万元) Expenditure on new products Development (10 000 yuan)
其他采矿业	Mining of Other Ores			
农副食品加工业	Processing of Food from Agricultural Products	5226	90	7104
食品制造业	Manufacture of Foods	14023	219	21007
酒、饮料和精制茶制造业	Manufacture of Wine, Drinks and Refined Tea	2579	44	2628
烟草制品业	Manufacture of Tobacco	589	27	4306
纺织业	Manufacture of Textile	7566	88	9317
纺织服装、服饰业	Manufacture of Textile Wearing Apparel and Finery	64	2	41
皮革、毛皮、羽毛及其制品和制鞋业	Manufacture of Leather, Fur, Feather & Its Products and Footwear	386	6	279
木材加工和木、竹、藤、棕、草制品业	Processing of Timbers, Manufacture of Wood,Bamboo, Rattan, Palm, and Straw Products	1665	17	1933
家具制造业	Manufacture of Furniture	215	8	373
造纸和纸制品业	Manufacture of Paper and Paper Products	7967	74	9958
印刷和记录媒介复制业	Printing, Reproduction of Recording Media	5829	75	7573
文教、工美、体育和娱乐用品制造业	Manufacture of Culture, Education,Arts and crafts, Sport and Entertainment Goods	2681	110	3933
石油、煤炭及其他燃料加工业	Processing of Petroleum, Coal and Other Fuels	20906	40	13626
化学原料和化学制品制造业	Manufacture of Chemical Raw Material and Chemical Products	64899	577	82017
医药制造业	Manufacture of Medicines	253031	1291	263675
化学纤维制造业	Manufacture of Chemical Fiber	10459	29	8725
橡胶和塑料制品业	Manufacture of Rubber and Plastic	9009	120	11607
非金属矿物制品业	Manufacture of Non-metallic Mineral Products	40634	427	59132
黑色金属冶炼和压延加工业	Manufacture and Processing of Ferrous Metals	296171	360	263531
有色金属冶炼和压延加工业	Manufacture & Processing of Non-ferrous Metals	9051	83	7293
金属制品业	Manufacture of Metal Products	73550	669	90063
通用设备制造业	Manufacture of General Purpose Machinery	135581	1576	178217
专用设备制造业	Manufacture of Special Purpose Machinery	94649	1454	137391
汽车制造业	Manufacture of Automotive	137496	547	318340
铁路、船舶、航空航天和其他运输设备制造业	Manufacture of Railroad,Marine,Aerospace and Other Transportation Equipment	9956	120	23150
电气机械和器材制造业	Manufacture of Electrical Machinery & Equipment	120877	891	144996
计算机、通信和其他电子设备制造业	Manufacture of Computer, Communications and Other Electronic Equipment	257389	612	268136
仪器仪表制造业	Manufacture of Measuring Instrument	41318	581	55680
其他制造业	Other Manufacture		19	1048
废弃资源综合利用业	Comprehensive Utilization of Waste	775	10	627
金属制品、机械和设备修理业	Metal Products, Machinery and Equipment Repair Industry	2662	31	4791
电力、热力生产和供应业	Production and Supply of Electric Power and Heat Power	50879	596	46196
燃气生产和供应业	Production and Supply of Gas	130	7	410
水的生产和供应业	Production and Supply of Water	1081	19	830

17-7 规模以上工业企业R&D经费情况(2021年)

R&D Funds of Industrial Enterprises Above Designated Size(2021)

单位：万元

指标	Item	合计 Total	按支出用途分组 By Object of Expenditure	
			经常费支出 Daily Expenditure	资产性支出 Capital Expenditure
总计	**Total**	**1704514**	**1630751**	**73762**
按登记注册类型分	**By Status of Registration**			
内资企业	Domestic Invested Enterprises	1485726	1420234	65493
国有企业	State-owned Enterprises	51982	50841	1142
集体企业	Collective-owned Enterprises	1874	1198	676
股份合作企业	Cooperative Enterprises	142	142	
联营企业	Joint Ownership Enterprises			
有限责任公司	Limited Liability Corporations	569160	541973	27187
国有独资公司	State Sole-proprietorship Corporations	33867	33365	502
其他有限责任公司	Other Limited Liability Corporations	535293	508608	26685
股份有限公司	Share-holding Corporations Ltd.	348660	341499	7160
私营企业	Private Enterprises	513909	484581	29327
私营独资企业	Private Sole-proprietorship Enterprises	740	699	41
私营合伙企业	Private Partnership Enterprises	49	49	
私营有限责任公司	Private Limited Liability Corporations	476701	452127	24573
私营股份有限公司	Private Share-holding Corporations Ltd.	36420	31706	4713
其他企业	Other Enterprises			
港、澳、台商投资企业	Enterprises with Funds from Hong Kong, Macao and Taiwan	144542	143264	1278
合资经营企业	Joint-venture Enterprises	45241	44156	1084
合作经营企业	Cooperative Enterprises			
独资经营企业	Sole-proprietorship Enterprises	98768	98575	193
投资股份有限公司	Share-holding Corporations Ltd.			
其他港澳台投资企业	Other Enterprises with Funds from Hong Kong, Macao and Taiwan	533	533	
外商投资企业	Foreign Funded Enterprises	74246	67253	6992
中外合资经营企业	Joint-venture Enterprises	31712	29686	2026
中外合作经营企业	Cooperative Enterprises	32	32	
外资企业	Sole-proprietorship Enterprises	21460	17849	3611
外商投资股份有限公司	Share-holding Corporations Ltd. with Foreign Investment	21042	19687	1355
其他外商投资企业	Other Foreign Funded Enterprises			
按工业行业大类分	**By Sector**			
煤炭开采和洗选业	Mining and Washing of Coal			
石油和天然气开采业	Extraction of Petroleum and Natural Gas			
黑色金属矿采选业	Mining and Processing of Ferrous Metal Ores	22608	22559	49
有色金属矿采选业	Mining and Processing of Non-Ferrous Metal Ores			
非金属矿采选业	Mining and Processing of Nonmetal Ores	2614	1860	754
开采专业及辅助性活动	Professional and Support Activities for Mining			

(10 000 yuan)

R&D经费支出 Expenditure on R&D				R&D经费外部支出 External expenditure on R&D
按资金来源分组 By Capital Source				
政府资金 Government Appropriation Funds	企业资金 Self-raised Funds by Enterprises	境外资金 Foreign funds	其他资金 Other Funds	
61734	**1641288**	**170**	**1321**	**181972**
58250	1426155		1321	166595
223	51760			23060
	1874			
39	103			
13082	555415		663	12601
314	33286		267	915
12768	522129		396	11686
12361	336299			99493
32545	480705		659	31441
	740			
	49			
30762	445280		659	30800
1783	34636			642
2181	142361			12994
1907	43333			9528
274	98494			3456
	533			11
1303	72772	170		2383
255	31286	170		384
	32			
96	21363			685
952	20091			1314
	22059		549	124
	2614			394

17-7 续表 continued

单位：万元

指标	Item	合计 Total	按支出用途分组 By Object of Expenditure	
			经常费支出 Daily Expenditure	资产性支出 Capital Expenditure
其他采矿业	Mining of Other Ores			
农副食品加工业	Processing of Food from Agricultural Products	5226	5044	181
食品制造业	Manufacture of Foods	14023	13231	793
酒、饮料和精制茶制造业	Manufacture of Wine, Drinks and Refined Tea	2579	2325	254
烟草制品业	Manufacture of Tobacco	589	486	103
纺织业	Manufacture of Textile	7566	7556	10
纺织服装、服饰业	Manufacture of Textile Wearing Apparel and Finery	64	64	
皮革、毛皮、羽毛及其制品和制鞋业	Manufacture of Leather, Fur, Feather & Its Products and Footwear	386	386	
木材加工和木、竹、藤、棕、草制品业	Processing of Timbers, Manufacture of Wood,Bamboo, Rattan, Palm, and Straw Products	1665	1665	
家具制造业	Manufacture of Furniture	215	215	
造纸和纸制品业	Manufacture of Paper and Paper Products	7967	7523	445
印刷和记录媒介复制业	Printing, Reproduction of Recording Media	5829	5791	38
文教、工美、体育和娱乐用品制造业	Manufacture of Culture, Education,Arts and crafts, Sport and Entertainment Goods	2681	2659	22
石油、煤炭及其他燃料加工业	Processing of Petroleum, Coal and Other Fuels	20906	20124	782
化学原料和化学制品制造业	Manufacture of Chemical Raw Material and Chemical Products	64899	58284	6615
医药制造业	Manufacture of Medicines	253031	232530	20500
化学纤维制造业	Manufacture of Chemical Fiber	10459	10107	352
橡胶和塑料制品业	Manufacture of Rubber and Plastic	9009	7810	1198
非金属矿物制品业	Manufacture of Non-metallic Mineral Products	40634	39711	923
黑色金属冶炼和压延加工业	Manufacture and Processing of Ferrous Metals	296171	295767	404
有色金属冶炼和压延加工业	Manufacture & Processing of Non-ferrous Metals	9051	9050	1
金属制品业	Manufacture of Metal Products	73550	70156	3394
通用设备制造业	Manufacture of General Purpose Machinery	135581	126855	8726
专用设备制造业	Manufacture of Special Purpose Machinery	94649	89590	5059
汽车制造业	Manufacture of Automotive	137496	134167	3330
铁路、船舶、航空航天和其他运输设备制造业	Manufacture of Railroad,Marine,Aerospace and Other Transportation Equipment	9956	8835	1120
电气机械和器材制造业	Manufacture of Electrical Machinery & Equipment	120877	114107	6770
计算机、通信和其他电子设备制造业	Manufacture of Computer, Communications and Other Electronic Equipment	257389	248210	9178
仪器仪表制造业	Manufacture of Measuring Instrument	41318	40085	1234
其他制造业	Other Manufacture			
废弃资源综合利用业	Comprehensive Utilization of Waste	775	775	
金属制品、机械和设备修理业	Metal Products, Machinery and Equipment Repair Industry	2662	2277	386
电力、热力生产和供应业	Production and Supply of Electric Power and Heat Power	50879	49871	1008
燃气生产和供应业	Production and Supply of Gas	130	130	
水的生产和供应业	Production and Supply of Water	1081	947	133

(10 000 yuan)

R&D经费支出 Expenditure on R&D				R&D经费外部支出 External expenditure on R&D
按资金来源分组 By Capital Source				
政府资金 Government Appropriation Funds	企业资金 Self-raised Funds by Enterprises	境外资金 Foreign funds	其他资金 Other Funds	
79	5147			44
121	13902			1174
63	2516			109
	553		36	169
32	7534			
	64			
	386			
	1665			
	215			
	7967			189
	5829			30
	2681			6
	20906			301
527	64372			1769
32390	220641			34603
	10459			
218	8791			7
450	40184			383
778	295393			661
15	9036			163
458	72888		204	76
5040	130536		5	1346
3836	90813			946
470	136499		527	49967
477	9308	170		551
920	119956			2269
13957	243432			59958
1292	40026			2426
66	709			
	2662			
534	50345			23581
	130			
13	1068			727

17-8 规模以上工业企业办科技机构情况(2021年)
Science and Technology Institutions of Industrial Enterprises Above Designated Size (2021)

指标	Item	机构数(个) Number (unit)
总计	**Total**	**506**
按登记注册类型分	**By Status of Registration**	
内资企业	Domestic Invested Enterprises	471
国有企业	State-owned Enterprises	4
集体企业	Collective-owned Enterprises	1
股份合作企业	Cooperative Enterprises	
联营企业	Joint Ownership Enterprises	
有限责任公司	Limited Liability Corporations	186
国有独资公司	State Sole-proprietorship Corporations	22
其他有限责任公司	Other Limited Liability Corporations	164
股份有限公司	Share-holding Corporations Ltd.	65
私营企业	Private Enterprises	215
私营独资企业	Private Sole-proprietorship Enterprises	1
私营合伙企业	Private Partnership Enterprises	
私营有限责任公司	Private Limited Liability Corporations	182
私营股份有限公司	Private Share-holding Corporations Ltd.	32
其他企业	Other Enterprises	
港、澳、台商投资企业	Enterprises with Funds from Hong Kong,Macao and Taiwan	10
合资经营企业	Joint-venture Enterprises	4
合作经营企业	Cooperative Enterprises	
独资经营企业	Sole-proprietorship Enterprises	6
投资股份有限公司	Share-holding Corporations Ltd.	
其他港澳台投资企业	Other Enterprises with Funds from Hong Kong,Macao and Taiwan	
外商投资企业	Foreign Funded Enterprises	25
中外合资经营企业	Joint-venture Enterprises	11
中外合作经营企业	Cooperative Enterprises	
外资企业	Sole-proprietorship Enterprises	11
外商投资股份有限公司	Share-holding Corporations Ltd. with Foreign Investment	3
其他外商投资企业	Other Foreign Funded Enterprises	
按工业行业大类分	**By Sector**	
煤炭开采和洗选业	Mining and Washing of Coal	
石油和天然气开采业	Extraction of Petroleum and Natural Gas	
黑色金属矿采选业	Mining and Processing of Ferrous Metal Ores	4
有色金属矿采选业	Mining and Processing of Non-Ferrous Metal Ores	
非金属矿采选业	Mining and Processing of Nonmetal Ores	
开采专业及辅助性活动	Professional and Support Activities for Mining	

机构人员(人) Research Personnel(Person)			机构经费支出(万元) Agency Expenditure (10 000 yuan)	仪器和设备原价(万元) Original price of Equipment (10 000 yuan)
合计 Total	博士毕业 Doctor	硕士毕业 Master		
23961	**375**	**3816**	**1241099**	**794085**
19293	316	2671	927642	624361
100		14	625	976
			1838	233
8261	163	1262	421711	346908
1212	46	290	59869	149928
7049	117	972	361842	196980
4907	76	958	211331	158154
6025	77	437	292138	118091
5			20	7
5057	64	339	261058	97595
963	13	98	31060	20489
2926	37	866	261413	74455
589	1	37	24844	10595
2337	36	829	236569	63861
1742	22	279	52044	95268
544	3	52	17005	17408
840	13	60	13639	71930
358	6	167	21400	5930
289	5	5	42987	8975

17-8 续表 continued

指标	Item	机构数（个）Number (unit)
其他采矿业	Mining of Other Ores	
农副食品加工业	Processing of Food from Agricultural Products	13
食品制造业	Manufacture of Foods	9
酒、饮料和精制茶制造业	Manufacture of Wine, Drinks and Refined Tea	3
烟草制品业	Manufacture of Tobacco	3
纺织业	Manufacture of Textile	3
纺织服装、服饰业	Manufacture of Textile Wearing Apparel and Finery	1
皮革、毛皮、羽毛及其制品和制鞋业	Manufacture of Leather, Fur, Feather & Its Products and Footwear	
木材加工和木、竹、藤、棕、草制品业	Processing of Timbers, Manufacture of Wood,Bamboo, Rattan, Palm, and Straw Products	
家具制造业	Manufacture of Furniture	
造纸和纸制品业	Manufacture of Paper and Paper Products	2
印刷和记录媒介复制业	Printing, Reproduction of Recording Media	5
文教、工美、体育和娱乐用品制造业	Manufacture of Culture, Education,Arts and crafts， Sport and Entertainment Goods	2
石油、煤炭及其他燃料加工业	Processing of Petroleum, Coal and Other Fuels	1
化学原料和化学制品制造业	Manufacture of Chemical Raw Material and Chemical Products	39
医药制造业	Manufacture of Medicines	45
化学纤维制造业	Manufacture of Chemical Fiber	3
橡胶和塑料制品业	Manufacture of Rubber and Plastic	8
非金属矿物制品业	Manufacture of Non-metallic Mineral Products	29
黑色金属冶炼和压延加工业	Manufacture and Processing of Ferrous Metals	6
有色金属冶炼和压延加工业	Manufacture & Processing of Non-ferrous Metals	4
金属制品业	Manufacture of Metal Products	39
通用设备制造业	Manufacture of General Purpose Machinery	53
专用设备制造业	Manufacture of Special Purpose Machinery	46
汽车制造业	Manufacture of Automotive	33
铁路、船舶、航空航天和其他运输设备制造业	Manufacture of Railroad,Marine,Aerospace and Other Transportation Equipment	5
电气机械和器材制造业	Manufacture of Electrical Machinery & Equipment	37
计算机、通信和其他电子设备制造业	Manufacture of Computer, Communications and Other Electronic Equipment	45
仪器仪表制造业	Manufacture of Measuring Instrument	46
其他制造业	Other Manufacture	
废弃资源综合利用业	Comprehensive Utilization of Waste	
金属制品、机械和设备修理业	Metal Products, Machinery and Equipment Repair Industry	3
电力、热力生产和供应业	Production and Supply of Electric Power and Heat Power	18
燃气生产和供应业	Production and Supply of Gas	
水的生产和供应业	Production and Supply of Water	1

机构人员(人) Research Personnel(Person)			机构经费支出(万元) Agency Expenditure (10 000 yuan)	仪器和设备原价(万元) Original price of Equipment (10 000 yuan)
合计 Total	博士毕业 Doctor	硕士毕业 Master		
146	2	12	2892	2693
655		11	11518	63453
110	2	5	1789	1863
204	7	56	17288	24046
68		2	4136	6171
2			25	1
37			1172	590
289		3	5885	14453
29		4	865	1166
101	1	1	16623	1774
1356	15	194	61543	44749
2793	66	698	105750	74565
100	2	8	8111	4266
258	6	11	4782	5149
751	6	20	29547	25169
1882	27	80	258151	54206
110	4	2	3028	1557
1423	32	36	38300	36852
2568	19	338	70250	87162
1569	24	214	63041	38523
2910	54	899	239387	71322
400	5	60	15093	8468
1333	8	249	68941	95157
2852	41	700	126067	64130
1373	7	109	30808	14987
64		14	1281	3224
201	42	70	7832	37231
88		15	4008	2185

17-9 规模以上工业企业自主知识产权及相关情况(2021年)

Independent Intellectual Property Rights of Industrial Enterprises Above Designated Size(2021)

单位：件

指标	Item	专利申请数 Number of Patent Applications
总计	**Total**	**14825**
按登记注册类型分	**By Status of Registration**	
内资企业	Domestic Invested Enterprises	12866
国有企业	State-owned Enterprises	2597
集体企业	Collective-owned Enterprises	31
股份合作企业	Cooperative Enterprises	3
联营企业	Joint Ownership Enterprises	
有限责任公司	Limited Liability Corporations	3467
国有独资公司	State Sole-proprietorship Corporations	390
其他有限责任公司	Other Limited Liability Corporations	3077
股份有限公司	Share-holding Corporations Ltd.	1560
私营企业	Private Enterprises	5208
私营独资企业	Private Sole-proprietorship Enterprises	49
私营合伙企业	Private Partnership Enterprises	8
私营有限责任公司	Private Limited Liability Corporations	4607
私营股份有限公司	Private Share-holding Corporations Ltd.	544
其他企业	Other Enterprises	
港、澳、台商投资企业	Enterprises with Funds from Hong Kong,Macao and Taiwan	390
合资经营企业	Joint-venture Enterprises	225
合作经营企业	Cooperative Enterprises	
独资经营企业	Sole-proprietorship Enterprises	147
投资股份有限公司	Share-holding Corporations Ltd.	
其他港澳台投资企业	Other Enterprises with Funds from Hong Kong,Macao and Taiwan	18
外商投资企业	Foreign Funded Enterprises	1569
中外合资经营企业	Joint-venture Enterprises	182
中外合作经营企业	Cooperative Enterprises	5
外资企业	Sole-proprietorship Enterprises	101
外商投资股份有限公司	Share-holding Corporations Ltd. with Foreign Investment	1281
其他外商投资企业	Other Foreign Funded Enterprises	
按工业行业大类分	**By Sector**	
煤炭开采和洗选业	Mining and Washing of Coal	10
石油和天然气开采业	Extraction of Petroleum and Natural Gas	
黑色金属矿采选业	Mining and Processing of Ferrous Metal Ores	15
有色金属矿采选业	Mining and Processing of Non-Ferrous Metal Ores	
非金属矿采选业	Mining and Processing of Nonmetal Ores	15
开采专业及辅助性活动	Professional and Support Activities for Mining	

(piece)

#发明专利 Inventions	有效发明专利数 Number of Effective Inventions	拥有注册商标数 Registered Trademarks	形成国家或行业标准数(项) Industry or National Standards(unit)
5718	**19626**	**14517**	**539**
5239	18156	11094	513
2073	5869	12	25
9	14	1	
1213	3301	4192	120
155	473	1646	8
1058	2828	2546	112
823	4003	2260	113
1121	4969	4629	255
10	48	144	
8	10	1	
970	4096	3882	244
133	815	602	11
163	582	34	16
136	343	19	1
16	193	11	15
11	46	4	
316	888	3389	10
53	264	497	10
	2		
53	124	73	
210	498	2819	
1	1		
2	3		
3	1		

17-9 续表 continued

单位：件

指标	Item	专利申请数 Number of Patent Applications
其他采矿业	Mining of Other Ores	
农副食品加工业	Processing of Food from Agricultural Products	99
食品制造业	Manufacture of Foods	198
酒、饮料和精制茶制造业	Manufacture of Wine, Drinks and Refined Tea	27
烟草制品业	Manufacture of Tobacco	227
纺织业	Manufacture of Textile	94
纺织服装、服饰业	Manufacture of Textile Wearing Apparel and Finery	17
皮革、毛皮、羽毛及其制品和制鞋业	Manufacture of Leather, Fur, Feather & Its Products and Footwear	5
木材加工和木、竹、藤、棕、草制品业	Processing of Timbers, Manufacture of Wood,Bamboo, Rattan, Palm, and Straw Products	8
家具制造业	Manufacture of Furniture	34
造纸和纸制品业	Manufacture of Paper and Paper Products	99
印刷和记录媒介复制业	Printing, Reproduction of Recording Media	107
文教、工美、体育和娱乐用品制造业	Manufacture of Culture, Education,Arts and crafts，Sport and Entertainment Goods	100
石油、煤炭及其他燃料加工业	Processing of Petroleum, Coal and Other Fuels	34
化学原料和化学制品制造业	Manufacture of Chemical Raw Material and Chemical Products	340
医药制造业	Manufacture of Medicines	714
化学纤维制造业	Manufacture of Chemical Fiber	70
橡胶和塑料制品业	Manufacture of Rubber and Plastic	186
非金属矿物制品业	Manufacture of Non-metallic Mineral Products	618
黑色金属冶炼和压延加工业	Manufacture and Processing of Ferrous Metals	550
有色金属冶炼和压延加工业	Manufacture & Processing of Non-ferrous Metals	113
金属制品业	Manufacture of Metal Products	761
通用设备制造业	Manufacture of General Purpose Machinery	1755
专用设备制造业	Manufacture of Special Purpose Machinery	1609
汽车制造业	Manufacture of Automotive	488
铁路、船舶、航空航天和其他运输设备制造业	Manufacture of Railroad,Marine,Aerospace and Other Transportation Equipment	93
电气机械和器材制造业	Manufacture of Electrical Machinery & Equipment	1996
计算机、通信和其他电子设备制造业	Manufacture of Computer, Communications and Other Electronic Equipment	1093
仪器仪表制造业	Manufacture of Measuring Instrument	663
其他制造业	Other Manufacture	4
废弃资源综合利用业	Comprehensive Utilization of Waste	48
金属制品、机械和设备修理业	Metal Products, Machinery and Equipment Repair Industry	21
电力、热力生产和供应业	Production and Supply of Electric Power and Heat Power	2608
燃气生产和供应业	Production and Supply of Gas	
水的生产和供应业	Production and Supply of Water	6

(piece)

#发明专利 Inventions	有效发明专利数 Number of Effective Inventions	拥有注册商标数 Registered Trademarks	形成国家或行业标准数(项) Industry or National Standards(unit)
25	162	172	3
32	303	483	1
9	8	114	5
75	255	1536	3
18	130	27	3
5	2	48	
	2	7	3
3	2	3	
	70	4	
19	119	28	
12	53	39	6
34	171	155	1
3	67	4	
116	817	3603	16
444	1154	5142	177
29	63	15	1
32	202	79	16
146	756	124	41
223	1039	41	16
17	33	14	1
192	778	180	20
355	1384	821	28
373	1253	522	39
71	504	260	12
52	154	36	5
312	1753	374	30
792	1920	376	52
184	521	296	28
2	1	8	4
23	21		
6	60	2	
2104	5860	4	27
4	4		1

主要统计指标解释

研究与试验发展(R&D) 指为增加知识存量（也包括有关人类、文化和社会的知识）以及设计已有知识的新应用而进行的创造性、系统性工作，包括基础研究、应用研究和试验发展三种类型。国际上通常采用R&D活动的规模和强度指标反映一国的科技实力和核心竞争力。

基础研究 指一种不预设任何特定应用或使用目的的实验性或理论性工作，其主要目的是为获得（已发生）现象和可观察事实的基本原理、规律和新知识。其成果通常表现为提出一般原理、理论或规律，并以论文、著作、研究报告等形式为主。

应用研究 指为获取新知识，达到某一特定的实际目的或目标而开展的初始性研究。应用研究是为了确定基础研究成果的可能用途，或确定实现特定和预定目标的新方法。其研究成果以论文、著作、研究报告、原理性模型或发明专利等形式为主。

试验发展 指利用从科学研究、实际经验中获取的知识和研究过程中产生的其他知识，开发新的产品、工艺或改进现有产品、工艺而进行的系统性研究。其研究成果以专利、专有技术，以及具有新颖性的产品原型、原始样机及装置等形式为主。

R&D人员 指报告期R&D活动单位中从事基础研究、应用研究和试验发展活动的人员。包括直接参加上述三类R&D活动的人员，以及与上述三类R&D活动相关的管理人员和直接服务人员，即直接为R&D活动提供资料文献、材料供应、设备维护等服务的人员。不包括为R&D活动提供间接服务的人员，如餐饮服务、安保人员等。

R&D人员全时当量 指报告期R&D人员按实际从事R&D活动时间计算的工作量，以“人年”为计量单位。为国际上比较科技人力投入而制定的可比指标。

R&D经费支出 指报告期调查单位内部为实施R&D活动而实际发生的全部经费，按支出性质分为日常性支出和资产性支出。不包括调查单位委托其他单位或与其他单位合作开展R&D活动而转拨给其他单位的全部经费。

新产品销售收入 指报告期企业销售新产品实现的销售收入。新产品是指采用新技术原理、新设计构思研制、生产的全新产品，或在结构、材质、工艺等某一方面比原有产品有明显改进，从而显著提高了产品性能或扩大了使用功能的产品。既包括经政府有关部门认定并在有效期内的新产品，也包括企业自行研制开发，未经政府有关部门认定，从投产之日起一年之内的新产品。

专利 是专利权的简称，是对发明人的发明创造经审查合格后，由国家知识产权局依据专利法授予发明人和设计人对该项发明创造享有的专有权。包括发明、实用新型和外观设计。反映拥有自主知识产权的科技和设计成果情况。

发明（专利） 指对产品、方法或者其改进所提出的新的技术方案。是国际通行的反映拥有自主知识产权技术的核心指标。

Explanatory Notes on Main Statistical Indicators

Research and Experimental Development (R&D) refers to creative and systematic work undertaken in order to increase the stock of knowledge (including knowledge of humankind, culture and society) and to devise new applications of available knowledge. R&D includes 3 categories of activities: basic research, applied research and experimental development. The scale and intensity of R&D are widely used internationally to reflect the strength of S&T and the core competitiveness of a country in the world.

Basic Research refers to experimental or theoretical work undertaken primarily to acquire new knowledge of the underlying foundations of phenomena and observable facts, without any particular application or use in view. Basic research usually formulates hypotheses, theories or laws, and its results are mainly released or disseminated in the form of scientific papers or monographs or research reports.

Applied Research refers to original investigation undertaken in order to acquire new knowledge. It is directed primarily towards a specific, practical aim or objective. Purpose of the applied research is to identify the possible uses of results from basic research, or to explore new (fundamental) methods or new approaches. Results of applied research are expressed in the form of scientific papers, monographs, fundamental models or invention patents.

Experimental Development refers to systematic work, drawing on knowledge gained from research and practical experience and producing additional knowledge, which is directed to producing new products or processes or to improving existing products or processes. Results of experimental development activities are embodied in patents, exclusive technology, and monotype of new products or equipment.

R&D Personnel refer to persons of R&D activities units engaged in basic research, applied research, and experimental development at the reference period, including persons of directly participating in the three activities above, as well as management and direct service staff related to R&D activities, such as literature provision, material supply, equipment maintenance staff, it excludes persons providing indirect support and ancillary services, such as canteen and security staff.

Full-time Equivalent of R&D Personnel refers to the ratio of working hours actually spent on R&D during a specific reference period (usually a calendar year) divided by the total number of hours conventionally worked in the same period by an individual or by a group. The measurement unit of the ratio is "man-years". This is an internationally comparable indicator of S&T manpower input.

Expenditure on R&D refers to the real expenditure of surveyed units on their own R&D activities in reporting period. It is divided into current expenditures and gross fixed capital expenditures for R&D according to the nature of expenditure. It doesn't include the fees transferred to cooperated or entrusted agencies on R&D activities.

Sales Income of New Products refers to the sales income of new products of the enterprises at the reference period. New products refer to products developed and produced with new technologies and designs or improved in structure, material, process or other aspects so that their performance are improved or their functions expanded. New products include those affirmed by government authorities in their validity period and also those developed by enterprises without the affirmation of government authorities within one year after they are put into production.

Patent is an abbreviation for the patent right and refers to the exclusive right of ownership by the inventors or designers for the creation or inventions, given from the China National Intellectual Property Administration after due process of assessment and approval in accordance with the Patent Law. Patents are granted for inventions, utility models and designs. This indicator reflects the achievements of S&T and design with independent intellectual property.

Patented Inventions refer to new technical proposals to the products or methods or their modifications. This is universal core indicator reflecting the technologies with independent intellectual property.

18

教育与文化

EDUCATION AND CULTURE

18-1 教育事业基本情况
Basic Statistics on Education

指标	Item	1952年	1957年	1962年	1965年	1970年
学校数(所)	**Number of Schools(unit)**	**2679**	**3106**	**3731**	**4318**	**5359**
#驻济高等学校	Colleges and Universities in Jinan	5	4	12	8	2
中等教育	Secondary Education	37	67	112	410	1204
#中等职业学校	Vocational Secondary Education	16	16	15	15	17
普通中学	Ordinary middle school	21	51	93	159	1024
小　学	Elementary school	2636	3034	3606	3899	4152
专任教师(人)	**Full-time Teachers(person)**	**8555**	**13452**	**19606**	**26760**	**32508**
#驻济高等学校	Colleges and Universities in Jinan	671	1325	2598	2451	922
中等教育	Secondary Education	1108	2569	3418	5321	9607
#中等职业学校	Vocational Secondary Education	311	787	765	685	914
普通中学	Ordinary middle school	797	1782	2629	3502	8445
小　学	Elementary school	6773	9550	13571	18971	21954
在校学生(万人)	**Total Enrollment(10 000 persons)**	**26.87**	**31.95**	**49.82**	**68.27**	**80.20**
#驻济高等学校	Colleges and Universities in Jinan	0.43	0.82	1.65	1.40	0.30
中等教育	Secondary Education	2.73	5.14	5.80	10.43	18.97
#中等职业学校	Vocational Secondary Education	0.69	0.93	0.51	0.65	0.12
普通中学	Ordinary middle school	2.04	4.21	5.22	7.50	17.81
小　学	Elementary school	23.70	25.98	42.35	56.42	60.91
各类学校毕业生数(万人)	**Graduates(10 000 persons)**	**4.38**	**8.58**	**10.60**	**10.45**	**12.09**
#驻济高等学校	Colleges and Universities in Jinan	0.14	0.11	0.31	0.43	
中等教育	Secondary Education	0.60	1.14	1.72	1.90	1.02
#中等职业学校	Vocational Secondary Education	0.13	0.14	0.32	0.03	
普通中学	Ordinary middle school	0.46	1.00	1.40	1.80	0.38
每一教师负担学生数(人)	**Each Teacher Burden Number of Students(person)**	**31.41**	**23.75**	**25.41**	**23.27**	**24.67**
#驻济高等学校	Colleges and Universities in Jinan	6.41	6.19	6.35	5.71	3.25
中等教育	Secondary Education	24.64	20.01	16.97	19.60	19.75
#中等职业学校	Vocational Secondary Education	22.33	11.84	6.64	9.51	1.36
普通中学	Ordinary middle school	25.63	23.64	19.84	21.41	21.09
小　学	Elementary school	34.99	27.20	31.21	29.74	27.74
平均每万人口在校学生(人)	**Number of Enrollment Per 10000 Population(person)**	**843**	**922**	**1418**	**1829**	**1968**
#大学生	Undergraduate	14	24	47	38	7
中专生	Secondary Students	22	27	14	17	3
中学生	Middle School Students	64	122	150	256	463
小学生	Elementary School Students	743	750	1206	1513	1494

注：1.驻济高等学校在校生含普通专本科、成人本专科、研究生在校生。
　　2.驻济高等学校毕业生为普通本专科毕业生。
　　3.“中等职业学校”中相关教师、学生数据不含技工学校。

1975年	1980年	1985年	1990年	1995年	2000年	2005年	2010年	2015年	2020年	2021年	2022年
5412	**5066**	**4511**	**3924**	**3360**	**1725**	**1251**	**1025**	**946**	**1108**	**1066**	**1031**
4	11	16	16	16	16	59	66	72	52	52	52
922	759	593	529	440	423	348	302	280	390	373	371
21	30	40	39	41	40	91	73	41	41	66	65
783	710	491	417	312	297	247	209	214	320	332	334
4485	4295	3899	3368	2890	1273	832	645	582	666	641	608
42432	**49608**	**46806**	**55978**	**58779**	**62869**	**77334**	**83106**	**88487**	**121438**	**123004**	**122248**
2468	3744	4614	7245	7500	8269	24341	29526	31693	42202	41894	41936
15274	19062	17530	21618	23946	26817	27435	28370	30589	42017	42643	40438
985	1338	2367	2890	2941	2916	4738	4511	4068	3642	4040	4273
13571	17294	13572	16065	17621	20585	21915	21943	23643	34796	35587	36165
24654	26775	24579	26922	27417	27417	25201	24801	25795	37219	38467	39874
90.28	**83.56**	**78.38**	**79.48**	**91.69**	**95.79**	**129.28**	**144.60**	**153.71**	**201.27**	**183.14**	**180.08**
0.61	1.58	3.02	3.73	5.66	9.30	48.71	64.25	71.40	89.85	69.40	67.07
25.43	20.24	25.34	28.08	36.64	44.99	42.50	41.76	40.77	54.41	52.74	48.59
0.58	0.31	1.92	2.51	4.79	5.75	9.88	8.10	5.93	6.28	6.40	6.49
23.86	19.63	21.49	22.45	27.15	33.82	30.91	30.18	30.16	39.84	40.70	42.10
64.22	61.47	49.98	47.57	49.23	41.40	37.88	38.40	41.44	57.01	61.00	64.42
22.66	**18.07**	**17.31**	**17.12**	**20.88**	**23.65**	**33.58**	**38.10**	**39.83**	**43.89**	**41.35**	**41.99**
0.20	0.03	0.45	1.03	1.68	1.55	13.49	17.57	19.48	18.37	17.86	18.09
11.83	8.41	7.36	8.24	10.39	10.80	14.03	13.55	14.22	17.12	15.27	14.79
0.20	0.46	0.52	0.62	1.16	1.84	3.29	3.13	2.75	1.73	1.72	1.91
11.58	7.89	6.39	6.66	7.78	8.16	10.40	9.20	10.23	12.97	12.28	12.87
21.28	**16.84**	**16.75**	**14.20**	**15.60**	**15.24**	**16.72**	**17.40**	**17.37**	**16.58**	**14.89**	**14.73**
2.47	4.22	6.55	5.15	7.54	11.25	20.01	21.76	22.53	21.29	16.57	15.99
16.65	10.62	14.46	12.99	15.30	16.78	15.49	14.72	13.33	11.00	12.37	12.02
5.95	2.29	8.12	8.69	16.30	18.84	20.86	17.96	14.58	17.24	15.80	15.19
17.58	11.35	15.83	13.98	15.41	16.43	14.10	13.75	12.76	11.45	11.43	11.64
26.05	22.96	20.33	17.67	18.20	15.10	15.03	15.48	16.07	15.32	15.87	16.16
2062	**1822**	**1605**	**1518**	**1691**	**1702**	**2177**	**2395**	**2465**	**2510**	**1962**	**2201**
14	34	62	71	104	165	820	1064	1145	1121	855	820
13	7	39	48	88	102	195	192	170	182	184	183
566	429	473	473	553	601	521	500	484	497	501	514
1466	1339	1024	908	908	736	638	636	664	711	752	787

Notes: 1.Students under high education in Jinan include regular college students, regular junior college students, adult college students, adult junior students and postgraduate students.

2.Graduates under high education in Jinan are Undergraduates and Short-cycle Courses in Regular HEIs.

3.Data related to teachers and students in the "Secondary Vocational Schools" do not include Skilled Workers Schools.

18-2 普通高等院校一览(2022年)
Basic Statistics on Institutions of Higher Education(2022)

单位：人 (person)

名称 Name	普通本专科在校学生数 Total Enrollment	普通本专科毕业生数 Graduates	普通本专科招生数 New Enrollment	教职工人数 Teachers and Staff	#专任教师 Full-time Teachers 合计 Total	 #正高级 Senior	 #副高级 Sub-Senior
总计(Total)	**644302**	**180926**	**202721**	**53336**	**38636**	**5535**	**12296**
综合性大学(Comprehensive Universities)	**92276**	**24512**	**25919**	**10881**	**7210**	**1865**	**2611**
山东大学	22751	5175	5735	5973	3375	1347	1274
济南大学	33067	8358	7841	2901	2304	355	843
山东青年政治学院	19761	5360	6557	1112	861	80	257
山东女子学院	16697	5619	5786	895	670	83	237
理工院校(Universities of Science and Engineering)	**79997**	**21408**	**21187**	**8442**	**5728**	**834**	**2029**
山东建筑大学	23564	6097	6001	2244	1706	276	638
山东科技大学	2251	746	544	206	91	8	36
齐鲁工业大学	27191	6697	7170	3503	2170	402	726
山东交通学院	23244	6638	6112	1855	1491	117	498
山东电力高等专科学校	3747	1230	1360	634	270	31	131
医药院校(Medical Colleges and Universities)	**61585**	**12798**	**14838**	**5772**	**3956**	**638**	**1311**
山东第一医科大学	22295	1762	2037	3228	1866	268	571
山东中医药大学	18075	4406	4177	1562	1360	307	389
山东医学高等专科学校	13787	4641	5655	522	444	38	257
济南护理职业学院	7428	1989	2969	460	286	25	94
师范院校(Normal Colleges and Schools)	**50019**	**15450**	**13845**	**4410**	**3377**	**525**	**1069**
山东师范大学	25456	7257	5903	2831	2118	401	699
齐鲁师范学院	17519	5644	5474	1019	855	93	262
济南幼儿师范专科学校	7044	2549	2468	560	404	31	108
财经院校(Colleges and Universities of Finance and Economics)	**32499**	**9224**	**8619**	**2893**	**2127**	**457**	**862**
山东财经大学	26460	6995	6545	2441	1730	388	695
山东财经大学燕山学院	6039	2229	2074	452	397	69	167
政法院校(Colleges and Universities of Politics and Law)	**25960**	**6282**	**7280**	**1780**	**1185**	**112**	**331**
山东警察学院	5777	1151	1502	558	319	37	127
山东司法警官职业学院	8627	2478	2858	297	166	2	40
山东政法学院	11556	2653	2920	925	700	73	164
体育院校(Sports Colleges and Universities)	**4097**	**1088**	**972**	**703**	**601**	**72**	**239**
山东体育学院	4097	1088	972	703	601	72	239
艺术院校(Art Schools)	**16625**	**4130**	**4546**	**1827**	**1474**	**153**	**502**
山东艺术学院	8995	2287	2498	1048	893	96	311
山东工艺美术学院	7630	1843	2048	779	581	57	191
职业技术学院(Vocational Technical Institutes)	**281244**	**86034**	**105515**	**16628**	**12978**	**879**	**3342**
山东协和学院	32584	10077	11848	1565	1409	112	414
山东商业职业技术学院	17240	4814	5643	1097	1015	49	258
山东劳动职业技术学院	13548	4180	5175	693	535	32	136
山东职业学院	12283	4764	3772	655	585	27	164
山东圣翰财贸职业学院	10733	4454	6265	675	438	4	89
山东艺术设计职业学院	5464	1390	2532	435	342	15	49
山东英才学院	21131	7461	8153	1247	940	76	224
山东旅游职业学院	9476	3547	3585	507	428	20	66
济南工程职业技术学院	13912	4345	5131	748	630	58	162
山东电子职业技术学院	10606	3029	3856	609	480	9	120
济南职业学院	15119	4876	5930	1051	811	70	295
山东现代学院	21388	6139	8056	889	615	36	155
山东工程职业技术大学	22890	4398	8134	945	764	53	198
山东城市建设职业学院	13777	4557	4956	711	598	10	184
山东管理学院	11309	2915	4040	820	595	47	127
齐鲁理工学院	22711	5889	8648	1702	1151	147	276
山东农业工程学院	3047	1250	832	895	623	55	168
山东特殊教育职业学院	1423	563	594	201	110	11	30
山东传媒职业学院	10457	3456	3553	411	389	18	74
莱芜职业技术学院	12146	3930	4812	772	520	30	153

18-3 中等专业学校一览(2022年)

Basic Statistics on Specialized Secondary Schools(2022)

单位：人 (person)

名称 Name	在校学生数 Total Enrollment	毕业生数 Graduates	招生数 New Enrollment	教职工人数 Teachers and Staff	#专任教师 Full-time Teachers		
					合计 Total	#正高级 Senior	#副高级 Sub-Senior
总计(Total)	**14323**	**3122**	**4460**	**1366**	**967**	**15**	**285**
工科学校(Engineering Schools)							
济南信息工程学校	3335	958	1080	207	181	1	69
济南电子机械工程学校	2764	542	944	219	182	5	61
济南铁路学校	263	39	119	69	68	3	16
山东冶金中等专业学校	884	215	354	135	61	1	30
财经学校(Finance and Economics Schools)							
山东省济南商贸学校	2479	424	750	227	186	3	58
体育学校(Sports Schools)							
济南市体育运动学校	958	290	225	123	62	0	16
济南市第二体育运动学校	173	124	51		29	1	6
山东体育学院附属中学	1610	160	437				
艺术学校(Art Schools)							
山东省文化艺术学校	944	141	230	198	125	0	11
山东工艺美术学院附属中等美术学校	143	48	43	22	19	1	4
济南艺术学校	770	181	227	166	54	0	14

18-4 分县区学前教育基本情况(2022年)

Statistics in Pre-school Education Institutions by Region(2022)

单位：人 (person)

县区	Region	幼儿园数(所) Number of Kindergartens (unit)	在园人数 Enrolment	入园人数 Entrants	教职工数 Teachers and Staff	#专任教师 Full-time Teachers
全市	Total	2190	362831	101997	48175	27217
历下区	Li xia	132	33858	9110	5293	2959
市中区	Shi zhong	189	36522	10407	5885	3066
槐荫区	Huai yin	169	36827	10998	5020	2670
天桥区	Tian qiao	169	31336	8631	4680	2278
历城区	Li cheng	234	56450	18246	7575	4136
长清区	Chang qing	119	17448	5025	1840	1143
章丘区	Zhang qiu	193	28068	8138	3560	2077
济阳区	Ji yang	161	19836	4805	2171	1300
莱芜区	Lai wu	325	31864	7689	3827	2687
钢城区	Gang cheng	76	9635	2370	1190	806
济南高新区	Jinan Gao xin	105	22565	7062	3151	1517
南部山区	Nan shan	68	6724	2019	862	436
平阴县	Ping yin	54	10803	2767	1052	771
商河县	Shang he	196	20895	4730	2069	1371

18-5 文化事业机构和人员
Number of Cultural Institutions and Persons in Culture

指标	Item	2018年	2019年	2020年	2021年	2022年
机构数(个)	**Institutions (unit)**					
电影业	Movies	54	65	64	65	72
艺术业	Arts	27	25	27	26	26
文物业	Cultural Relics	48	67	64	80	91
图书馆业	Libraries	12	14	14	14	14
群众文化业	Mass Culture	153	175	174	174	174
艺术教育业	Art Education	1	1	1	1	1
文艺科研业	Culture Research	1	1	1	1	1
从业人员数(人)	**Employed Persons(person)**					
电影业	Movies	1380	1075	641	588	528
艺术业	Arts	1537	1475	1512	1492	1480
文物业	Cultural Relics	1068	1365		1637	1604
图书馆业	Libraries	472	507	567	756	730
群众文化业	Mass Culture	695	745	801	723	775
艺术教育业	Art Education	170	175	181	180	238
文艺科研业	Culture Research	47	47	50	49	54

注：电影业机构、从业人员数据为城市电影院线数据，不含农村。
Note: The data of the film industry institutions and employees are urban cinema line data, excluding rural areas.

主要统计指标解释

普通高等学校 指通过国家普通高等教育招生考试，招收高中毕业生为主要培养对象，实施高等学历教育的全日制大学、独立设置的学院、独立学院和高等专科学校、高等职业学校及其他普通高教机构。

大学、独立设置的学院主要实施本科及本科层次以上的教育。独立学院主要实施本科层次的教育。高等专科学校、高等职业学校实施专科层次的教育。其他普通高教机构是指承担国家普通招生计划任务不计校数的机构，包括普通高等学校分校、大专班等。

文化事业机构 指从事专业文化工作和为专业文化工作服务的独立建制的单位。不包括这些单位另外举办独立核算的其他机构和各部门的业余文化组织。

Explanatory Notes on Main Statistical Indicators

Regular Higher Education Institutions refer to educational establishments recruiting graduates from senior secondary schools as the main target through National Matriculation TEST. They include full-time universities, independently established schools, independent colleges, higher professional colleges, higher vocational colleges and other regular higher education institutions.

Universities and independently established schools primarily provide normal courses at undergraduate and higher levels. Independent colleges mainly provide normal undergraduate courses. Higher professional colleges and higher vocational colleges primarily provide undergraduate of short-cycle courses. Other regular higher education institutions refer to educational establishments, which are responsible for enrolling higher education students under the State Plan but not enumerated in the total number of schools, including: branch schools of regular higher education institutions and junior colleges.

Cultural Institutions refer to units which have their own organizational system, work on professional culture work and serve the professional culture work, excluding other institutions for independent accounting established by such units separately and amateur cultural organizations of all departments.

19

体育与卫生

SPORTS AND PUBLIC HEALTH

19–1 体育事业
Statistics of Sports Institutions

指标	Item	2018年	2019年	2020年	2021年	2022年
体育部门职工人数(人)	**Number of Persons of Physical System(person)**	**591**	**672**	**677**	**550**	**548**
#业余体育学校	Spare-time Sports School	423	402	410	375	375
总计中:教练员	Referees	191	183	181	251	232
等级裁判员(人)	**Number of Referees in Grades(person)**					
一级裁判员	First Grade Referees					
二级裁判员	Second Grade Referees	268	344	155	169	90
三级裁判员	Third Grade Referees					
二级运动员发展人数(人)	**Number of Second Grade Sportsmen(person)**	**279**	**534**	**564**	**637**	**293**
少年儿童业余体校在校学生(人)	Enrollment Spare-time Sports School(person)	1140	1286	1010	1961	1666
业余体校(所)	Spare-time Sports School(unit)	5	10	10	10	7
运动员获奖牌数(枚)	**Number of Medals Won by Athletes(unit)**	**1186**	**1353**	**715.5**	**784**	**717**
#世界级 金牌	World Gold Medals	3	13		3	2
银牌	Silver Medals	1	7			
铜牌	Copper Medal	2	8		2	
#洲 际 金牌	Intercontinental Gold Medals	3	10		1	1
银牌	Silver Medals	2	11			2
铜牌	Copper Medal	1	7		1	
#全 国 金牌	Country Gold Medals	50	100	15	39	26
银牌	Silver Medals	36	91	7	28	30
铜牌	Copper Medal	41	132	10	27	26
#全 省 金牌	Province Gold Medals	430	442	285.5	298	258
银牌	Silver Medals	319	248	182	162	181
铜牌	Copper Medal	288	284	216	223	191
体育设施(个)	**Sports Facility(unit)**					
体育场	Stadium	12	14	14	124	119
体育馆	Gymnasium	9	10	11	28	32
游泳馆	Natatorium	5	9	10	79	122
室内外游泳池	Indoor Swimming Pool	4	10	10	90	13
有固定看台的灯光球场	Light Count With Fixed Stand	2	5	5	8	8

注：等级裁判员为当年新评定的人数。
Note: The number of referees is the number of new assessments in the current year.

19–2 各时期卫生事业情况

Statistics of Health Institutions in Major Years

年份 Year	卫生机构(个) Number of Health Institutions (unit)		卫生工作人员(人) Medical Technical Personnel (person)		卫生机构床位(张) Number of Health Institutions Beds (set)	
	小计 Total	#医院及卫生院 Hospitals and Township Hospitals	小计 Total	#卫生技术人员 Medical Technical Personnel	小计 Total	#医院及卫生院 Hospitals and Township Hospitals
1952	208	22	6277	4778	3160	1906
1957	708	45	10740	7991	5972	3401
1962	1191	98	13705	9648	7917	5662
1965	1144	114	18885	14881	9035	6438
1970	682	130	13273	10341	7878	6462
1975	934	137	20021	14956	9066	8050
1978	1017	148	24949	19198	11496	9856
1979	1078	152	26385	20110	11902	10781
1980	1091	151	27843	21295	12301	11052
"六五"时期						
1981	1188	152	29597	22559	12428	11436
1982	1159	151	30636	22814	12379	11383
1983	1177	156	31924	23948	12966	11674
1984	1160	157	32967	24502	13728	12960
1985	1175	165	34232	26185	14356	13791
"七五"时期						
1986	1184	167	35803	27360	14757	14165
1987	1137	166	37129	28159	15457	14721
1988	1103	171	38384	29167	16165	15580
1989	1137	180	39926	29878	16698	16176
1990	1300	178	41444	31130	18214	17216
"八五"时期						
1991	1233	177	40957	30815	18439	17538
1992	1331	180	41996	31541	18818	18178
1993	1285	193	43274	32871	20243	19320
1994	1228	213	43630	33007	20001	19064
1995	1185	216	43648	32848	20747	19534
"九五"时期						
1996	1674	214	45765	35219	20428	19716
1997	1567	220	44664	34188	21422	20706
1998	1574	227	45110	34596	21965	21130

19-2 续表 continued

年份 Year	卫生机构(个) Number of Health Institutions (unit)		卫生工作人员(人) Medical Technical Personnel (person)		卫生机构床位(张) Number of Health Institutions Beds (set)	
	小计 Total	#医院及卫生院 Hospitals and Township Hospitals	小计 Total	#卫生技术人员 Medical Technical Personnel	小计 Total	#医院及卫生院 Hospitals and Township Hospitals
1999	1570	226	45121	34000	21735	21086
2000	1414	231	45166	35669	21698	20830
"十五"时期						
2001	1414	231	45296	35790	21906	21033
2002	1708	243	39386	31945	21576	21042
2003	1868	246	41925	33803	22674	22262
2004	1917	243	41625	33998	24044	22588
2005	2138	246	41499	34129	24695	23524
"十一五"时期						
2006	2285	240	43023	35124	27695	26101
2007	2265	243	42513	34579	26055	25328
2008	5092	286	44416	36143	28939	27555
2009	5163	281	46311	37648	30920	28749
2010	5086	277	54711	39366	31947	29844
"十二五"时期						
2011	5159	262	58590	42116	34920	31545
2012	5239	243	60426	44331	38834	35194
2013	5368	255	76955	57700	45465	41287
2014	5784	265	84515	63604	48280	44058
2015	5947	269	89117	71778	49311	45195
"十三五"时期						
2016	6188	270	92060	76447	52191	47524
2017	5770	289	97663	76273	54855	50142
2018	6030	293	104347	82834	57460	51207
2019	7487	351	122370	97532	66623	59697
2020	7514	343	126681	102172	68831	62072
"十四五"时期						
2021	7515	336	131269	108401	72832	66258
2022	7665	329	137111	113536	76367	69642

注：2015年及2016年的卫生技术人员为注册卫生技术人员，其他年份为在岗卫生技术人员。
Note: Health technicians in 2015 and 2016 are registered health technicians, and other years are on-the-job health technicians.

19–3 卫生事业机构及床位
Number of Health Institutions and Beds

指标	Item	2018年	2019年	2020年	2021年	2022年
各类卫生机构数(个)	**Number of Health Institutions (unit)**	**6030**	**7487**	**7514**	**7515**	**7665**
医院	Hospital	246	289	284	279	280
社区卫生服务中心(站)	Health Service Center for Community	314	352	379	385	399
卫生院	Health Centers	47	62	59	57	49
门诊部	Outpatient Department	135	156	163	177	184
急救中心(站)	First-Aid Center	1	1	1	1	1
采血供应机构	Pick and Supply Blood Institution	2	3	2	2	2
妇幼保健院(所、站)	Women and Children Care Agencies	12	15	15	15	15
专科疾病防治院(所、站)	Specialized Disease Prevention &Treatment Institution	11	13	9	8	7
疾病预防控制中心(防疫站)	Center for Disease Control and Prevention	12	15	14	14	14
医学科学研究机构	Medical Science Research Institutes	2	2	2	2	2
其他卫生机构	Other Medical Institutions	29	39	32	30	40
各类卫生机构病床数(张)	**Number of Health Institutions Beds(set)**	**57460**	**66623**	**68831**	**72832**	**76367**
医院	Number of Medals Won by Athletes(unit)	48843	56315	58790	62887	66157
社区卫生服务中心(站)	Health Service Center for Community	3361	3791	3899	3873	4371
卫生院	Health Centers	2364	3382	3282	3371	3485
门诊部	Outpatient Department	65	33	43	138	73
妇幼保健院(所、站)	Women and Children Care Agencies	1158	1444	1533	1592	1591
专科疾病防治院(所、站)	Specialized Disease Prevention	1669	1658	1284	932	595
千人拥有量(张、人)	**Number Per 1000 Population(set.person)**					
平均每千人拥有病床	Number Of Beds Per 1000 Population	7.70	7.48	7.48	7.80	8.11
每千人拥有卫生技术人员	Number Of Medical Technical Personnel Per 1000 Population	11.10	10.95	11.10	11.61	12.06
每千人拥有医生	Number Of Doctors Per 1000 Population	4.31	4.30	4.37	4.55	4.67
每千人拥有护士	Number Of Nurses Per 1000 Population	5.03	4.91	4.97	5.30	5.51

19–4 分地区卫生事业机构及床位(2022年)
Number of Health Institutions and Beds by District(2022)

指标	Item	全市 Total	市区 Districts	平阴县 Ping yin	商河县 Shang he
各类卫生机构数(个)	**Number of Institutions(unit)**	**7665**	**6955**	**263**	**447**
医院	Hospital	280	270	4	6
疗养院	Sanatorium				
社区卫生服务中心(站)	Health Service Center for Community	399	382	8	9
卫生院	Health Centers	49	32	6	11
门诊部	Outpatient Department	184	177		7
诊所、卫生所、医务室	Infirmaries and Clinics	3071	2910	75	86
急救中心(站)	First-Aid Center	1	1		
采血供应机构	Pick and Supply Blood Institution	2	2		
妇幼保健院(所、站)	Women and Children Care Agencies	15	13	1	1
专科疾病防治院(所、站)	Specialized Disease Prevention &Treatment Institution	7	6	1	
疾病预防控制中心(防疫站)	Center for Disease Control and Prevention	14	12	1	1
卫生监督所	Number of Medals Won by Athletes(unit)	14	12	1	1
医学科学研究机构	Medical Science Research Institutes	2	2		
其他卫生构	Other Medical Institutions	40	40		
各类卫生机构病床数(张)	**Number of Institutions Beds(set)**	**76367**	**71066**	**2491**	**2810**
医院	Hospital	66157	62281	1736	2140
疗养院	Sanatorium				
社区卫生服务中心(站)	Health Service Center for Community	4371	4290	20	61
卫生院	Health Centers	3485	2276	609	600
门诊部	Outpatient Department	73	73		
妇幼保健院(所、站)	Women and Children Care Agencies	1636	1621	6	9
专科疾病防治院(所、站)	Specialized Disease Prevention&Treatment Institution	595	475	120	
千人拥有量(张、人)	**Number Per 1000 Population(set.person)**				
平均每千人拥有病床	Number Of Beds Per 1000 Population	8.11	8.30	7.54	5.34
每千人拥有卫生技术人员	Number Of Medical Technical Personnel Per 1000 Population	12.06	12.60	7.89	5.95
每千人拥有医生	Number Of Doctors Per 1000 Population	4.67	4.89	2.92	2.26
每千人拥有护士	Number Of Nurses Per 1000 Population	5.51	5.76	3.71	2.63

19–5 医疗机构年收入与支出 (2022年)
Revenue and Expenditure in Health Institutions(2022)

单位:万元 (10 000 yuan)

机构分类	Institutions	总收入 Total Income 合计 Total	财政补助收入 Financial Subsidy Income	上级补助收入 Grant From Higher Authority	业务收入/事业收入 Business Income
合计	**Total**	**7218264.4**	**975025.7**	**23081.2**	**5812630.1**
医院	Hospital	5856398.8	525865.7	1255.6	5072019.5
社区卫生服务中心(站)	Health Service Center for Community	390810.7	133648.1	4267.7	239606.5
卫生院	Health Centers	118134.4	58152.6	942.3	57107.0
门诊部	Outpatient Department	50753.6	-	-	43333.6
诊所.卫生所.医务室	Infirmaries and Clinics	79871.7	-	-	70535.2
急救中心(站)	First-Aid Center	7805.8	4732.4		112.5
妇幼保健院(所、站)	Women and Children Care Agencies	211367.0	45224.9	4.2	156625.3
专科疾病防治院(所、站)	Specialized Disease Prevention&Treatment Institution	14989.6	5192.1	583.8	8984.8

19–5 续表 continued

单位:万元 (10 000 yuan)

机构分类	Institutions	总支出 Total Expenditure 合计 Total	单位管理费 Unit Management Fee	业务活动费 Business Activity Fee	总费用中:人员费用 Staff Expenditure
合计	**Total**	**6766425.9**	**801413.2**	**5625395.6**	**2454228.4**
医院	Hospital	5575111.1	700583.0	4758404.6	1994555.6
社区卫生服务中心(站)	Health Service Center for Community	398522.3	11487.5	328788.5	126809.1
卫生院	Health Centers	117812.3	3531.1	111805.3	57313.0
门诊部	Outpatient Department	36843.0	-	-	20199.7
诊所.卫生所.医务室	Infirmaries and Clinics	62884.5	-	-	35495.1
急救中心(站)	First-Aid Center	4004.5	790.2	3213.3	360.7
妇幼保健院(所、站)	Women and Children Care Agencies	205516.8	27481.0	176281.6	98508.9
专科疾病防治院(所、站)	Specialized Disease Prevention&Treatment Institution	14101.8	2737.6	11364.1	7627.7

注:门诊部及诊所.卫生所.医务室不填报财政补助收入、上级补助收入、单位管理费、业务活动费四项指标。

Note:Outpatient department and clinic. Health clinic. The medical office does not report four indicators: financial subsidy income, superior subsidy income, Unit Management Fee, Business Activity Fee.

19-6 医院卫生院工作情况
Basic Statistics on Hospitals and Health Centers

指标	Item	2018年	2019年	2020年	2021年	2022年
医院	**Hospital**					
单位数(个)	Number(unit)	246	289	284	279	280
诊疗人次数(万人次)	Visits (10 000 person-times)	3309	3922	3397	3993	3584
#门诊人次数	Outpatient Visits	2960	3449	3018	3504	3148
急诊人次数	Emergency Visits	228	300	235	327	314
健康检查人数(万人次)	check-up(10 000 person-times)	201	260	235	271	253
入院人数(万人)	Inpatients(10 000 persons)	150.0	182.2	172.3	204.3	203.1
出院人数(万人)	Patients Discharged(10 000 persons)	149.4	181.5	171.8	203.6	202.7
平均开放病床数(张)	Average Bed Opened(set)	45132	52359	54692	58399	62570
病床使用率(%)	Utilization Rate of Beds(%)	87.28	87.27	77.71	82.71	71.42
病床周转次数(次)	Number of Medals Won by Athletes(unit)	33.10	34.70	31.40	34.90	32.40
出院者平均住院日(日)	Average Stay Days in Hospital(day)	9.40	9.20	9.10	8.50	8.00
卫生院	**Health Centers**					
单位数(个)	Number(unit)	47	62	59	57	49
诊疗人次数(万人次)	Visits (10 000 person-times)	195.2	301.9	304.1	349.4	310.4
#门诊人次数	Outpatient Visits	190.3	292.1	292.7	334.2	302.7
急诊人次数	Emergency Visits	3.3	3.6	5.0	4.5	3.9
健康检查人数(万人次)	check-up(10 000 person-times)	20.4	35.8	25.5	28.3	24.5
入院人数(万人)	Inpatients(10 000 persons)	4.4	7.2	5.8	6.5	6.6
出院人数(万人)	Patients Discharged(10 000 persons)	4.4	7.2	5.7	6.5	6.5
平均开放病床数(张)	Average Bed Opened(set)	2277	3187	3203	3240	3153
病床使用率(%)	Occupancy Rate of Hospital Beds(%)	54.85	58.03	47.37	51.77	51.27
病床周转次数(次)	Turnover of Hospital Beds(time)	19.40	22.70	17.90	20.00	20.60
出院者平均住院日(日)	Average Length of Stay in Hospital(day)	9.70	7.80	8.50	8.80	8.80

19-7 分地区卫生技术人员分类情况(2022年)
Medical Technical Personnel by Region(2022)

单位：人 (person)

指标	Item	全市 Total	市区 Districts	平阴县 Ping yin	商河县 Shang he
各类卫生机构工作人员合计	**Total of Personnel in Health Institutions**	**137111**	**129496**	**3440**	**4175**
#卫生技术人员小计	Health Technical Personnel	113536	107795	2607	3134
医生	Licensed Physicians	43984	41827	966	1191
注册护士	Registered Nurses	51911	49300	1225	1386
其他	Others	4344	4001	122	221

主要统计指标解释

医疗卫生机构 指从卫生健康行政部门取得《医疗机构执业许可证》，或从民政、工商行政、机构编制管理部门取得法人单位登记证书，为社会提供医疗保健、疾病控制、卫生监督服务或从事医学科研和医学在职培训等工作的单位。医疗卫生机构包括医院、基层医疗卫生机构、专业公共卫生机构、其他医疗卫生机构。

医院 包括综合医院、中医医院、中西医结合医院、民族医院、各类专科医院和护理院，不包括专科疾病防治院、妇幼保健院和疗养院。

卫生技术人员 包括执业医师、执业助理医师、注册护士、药师（士）、检验技师（士）、影像技师、卫生监督员和见习医（药、护、技）师（士）等卫生专业人员。不包括从事管理工作的卫生技术人员(如院长、副院长、党委书记等)。

执业医师 指《医师执业证》“级别”为“执业医师”且实际从事医疗、预防保健工作的人员，不包括实际从事管理工作的执业医师。执业医师类别分为临床、中医、口腔和公共卫生四类。

床位数 指年末医疗卫生机构实有床位，又称实有床位数、病床数。实有床位包括正规床、简易床、监护床、超过半年的加床、正在消毒和修理的床位、因扩建或大修而停用的床位。不包括产科新生儿床、接产室待产床、库存床、观察床、临时加床和病人家属陪待床。

Explanatory Notes on Main Statistical Indicators

Health Care Institutions refer to the units which have been qualified with the Certification of Health Care Institution,, or qualified with the Certification of Corporate Unit by the civil affairs, administration for industry and commerce, and engaging in medical care services, disease control services, health supervision services, or medicine research and on-job training, etc., including: hospitals, health care institutions at grass-root level, specialized public health institutions, and other health care institutions.

Hospitals include general hospitals, traditional Chinese medicine hospitals, hospitals of integrated traditional Chinese and western medicine, nationalities hospitals, specialized hospitals and nursing hospitals, as well as affiliated hospitals of medical colleges, excluding specialized disease prevention and treatment institutes, maternal and child health centers and convalescent hospitals.

Health Technical Personnel refer to the professional staff engaged in health care, including licensed physicians and physician assistants, registered nurses, pharmacists, laboratory and imaging technicians, health care supervisors and intern doctors, pharmacists, nurses, and technical personnel, excluding health technical personnel engaged in management (e.g. president, vice president and secretary of the party committee etc).

Licensed Physicians refer to the medical workers with licenses of qualified doctors and are employed in medical treatment, disease prevention or healthcare institutions, excluding the licensed doctors engaged in management. The physicians are divided into 4 categories: clinician, Chinese medicine, stomatology and public health.

Number of Beds refer to the actual number of beds in health care institutions at year-end, also known as the actual number of beds or hospital beds, including regular beds, simple beds, monitoring beds, extra bed over 6 months, beds under disinfection or repairing, beds deactivated due to expansion or overhaul, not including neonatal beds, pre-delivery beds, inventory beds, observation beds, temporary beds and family accompany beds.

20

民政、司法和其他

SOCIAL WELFARE CIVIL ADMINISTRATION AND JUSTICE

20-1 社会治安主要指标
Main Indicators of Public Order

指标	Item	2018年	2019年	2020年	2021年	2022年
刑事案件(件)	**Criminal Cases(case)**					
当年全部立案数	Put on Record	18594	25382	32965	40583	36275
破获当年刑事案件数	Cracked the Number of Criminal Cases	7103	9259	18983	17316	16099
治安案件(件)	**Public Security Cases(case)**					
受理数	Cases Accepted	75393	79355	68614	64550	63708
查处数	Cases Investigated and Treated	73700	72593	60633	58043	62628
城市交通事故	**Traffic Accidents**					
交通事故(起)	Number of Traffic Accidents(case)	3071	3334	3313	3317	3257
伤亡人数(人)	Number of Injuries and Deaths(person)	3618	3925	3747	3631	3771
#死亡人数(人)	Number of Deaths(person)	419	472	465	447	439
损失折款(万元)	Direct Losses(10 000 yuan)	947	905	1006	1207	857
火灾事故	**Fires**					
火灾起数(起)	Number of Fire Accidents(case)	1539	4577	4319	5907	5892
伤亡人数(人)	Number of Injuries and Deaths(person)	12	12	16	35	13
#死亡人数(人)	Number of Deaths(person)	10	10	13	24	9
损失折款(万元)	Direct Losses(10 000 yuan)	827	1529	2153	6231.8	3817

20-2 分地区社会治安主要指标(2022年)
Main Indicators of Public Order by District(2022)

指标	Item	全市 Total	其中 of which		
			市区 Districts	平阴县 Ping yin	商河县 Shang he
刑事案件(件)	Criminal Cases(case)				
当年全部立案数	Put on Record	36275	34301	933	1041
破获当年刑事案件数	Cracked the Number of Criminal Cases	16099	15122	472	505
治安案件(件)	Public Security Cases(case)				
受理数	Cases Accepted	63708	60702	977	2029
查处数	Cases Punished	62628	59836	976	1816
城市交通事故	Traffic Accidents				
交通事故(起)	Number of Traffic Accidents(case)	3257	3117	98	42
伤亡人数(人)	Number of Injuries and Deaths(person)	3771	3562	160	49
#死亡人数(人)	Number of Deaths(person)	439	410	19	10
损失折款(万元)	Direct Losses(10 000 yuan)	857	846	5	6
火灾事故	Fires				
火灾起数(起)	Number of Fire Accidents(case)	5892	5114	277	501
伤亡人数(人)	Number of Injuries and Deaths(person)	13	10	1	2
#死亡人数(人)	Number of Deaths(person)	9	8	1	
损失折款(万元)	Direct Losses(10 000 yuan)	3817	2899	261	657.0

20-3 社会保障和救济
Basic Statistics on Social Security and Receiving Relief Flinds

指标	Item	2018年	2019年	2020年	2021年	2022年
优抚情况(人)	**Veteran Benefit and Placement(person)**					
享受定期抚恤金人数	Number of Receiving Periodic Pensions	784	914			
在乡复员军人	Demobilized Soldiers in Countryside	1486	1727			
参战退役人员	Veterans	4630	5636			
社会救济情况(人)	**Social Relief(person)**					
城镇居民最低生活保障人数	Number of Urban Residents for Minimum Livelihood Guarantee	13364	15491	14159	13063	10932
农村居民最低生活保障人数	Number of Rural residents for Minimum Livelihood Guarantee	64271	73305	84209	84367	83049
民政经费(万元)	**Civil Affairs Expenditures(10 000 yuan)**					
城市居民最低生活保障费	Urban Residents for Minimum Livelihood Guarantee	9563	9657	11030	11774	12952
农村最低生活保障费	Rural residents for Minimum Livelihood Guarantee	26439	26039	39218	51177	66311
其它社会救助费	Other Social Assistance Expenses	3088	1158	1175	1367	1214
社会福利费	Social Welfare Funds	47654	60731	69771	92454	96830
退役安置费(万元)	**Decommissioning Costs(10 000 yuan)**	**12656**	**13538**			
自然灾害生活救助费(万元)	**Natural Disaster Assistance Expenses(10 000 yuan)**	**69**	**2450**			
医疗救助费(万元)	**Medical Assistance Expenses(10 000 yuan)**	**7175**	**3680**	**9280**	**10409**	**9656**
社会保障及扶贫(个、元)	**Social Security and Poverty Alleviation(unit.yuan)**					
建立社会保障服务网络的乡镇数	Number of Towns With Social Security Service Network	29	40	29	29	192
城市市区居民最低生活保障金标准	Minimum Living Standards for Urban Residents	616	685	821	904	995

注：1.本表指标为“–”的，部门相关统计制度中已经不在进行统计。
2. 2022年，“建立社会保障服务网络的乡镇数”的口径为全市可以经办居民养老保险业务的乡镇。
Note:1.The indicator “-” in this table means statistics are no longer in the relevant statistical system of the department.
2.The unified standard for the "number of towns and villages establishing social security service networks" in 2022 refers to the towns and villages that can handle residents' endowment insurance business in the whole city.

20–4 分地区社会保障和救济(2022年)

Basic Statistics on Social Security and Receiving Relief Flinds by Region (2022)

指标	Item	济南市(汇总) Total	济南市(市本级) Cities	历下区 Li xia	市中区 Shi zhong
社会救济情况(人)	**Social Relief(person)**				
城镇居民最低生活保障人数	Number of Urban Residents for Minimum Livelihood Guarantee	10932		1448	1582
农村居民最低生活保障人数	Number of Rural residents for Minimum Livelihood Guarantee	83049			1231
民政经费(万元)	**Civil Affairs Expenditures(10 000 yuan)**				
城市居民最低生活保障费	Urban Residents for Minimum Livelihood Guarantee	12951.5		1954.2	1931.7
农村最低生活保障费	Rural residents for Minimum Livelihood Guarantee	66311.4			1335.4
其它社会救助费	Other Social Assistance Expenses	1213.9		110.8	312.0
社会福利费	Social Welfare Funds	96830.4	20762.8	7023.6	2615.5
社会保障及扶贫(个、元)	**Social Security and Poverty Alleviation(unit.yuan)**				
建立社会保障服务网络的乡镇数	Number of Towns With Social Security Service Network	192		13	17
城市市区居民最低生活保障金标准	Minimum Living Standards for Urban Residents	995		995	995

槐荫区 Huai yin	天桥区 Tian qiao	历城区 Li cheng	长清区 Chang qing	章丘区 Zhang qiu	济阳区 Ji yang	莱芜区 Lai wu	钢城区 Gang cheng	济南高新区 Jinan Gao xin	济南起步区（直管） Jinan Start-up Area (Directly under)	南部山区 Nan shan	平阴县 Ping yin	商河县 Shang he
1194	2501	400.0	546	563	62	1355	603	17	112	45	158	346
472	464	1793.0	10160	17704	5189	16869	3558	862	2214	4531	4011	13991
1408.0	3051.2	513.5	524.0	609.0	58.9	1500.5	707.5	24.8	132.7	57.6	166.2	311.7
508.7	348.5	2203.1	7493.3	13621.0	3709.6	13571.0	3058.8	950.3	2000.2	4281.8	2986.4	10243.3
11.4	47.4	198.3		350.0	155.4		1.2	4.8		0.4	3.1	19.1
2392.2	2016.4	2831.2	4718.0	13748.7	8096.3	7627.1	9022.5	2952.5	2547.6	1954.7	3671.4	4849.9
17	14	21	10	20	8	20	13	9	4	5	8	13
995	995	995	995	995	995	995	995	995	995	995	995	995

20-5 律师、公证、司法基本情况(2022年)
Basic Statistics on Law, Notarizations and Mediation (2022)

指标	Item	单位 Unit	全市 Total	市区 Districts	平阴县 Ping yin	商河县 Shang he
律师工作	**Lawyers**					
律师事务所	Number of Law Offices	个(unit)	500	490	8	2
执业律师	Number of Lawyers	人(person)	9024	8930	58	36
担任常年法律顾问	Permanent Legal Advisor	家(unit)	11000	10822	147	31
民事诉讼代理	Civil Agent	件(case)	105463	104388	834	241
刑事诉讼辩护及代理	Criminal Defense and Agent	件(case)	8903	8637	117	149
行政诉讼代理	Administrative Agent	件(case)	5682	5646	24	12
非诉讼法律事务	Non-litigation Legal Matters	件(case)	22013	21987	26	
公证工作	**Notarization**					
公证处	Number of Notary Offices	个(unit)	15	8	1	1
公证处人员	Personnel of Notary Offices	人(person)	493	415	8	6
#公证员	Notaries	人(person)	175	148	4	2
办理公证总数	Number of Notarized Affair	件(case)	207026	193004	883	1017
#国内民事公证	Domestic Civil Notarization	件(case)	56050	44559	463	475
国内经济公证	Domestic Commerce Notarization	件(case)	93133	90675	420	529
涉外公证	Foreign-related Notarization	件(case)	67055	66974		13
办理经济公证涉及金额	Money of Commerce Notarization	亿元(100 million yuan)	145.90	45	5.16	0.05
基层司法行政工作	**Basic Mediation Administration**					
人民调解委员会	People's Mediation Committee	个(unit)	6011	5101	348	562
人民调解员	People's Mediators	人(person)	23947	19963	1316	2668
调解纠纷总数	Number of Mediation Disputes	件(case)	27339	23431	1940	1968
#调解成功	Success Mediation	件(case)	26576	22671	1940	1968
法律服务所	Legal Service Office	个(unit)	149	137	9	3
基层法律工作者	Grassroots Legal Workers	人(person)	826	779	34	13
担任法律顾问	Legal Advisor	家(unit)	826	752	66	8
民事诉讼代理	Civil Agent	件(case)	8710	6158	621	931
非诉讼代理	Non-litigation Agent	件(case)	3530	3365	143	22
法律援助工作	**Legal Aid**					
法律援助机构	Legal Aid Institution	个(unit)	13	1	1	1
执业人员	Practitioners	人(person)	17	4		
办理法律援助案件	Legal Aid Cases	件(case)	21519	1248	822	820

主要统计指标解释

律师 是指依法取得律师执业证书，接受委托或指定，为当事人提供法律服务的执业人员。

公证员 是指符合法定条件，在公证机构从事公证业务的执业人员。

调解人员 指在人民调解委员会担负调解民间一般民事纠纷和轻微违法行为引起纠纷的工作人员，包括调解委员会的委员和调解小组的调解员。

Explanatory Notes on Main Statistical Indicators

Lawyers refer to practitioners who have obtained a lawyer's practice certificate in accordance with the law, accept commissions or appointments, and provide legal services to clients.

Notary refers to a practitioner who meets the legal requirements and engages in notarization business at a notary institution.

Mediation Personnel refers to staff taking charge of mediating ordinary civil disputes among the people and disputes arising from minor infraction at the people's mediation committee, including the member of the mediation committee and the mediator of the mediation team.

附录

APPENDIX

附录一 山东省十六城市主要经济指标(2022年)
Main Statistical Indicators Indicators of 16 Cities in Shandong(2022)

单位：亿元

城市名称	Region	地区生产总值 Gross Domestic Product	第一产业 Primary Industry	第二产业 Secondary Industry	第三产业 Tertiary Industry	固定资产投资比上年增长(%) Growth Rate Investment in Fixed Assets (%)	房地产开发投资额 Estate Development Investment	一般公共预算收入 General Public Budget Revenue	一般公共预算支出 General Public Budget Expenditure	金融机构本外币存款余额 The Balance of RMB and Foreign Currencies Deposits in Financial Institutions
全 省	**Total**	**87435.0**	**6298.6**	**35014.2**	**46122.3**	**6.1**	**9225.9**	**7104.0**	**12131.5**	**146076.0**
济南市	**Jinan**	**12027.5**	**420.5**	**4180.2**	**7426.7**	**3.8**	**1830.8**	**1001.1**	**1225.6**	**25941.0**
青岛市	Qingdao	14920.8	478.1	5197.3	9245.4	4.5	1789.1	1273.2	1696.2	24992.7
淄博市	Zibo	4402.6	188.6	2193.7	2020.3	18.1	356.6	375.9	526.4	6868.7
枣庄市	Zaozhuang	2039.0	194.3	804.1	1040.7	10.1	334.8	168.9	325.5	2930.2
东营市	Dongying	3620.7	191.6	2092.1	1337.0	12.4	200.7	265.5	369.5	5352.8
烟台市	Yantai	9515.9	662.5	4022.2	4831.1	8.5	701.6	635.4	923.5	12344.8
潍坊市	Weifang	7306.5	647.0	3066.6	3592.9	12.7	778.1	608.0	842.5	12352.2
济宁市	Jining	5316.9	610.9	2068.1	2637.8	-16.1	506.6	447.7	746.9	8069.6
泰安市	Taian	3198.1	350.9	1286.0	1561.3	17.4	263.5	222.7	441.7	5597.1
威海市	Weihai	3408.2	354.8	1313.7	1739.8	-18.9	256.1	225.2	417.4	5886.4
日照市	Rizhao	2306.8	208.0	938.8	1160.0	3.1	229.4	185.5	289.1	3720.4
临沂市	Linyi	5778.5	511.0	2294.4	2973.2	12.3	704.4	420.2	874.8	9797.1
德州市	Dezhou	3633.1	370.4	1509.2	1753.5	18.5	352.1	235.0	573.3	5409.5
聊城市	Liaocheng	2779.9	400.1	1044.5	1335.3	16.3	355.9	230.6	514.9	5546.6
滨州市	Binzhou	2975.2	296.8	1266.7	1411.7	14.1	190.4	275.7	481.7	4358.2
菏泽市	Heze	4205.3	413.1	1736.6	2055.6	18.3	375.7	300.6	692.2	6413.9
济南位次	Position	2	6	2	2	13	1	2	2	1

注：本表内其他城市数据根据内部资料整理，不做正式发布，仅供参考。各项指标最终数据，敬请关注各城市官方发布机构。

(100 million yuan)

#住户存款 Household Deposits	金融机构本外币贷款余额 The Balance of RMB and Foreign Currencies Loans in Financial Institutions	社会消费品零售总额比上年增长(%) Growth Rate Total Retail Sales of Consumer Goods (%)	货物进出口总额 Total Import & Export	#出口总额 Total Export	实际使用外资(亿美元) Actual Use of Foreign Capital (100 million USD)	城镇居民人均可支配收入(元) Per Capita Disposable Income of Urban Households (yuan)	城镇居民人均消费支出(元) Per Capita Consumption Expenditure of Urban Households (yuan)	农村居民人均可支配收入(元) Per Capita Disposable Income of Rural Households (yuan)	农村居民人均消费支出(元) Per Capita Consumption Expenditure of Rural Households (yuan)	居民消费价格指数 Consumer Price Indices
85033.3	**123994.8**	**-1.4**	**33324.9**	**20355.8**	**228.7**	**49050**	**28555**	**22110**	**14687**	**101.7**
10291.7	**26112.3**	**-4.8**	**2208.9**	**1431.8**	**31.4**	**59459**	**35788**	**23844**	**14883**	**101.4**
11081.7	26782.5	-1.4	9117.2	5361.1	55.1	62584	37592	27701	17508	102.0
4700.6	4716.7	-1.1	1234.1	731.6	10.3	52684	30999	24572	17319	101.3
2126.4	2313.4	-2.6	431.0	397.5	6.7	39727	21490	20858	13038	101.2
2899.7	3723.2	1.9	2626.5	674.8	8.0	58794	32723	23642	16994	101.4
7538.1	8097.9	0.5	4547.4	2750.9	29.8	55700	33577	26286	18042	101.4
7987.6	10007.2	-1.3	3419.9	2477.2	13.0	48989	27835	25639	15901	101.6
5597.8	6410.4	0.1	848.2	637.8	12.9	42989	23529	22137	13554	101.7
4036.1	3969.6		405.9	352.4	5.6	43435	24101	23149	14404	101.3
3813.6	4655.1	-4.4	2095.6	1567.5	10.8	56024	32772	27027	15845	101.4
2324.2	3785.6	0.3	1397.7	545.3	7.0	40798	23211	21302	10992	101.2
6792.1	9013.6	-0.4	1875.1	1711.3	13.9	44457	19951	19000	11728	101.6
4045.2	3303.2	-0.3	622.1	489.1	6.4	33495	18730	20413	15338	101.4
4015.1	3482.6		614.0	408.3	4.8	33778	18537	18674	12867	101.6
2651.9	3475.5	-0.3	1227.1	506.3	6.8	43421	25788	21862	14316	100.9
5131.1	3943.5	-1.4	654.3	313.0	6.2	33334	19600	18040	13918	101.1
2	2	16	5	6	2	2	2	6	8	6

Note: The data regarding other cities in this table is sorted out according to internal data which is for reference only instead of being released officially. As for final data regarding various indicators, refer to official release mechanism in each city.

附录二 十五副省级城市主要经济指标(2022年)
Main Statistical Indicators of 15 Vice-provincial Cities(2022)

单位：亿元

城市名称	Region	地区生产总值 Gross Domestic Product	第一产业 Primary Industry	第二产业 Secondary Industry	第三产业 Tertiary Industry	固定资产投资比上年增长(%) Growth Rate Investment in Fixed Assets (%)	房地产开发投资上年增长(%) Growth rate Estate Development Investment (%)	一般公共预算收入 General Public Budget Revenue	一般公共预算支出 General Public Budget Expenditure
济南	**Jinan**	**12027.5**	**420.5**	**4180.2**	**7426.7**	**3.8**	**-5.0**	**1001.1**	**1225.6**
沈阳	Shenyang	7695.8	335.2	2885.5	4475.1	6.1	-23.1	713.7	1048.9
大连	Dalian	8430.9	563.0	3712.5	4155.4	6.5	-16.5	669.7	991.1
长春	Changchun	6744.6	551.3	2695.0	3498.3	-11.8	-37.1	459.7	976.7
哈尔滨	Harbin	5490.1	672.1	1285.0	3533.0	-7.6	-35.8	262.2	1065.5
南京	Nanjing	16907.9	315.6	6069.6	10522.7	3.5	1.4	1558.2	1828.7
杭州	Hangzhou	18753.0	346.0	5620.0	12787.0	6.0	7.2	2451.0	2542.0
宁波	Ningbo	15704.3	382.0	7413.5	7908.8	10.4	2.7	1680.2	2187.8
厦门	Xiamen	7802.7	29.3	3233.6	4539.8	9.9	-0.5	883.8	1088.7
青岛	Qingdao	14920.8	478.1	5197.3	9245.4	4.5	-9.7	1273.2	1696.2
武汉	Wuhan	18866.4	475.8	6716.7	11674.0	10.8	5.5	1504.7	2227.2
广州	Guangzhou	28839.0	318.3	7909.3	20611.4	-2.1	-5.4	1854.7	3014.2
深圳	Shenzhen	32387.7	25.6	12405.9	19956.2	8.4	13.3	4012.3	4997.2
成都	Chengdu	20817.5	588.4	6404.1	13825.0	5.0	7.0	1722.4	2435.0
西安	Xi'an	11486.5	323.6	4071.6	7091.4	10.5	6.5	834.1	1573.1
济南位次	Position	9	7	9	9	11	9	9	10

注：1.为便于排序，广州实际使用外资数据为人民币口径根据平均汇率推算；武汉、成都、西安实际使用外资为FDI口径。
2.本表内其他城市数据根据内部资料整理，不做正式发布，仅供参考。各项指标最终数据，敬请关注各城市官方发布机构。

(100 million yuan)

金融机构本外币存款余额 The Balance of RMB and Foreign Currencies Deposits in Financial Institutions	金融机构本外币贷款余额 The Balance of RMB and Foreign Currencies Loans in Financial Institutions	社会消费品零售总额 Total Retail Sales of Consumer Goods	货物进出口总额 Total Import & Export	#出口总额 Total Export	实际使用外资(亿美元) Actual Use of Foreign Capital (100 million USD)	城镇居民人均可支配收入(元) Per Capita Disposable Income of Urban Households (yuan)	农村居民人均可支配收入(元) Per Capita Disposable Income of Rural Households (yuan)	居民消费价格指数 Consumer Price Indices
25941.0	**26112.3**	**4878.1**	**2208.9**	**1431.8**	**31.4**	**59459**	**23844**	**101.4**
20855.0	20777.3	3864.5	1406.6	522.3	39.2	51702	22352	101.7
18911.4	14235.1	1846.9	4792.1	2086.7	20.3	51904	24759	102.2
16851.3	17122.1	1907.8	1107.6	208.5	3.1	43240	18919	101.9
16474.0	14396.5	2195.9	387.0	136.3		43981	22260	101.9
49531.3	48760.2	7832.4	6292.1	3827.9	48.5	76643	34664	102.2
69592.0	62306.0	7294.0	7565.0	5141.0	78.1	77043	45183	102.4
31302.7	32986.1	4896.7	12671.3	8230.6	37.3	76690	45487	102.3
16167.0	17319.3	2665.4	9225.6	4657.4	22.1	70467	32323	101.8
24992.8	26782.5	5891.8	9117.2	5361.1	55.1	62584	27701	102.0
35754.0	44383.8	6936.2	3532.2	2153.0	21.1	58449	29304	102.3
80495.1	68918.6	10298.2	10948.4	6194.8	86.0	76849	36292	102.4
123400.5	83423.0	9708.3	36737.5	21944.8	109.7	72718	-	102.3
53189.0	53053.0	9096.5	8346.4	5005.1	29.5	54897	30931	102.4
31763.1	32247.1	4642.1	4474.1	2801.5	11.7	48418	18285	102.2
9	10	9	12	12	8	8	10	15

Notes: 1.To facilitate ranking, the data regarding actual use of foreign capital actually used by Guangzhou is calculated as per RMB caliber and average annual rate; The actual Use of foreign capital in Wuhan Chengdu and Xi'an is Based on FDI Criteria

2.The data regarding other cities in this table is sorted out according to internal data which is for reference only instead of being released officially. As for final data regarding various indicators, refer to official release mechanism in each city.

附录三 二十六省会城市主要经济指标(2022年)
Main Statistical Indicators of 26 Provincial Capitals (2022)

单位：亿元

城市名称	Region	地区生产总值 Gross Domestic Product	第一产业 Primary Industry	第二产业 Secondary Industry	第三产业 Tertiary Industry	固定资产投资比上年增长(%) Growth Rate Investment in Fixed Assets (%)	房地产开发投资上年增长(%) Growth rate Estate Development Investment (%)
济南	**Jinan**	**12027.5**	**420.5**	**4180.2**	**7426.7**	**3.8**	**-5.0**
石家庄	Shijiazhuang	7100.6	558.3	2334.1	4208.2	10.0	-6.8
太原	Taiyuan	5571.2	48.1	2466.1	3057.0	0.2	-18.6
呼和浩特	Hohhot	3329.1	160.6	1155.8	2012.7	12.6	-19.1
沈阳	Shenyang	7695.8	335.2	2885.5	4475.1	6.1	-23.1
长春	Changchun	6744.6	551.3	2695.0	3498.3	-11.8	-37.1
哈尔滨	Harbin	5490.1	672.1	1285.0	3533.0	-7.6	-35.8
南京	Nanjing	16907.9	315.6	6069.6	10522.7	3.5	1.4
杭州	Hangzhou	18753.0	346.0	5620.0	12787.0	6.0	7.2
合肥	Hefei	12013.1	379.2	4394.5	7239.4	9.1	-0.6
福州	Fuzhou	12308.2	683.4	4656.9	6968.0	5.9	-15.0
南昌	Nanchang	7203.5	248.6	3484.6	3470.3	7.6	-19.3
郑州	Zhengzhou	12934.7	185.6	5174.6	7574.5	-8.5	-18.7
武汉	Wuhan	18866.4	475.8	6716.7	11674.0	10.8	5.5
长沙	Changsha	13966.1	451.3	5589.6	7925.2	5.1	8.4
广州	Guangzhou	28839.0	318.3	7909.3	20611.4	-2.1	-5.4
南宁	Nanning	5218.3	601.5	1182.8	3434.0	-17.8	-45.3
海口	Haikou	2134.8	99.2	406.3	1629.3	-12.7	-3.2
成都	Chengdu	20817.5	588.4	6404.1	13825.0	5.0	7.0
贵阳	Guiyang	4921.2	203.6	1739.6	2978.0	-4.2	-21.7
昆明	Kunming	7541.4	327.0	2413.4	4801.0	-3.1	-30.8
西安	Xi'an	11486.5	323.6	4071.6	7091.4	10.5	6.5
兰州	Lanzhou	3343.5	65.0	1150.8	2127.8	-3.5	-19.0
西宁	Xining	1644.4	63.0	618.5	962.9	-18.3	-36.1
银川	Yinchuan	2535.6	91.8	1261.7	1182.1	3.7	-16.0
乌鲁木齐	Urumqi	3893.0	31.0	1133.4	2728.8	0.3	-41.7
济南位次	Position	9	9	10	8	12	9

注：本表内其他城市数据根据内部资料整理，不做正式发布，仅供参考。各项指标最终数据，敬请关注各城市官方发布机构。

(100 million yuan)

一般公共预算收入 General Public Budget Revenue	一般公共预算支出 General Public Budget Expenditure	金融机构本外币存款余额 The Balance of RMB and Foreign Currencies Deposits in Financial Institutions	金融机构本外币贷款余额 The Balance of RMB and Foreign Currencies Loans in Financial Institutions	社会消费品零售总额 Total Retail Sales of Consumer Goods	货物进出口总额 Total Import & Export	#出口总额 Total Export	城镇居民人均可支配收入(元) Per Capita Disposable Income of Urban Households (yuan)	农村居民人均可支配收入(元) Per Capita Disposable Income of Rural Households (yuan)	居民消费价格指数 Consumer Price Indices
1001.1	**1225.6**	**25941.0**	**26112.3**	**4878.1**	**2208.9**	**1431.8**	**59459**	**23844**	**101.4**
718.0	1276.3	20723.0	16208.7	2548.4	1235.1	803.7	44745	19834	101.2
437.5	715.9	18288.0	18162.1	1761.4	1467.1	971.8	43694	22822	102.1
230.9	420.8	7788.4	10595.7	1059.8	182.7	93.0	54616	23938	102.1
713.7	1048.9	20855.0	20777.3	3864.5	1406.6	522.3	51702	22352	101.7
459.7	976.7	16851.3	17122.1	1907.8	1107.6	208.5	43240	18919	101.9
262.2	1065.5	16474.0	14396.5	2195.9	387.0	136.3	43981	22260	101.9
1558.2	1828.7	49531.3	48760.2	7832.4	6292.1	3827.9	76643	34664	102.2
2451.0	2542.0	69592.0	62306.0	7294.0	7565.0	5141.0	77043	45183	102.4
909.3	1380.2	25070.9	23952.1	5021.6	3611.0	2301.8	56177	28727	102.4
698.5	999.9	21258.8	23047.7	4679.5	3656.9	2564.6	55638	26826	102.4
457.7	939.0	16110.3	18949.1	3012.0	1345.6	954.9	52622	24218	101.8
1130.8	1456.4	29416.5	34814.0	5223.1	6069.7	3596.3	46287	28237	101.2
1504.7	2227.2	35754.0	44383.8	6936.2	3532.2	2153.0	58449	29304	102.3
1202.0	1566.3	27882.6	29853.4	5235.6	3315.6	2462.9	65190	40678	101.7
1854.7	3014.2	80495.1	68918.6	10298.2	10948.4	6194.8	76849	36292	102.4
392.7	838.9	13146.3	19877.7	2358.8	1510.1	742.7	42636	19001	101.7
204.8	332.3	6399.5	7073.3	1003.1	605.6	170.8	43535	20388	101.1
1722.4	2435.0	53189.0	53053.0	9096.5	8346.4	5005.1	54897	30931	102.4
402.2	726.4	14474.6	19293.1	2402.1	593.3	371.1	46242	21925	101.4
505.3	863.3	17740.7	23868.0	3385.3	1997.4	946.4	53832	20722	101.7
834.1	1573.1	31763.1	32247.1	4642.1	4474.1	2801.5	48418	18285	102.2
221.0	498.8	10109.1	15016.2	1598.2	168.8	65.3	45277	17178	102.3
131.7	339.0			531.7	32.4	16.5	40197	15797	102.5
168.9	352.3	5432.7	6527.9	791.6	156.6	122.6	44392	19349	102.0
314.8	455.8	11967.1	10603.0	1033.0	513.6	388.8	46972	25873	101.6
8	11	9	9	9	11	11	5	13	22

Note:The data regarding other cities in this table is sorted out according to internal data which is for reference only instead of being released officially. As for final data regarding various indicators, refer to official release mechanism in each city.

附录四

中华人民共和国统计法

Statistical Law of The People's Republic of China

（1983 年 12 月 8 日第六届全国人民代表大会常务委员会第三次会议通过　根据 1996 年 5 月 15 日第八届全国人民代表大会常务委员会第十九次会议《关于修改〈中华人民共和国统计法〉的决定》修正　2009 年 6 月 27 日第十一届全国人民代表大会常务委员会第九次会议修订）

目　录

第一章　总　则

第一条　为了科学、有效地组织统计工作，保障统计资料的真实性、准确性、完整性和及时性，发挥统计在了解国情国力、服务经济社会发展中的重要作用，促进社会主义现代化建设事业发展，制定本法。

第二条　本法适用于各级人民政府、县级以上人民政府统计机构和有关部门组织实施的统计活动。

统计的基本任务是对经济社会发展情况进行统计调查、统计分析，提供统计资料和统计咨询意见，实行统计监督。

第三条　国家建立集中统一的统计系统，实行统一领导、分级负责的统计管理体制。

第四条　国务院和地方各级人民政府、各有关部门应当加强对统计工作的组织领导，为统计工作提供必要的保障。

第五条　国家加强统计科学研究，健全科学的统计指标体系，不断改进统计调查方法，提高统计的科学性。

国家有计划地加强统计信息化建设，推进统计信息搜集、处理、传输、共享、存储技术和统计数据库体系的现代化。

第六条　统计机构和统计人员依照本法规定独立行使统计调查、统计报告、统计监督的职权，不受侵犯。

地方各级人民政府、政府统计机构和有关部门以及各单位的负责人，不得自行修改统计机构和统计人员依法搜集、整理的统计资料，不得以任何方式要求统计机构、统计人员及其他机构、人员伪造、篡改统计资料，不得对依法履行职责或者拒绝、抵制统计违法行为的统计人员打击报复。

第七条　国家机关、企业事业单位和其他组织以及个体工商户和个人等统计调查对象，必须依照本法和国家有关规定，真实、准确、完整、及时地提供统计调查所需的资料，不得提供不真实或者不完整的统计资料，不得迟报、拒报统计资料。

第八条　统计工作应当接受社会公众的监督。任何单位和个人有权检举统计中弄虚作假等违法行为。对检举有功的单位和个人应当给予表彰和奖励。

第九条　统计机构和统计人员对在统计工作中知悉的国家秘密、商业秘密和个人信息，应当予以保密。

第十条　任何单位和个人不得利用虚假统计资料骗取荣誉称号、物质利益或者职务晋升。

第二章　统计调查管理

第十一条　统计调查项目包括国家统计调查项目、部门统计调查项目和地方统计调查项目。

国家统计调查项目是指全国性基本情况的统计调查项目。部门统计调查项目是指国务院有关部门的专业性统计调查项目。地方统计调查项目是指县级以上地方人民政府及其部门的地方性统计调查项目。

国家统计调查项目、部门统计调查项目、地方统计调查项目应当明确分工，互相衔接，不得重复。

第十二条　国家统计调查项目由国家统计局制定，或者由国家统计局和国务院有关部门共同制定，报国务院备案；重大的国家统计调查项目报国务院审批。

部门统计调查项目由国务院有关部门制定。统计调查对象属于本部门管辖系统的，报国家统计局备案；统计调查对象超出本部门管辖系统的，报国家统计局审批。

地方统计调查项目由县级以上地方人民政府统计机构和有关部门分别制定或者共同制定。其中，由省级人民政府统计机构单独制定或者和有关部门共同制定的，报国家统计局审批；由省级以下人民政府统计机构单独制定或者和有关部门共同制定的，报省级人民政府统计机构审批；由县级以上地方人民政府有关部门制定的，报本级人民政府统计机构审批。

第十三条　统计调查项目的审批机关应当对调查项目的必

要性、可行性、科学性进行审查，对符合法定条件的，作出予以批准的书面决定，并公布；对不符合法定条件的，作出不予批准的书面决定，并说明理由。

第十四条 制定统计调查项目，应当同时制定该项目的统计调查制度，并依照本法第十二条的规定一并报经审批或者备案。

统计调查制度应当对调查目的、调查内容、调查方法、调查对象、调查组织方式、调查表式、统计资料的报送和公布等作出规定。

统计调查应当按照统计调查制度组织实施。变更统计调查制度的内容，应当报经原审批机关批准或者原备案机关备案。

第十五条 统计调查表应当标明表号、制定机关、批准或者备案文号、有效期限等标志。

对未标明前款规定的标志或者超过有效期限的统计调查表，统计调查对象有权拒绝填报；县级以上人民政府统计机构应当依法责令停止有关统计调查活动。

第十六条 搜集、整理统计资料，应当以周期性普查为基础，以经常性抽样调查为主体，综合运用全面调查、重点调查等方法，并充分利用行政记录等资料。

重大国情国力普查由国务院统一领导，国务院和地方人民政府组织统计机构和有关部门共同实施。

第十七条 国家制定统一的统计标准，保障统计调查采用的指标涵义、计算方法、分类目录、调查表式和统计编码等的标准化。

国家统计标准由国家统计局制定，或者由国家统计局和国务院标准化主管部门共同制定。

国务院有关部门可以制定补充性的部门统计标准，报国家统计局审批。部门统计标准不得与国家统计标准相抵触。

第十八条 县级以上人民政府统计机构根据统计任务的需要，可以在统计调查对象中推广使用计算机网络报送统计资料。

第十九条 县级以上人民政府应当将统计工作所需经费列入财政预算。

重大国情国力普查所需经费，由国务院和地方人民政府共同负担，列入相应年度的财政预算，按时拨付，确保到位。

第三章 统计资料的管理和公布

第二十条 县级以上人民政府统计机构和有关部门以及乡、镇人民政府，应当按照国家有关规定建立统计资料的保存、管理制度，建立健全统计信息共享机制。

第二十一条 国家机关、企业事业单位和其他组织等统计调查对象，应当按照国家有关规定设置原始记录、统计台账，建立健全统计资料的审核、签署、交接、归档等管理制度。

统计资料的审核、签署人员应当对其审核、签署的统计资料的真实性、准确性和完整性负责。

第二十二条 县级以上人民政府有关部门应当及时向本级人民政府统计机构提供统计所需的行政记录资料和国民经济核算所需的财务资料、财政资料及其他资料，并按照统计调查制度的规定及时向本级人民政府统计机构报送其组织实施统计调查取得的有关资料。

县级以上人民政府统计机构应当及时向本级人民政府有关部门提供有关统计资料。

第二十三条 县级以上人民政府统计机构按照国家有关规定，定期公布统计资料。

国家统计数据以国家统计局公布的数据为准。

第二十四条 县级以上人民政府有关部门统计调查取得的统计资料，由本部门按照国家有关规定公布。

第二十五条 统计调查中获得的能够识别或者推断单个统计调查对象身份的资料，任何单位和个人不得对外提供、泄露，不得用于统计以外的目的。

第二十六条 县级以上人民政府统计机构和有关部门统计调查取得的统计资料，除依法应当保密的外，应当及时公开，供社会公众查询。

第四章 统计机构和统计人员

第二十七条 国务院设立国家统计局，依法组织领导和协调全国的统计工作。

国家统计局根据工作需要设立的派出调查机构，承担国家统计局布置的统计调查等任务。

县级以上地方人民政府设立独立的统计机构，乡、镇人民政府设置统计工作岗位，配备专职或者兼职统计人员，依法管理、开展统计工作，实施统计调查。

第二十八条 县级以上人民政府有关部门根据统计任务的需要设立统计机构，或者在有关机构中设置统计人员，并指定统计负责人，依法组织、管理本部门职责范围内的统计工作，实施统计调查，在统计业务上受本级人民政府统计机构的指导。

第二十九条 统计机构、统计人员应当依法履行职责，如实搜集、报送统计资料，不得伪造、篡改统计资料，不得以任何方式要求任何单位和个人提供不真实的统计资料，不得有其他违反本法规定的行为。

统计人员应当坚持实事求是，恪守职业道德，对其负责搜集、审核、录入的统计资料与统计调查对象报送的统计资料的一致性负责。

第三十条 统计人员进行统计调查时，有权就与统计有关的问题询问有关人员，要求其如实提供有关情况、资料并改正不真实、不准确的资料。

统计人员进行统计调查时，应当出示县级以上人民政府统计机构或者有关部门颁发的工作证件；未出示的，统计调查对象有权拒绝调查。

第三十一条 国家实行统计专业技术职务资格考试、评聘制度，提高统计人员的专业素质，保障统计队伍的稳定性。

统计人员应当具备与其从事的统计工作相适应的专业知识和业务能力。

县级以上人民政府统计机构和有关部门应当加强对统计人员的专业培训和职业道德教育。

第五章 监督检查

第三十二条 县级以上人民政府及其监察机关对下级人民政府、本级人民政府统计机构和有关部门执行本法的情况，实施监督。

第三十三条 国家统计局组织管理全国统计工作的监督检查，查处重大统计违法行为。

县级以上地方人民政府统计机构依法查处本行政区域内发生的统计违法行为。但是，国家统计局派出的调查机构组织实施的统计调查活动中发生的统计违法行为，由组织实施该项统计调查的调查机构负责查处。

法律、行政法规对有关部门查处统计违法行为另有规定的，从其规定。

第三十四条 县级以上人民政府有关部门应当积极协助本级人民政府统计机构查处统计违法行为，及时向本级人民政府统计机构移送有关统计违法案件材料。

第三十五条 县级以上人民政府统计机构在调查统计违法行为或者核查统计数据时，有权采取下列措施：

（一）发出统计检查查询书，向检查对象查询有关事项；

（二）要求检查对象提供有关原始记录和凭证、统计台账、统计调查表、会计资料及其他相关证明和资料；

（三）就与检查有关的事项询问有关人员；

（四）进入检查对象的业务场所和统计数据处理信息系统进行检查、核对；

（五）经本机构负责人批准，登记保存检查对象的有关原始记录和凭证、统计台账、统计调查表、会计资料及其他相关证明和资料；

（六）对与检查事项有关的情况和资料进行记录、录音、录像、照相和复制。

县级以上人民政府统计机构进行监督检查时，监督检查人员不得少于二人，并应当出示执法证件；未出示的，有关单位和个人有权拒绝检查。

第三十六条 县级以上人民政府统计机构履行监督检查职责时，有关单位和个人应当如实反映情况，提供相关证明和资料，不得拒绝、阻碍检查，不得转移、隐匿、篡改、毁弃原始记录和凭证、统计台账、统计调查表、会计资料及其他相关证明和资料。

第六章 法律责任

第三十七条 地方人民政府、政府统计机构或者有关部门、单位的负责人有下列行为之一的，由任免机关或者监察机关依法给予处分，并由县级以上人民政府统计机构予以通报：

（一）自行修改统计资料、编造虚假统计数据的；

（二）要求统计机构、统计人员或者其他机构、人员伪造、篡改统计资料的；

（三）对依法履行职责或者拒绝、抵制统计违法行为的统计人员打击报复的；

（四）对本地方、本部门、本单位发生的严重统计违法行为失察的。

第三十八条 县级以上人民政府统计机构或者有关部门在组织实施统计调查活动中有下列行为之一的，由本级人民政府、上级人民政府统计机构或者本级人民政府统计机构责令改正，予以通报；对直接负责的主管人员和其他直接责任人员，由任免机关或者监察机关依法给予处分：

（一）未经批准擅自组织实施统计调查的；

（二）未经批准擅自变更统计调查制度的内容的；

（三）伪造、篡改统计资料的；

（四）要求统计调查对象或者其他机构、人员提供不真实的统计资料的；

（五）未按照统计调查制度的规定报送有关资料的。

统计人员有前款第三项至第五项所列行为之一的，责令改正，依法给予处分。

第三十九条 县级以上人民政府统计机构或者有关部门有下列行为之一的，对直接负责的主管人员和其他直接责任人员由任免机关或者监察机关依法给予处分：

（一）违法公布统计资料的；

（二）泄露统计调查对象的商业秘密、个人信息或者提供、泄露在统计调查中获得的能够识别或者推断单个统计调查对象身份的资料的；

（三）违反国家有关规定，造成统计资料毁损、灭失的。

统计人员有前款所列行为之一的，依法给予处分。

第四十条 统计机构、统计人员泄露国家秘密的，依法追究法律责任。

第四十一条 作为统计调查对象的国家机关、企业事业单位或者其他组织有下列行为之一的，由县级以上人民政府统计机构责令改正，给予警告，可以予以通报；其直接负责的主管人员和其他直接责任人员属于国家工作人员的，由任免机关或者监察机关依法给予处分：

（一）拒绝提供统计资料或者经催报后仍未按时提供统计资料的；

（二）提供不真实或者不完整的统计资料的；

（三）拒绝答复或者不如实答复统计检查查询书的；

（四）拒绝、阻碍统计调查、统计检查的；

（五）转移、隐匿、篡改、毁弃或者拒绝提供原始记录和凭证、统计台账、统计调查表及其他相关证明和资料的。

企业事业单位或者其他组织有前款所列行为之一的，可以并处五万元以下的罚款；情节严重的，并处五万元以上二十万元以下的罚款。

个体工商户有本条第一款所列行为之一的，由县级以上人民政府统计机构责令改正，给予警告，可以并处一万元以下的罚款。

第四十二条 作为统计调查对象的国家机关、企业事业单位或者其他组织迟报统计资料，或者未按照国家有关规定设置原始记录、统计台账的，由县级以上人民政府统计机构责令改正，给予警告。

企业事业单位或者其他组织有前款所列行为之一的，可以并处一万元以下的罚款。

个体工商户迟报统计资料的，由县级以上人民政府统计机构责令改正，给予警告，可以并处一千元以下的罚款。

第四十三条 县级以上人民政府统计机构查处统计违法行为时，认为对有关国家工作人员依法应当给予处分的，应当提出给予处分的建议；该国家工作人员的任免机关或者监察机关应当依法及时作出决定，并将结果书面通知县级以上人民政府统计机构。

第四十四条 作为统计调查对象的个人在重大国情国力普查活动中拒绝、阻碍统计调查，或者提供不真实或者不完整的普查资料的，由县级以上人民政府统计机构责令改正，予以批评教育。

第四十五条 违反本法规定，利用虚假统计资料骗取荣誉称号、物质利益或者职务晋升的，除对其编造虚假统计资料或者要求他人编造虚假统计资料的行为依法追究法律责任外，由作出有关决定的单位或者其上级单位、监察机关取消其荣誉称号，追缴获得的物质利益，撤销晋升的职务。

第四十六条 当事人对县级以上人民政府统计机构作出的行政处罚决定不服的，可以依法申请行政复议或者提起行政诉讼。其中，对国家统计局在省、自治区、直辖市派出的调查机构作出的行政处罚决定不服的，向国家统计局申请行政复议；对国家统计局派出的其他调查机构作出的行政处罚决定不服的，向国家统计局在该派出机构所在的省、自治区、直辖市派出的调查机构申请行政复议。

第四十七条 违反本法规定，构成犯罪的，依法追究刑事责任。

第七章 附 则

第四十八条 本法所称县级以上人民政府统计机构，是指国家统计局及其派出的调查机构、县级以上地方人民政府统计机构。

第四十九条 民间统计调查活动的管理办法，由国务院制定。

中华人民共和国境外的组织、个人需要在中华人民共和国境内进行统计调查活动的，应当按照国务院的规定报请审批。

利用统计调查危害国家安全、损害社会公共利益或者进行欺诈活动的，依法追究法律责任。

第五十条 本法自 2010 年 1 月 1 日起施行。

附录五

中华人民共和国统计法实施条例

Regulations for the Implementation of the Statistics Law of the People's Republic of China

中华人民共和国国务院令

第 681 号

《中华人民共和国统计法实施条例》已经 2017 年 4 月 12 日国务院第 168 次常务会议通过，现予公布，自 2017 年 8 月 1 日起施行。

总理　李克强

2017 年 5 月 28 日

中华人民共和国统计法实施条例

第一章　总　则

第一条　根据《中华人民共和国统计法》(以下简称统计法)，制定本条例。

第二条　统计资料能够通过行政记录取得的，不得组织实施调查。通过抽样调查、重点调查能够满足统计需要的，不得组织实施全面调查。

第三条　县级以上人民政府统计机构和有关部门应当加强统计规律研究，健全新兴产业等统计，完善经济、社会、科技、资源和环境统计，推进互联网、大数据、云计算等现代信息技术在统计工作中的应用，满足经济社会发展需要。

第四条　地方人民政府、县级以上人民政府统计机构和有关部门应当根据国家有关规定，明确本单位防范和惩治统计造假、弄虚作假的责任主体，严格执行统计法和本条例的规定。

地方人民政府、县级以上人民政府统计机构和有关部门及其负责人应当保障统计活动依法进行，不得侵犯统计机构、统计人员独立行使统计调查、统计报告、统计监督职权，不得非法干预统计调查对象提供统计资料，不得统计造假、弄虚作假。

统计调查对象应当依照统计法和国家有关规定，真实、准确、完整、及时地提供统计资料，拒绝、抵制弄虚作假等违法行为。

第五条　县级以上人民政府统计机构和有关部门不得组织实施营利性统计调查。

国家有计划地推进县级以上人民政府统计机构和有关部门通过向社会购买服务组织实施统计调查和资料开发。

第二章　统计调查项目

第六条　部门统计调查项目、地方统计调查项目的主要内容不得与国家统计调查项目的内容重复、矛盾。

第七条　统计调查项目的制定机关（以下简称制定机关）应当就项目的必要性、可行性、科学性进行论证，征求有关地方、部门、统计调查对象和专家的意见，并由制定机关按照会议制度集体讨论决定。

重要统计调查项目应当进行试点。

第八条　制定机关申请审批统计调查项目，应当以公文形式向审批机关提交统计调查项目审批申请表、项目的统计调查制度和工作经费来源说明。

申请材料不齐全或者不符合法定形式的，审批机关应当一次性告知需要补正的全部内容，制定机关应当按照审批机关的要求予以补正。

申请材料齐全、符合法定形式的，审批机关应当受理。

第九条　统计调查项目符合下列条件的，审批机关应当作出予以批准的书面决定：

（一）具有法定依据或者确为公共管理和服务所必需；

（二）与已批准或者备案的统计调查项目的主要内容不重复、不矛盾；

（三）主要统计指标无法通过行政记录或者已有统计调查资料加工整理取得；

（四）统计调查制度符合统计法律法规规定，科学、合理、

可行;

（五）采用的统计标准符合国家有关规定;

（六）制定机关具备项目执行能力。

不符合前款规定条件的，审批机关应当向制定机关提出修改意见；修改后仍不符合前款规定条件的，审批机关应当作出不予批准的书面决定并说明理由。

第十条 统计调查项目涉及其他部门职责的，审批机关应当在作出审批决定前，征求相关部门的意见。

第十一条 审批机关应当自受理统计调查项目审批申请之日起20日内作出决定。20日内不能作出决定的，经审批机关负责人批准可以延长10日，并应当将延长审批期限的理由告知制定机关。

制定机关修改统计调查项目的时间，不计算在审批期限内。

第十二条 制定机关申请备案统计调查项目，应当以公文形式向备案机关提交统计调查项目备案申请表和项目的统计调查制度。

统计调查项目的调查对象属于制定机关管辖系统，且主要内容与已批准、备案的统计调查项目不重复、不矛盾的，备案机关应当依法给予备案文号。

第十三条 统计调查项目经批准或者备案的，审批机关或者备案机关应当及时公布统计调查项目及其统计调查制度的主要内容。涉及国家秘密的统计调查项目除外。

第十四条 统计调查项目有下列情形之一的，审批机关或者备案机关应当简化审批或者备案程序，缩短期限:

（一）发生突发事件需要迅速实施统计调查;

（二）统计调查制度内容未作变动，统计调查项目有效期届满需要延长期限。

第十五条 统计法第十七条第二款规定的国家统计标准是强制执行标准。各级人民政府、县级以上人民政府统计机构和有关部门组织实施的统计调查活动，应当执行国家统计标准。

制定国家统计标准，应当征求国务院有关部门的意见。

第三章 统计调查的组织实施

第十六条 统计机构、统计人员组织实施统计调查，应当就统计调查对象的法定填报义务、主要指标涵义和有关填报要求等，向统计调查对象作出说明。

第十七条 国家机关、企业事业单位或者其他组织等统计调查对象提供统计资料，应当由填报人员和单位负责人签字，并加盖公章。个人作为统计调查对象提供统计资料，应当由本人签字。统计调查制度规定不需要签字、加盖公章的除外。

统计调查对象使用网络提供统计资料的，按照国家有关规定执行。

第十八条 县级以上人民政府统计机构、有关部门推广使用网络报送统计资料，应当采取有效的网络安全保障措施。

第十九条 县级以上人民政府统计机构、有关部门和乡、镇统计人员，应当对统计调查对象提供的统计资料进行审核。统计资料不完整或者存在明显错误的，应当由统计调查对象依法予以补充或者改正。

第二十条 国家统计局应当建立健全统计数据质量监控和评估制度，加强对各省、自治区、直辖市重要统计数据的监控和评估。

第四章 统计资料的管理和公布

第二十一条 县级以上人民政府统计机构、有关部门和乡、镇人民政府应当妥善保管统计调查中取得的统计资料。

国家建立统计资料灾难备份系统。

第二十二条 统计调查中取得的统计调查对象的原始资料，应当至少保存2年。

汇总性统计资料应当至少保存10年，重要的汇总性统计资料应当永久保存。法律法规另有规定的，从其规定。

第二十三条 统计调查对象按照国家有关规定设置的原始记录和统计台账，应当至少保存2年。

第二十四条 国家统计局统计调查取得的全国性统计数据和分省、自治区、直辖市统计数据，由国家统计局公布或者由国家统计局授权其派出的调查机构或者省级人民政府统计机构公布。

第二十五条 国务院有关部门统计调查取得的统计数据，由国务院有关部门按照国家有关规定和已批准或者备案的统计调查制度公布。

县级以上地方人民政府有关部门公布其统计调查取得的统计数据，比照前款规定执行。

第二十六条 已公布的统计数据按照国家有关规定需要进行修订的，县级以上人民政府统计机构和有关部门应当及时公布修订后的数据，并就修订依据和情况作出说明。

第二十七条 县级以上人民政府统计机构和有关部门应当及时公布主要统计指标涵义、调查范围、调查方法、计算方法、抽样调查样本量等信息，对统计数据进行解释说明。

第二十八条 公布统计资料应当按照国家有关规定进行。公布前，任何单位和个人不得违反国家有关规定对外提供，不得利用尚未公布的统计资料谋取不正当利益。

第二十九条 统计法第二十五条规定的能够识别或者推断单个统计调查对象身份的资料包括:

（一）直接标明单个统计调查对象身份的资料;

（二）虽未直接标明单个统计调查对象身份，但是通过已标明的地址、编码等相关信息可以识别或者推断单个统计调查对象身份的资料;

（三）可以推断单个统计调查对象身份的汇总资料。

第三十条 统计调查中获得的能够识别或者推断单个统计调查对象身份的资料应当依法严格管理，除作为统计执法依据外，不得直接作为对统计调查对象实施行政许可、行政处罚等具体行政行为的依据，不得用于完成统计任务以外的目的。

第三十一条 国家建立健全统计信息共享机制，实现县级以上人民政府统计机构和有关部门统计调查取得的资料共享。制定机关共同制定的统计调查项目，可以共同使用获取的统计资料。

统计调查制度应当对统计信息共享的内容、方式、时限、渠道和责任等作出规定。

第五章　统计机构和统计人员

第三十二条　县级以上地方人民政府统计机构受本级人民政府和上级人民政府统计机构的双重领导，在统计业务上以上级人民政府统计机构的领导为主。

乡、镇人民政府应当设置统计工作岗位，配备专职或者兼职统计人员，履行统计职责，在统计业务上受上级人民政府统计机构领导。乡、镇统计人员的调动，应当征得县级人民政府统计机构的同意。

县级以上人民政府有关部门在统计业务上受本级人民政府统计机构指导。

第三十三条　县级以上人民政府统计机构和有关部门应当完成国家统计调查任务，执行国家统计调查项目的统计调查制度，组织实施本地方、本部门的统计调查活动。

第三十四条　国家机关、企业事业单位和其他组织应当加强统计基础工作，为履行法定的统计资料报送义务提供组织、人员和工作条件保障。

第三十五条　对在统计工作中做出突出贡献、取得显著成绩的单位和个人，按照国家有关规定给予表彰和奖励。

第六章　监督检查

第三十六条　县级以上人民政府统计机构从事统计执法工作的人员，应当具备必要的法律知识和统计业务知识，参加统计执法培训，并取得由国家统计局统一印制的统计执法证。

第三十七条　任何单位和个人不得拒绝、阻碍对统计工作的监督检查和对统计违法行为的查处工作，不得包庇、纵容统计违法行为。

第三十八条　任何单位和个人有权向县级以上人民政府统计机构举报统计违法行为。

县级以上人民政府统计机构应当公布举报统计违法行为的方式和途径，依法受理、核实、处理举报，并为举报人保密。

第三十九条　县级以上人民政府统计机构负责查处统计违法行为；法律、行政法规对有关部门查处统计违法行为另有规定的，从其规定。

第七章　法律责任

第四十条　下列情形属于统计法第三十七条第四项规定的对严重统计违法行为失察，对地方人民政府、政府统计机构或者有关部门、单位的负责人，由任免机关或者监察机关依法给予处分，并由县级以上人民政府统计机构予以通报：

（一）本地方、本部门、本单位大面积发生或者连续发生统计造假、弄虚作假；

（二）本地方、本部门、本单位统计数据严重失实，应当发现而未发现；

（三）发现本地方、本部门、本单位统计数据严重失实不予纠正。

第四十一条　县级以上人民政府统计机构或者有关部门组织实施营利性统计调查的，由本级人民政府、上级人民政府统计机构或者本级人民政府统计机构责令改正，予以通报；有违法所得的，没收违法所得。

第四十二条　地方各级人民政府、县级以上人民政府统计机构或者有关部门及其负责人，侵犯统计机构、统计人员独立行使统计调查、统计报告、统计监督职权，或者采用下发文件、会议布置以及其他方式授意、指使、强令统计调查对象或者其他单位、人员编造虚假统计资料的，由上级人民政府、本级人民政府、上级人民政府统计机构或者本级人民政府统计机构责令改正，予以通报。

第四十三条　县级以上人民政府统计机构或者有关部门在组织实施统计调查活动中有下列行为之一的，由本级人民政府、上级人民政府统计机构或者本级人民政府统计机构责令改正，予以通报：

（一）违法制定、审批或者备案统计调查项目；

（二）未按照规定公布经批准或者备案的统计调查项目及其统计调查制度的主要内容；

（三）未执行国家统计标准；

（四）未执行统计调查制度；

（五）自行修改单个统计调查对象的统计资料。

乡、镇统计人员有前款第三项至第五项所列行为的，责令改正，依法给予处分。

第四十四条　县级以上人民政府统计机构或者有关部门违反本条例第二十四条、第二十五条规定公布统计数据的，由本级人民政府、上级人民政府统计机构或者本级人民政府统计机构责令改正，予以通报。

第四十五条　违反国家有关规定对外提供尚未公布的统计资料或者利用尚未公布的统计资料谋取不正当利益的，由任免机关或者监察机关依法给予处分，并由县级以上人民政府统计机构予以通报。

第四十六条　统计机构及其工作人员有下列行为之一的，由本级人民政府或者上级人民政府统计机构责令改正，予以通报：

（一）拒绝、阻碍对统计工作的监督检查和对统计违法行为的查处工作；

（二）包庇、纵容统计违法行为；

（三）向有统计违法行为的单位或者个人通风报信，帮助其逃避查处；

（四）未依法受理、核实、处理对统计违法行为的举报；

（五）泄露对统计违法行为的举报情况。

第四十七条　地方各级人民政府、县级以上人民政府有关部门拒绝、阻碍统计监督检查或者转移、隐匿、篡改、毁弃原始记录和凭证、统计台账、统计调查表及其他相关证明和资料的，由上级人民政府、上级人民政府统计机构或者本级人民政府统计机构责令改正，予以通报。

第四十八条 地方各级人民政府、县级以上人民政府统计机构和有关部门有本条例第四十一条至第四十七条所列违法行为之一的，对直接负责的主管人员和其他直接责任人员，由任免机关或者监察机关依法给予处分。

第四十九条 乡、镇人民政府有统计法第三十八条第一款、第三十九条第一款所列行为之一的，依照统计法第三十八条、第三十九条的规定追究法律责任。

第五十条 下列情形属于统计法第四十一条第二款规定的情节严重行为：

（一）使用暴力或者威胁方法拒绝、阻碍统计调查、统计监督检查；

（二）拒绝、阻碍统计调查、统计监督检查，严重影响相关工作正常开展；

（三）提供不真实、不完整的统计资料，造成严重后果或者恶劣影响；

（四）有统计法第四十一条第一款所列违法行为之一，1年内被责令改正3次以上。

第五十一条 统计违法行为涉嫌犯罪的，县级以上人民政府统计机构应当将案件移送司法机关处理。

第八章 附 则

第五十二条 中华人民共和国境外的组织、个人需要在中华人民共和国境内进行统计调查活动的，应当委托中华人民共和国境内具有涉外统计调查资格的机构进行。涉外统计调查资格应当依法报经批准。统计调查范围限于省、自治区、直辖市行政区域内的，由省级人民政府统计机构审批；统计调查范围跨省、自治区、直辖市行政区域的，由国家统计局审批。

涉外社会调查项目应当依法报经批准。统计调查范围限于省、自治区、直辖市行政区域内的，由省级人民政府统计机构审批；统计调查范围跨省、自治区、直辖市行政区域的，由国家统计局审批。

第五十三条 国家统计局或者省级人民政府统计机构对涉外统计违法行为进行调查，有权采取统计法第三十五条规定的措施。

第五十四条 对违法从事涉外统计调查活动的单位、个人，由国家统计局或者省级人民政府统计机构责令改正或者责令停止调查，有违法所得的，没收违法所得；违法所得50万元以上的，并处违法所得1倍以上3倍以下的罚款；违法所得不足50万元或者没有违法所得的，处200万元以下的罚款；情节严重的，暂停或者取消涉外统计调查资格，撤销涉外社会调查项目批准决定；构成犯罪的，依法追究刑事责任。

第五十五条 本条例自2017年8月1日起施行。1987年1月19日国务院批准、1987年2月15日国家统计局公布，2000年6月2日国务院批准修订、2000年6月15日国家统计局公布，2005年12月16日国务院修订的《中华人民共和国统计法实施细则》同时废止。

附录六

统计违法违纪行为处分规定

Statistics Regulation Violations of Law

中华人民共和国监察部
中华人民共和国人力资源和社会保障部 令
国家统计局

第 18 号

《统计违法违纪行为处分规定》已经监察部2009年2月9日第一次部长办公会议、人力资源社会保障部2008年12月30日第十六次部务会议、国家统计局2008年11月6日第十八次局务会议审议通过。现予公布，自2009年5月1日起施行。

监察部部长 马馼
人力资源社会保障部部长 尹蔚民
国家统计局局长 马建堂
二〇〇九年三月二十五日

统计违法违纪行为处分规定

第一条 为了加强统计工作，提高统计数据的准确性和及时性，惩处和预防统计违法违纪行为，促进统计法律法规的贯彻实施，根据《中华人民共和国统计法》、《中华人民共和国行政监察法》、《中华人民共和国公务员法》、《行政机关公务员处分条例》及其他有关法律、行政法规，制定本规定。

第二条 有统计违法违纪行为的单位中负有责任的领导人员和直接责任人员，以及有统计违法违纪行为的个人，应当承担纪律责任。属于下列人员的（以下统称有关责任人员），由任免机关或者监察机关按照管理权限依法给予处分：

（一）行政机关公务员；

（二）法律、法规授权的具有公共事务管理职能的事业单位中经批准参照《中华人民共和国公务员法》管理的工作人员；

（三）行政机关依法委托的组织中除工勤人员以外的工作人员；

（四）企业、事业单位、社会团体中由行政机关任命的人员。

法律、行政法规、国务院决定和国务院监察机关、国务院人力资源社会保障部门制定的处分规章对统计违法违纪行为的处分另有规定的，从其规定。

第三条 地方、部门以及企业、事业单位、社会团体的领导人员有下列行为之一的，给予记过或者记大过处分；情节较重的，给予降级或者撤职处分；情节严重的，给予开除处分：

（一）自行修改统计资料、编造虚假数据的；

（二）强令、授意本地区、本部门、本单位统计机构、统计人员或者其他有关机构、人员拒报、虚报、瞒报或者篡改统计资料、编造虚假数据的；

（三）对拒绝、抵制篡改统计资料或者对拒绝、抵制编造虚假数据的人员进行打击报复的；

（四）对揭发、检举统计违法违纪行为的人员进行打击报复的。

有前款第（三）项、第（四）项规定行为的，应当从重处分。

第四条 地方、部门以及企业、事业单位、社会团体的领导人员，对本地区、本部门、本单位严重失实的统计数据，应当发现而未发现或者发现后不予纠正，造成不良后果的，给予警告或者记过处分；造成严重后果的，给予记大过或者降级处分；造成特别严重后果的，给予撤职或者开除处分。

第五条 各级人民政府统计机构、有关部门及其工作人员在实施统计调查活动中，有下列行为之一的，对有关责任人员，给予记过或者记大过处分；情节较重的，给予降级或者撤职处分；情节严重的，给予开除处分：

（一）强令、授意统计调查对象虚报、瞒报或者伪造、篡改统计资料的；

（二）参与篡改统计资料、编造虚假数据的。

第六条 各级人民政府统计机构、有关部门及其工作人员在实施统计调查活动中，有下列行为之一的，对有关责任人员，给予警告、记过或者记大过处分；情节较重的，给予降级处分；情节严重的，给予撤职处分：

（一）故意拖延或者拒报统计资料的；

（二）明知统计数据不实，不履行职责调查核实，造成不良后果的。

第七条 统计调查对象中的单位有下列行为之一，情节较重的，对有关责任人员，给予警告、记过或者记大过处分；情节严重的，给予降级或者撤职处分；情节特别严重的，给予开除处分：

（一）虚报、瞒报统计资料的；

（二）伪造、篡改统计资料的；

（三）拒报或者屡次迟报统计资料的；

（四）拒绝提供情况、提供虚假情况或者转移、隐匿、毁弃原始统计记录、统计台账、统计报表以及与统计有关的其他资料的。

第八条 违反国家规定的权限和程序公布统计资料，造成不良后果的，对有关责任人员，给予警告或者记过处分；情节较重的，给予记大过或者降级处分；情节严重的，给予撤职处分。

第九条 有下列行为之一，造成不良后果的，对有关责任人员，给予警告、记过或者记大过处分；情节较重的，给予降级或者撤职处分；情节严重的，给予开除处分：

（一）泄露属于国家秘密的统计资料的；

（二）未经本人同意，泄露统计调查对象个人、家庭资料的；

（三）泄露统计调查中知悉的统计调查对象商业秘密的。

第十条 包庇、纵容统计违法违纪行为的，对有关责任人员，给予记过或者记大过处分；情节较重的，给予降级或者撤职处分；情节严重的，给予开除处分。

第十一条 受到处分的人员对处分决定不服的，依照《中华人民共和国行政监察法》、《中华人民共和国公务员法》、《行政机关公务员处分条例》等有关规定，可以申请复核或者申诉。

第十二条 任免机关、监察机关和人民政府统计机构建立案件移送制度。

任免机关、监察机关查处统计违法违纪案件，认为应当由人民政府统计机构给予行政处罚的，应当将有关案件材料移送人民政府统计机构。人民政府统计机构应当依法及时查处，并将处理结果书面告知任免机关、监察机关。

人民政府统计机构查处统计行政违法案件，认为应当由任免机关或者监察机关给予处分的，应当及时将有关案件材料移送任免机关或者监察机关。任免机关或者监察机关应当依法及时查处，并将处理结果书面告知人民政府统计机构。

第十三条 有统计违法违纪行为，应当给予党纪处分的，移送党的纪律检查机关处理。涉嫌犯罪的，移送司法机关依法追究刑事责任。

第十四条 本规定由监察部、人力资源社会保障部、国家统计局负责解释。

第十五条 本规定自 2009 年 5 月 1 日起施行。

附录七

济南市统计局2022年统计大事要事

Chronicle of Events of Jinan Statistical Undertaking

1月5日，济南市统计局组织召开全市地区生产总值统一核算暨金融业统计年报培训会议。

1月26日，济南市统计局组织开展“送温暖过大年”一线走访慰问生活困难党员群众主题党日系列活动。市统计局党组书记、局长程伟到“双报到”洪北社区参加活动。

2月7日，济南市统计局组织开展春节后促进农民工返岗和企业复工复产情况快速调研。

2月9日，济南市统计局组织召开国家安全和保密工作会议。

2月14日，济南市统计局党组召开理论中心组（扩大）集体学习，贯彻落实中央、省、市纪委全会精神。市统计局党组书记、局长程伟主持会议。

2月23日，省统计局党组书记、局长辛树人来济开展经济运行情况调研。市统计局党组书记、局长程伟陪同调研并参加座谈。

3月2日，省统计局执法监督局调研组来济南组织座谈调研。

3月4日，《2021年济南市国民经济和社会发展统计公报》对外发布，同时配发专业解读，被济南发布、新黄河等媒体转载。

3月8日，济南市统计局以“四不两直”方式开展重点贸易企业实地数据核查，并就企业经营情况开展调研。

3月18日，济南市统计局组织召开社情民意专项调查工作推进会。

4月21日，济南市统计局圆满完成市人代会服务保障工作。

4月22日，济南市统计局组织召开一季度经济运行调度分析会。市统计局党组书记、局长程伟主持会议，各专业处室负责同志、业务骨干参加会议并交流发言。

5月11日，济南市统计局第五次全国经济普查筹备领导小组办公室召开专题工作研讨会。

5月13日，济南市统计局召开全面从严治党暨党风廉政建设工作会议。市统计局市管干部，总统计师，总经济师，各处室、局属事业单位负责人参加会议，市纪委监委派驻第六纪检监察组组长、副组长到会指导。

5月20日，济南市统计局召开济南新旧动能转换起步区全域统计工作会议，建立起步区全域核算体系。

5月24日，济南市统计局到部分铸造企业开展现场调研，了解五经普数据采集模板制作情况。

5月25日，济南市统计局到驻村“第一书记”工作村汪家场村走访调研，看望驻村“第一书记”，了解驻村工作情况，并送去防疫物资。

6月6日，济南市统计局召开落实政府系统作风建设专项行动专题会议精神推进会。

6月20日，省统计局、省发展改革委联合调研组到济南开展投资领域专题调研。

6月27日，济南市统计局组织召开全体党员大会进行换届选举，选举产生新一届局机关党委、机关纪委。

7月4日，济南市统计局联合自贸区济南片区管委会召开自贸区济南片区综合统计磋商会议。

7月5日，省统计局党组书记、局长辛树人来济调研专业市场业户生产经营及经济运行情况。市统计局党组书记、局长程伟陪同调研。

7月19日，济南市统计局组织召开第五次全国经济普查筹备阶段重点区域清查和专项试点工作培训会。

7月20日，济南市统计局、济南市社会经济调查中心召开上半年规下（限下）调查单位运行分析会议。

7月20日，济南市统计局到槐荫区五里沟街道办事处开展“三联系三调研”专题对接调研活动。

7月21日，济南市统计局印发《济南市统计局贯彻落实<关于更加有效发挥统计监督职能作用的意见>的实施方案》。

7月28日，济南市统计局举办学习习近平新时代中国特色社会主义思想知识竞赛。

8月3日，济南市统计局印发《济南市统计造假不收手不收敛问题专项纠治实施方案》。

8月12日，济南市统计局召开重点企业集团统计工作培训会，启动重点企业集团摸底工作。

8月29日，济南市统计局启动局领导包挂联系点统计造假不收手不收敛督导工作。

9月13日，省统计局督导组来济督导统计造假不收手不收敛专项纠治工作。

9月14日，济南市统计局组织召开全市统计“双随机”执法检查工作培训班。

9月20日，济南市统计局、国家统计局济南调查队联合开展第十三届“中国统计开放日”宣传进社区活动。

9月28日，市统计局组织召开全市五经普筹备阶段区域清查和专项试点工作总结会。

9月30日，省委常委、市委书记刘强在济南市统计局《庆祝第十三届统计开放日“数说新时代 奋进新征程”汇编》上作出批示。

9月30日，济南市统计局组织收听收看全省统计造假不收手不收敛问题专项纠治工作推进视频会议，并接续召开全市统计造假不收手不收敛问题专项纠治工作专题推进会议。

10月16日，济南市统计局组织党员干部集中收听收看党的二十大开幕盛况，聆听习近平总书记代表十九届中央委员会所作的工作报告。市统计局党组成员、市管干部、两总师，副处级以上领导干部集中观看，其他党员干部以处室为单位组织收听收看。

10月19日，济南市统计局、市金融局联合召开三季度金融运行分析座谈会。

10月26日，济南市统计局组织召开全市基本公共服务满意度调查工作推进会议，通报反馈全市基本公共服务满意度快速调查情况。

11月2日，济南市统计局召开政务公开业务培训会议。

11月10日，济南市统计局举办全市综合统计业务培训班。

11月15日，济南市统计局参加济南广播电视台“作风监督面对面”2022年度党风政风行风正风肃纪民主评议电视问政特别节目。

12月1日，济南市统计局统筹疫情防控和业务工作，有序组织开展值班和居家办公。

12月26日，济南市统计局完成市“两会”服务保障工作。